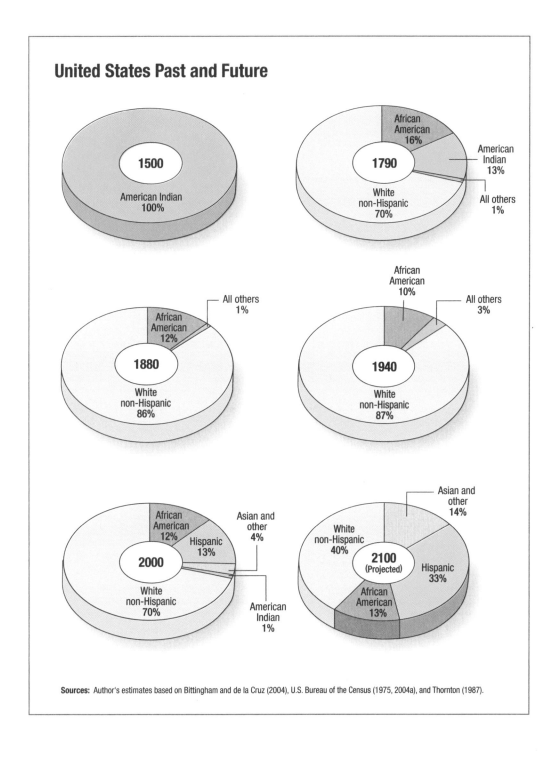

United States Past and Future

1500
American Indian
100%

1790
African American 16%
American Indian 13%
White non-Hispanic 70%
All others 1%

1880
All others 1%
African American 12%
White non-Hispanic 86%

1940
African American 10%
All others 3%
White non-Hispanic 87%

2000
African American 12%
Hispanic 13%
Asian and other 4%
White non-Hispanic 70%
American Indian 1%

2100 (Projected)
Asian and other 14%
White non-Hispanic 40%
Hispanic 33%
African American 13%

Sources: Author's estimates based on Bittingham and de la Cruz (2004), U.S. Bureau of the Census (1975, 2004a), and Thornton (1987).

TENTH EDITION

RACIAL *and* ETHNIC GROUPS

RICHARD T. SCHAEFER

DePaul University

PEARSON

Prentice
Hall

Upper Saddle River, NJ 07458

Library of Congress Cataloging-in-Publication Data

Schaefer, Richard T.
    Racial and ethnic groups / Richard T. Schaefer.— 10th ed.
        p. cm.
    Includes bibliographical references and index.
    ISBN 0-13-192897-X (alk. paper)
        1. Minorities—United States. 2. United States—Ethnic relations. 3. United States—Race
relations. 4. Prejudices—United States. I. Title.

E184.A1S3 2006
305.8'00973—dc22

2004029330

Editorial Director: Leah Jewell
AVP/Publisher: Nancy Roberts
VP, Director of Production and Manufacturing: Barbara
    Kittle
Managing Editor: Ann Marie McCarthy
Full-Service Project Management: Katie Ostler and
    Sandy Reinhard, Seven Worldwide
Prepress and Manufacturing Manager: Nick Sklitsis
Prepress and Manufacturing Buyer: Mary Ann Gloriande
Director of Marketing: Brandy Dawson
Senior Marketing Manager: Marissa Feliberty
Marketing Assistant: Jennifer Lang
Editorial Assistant: Lee Peterson

Creative Design Director: Leslie Osher
Art Director/Interior and Cover Design: Kathryn Foot
Line Art Illustrations: Seven Worldwide
Director, Image Resource Center: Melinda Reo
Manager, Rights and Permissions: Zina Arabia
Manager, Visual Research: Beth Brenzel
Image Permissions Coordinator: Joanne Dippel
Photo Researcher: Beaura Kathy Ringrose
Cover Photo: Jane Sterrett / Stock Illustration Source /
    Images.com
Media Editor: Kate Ramunda
Manager of Media Production: Lynn Pearlman

This book was set in 10/12 New Baskerville by Seven Worldwide Publishing Solutions, and was printed and bound
by Courier Companies, Inc. The cover was printed by The Lehigh Press.

For permission to use copyrighted material, grateful acknowledgment is made to the copyright holders listed on
pages 487–488, which is considered an extension of this copyright page.

Pearson Education LTD.
Pearson Education Singapore, Pte. Ltd
Pearson Education, Canada, Ltd.
Pearson Education—Japan
Pearson Education Australia PTY, Limited

Pearson Education North Asia Ltd
Pearson Educación de México, S.A. de C.V.
Pearson Education Malaysia, Pte. Ltd
Pearson Education, Upper Saddle River, New Jersey

10 9 8 7 6 5 4 3 2
ISBN: 0-13-192897-X

To the students in my classes who assist me in understanding a multicultural society

Brief Contents

Contents

Prejudice   32

 Discrimination   64

PART II
ETHNIC AND RELIGIOUS SOURCES OF CONFLICT

PART III
MAJOR RACIAL AND ETHNIC MINORITY GROUPS IN THE UNITED STATES

African Americans Today   208

Hispanic Americans   234

Chinese Americans and Japanese Americans 332

Jewish Americans: Quest to Maintain Identity 354

PART IV
OTHER PATTERNS OF DOMINANCE

Women: The Oppressed Majority   382

Beyond the United States:
The Comparative Perspective   406

17   Overcoming Exclusion   432

Preface

"Minorities Majority" read first-page newspaper headlines in Fall 2004; when the Census Bureau released their annual population estimates. Now in 280 counties, Whites who are not Hispanic are outnumbered by Latinos, African Americans, Asian Americans, Native American tribal members, and others. However, do these groups wield the power in all these counties? In any of these counties? Does the United States' becoming more diverse signify a significant advancement in the quality of life of people of color relative to gains made by White Americans? These are the real questions, and rarely are they asked and almost never answered. Some people who have not followed these trends seemed stunned that in 2003, Orange County, surf 'n sun capital of southern California and home of Disneyland, now has minority majority. Although these changes may not signify a major shift in social inequality among groups, they do underscore the importance of being familiar with the nature of race and ethnicity in the United States.

Race and ethnicity are an important part of the national agenda. Twenty-seven years ago, when the first edition of this book was being written, it was noted that race is not a static phenomenon and that although it is always a part of the social reality, specific aspects change. At that time, the presence of a new immigrant group, the Vietnamese, was duly noted, and the efforts to define affirmative action were described. Today we seek to describe the growing presence of El Salvadorans, Haitians, and Arab Americans, and the attempts to dismantle affirmative action.

Specific issues may change over time, but they continue to play out against a backdrop of discrimination that is rooted in the social structure and changing population composition, as influenced by immigration patterns and reproduction patterns. One unanticipated change is that the breakup of the Soviet Union and further disinterest of the major industrial powers in the political and social events in Africa, Latin America, and much of Asia have made ethnic, language, and religious divisions even more significant sources of antagonism between and within nations. The old ideological debates about communism and capitalism have been replaced by emotional divisions over religious dogma and cultural traditions.

We continue to be reminded about the importance of the social construction of many aspects of racial and ethnic relations. What constitutes a race in terms of identity? What meaning do race and ethnicity have amid the growing number of interracial marriages and marriages across cultural boundaries? Beyond the spectrum of race and ethnicity, we see the socially constructed meaning attached to all religions as members debate who is the "true" keeper of the faith. As we consider matters of gender, we see again that differences are largely the result of social constructions. And finally, as we consider all groups that have been subjected to discrimination, such as the disabled, the elderly, and gays and lesbians, we see, in a similar manner, the power of labeling. The very issue of national identity is also a part of the agenda. The public and politicians alike ask, "How many immigrants can we accept?" and "How much should be done to make up for past discrimination?" We are also witnessing the emergence of race, ethnicity, and national identity as global issues.

Changes in the Tenth Edition

As with all previous editions, every line, every source, and every number have been rechecked for its currency. We pride ourselves on providing the most current information possible to document the patterns in intergroup relations both in the United States and abroad.

Relevant scholarly findings in a variety of disciplines, including economics, anthropology, and communication sciences, have been incorporated. The feature *"Listen to Our Voices"* appears in every chapter. These selections include excerpts from the writings or speeches of noted members of racial and ethnic groups such as Martin Luther King, Jr., Elie Wiesel, Patricia J. Williams, and Nelson Mandela. Their writings will help students appreciate the emotional and the intellectual energies felt by subordinate groups.

The tenth edition includes a new chapter—*Muslim and Arab Americans*—Chapter 11. There is a critical need to understand the diversity among both people of Arab ethnicity and followers of Islam in the United States. A full chapter-length treatment is a requirement of any book-length treatment of race and ethnicity of the United States in the 21st century.

In addition to this feature, the tenth edition includes the following additions and changes:

■ New key terms such as *asylees* (Chapter 4), *blaming the victim* (Chapter 3), *glass escalator* (Chapter 3), *sovereignty* (Chapter 6), and *blended identity, deficit model of ethnic identity, hajib, hajj, jihad,* and *Orientalism* (Chapter 11)

■ The section on race is now revamped and titled "Does Race Matter?" to emphasize that race is socially constructed (Chapter 1)

■ A new "Research Focus" on how potential employers respond to ethnic-sounding names (Chapter 2)

Voices Listen to Our Voices Listen to

- Problem of the Color Line, W. E. B. DuBois (Chapter 1)
- National Media Should Stop Using Obscene Words, Tim Giago (Chapter 2)
- When Work Disappears, William Julius Wilson (Chapter 3)
- Imagining Life Without Illegal Immigrants, Dean E. Murphy (Chapter 4)
- When the Boats Arrived, Diane Glancy (Chapter 5)
- The Scalpel and the Silver Bear, Lori Arviso Alvord (Chapter 6)
- Letter from Birmingham Jail, Martin Luther King, Jr. (Chapter 7)
- Of Race and Risk, Patricia J. Williams (Chapter 8)
- Leaving Cuba, Alfredo Jimenez (Chapter 9)

- "¡Viva Vieques!", Martín St. Espada (Chapter 10)
- Pendulum Swings on Civil Rights, James Zogby (Chapter 11)
- Racial Hatred, Madhu S. Chawla (Chapter 12)
- Gangsters, Gooks, Geishas, and Geeks, Helen Zia (Chapter 13)
- Night, Elie Wiesel (Chapter 14)
- Time for Change, Arlie Russell Hochschild (Chapter 15)
- Africa, It Is Ours! Nelson Mandela (Chapter 16)
- Debunk Those Stereotypes, Kathi Wolfe (Chapter 17)

- A new section on low-wage labor emphasizes that a large proportion of racial and ethnic minorities are among the working poor (Chapter 3)
- A new "Listen to Our Voices" box entitled "Imagining Life Without Illegal Immigrants" by Dean E. Murphy (Chapter 4)
- A new United States map showing percentage of foreign born by state (Chapter 4)
- A new section on sovereignty underscores the complexity of tribal identity both for the individual and the federal government (Chapter 6)
- A dramatic income pyramid representing the contrasting incomes in 2003 between Black and White households (Chapter 8)
- A new "Research Focus" box on race and the implementation of the death penalty in the United States (Chapter 8)
- A separate section on the overall economic picture of Latinos as a group (Chapter 9)
- A new "Listen to Our Voices" box entitled "Leaving Cuba" by Alfredo Jimenez (Chapter 9)
- The impact of September 11, 2001 on immigration (Chapter 4) in general and specifically, the Arab and Muslim American community (Chapter 11)
- A new "Research Focus" box on gender roles, comparing Christian and Muslim Arab American women (Chapter 11)
- A new "Listen to Our Voices" box entitled "Pendulum Swings on Civil Rights" by James Zogby (Chapter 11)
- Maps showing the countries of the world that have been the source of Arab immigrants to the United States, and the Arab American population in the United States by state (Chapter 11)
- An ethnic diversity worldwide map illustrating that multiculturalism is a global phenomenon (Chapter 16)

In addition, tables, figures, maps, political cartoons, and Internet Exercises have been updated.

Focus Research Focus Research Focus

- Measuring Multiculturalism (Chapter 1)
- What's in a Name? (Chapter 2)
- Redlining (Chapter 3)
- How Well Are Immigrants Doing? (Chapter 4)
- Measuring the Importance of Religion (Chapter 5)
- Learning the Navajo Way (Chapter 6)
- The Black Church as a Change Agent (Chapter 7)
- The Ultimate Penalty: Execution (Chapter 8)
- Latinas: American Style (Chapter 9)

- Assimilation May Be Hazardous to Your Health (Chapter 10)
- Christian and Muslim Arab American Women's Gender Roles (Chapter 11)
- Aging in America (Chapter 12)
- Chinese Christians or Christian Chinese? (Chapter 13)
- Intermarriage: The Final Step to Assimilation? (Chapter 14)
- Housework and the Gender Divide (Chapter 15)
- Listening to the People (Chapter 16)
- The Face of Ageism (Chapter 17)

Complete Coverage in Four Parts

Any constructive discussion of racial and ethnic minorities must do more than merely describe events. Part I, "Perspectives on Racial and Ethnic Groups," includes the relevant theories and operational definitions that ground the study of race and ethnic relations in the social sciences. We specifically present the functionalist, conflict, and labeling theories of sociology in relation to the study of race and ethnicity. We show the relationship between subordinate groups and the study of stratification. We also introduce the dual labor market theory and the irregular economy from economics and the reference group theory from psychology. The extensive treatment of prejudice and discrimination covers anti-White prejudice as well as the more familiar topic of bigotry aimed at subordinate groups. Discrimination is analyzed from an economic perspective, including the latest efforts to document discrimination in environmental issues such as location of toxic waste facilities and the move to dismantle affirmative action.

In Part II, "Ethnic and Religious Sources of Conflict," we examine some often-ignored sources of intergroup conflict in the United States: White ethnic groups and religious minorities. Diversity in the United States is readily apparent when we look at the ethnic and religious groups that have resulted from waves of immigration. Refugees, now primarily from Haiti and Central America, also continue to raise major issues.

Any student needs to be familiar with the past to understand present forms of discrimination and subordination. Part III, "Major Racial and Ethnic Minority Groups in the United States," brings into sharper focus the history and contemporary status of Native Americans, African Americans, Latinos, Arab and Muslim Americans, Asian Americans, and Jews in the United States. Social institutions such as family, education, politics, health care, religion, and the economy receive special attention for the subordinate groups. The author contends that institutional discrimination, rather than individual action, is the source of conflict between the subordinate and dominant elements in the United States.

Part IV, "Other Patterns of Dominance," includes topics related to American racial and ethnic relations. The author recognizes, as have Gunnar Myrdal and Helen Mayer Hacker before, that relations between women and men resemble those between Blacks and Whites. Therefore, in this book, we consider the position of women as a subordinate group. Since the first edition of *Racial and Ethnic Groups*, published more than 20 years ago, debates over equal rights and abortion have shown no sign of resolution. For women of color, we document the double jeopardy suffered because of their dual subordinate status of race and gender.

Perhaps we can best comprehend intergroup conflict in the United States by comparing it with the ethnic hostilities in other nations. The similarities and differences between the United States and other societies treated in this book are striking. Again, as in the ninth edition, we examine the tensions in Canada, Israel, Mexico, Northern Ireland, and South Africa to document further the diversity of intergroup conflict.

The final chapter highlights other groups that have been the subject of exclusion: the aged, people with disabilities, and gay men and lesbians. This chapter also includes a concluding section that ties together thematically the forces of dominance and subordination that have been the subject of this book.

Features to Aid Students

Several features are included in the text to facilitate student learning. A Chapter Outline appears at the beginning of each chapter and is followed by Highlights, a short section alerting students to important issues and topics to be addressed. To help students review, each chapter ends with a summary Conclusion. The Key Terms are highlighted in bold when they are first introduced in the text and are listed with page numbers at the end of each chapter. Periodically throughout the book, the Intergroup Relations Continuum first presented in Chapter 1 is repeated to reinforce major concepts while addressing the unique social circumstances of individual racial and ethnic groups.

In addition, there is an end-of-book Glossary with full definitions referenced to page numbers. This edition includes both Review Questions and Critical Thinking Questions. The Review Questions are intended to remind the reader of major points, whereas the Critical Thinking Questions encourage students to think more deeply about some of the major issues raised in the chapter. Updated Internet Exercises allow students to do some critical thinking and research on the Web. An Internet Resource Directory has been expanded to allow access to the latest electronic sources. An extensive illustration program, which includes maps and political cartoons, expands the text discussion and provokes thought.

Ancillary Materials

The ancillary materials that accompany this textbook have been carefully created to enhance the topics being discussed.

FOR THE INSTRUCTOR

Instructor's Manual with Tests This carefully prepared manual includes chapter overviews, key term identification exercises, discussion questions, topics for class discussion, audio-visual resources, and test questions in both multiple-choice and essay format.

TestGEN-EQ This computerized software allows instructors to create their own personalized exams, to edit any or all of the existing test questions, and to add new questions. Other special features of this program include random generation of test questions, creation of alternate versions of the same test, a scrambling question sequence, and test preview before printing.

OneKey A one-stop shop for both professors and students, this innovative premium Web site will help professors more effectively prepare lectures and help students more efficiently review the course material. For professors, it will include PowerPoint® presentations, all of the instructor supplements, and testing software. For students, it will include an e-book tied to chapter assessment, flashcards, and self-graded chapter review quizzes. Professor access to OneKey can be gained by contacting your Prentice Hall representative or by visiting www.prenhall.com/onekey for registration. Students can access OneKey when professors order a special package of *Racial and Ethnic Groups 10/E* with a free OneKey access code wrapped with the text.

ABCNEWS *ABC News*/Prentice Hall Video Library for Race and Ethnic Relations Selected video segments from award-winning *ABC News* programs such as *Nightline*, *ABC World News Tonight*, and *20/20* accompany topics featured in the text. An Instructor's Guide is also available. Please contact your Prentice Hall representative for more details.

FOR THE STUDENT

Census 2000 CD-ROM In the back of every new copy of *Racial and Ethnic Groups, 10/E*, is a CD-ROM offering a fun, easy-to-use learning tool that allows the students to view and think critically about the most relevant census documents as they relate to the key concepts and racial and ethnic groups discussed in the text.

The easily accessible format enhances the information with video and audio clips, photos, and detailed maps from the U.S. Census Bureau. Students are given the opportunity to draw conclusions and answer questions about the data. Exercises and activities based on the CD-ROM are indicated in the margins of the text.

SocNote Plus A useful and exciting super study guide, *SocNotes Plus* is Prentice Hall's one-stop resource for students studying racial and ethnic relations. Designed around the chapters in *Racial and Ethnic Groups,* 10/E, it helps students keep their course notes and lecture information in order.

Easy to use and portable, *SocNotes Plus* includes the following for each chapter of this text:

Chapter outline
Learning objectives
Key terms
A notetaking section that includes key concepts and art from the chapter presented in PowerPoint® slide format
Two chapter review tests that include multiple-choice and true-false questions

SocNotes Plus is FREE when packaged with new copies of this text. Please see your local Prentice Hall representative for more details.

OneKey. A one-stop shop for both professors and students, this innovative, premium Web site will help professors more effectively prepare lectures and help students more efficiently review the course material. For professors, it will include PowerPoint® presentations, all of the instructor supplements, and testing software. For students, it will include an e-book tied to chapter assessment, flashcards, and self-graded chapter review quizzes. Professor access to OneKey can be gained by contacting your Prentice Hall representative or by visiting www.prenhall.com/onekey for registration. Students can access OneKey when professors order a special package of *Racial and Ethnic Groups,* 10/E, with a free OneKey access code wrapped with the text.

Companion Website™ In tandem with the text, students can now take full advantage of the World Wide Web to enrich their study of material found in the text. This resource correlates the text with related material available on the Internet. Features of the Web site include chapter objectives, study questions, census updates, and links to interesting material and information from other sites on the Web that can reinforce and enhance the content of each chapter. **Address**: www.prenhall.com/schaefer

*The New York Times/***Prentice Hall** *eThemes of the Times* *The New York Times* and Prentice Hall are sponsoring *eThemes of the Times,* a program designed to enhance student access to current information relevant to the classroom. Through this program, the core subject matter provided in the text is supplemented by a collection of timely articles downloaded from one of the world's most distinguished newspapers, *The New York Times.* These articles demonstrate the vital, ongoing connection between what is learned in the classroom and what is happening in the world around us. Access to *The New York Times/*Prentice Hall *eThemes of the Times* is available on the Schaefer Companion Website™.

 **OneSearch with Research Navigator™: Sociology** This guide focuses on using **Research Navigator™**—Prentice Hall's own gateway to databases—including *The New York Times* Search-by-Subject Archive, ContentSelect™ Academic Journal Database powered by EBSCO, *The Financial Times*, and the *Best of the Web* Link Library. It also includes extensive appendices on documenting online sources and on avoiding plagiarism. This guide, along with the Research Navigator™ access code, is free to students when packaged with *Racial and Ethnic Groups*, 10/E.

TIME **TIME Special Edition: Sociology** Prentice Hall and TIME Magazine are pleased to offer you and your students a chance to examine today's most current and compelling issues in an exciting new way. TIME Special Edition: Sociology offers a selection of 20 TIME articles on today's most current issues and debates in Sociology. TIME Special Edition provides your students the full coverage, accessible writing, and bold photographs that TIME is known for. Free when packaged with *Racial and Ethnic Groups*, 10/E, it is perfect for discussion groups, in-class debates, or research assignments. Please see your local Prentice Hall representative.

"10 Ways to Fight Hate" brochure Produced by the Southern Poverty Law Center, the leading hate-crime and crime-watch organization in the United States, this brochure walks students through ten steps that they can take on their own campus or in their own neighborhood to fight hate every day. Free when packaged with *Racial and Ethnic Groups*, 10/E.

Acknowledgments

The tenth edition benefited from the thoughtful reaction of my students in classes. Data analysis of the General Social Survey and Census Bureau data sets was provided by my faculty colleague Kiljoong Kim of DePaul University. Kellie Small, a student at DePaul, assisted with special tasks related to the preparation of the manuscript.

The tenth edition was improved by the suggestions of Deborah Brunson, University of North Carolina–Wilmington; Jac D. Bulk, University of Wisconsin–La Crosse; Efren N. Padilla, California State University–Hayward; and Kristen M. Wallingford, Davidson College. In addition, an early draft of the new material on Muslim and Arab Americans benefited from the comments of Seif Da'Na, University of Wisconsin–Parkside; Gary David, Bentley College; Aminah McCloud, DePaul University; and Gina Petonito, Western Illinois University.

I would also like to thank my editors, Sharon Chambliss and Nancy Roberts, for developing this tenth edition. They make a great team in the production of academic books.

The truly exciting challenge of writing and researching has always been for me an enriching experience, mostly because of the supportive home I share with my wife, Sandy. She knows so well my appreciation and gratitude, now as in the past and in the future.

Richard T. Schaefer
schaeferrt@aol.com
www.schaefersociology.net

About the Author

Richard T. Schaefer grew up in Chicago at a time when neighborhoods were going through transitions in ethnic and racial composition. He found himself increasingly intrigued by what was happening, how people were reacting, and how these changes were affecting neighborhoods and people's jobs. In high school, he took a course in sociology. His interest in social issues caused him to gravitate to more sociology courses at Northwestern University, where he eventually received a B.A. in sociology.

"Originally as an undergraduate I thought I would go on to law school and become a lawyer. But after taking a few sociology courses, I found myself wanting to learn more about what sociologists studied, and fascinated by the kinds of questions they raised," Dr. Schaefer says. "Perhaps the most fascinating and, to me, relevant to the 1960s was the intersection of race, gender, and social class." This interest led him to obtain his M.A. and Ph.D. in sociology from the University of Chicago. Dr. Schaefer's continuing interest in race relations led him to write his master's thesis on the membership of the Ku Klux Klan and his doctoral thesis on racial prejudice and race relations in Great Britain.

Dr. Schaefer went on to become a professor of sociology. He has taught sociology and courses on multiculturalism for 30 years. He has been invited to give special presentations to students and faculty on racial and ethnic diversity in Illinois, Indiana, Missouri, North Carolina, Ohio, and Texas.

Dr. Schaefer is author of *Race and Ethnicity in the United States*, Third Edition (Prentice Hall). Dr. Schaefer is also the author of the ninth edition of *Sociology* (2005), the sixth edition of *Sociology: A Brief Introduction* (2006), and the second edition of *Sociology Matters* (2006). His articles and book reviews have appeared in many journals, including *American Journal of Sociology*, *Phylon: A Review of Race and Culture*, *Contemporary Sociology*, *Sociology and Social Research*, *Sociological Quarterly*, and *Teaching Sociology*. He served as president of the Midwest Sociological Society from 1994–1995. In recognition of his achievements in undergraduate teaching, he was named Vincent de Paul Professor of Sociology in 2004.

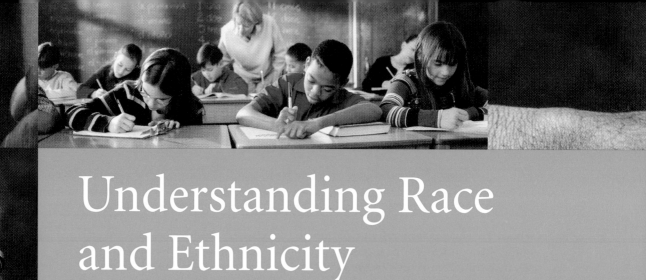

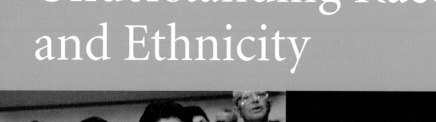

1

Understanding Race and Ethnicity

CHAPTER OUTLINE

MINORITY GROUPS ARE SUBORDINATED IN TERMS OF POWER and privilege to the majority, or dominant, group. A minority is defined not by being outnumbered but by five characteristics: unequal treatment, distinguishing physical or cultural traits, involuntary membership, awareness of subordination and in-group marriage. Subordinate groups are classified in terms of race, ethnicity, religion, and gender. The social importance of race is derived from a process of racial formation; its biological significance is uncertain. The theoretical perspectives of functionalism, conflict theory, and labeling offer insights into the sociology of intergroup relations.

Immigration, annexation, and colonialism are processes that may create subordinate groups. Other processes such as expulsion may remove the presence of a subordinate group. Significant for racial and ethnic oppression in the United States today is the distinction between assimilation and pluralism. Assimilation demands subordinate-group conformity to the dominant group, and pluralism implies mutual respect between diverse groups.

In the wake of the September 11, 2001, terrorist attacks in the United States, Alexandr Manin, a citizen of Kazakhstan, joined the military in October 2001. He was not joining some far-flung military effort of his country of birth: The 25-year-old from Brooklyn was joining the U.S. Marine Corps. A legal permanent resident, Alexandr can join the U.S. military even though he is not a citizen. His decision is not that unusual. Thousands of immigrants join each year; indeed, recently in cities such as New York, Miami, and Los Angeles immigrant enlistees have been joining in higher proportions than their peers in the general population. Some do it for the training or employment possibilities, but others are motivated by allegiance to their new country. As Alexandr said, "It doesn't matter that America is not my country; New York is my city, and what happened shook my life. I feel patriotic, and I have this itch now to go sooner" (Chen and Sengupta 2001:A1).

So the United States, with its diverse racial and ethnic heritage and new immigrants, is a country that respects its multiculturalism. Or does it?

In July 2004, Jefferson County in Texas tried to bring to a close a century of debate. Over the objections of many residents, the County Board decided to rename a stretch of road known as "Jap Road." Named for the Japanese rice farmers who had settled there in the 19TH century, the name had stuck despite generations of objections by Asian Americans and others. Finally change came (T. Marshall 2004).

Lewiston, Maine, is also adjusting. In this old New England town, hundreds of Somalis have arrived seeking work and affordable housing thousands of miles from their African hometowns, which were torn apart by civil strife and famine. Residents expressed alarm over this influx, prompting the mayor to send a letter to all the Somalis already in Lewiston to discourage friends and relatives from relocating there. The pace of Somalis resettling to the Lewistown, many of them American citizens, slowed significantly amidst the furor (C. Jones 2003).

Relations between racial and ethnic groups are not like relations between family members. The history of the United States is one of racial oppression. It goes well beyond a mayor in Maine or people living on a road in Texas not liking people of a certain color or national origin. Episodes of a new social identity developing, as in the case of Alexandr Manin, are not unusual, but that does not mean that the society is not structured to keep some groups of people down and extend privileges automatically to other groups based on race, ethnicity, or gender.

People in the United States and elsewhere are beginning to consider that the same principles that guarantee equality based on race or gender can apply to other groups who are discriminated against. There have been growing efforts to ensure that the same rights and privileges are available to all people, regardless of age, disability, or sexual orientation. These concerns are emerging even as the old divisions over race, ethnicity, and religion continue to fester and occasionally explode into violence that envelops entire nations.

CD-ROM *Activity 1.0*

The United States is a very diverse nation, as shown in Table 1.1. According to the 2000 census, about 17 percent of the population are members of racial minorities, and about another 13 percent are Hispanic. These percentages represent almost one of three people in the United States, without counting White ethnic groups. As shown in Figure 1.1, between 2000 and 2100 the population in the United States is expected to rise from 30 percent Black, Hispanic, Asian, and Native American to 60 percent.

TABLE 1.1
Racial and Ethnic Groups in the United States, 2000

Classification	Number in Thousands	Percentage of Total Population
RACIAL GROUPS		
Whites (includes 16.9 million White Hispanic)	211,461	75.1
Blacks/African Americans	34,658	12.3
Native Americans, Alaskan Native	2,476	0.9
Asian Americans	10,243	3.6
Chinese	2,433	0.9
Filipinos	1,850	0.7
Asian Indians	1,679	0.6
Vietnamese	1,123	0.4
Koreans	1,077	0.4
Japanese	797	0.2
Other	1,285	0.5
ETHNIC GROUPS		
White ancestry (single or mixed)		
Germans	42,842	15.2
Irish	30,525	10.8
English	24,509	8.7
Italians	15,638	5.6
Poles	8,977	3.2
French	8,310	3.0
Jews	5,200	1.8
Hispanics (or Latinos)	35,306	12.5
Mexican Americans	23,337	8.3
Central and South Americans	5,119	1.8
Puerto Ricans	3,178	1.1
Cubans	1,412	0.5
Other	2,260	0.8
TOTAL (ALL GROUPS)	281,422	

Note: Percentages do not total 100 percent, and subheads do not add up to figures in major heads because of overlap between groups (e.g., Polish American Jews or people of mixed ancestry, such as Irish and Italian).

Source: Brittingham and de la Cruz 2004; Bureau of the Census 2003a; Grieco and Cassidy 2001; Therrien and Ramirez 2001; United Jewish Communities 2001.

Although the composition of the population is changing, the problems of prejudice, discrimination, and mistrust remain.

What Is a Subordinate Group?

Identifying a subordinate group or a minority in a society seems to be a simple enough task. In the United States, the groups readily identified as minorities—Blacks and Native Americans, for example—are outnumbered by non-Blacks and non-Native Americans. However, minority status is not necessarily the result of being outnumbered. A social minority need not be a mathematical one. A **minority group** is a subordinate group whose members have significantly less control or power over their own lives than do the members of a dominant or majority group. In sociology, *minority* means the same as *subordinate*, and *dominant* is used interchangeably with *majority*.

minority group
A subordinate group whose members have significantly less control or power over their own lives than do the members of a dominant or majority group.

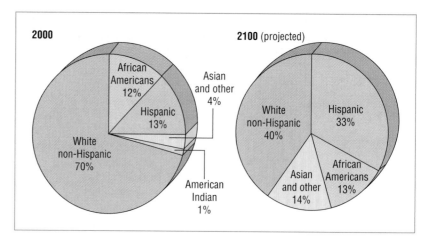

FIGURE 1.1   Population of the United States by Race and Ethnicity, 2000 and 2100 (Projected)

According to projections by the Census Bureau, the proportion of residents of the United States who are White and non-Hispanic will decrease significantly by the year 2050. By contrast, there will be a striking rise in the proportion of both Hispanic Americans and Asian Americans.

Source: Bureau of the Census 2004b.

Confronted with evidence that a particular minority in the United States is subordinate to the majority, some people respond, "Why not? After all, this is a democracy, so the majority rules." However, the subordination of a minority involves more than its inability to rule over society. A member of a subordinate or minority group experiences a narrowing of life's opportunities—for success, education, wealth, the pursuit of happiness—that goes beyond any personal shortcoming he or she may have. A minority group does not share in proportion to its numbers what a given society, such as the United States, defines as valuable.

Being superior in numbers does not guarantee a group control over its destiny and ensure majority status. In 1920, the majority of people in Mississippi and South Carolina were African Americans. Yet African Americans did not have as much control over their lives as Whites, let alone control of the states of Mississippi and South Carolina. Throughout the United States today are counties or neighborhoods in which the majority of people are African American, Native American, or Hispanic, but White Americans are the dominant force. Nationally, 50.8 percent of the population is female, but males still dominate positions of authority and wealth well beyond their numbers.

A minority or subordinate group has five characteristics: unequal treatment, distinguishing physical or cultural traits, involuntary membership, awareness of subordination, and in-group marriage (Wagley and Harris 1958):

1. Members of a minority experience unequal treatment and have less power over their lives than members of a dominant group have over theirs. Prejudice, discrimination, segregation, and even extermination create this social inequality.

2. Members of a minority group share physical or cultural characteristics that distinguish them from the dominant group, such as skin color or language. Each society has its own arbitrary standard for determining which characteristics are most important in defining dominant and minority groups.

3. Membership in a dominant or minority group is not voluntary: People are born into the group. A person does not choose to be African American or White.

4. Minority-group members have a strong sense of group solidarity. William Graham Sumner, writing in 1906, noted that people make distinctions between members

of their own group (the in-group) and everyone else (the out-group). When a group is the object of long-term prejudice and discrimination, the feeling of "us versus them" often becomes intense.

5. Members of a minority generally marry others from the same group. A member of a dominant group often is unwilling to join a supposedly inferior minority by marrying one of its members. In addition, the minority group's sense of solidarity encourages marriage within the group and discourages marriage to outsiders.

racial group
A group that is socially set apart because of obvious physical differences.

ethnic group
A group set apart from others because of its national origin or distinctive cultural patterns.

Types of Subordinate Groups

There are four types of minority or subordinate groups. All four, except where noted, have the five properties previously outlined. The four criteria for classifying minority groups are race, ethnicity, religion, and gender.

Racial Groups

The term **racial group** is reserved for minorities and the corresponding majorities that are socially set apart because of obvious physical differences. Notice the two crucial words in the definition: *obvious* and *physical*. What is obvious? Hair color? Shape of an earlobe? Presence of body hair? To whom are these differences obvious, and why? Each society defines what it finds obvious.

In the United States, skin color is one obvious difference. On a cold winter day when one has clothing covering all but one's head, however, skin color may be less obvious than hair color. Yet people in the United States have learned informally that skin color is important, and hair color is unimportant. We need to say more than that. In the United States, people have traditionally classified and classify themselves as either Black or White. There is no in-between state except for people readily identified as Native Americans or Asian Americans. Later in this chapter we will explore this issue more deeply and see how such assumptions have very complex implications.

Other societies use skin color as a standard but may have a more elaborate system of classification. In Brazil, where hostility between races is less than in the United States, numerous categories identify people on the basis of skin color. In the United States, a person is Black or White. In Brazil, a variety of terms, such as *cafuso, mazombo, preto,* and *escuro,* are applied to describe various combinations of skin color, facial features, and hair texture. What makes differences obvious is subject to a society's definition.

The designation of a racial group emphasizes physical differences as opposed to cultural distinctions. In the United States, minority races include Blacks, Native Americans (or American Indians), Japanese Americans, Chinese Americans, Arab Americans, Filipinos, Hawaiians, and other Asian peoples. The issue of race and racial differences has been an important one, not only in the United States but throughout the entire sphere of European influence. Later in this chapter we will examine race and its significance more closely. We should not forget that Whites are a race, too. As we will consider in Chapter 5, who is White has been subject to change over time as certain European groups were felt historically not to deserve being considered White, but over time, partly to compete against a growing Black population, the whiting of some European Americans has occurred.

Ethnic Groups

Ethnic minority groups are differentiated from the dominant group on the basis of cultural differences, such as language, attitudes toward marriage and parenting, and food habits. **Ethnic groups** are groups set apart from others because of their national origin or distinctive cultural patterns.

Ethnic Groups [handwritten marginal note]

Ethnic groups in the United States include a grouping that we call Hispanics or Latinos, which includes Mexican Americans, Puerto Ricans, Cubans, and other Latin Americans in the United States. Hispanics can be either Black or White, as in the case of a dark-skinned Puerto Rican who may be taken as Black in central Texas but be viewed as a Puerto Rican in New York City. The ethnic group category also includes White ethnics, such as Irish Americans, Polish Americans, and Norwegian Americans.

The cultural traits that make groups distinctive usually originate from their homeland or, for Jews, from a long history of being segregated and prohibited from becoming a part of the host society. Once in the United States, an immigrant group may maintain distinctive cultural practices through associations, clubs, and worship. Ethnic enclaves such as a Little Haiti or a Greektown in urban areas also perpetuate cultural distinctiveness.

Some racial groups may also have unique cultural traditions, as we can readily see in the many Chinatowns throughout the United States. For racial groups, however, the physical distinctiveness and not the cultural differences generally prove to be the barrier to acceptance by the host society. For example, Chinese Americans who are faithful Protestants and know the names of all the members of the Baseball Hall of Fame may be bearers of American culture. Yet these Chinese Americans are still part of a minority because they are seen as physically different.

Ethnicity continues to be important, as recent events in Bosnia and other parts of Eastern Europe have demonstrated. Almost a century ago, African American sociologist W. E. B. Du Bois, addressing an audience in London, called attention to the overwhelming importance of the color line throughout the world. In "Listen to Our Voices," we read the remarks of Du Bois, the first Black person to receive a doctorate from Harvard, who later helped to organize the National Association for the Advancement of Colored People (NAACP). Du Bois's observances give us a historic perspective on the struggle for equality. We can look ahead, knowing how far we have come and speculating on how much further we have to go.

Religious Groups

Association with a religion other than the dominant faith is the third basis for minority-group status. In the United States, Protestants, as a group, outnumber members of all other religions. Roman Catholics form the largest minority religion. Chapter 5 focuses on the increasing Judeo-Christian-Islamic diversity of the United States. For people who are not a part of the Christian tradition, such as followers of Islam, allegiance to the faith often is misunderstood and stigmatizes people. This stigmatization became especially widespread and legitimated by government action in the aftermath of the 9/11 attacks.

Religious minorities [handwritten marginal note]

Religious minorities include such groups as the Church of Jesus Christ of Latter-day Saints (the Mormons), Jehovah's Witnesses, Amish, Muslims, and Buddhists. Cults or sects associated with such practices as animal sacrifice, doomsday prophecy, demon worship, or the use of snakes in a ritualistic fashion would also constitute minorities. Jews are excluded from this category and placed among ethnic groups. Culture is a more important defining trait for Jewish people worldwide than is religious dogma. Jewish Americans share a cultural tradition that goes beyond theology. In this sense, it is appropriate to view them as an ethnic group rather than as members of a religious faith.

Gender Groups

Gender is another attribute that creates dominant and subordinate groups. Males are the social majority; females, although more numerous, are relegated to the position of the social minority—a subordinate status to be explored in detail in Chapter 15. Women are considered a minority even though they do not exhibit all the characteristics outlined earlier (e.g., there is little in-group marriage). Women encounter preju-

Voices Listen to Our Voices Listen to

PROBLEM OF THE COLOR LINE

In the metropolis of the modern world, in this the closing year of the nineteenth century, there has been assembled a congress of men and women of African blood, to deliberate solemnly upon the present situation and outlook of the darker races of mankind. The problem of the twentieth century is the problem of the color line, the question as to how far differences of race—which show themselves chiefly in the color of the skin and the texture of the hair—will hereafter be made the basis of denying to over half the world the right of sharing to their utmost ability the opportunities and privileges of modern civilization. . . .

Let the world take no backward step in that slow but sure progress which has succes-

W. E. B. Du Bois

sively refused to let the spirit of class, of caste, of privilege, or of birth, debar from life, liberty and the pursuit of happiness a striving human soul.

Let not color or race be a feature of distinction between white and black men, regardless of worth or ability. . . .

Thus we appeal with boldness and confidence to the Great Powers of the civilized world, trusting in the wide spirit of humanity, and the deep sense of justice of our age, for a generous recognition of the righteousness of our cause. ▪

Source: Du Bois [1969a]. From pp. 20–21, 23, in *An ABC of Color*, by W. E. B. Du Bois. Copyright 1969 by International Publishers.

---

dice and discrimination and are physically distinguishable. Group membership is involuntary, and many women have developed a sense of sisterhood. Women who are members of racial and ethnic minorities face a special challenge to achieving equality. They suffer from double jeopardy because they belong to two separate minority groups: a racial or ethnic group plus a subordinate gender group.

Other Subordinate Groups

This book focuses on groups that meet a set of criteria for subordinate status. People encounter prejudice or are excluded from full participation in society for many reasons. Racial, ethnic, religious, and gender barriers are the main ones, but there are others. Age, disabilities, and sexual orientation are among the factors that are used to subordinate groups of people. As a result, in Chapter 17 we will go beyond the title of the book and consider other groups of people who have been excluded from all that society offers and witness their fight against prejudice and discrimination.

Does Race Matter?

We see people around us—some of whom may look quite different from us. Do these differences matter? The simple answer is no, but because so many people have for so long acted as if difference in physical characteristics as well geographic origin and shared culture do matter, distinct groups have been created in people's minds. Race

Given the diversity in the nation, the workplace is increasingly a place where intergroup tensions may develop.

has many meanings for many people. Often these meanings are inaccurate and based on theories discarded by scientists generations ago. As we will see, race is a socially constructed concept (J. Young 2003).

Biological Meaning

The way the term *race* has been used by some people to apply to human beings lacks any scientific meaning. We cannot identify distinctive physical characteristics for groups of human beings the way scientists do to distinguish one animal species from another. The idea of **biological race** is based on the mistaken notion of a genetically isolated human group.

Even among past proponents that sharp, scientific divisions exist among humans, there were endless debates over what the races of the world were. Given people's frequent migration, exploration, and invasions, pure genetic types have not existed for some time, if they ever did. There are no mutually exclusive races. Skin color among African Americans varies tremendously, as it does among White Americans. There is even an overlapping of dark-skinned Whites and light-skinned African Americans. If we grouped people by genetic resistance to malaria and by fingerprint patterns, Norwegians and many African groups would be of the same race. If we grouped people by some digestive capacities, some Africans, Asians, and southern Europeans would be of one group and West Africans and northern Europeans of another (Leehotz 1995; Shanklin 1994).

Biologically there are no pure, distinct races. For example, blood type cannot distinguish racial groups with any accuracy. Furthermore, applying pure racial types to humans is problematic because of interbreeding. Despite continuing prejudice about Black-White marriages, a large number of Whites have African American ancestry. Scientists, using various techniques, maintain that the proportion of African Americans with White ancestry is between 20 and 75 percent. Despite the wide range of these estimates, the mixed ancestry of today's Blacks and Whites is part of the biological reality of race (Herskovits 1930:15; Roberts 1955).

biological race
The mistaken notion of a genetically isolated human group.

Even the latest research as a part of the Human Genome Project mapping human DNA has only served to confirm genetic diversity with differences within traditionally regarded racial groups (e.g., Black Africans) much greater than that between groups (e.g., between Black Africans and Europeans). Research has also been conducted to determine whether personality characteristics such as temperament and nervous habits are inherited among minority groups. Not surprisingly, the question of whether races have different innate levels of intelligence has led to the most explosive controversy (Bamshad and Olson 2003).

Typically, intelligence is measured as an **intelligence quotient** (IQ), the ratio of a person's mental age to his or her chronological age, multiplied by 100, where 100 represents average intelligence and higher scores represent greater intelligence. It should be noted that there is little consensus over just what intelligence is, other than as defined by such IQ tests. Intelligence tests are adjusted for a person's age, so that 10-year-olds take a very different test from someone aged 20. Although research shows that certain learning strategies can improve a person's IQ, generally IQ remains stable as one ages.

A great deal of debate continues over the accuracy of these tests. Are they biased toward people who come to the tests with knowledge similar to that of the test writers? Consider the following two questions used on standard tests.

1. Runner: marathon (A) envoy: embassy, (B) oarsman: regatta, (C) martyr: massacre, (D) referee: tournament.
2. Your mother sends you to a store to get a loaf of bread. The store is closed. What should you do? (A) return home, (B) go to the next store, (C) wait until it opens, (D) ask a stranger for advice.

Both correct answers are B. But is a lower-class youth likely to know, in the first question, what a regatta is? Skeptics argue that such test questions do not truly measure intellectual potential. Inner-city youths often have been shown to respond with A to the second question because that may be the only store with which the family has credit. Youths in rural areas, where the next store may be miles away, are also unlikely to respond with the designated correct answer. The issue of culture bias in tests remains an unresolved concern. The most recent research shows that differences in intelligence scores between Blacks and Whites are almost eliminated when adjustments are made for social and economic characteristics (Brooks-Gunn et al. 1996; Herrnstein and Murray 1994:30; Kagan 1971; J. Young 2003).

The second issue, trying to associate these results with certain subpopulations such as races, also has a long history. In the past, a few have contended that Whites have more intelligence on average than Blacks. All researchers agree that within-group differences are greater than any speculated differences between groups. The range of intelligence among, for example, Korean Americans is much greater than any average difference between them as a group and Japanese Americans.

The third issue relates to the subpopulations themselves. If Blacks or Whites are not mutually exclusive biologically, how can there be measurable differences? Many Whites and most Blacks have mixed ancestry that complicates any supposed inheritance of intelligence issue. Both groups reflect a rich heritage of very dissimilar populations, from Swedes to Slovaks and Zulus to Tutus.

In 1994, an 845-page book unleashed a new national debate on the issue of IQ. The latest research effort of psychologist Richard J. Herrnstein and social scientist Charles Murray (1994), published in *The Bell Curve*, concluded that 60 percent of IQ is inheritable and that racial groups offer a convenient means to generalize about any differences in intelligence. Unlike most other proponents of the race-IQ link, the authors offered policy suggestions that include ending welfare to discourage births among low-IQ poor women and changing immigration laws so that the IQ pool in the United States is not diminished. Herrnstein and Murray even made generalizations

intelligence quotient
The ratio of a person's mental age (as computed by an IQ test) to his or her chronological age, multiplied by 100.

about IQ levels among Asians and Hispanics in the United States, groups subject to even more intermarriage. It is not possible to generalize about absolute differences between groups, such as Latinos versus Whites, when almost half of Latinos in the United States marry non-Hispanics.

Years later, the mere mention of "the bell curve" signals to many the belief in a racial hierarchy with Whites toward the top and Blacks near the bottom. The research present then and repeated today points to the difficulty in definitions: What is intelligence, and what constitutes a racial group, given generations, if not centuries, of intermarriage? How can we speak of definitive inherited racial differences if there has been intermarriage between people of every color? Furthermore, as people on both sides of the debate have noted, regardless of the findings, we would still want to strive to maximize the talents of each individual. All research shows that the differences within a group are much greater than any alleged differences between group averages.

All these issues and controversial research have led to the basic question of what difference it would make if there were significant differences. No researcher believes that race can be used to predict one's intelligence. Also, there is a general agreement that certain intervention strategies can improve scholastic achievement and even intelligence as defined by standard tests. Should we mount efforts to upgrade the abilities of those alleged to be below average? These debates tend to contribute to a sense of hopelessness among some policy makers who think that biology is destiny, rather than causing them to rethink the issue or expand positive intervention efforts.

Why does such IQ research re-emerge if the data are subject to different interpretations? The argument that "we" are superior to "them" is very appealing to the dominant group. It justifies receiving opportunities that are denied to others. For example, the authors of *The Bell Curve* argue that intelligence significantly determines the poverty problem in the United States. We can anticipate that the debate over IQ and the allegations of significant group differences will continue. Policy makers need to acknowledge the difficulty in treating race as a biologically significant characteristic.

Social Construction of Race

If race does not distinguish humans from one another biologically, why does it seem to be so important? It is important because of the social meaning people have attached to it. The 1950 (UNESCO) Statement on Race maintains that "for all practical social purposes 'race' is not so much a biological phenomenon as a social myth" (Montagu 1972:118). Adolf Hitler expressed concern over the "Jewish race" and translated this concern into Nazi death camps. Winston Churchill spoke proudly of the "British race" and used that pride to spur a nation to fight. Evidently, race was a useful political tool for two very different leaders in the 1930s and 1940s.

Race is a social construction, and this process benefits the oppressor, who defines who is privileged and who is not. The acceptance of race in a society as a legitimate category allows racial hierarchies to emerge to the benefit of the dominant "races." For example, inner-city drive-by shootings have come to be seen as a race-specific problem worthy of local officials cleaning up troubled neighborhoods. Yet schoolyard shoot-outs are viewed as a societal concern and placed on the national agenda.

People could speculate that if human groups have obvious physical differences, then they could have corresponding mental or personality differences. No one disagrees that people differ in temperament, potential to learn, and sense of humor. In its social sense, race implies that groups that differ physically also bear distinctive emotional and mental abilities or disabilities. These beliefs are based on the notion that humankind can be divided into distinct groups. We have already seen the difficulties associated with pigeonholing people into racial categories. Despite these difficulties, belief in the inheritance of behavior patterns and in an association between physical and cultural traits is widespread. It is called **racism** when this belief is coupled with the feeling that certain

racism
A doctrine that one race is superior.

groups or races are inherently superior to others. Racism is a doctrine of racial supremacy, stating that one race is superior to another (Bash 2001; Bonilla-Silva 1996).

We questioned the biological significance of race in the previous section. In modern complex industrial societies, we find little adaptive utility in the presence or absence of prominent chins, epicanthic folds of the eyelids, or the comparative amount of melanin in the skin. What is important is not that people are genetically different but that they approach one another with dissimilar perspectives. It is in the social setting that race is decisive. Race is significant because people have given it significance.

Race definitions are crystallized through what Michael Omi and Howard Winant (1994) called racial formation. **Racial formation** is a sociohistorical process by which racial categories are created, inhibited, transformed, and destroyed. Those in power define groups of people in a certain way that depends on a racist social structure. The Native Americans and the creation of the reservation system for Native Americans in the late 1800s is an example of this racial formation. The federal American Indian policy combined previously distinctive tribes into a single group. No one escapes the extent and frequency to which we are subjected to racial formation.

In the southern United States, the social construction of race was known as the "one-drop rule." This tradition stipulated that if a person had even a single drop of "Black blood," that person was defined and viewed as Black. Today children of biracial or multiracial marriages try to build their own identity in a country that seems intent on placing them in some single, traditional category.

Who are we in terms of race or ethnicity? These concepts in the United States are socially constructed and while most of the time we think we can correctly identify people around us, sometimes we cannot.

Sociology and the Study of Race and Ethnicity

Before proceeding further with our study of racial and ethnic groups, let us consider several sociological perspectives that provide insight into dominant-subordinate relationships. **Sociology** is the systematic study of social behavior and human groups and therefore is aptly suited to enlarge our understanding of intergroup relations. There is a long, valuable history of the study of race relations in sociology. Admittedly, it has not always been progressive; indeed, at times it has reflected the prejudices of society. In some instances, scholars who are members of racial, ethnic, and religious minorities, as well as women, have not been permitted to make the kind of contributions they are capable of making to the field.

Stratification by Class and Gender

All societies are characterized by members having unequal amounts of wealth, prestige, or power. Sociologists observe that entire groups may be assigned less or more of what a society values. The hierarchy that emerges is called stratification. **Stratification** is the structured ranking of entire groups of people that perpetuates unequal rewards and power in a society.

Much discussion of stratification identifies the **class**, or social ranking, of people who share similar wealth, according to sociologist Max Weber's classic definition. Mobility from one class to another is not easy. Movement into classes of greater wealth may be particularly difficult for subordinate-group members faced with lifelong prejudice and discrimination (Gerth and Mills 1958).

Recall that the first property of subordinate-group standing is unequal treatment by the dominant group in the form of prejudice, discrimination, and segregation. Stratification is intertwined with the subordination of racial, ethnic, religious, and gender groups. Race has implications for the way people are treated; so does class. One also has to add the effects of race and class together. For example, being poor and Black is not the same as being either one by itself. A wealthy Mexican American is not the same as an affluent Anglo or as Mexican Americans as a group.

racial formation
A sociohistorical process by which racial categories are created, inhibited, transformed, and destroyed.

sociology
The systematic study of social behavior and human groups.

stratification
A structured ranking of entire groups of people that perpetuates unequal rewards and power in a society.

class
As defined by Max Weber, people who share similar levels of wealth.

functionalist perspective
A sociological approach emphasizing how parts of a society are structured to maintain its stability.

Public discussion of issues such as housing or public assistance often is disguised as discussion of class issues, when in fact the issues are based primarily on race. Similarly, some topics such as the poorest of poor or the working poor are addressed in terms of race when the class component should be explicit. Nonetheless, the link between race and class in society is abundantly clear (Winant 1994).

Another stratification factor that we need to consider is gender. How different is the situation for women as contrasted with men? Returning again to the first property of minority groups—unequal treatment and less control—treatment of women is not equal to that received by men. Whether the issue is jobs or poverty, education or crime, the experience of women typically is more difficult. In addition, the situation faced by women in such areas as health care and welfare raises different concerns than it does for men. Just as we need to consider the role of social class to understand race and ethnicity better, we also need to consider the role of gender.

Theoretical Perspectives

Sociologists view society in different ways. Some see the world basically as a stable and ongoing entity. They are impressed by the endurance of a Chinatown, the general sameness of male-female roles over time, and other aspects of intergroup relations. Some sociologists see society as composed of many groups in conflict, competing for scarce resources. Within this conflict, some people or even entire groups may be labeled or stigmatized in a way that blocks their access to what a society values. We will examine three theoretical perspectives that are widely used by sociologists today: the functionalist, conflict, and labeling perspectives.

Functionalist Perspective   In the view of a functionalist, a society is like a living organism in which each part contributes to the survival of the whole. The **functionalist perspective** emphasizes how the parts of society are structured to maintain its stability. According to this approach, if an aspect of social life does not contribute to a society's stability or survival, it will not be passed on from one generation to the next.

It seems reasonable to assume that bigotry between races offers no such positive function, and so we ask, why does it persist? Although agreeing that racial hostility is hardly to be admired, the functionalist would point out that it serves some positive functions from the perspective of the racists. We can identify five functions that racial beliefs have for the dominant group.

Diversity brings new challenges but also new opportunities. California-based Network Omni provides translation services in 150 languages to a variety of corporations and government agencies.

1. Racist ideologies provide a moral justification for maintaining a society that routinely deprives a group of its rights and privileges.
2. Racist beliefs discourage subordinate people from attempting to question their lowly status; to do so is to question the very foundations of the society.
3. Racial ideologies not only justify existing practices but also serve as a rallying point for social movements, as seen in the rise of the Nazi party.
4. Racist myths encourage support for the existing order. Some argue that if there were any major societal change, the subordinate group would suffer even greater poverty, and the dominant group would suffer lower living standards (Nash 1962).
5. Racist beliefs relieve the dominant group of the responsibility to address the economic and educational problems faced by subordinate groups.

As a result, racial ideology grows when a value system (e.g., that underlying a colonial empire or slavery) is being threatened.

There are also definite dysfunctions caused by prejudice and discrimination. **Dysfunctions** are elements of society that may disrupt a social system or decrease its stability. There are six ways in which racism is dysfunctional to a society, including to its dominant group.

1. A society that practices discrimination fails to use the resources of all individuals. Discrimination limits the search for talent and leadership to the dominant group.
2. Discrimination aggravates social problems such as poverty, delinquency, and crime and places the financial burden of alleviating these problems on the dominant group.
3. Society must invest a good deal of time and money to defend the barriers that prevent the full participation of all members.
4. Racial prejudice and discrimination undercut goodwill and friendly diplomatic relations between nations. They also negatively affect efforts to increase global trade.
5. Social change is inhibited because change may assist a subordinate group.
6. Discrimination promotes disrespect for law enforcement and for the peaceful settlement of disputes.

That racism has costs for the dominant group as well as for the subordinate group reminds us that intergroup conflict is exceedingly complex (Bowser and Hunt 1996; Feagin et al. 2000; Rose 1951).

Conflict Perspective   In contrast to the functionalists' emphasis on stability, conflict sociologists see the social world as being in continual struggle. The **conflict perspective** assumes that the social structure is best understood in terms of conflict or tension between competing groups. Specifically, society is a struggle between the privileged (the dominant group) and the exploited (the subordinate groups). Such conflicts need not be physically violent and may take the form of immigration restrictions, real estate practices, or disputes over cuts in the federal budget.

The conflict model often is selected today when one is examining race and ethnicity because it readily accounts for the presence of tension between competing groups. According to the conflict perspective, competition takes place between groups with unequal amounts of economic and political power. The minorities are exploited or, at best, ignored by the dominant group. The conflict perspective is viewed as more radical and activist than functionalism because conflict theorists emphasize social change and the redistribution of resources. Functionalists are not necessarily in favor of inequality; rather, their approach helps us to understand why such systems persist.

Those who follow the conflict approach to race and ethnicity have remarked repeatedly that the subordinate group is criticized for its low status. That the dominant group

dysfunction
An element of society that may disrupt a social system or decrease its stability.

conflict perspective
A sociological approach that assumes that the social structure is best understood in terms of conflict or tension between competing groups.

blaming the victim
Portraying the problems of racial and ethnic minorities as their fault rather than recognizing society's responsibility.

labeling theory
A sociological approach introduced by Howard Becker that attempts to explain why certain people are viewed as deviants and others engaging in the same behavior are not.

stereotypes
Unreliable, exaggerated generalizations about all members of a group that do not take individual differences into account.

self-fulfilling prophecy
The tendency to respond to and act on the basis of stereotypes, a predisposition that can lead one to validate false definitions.

is responsible for subordination is often ignored. William Ryan (1976) calls this an instance of **blaming the victim**: portraying the problems of racial and ethnic minorities as their fault rather than recognizing society's responsibility.

The recognition that many in society fault the weak rather than embrace the need for restructuring society is not new. Gunnar Myrdal, a Swedish social economist of international reputation, headed a project that produced the classic 1944 work on Blacks in the United States, *The American Dilemma*. Myrdal concluded that the plight of the subordinate group is the responsibility of the dominant majority. It is not a Black problem but a White problem. Similarly, we can use the same approach and note that it is not a Hispanic problem or a Haitian refugee problem but a White problem. Myrdal and others since then have reminded the public and policy makers alike that the ultimate responsibility for society's problems must rest with those who possess the most authority and the most economic resources (Hochschild 1995; Southern 1987).

Labeling Approach   Related to the conflict perspective and its concern over blaming the victim is labeling theory. **Labeling theory,** a concept introduced by sociologist Howard Becker, is an attempt to explain why certain people are viewed as deviant and others engaging in the same behavior are not. Students of crime and deviance have relied heavily on labeling theory. According to labeling theory, a youth who misbehaves may be considered and treated as a delinquent if she or he comes from the "wrong kind of family." Another youth, from a middle-class family, who commits the same sort of misbehavior might be given another chance before being punished.

The labeling perspective directs our attention to the role negative stereotypes play in race and ethnicity. The image that prejudiced people maintain of a group toward which they hold ill feelings is called a stereotype. **Stereotypes** are unreliable generalizations about all members of a group that do not take individual differences into account. The warrior image of American Indian people is perpetuated by the frequent use of tribal names or even terms such as "Indians" and "Redskins" as sports team mascots. In Chapter 2, we will review some of the research on the stereotyping of minorities. This labeling is not limited to racial and ethnic groups, however. For instance, age can be used to exclude a person from an activity in which he or she is qualified to engage. Groups are subjected to stereotypes and discrimination in such a way that their treatment resembles that of social minorities. Social prejudice exists toward ex-convicts, gamblers, alcoholics, lesbians, gays, prostitutes, people with AIDS, and people with disabilities, to name a few.

The labeling approach points out that stereotypes, when applied by people in power, can have very negative consequences for people or groups identified falsely. A crucial aspect of the relationship between dominant and subordinate groups is the prerogative of the dominant group to define society's values. American sociologist William I. Thomas (1923), an early critic of racial and gender discrimination, saw that the "definition of the situation" could mold the personality of the individual. In other words, Thomas observed that people respond not only to the objective features of a situation (or person) but also to the meaning these features have for them. So, for example, a lone walker seeing a young Black man walking toward him may perceive the situation differently than if the oncoming person is an older woman. In this manner, we can create false images or stereotypes that become real in their social consequences.

In certain situations, we may respond to negative stereotypes and act on them, with the result that false definitions become accurate. This is known as a **self-fulfilling prophecy**. A person or group described as having particular characteristics begins to display the very traits attributed to him or her. Thus, a child who is praised for being a natural comic may focus on learning to become funny to gain approval and attention.

Self-fulfilling prophecies can be devastating for minority groups (Figure 1.2). Such groups often find that they are allowed to hold only low-paying jobs with little prestige or opportunity for advancement. The rationale of the dominant society is that these

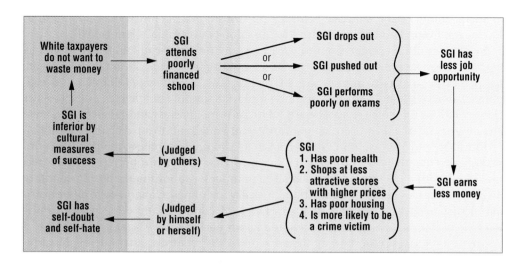

FIGURE 1.2 Self-Fulfilling Prophecy
The self-validating effects of dominant-group definitions are shown in this figure. The subordinate-group individual (SGI) attends a poorly financed school and is left unequipped to perform jobs that offer high status and pay. He or she then gets a low-paying job and must settle for a standard of living far short of society's standards. Because the person shares these societal standards, he or she may begin to feel self-doubt and self-hatred.

minority people lack the ability to perform in more important and lucrative positions. Training to become scientists, executives, or physicians is denied to many subordinate-group individuals, who are then locked into society's inferior jobs. As a result, the false definition becomes real. The subordinate group has become inferior because it was defined at the start as inferior and was therefore prevented from achieving the levels attained by the majority.

Because of this vicious circle, a talented subordinate-group person may come to see the worlds of entertainment and professional sports as his or her only hope for achieving wealth and fame. Thus, it is no accident that successive waves of Irish, Jewish, Italian, African American, and Hispanic performers and athletes have made their mark on culture in the United States. Unfortunately, these very successes may convince the dominant group that its original stereotypes were valid—that these are the only areas of society in which subordinate-group members can excel. Furthermore, athletics and the arts are highly competitive areas. For every Michael Jordan and Jennifer Lopez who makes it, many, many more will end up disappointed.

The Creation of Subordinate-Group Status

Three situations are likely to lead to the formation of a subordinate-group-dominant-group relationship. A subordinate group emerges through migration, annexation, and colonialism.

Migration

People who immigrate to a new country often find themselves a minority in that new country. Cultural or physical traits or religious affiliation may set the immigrant apart from the dominant group. Immigration from Europe, Asia, and Latin America has been a powerful force in shaping the fabric of life in the United States. **Migration** is the general term used to describe any transfer of population. **Emigration** (by emigrants) describes leaving a country to settle in another; **immigration** (by immigrants) denotes coming into the new country. From Vietnam's perspective, the "boat people" were emigrants from Vietnam to the United States, but in the United States they were counted among this nation's immigrants.

Although people may migrate because they want to, leaving the home country is not always voluntary. Conflict or war has displaced people throughout human history. In the 20th century, we saw huge population movements caused by two world wars; revolutions

migration
A general term that describes any transfer of population.

emigration
Leaving a country to settle in another.

immigration
Coming into a new country as a permanent resident.

globalization
Worldwide integration of government policies, cultures, social movements, and financial markets through trade, movements of people, and the exchange of ideas.

colonialism
A foreign power's maintenance of political, social, economic, and cultural dominance over people for an extended period.

in Spain, Hungary, and Cuba; the partition of British India; conflicts in Southeast Asia, Korea, and Central America; and the confrontation between Arabs and Israelis.

In all types of movement, even the movement of an American family from Ohio to Florida, two sets of forces operate: push factors and pull factors. Push factors discourage a person from remaining where he or she lives. Religious persecution and economic factors such as dissatisfaction with employment opportunities are possible push factors. Pull factors, such as a better standard of living, friends and relatives who have already emigrated, and a promised job, attract an immigrant to a particular country.

Although generally we think of migration as a voluntary process, much of the population transfer that has occurred in the world has been involuntary. The forced movement of people into another society guarantees a subordinate role. Involuntary migration is no longer common; although enslavement has a long history, all industrialized societies today prohibit such practices. Of course, many contemporary societies, including the United States, bear the legacy of slavery.

Migration has taken on new significance in the 21st century partly due to globalization. **Globalization** refers to the worldwide integration of government policies, cultures, social movements, and financial markets through trade and the exchange of ideas. The increased movement of people and money across borders has made the distinction between temporary and permanent migration less meaningful. Although migration has always been fluid, in today's global economy, people are connected across societies culturally and economically like they have never been before. Even after they have relocated, people maintain global linkages to their former country and with a global economy (A. Richmond 2002).

Annexation

Nations, particularly during wars or as a result of war, incorporate or attach land. This new land is contiguous to the nation, as in the German annexation of Austria and Czechoslovakia in 1938 and 1939 and in the United States' Louisiana Purchase of 1803. The Treaty of Guadalupe Hidalgo that ended the Mexican-American War in 1848 gave the United States California, Utah, Nevada, most of New Mexico, and parts of Arizona, Wyoming, and Colorado. The indigenous peoples in some of this huge territory were dominant in their society one day, only to become minority-group members the next.

When annexation occurs, the dominant power generally suppresses the language and culture of the minority. Such was the practice of Russia with the Ukrainians and Poles, and of Prussia with the Poles. Minorities try to maintain their cultural integrity despite annexation. Poles inhabited an area divided into territories ruled by three countries but maintained their own culture across political boundaries.

Colonialism

Colonialism has been the most common way for one group of people to dominate another. **Colonialism** is the maintenance of political, social, economic, and cultural dominance over people by a foreign power for an extended period (Bell 1991). Colonialism is rule by outsiders but, unlike annexation, does not involve actual incorporation into the dominant people's nation. The long control exercised by the British Empire over much of North America, parts of Africa, and India is an example of colonial domination.

Societies gain power over a foreign land through military strength, sophisticated political organization, and investment capital. The extent of power may also vary according to the dominant group's scope of settlement in the colonial land. Relations between the colonial nation and the colonized people are similar to those between a dominant group and exploited subordinate groups. The colonial subjects generally are limited to menial jobs and the wages from their labor. The natural resources of their land benefit the members of the ruling class.

Colonialism in India and elsewhere established for generations a hierarchical relationship between Europeans and much of the rest of the world. Pictured here is a British officer being fanned and pampered by two Indian attendants.

By the 1980s, colonialism, in the sense of political rule, had become largely a phenomenon of the past, yet industrial countries of North America and Europe still dominated the world economically and politically. Drawing on the conflict perspective, sociologist Immanuel Wallerstein (1974) views the global economic system of today as much like the height of colonial days. Wallerstein has advanced the **world systems theory**, which views the global economic system as divided between nations that control wealth and those that provide natural resources and labor. Many of the ethnic, racial, and religious conflicts noted at the beginning of the chapter are exacerbated by the limited economic resources available in developing nations. In addition the presence of massive inequality between nations only serves to encourage immigration generally and more specifically the movement of many of the most skilled from developing nations to the industrial nations.

A significant exception to the end of foreign political rule is Puerto Rico, whose territorial or commonwealth status with the United States is basically that of a colony. The nearly 4 million people on the island are U.S. citizens but are unable to vote in presidential elections unless they migrate to the mainland. In 1998, 50 percent of Puerto Ricans on the island voted for options favoring continuation of commonwealth status, 47 percent favored statehood, and less than 3 percent voted for independence. Despite their poor showing, proindependence forces are very vocal and enjoy the sympathies of others concerned about the cultural and economic dominance of the U.S. mainland (Navarro 1998; Saad 1998).

Colonialism is domination by outsiders. Relations between the colonizer and the colony are similar to those between the dominant and subordinate peoples within the same country. This distinctive pattern of oppression is called **internal colonialism.** Among other cases, it has been applied to the plight of Blacks in the United States and Mexican Indians in Mexico, who are colonial peoples in their own country. Internal colonialism covers more than simple economic oppression. Nationalist movements in African colonies struggled to achieve political and economic independence from Europeans. Similarly, some African Americans also call themselves nationalists in trying to gain more autonomy over their lives (Blauner 1969, 1972).

The Consequences of Subordinate-Group Status

There are several consequences for a group of subordinate status. These differ in their degree of harshness, ranging from physical annihilation to absorption into the dominant group. In this section, we will examine six consequences of subordinate-group

world systems theory
A view of the global economic system as divided between nations that control wealth and those that provide natural resources and labor.

internal colonialism
The treatment of subordinate peoples as colonial subjects by those in power.

genocide
The deliberate, systematic killing of an entire people or nation.

ethnic cleansing
Policy of ethnic Serbs to eliminate Muslims from parts of Bosnia.

status: extermination, expulsion, secession, segregation, fusion, and assimilation. Figure 1.3 illustrates how these consequences can be defined.

Extermination

The most extreme way of dealing with a subordinate group is to eliminate it. One historical example is the British destruction of the people of Tasmania, an island off the coast of Australia. There were 5,000 Tasmanians in 1800, but because they were attacked by settlers and forced to live on less habitable islands, the last full-blooded Tasmanian died in 1876. A human group had become extinct, totally eliminated.

Today the term **genocide** is used to describe the deliberate, systematic killing of an entire people or nation. This term is often used in reference to the Holocaust, Nazi Germany's extermination of 12 million European Jews and other ethnic minorities during World War II. The term **ethnic cleansing** was introduced into the world's vocabulary as ethnic Serbs instituted a policy intended to "cleanse"—eliminate—Muslims from parts of Bosnia. More recently, a genocidal war between the Hutu and Tutsi people in Rwanda left 300,000 school-age children orphaned (Chirot and Edwards 2003).

However, *genocide* also appropriately describes White policies toward Native Americans in the 19th century. In 1800, the American Indian population in the United States was about 600,000; by 1850 it had been reduced to 250,000 through warfare with the U.S. Army, disease, and forced relocation to inhospitable environments.

Expulsion

Dominant groups may choose to force a specific subordinate group to leave certain areas or even vacate a country. Expulsion, therefore, is another extreme consequence of minority-group status. European colonial powers in North America and eventually the U.S. government itself drove almost all Native Americans out of their tribal lands into unfamiliar territory.

More recently, Vietnam in 1979 expelled nearly 1 million ethnic Chinese from the country, partly as a result of centuries of hostility between the two Asian neighbors. These "boat people" were abruptly eliminated as a minority within Vietnamese society. This expulsion meant that they were uprooted and became a new minority group in many nations, including Australia, France, the United States, and Canada. Thus, expulsion may remove a minority group from one society; however, the expelled people merely go to another nation, where they are again a minority group.

Secession

A group ceases to be a subordinate group when it secedes to form a new nation or moves to an already established nation, where it becomes dominant. After Great Britain withdrew from Palestine, Jewish people achieved a dominant position in 1948, attracting Jews from throughout the world to the new state of Israel. In a similar fashion, Pakistan was created in 1947 when India was partitioned. The predominantly Mus-

FIGURE 1.3 Intergroup Relations Continuum

The social consequences of being in a subordinate group can be viewed along a continuum ranging from extermination to forms of mutual acceptance such as pluralism.

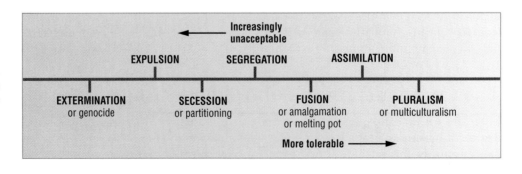

lim areas in the north became Pakistan, making India predominantly Hindu. Throughout this century, minorities have repudiated dominant customs. In this spirit, the Estonian, Latvian, Lithuanian, and Armenian peoples, not content to be merely tolerated by the majority, all seceded to form independent states after the demise of the Soviet Union in 1991. In 1999, ethnic Albanians fought bitterly for their cultural and political recognition in the Kosovo region of Yugoslavia.

Some African Americans have called for secession. Suggestions dating back to the early 1700s supported the return of Blacks to Africa as a solution to racial problems. The settlement target of the American Colonization Society was Liberia, but proposals were also advanced to establish settlements in other areas. Territorial separatism and the emigrationist ideology were recurrent and interrelated themes among African Americans from the late 19th century well into the 1980s. The Black Muslims, or Nation of Islam, once expressed the desire for complete separation in their own state or territory within the present borders of the United States. Although a secession of Blacks from the United States has not taken place, it has been proposed.

Segregation

segregation
The physical separation of two groups, often imposed on a subordinate group by the dominant group.

Segregation is the physical separation of two groups in residence, workplace, and social functions. Generally, the dominant group imposes segregation on a subordinate group. Segregation is rarely complete, however; intergroup contact inevitably occurs even in the most segregated societies.

Sociologists Douglas Massey and Nancy Denton (1993) wrote *American Apartheid*, which described segregation in U.S. cities based on 1990 data. The title of their book was meant to indicate that neighborhoods in the United States resembled the segregation of the rigid government-imposed racial segregation that prevailed for so long in the Republic of South Africa.

Analyzing the 2000 census results shows little change despite growing racial and ethnic diversity in the nation. Sociologists measure racial segregation using a segregation index or index of dissimilarity. The index ranges from 0 to 100, giving the percentage of a group that would have to move to achieve even residential patterns. For example, Atlanta has an index of 65.6 for Black-White segregation, which means that about 66 percent of either Blacks or Whites would have to move so that each small neighborhood (or census tract) would have the same racial balance as the metropolitan area as a whole. In Figure 1.4, we give the index values for the most and least segregated metropolitan areas among the 50 largest in the nation with respect to the Black-White racial divide.

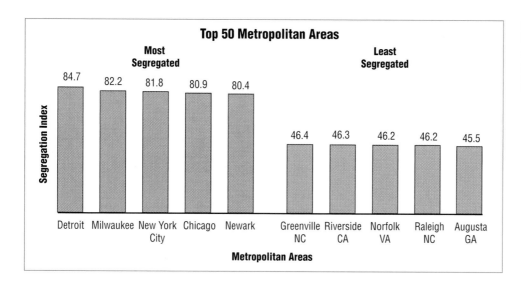

FIGURE 1.4 White-Black Segregation, 2000

Source: From *"Ethnic Diversity Grows, Neighborhood Integration Lags Behind."* Reprinted by permission of John Logan, Brown University, http://www.s4.brown.edu.

fusion
A minority and a majority group combining to form a new group with characteristics of the initial groups.

amalgamation
The process by which a dominant group and a subordinate group combine through intermarriage to form a new group.

melting pot
Diverse racial or ethnic groups or both forming a new creation, a new cultural entity.

Overall, the least segregated metropolitan areas tend to be those with smallest African American populations. For Latinos, the separation patterns are similar, with the highest patterns of isolation occurring in the cities with the larger number of Hispanics (Figure 1.5). There has been little change in overall levels of racial and ethnic segregation from 1990 to 2000. Similarly, Asian-White segregation remains high and showed little change during the 1990s (Lewis Mumford Center 2001).

This focus on metropolitan areas should not cause us to ignore the continuing legally sanctioned segregation of Native Americans on reservations. Although the majority of our nation's first inhabitants live outside these tribal areas, the reservations play a prominent role in the identity of Native Americans. Although it is easier to maintain tribal identity on the reservation, economic and educational opportunities are more limited in these areas segregated from the rest of society.

The social consequences of residential segregation are significant. Given the elevated rates of poverty experienced by racial and ethnic minorities, their patterns of segregation mean that the consequences of poverty (dismal job opportunities, poor health care facilities, delinquency, and crime) are much more likely to be experienced by even the middle-class Blacks, Latinos, and tribal people than it is by middle-class Whites (Massey 2004).

Fusion

Fusion occurs when a minority and a majority group combine to form a new group. This combining can be expressed as $A + B + C \rightarrow D$ where A, B, and C represent the groups present in a society, and D signifies the result, an ethnocultural-racial group sharing some of the characteristics of each initial group. Mexican people are an example of fusion, originating as they do out of the mixing of the Spanish and indigenous Indian cultures. Theoretically, fusion does not entail intermarriage, but it is very similar to **amalgamation,** or the process by which a dominant group and a subordinate group combine through intermarriage into a new people. In everyday speech, the words *fusion* and *amalgamation* are rarely used, but the concept is expressed in the notion of a human **melting pot,** in which diverse racial or ethnic groups form a new creation, a new cultural entity (Newman 1973).

The analogy of the cauldron, the "melting pot," was first used to describe the United States by the French observer Crèvecoeur in 1782. The phrase dates back to the

FIGURE 1.5 White-Latino Segregation, 2000

Source: From *"Ethnic Diversity Grows, Neighborhood Integration Lags Behind."* Reprinted by permission of John Logan, Brown University http://www.s4.brown.edu.

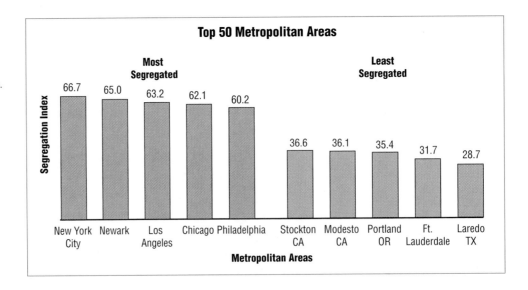

Middle Ages, when alchemists attempted to change less valuable metals into gold and silver. Similarly, the idea of the human melting pot implied that the new group would represent only the best qualities and attributes of the different cultures contributing to it. The belief in the United States as a melting pot became widespread in the early 20th century. This belief suggested that the United States had an almost divine mission to destroy artificial divisions and create a single kind of human. However, the dominant group had indicated its unwillingness to welcome such groups as Native Americans, Blacks, Hispanics, Jews, Asians, and Irish Roman Catholics into the melting pot. It is a mistake to think of the United States as an ethnic mixing bowl. Although there are superficial signs of fusion, as in a cuisine that includes sauerkraut and spaghetti, most contributions of subordinate groups are ignored (Gleason 1980).

Marriage patterns indicate the resistance to fusion. People are unwilling, in varying degrees, to marry outside their own ethnic, religious, and racial groups. Surveys show that 20 to 50 percent of various White ethnic groups report single ancestry. When White ethnics do cross boundaries, they tend to marry within their religion and social class. For example, Italians are more likely to marry Irish, who are also Catholic, than they are to marry Protestant Swedes.

There is only modest evidence of a fusion of races in the United States. Racial intermarriage has been increasing, and the number of interracial couples immigrating to the United States has also grown. In 1980, there were 167,000 Black-White couples, but by 2002 there were 395,000. Taken together, interracial couples still account for about 5 percent of all married couples. Among couples in which at least one member is Hispanic, marriages with a non-Hispanic partner account for about one out of four (Bureau of the Census 2003a:59).

√ Assimilation

Assimilation is the process by which a subordinate individual or group takes on the characteristics of the dominant group and is eventually accepted as part of that group. Assimilation is a majority ideology in which $A + B + C = A$. The majority (A) dominates in such a way that the minorities (B and C) become indistinguishable from the dominant group. Assimilation dictates conformity to the dominant group, regardless of how many racial, ethnic, or religious groups are involved (Bash 1979; Gordon 1964, 1996; Hirschman 1983; Newman 1973:53).

Neg

neg

To be complete, assimilation must entail an active effort by the minority-group individual to shed all distinguishing actions and beliefs and the unqualified acceptance of that individual by the dominant society. In the United States, dominant White society encourages assimilation. The assimilation perspective tends to devalue alien culture and to treasure the dominant. For example, assimilation assumes that whatever is admirable among Blacks was adapted from Whites and that whatever is bad is inherently Black. The assimilation solution to Black-White conflict is the development of a consensus around White American values.

positive

Neg.

Assimilation is very difficult. The person must forsake his or her cultural tradition to become part of a different, often antagonistic culture. Members of the subordinate group who choose not to assimilate look on those who do as deserters.

Assimilation does not occur at the same pace for all groups or for all individuals in the same group. Assimilation tends to take longer under the following conditions:

- The differences between the minority and the majority are large.
- The majority is not receptive or the minority retains its own culture.
- The minority group arrives over a short period of time.
- The minority-group residents are concentrated rather than dispersed.
- The arrival is recent, and the homeland is accessible.

assimilation
The process by which a subordinate individual or group takes on the characteristics of the dominant group.

pluralism
Mutual respect between the various groups in a society for one another's cultures, allowing minorities to express their own culture without experiencing prejudice or hostility.

positive

Assimilation is not a smooth process (Warner and Srole 1945).

Assimilation is viewed by many as unfair or even dictatorial. However, members of the dominant group see it as reasonable that people shed their distinctive cultural traditions. In public discussions today, assimilation is the ideology of the dominant group in forcing people how to act. Consequently, the social institutions in the United States, such as the educational system, economy, government, religion, and medicine, all push toward assimilation, with occasional references to the pluralist approach.

✓ The Pluralist Perspective

Thus far, we have concentrated on how subordinate groups cease to exist (removal) or take on the characteristics of the dominant group (assimilation). The alternative to these relationships between the majority and the minority is pluralism. **Pluralism** implies that various groups in a society have mutual respect for one another's culture, a respect that allows minorities to express their own culture without suffering prejudice or hostility. Whereas the assimilationist or integrationist seeks the elimination of ethnic boundaries, the pluralist believes in maintaining many of them.

There are limits to cultural freedom. A Romanian immigrant to the United States could not expect to avoid learning English and still move up the occupational ladder. To survive, a society must have a consensus among its members on basic ideals, values, and beliefs. Nevertheless, there is still plenty of room for variety. Earlier, fusion was described as $A + B + C \rightarrow D$ and assimilation as $A + B + C \rightarrow A$. Using this same scheme, we can think of pluralism as $A + B + C \rightarrow A + B + C$, where groups coexist in one society (Manning 1995; Newman 1973; Simpson 1995).

In the United States, cultural pluralism is more an ideal than a reality. Although there are vestiges of cultural pluralism—in the various ethnic neighborhoods in major cities, for instance—the rule has been for subordinate groups to assimilate. Yet as the minority becomes the numerical majority, the ability to live out one's identity becomes a bit easier. African Americans, Hispanics, and Asian Americans already outnumber Whites in 9 of the 10 largest cities (Figure 1.6). The trend is toward even greater diversity. Nonetheless the cost of cultural integrity throughout the nation's history has been high. The various Native American tribes have succeeded to a large extent in maintaining their heritage, but the price has been bare subsistence on federal reservations.

In the United States, there is a reemergence of ethnic identification by groups that had previously expressed little interest in their heritage. Groups that make up the dominant majority are also reasserting their ethnic heritage. Various nationality groups are

Faced with new laws restricting rights of noncitizens, people representing countries from around the world participate in naturalization ceremonies in Seattle, Washington on the Fourth of July, 1997.

rekindling interest in almost forgotten languages, customs, festivals, and traditions. In some instances, this expression of the past has taken the form of a protest against exclusion from the dominant society. For example, Chinese youths chastise their elders for forgetting the old ways and accepting White American influence and control.

The most visible controversy about pluralism is the debate surrounding bilingualism. **Bilingualism** is the use of two or more languages in places of work or education, with each language being treated as equally legitimate.

As of 2000, about one of every six people (17 percent) speaks a native language other than English at home. Reflecting this diversity, the demand for interpreters is now unprecedented. One private company, NetworkOmni, provides services to both government and private clients seeking translation services. To meet the need, the business offers interpreters to 911 services, hospitals, and private corporations in 150 languages and dialects ranging from widely spoken languages like Arabic, Spanish, Chinese, and Russian to dozens of lesser-known ones such as Akan, Oromo, and Telagu (D. Kelly 2003).

The passionate debate under way in the United States over bilingualism often acknowledges the large number of people who do not speak English at home. In education, bilingualism has seemed to be one way of helping millions of people who want to learn English to function more efficiently within the United States.

Bilingualism for almost two decades has been a political issue. A proposed Constitutional amendment has been introduced that designates English as the "official language of the nation." A major force behind the proposed amendment and other efforts to restrict bilingualism is U.S. English, a nationwide organization that views the English language as the "social glue" that keeps the nation together. This organization supports assimilation. By contrast, Hispanic leaders see the U.S. English campaign as a veiled expression of racism.

bilingualism
The use of two or more languages in places of work or education and the treatment of each language as legitimate.

Who Am I?

When Tiger Woods first appeared on *The Oprah Winfrey Show,* he was asked whether it bothered him, the only child of a Black American father and a Thai mother, to be called an African American. He replied, "It does. Growing up, I came up with this

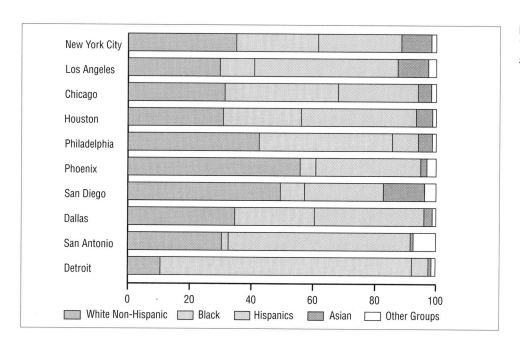

FIGURE 1.6   Race and Ethnicity, 10 Largest Cities, 2000

Source: Bureau of the Census 2001c.

Focus Research Focus *Research Focus Res*

MEASURING MULTICULTURALISM

Approaching Census 2000, a movement was spawned by people who were frustrated by government questionnaires that forced them to indicate only one race. Take the case of Stacey Davis in New Orleans. The young woman's mother is Thai and her father is Creole, a blend of Black, French, and German. People seeing Stacey confuse her for a Latina, Filipina, or Hawaiian. Officially, she has been "White" all her life because she looked White. Congress was lobbied by groups such as Project RACE (Reclassify All Children Equally) for a category "biracial" or "multiracial" that one could select on census forms instead of a specific race.

Race is only one of six questions asked of every person in the United States on census day every 10 years. After various trial runs with different wordings on the race question, Census 2000 for the first time gave people the option to check off one or more racial groups. "Biracial" or "multiracial" was not an option because pretests showed very few people would use it. This meant that the government recognized in Census 2000 dif-

ferent social constructions of racial identity—that is, a person could be Asian American and White.

Most people did select one racial category in the Census 2000. Overall, about 7 million people, or 2.4 percent of the total population, selected two or more racial groups. This was a smaller proportion than many had anticipated. In fact, not even the majority of mixed-race couples identified their children with more than one racial classification. As shown in Figure 1.7, White and American Indian was the most common multiple identity, with about a million people selecting that response. As a group, American Indians were most likely to select a second category and Whites least likely. Race is socially defined.

Complicating the situation is that people are asked separately whether they are Hispanic or non-Hispanic. So a Hispanic person can be any race. In the 2000 Census 94 percent indicated they were one race but 6 percent indicated two or more races; this proportion was three times higher than among non-Hispanics. Therefore, Latinos

name: I'm a Cabalinasian" (White 1997:34). This is a self-crafted acronym to reflect that Tiger Woods is one-eighth Caucasian, one-fourth Black, one-eighth American Indian, one-fourth Thai, and one-fourth Chinese. Soon after he achieved professional stardom, another golfer was strongly criticized for making racist remarks based on seeing Woods only as African American. If Tiger Woods was not so famous, would most people, upon meeting him, see him as anything but an African American? Probably not. Tiger Woods's problem is really the challenge to a diverse society that continues to try to place people in a few socially constructed racial and ethnic boxes.

The diversity of the United States today has made it more difficult for many people to place themselves on the racial and ethnic landscape. It reminds us that racial formation continues to take place. Obviously, the racial and ethnic landscape, as we have seen, is constructed not naturally but socially, and therefore is subject to change and different interpretations. Although our focus is on the United States, almost every nation faces the same problems.

The United States tracks people by race and ethnicity for myriad reasons, ranging from attempting to improve the status of oppressed groups to diversifying classrooms.

Focus Research Focus Research Focus Research

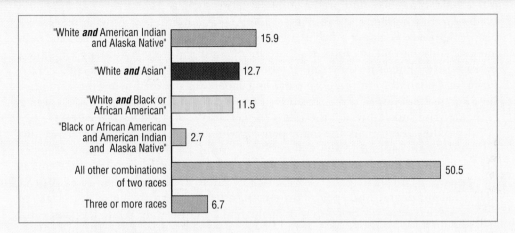

FIGURE 1.7   Multiple Race Choices in Census 2000

This figure shows the percentage distribution of the 6.8 million people who chose two or more races out of 281.4 million total population.

Source: Grieco and Cassidy 2001.

are more likely than non-Hispanics to indicate a multiracial ancestry.

The Census Bureau's decision does not necessarily resolve the frustration of hundreds of thousands of people such as Stacey Davis who face on a daily basis people trying to place them in some racial or ethnic catego— ry convenient for them. However, it does underscore the complexity of social construction and trying to apply arbitrary definitions to the diversity of the human population. ■

Sources: El Nasser 1997; Grieco and Cassidy 2001; Jones and Smith 2001; Tafoya et al. 2004.

 CD-ROM *Activity 1.1*

But how can we measure the growing number of people whose ancestry is mixed by anyone's definition? In Research Focus we consider how this problem was resolved by the U. S. Census Bureau.

Within little more than a generation, we have witnessed changes in labeling subordinate groups from Negroes to Blacks to African Americans, from American Indians to Native Americans or Native Peoples. However, more Native Americans prefer the use of their tribal name, such as *Seminole,* instead of a collective label. The old 1950s statistical term of "people with a Spanish surname" has long been discarded, yet there is disagreement over a new term: *Latino* or *Hispanic.* Like Native Americans, Hispanic Americans avoid such global terms and prefer their native names, such as *Puerto Ricans* or *Cubans.* People of Mexican ancestry indicate preferences for a variety of names, such as *Mexican American, Chicano,* or simply *Mexican.*

In the United States and other multiracial, multiethnic societies, panethnicity has emerged. **Panethnicity** is the development of solidarity between ethnic subgroups. The coalition of tribal groups as Native Americans or American Indians to confront outside forces, notably the federal government, is one example of panethnicity. His-

panethnicity
The development of solidarity between ethnic subgroups, as reflected in the terms *Hispanic* or *Asian American.*

marginality
The status of being between two cultures at the same time, such as the status of Jewish immigrants in the United States.

panics or Latinos and Asian Americans are other examples of panethnicity. Although it is rarely recognized by dominant society, the very term *Black* or *African American* represents the descendants of many different ethnic or tribal groups, such as Akamba, Fulani, Hausa, Malinke, and Yoruba (Lopez and Espiritu 1990).

Is panethnicity a convenient label for "outsiders" or a term that reflects a mutual identity? Certainly, many people outside the group are unable or unwilling to recognize ethnic differences and prefer umbrella terms such as *Asian Americans*. For some small groups, combining with others is emerging as a useful way to make themselves heard, but there is always a fear that their own distinctive culture will become submerged. Although many Hispanics share the Spanish language and many are united by Roman Catholicism, only one in four native-born people of Mexican, Puerto Rican, or Cuban descent prefers a panethnic label over nationality or ethnic identity. Yet the growth of a variety of panethnic associations among many groups, including Hispanics, continued through the 1990s (de la Garza et al. 1992; Espiritu 1992).

Add to this cultural mix the many peoples with clear social identities who are not yet generally recognized in the United States. Arabs are a rapidly growing segment whose identity is heavily subject to stereotypes or, at best, is still ambiguous. Haitians and Jamaicans affirm that they are Black but rarely accept the identity of African American. Brazilians, who speak Portuguese, often object to being called Hispanic because of that term's association with Spain. Similarly, there are White Hispanics and non-White Hispanics, some of the latter being Black and others Asian (Bennett 1993; Omi and Winant 1994:162).

Another challenge to identity is **marginality,** the status of being between two cultures, as in the case of a person whose mother is a Jew and whose father is a Christian. Du Bois (1903) spoke eloquently of the "double consciousness" that Black Americans feel—caught between the conception of being a citizen of the United States but viewed as something quite apart from the dominant social forces of society. Incomplete assimilation by immigrants also results in marginality. Although a Filipino woman migrating to the United States may take on the characteristics of her new host society, she may not be fully accepted and may therefore feel neither Filipino nor American. The marginal person finds himself or herself being perceived differently in different environments, with varying expectations (Billson 1988; Park 1928; Stonequist 1937).

As we seek to understand diversity in the United States, we must be mindful that ethnic and racial labels are just that: labels that have been socially constructed. Yet these social constructs can have a powerful impact, whether self-applied or applied by others.

Resistance and Change

By virtue of wielding power and influence, the dominant group may define the terms by which all members of society operate. This is particularly evident in a slave society, but even in contemporary industrialized nations, the dominant group has a disproportionate role in shaping immigration policy, the curriculum of the schools, and the content of the media.

Subordinate groups do not merely accept the definitions and ideology proposed by the dominant group. A continuing theme in dominant-subordinate relations is the minority group's challenge to their subordination. We will see throughout this book the resistance of subordinate groups as they seek to promote change that will bring them more rights and privileges, if not true equality (Moulder 1996).

Resistance can be seen in efforts by racial and ethnic groups to maintain their identity through newspapers, organizations, and in today's technological age, cable television stations and Internet sites. Resistance manifests itself in social movements such as the civil rights movement, the feminist movement, and gay rights efforts. The

Children of biracial or multiracial couples face special challenges in the United States where there remains a strong desire to place everyone in just a few socially constructed racial and ethinic categories.

passage of such legislation as the Age Discrimination Act or the Americans with Disabilities Act marks the success of oppressed groups in lobbying on their own behalf.

Resistance efforts may begin through small actions. For example, residents of a reservation question a second toxic waste dump being located on their land. Although it may bring in money, they question the wisdom of such a move. Their concerns lead to further investigations of the extent to which American Indian lands are used disproportionately to house dangerous materials. This action in turn leads to a broader investigation of the way in which minority-group people often find themselves "hosting" dumps and incinerators. As we will discuss later, these local efforts eventually led the Environmental Protection Agency to monitor the disproportionate placement of toxic facilities in or near racial and ethnic minority communities. There is little reason to expect that such reforms would have occurred if we had relied on traditional decision-making processes alone.

An even more basic form of resistance is to question societal values. In this book, we avoid using the term *American* to describe people of the United States because geographically Brazilians, Canadians, and El Salvadorans are Americans as well. It is very easy to overlook how our understanding of today has been shaped by the way institutions and even the very telling of history have been presented by members of the dominant group. African American studies scholar Molefi Kete Asante (2000) has called for an **Afrocentric perspective** that emphasizes the customs of African cultures and how they have pervaded the history, culture, and behavior of Blacks in the United States and around the world. Afrocentrism counters Eurocentrism and works toward a multiculturalist or pluralist orientation in which no viewpoint is suppressed. The Afrocentric approach could become part of our school curriculum, which has not adequately acknowledged the importance of this heritage.

The Afrocentric perspective has attracted much attention in colleges. Opponents view it as a separatist view of history and culture that distorts both past and present. Its supporters counter that African peoples everywhere can come to full self-determination only when they are able to overthrow White or Eurocentric intellectual interpretations (Early 1994).

In considering the inequalities present today, as we will in the chapters that follow, it is easy to forget how much change has taken place. Much of the resistance to prejudice and discrimination in the past, whether to slavery or to women's prohibition from voting, took the active support of members of the dominant group. The indignities still experienced by subordinate groups continue to be resisted as subordinate groups and their allies among the dominant group seek further change.

afrocentric perspective
An emphasis on the customs of African cultures and how they have pervaded the history, culture, and behavior of Blacks in the United States and around the world.

Conclusion

One hundred years ago, sociologist and activist W. E. B. Du Bois took another famed Black activist, Booker T. Washington, to task for saying that the races could best work together apart, like fingers on a hand. Du Bois felt that Black people had to be a part of all social institutions and not create their own. Today among African Americans, Whites, and other groups, the debate persists as to what form society should take. Should we seek to bring everyone together into an integrated whole? Or do we strive to maintain as much of our group identities as possible while working cooperatively as necessary?

In this first chapter, we have attempted to organize our approach to subordinate-dominant relations in the United States. We observed that subordinate groups do not necessarily contain fewer members than the dominant group. Subordinate groups are classified into racial, ethnic, religious, and gender groups. Racial classification has been of interest, but scientific findings do not explain contemporary race relations. Biological differences of race are not supported by scientific data. Yet as the continuing debate over standardized tests demonstrates, attempts to establish a biological meaning of race have not been swept entirely into the dustbin of history. However, the social meaning given to physical differences is very significant. People have defined racial differences in such a way as to encourage or discourage the progress of certain groups.

The oppression of selected racial and ethnic groups may serve some people's vested interests. However, denying opportunities or privileges to an entire group only leads to conflict between dominant and subordinate groups. Societies such as the United States develop ideologies to justify privileges given to some and opportunities denied to others. These ideologies may be subtle, such as assimilation (i.e., "You should be like us"), or overt, such as racist thought and behavior.

Subordinate groups generally emerge in one of three ways: migration, annexation, or colonialism. Once a group is given subordinate status, it does not necessarily keep it indefinitely. Extermination, expulsion, secession, segregation, fusion, and assimilation remove the status of subordination, although inequality still persists.

Subordinate-group members' reactions include the seeking of an alternative avenue to acceptance and success: "Why should we forsake what we are to be accepted by them?" In response to this question, there has been a resurgence of ethnic identification. *Pluralism* describes a society in which several different groups coexist, with no dominant or subordinate groups. The hope for such a society remains unfulfilled, except perhaps for isolated exceptions.

Subordinate groups have not and do not always accept their second-class status passively. They may protest, organize, revolt, and resist society as defined by the dominant group. Patterns of race and ethnic relations are changing, not stagnant. Furthermore, in many nations, including the United States, the nature of race and ethnicity changes through migration. Indicative of the changing landscape, biracial and multiracial children present us with new definitions of identity emerging through a process of racial formation, reminding us that race is socially constructed.

The two significant forces that are absent in a truly pluralistic society are prejudice and discrimination. In an assimilation society, prejudice disparages out-group differences, and discrimination financially rewards those who shed their past. In the next two chapters, we will explore the nature of prejudice and discrimination in the United States.

Key Terms

Afrocentric perspective 29	biological race 10	emigration 17
amalgamation 22	class 13	ethnic cleansing 20
assimilation 23	colonialism 18	ethnic group 7
bilingualism 25	conflict perspective 15	functionalist perspective 14
blaming the victim 16	dysfunction 15	fusion 22

genocide 20	melting pot 22	racism 12
globalization 18	migration 17	segregation 21
immigration 17	minority group 5	self-fulfilling prophecy 16
intelligence quotient 11	panethnicity 27	sociology 13
internal colonialism 19	pluralism 24	stereotypes 16
labeling theory 16	racial formation 13	stratification 13
marginality 28	racial group 7	world systems theory 19

Review Questions

1. In what ways have you seen issues of race and ethnicity emerge? Identify groups that have been subordinated for reasons other than race, ethnicity, or gender.

2. How can a significant political or social issue (such as bilingual education) be viewed in assimilationist and pluralistic terms?

3. How does the concept of "double consciousness" popularized by W. E. B. Du Bois relate to the question "Who am I?"

Critical Thinking

 **CD-ROM** *Activity 1.2*

1. How diverse is your city? Can you see evidence that some group is being subordinated? What social construction of categories do you see that may be different in your community as compared to elsewhere?

2. In 1996 Denny Mendéz was crowned Miss Italy, but many people protested her selection because they said she did not reflect the appropriate physical image of the Italian people. Mendéz had moved to Italy from the Dominican Republic when her mother married an Italian and has since become a citizen. What does this controversy around a beauty pageant tell us about the social construction of race? What similar situations have you witnessed in which race and ethnicity can be seen in their social context?

3. Identify some protest and resistance efforts by subordinated groups in your area. Have they been successful? Why are some people who say they favor equality uncomfortable with such efforts? How can people unconnected with such efforts either help or hinder such protests?

Internet Connections—Research Navigator™

To access the full resources of Research Navigator™, please find the access code printed on the inside cover of One-Search with Research Navigator ™: Sociology. You may have received this booklet if your instructor recommended this guide be packaged with new textbooks. (If your book did not come with this printed guide, you can purchase one through your college bookstore). Visit our Research Navigator ™ site at www.ResearchNavigator.com. Once at this site click on REGISTER under New Users and enter your access code to create a personal Login Name and Password. (When revisiting the site, use the same Login Name and Password.) Browse the features of the Research Navigator ™ Web site and search the databases of academic journals, newspapers, magazines, and Web links.

For further information relevant to Chapter One, you may wish to use such keywords as "ethnicity," "I.Q.," and "biracial," and the search engine will supply relevant and recent scholarly and popular press publications. Use the *New York Times* Search-by-Subject Archive to find recent news articles related to sociology and the Link Library feature to locate relevant Web links organized by the key terms associated with this chapter.

2

Prejudice

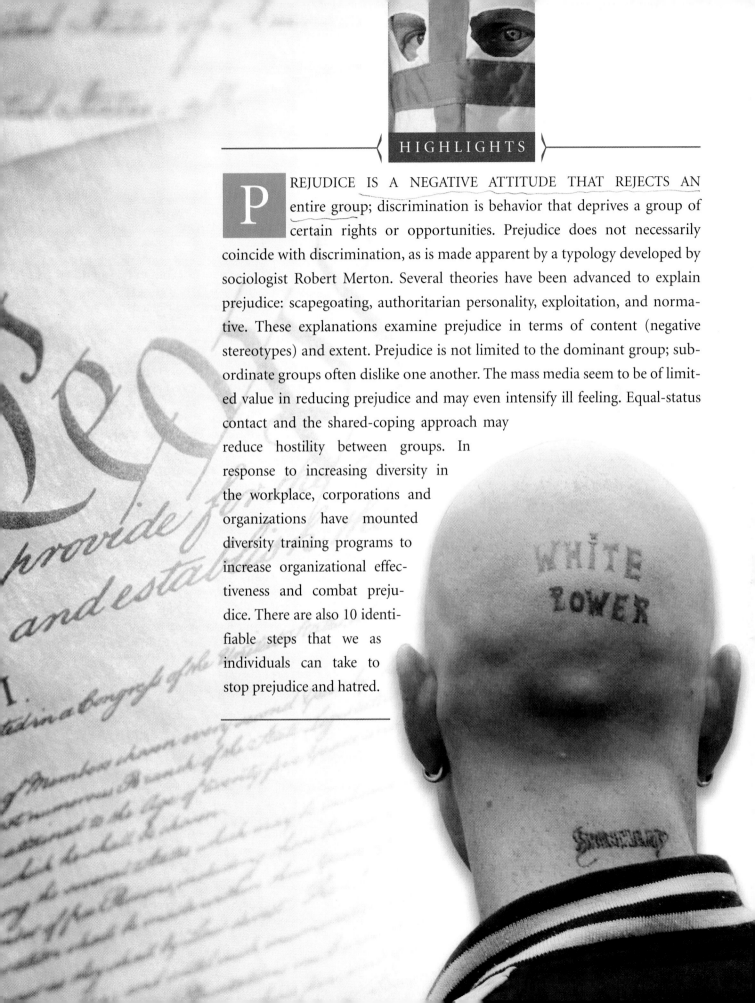

PREJUDICE IS A NEGATIVE ATTITUDE THAT REJECTS AN entire group; discrimination is behavior that deprives a group of certain rights or opportunities. Prejudice does not necessarily coincide with discrimination, as is made apparent by a typology developed by sociologist Robert Merton. Several theories have been advanced to explain prejudice: scapegoating, authoritarian personality, exploitation, and normative. These explanations examine prejudice in terms of content (negative stereotypes) and extent. Prejudice is not limited to the dominant group; subordinate groups often dislike one another. The mass media seem to be of limited value in reducing prejudice and may even intensify ill feeling. Equal-status contact and the shared-coping approach may reduce hostility between groups. In response to increasing diversity in the workplace, corporations and organizations have mounted diversity training programs to increase organizational effectiveness and combat prejudice. There are also 10 identifiable steps that we as individuals can take to stop prejudice and hatred.

African American artist Jacob Lawrence portrays the separate facilities typical of the treatment received by blacks in the first half of the twentieth century.

"The Phillips Collection," Washington D.C., ARS (Artists Rights Society)

In a social science laboratory at the University of Colorado, Boulder, subjects in an experiment played video games as researchers recorded their moves. Presented with a rapid-fire series of pictures showing Black and White men holding various objects—cell phones, cameras, wallets, guns—subjects pressed one button if they considered a character harmless and another button to "shoot" characters they believed to be armed. Researchers were studying people's split-second reactions to tests of decision making involving race and the potential for violence. When they analyzed the results, they found that the subjects, most of whom were White, had reacted more quickly to pictures of Black men with guns than to pictures of White men with guns. Subjects were also more likely to mistakenly shoot an unarmed Black character than an unarmed White character. The results were the same for Black subjects as for White subjects.

These results were not unusual. In a similar study at the University of Washington, psychologists asked college students to distinguish virtual citizens and police officers from armed criminals. They found that subjects were more likely to misperceive and shoot images of Black men than of White men in the video game they created. For the last three decades, in fact, research has suggested that people in the United States are more likely to see Black men as being violent than White men, which translated in this study for the Black men to be more likely to be "shot" at.

Are there limits for this hostility? Apparently not. In the commercially successful "Grand Theft Auto: Vice City" video-game players are encouraged to take very violent actions against a variety of images. At one point players are informed that they have come across a "Stinking nest of Haitians. We gonna kill them all. Kill all the Haitians." Why? "Kill all the Haitians, they are all drug dealers." This game, released by Rockstar Video in 2003, bore a parental code declaring that use was inappropriate for children under 17, but aside from the fact that so many youth access such games, we might be left to ponder why such a "game" with this dialogue would be marketed even to young adults (CBS New York 2003; Correll et al. 2002; Greenwald et al. 2003).

Prejudice is so prevalent that it is tempting to consider it inevitable or, even more broadly, just part of human nature. Such a view ignores its variability from individual to individual and from society to society. People must learn prejudice as children before they exhibit it as adults. Therefore, prejudice is a social phenomenon, an acquired characteristic. A truly pluralistic society would lack unfavorable distinctions made through prejudicial attitudes among racial and ethnic groups.

Ill feeling between groups may result from ethnocentrism. **Ethnocentrism** is the tendency to assume that one's culture and way of life are superior to all others. The ethnocentric person judges other groups and other cultures by the standards of his or her own group. This attitude leads people quite easily to view other cultures as inferior. We see a woman with a veil and many regard it as strange and backward, yet find it baffling when other societies see American women in short skirts and view the dress as inappropriate. Ethnocentrism and other expressions of prejudice are voiced very often, but unfortunately they also become the motivation for criminal acts.

ethnocentrism
The tendency to assume that one's culture and way of life are superior to all others.

Hate Crimes

Although prejudice certainly is not new in the United States, it is receiving increased attention as it manifests itself in neighborhoods, at meetings, and on college campuses. The Hate Crime Statistics Act, which became law in 1990, directs the Department of Justice to gather data on hate or bias crimes. The government defines a **hate crime** as

> *a criminal offense committed against a person, property, or society which is motivated, in whole or in part, by the offender's bias against a race, religion, ethnic/national origin group, or sexual-orientation group. (Department of Justice 2001c:58)*

This law created a national mandate to identify such crimes, whereas previously only 12 states had monitored hate crimes. In 1994, the act was amended to include disabilities, both physical and mental, as factors that could be considered a basis for hate crimes.

In 2003 law enforcement agencies released hate crime data submitted by police agencies covering 86 percent of the United States. Even though many, many hate crimes are not reported, a staggering number of offenses that come to law agencies' attention were motivated by hate. There were official reports of more than 8,800 hate crimes and bias-motivated incidents. As indicated in Figure 2.1, race was the apparent motivation for the bias in about 49 percent of the reports, and religion, sexual orientation, and ethnicity accounted for 14 to 19 percent each. Vandalism and intimidation were the most common, but 43 percent of the incidents against people involved assault, rape, or murder.

National legislation and publicity have made *hate crime* a meaningful term, and we are beginning to recognize the victimization associated with such incidents. A current proposal would make a violent crime into a federal crime if it were motivated by racial or religious bias. Although passage is uncertain, the serious consideration of the proposal indicates a willingness to consider a major expansion of federal jurisdiction. Currently, federal law prohibits crimes motivated by race, color, religion, or national origin only if they involve violation of a federally guaranteed right, such as voting.

Most hate crimes are the result of people acting alone or with a few others, but there is a troubling pattern of organized hate groups that dates back more than 130 years in the United States to the founding of the Ku Klux Klan. As shown in Figure 2.2, some people organize into groups with the express purpose of showing their hatred toward other groups of people. Law enforcement agencies attempt to monitor such groups but are limited in their actions by constitutional freedoms of speech and assembly.

Victimized groups are not merely observing these events. Watchdog organizations play an important role in documenting bias-motivated violence; among such groups are the Anti-Defamation League (ADL), the National Institute Against Prejudice and Violence, the Southern Poverty Law Center, and the National Gay and Lesbian Task Force.

hate crimes
Criminal offense committed because of the offender's bias against a race, religion, ethnic/national origin group, or sexual orientation group.

CD-ROM *Activity 2.3*

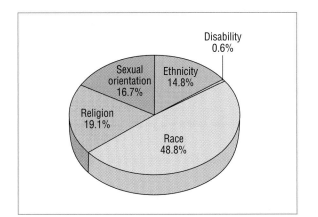

FIGURE 2.1 Distribution of Reported Hate Crimes in 2002

Source: Department of Justice 2003a.

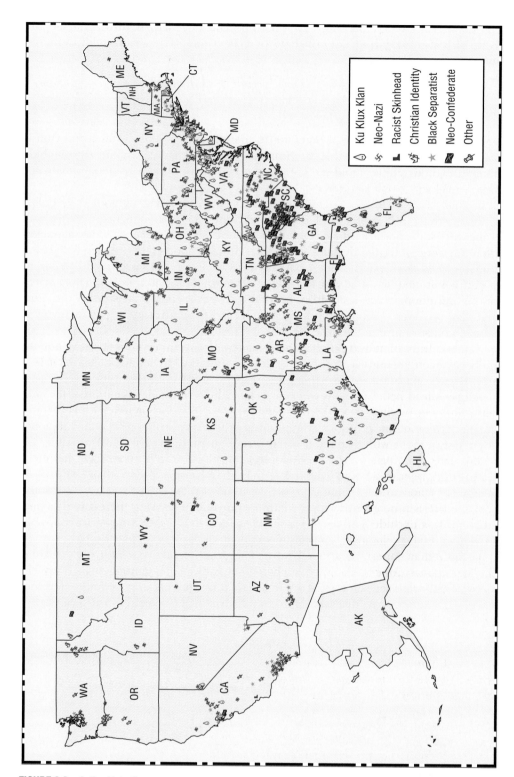

FIGURE 2.2 Active Hate Groups

Source: Map, "*Active Hate Groups in the U.S. in the Year 2003,*" The Intelligence Project of the Southern Poverty Law Center (2004). Reprinted by permission of Southern Poverty Law Center, Montgomery, AL.

Established hate groups have even set up propaganda sites on the World Wide Web. This also creates opportunities for previously unknown haters and hate groups to promote themselves. However, hate crime legislation does not affect such outlets because of legal questions involving freedom of speech. An even more recent technique has been to use instant messaging software, which enables Internet users to create a private chat room with another individual. Enterprising bigots use directories to target their attacks through instant messaging, much as harassing telephone calls were placed in the past (ADL 1996; Grattet and Jenness 2001; McDevitt et al. 2002).

What causes people to dislike entire groups of other people? Is it possible to change attitudes? This chapter tries to answer these questions about prejudice. Chapter 3 focuses on discrimination.

Prejudice and Discrimination

Prejudice and discrimination are related concepts but are not the same. **Prejudice** is a negative attitude toward an entire category of people. The two important components in this definition are *attitude* and *entire category*. Prejudice involves attitudes, thoughts, and beliefs, not actions. Prejudice often is expressed through the use of **ethnophaulisms**, or ethnic slurs, which include derisive nicknames such as *honky, gook*, or *wetback*. Ethnophaulisms also include speaking about or to members of a particular group in a condescending way ("José does well in school for a Mexican American") or referring to a middle-aged woman as "one of the girls."

A prejudiced belief leads to categorical rejection. Prejudice is not disliking someone you meet because you find his or her behavior objectionable. It is disliking an entire racial or ethnic group, even if you have had little or no contact with that group. A college student who requests a room change after three weeks of enduring his roommate's sleeping all day, playing loud music all night, and piling garbage on his desk is not prejudiced. However, he is displaying prejudice if he requests a change on arriving at school and learning that his new roommate is of a different nationality.

Prejudice is a belief or attitude; discrimination is action. **Discrimination** involves behavior that excludes all members of a group from certain rights, opportunities, or privileges. Like prejudice, it must be categorical. If an employer refuses to hire as a typist an Italian American who is illiterate, it is not discrimination. If she refuses to hire any Italian Americans because she thinks they are incompetent and does not make the effort to see whether an applicant is qualified, it is discrimination.

Merton's Typology

Prejudice does not necessarily coincide with discriminatory behavior. In exploring the relationship between negative attitudes and negative behavior, sociologist Robert Merton (1949, 1976) identified four major categories (Figure 2.3). The label added to each of Merton's categories may more readily identify the type of person being described. These are

1. The unprejudiced nondiscriminator: all-weather liberal
2. The unprejudiced discriminator: reluctant liberal
3. The prejudiced nondiscriminator: timid bigot
4. The prejudiced discriminator: all-weather bigot

As the term is used in types 1 and 2, liberals are committed to equality among people. The all-weather liberal believes in equality and practices it. Merton was quick to observe that all-weather liberals may be far removed from any real competition with

prejudice
A negative attitude toward an entire category of people, such as a racial or ethnic minority.

ethnophaulism
Ethnic or racial slurs, including derisive nicknames.

discrimination
The denial of opportunities and equal rights to individuals and groups because of prejudice or for other arbitrary reasons.

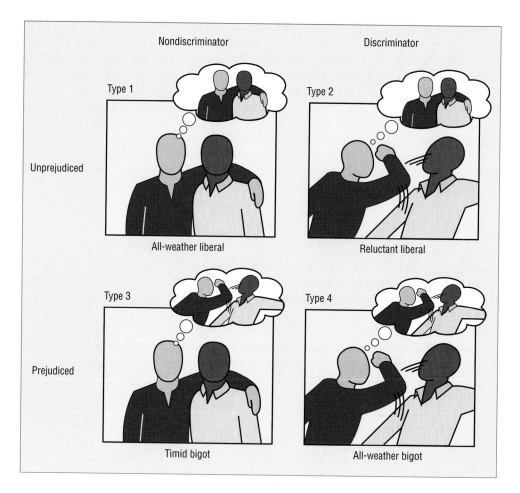

FIGURE 2.3   Prejudice and Discrimination

As sociologist Robert Merton's formulation shows, prejudice and discrimination are related to each other but are not the same.

subordinate groups such as African Americans or women. Furthermore, such people may be content with their own behavior and may do little to change themselves. The reluctant liberal is not this committed to equality between groups. Social pressure may cause such a person to discriminate. Fear of losing employees may lead a manager to avoid promoting women to supervisory capacities. Equal-opportunity legislation may be the best way to influence the reluctant liberals.

Types 3 and 4 do not believe in equal treatment for racial and ethnic groups, but they vary in their willingness to act. The timid bigot, type 3, will not discriminate if discrimination costs money or reduces profits or if he or she is pressured not to by peers or the government. The all-weather bigot unhesitatingly acts on the prejudiced beliefs he or she holds.

LaPiere's Study

Merton's typology points out that attitudes should not be confused with behavior. People do not always act as they believe. More than a half century ago, Richard LaPiere (1934, 1969) exposed the relationship between racial attitudes and social conduct. From 1930 to 1932 LaPiere traveled throughout the United States with a Chinese couple. Despite an alleged climate of intolerance of Asians, LaPiere observed that the couple were treated courteously at hotels, motels, and restaurants. He was puzzled by the good reception they received; all the conventional attitude surveys showed extreme prejudice by Whites toward the Chinese.

Was it possible that LaPiere had been fortunate during his travels and consistently stopped at places operated by the tolerant members of the dominant group? To test this possibility, he sent questionnaires asking the very establishments at which they had been served whether the owner would "accept members of the Chinese race as guests in your establishment." More than 90 percent responded no, even though LaPiere's Chinese couple had been treated politely at all the establishments. How can this inconsistency be explained? People who returned questionnaires reflecting prejudice were unwilling to act based on those asserted beliefs; they were timid bigots.

The LaPiere study is not without flaws. First, he had no way of knowing whether the respondent to the questionnaire was the same person who had served him and the Chinese couple. Second, he accompanied the couple, but the questionnaire suggested that the arrival would be unescorted (and, in the minds of some, uncontrolled) and perhaps would consist of many Chinese people. Third, personnel may have changed between the time of the visit and the mailing of the questionnaire (Deutscher et al. 1993).

The LaPiere technique has been replicated with similar results. This technique raises the question of whether attitudes are important if they are not completely reflected in behavior. But if attitudes are not important in small matters, they are important in other ways: Lawmakers legislate and courts may reach decisions based on what the public thinks.

This is not just a hypothetical possibility. Legislators in the United States often are persuaded to vote in a certain way by what they perceive as changed attitudes toward immigration, affirmative action, and prayer in public schools. Sociologists have enumerated some of prejudice's functions. For the majority group, it serves to maintain privileged occupations and more power for its members.

The following sections examine the theories of why prejudice exists and discuss the content and extent of prejudice today.

Theories of Prejudice

Prejudice is learned. Friends, relatives, newspapers, books, movies, television, and the Internet all teach it. Awareness begins at an early age that there are differences between people that society judges to be important. Several theories have been advanced to explain the rejection of certain groups in a society. We will examine four theoretical explanations. The first two (scapegoating and authoritarian personality) tend to be psychological, emphasizing why a particular person harbors ill feelings. The second two are more sociological (exploitation and normative), viewing prejudice in the context of our interaction in a larger society.

Scapegoating Theory ①

Scapegoating theory says that prejudiced people believe they are society's victims. The term *scapegoat* comes from a biblical injunction telling the Hebrews to send a goat into the wilderness to symbolically carry away the people's sins. Similarly, the theory of scapegoating suggests that, rather than accepting guilt for some failure, a person transfers the responsibility for failure to some vulnerable group. In the major tragic 20th-century example, Adolf Hitler used the Jews as the scapegoat for all German social and economic ills in the 1930s. This premise led to the passage of laws restricting Jewish life in pre–World War II Germany and eventually escalated into the mass extermination of Europe's Jews.

Today in the United States, immigrants, whether legal or illegal, often are blamed by "real Americans" for their failure to get jobs or secure desirable housing. The immigrant becomes the scapegoat for one's own lack of skills, planning, or motivation. It is so much easier to blame someone else.

scapegoating theory
A person or group blamed irrationally for another person's or group's problems or difficulties.

Many would regard this statue of colonist Hannah Duston in Massachusetts as perpetuating stereotypes about American Indians. She is honored for killing and scalping ten Abeenaki Indians in 1697 while defending her family. Believed to be the first woman ever honored in the United States with a monument, it portrays her holding a hatchet in her right hand.

Like exploitation theory (page 41), scapegoating theory adds to our understanding of why prejudice exists but does not explain all its facets. For example, scapegoating theory offers little explanation of why a specific group is selected or why frustration is not taken out on the real culprit when possible. Also, both the exploitation and the scapegoating theories suggest that every person sharing the same general experiences in society would be equally prejudiced, but that is not the case. Prejudice varies between individuals who seem to benefit equally from the exploitation of a subordinate group or who have experienced equal frustration. In an effort to explain these personality differences, social scientists developed the concept of the authoritarian personality.

 ## Authoritarian Personality Theory

A number of social scientists do not see prejudice as an isolated trait that anyone can have. Several efforts have been made to detail the prejudiced personality, but the most comprehensive effort culminated in a volume titled *The Authoritarian Personality* (Adorno et al. 1950). Using a variety of tests and relying on more than 2,000 respondents, ranging from middle-class Whites to inmates of San Quentin (California) State Prison, the authors claimed they had isolated the characteristics of the authoritarian personality.

In these authors' view, the basic characteristics of the **authoritarian personality** are adherence to conventional values, uncritical acceptance of authority, and concern with power and toughness. With obvious relevance to the development of intolerance, the authoritarian personality was also characterized by aggressiveness toward people who did not conform to conventional norms or obey authority. According to

authoritarian personality
A psychological construct of a personality type likely to be prejudiced and to use others as scapegoats.

the researchers, this personality type developed from an early childhood of harsh discipline. A child with an authoritarian upbringing obeyed and then later treated others as he or she had been raised.

This study has been widely criticized, but the very existence of such wide criticism indicates the influence of the study. Critics have attacked the study's equation of authoritarianism with right-wing politics (although liberals can also be rigid); its failure to see that prejudice is more closely related to other individual traits, such as social class, than to authoritarianism as it was defined; and the research methods used. Graham Kinloch (1974), discussing personality research, added a fourth criticism: The authors concentrated on factors behind extreme racial prejudice rather than on more common expressions of hostility.

Exploitation Theory ✓ ③

exploitation theory
A Marxist theory that views racial subordination in the United States as a manifestation of the class system inherent in capitalism.

Racial prejudice often is used to justify keeping a group in a subordinate position, such as a lower social class. Conflict theorists, in particular, stress the role of racial and ethnic hostility as a way for the dominant group to keep its position of status and power intact. Indeed, this approach maintains that even the less affluent White working class uses prejudice to minimize competition from upwardly mobile minorities.

This exploitation theory is clearly part of the Marxist tradition in sociological thought. Karl Marx emphasized exploitation of the lower class as an integral part of capitalism. Similarly, the exploitation or conflict approach explains how racism can stigmatize a group as inferior so that the exploitation of that group can be justified. As developed by Oliver Cox (1942), exploitation theory saw prejudice against Blacks as an extension of the inequality faced by the entire lower class.

The **exploitation theory** of prejudice is persuasive. Japanese Americans were the object of little prejudice until they began to enter occupations that brought them into competition with Whites. The movement to keep Chinese out of the country became strongest during the late 19th century, when Chinese immigrants and Whites fought over dwindling numbers of jobs. Both the enslavement of African Americans and the removal westward of Native Americans were to a significant degree economically motivated.

Although many cases support the exploitation theory, it is too limited to explain prejudice in all its forms. First, not all minority groups are exploited economically to the same extent. Second, many groups that have been the victims of prejudice have

Preserving culture or expressing pride can sometimes cross the line and intimidate others. In Laurens, South Carolina, one finds the "World Famous Redneck Shop and Klan Museum" where one can pick up souvenirs that often carry symbolism that is regarded as racist by many.

TABLE 2.1
Theories of Prejudice

There is no one explanation of why prejudice exists, but several approaches taken together offer insight.

Theory	Proponent	Explanation	Example
Scapegoating	Bruno Bettelheim Morris Janowitz	People blame others for their own failures.	An unsuccessful applicant assumes that a minority member or a woman got "his" job.
Authoritarian personality	Adorno and associates	Child rearing leads one to develop intolerance as an adult.	The rigid personality type dislikes people who are different.
Exploitation	Oliver C. Cox Marxist theory	People use others unfairly for economic advantage.	A minority member is hired at a lower wage level.
Normative	Thomas Pettigrew	Peer and social influences encourage tolerance or intolerance.	A person from an intolerant household is more likely to be openly prejudiced.

not been persecuted for economic reasons, such as the Quakers or gays and lesbians. Nevertheless, as Gordon Allport (1979) concludes, the exploitation theory correctly points a finger at one of the factors in prejudice, that is, the rationalized self-interest of the privileged.

Normative Approach

Although personality factors are important contributors to prejudice, normative or situational factors must also be given serious consideration. The **normative approach** takes the view that prejudice is influenced by societal norms and situations that encourage or discourage the tolerance of minorities.

Analysis reveals how societal influences shape a climate for tolerance or intolerance. Societies develop social norms that dictate not only what foods are desirable (or forbidden) but also what racial and ethnic groups are to be favored (or despised). Social forces operate in a society to encourage or discourage tolerance. The force may be widespread, such as the pressure on White Southerners to oppose racial equality while there was slavery or segregation. The influence of social norms may be limited, as when one man finds himself becoming more sexist as he competes with three women for a position in a prestigious law firm.

We should not view the four approaches to prejudice summarized in Table 2.1 as mutually exclusive. Social circumstances provide cues for a person's attitudes; personality determines the extent to which people follow social cues and the likelihood that they will encourage others to do the same. Societal norms may promote or deter tolerance; personality traits suggest the degree to which a person will conform to norms of intolerance. To understand prejudice, we need to use all four approaches together.

The Content of Prejudice: Stereotypes

normative approach
The view that prejudice is influenced by societal norms and situations that encourage or discourage the tolerance of minorities.

On Christmas Day 2001, Arab American Walied Shater boarded an American Airlines flight from Baltimore to Dallas carrying a gun. Immediately, the cockpit crew refused to let him fly, fearing that Shater would take over the plane and use it as a weapon of mass destruction. Yet Walied Shater carried documentation that he was a Secret Service agent, and calls to Washington, D.C., confirmed that he was flying to join a presidential protection force at President George W. Bush's ranch in Texas. Nevertheless, the crew could not get past the stereotype of Arab American men posing a lethal threat (Leavitt 2002).

What Are Stereotypes?

stereotype
Unreliable, exaggerated generalizations about all members of a group that do not take individual differences into account.

In Chapter 1, we saw that stereotypes play a powerful role in how people come to view dominant and subordinate groups. **Stereotypes** are unreliable generalizations about all members of a group that do not take individual differences into account. Numerous scientific studies have been made of these exaggerated images. This research has shown the willingness of people to assign positive and negative traits to entire groups of people, which are then applied to particular individuals. Stereotyping causes people to view Blacks as superstitious, Whites as uncaring, and Jews as shrewd. Over the last 70 years of such research, social scientists have found that people have become less willing to express such views openly, but as we will see later, prejudice persists (MacRae et al. 1996).

In "Listen to Our Voices," journalist and Lakota Sioux member Tim Giago speaks strongly against the widely accepted, commercially successful use of stereotypes: the continued use of Indians as mascots for athletic teams.

If stereotypes are exaggerated generalizations, why are they so widely held, and why are some traits more often assigned than others? Evidence for traits may arise out of real conditions. For example, more Puerto Ricans live in poverty than Whites, and so the prejudiced mind associates Puerto Ricans with laziness. According to the New Testament, some Jews were responsible for the crucifixion of Jesus, and so, to the prejudiced mind, all Jews are Christ killers. Some activists in the women's movement are lesbians, and so all feminists are seen as lesbians. From a kernel of fact, faulty generalization creates a stereotype.

Voices Listen to Our Voices Listen to

NATIONAL MEDIA SHOULD STOP USING OBSCENE WORDS

I am just sick and tired of hearing students and faculty from school using Indians as mascots say they are doing it to "honor us. . . ."

Who or what is a Redskin? It is a derogatory name for a race of people. It's as simple as that. It is akin to the racist names "nigger" or "gook" or "kike" or "wop." It is not, I repeat NOT, an honor to be called a racist name nor is it an honor to see football fans dressed in supposed Indian attire nor to hear them trumpeting some ludicrous war chant nor to see them mimic or ape our dress, culture, or person.

When I saw the Florida State fans doing the ridiculous "tomahawk chop" and heard their Johnny-one-note band play that asinine version of an Indian song over and over, I was heartsick. I was also highly embarrassed for the people of the Seminole Nation of Florida for allowing their good name to be taken in vain.

I am also sick and tired of fanatical sports fans telling Indians who object to this kind of treatment to "lighten up." You know, I didn't hear those same white folks saying this to African-Americans in the 1960s when they were objecting to the hideous black caricature at the Sambo Restaurants or to the Step-in-Fetch-It character used so often in the early movie days to portray blacks as dimwitted, shiftless people. I didn't hear anybody tell them to "lighten up."

Tim Giago

However, 2000 did give us (Indians) a little reprieve. The Cleveland Indians and their hideous mascot were clobbered and didn't make the playoffs. The Washington Redskins turned into the Washington "Deadskins." The Kansas City Chiefs were real losers. And almost best of all, the Florida State Seminoles were steamrolled by an Oklahoma team with real Indians serving as bodyguards to the Oklahoma coach Bob Stoops. My thrill at watching the Seminoles lose was topped only by watching Ted Turner's Atlanta Braves get "tomahawked" this year. Now that was truly an "honor. . . ."

Webster's Ninth New Collegiate Dictionary, note the word "collegiate" here, reads the word redskin quite simply as "American Indian usually taken to be offensive."

"Usually taken to be offensive." Now what is so hard to understand about this literal translation of the word "redskin"?

Attention major newspapers, CNN, Fox, ABC, CBS and NBC: the word "redskin" is an obscenity to Indians and to people who are sensitive to racism. It is translated by *Webster's* to be offensive. Now what other proof do you need to discontinue its usage? ■

Labels take on such strong significance that people often ignore facts that contradict their previously held beliefs. People who believe many Italian Americans to be members of the Mafia disregard law-abiding Italian Americans. Muslims are regularly portrayed in a violent, offensive manner that contributes to their being misunderstood and distrusted. We will consider later in the chapter how this stereotype about Muslims has become widespread since the mid-1970s but intensified after the attack on the World Trade Center on September 11, 2001.

Trends in Stereotypes

In the last 30 years, we have become more and more aware of the power of the mass media to introduce stereotypes into everyday life. Television is a prime example. Almost all television roles showing leadership feature Whites. Even urban-based programs such as *Seinfeld* and *Friends* prospered without any major Black, Hispanic, or Asian American characters. A 1998 national survey of boys and girls aged 10 to 17 asked a very simple question and came up with some disturbing findings. The children were asked, "How often do you see your race on television?" The results showed that 71 percent of White children said "very often," compared with only 42 percent of African Americans, 22 percent of Latinos, and 16 percent of Asian Americans. Even more troubling is that generally the children view the White characters as affluent and well educated, whereas they see the minority characters as "breaking the law or rules," "being lazy," and "acting goofy." Later in this chapter we will consider the degree to which the media have changed in presenting stereotyped images (Children Now 1998).

The labeling of individuals has strong implications for the self-fulfilling prophecy. Studies show that people are all too aware of the negative images other people have of them. When asked to estimate the prevalence of hard-core racism among Whites, one in four Blacks agrees that more than half "personally share the attitudes of groups like the Ku Klux Klan toward Blacks"; only one Black in ten says "only a few" share such views. Stereotypes not only influence how people feel about themselves but, perhaps equally important, also affect how people interact with others. If people feel that others hold incorrect, disparaging attitudes toward them, it undoubtedly will make it difficult to have harmonious relations (Sigelman and Tuch 1997).

Are stereotypes held only by dominant groups about subordinate groups? The answer is clearly no. White Americans even believe generalizations about themselves, although admittedly these are usually positive. Subordinate groups also hold exaggerated images of themselves. Studies before World War II showed a tendency for Blacks to assign to themselves many of the same negative traits assigned by Whites. Today, stereotypes of themselves are largely rejected by African Americans, Jews, Asians, and other minority groups.

Stereotyping in Action: Racial Profiling

A Black dentist, Elmo Randolph, testified before a state commission that he was stopped dozens of times in the 1980s and 1990s while traveling the New Jersey Turnpike to work. Invariably state troopers asked, "Do you have guns or drugs?" "My parents always told me, be careful when you're driving on the turnpike" said Dr. Randolph, 44. "White people don't have that conversation" (Purdy 2001:37).

Little wonder that Dr. Randolph was pulled over. African Americans accounted for 17 percent of the motorists on that turnpike but 80 percent of the motorists pulled over. Such occurrences gave rise to the charge that we had added a new traffic offense to the books: DWB, or Driving While Black (Bowles 2000).

In recent years government attention has been given to a social phenomenon with a long history: racial profiling. According to the Department of Justice, **racial profiling** is any police-initiated action based on race, ethnicity, or national origin rather than the person's behavior. Generally, profiling occurs when law enforcement officers, including customs officials, airport security, and police, assume that people fitting certain descriptions are likely to be engaged in something illegal. Beginning in the 1980s with the emergence of the crack cocaine market, skin color became a key characteristic. This profiling can be a very explicit use of stereotypes. For example, the federal antidrug initiative, Operation Pipeline, specifically encouraged officers to look for people with dreadlocks or for Latino men traveling together.

racial profiling
Any arbitrary police-initiated action based on race, ethnicity, or natural origin rather than a person's behavior.

Actor Danny Glover with his daughter, holds a press briefing after filing a discrimination complaint with a New York taxi company in 1999. A driver refused to let him sit in the front of the car while his daughter and a friend sat in the back.

The reliance on racial profiling persists despite overwhelming evidence that it is misleading. Whites are more likely to be found with drugs in the areas in which minority group members are disproportionately targeted. Nationwide, 80 percent of the country's cocaine users are White, but law enforcement tactics concentrate on the inner-city drug trade. Of course, there is a self-fulfilling nature to racial profiling. If, overwhelmingly, Blacks and Latinos are investigated, they will account for the majority of successful arrests. Data presented in 1999 indicated that Blacks constitute 13 percent of the country's drug users, 37 percent of those arrested on drug charges, 55 percent of those convicted, and 74 percent of all drug offenders sentenced to prison (Harris 1999).

In the 1990s increased attention to racial profiling led not only to special reports and commissions but also to talk of legislating against it. This proved difficult. The U.S. Supreme Court in *Whren v. United States* (1996) upheld the constitutionality of using a minor traffic infraction as an excuse to stop and search a vehicle and its passengers. Nonetheless, states and other government units are discussing policies and training that would discourage racial profiling. At the same time, most law enforcement agencies reject the idea of compiling racial data on traffic stops, arguing that it would be a waste of money and staff time.

The effort to stop racial profiling came to an abrupt end after the September 11, 2001, terrorist attacks on the United States. Suspicions about Muslims and Arabs in the United States became widespread. Foreign students from Arab countries were summoned for special questioning. Legal immigrants identified as Arab or Muslim were scrutinized for any illegal activity and were prosecuted for routine immigration violations that were ignored for people of other ethnic backgrounds and religious faiths. In 2003, President George W. Bush issued guidelines that barred federal agents from using race and ethnicity in investigations but specifically exempted cases involving terrorism and national security matters.

National surveys showed that those groups most likely to be stigmatized were not as supportive of using profiling. In a national 2004 survey, people were asked if racial profiling was ever justified when passengers are stopped at airport security checkpoints. Less than a third of all African Americans and 40 percent of Latinos supported such profiling compared to 46 percent of non-hispanic Whites. Nonetheless, racial profiling moved from a questionable local police action to a reaffirmed matter of national policy (Carlson 2004; Coates 2004; Harris 1999; Lictblau 2003).

The Extent of Prejudice

Interest in developing theories of prejudice or studying the concept has been exceeded only by interest in measuring it. From the outset, efforts to measure prejudice have suffered from disagreement over exactly what constitutes intolerance and whether there is such a phenomenon as no prejudice at all. Add to these uncertainties the methodological problems of attitude measurement, and the empirical study of prejudice becomes fraught with difficulty.

The extent of prejudice can be measured only in relative differences. For example, we cannot accurately say that prejudice toward Puerto Ricans is four times greater than that toward Portuguese Americans. We can conclude that prejudice is greater toward one group than toward the other; we just cannot quantify how much greater. The social distance scale is especially appropriate to assess differences in prejudice.

The Social Distance Scale

Robert Park and Ernest Burgess first defined **social distance** as the tendency to approach or withdraw from a racial group (1921:440). Emory Bogardus (1968) conceptualized a scale that could measure social distance empirically. His social distance scale is so widely used that it is often called the **Bogardus scale.**

The scale asks people how willing they would be to interact with various racial and ethnic groups in specified social situations. The situations describe different degrees of social contact or social distance. The seven items used, with their corresponding distance scores, follow. People are asked whether they would be willing to admit each group

- To close kinship by marriage (1.00)
- To my club as personal chums (2.00)
- To my street as neighbors (3.00)
- To employment in my occupation (4.00)
- To citizenship in my country (5.00)
- As only visitors to my country (6.00)
- Would exclude from my country (7.00)

A score of 1.00 for any group would indicate no social distance and therefore no prejudice. The social distance scale has been administered to many different groups in other countries as well. Despite some minor flaws and certain refinements needed in the scale, the results of these studies are useful and can be compared.

The data in Table 2.2 summarize the results of studies using the social distance scale in the United States at three points in time over a 65-year period. In the top third of the hierarchy are White Americans and northern Europeans. In the middle are eastern and southern Europeans, and generally near the bottom are racial minorities. This prestige hierarchy resembles the relative proportions of the various groups in the population.

social distance
Tendency to approach or withdraw from a racial group.

Bogardus scale
Technique to measure social distance toward different racial and ethnic groups.

TABLE 2.2
Changes in Social Distance

The social distance scale developed by Emory Bogardus has been a useful measure of people's feelings of hostility toward different racial and ethnic groups.

1926		1966		1991	
1. English	1.06	1. Americans		1. Americans	1.00
2. Americans	1.10	(U.S. White)	1.07	(U.S. White)	
(U.S. White)		2. English	1.14	2. English	1.08
3. Canadians	1.13	3. Canadians	1.15	3. French	1.16
4. Scots	1.13	4. French	1.36	4. Canadians	1.21
5. Irish	1.30	5. Irish	1.40	5. Italians	1.27
6. French	1.32	6. Swedish	1.42	6. Irish	1.30
7. Germans	1.46	7. Norwegians	1.50	7. Germans	1.36
8. Swedish	1.54	8. Italians	1.51	8. Swedish	1.38
9. Hollanders	1.56	9. Scots	1.53	9. Scots	1.50
10. Norwegians	1.59	10. Germans	1.54	10. Hollanders	1.56
11. Spanish	1.72	11. Hollanders	1.54	11. Norwegians	1.66
12. Finns	1.83	12. Finns	1.67	12. Native	1.70
13. Russians	1.88	13. Greeks	1.82	Americans	
14. Italians	1.94	14. Spanish	1.93	13. Greeks	1.73
15. Poles	2.01	15. Jews	1.97	14. Finns	1.73
16. Armenians	2.06	16. Poles	1.98	15. Poles	1.74
17. Czechs	2.08	17. Czechs	2.02	16. Russians	1.76
18. Native	2.38	18. Native	2.12	17. Spanish	1.77
Americans		Americans		18. Jews	1.84
19. Jews	2.39	19. Japanese	2.14	19. Mexicans (U.S.)	1.84
20. Greeks	2.47	Americans		20. Czechs	1.90
21. Mexicans	2.69	20. Armenians	2.18	21. Americans	1.94
22. Mexican	–	21. Filipinos	2.31	(U.S. Black)	
Americans		22. Chinese	2.34	22. Chinese	1.96
23. Japanese	2.80	23. Mexican	2.37	23. Filipinos	2.04
24. Japanese	–	Americans		24. Japanese (U.S.)	2.06
Americans		24. Russians	2.38	25. Armenians	2.17
25. Filipinos	3.00	25. Japanese	2.41	26. Turks	2.23
26. Negroes	3.28	26. Turks	2.48	27. Koreans	2.24
27. Turks	3.30	27. Koreans	2.51	28. Mexicans	2.27
28. Chinese	3.36	28. Mexicans	2.56	29. Japanese	2.37
29. Koreans	3.60	29. Negroes	2.56	30. Indians	2.39
30. Indians	3.91	30. Indians	2.62	(from India)	
(from India)		(from India)			
Arithmetic mean	2.14	Arithmetic mean	1.92	Arithmetic mean	1.76
Spread in distance	2.85	Spread in distance	1.56	Spread in distance	1.39

(*Source:* Emory S. Bogardus, "Comparing Racial Distance in Ethiopia, South Africa, and the United States," *Sociology and Social Research,* 52 [January 1968]. Copyright, University of Southern California, 1968. All rights reserved; and Tae-Hyon Song, "Social Contact and Ethnic Distance Between Koreans and the U.S. Whites in the United States," paper, Macomb, Western Illinois University, 1991. Reprinted by permission.)

The similarity in the hierarchy during the 65 years was not limited to White respondents. Several times, the scale was administered to Jewish, Mexican-American, Asian, Puerto Rican, Black-African, and Black-American groups. These groups generally shared the same hierarchy, although they placed their own group at the top. The extent of prejudice as illustrated in the ranking of racial and ethnic groups seems to be widely shared. Studies have also been performed in other societies and show that they have a racial and ethnic hierarchy as well.

A tentative conclusion that we can draw from these studies is that the extent of prejudice is decreasing. At the bottom of Table 2.2 is the arithmetic mean of the racial reactions on a scale of 1.0 to 7.0. Although the change was slight from survey to survey, it is generally downward. However, many specific nationalities and races experienced little change. The spread in social distance (the difference between the top- and bottom-ranked groups) also decreased from 1926 to 1991, a finding indicating that fewer distinctions were being made. This result was also confirmed empirically in research on stereotypes (Crull and Bruton 1985; Owen et al. 1981).

Trends in Prejudice

We hold certain images or stereotypes of each other, and we also may be more prejudiced toward some groups of people than others. However, is prejudice less than it used to be? The evidence we will see is mixed, with some indications of willingness to give up some old prejudices while new negative attitudes emerge.

Over the years, nationwide surveys have consistently shown growing support by Whites for integration, even during the Southern resistance and Northern turmoil of the 1960s. National opinion surveys conducted from the 1950s through the 1990s, with few exceptions, show an increase in the number of Whites responding positively to hypothetical situations of increased contact with African Americans. For example, 30 percent of the Whites sampled in 1942 felt that Blacks should not attend separate schools, but by 1970, 74 percent supported integrated schools, and fully 93 percent responded in that manner in 1991 (Davis and Smith 2001).

Attitudes are still important, however. A change of attitude may create a context in which legislative or behavioral change can occur. Such attitude changes leading to behavior changes did occur in some areas in the 1960s. Changes in intergroup behavior mandated by law in housing, schools, public places of accommodation, and the workplace appear to be responsible for making some new kinds of interracial contact a social reality. Attitudes translate into votes, peer pressure, and political clout, each of which can facilitate efforts to undo racial inequality. However, attitudes can work in the opposite direction. In the mid-1990s, surveys showed resistance to affirmative action and immigration. Policy makers quickly developed new measures to respond to these concerns, voiced largely by Whites.

When we survey White attitudes toward African Americans, two conclusions are inescapable. First, attitudes are subject to change, and in periods of dramatic social upheaval, dramatic shifts can occur within one generation. Second, less progress has been made in the late 20th century than was made in the 1950s and 1960s. Researchers have variously called these subtle forms of prejudice symbolic racism, modern racism, or laissez-faire racism. People today may not be as openly racist or prejudiced as in the past in expressing the notion that they are inherently superior to others. Yet much of the opposition to policies related to eradicating poverty or immigration is a smoke screen for those who dislike entire groups of racial and ethnic minorities (Bobo et al. 1997; Sniderman and Carmines 1997).

In the 1990s, White attitudes hardened still further as issues such as affirmative action, immigration, and crime provoked strong emotions among members of this dominant group as well as members of subordinate groups. Economically less-successful groups such as African Americans and Latinos have been associated with negative traits to the point where issues such as welfare and crime are now viewed as race issues. Besides making the resolution of very difficult social issues even harder, this is another instance of blaming the victim. These perceptions come at a time when the willingness of government to address domestic ills is limited by increasing opposition to new taxes. Although there is some evidence that fewer Whites are consistently prejudiced on all issues from interracial marriage to school integration, it is also apparent that many Whites continue to endorse some anti-Black statements and that negative images are widespread as they relate to the major domestic issues of the 21st century (Gilens 1996; Hughes 1998; Schaefer 1996).

The Mood of the Oppressed

Sociologist W. E. B. DuBois relates an experience from his youth in a largely White community in Massachusetts. He tells how, on one occasion, the boys and girls were exchanging cards, and everyone was having a lot of fun. One girl, a newcomer, refused his card as soon as she saw that DuBois was Black. He wrote,

> *Then it dawned upon me with a certain suddenness that I was different from others...shut out from their world by a vast veil. I had therefore no desire to tear down that veil, to creep through; I held all beyond it in common contempt and lived above it in a region of blue sky and great wandering shadows. (DuBois 1903:2)*

In using the image of a veil, DuBois describes how members of subordinate groups learn that they are being treated differently. In his case and that of many others, this leads to feelings of contempt toward all Whites that continue for a lifetime.

Opinion pollsters have been interested in White attitudes on racial issues longer than they have measured the views of subordinate groups. This neglect of minority attitudes reflects, in part, the bias of the White researchers. It also stems from the contention that the dominant group is more important to study because it is in a better position to act on its beliefs. The results of nationwide surveys conducted in the United States in 2003 offer insight into sharply different views on the state of race relations today (Figure 2.4). African Americans are much less satisfied with the current situation than are White Americans and Hispanics.

We have focused so far on what usually comes to mind when we think about prejudice: one group hating another group. But there is another form of prejudice: A group may come to hate itself. Members of groups held in low esteem by society may, as a result, have low self-esteem themselves. Many social scientists once believed that members of subordinate groups hated themselves or at least had low self-esteem. Similarly, they argued that Whites had high self-esteem. High self-esteem means that an individual has fundamental respect for himself or herself, appreciates his or her own merits, and is aware of personal faults and will strive to overcome them.

The research literature of the 1940s through the 1960s emphasized the low self-esteem of minorities. Usually, the subject was African Americans, but the argument has also been generalized to include any subordinate racial, ethnic, or nationality group. This view is no longer accepted. We should not assume that minority status influences personality traits in either a good or a bad way. First, such assumptions may create a stereotype. We cannot describe a Black personality any more accurately than we can a White personality. Second, characteristics of minority-group members are not entirely the result of subordinate racial status; they are also influenced by low incomes, poor neighborhoods, and so forth. Third, many studies of personality imply that certain values are normal or preferable, but the values chosen are those of dominant groups.

If assessments of a subordinate group's personality are so prone to misjudgments, why has the belief in low self-esteem been so widely held? Much of the research rests on studies with preschool-age Black children asked to express preferences among dolls with different facial colors. Indeed, one such study, by psychologists Kenneth and Mamie Clark (1947), was cited in the arguments before the U.S. Supreme Court in the landmark 1954 case *Brown v. Board of Education*. The Clarks' study showed that Black children preferred White dolls, a finding suggesting that the children had developed a negative self-image. Although subsequent doll studies have sometimes shown Black children's preference for white-faced dolls, other social scientists contend that this shows a realization of what most commercially sold dolls look like rather than documenting low self-esteem (Bloom 1971; Powell-Hopson and Hopson 1988).

Because African American children, as well as other subordinate groups' children, can realistically see that Whites have more power and resources and therefore rate

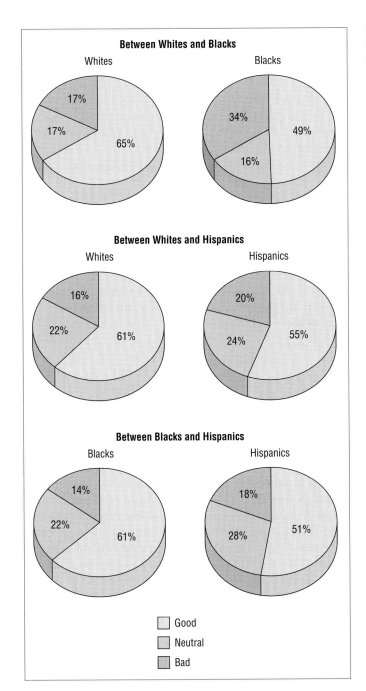

FIGURE 2.4 What Is the State of Race Relations?

Source: AARP 2004: 36, 41, 44.

them higher does not mean that they personally feel inferior. Indeed, studies, even with children, show that when the self-images of middle-class or affluent African Americans are measured, their feelings of self-esteem are more positive than those of comparable Whites (Gray-Little and Hafdahl 2000).

Intergroup Hostility

CD-ROM *Activity 2.1*

Prejudice is as diverse as the nation's population. It exists not only between dominant and subordinate peoples but also between specific subordinate groups. Unfortunately, until recently little research existed on this subject except for a few social distance scales administered to racial and ethnic minorities.

A national survey revealed that, like Whites, many African Americans, Hispanic Americans, and Asian Americans held prejudiced and stereotypical views of other racial and ethnic minority groups:

- Majorities of Black, Hispanic, and Asian American respondents agreed that Whites are "bigoted, bossy, and unwilling to share power." Majorities of these non-White groups also believed that they had less opportunity than Whites to obtain a good education, a skilled job, or decent housing.
- Forty-six percent of Hispanic Americans and 42 percent of African Americans agreed that Asian Americans are "unscrupulous, crafty, and devious in business."
- Sixty-eight percent of Asian Americans and 49 percent of African Americans believed that Hispanic Americans "tend to have bigger families than they are able to support."
- Thirty-one percent of Asian Americans and 26 percent of Hispanic Americans agreed that African Americans "want to live on welfare."

Members of oppressed groups obviously have adopted the widely held beliefs of the dominant culture concerning oppressed groups. At the same time, the survey also revealed positive views of major racial and ethnic minorities:

- More than 80 percent of respondents admired Asian Americans for "placing a high value on intellectual and professional achievement" and "having strong family ties."
- A majority of all groups surveyed agreed that Hispanic Americans "take deep pride in their culture and work hard to achieve a better life."
- Large majorities from all groups stated that African Americans "have made a valuable contribution to American society and will work hard when given a chance" (National Conference of Christians and Jews 1994).

Do we get along? Although this question often is framed in terms of the relationships between White Americans and other racial and ethnic groups, we should recognize the prejudice between groups. In a national survey conducted in 2000, people were asked whether they felt they could generally get along with members of other groups. In Figure 2.5, we can see that Whites felt they had the most difficulty getting along with Blacks. We also see the different views that Blacks, Latinos, Asian Americans, and American Indians hold toward other groups.

Curiously, we find that some groups feel they get along better with Whites than with other minority groups. Why would that be? Often, low-income people are competing on a daily basis with other low-income people and do not readily see the larger societal forces that contribute to their low status. As we can see from the survey results, many Hispanics are more likely to see Asian Americans as getting in their way than the White Americans who are actually the real decision makers in their community.

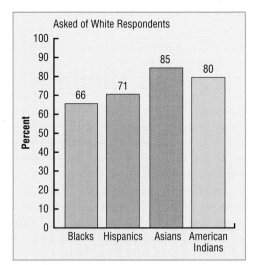

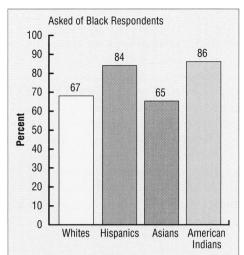

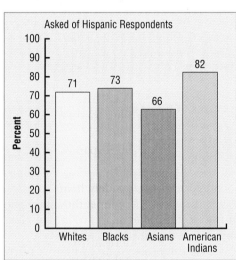

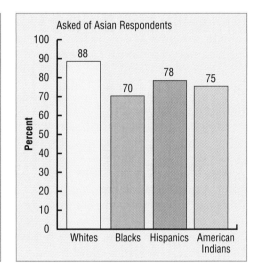

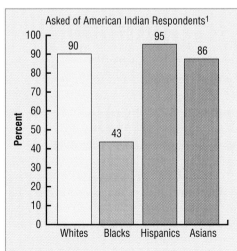

FIGURE 2.5 Do We Get Along?

Percentage saying groups get along with each other (Don't Knows excluded).
Note: The wording of the question was: "We hear a lot these days about how various groups in society get along with each other. I'm going to mention several groups and ask whether you think they generally get along with each other or generally do not get along with each other." So, in the Asked of White Respondents graph, Whites are asked how Whites get along with each ethnic group; in the Asked of Black Respondents graph, Blacks are asked how Blacks get along with each ethnic group etc.

(Source: From Taking America's Pulse II: NCCJ's 2000 Survey of Intergroup Relations in the United States, by T. Smith 2000:54) National Conference for Community Justice.

[1] Sample size for American Indians is very small and subject to large sample variance.

Reducing Prejudice

Focusing on how to eliminate prejudice involves an explicit value judgment: Prejudice is wrong and causes problems for those who are prejudiced and for their victims. The obvious way to eliminate prejudice is to eliminate its causes: the desire to exploit, the fear of being threatened, and the need to blame others for one's own failure. These might be eliminated by personal therapy, but therapy, even if it works for every individual, is no solution for an entire society in which prejudice is a part of everyday life.

The answer appears to rest with programs directed at society as a whole. Prejudice is attacked indirectly when discrimination is attacked. Despite prevailing beliefs to the contrary, we can legislate against prejudice: Statutes and decisions do affect attitudes. In the past, people firmly believed that laws could not overcome norms, especially racist ones. Recent history, especially after the civil rights movement began in 1954, has challenged that common wisdom. Laws and court rulings that have equalized the treatment of Blacks and Whites have led people to reevaluate their beliefs about what is right and wrong. The increasing tolerance by Whites during the civil rights era, from 1954 to 1965, seems to support this conclusion.

Much research has been done to determine how to change negative attitudes toward groups of people. The most encouraging findings point to education, mass media, intergroup contact, and workplace training programs.

Education and Mass Media

Research on the mass media and education consists of two types: research performed in artificially (experimentally) created situations and studies examining the influence on attitudes of motion pictures, television, and advertisements.

Leaflets, radio commercials, comic books, billboards, Web pages, and classroom posters bombard people with the message of racial harmony. Television audiences watch a public service message that for 30 seconds shows smiling White and African American infants reaching out toward each other. Law enforcement and military personnel attend in-service training sessions that preach the value of a pluralistic society. Does this publicity do any good? Do these programs make any difference?

Most research studies show that well-constructed programs do have some positive effect in reducing prejudice, at least temporarily. The reduction is rarely as much as one might wish, however. The difficulty is that a single program is insufficient to change lifelong habits, especially if little is done to reinforce the program's message once it ends. Persuasion to respect other groups does not operate in a clear field because, in their ordinary environments, people are still subjected to situations that promote prejudicial feelings. Children and adults are encouraged to laugh at Polish jokes and cheer for a team named "Redskins." Black adolescents may be discouraged by peers from befriending a White youth. All this undermines the effectiveness of prejudice reduction programs (Allport 1979).

Studies consistently document that increased formal education, regardless of content, is associated with racial tolerance. Research data show that more highly educated people are more likely to indicate respect and liking for groups different from themselves. Why should more years of schooling have this effect? It could be that more education gives a broader outlook and makes a person less likely to endorse myths that sustain racial prejudice. Formal education teaches the importance of qualifying statements and the need to question rigid categorizations, if not reject them altogether. Colleges are increasingly including as a graduation requirement a course that explores diversity or multiculturalism. Another explanation is that education does not actually reduce intolerance but simply makes people more careful about revealing it. Formal education may simply instruct people in the appropriate responses, which in some settings could even be prejudiced views. Despite the lack of a clear-cut explanation, either theory suggests that the continued trend toward a better-educated population will contribute to a reduction in overt prejudice.

However, college education may not reduce prejudice uniformly. For example, some White students will come to believe that minority students did not earn their admission into college. Students may feel threatened to see large groups of people of different racial and cultural backgrounds congregating together and forming their own groups. Racist confrontations do occur outside the classroom and, even if they do involve only a few, the events themselves will be followed by hundreds. Therefore, some aspects of the college experience may only foster "we" and "they" attitudes (Schaefer 1986, 1996).

The mass media, like schools, may reduce prejudice without the need for specially designed programs. Television, radio, motion pictures, newspapers, magazines, and the Internet present only a portion of real life, but what effect do they have on prejudice if the content is racist or antiracist, sexist or antisexist? As with measuring the influence of programs designed to reduce prejudice, coming to strong conclusions on the mass media's effect is hazardous, but the evidence points to a measurable effect.

In late spring 1999, as the television networks prepared their schedules for the 1999–2000 season, an article in the *Los Angeles Times* hit the broadcasting industry like a bombshell. In every new prime time series—26 of them—set to debut in the coming season, the *Times* reported, all the leading characters and most of the supporting casts would be White. The public response was immediate. The NAACP, alarmed by the "virtual whitewash in programming," threatened a lawsuit, and a national coalition of Latino groups urged viewers to boycott network TV.

By 2004, reports showed improvement in the representation on Blacks on television but little improvement in Hispanic represension (especially if the *George Lopez* show is excluded). Asian Americans, Arab Americans, and Native Americans continue to be virtually nonexistent.

Why the underrepresentation? Incredibly, network executives seemed surprised by the research demonstrating an all-White season. Producers, writers, executives, and advertisers blamed each other for the alleged oversight. In recent years, the rise of both cable TV and the Internet has fragmented the broadcast entertainment market,

Source: JEFF STAHER reprinted by permission of Newspaper Enterprise Association, Inc.

siphoning viewers away from the general-audience sitcoms and dramas of the past. With the proliferation of cable channels such as Black Entertainment Television (BET) and the Spanish-language Univision and Web sites that cater to every imaginable taste, there no longer seems to be a need for broadly popular series such as *The Cosby Show,* whose tone and content appealed to Whites as well as Blacks in a way that the newer series do not. The UPN and WB networks produce situation comedies and even full nights geared toward African American audiences. The result of these sweeping technological changes has been a sharp divergence in viewer preferences.

While BET and Univision were grabbing minority audiences and offering new outlets for minority talent, network executives and writers remained overwhelmingly White. It is not surprising that these mainstream writers and producers, most of whom live far from ethnically and racially diverse inner-city neighborhoods, tend to write and prefer stories about people like themselves. Even urban-based programs such as the successful *Seinfeld* and *Frazier* lasted years on television with almost no people of color crossing the screen. Television series are only part of the picture. Newscasting is overwhelmingly done by Whites: Eighty-nine percent in 2000. Among the top 30 correspondents on the major network evening news shows, one was a Latino, one was an African American, and 28 were White. Ironically, this means that if television were to report the research on television and race, the news correspondent probably would be White (Braxton 1999; Carter 2001; Bunche Center 2004; Children Now 2004; P. Johnson 2001).

Because we acquire prejudice from our social environment, it follows that the mass media and educational programs, as major elements of that environment, influence the level of prejudice. The movement to eliminate the stereotyping of minorities and the sexes in textbooks and on television recognizes this influence. Most of the effort has been to avoid contributing to racial hostility; less effort has been made to attack prejudice actively, primarily because no one knows how to do that effectively. In looking for a way to attack prejudice directly, many people advocate intergroup contact.

Equal-Status Contact

An impressive number of research studies have confirmed the **contact hypothesis,** which states that intergroup contact between people of equal status in harmonious circumstances will cause them to become less prejudiced and to abandon previously held stereotypes. Most studies indicate that such contact also improves the attitude of subordinate-group members. The importance of equal status in the interaction cannot be stressed enough. If a Puerto Rican is abused by his employer, little interracial harmony is promoted. Similarly, the situation in which contact occurs must be pleasant, making a positive evaluation likely for both individuals. Contact between two nurses, one Black and the other White, who are competing for one vacancy as a supervisor may lead to greater racial hostility (Schaefer 1976).

The key factor in reducing hostility, in addition to equal-status contact, is the presence of a common goal. If people are in competition, as already noted, contact may heighten tension. However, bringing people together to share a common task has been shown to reduce ill feeling when these people belong to different racial, ethnic, or religious groups. A study released in 2004 traced the transformations that occurred over the generations in the composition of the Social Service Employees Union in New York City. Always a mixed membership, the union was founded by Jews and Italian Americans, only to experience an influx of Black Americans, but more recently comprised of Latin Americans, Africans, West Indians, and South Asians. At each point, the common goals of representing the workers effectively overcame the very real cultural differences among the rank-and-file of Mexican and El Salvadoran immigrants in Houston. The researchers found when the new arrivals had contact

contact hypothesis
An interactionist perspective stating that intergroup contact between people of equal status in noncompetitive circumstances will reduce prejudice.

with African Americans, intergroup relations generally improved relations, and the absence of contact tended to foster ambivalent, even negative attitudes (Foerster 2004; Sherif and Sherif 1969).

Researchers in a housing study examined the harassment, threats, and fears that Blacks face in White schools in which low-income Black students are in the minority. Did these African American youths experience acceptance, friendships, and positive interactions with their White classmates? The researchers interviewed youth who had moved to the suburbs and those who had relocated within the city of Chicago under the auspices of a federally funded program. In this program, low-income Black families received housing subsidies that allowed them to move from inner-city housing projects into apartment buildings occupied largely by middle-income Whites and located in middle-income, mostly White suburbs. The study found that these low-income Black youth did experience some harassment and some difficulty in gaining acceptance in the suburban schools, but the findings also suggested that they eventually experienced great success in social integration and felt that they fit into their new environments (Rosenbaum and Meaden 1992).

As African Americans and other subordinate groups slowly gain access to better-paying and more responsible jobs, the contact hypothesis takes on greater significance. Usually, the availability of equal-status interaction is taken for granted, yet in everyday life intergroup contact does not conform to the equal-status idea of the contact hypothesis as often as we are assured by researchers, who hope to see a lessening of tension. Furthermore, in a highly segregated society such as the United States, contact, especially between Whites and minorities, tends to be brief and superficial (N. Miller 2002).

Corporate Response: Diversity Training

Prejudice carries a cost. This cost is not only to the victim but also to any organization that allows prejudice to interfere with its functioning. Workplace hostility can lead to lost productivity and even attrition. Furthermore, if left unchecked, an organization, whether a corporation, government agency, or nonprofit enterprise, can develop a reputation for having a "chilly climate." This reputation as a business unfriendly to people of color or to women discourages both qualified people from applying for jobs and potential clients from seeking products or services.

 **CD-ROM** *Activity 2.2*

In an effort to improve workplace relations, most organizations have initiated some form of diversity training. These programs are aimed at eliminating circum-

Efforts are beginning in the workplace to reduce hostility among workers based on prejudice.

stances and relationships that cause groups to receive fewer rewards, resources, or opportunities. Typically, programs aim to reduce ill treatment based on race, gender, and ethnicity. In addition, diversity training may deal with (in descending order of frequency) age, disability, religion, and language, as well as other aspects, including citizenship status, marital status, and parental status (Society for Human Resource Management).

It is difficult to make any broad generalization about the effectiveness of diversity training programs because they vary so much in structure between organizations. At one extreme are short presentations that seem to have little support from management. People file into the room feeling that this is something they need to get through quickly. Such training is unlikely to be effective and may actually be counterproductive by heightening social tensions. At the other end of the continuum is a diversity training program that is integrated into initial job training, reinforced periodically, and presented as part of the overall mission of the organization, with full support from all levels of management. In these businesses, diversity is a core value, and management demands a high degree of commitment from all employees (ADL 2001; Lindsley 1998).

As shown in Figure 2.6, the workforce is becoming more diverse, and management is taking notice. It is not in an organization's best interests if employees start to create barriers based on, for example, racial lines. We saw in the previous section that equal-status contact can reduce hostility. However, in the workplace, people compete for promotions, desirable work assignments, and better office space, to name a few sources of friction. When done well, an organization undertakes diversity training to remove ill feelings among workers, often reflected in the prejudices present in larger society.

The content of diversity training also varies. Generally, it includes sharing information about the diverse composition of the service region, the company, and potential clientele, today and in the future. Videotapes are sometimes used, which usually com-

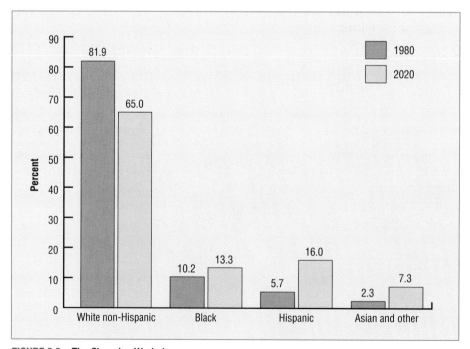

FIGURE 2.6   The Changing Workplace
Racial and ethnic composition of the labor force in 1990 and projected to 2015.
Source: Toossi 2002: 24.

Focus Research Focus Research Focus

WHAT'S IN A NAME?

As a job applicant, you revise and rework that résumé. Do you include that summer job three years ago? Who should you list as a reference? Do you state specific career objectives? But one thing you never ponder—your name.

Yet recent research shows your name may be a big factor if the potential interviewer is able to use it as a means to determine your race or nationality. Would a Mohammad be as likely to get a chance to work as a Michael in the United States? Most likely not in what could be seen as yet another form of profiling, but only this one occurs in the job market. Two economists, Marianne Bertrand and Sendhil Mullainathan, sent out 5,000 job applications for 1,300 job openings advertised in the *Boston Globe* and *Chicago Tribune.* The vacancies covered the gamut of the classified advertisements from cashier jobs to sales management positions. Among this massive undertaking, the researchers decided to see if the name of the job applicant made a difference. Carefully they tracked responses to two different sets of applicants—one with first names most likely to be African American and the other set being more typical of Whites. Names were

selected by examining a random sample of Boston birth certificates that identifed a person's race as well as his or her name.

The results of this job-seeking experiment were even startling to the researchers. Applicants with White-sounding names were 50 percent more likely to be called for an interview than those with Black-sounding names. Put another way, the typical White applicant was contacted for an interview for every 10 résumés they sent out, while the "African American" applicant had to send out 15 applications. Where employers responded positively to more than one résumé, rarely did they contact a "Black" applicant and not also contact a "White" applicant.

Because these were hypothetical applicants, we have no way of knowing to what degree these disturbing job results would have continued during the interview, job offer, and salary offered. Yet, clearly, the biggest constraining factor in any person's attempt to get a job is to get that interview.

The researchers took their study one step further. They made conscious efforts to make a portion of the applicants better qualified or to list addresses in more affluent neighborhoods. In both instances, resumes with White-sounding names were given even further advantages but this had much less positive impact on callbacks to the résumés bearing Black-sounding names. They did find that the apparent pro-White bias was less when employers where located in minority neighborhoods.

This study showed, using a clever, if simple, methodology, that people's prejudices seem to surface even when they scan that top line of the résumé Many business people apparently read no further if they detect that the applicant is from the wrong group. ■

Source: Bertand and Mullainathan 2003 and Krueger 2002.

TABLE 2.3
Names and Interview Success

Name on resume	Callback (%)
Brad	15.0
Kristen	13.6
Meredith	10.6
Mathew	9.0
Emily	8.3
Tanisha	6.3
Darnell	4.8
Keisha	3.8
Rasheed	3.0
Aisha	2.2

pare proper and awkward ways to handle a situation. Training sessions may break up into smaller group interactions where problem solving and team building are also encouraged.

If it is to have lasting impact on an organization, diversity training should not be separated from other aspects of the organization. For example, even the most inspired program will have little effect on prejudice if the organization promotes a sexist or ethnically offensive image in its advertising. As we heard in "Listen to Our Voices," Tim Giago expresses anger about continued use of Indians as mascots. The University of North Dakota launched an initiative in 2001 to become one of the top institutions for American Indians in the nation. Yet at almost the same time, the administration reaffirmed its commitment, despite tribal objections, to having as its mascot for athletic teams the "Fighting Sioux." It does little to do diversity training if overt actions by an organization propel it in the opposite direction (Brownstein 2001).

A central function that businesses can perform is to monitor prejudice that may deny opportunities to people largely because of their race, ethnicity, or nationality. In "Research Focus," (see page 59) we consider a recent and innovative experiment to measure prejudice in the workplace.

Although diversity training is increasingly common in the workplace, it may be undertaken primarily in response to major evidence of wrongdoing. In recent years, companies as diverse as Avis Rent-a-Car, Circuit City, Coca-Cola, Mitsubishi, Denny's Restaurants, Morgan Stanley, and Texaco have become synonymous with racism or sexual harassment. Generally, as a part of multimillion-dollar settlements, organizations agree to conduct comprehensive diversity training programs. So common is this pattern that a human resources textbook even cautions that a company should "avoid beginning such training too soon" after a complaint of workplace prejudice or discrimination (Carrell et al. 2000:266).

Despite the problems inherent in confronting prejudice, an organization with a comprehensive, management-supported program of diversity training can go a long way toward reducing prejudice in the workplace. The one major qualifier is that the rest of the organization must also support mutual respect.

Ways to Fight Hate

What can schools do? Television and movie producers? Corporate big shots? It is easy to shift the responsibility for confronting prejudice to the movers and shakers and certainly they do play a critical role. Yet there are definitely actions one can take in the course of everyday day life to challenge intergroup hostility.

The Southern Poverty Law Center (SPLC), founded in 1971 and based in Montgomery, Alabama, organized committed activists all over the country to mount legal cases and challenges against hate groups such as the Ku Klux Klan. The center's courtroom challenges led to the end of many discriminatory practices. Their cases have now gone beyond conventional race-based cases as they have won equal benefits for women in the armed forces, ended involuntary sterilization of women on welfare, and reformed prison and mental health conditions.

Recognizing that social change can also begin at the individual level, the SPLC has identified ten ways to fight hate based on their experience working at the community level (Carrier 2000).

1. Act. Do something. In the face of hatred, apathy will be taken as acceptance even by the victims of prejudice themselves. The SPLC tells of a time when a cross was burned in the yard of a single mother of Portuguese descent in Missouri; one person acted and set in motion a community uprising against hatred.

2. Unite. Call a friend or coworker. Organize a group of like-thinking friends from school or your place of worship or club. Create a coalition that is a diverse coalition and includes the young, the old, law enforcement representatives, and the media. Frustrated when a neo-Nazi group got permission to march in Springfield, Illinois, in 1994, a Jewish couple formed Project Lemonade. Money raised helps to create education projects or monuments in communities that witness such decisive events.

3. Support the Victims. Victims of hate crimes are especially vulnerable. Let them know you care by words, by e-mail. If you or your friend is a victim, report it. In the wake of an outbreak of anti-Native American and anti-Jewish activity in Billings, Montana, a manager of a local sports shop replaced all his usual outdoor advertising and print ads with "Not in Our Town," which soon became a community rallying point for a support network of hate victims.

4. Do Your Homework. If you suspect a hate crime has been committed, do your research to document it. An Indiana father spotted his son receiving a "pastor's license," did some research, and found that the source was a White supremacist group disguised as a church. It helped explain the boy's recent fascination with Nazi symbols. The father wrote the "church," demanded that the contacts be stopped, and threatened suit.

5. Create an Alternative. Never attend a rally where hate is a part of the agenda. Find another outlet for your frustration, whatever the cause. When the Ku Klux Klan held a rally in Madison, Wisconsin, a coalition of ministers organized citizens to spend the day in minority neighborhoods.

6. Speak Up. You too have First Amendment rights. Denounce the hatred, the cruel jokes. If you see a news organization misrepresenting a group, speak up. When a newspaper exposed the 20-year-old national leader of the Aryan Nation in Canada, he resigned and closed his Web site.

7. Lobby Leaders. Persuade policy makers, business heads, community leaders, and executives of media outlets to take a stand against hate. Levi Strauss contributed $5 million to an antiprejudice project and a program that helps people of color get loans in communities where it has plants: Knoxville, Albuquerque, El Paso, and Valdosta, Georgia.

8. Look Long Range. Participate or organize events such as annual parades or cultural fairs to celebrate diversity and harmony. Supplement it with a Web site that can be a 24/7 resource. In Selma, Alabama, a major weekend street fair is held on the anniversary of Bloody Sunday, when voting-rights activists attempting to walk across a bridge to Montgomery were beaten back by police.

9. Teach Tolerance. Prejudice is learned and parents and teachers can influence the content of curriculum. In Brooklyn, New York, an interracial basketball program called Flames was founded in the mid-1970s. Since then, it has brought together more than 10,000 youths of diverse backgrounds.

10. Dig Deeper. Look into the issues that divide us—social inequality, immigration, and sexual orientation. Work against prejudice. Dig deep inside yourself for prejudices and stereotypes you may embrace. Find out what is happening and act! As former White supremacist Floyd Cochran declared, "It is not enough to hold hands and sing Kumbaya" (Carrier 2000:22).

Expressing prejudice and expressing tolerance are fundamentally personal decisions. These steps recognize that we have the ability to change our attitudes and resist ethnocentrism and prejudice and avoid the use of ethnophaulisms and stereotypes.

Conclusion

This chapter has examined theories of prejudice and measurements of its extent. Prejudice should not be confused with discrimination. The two concepts are not the same: Prejudice consists of negative attitudes, and discrimination consists of negative behavior toward a group.

Several theories try to explain why prejudice exists. Some emphasize economic concerns (the exploitation and scapegoating theories), whereas other approaches stress personality or normative factors. No one explanation is sufficient. Surveys conducted in the United States over the past 60 years point to a reduction of prejudice as measured by the willingness to express stereotypes or maintain social distance. Survey data also show that African Americans, Latinos, Asian Americans, and American Indians do not necessarily feel comfortable with each other. They have adopted attitudes toward other oppressed groups similar to those held by many White Americans. Prejudice aimed at Hispanics, Asian Americans, and large recent immigrant groups such as Arab Americans and Muslim Americans is well documented. Issues such as immigration and affirmative action reemerge and cause bitter resentment. Furthermore, ill feelings exist between subordinate groups in schools, in the streets, and in the workplace.

Equal-status contact may reduce hostility between groups. However, in a highly segregated society defined by inequality, such opportunities are not typical. The mass media can be of value in reducing discrimination but have not done enough and may even intensify ill feeling by promoting stereotypical images. Although strides are being made in increasing the appearance of minorities in positive roles in television and films, one would not realize how diverse our society is by sampling advertisements, TV programs, or movies.

Even though we can be encouraged by the techniques available to reduce intergroup hostility, there are still sizable segments of the population that do not want to live in integrated neighborhoods, that do not want to work for or be led by someone of a different race, and that certainly object to the idea of their relatives' marrying outside their own group. People still harbor stereotypes toward one another, and this tendency includes racial and ethnic minorities having stereotypes about one another.

Reducing prejudice is important because it can lead to support for policy change. There are steps we can take as individuals to confront prejudice and overcome hatred. Another real challenge and the ultimate objective is to improve the social condition of oppressed groups in the United States. To consider this challenge, we turn to discrimination in Chapter 3. Discrimination's costs are high to both dominant and subordinate groups. With that fact in mind, we will examine some techniques for reducing discrimination.

Key Terms

authoritarian personality 40
Bogardus scale 47
contact hypothesis 56
discrimination 37
ethnocentrism 34

ethnophaulism 37
exploitation theory 41
hate crimes 35
normative approach 42
prejudice 37

racial profiling 45
scapegoating theory 39
social distance 47
stereotype 43

Review Questions

1. How are prejudice and discrimination both related and unrelated to each other?
2. How do theories of prejudice relate to different expressions of prejudice?
3. Why does prejudice develop even toward groups with whom people have little contact?
4. Are there steps that you can identify that have been taken against prejudice in your community?

Critical Thinking

1. Identify stereotypes associated with a group of people, such as older adults or people with physical handicaps.
2. What social issues do you think are most likely to engender hostility along racial and ethnic lines?
3. Consider the television programs you have watched the most. In terms of race and ethnicity, how well do the programs you watch tend to reflect the diversity of the population in the United States?

Internet Connections—Research Navigator™

Follow the instructions found on page 31 of this text to access the features of Research Navigator™. Once at the Website, enter your Login Name and Password. Then, to use the ContentSelect database, enter keywords such as "racism," "racial profiling," and "diversity training," and the research engine will supply relevant and recent scholarly and popular press publications. Use the *New York Times* Search-by-Subject Archive to find recent news articles related to sociology and the Link Library feature to locate relevant Web links organized by the key terms associated with this chapter.

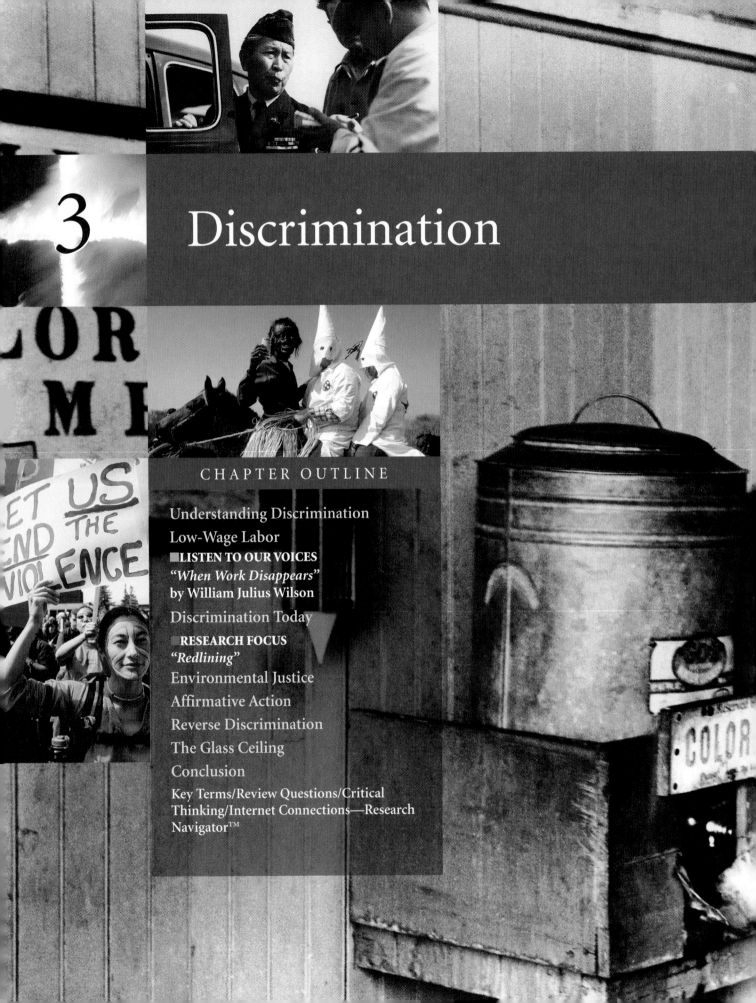

3 Discrimination

JUST AS SOCIAL SCIENTISTS HAVE ADVANCED THEORIES TO explain why prejudice exists, they have also presented explanations of why discrimination occurs. Social scientists look more and more at the manner in which institutions, not individuals, discriminate. Institutional discrimination is a pattern in social institutions that produces or perpetuates inequalities, even if individuals in the society do not intend to be racist or sexist. Income data document that gaps exist between racial and ethnic groups. Historically, attempts have been made to reduce discrimination, usually as a result of strong lobbying efforts by minorities themselves. Patterns of total discrimination make solutions particularly difficult for people in the informal economy or the underclass. Affirmative action was designed to equalize opportunity but has encountered significant resentment by those who charge that it constitutes reverse discrimination. Despite many efforts to end discrimination, glass ceilings and glass walls remain in the workplace.

CD-ROM *Activity 3.1*

Discrimination can take many forms. As the next two incidents indicate, discrimination can be either direct or the result of a complex combination of factors. It can lead to indignities or death.

Lawrence Otis Graham (1995) had "arrived" by the standards of most people in the United States. He was a graduate of Harvard Law School, married, and had become a well-regarded member of a Manhattan law firm. But he was also Black. Despite his success in securing clients for himself and his firm, Graham had noticed that White attorneys seemed to get a jump on him because of their associations with corporate leaders at private clubs. By tradition, the clubs were exclusively White. Graham decided to take time out from his law firm and learn more about the workings of these private clubs, which allowed some Whites to mingle in an informal atmosphere and so contributed to their establishing networks. These networks, in turn, allowed people to establish contacts that advanced their success in the business world. Rather than present himself as a successful Ivy League college graduate to become a member, he presented himself as a working-class African American seeking a job as a waiter. From the vantage point of a server, Graham figured he could observe the network of these predominantly White country club members. This was not to be the case. He was not given a job at club after club. Despite all sorts of encouragement when he talked to employers over the phone, he was denied a job when he presented himself and they saw that this articulate, well-mannered young man was Black. Eventually, he obtained a job as a bus boy, clearing tables in a club where the White servers commented that he could do their job better than they could.

Harvard-educated lawyer Lawrence Otis Graham sought a position as a waiter in exclusive clubs to learn more about contemporary discrimination.

Cynthia Wiggins was also African American, but she lived in a different world from Lawrence Otis Graham. She was a 17-year-old single mother struggling to make a living. She had sought jobs near her home but had found no employment opportunities. Eventually she found employment as a cashier, but it was far from her home, and she could not afford a car. Still, she was optimistic and looked forward to marrying the man to whom she was engaged. In 1995, she made the 50-minute bus ride from her predominantly Black neighborhood in Buffalo, New York, to her job at the Galleria, a fancy suburban shopping mall. Every day, charter buses unloaded shoppers from as far away as Canada, but city buses were not allowed on mall property. The bus Wiggins rode was forced to stop across the lot and across a seven-lane highway without sidewalks. On a December day, with the roadway lined with mounds of snow, she tried to cross the highway, only to be struck by a dump truck. She died three weeks later. Later investigation showed that the bus company had been trying to arrange for the bus to stop in the mall parking lot, but the shopping center authorities had blocked the move. Before the incident, the mall said they would consider allowing in suburban buses but not public buses from the city. As one mall store owner put it, "You'll never see an inner-city bus on the mall premises" (Barnes 1996:33; Gladwell 1996).

Discrimination has a long history, right up to the present, of taking its toll on people. For some, such as Lawrence Otis Graham, discrimination is being reminded that even when you do try to seek employment, you may be treated like a second-class citizen. For others, such as Cynthia Wiggins, discrimination meant suffering for the unjust decisions made in a society that quietly discriminated. Williams lost her life not because anyone actually intended to kill her but because decisions made it more likely that an inner-city resident would be an accident victim. Despite legislative and court efforts to eliminate discrimination, members of dominant and subordinate groups pay a price for continued intolerance.

Understanding Discrimination

Discrimination is the denial of opportunities and equal rights to individuals and groups because of prejudice or for other arbitrary reasons. Some people in the United States find it difficult to see discrimination as a widespread phenomenon. "After all," it is often said, "these minorities drive cars, hold jobs, own their homes, and even go to college." This does not mean that discrimination is rare. An understanding of discrimination in modern industrialized societies such as the United States must begin by distinguishing between relative and absolute deprivation.

Relative Versus Absolute Deprivation

Conflict theorists have said correctly that it is not absolute, unchanging standards that determine deprivation and oppression. Although minority groups may be viewed as having adequate or even good incomes, housing, health care, and educational opportunities, it is their position relative to some other group that offers evidence of discrimination.

Relative deprivation is defined as the conscious experience of a negative discrepancy between legitimate expectations and present actualities. After settling in the United States, immigrants often enjoy better material comforts and more political freedom than were possible in their old country. If they compare themselves with most other people in the United States, however, they will feel deprived because, although their standard has improved, the immigrants still perceive relative deprivation.

discrimination
The denial of opportunities and equal rights to individuals and groups because of prejudice or for other arbitrary reasons.

relative deprivation
The conscious experience of a negative discrepancy between legitimate expectations and present actualities.

absolute deprivation
The minimum level of subsistence below which families or individuals should not be expected to exist.

total discrimination
The combination of current discrimination with past discrimination created by poor schools and menial jobs.

Absolute deprivation, on the other hand, implies a fixed standard based on a minimum level of subsistence below which families should not be expected to exist. Discrimination does not necessarily mean absolute deprivation. A Japanese American who is promoted to a management position may still be a victim of discrimination if he or she had been passed over for years because of corporate reluctance to place an Asian American in a highly visible position.

Dissatisfaction is also likely to arise from feelings of relative deprivation. The members of a society who feel most frustrated and disgruntled by the social and economic conditions of their lives are not necessarily worse off in an objective sense. Social scientists have long recognized that what is most significant is how people perceive their situations. Karl Marx pointed out that, although the misery of the workers was important in reflecting their oppressed state, so was their position relative to the ruling class. In 1847, Marx wrote,

Although the enjoyment of the workers has risen, the social satisfaction that they have has fallen in comparison with the increased enjoyment of the capitalist.
(Marx and Engels 1955:94)

This statement explains why the groups or individuals who are most vocal and best organized against discrimination are not necessarily in the worst economic and social situation. However, they are likely to be those who most strongly perceive that, relative to others, they are not receiving their fair share. Resistance to perceived discrimination, rather than the actual amount of absolute discrimination, is the key.

Total Discrimination

Social scientists—and increasingly policy makers—have begun to use the concept of total discrimination. **Total discrimination**, as shown in Figure 3.1, refers to current discrimination operating in the labor market and past discrimination. Past discrimination experienced by an individual includes the poorer education and job experiences of racial and ethnic minorities compared with those of many White Americans. When considering discrimination, therefore, it is not enough to focus only on what is being done to people now. Sometimes a person may be dealt with fairly but may still be at a disadvantage because he or she suffered from poorer health care, inferior counseling in the school system, less access to books and other educational materials, or a poor job record resulting from absences to take care of brothers and sisters.

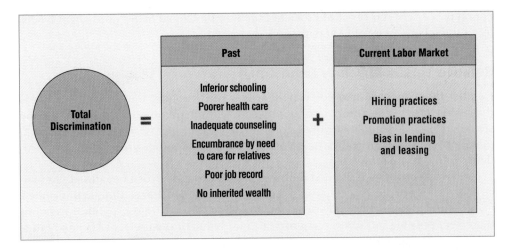

FIGURE 3.1 Total Discrimination

We find another variation of this past-in-present discrimination when apparently nondiscriminatory present practices have negative effects because of prior intentionally biased practices. Although unions that purposely discriminated against minority members in the past may no longer do so, some people are still prevented from achieving higher levels of seniority because of those past practices. Personnel records include a cumulative record that is vital in promotion and selection for desirable assignments. Blatantly discriminatory judgments and recommendations in the past remain part of a person's record.

Institutional Discrimination

Individuals practice discrimination in one-to-one encounters, and institutions practice discrimination through their daily operations. Indeed, a consensus is growing today that this institutional discrimination is more significant than that committed by prejudiced individuals.

Social scientists are particularly concerned with the ways in which patterns of employment, education, criminal justice, housing, health care, and government operations maintain the social significance of race and ethnicity. **Institutional discrimination** is the denial of opportunities and equal rights to individuals and groups that results from the normal operations of a society.

Civil rights activist Stokely Carmichael and political scientist Charles Hamilton are credited with introducing the concept of institutional racism. Individual discrimination refers to overt acts of individual Whites against individual Blacks; Carmichael and Hamilton reserved the term *institutional racism* for covert acts committed collectively against an entire group. From this perspective, discrimination can take place without an individual's intending to deprive others of privileges and even without the individual's being aware that others are being deprived (Ture and Hamilton 1992).

How can discrimination be widespread and unconscious at the same time? The following are a few documented examples of institutional discrimination.

1. Standards for assessing credit risks work against African Americans and Hispanics seeking to establish businesses because many lack conventional credit references. Businesses in low-income areas where these groups often reside also have much higher insurance costs. *Blacks*

2. IQ testing favors middle-class children, especially the White middle class, because of the types of questions included. *Blacks*

3. The entire criminal justice system, from the patrol officer to the judge and jury, is dominated by Whites who find it difficult to understand life in poverty areas.

4. Hiring practices often require several years' experience at jobs only recently opened to members of subordinate groups. *Women + blacks*

5. Many jobs automatically eliminate people with felony records or past drug offenses, which disproportionately reduces employment opportunities for people of color.

In some cases, even apparently neutral institutional standards can turn out to have discriminatory effects. In 1992, African American students at a Midwestern state university protested a policy under which fraternities and sororities that wanted to use campus facilities for a dance were required to post a $150 security deposit to cover possible damage. The Black students complained that this policy had a discriminatory impact on minority student organizations. Campus police countered that the university's policy applied to all student groups interested in using these facilities. However, because, overwhelmingly, White fraternities and sororities at the school had their own houses, which they used for dances, the policy affected only African American and other subordinate groups' organizations.

institutional discrimination
A denial of opportunities and equal rights to individuals or groups resulting from the normal operations of a society.

Ten years later, the entire nation scrambled to make aviation safer in the wake of the 9/11 terrorist attacks. The government saw airport security as a weak link and federalized airport screeners under the newly formed Transport Security Administration. Wages improved and training strengthened. The new screeners also had to be U.S. citizens. This latter provision eliminated the many legal immigrants from Asia, Africa, and Latin America who had previously worked as screeners. Airport screening went from overwhelmingly minority to 61 percent White. Clearly, this measure had the unintended consequences of discriminating against people of color (Alonso-Zaldivar and Oldham 2002).

The U.S. population is becoming more diversified, and examples of institutional discrimination are confronting more and different groups. Many Asian peoples have distinctive customs honoring their deceased family members. Among these traditions is the burning of incense at the gravesite, placing food on the grave markers, and leaving fake money. These practices stem from ancestor worship but often are followed by Christian Chinese Americans who try to hold on to some of the "old ways." Cemetery proprietors maintain standards of what they regard as proper grave decoration to maintain a tidy appearance. Consequently, people of Asian descent find they are unable to bury their loved ones in the cemeteries most convenient to them and must travel to cemeteries that are more open to different ways of memorializing the dead. Cemeteries do not consciously seek to keep people out because they are Asian, but they develop policies, often with little thought, that fail to recognize the pluralistic nature of society (Eng 1998).

The 2000 presidential election created headlines as it took weeks to resolve who won—Bush or Gore. Yet for 1.4 million African Americans who were denied the right to vote, this seemed like a national issue that had left them on the sidelines. The prohibition was not because they were Black, which would have been clearly racist and legally discriminatory, but because they were convicted felons. Twelve states prohibit felons from voting even *after* their prison sentence, although thousands have their sentences suspended. Because many of these states are in the South and have large Black populations, disproportionately, the voting prohibition covers African American men. Currently 13 percent of the nation's Black male population is precluded from voting by such laws. Florida was the deciding state in the close 2000 elections, and more than 200,000 potential Black voters were excluded. This case of institutional discrimination may have changed the outcome of a presidential election (Human Rights Watch 1998, 2002).

Institutional discrimination continuously imposes more hindrances on and awards fewer benefits to certain racial and ethnic groups than it does to others. This is the underlying and painful context of American intergroup relations.

Low-Wage Labor

A disproportionate share of racial and ethnic minority members are either unemployed or employed in low wage labor. Much of this low-wage labor is in a part of the labor market that provides little opportunities of improvement during one's time working and virtually no protection in terms of health insurance or retirement benefits.

The secondary labor market affecting many members of racial and ethnic minorities has come to be called the informal economy. The **informal economy** (also called the **irregular or underground economy**) consists of transfers of money, goods, or services that are not reported to the government. This label describes much of the work in inner-city neighborhoods and poverty-stricken rural areas, in sharp contrast to the rest of the marketplace. Workers are employed in the informal economy seasonally or infrequently. The work they do may resemble the work of traditional occupations,

informal economy
Transfers of money, goods, or services that are not reported to the government. Common in inner-city neighborhoods and poverty-stricken rural areas.

such as mechanic, cook, or electrician, but these workers lack the formal credentials to enter such employment. Indeed, workers in the informal economy may work sporadically or may moonlight in the regular economy. The informal economy also includes unregulated child-care services, garage sales, and the unreported income of craftspeople and street vendors.

The informal economy exists worldwide and networks nations though globalization. Recently, wide publicity was given to the presence of sweatshops throughout the world and in urban America that supplied clothing for major retailers such as Wal-Mart. Concern has targeted the apparel industry and working conditions of employees. Students have formed a nationwide coalition called United Students Against Sweatshops that brings attention to exploited workers here and abroad. Research also documents that Latinos and African Americans are much more likely than Whites to work "nonstandard shifts" (nights and weekends) without receiving premium wages (Appelbaum and Dreier 1999; Bonacich and Appelbaum 2000; Presser 2003).

According to the **dual labor market** model, minorities have been relegated to the informal economy. Although the informal economy may offer employment to the jobless, it provides few safeguards against fraud or malpractice that victimizes the workers. There are also few of the fringe benefits of health insurance and pensions that are much more likely to be present in the conventional marketplace. Therefore, informal economies are criticized for promoting highly unfair and dangerous working conditions. To be consigned to the informal economy is yet another example of social inequality.

Sociologist Edna Bonacich (1972, 1976) outlined the dual or split labor market that divides the economy into two realms of employment, the secondary one being populated primarily by minorities working at menial jobs. Even when not manual, labor is still rewarded less when performed by minorities. In keeping with the conflict model, this dual market model emphasizes that minorities fare unfavorably in the competition between dominant and subordinate groups.

The workers in the informal economy are ill prepared to enter the regular economy permanently or to take its better-paying jobs. Frequent changes in employment or lack of a specific supervisor leaves them without the kind of résumé that employers in the regular economy expect before they hire. Some of the sources of employment in the informal economy are illegal, such as fencing stolen goods, narcotics peddling, pimping, and prostitution. More likely, the work is legal but not transferable to a more traditional job. An example is an "information broker," who receives cash in

dual labor market
Division of the economy into two areas of employment, the secondary one of which is populated primarily by minorities working at menial jobs.

2 of minorities
menial jobs

Many people work in the informal economy with little prospect of moving into the primary, better-paying economy. Pictured is a street vendor in New York City.

Voices **Listen to Our Voices** Listen to Our

WHEN WORK DISAPPEARS

William Julius Wilson

It is interesting to note how the media perceptions of "underclass" values and attitudes contrast sharply with the views actually expressed by the residents of the inner-city ghetto. For example, a 28-year-old unmarried welfare mother of two children who lives in one of Chicago's large public housing projects described to one of the Urban Poverty and Family Life Study (UPFLS) interviewers how the media create the impression that the people who live in her housing project are all bad or are thugs and killers.

OK, I don't know where you live at, but you read the papers . . . they say, . . . Oh, Cabrini! Oh, they have gang killings . . . they have gang killings on the South Side! But the media and . . . and I guess the

public, you know, they build it up so big. I mean, it's bad everywhere. Did anyone offend you when you came up here? My neighbor stopped you and gave you the message. You're white, you're white and they don't know you here, see, see, but you read the paper and your parents will say "don't go over there, girl!" I read where they said, you know, well, I read where there they kill blacks . . . whites, and they do this and they do that, and they, I mean, we're people, too. But it's . . . that's just the system. It makes us look like we're all the same, and we're all bad. . . . But that's not true.

A 28-year-old welfare mother from another South Side housing project raised a similar point:

exchange for such information about where to find good buys or how to receive maximum benefits from public assistance programs (Pedder 1991).

Workers in the informal economy have not necessarily experienced direct discrimination. Because of past discrimination, they are unable to secure traditional employment. Working in the informal economy provides income but does not lead them into the primary labor market. A self-fulfilling cycle continues that allows past discrimination to create a separate work environment.

Not all low-wage laborers are a part of the informal economy, but many workers are driven into such jobs as better-paying jobs either move far away from where African Americans and Latinos live or even move abroad as globalization creates more and more of an international labor market. Sociologist William Wilson (1988, 1996, 2003) drew attention to the growth of families and individuals who are outside the mainstream of the occupational structure in the United States. In "Listen to Our Voices," sociologist and former president of the American Sociological Association William Julius Wilson presents the findings of his research. In this selection Wilson shows how the poor are very aware of how larger society sees them, labels them, and stereotypes them.

It is commonly believed that there are jobs available for the inner-city poor, but they just do not seek them. A study looked at jobs that were advertised in a help-wanted section of the *Washington Post*. The analysis showed that most of the jobs were beyond the reach of the underclass; perhaps 5 percent of all openings could even remotely be cons Listen to Our Voices Listen to Our Voices Listen

'Cause a lot of people when they meet me, they say, "You live in a project?" I say "yeah." "Well, you don't look like the type of person." "How is a person supposed to look?" You know, like I tell them, the project don't make nobody, you make yourself. Now, if you want to get out there and carry that project name, be tough and rowdy and sloppy, disrespectful, well, shoot, that's lowlife. "You don't look like the type that lives in a project!" "Well, how am I supposed to look?" Just because I live in a project, that don't mean I have to come outside looking like a tramp, because I'm not. But they all, they like, "You too nice to be living in a project." You know, sometimes I get offended. . . . . .That just really gets on my nerves. You know, don't no building make you, you make yourself. You live in a home, you know. Look at all these people that's got Hollywood kids, busted for cocaine, o.d.'in' on it, you know, what's happened to them?

Our research reveals that the beliefs of inner-city residents bear little resemblance to the blanket media reports asserting that values have plummeted in impoverished inner-city neighborhoods or that people in the inner city have an entirely different value system. What is so striking is that despite the overwhelming joblessness and poverty, black residents in inner-city ghetto neighborhoods actually verbally endorse, rather than undermine, the basic American values concerning individual initiative. ■

Source: Excerpt from *When Work Disappears* by William Julius Wilson. Copyright © 1996 by William Julius Wilson. Reprinted by permission of Alfred A. Knopf, a division of Random House, Inc.

sidered reasonable job prospects for people without skills or experience. During interviews with the employers, researchers found that an average of 21 people applied for each position, which typically was filled within three days of when the advertisement appeared. The mean hourly wage was $6.12, 42 percent offered no fringe benefits, and the remaining positions offered meager fringe benefits after six months or one year of employment. This study, like others before it, counters the folk wisdom that there are plenty of jobs around for the underclass (Pease and Martin 1997).

Discrimination Today

In 2003, the Legal Assistance Foundation of Metropolitan Chicago sent matched pairs of a White woman and a Black woman to seek jobs in suburban Chicago. They applied for a variety of jobs that were advertised or that posted "Help Wanted" signs in the window. Many of the jobs were retail positions in shopping centers or malls. Employers were 16 percent more likely to offer jobs to Whites than to Blacks, even though the Black applicant always applied first and presented stronger job-related qualifications. Black applicants were four times as likely to be asked about their absenteeism record and nearly twice as likely to be specifically asked why they left their previous job. This was in 2003, not 1953. It was also where jobs in urban American tend to be available—the suburbs (Lodder et al. 2003).

double jeopardy
The subordinate status twice defined, as experienced by women of color.

Discrimination is widespread in the United States. It sometimes results from prejudices held by individuals. More significantly, it is found in institutional discrimination and the presence of the informal economy. The presence of an underclass is symptomatic of many social forces, and total discrimination—past and present discrimination taken together—is one of them.

Measuring Discrimination

How much discrimination is there? As in measuring prejudice, problems arise in quantifying discrimination. Measuring prejudice is hampered by the difficulties in assessing attitudes and by the need to take many factors into account. It is further limited by the initial challenge of identifying different treatment. A second difficulty of measuring discrimination is assigning a cost to the discrimination.

Some tentative conclusions about discrimination can be made, however. Figure 3.2 uses income data to show vividly the disparity in income between African Americans and Whites, and also between men and women. This encompasses all full-time workers. White men, with a median income of $46,579, earn one-third more than Black men and nearly twice what Hispanic women earn in wages.

Clearly, White men earn most, followed by Black men, White women, Hispanic men, and Hispanic women. The sharpest drop is between White and Black men. Even worse, relatively speaking, is the plight of women. **Double jeopardy** refers to the combination of two subordinate statuses, defined as experienced by women of color. This disparity between the incomes of Black women and White men has remained unchanged over the more than 50 years during which such data have been tabulated. It illustrates yet another instance of the double jeopardy experienced by minority women. Also, Figure 3.2 includes only data for full-time, year-round workers; it excludes homemakers and the unemployed. Even in this comparison, the deprivation of Blacks, Hispanics, and women is confirmed again.

CD-ROM *Activity 3.3*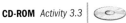

Are these differences entirely the result of discrimination in employment? No, individuals within the four groups are not equally prepared to compete for high-paying jobs. Past discrimination is a significant factor in a person's present social

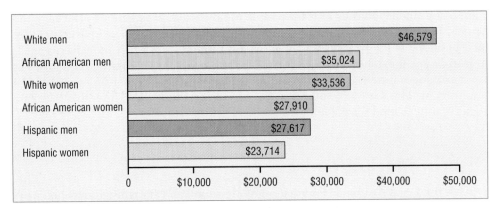

FIGURE 3.2   Median Income by Race, Ethnicity, and Gender, 2003
Even at the very highest levels of schooling, the income gap remains between Whites and Blacks. Education also has little apparent effect on the income gap between male and female workers. Even a brief analysis reveals striking differences in earning power between White men and other groups in the United States. Furthermore, the double jeopardy is apparent for African American and Hispanic women.
Note: Median income is from all sources and is limited to year-round, full-time workers over 25 years old. Data for White men and women are for non-Hispanics.
Source: DeNavas-Walt et al. 2004: FINC-01 and PINC-03.

TABLE 3.1
Median Income by Race and Sex, Holding Education Constant, 2003

Even at the very highest levels of schooling, the income gap remains between Whites and Blacks. Education also has little apparent effect on the income gap between male and female workers.

	Race		Sex	
	White Families	Black Families	Male	Female
Total	$61,036	$36,688	$41,939	$31,565
HIGH SCHOOL				
Nongraduate	30,841	19,956	26,468	18,938
Graduate	48,901	31,670	35,412	26,074
COLLEGE				
Some college	58,178	39,214	41,348	30,142
Bachelor's degree	84,227	64,977	56,502	41,327
Master's degree	95,214	77,453	70,640	50,163
Doctorate degree	100,000	81,346	87,131	66,491

Notes: Figures are median income from all sources except capital gains. Included are public assistance payments, dividends, pensions, unemployment compensation, and so on. Incomes are for all workers over 25 years of age. High school graduates include those with GEDs. Data for Whites are for White non-Hispanics. "Some college" excludes associate degree holders. Black data for doctorate is author's estimate.

Source: DeNavas-Walt et al. 2004: FINC-01 and PINC-03.

position. As discussed previously and illustrated in Figure 3.1, past discrimination continues to take its toll on modern victims. Taxpayers, predominantly White, were unwilling to subsidize the public education of African Americans and Hispanics at the same levels as White pupils. Even as these actions have changed, today's schools show the continuing results of this uneven spending pattern from the past. Education clearly is an appropriate variable to control.

In Table 3.1, median income is compared, holding education constant, which means that we can compare Blacks and Whites and men and women with approximately the same amount of formal schooling. More education means more money, but the disparity remains. The gap between races does narrow somewhat as education increases. However, both African Americans and women lag behind their more affluent counterparts. The contrast remains dramatic: Women with a master's degree typically receive $50,163, which means they earn over $6,500 less than men who complete only a bachelor's degree.

What do these individual differences look like if we consider them on a national level? Economist Andrew Brimmer (1995), citing numerous government studies, estimates that about 3 or 4 percent of the gross domestic product (GDP, or the value of goods and services) is lost annually by the failure to use African Americans' existing education. There had been little change in this economic cost from the mid-1960s to the mid-1990s. This estimate would be even higher if we took into account economic losses caused by the underuse of the academic talents of women and other minorities.

Now that education has been held constant, is the remaining gap caused by discrimination? No, not necessarily. Table 3.1 uses only the amount of schooling, not its quality. Racial minorities are more likely to attend inadequately financed schools. Some efforts have been made to eliminate disparities between school districts in the amount of wealth available to tax for school support, but with little success. The inequality of educational opportunity may seem less important in explaining sex discrimination. Although women usually are not segregated from men, educational institutions encourage talented women to enter fields that pay less (nursing or elementary education) than other occupations requiring similar amounts of training.

Eliminating Discrimination

Two main agents of social change work to reduce discrimination: voluntary associations organized to solve racial and ethnic problems, and the federal government, including the courts. The two are closely related: Most efforts initiated by the government were urged by associations or organizations representing minority groups, following vigorous protests against racism by African Americans. Resistance to social inequality by subordinate groups has been the key to change. Rarely has any government of its own initiative sought to end discrimination based on such criteria as race, ethnicity, and gender.

All racial and ethnic groups of any size are represented by private organizations that are to some degree trying to end discrimination. Some groups originated in the first half of the 20th century, but most have been founded since World War II or have become significant forces in bringing about change only since then. These include church organizations, fraternal social groups, minor political parties, and legal defense funds, as well as more militant organizations operating under the scrutiny of law enforcement agencies. The purposes, membership, successes, and failures of these resistance organizations dedicated to eliminating discrimination are discussed throughout this book.

Government action toward eliminating discrimination is also recent. Antidiscrimination actions have been taken by each branch of the government: the executive, the judicial, and the legislative.

The first antidiscrimination action at the executive level was President Franklin D. Roosevelt's 1943 creation of the Fair Employment Practices Commission (FEPC), which handled thousands of complaints of discrimination, mostly from African Americans, despite strong opposition by powerful economic and political leaders and many southern Whites. The FEPC had little actual power. It had no authority to compel employers to stop discriminating but could only ask for voluntary compliance. Its jurisdiction was limited to federal government employees, federal contractors, and labor unions. State and local governments and any business without a federal contract

Relatively few workers are hired due to affirmative action pressure, yet many minority workers are viewed by their colleagues at work as taking the place of someone "more qualified."

were not covered. Furthermore, the FEPC never enjoyed vigorous support from the White House, was denied adequate funds, and was part of larger agencies that were hostile to the commission's existence. This weak antidiscrimination agency was finally dropped in 1946, to be succeeded by an even weaker one in 1948.

The judiciary, charged with interpreting laws and the U.S. Constitution, has a much longer history of involvement in the rights of racial, ethnic, and religious minorities. However, its early decisions protected the rights of the dominant group, as in the 1857 U.S. Supreme Court's *Dred Scott* decision, which ruled that slaves remained slaves even when living or traveling in states where slavery was illegal. Not until the 1940s did the Supreme Court revise earlier decisions and begin to grant African Americans the same rights as those held by Whites. The 1954 *Brown v. Board of Education* decision, which stated that "separate but equal" facilities, including education, were unconstitutional, heralded a new series of rulings, arguing that distinguishing between races in order to segregate was inherently unconstitutional.

It was assumed incorrectly by many that *Brown* and other judicial actions would lead quickly to sweeping change. In fact, little change occurred initially, and resistance to racism continued. The immediate effect of many court rulings was minimal because the executive branch and the Congress did not want to violate the principle of **states' rights,** which holds that each state is sovereign in most of its affairs and has the right to order them without interference from the federal government. In other words, supporters of states' rights felt that the federal government had to allow state governments to determine how soon the rights of African Americans would be protected. Gradually, U.S. society became more committed to the rights of individuals. Legislation in the 1960s committed the federal government to protecting civil rights actively rather than merely leaving action up to state and local officials.

The most important legislative effort to eradicate discrimination was the Civil Rights Act of 1964. This act led to the establishment of the Equal Employment Opportunity Commission (EEOC), which had the power to investigate complaints against employers and to recommend action to the Department of Justice. If the Justice Department sued and discrimination was found, the court could order appropriate compensation. The act covered employment practices of all businesses with more than 25 employees and nearly all employment agencies and labor unions. A 1972 amendment broadened the coverage to employers with as few as fifteen employees.

The act also prohibited different voting registration standards for White and Black voting applicants. It also prohibited discrimination in public accommodations: that is, hotels, motels, restaurants, gasoline stations, and amusement parks. Publicly owned facilities, such as parks, stadiums, and swimming pools, were also prohibited from discriminating. Another important provision forbade discrimination in all federally supported programs and institutions, such as hospitals, colleges, and road construction projects.

The Civil Rights Act of 1964 covered discrimination based on race, color, creed, national origin, and sex. Although the inclusion of gender in employment criteria had been prohibited in the federal civil service since 1949, most laws and most groups pushing for change showed little concern about sex discrimination. There was little precedent for attention to sex discrimination even at the state level. Only Hawaii and Wisconsin had enacted laws against sex discrimination before 1964. As first proposed, the Civil Rights Act did not include mention of gender. One day before the final vote, opponents of the measure offered an amendment on gender bias in an effort to defeat the entire act. The act did pass with prohibition against sex bias included, an event that can only be regarded as a milestone for women seeking equal employment rights with men.

The Civil Rights Act of 1964 was not perfect. Since 1964, several acts and amendments to the original act have been added to cover the many areas of discrimination it left untouched, such as criminal justice and housing. Even in areas singled out for enforcement in the Civil Rights Act of 1964, discrimination still occurs. Federal agen-

states' rights
The principle, reinvoked in the late 1940s, that holds that each state is sovereign and has the right to order its own affairs without interference by the federal government.

cies charged with its enforcement complain that they are underfunded or are denied wholehearted support by the White House. Also, regardless of how much the EEOC may want to act in a particular case, the person who alleges discrimination has to pursue the complaint over a long time, marked by long periods of inaction.

Despite these efforts, devastating forms of discrimination persist. African Americans, Latinos, and others fall victim to redlining. **Redlining** is the pattern of discrimination against people trying to buy homes in minority and racially changing neighborhoods. In "Research Focus" we consider the extent of redlining today.

Although civil rights laws often have established rights for other minorities, the Supreme Court made them explicit in two 1987 decisions involving groups other than African Americans. In the first of the two cases, an Iraqi-American professor asserted that he had been denied tenure because of his Arab origins; in the second, a Jewish congregation brought suit for damages in response to the defacing of its synagogue with derogatory symbols. The Supreme Court ruled unanimously that, in effect, any member of an ethnic minority may sue under federal prohibitions against discrimination. These decisions paved the way for almost all racial and ethnic groups to invoke the Civil Rights Act of 1964 (Taylor 1987).

A particularly insulting form of discrimination seemed finally to be on its way out in the late 1980s. Many social clubs had limitations forbidding membership to minorities, Jews, and women. For years, exclusive clubs argued that they were merely selecting friends, but, in fact, a principal function of these clubs is as a forum to transact business. Denial of membership meant more than the inability to attend a luncheon; it also seemed to exclude one from part of the marketplace, as Lawrence Otis Graham observed at the beginning of this chapter. The Supreme Court ruled unanimously in the 1988 case *New York State Clubs Association v. City of New York* that states and cities may ban sex discrimination by large private clubs where business lunches and similar activities take place. Although the ruling does not apply to all clubs and leaves the issue of racial and ethnic barriers unresolved, it did chip away at the arbitrary exclusiveness of private groups (Taylor 1988).

Memberships and restrictive organizations remain perfectly legal. The rise to national attention of professional golfer Tiger Woods, of mixed Native American,

redlining
The pattern of discrimination against people trying to buy homes in minority and racially changing neighborhoods.

REDLINING

A home is the typical family's most important financial asset and the most important means of transmitting wealth from generation to generation. Historically, minority homebuyers found themselves unable to secure home loans. Lenders circled areas on a city map in red pencil (hence, the term *redlining*) that they regarded as too insecure to grant mortgages. If loans were granted in redlined neighborhoods, interest rates were much higher, and greater demands were made on the family to prove its financial ability to maintain payments. These neighborhoods were almost always minority residential areas and, because of racial segregation, the areas in which African Americans and other minority buyers were most able to find housing open to them. Legislation now prevents such explicit forms of racial bias, but does redlining persist in a more subtle fashion?

Research finds that in 25 metropolitan areas, housing agents showed fewer housing units to Blacks and Latinos, steered them to minority neighborhoods, and gave them far less assistance in finding housing that met their needs. Other recent studies reveal that lenders are more likely to turn down a mortgage request from a minority applicant than from an equally qualified White and that lenders give minority applicants far less assistance in filling out their forms.

Successful African American homebuyers find that they receive less for their homes.

Controlling for a variety of factors except race of neighborhood, Black homeowners received 18 percent less value for their homes than White homeowners. The Brookings Institution has called this "the segregation tax," the price Blacks pay for living in all-Black neighborhoods.

The concept of redlining is now being applied to areas other than homebuying. People living in predominantly minority neighborhoods have found that service deliverers refuse to go to their area. In one case that attracted national attention, in 1997, Kansas City's Pizza Hut refused to deliver 40 pizzas to an honor program at a high school in an all-Black neighborhood. A Pizza Hut spokesperson called the neighborhood unsafe and said that almost every city has "restricted areas" to which the company will not deliver. This admission was particularly embarrassing because the high school already had a $170,000-a-year contract with Pizza Hut to deliver pizzas as a part of their school lunch program.

Service redlining covers everything from parcel deliveries to repair people as well as food deliveries. The red pencil appears not be have been set aside in cities throughout the United States. ■

Sources: Fuller 1998; Rusk 2001; A. Schwartz 2001; Turner et al. 2002; Yinger 1995.

African, and Asian ancestry, made the public aware that there were at least 23 golf courses he would be prohibited from playing by virtue of race. In 2002, women's groups tried unsuccessfully to have the golf champion speak out as the Master's and British Open played on courses closed to women as members (Scott 2003).

The inability of the Civil Rights Act, similar legislation, and court decisions to end discrimination does not result entirely from poor financial and political support, although they played a role. The number of federal employees assigned to investigate and prosecute bias cases is insufficient. Many discriminatory practices, such as those described as institutional discrimination, are seldom subject to legal action.

environmental justice
Efforts to ensure that hazardous substances are controlled so that all communities receive protection regardless of race or socioeconomic circumstances.

Environmental Justice

Discrimination takes many forms and is not necessarily apparent, even when its impact can be far reaching. Take the example of Kennedy Heights, a well-kept working-class neighborhood nestled in southeastern Houston. This community faces a real threat and it is not from crime or drugs. The threat they fear is under their feet, in the form of three oil pits abandoned by Gulf Oil in 1927. The residents, most of whom are African American, argue that they have suffered high rates of cancer, lupus, and other illnesses because the chemicals from the oil fields poison their water supply. The residents first sued Chevron USA in 1985, and the case is still making its way through the courtrooms of no less than six states and the federal judiciary.

Lawyers and other representatives for the residents say that the oil company is guilty of environmental racism because it knowingly allowed a predominantly Black housing development to be built on the contaminated land. They are able to support this charge with documents, including a 1954 memorandum from an appraiser who suggested that the oil pits be drained of any toxic substances and the land filled for "low-cost houses for White occupancy." When the land did not sell right away, an oil company official in a 1967 memorandum suggested a tax-free land exchange with a developer who intended to use the land for "Negro residents and commercial development." For this latter intended use by African Americans, there was no mention of environmental cleanup of the land. The oil company counters that it just assumed the developer would do the necessary cleanup of the pits (Manning 1997; Verhovek 1997).

The conflict perspective sees the case of the Houston suburb as one in which pollution harms minority groups disproportionately. **Environmental justice** refers to the efforts to ensure that hazardous substances are controlled so that all communities receive protection regardless of race or socioeconomic circumstance. After the Environmental Protection Agency (EPA) and other organizations documented discrimination in the locating of hazardous waste sites, an Executive Order was issued in 1994 that requires all federal agencies to ensure that low-income and minority communities have access to better information about their environment and have an opportunity to participate in shaping government policies that affect their community's health. Initial efforts to implement the policy have met widespread opposition, including criticism from some proponents of economic development who

The location of health hazards near minority and low-income neighborhoods is regarded as a concern of environmental justice. Pictured here is a youth basketball court next to an oil refinery in Norco, Louisiana, which has been dubbed "cancer alley."

argue that the guidelines unnecessarily delay or block altogether locating new industrial sites.

Sociologist Robert Bullard (1990) has shown that low-income communities and areas with significant minority populations are more likely to be adjacent to waste sites than are affluent White communities. Undergraduate student researchers at Occidental College in California found in 1995 that the poor, African Americans, Latinos, Asian Americans, and Native Americans were especially likely to be living near Los Angeles County's 82 potential environmental hazards. Another study in 2001 also showed the higher probability that people of color live closer to sources of air pollution. Yet a third study, released in 2003, found that grade schools in Florida nearer environmental hazards are disproportionately Black or Latino. People of color jeopardized by environmental problems also lack the resources and political muscle to do something about it (Institute of Medicine 1999; Moffat 1995; Polakovic 2001; Streteksy and Lynch 2002).

Issues of environmental justice are not limited to metropolitan areas. Another continuing problem is abuse of Native American reservation land. Many American Indian leaders are concerned that tribal lands are too often regarded as dumping grounds for toxic waste that go to the highest bidder.

As with other aspects of discrimination, experts disagree. There is controversy within the scientific community over the potential hazards of some of the problems, and there is even some opposition within the subordinate communities being affected. This complexity of the issues in terms of social class and race is apparent, as some observers question the wisdom of an executive order that slows economic development coming to areas in dire need of employment opportunities. On the other hand, some counter that such businesses typically employ few less-skilled workers and only make the environment less livable for those left behind. Despite such varying viewpoints, environmental justice is an excellent example of resistance and change in the 1990s that could not have been foreseen by the civil rights workers of the 1950s.

Affirmative Action

Affirmative action is the positive effort to recruit subordinate-group members, including women, for jobs, promotions, and educational opportunities. The phrase *affirmative action* first appeared in an executive order issued by President Kennedy in 1961. The order called for contractors to "take affirmative action to ensure that applicants are employed, and that employees are treated during employment, without regard to their race, creed, color, or national origin." However, at this early time, no enforcement procedures were specified. Six years later, the order was amended to prohibit discrimination on the basis of sex, but affirmative action was still defined vaguely.

Today, affirmative action has become a catch-all term for racial preference programs and goals. It has also become a lightning rod for opposition to any programs that suggest special consideration of women or racial minorities.

Affirmative Action Explained

Affirmative action has been viewed as an important tool for reducing institutional discrimination. Whereas previous efforts were aimed at eliminating individual acts of discrimination, federal measures under the heading of affirmative action have been aimed at procedures that deny equal opportunities, even if they are not intended to be overtly discriminatory. This policy has been implemented to deal with both the current discrimination and the past discrimination outlined earlier in this chapter.

affirmative action
Positive efforts to recruit subordinate group members, including women, for jobs, promotions, and educational opportunities.

Affirmative action has been aimed at institutional discrimination in such areas as:

- Height and weight requirements that are unnecessarily geared to the physical proportions of White men without regard to the actual characteristics needed to perform the job and therefore exclude women and some minorities.

- Seniority rules, when applied to jobs historically held only by White men, that make more recently hired minorities and females more subject to layoff—the "last hired, first fired" employee—and less eligible for advancement.

- Nepotism-based membership policies of some unions that exclude those who are not relatives of members, who, because of past employment practices, are usually White.

- Restrictive employment leave policies, coupled with prohibitions on part-time work or denials of fringe benefits to part-time workers, that make it difficult for the heads of single-parent families, most of whom are women, to get and keep jobs and also meet the needs of their families.

- Rules requiring that only English be spoken at the workplace, even when not a business necessity, which result in discriminatory employment practices toward people whose primary language is not English.

- Standardized academic tests or criteria geared to the cultural and educational norms of middle-class or White men when these are not relevant predictors of successful job performance.

- Preferences shown by law and medical schools in admitting children of wealthy and influential alumni, nearly all of whom are White.

- Credit policies of banks and lending institutions that prevent the granting of mortgages and loans in minority neighborhoods or prevent the granting of credit to married women and others who have previously been denied the opportunity to build good credit histories in their own names.

Employers have also been cautioned against asking leading questions in interviews, such as "Did you know you would be the first Black to supervise all Whites in that factory?" or "Does your husband mind your working on weekends?" Furthermore, the lack of minority-group (Blacks, Asians, Native Americans, and Hispanics) or female employees may in itself represent evidence for a case of unlawful exclusion (Commission on Civil Rights 1981).

The Legal Debate

How far can an employer go in encouraging women and minorities to apply for a job before it becomes unlawful discrimination against White men? Since the late 1970s, a number of bitterly debated cases on this difficult aspect of affirmative action have reached the U.S. Supreme Court. The most significant cases are summarized in Table 3.2. Furthermore, as we will see, the debate has moved into party politics.

In the 1978 Bakke case (*Regents of the University of California v. Bakke*), by a narrow 5–4 vote, the Court ordered the medical school of the University of California at Davis to admit Allan Bakke, a qualified White engineer who had originally been denied admission solely on the basis of his race. The justices ruled that the school had violated Bakke's constitutional rights by establishing a fixed quota system for minority students. However, the Court added that it was constitutional for universities to adopt flexible admission programs that use race as one factor in making decisions.

Colleges and universities responded with new policies designed to meet the Bakke ruling while broadening opportunities for traditionally underrepresented minority students. However, in 1996 the Supreme Court allowed a lower court decision to stand that affirmative action programs for African American and Mexican American students at the University of Texas law school were unconstitutional. The ruling effec-

---

TABLE 3.2
Key Decisions on Affirmative Action

In a series of split and often very close decisions, the Supreme Court has expressed a variety of reservations in specific situations.

Year	Favorable/ Unfavorable to Policy	Case	Vote	Ruling
1971	+	*Griggs v. Duke Power Co.*	9–0	Private employers must provide a remedy where minorities were denied opportunities, even if unintentional
1978	−	*Regents of the University of California v. Bakke*	5–4	Prohibited specific number of places for minorities in college admissions
1979	+	*United Steelworkers of America v. Weber*	5–2	Okay for union to favor minorities in special training programs
1984	−	*Firefighters Local Union No 1784 (Memphis, TN) v. Stotts*	6–1	Seniority means recently hired minorities may be laid off first in staff reductions
1986	+	*International Association of Firefighters v. City of Cleveland*	6–3	May promote minorities over more senior Whites
1986	+	*New York City v. Sheet Metal*	5–4	Approved specific quota of minority workers for union
1987	+	*United States v. Paradise*	5–4	Endorsed quotas for promotions of state troopers
1987	+	*Johnson v. Transportation Agency, Santa Clara, CA*	6–3	Approved preference in hiring for minorities and women over better-qualified men and Whites
1989	−	*Richmond v. Croson Company*	6–3	Ruled a 30 percent set-aside program for minority contractors unconstitutional
1989	−	*Martin v. Wilks*	5–4	Ruled Whites may bring reverse discrimination claims against court-approved affirmative action plans
1990	+	*Metro Broadcasting v. FCC*	5–4	Supported federal programs aimed at increasing minority ownership of broadcast licenses
1995	−	*Adarand Constructors Inc. v. Peña*	5–4	Benefits based on race are constitutional only if narrowly defined to accomplish a compelling interest
1996	−	*Texas v. Hopwood*	*	Let stand a lower court decision covering Louisiana, Mississippi, and Texas that race could not be used in college admissions
2003	+	*Grutter v. Bollinger*	5–4	Race can be a factor in admissions at the University of Michigan Law School
2003	−	*Gratz v. Bollinger*	6–3	Cannot use a strict formula awarding advantage based on race for admissions to the University of Michigan

*5th U.S. Circuit Court of Appeals decision.

---

tively prohibited schools in the lower court's jurisdiction of Louisiana, Mississippi, and Texas from taking race into account in admissions. In 2003, the Supreme Court made two rulings concerning the admissions policies at the University of Michigan. In one case involving the law school, the Court upheld the right of the school to use applicants' race as criteria for admission decisions but found against a strict admissions formula awarding points to minority applicants who applied to the university's undergraduate school. Given the various legal actions, further challenges to affirmative action can be expected (Greenhouse 2003a).

Even if the U.S. public acknowledges the disparity in earnings between White men and others, growing numbers of people doubt that everything done in the name of affirmative action is desirable. In 2001, national surveys showed that 58 percent thought that affirmative action had been good for the country, but 35 percent felt programs should be decreased, whereas 24 percent advocated an expansion of affirmative action (Gallup 2002).

Has affirmative action actually helped alleviate employment inequality on the basis of race and gender? This is a difficult question to answer, given the complexity of the labor market and the fact that there are other antidiscrimination measures, but it does appear that affirmative action has had significant impact in the sectors where it has been applied. Sociologist Barbara Reskin (1998) reviewed available studies looking at workforce composition in terms of race and gender in light of affirmative action policies. She found that gains in minority employment can be attributed to affirmative action policies. This includes both firms mandated to follow affirmative action guidelines and those that took them on voluntarily. There is also evidence that some earnings gains can be attributed to affirmative action. Economists M. V. Lee Badgett and Heidi Hartmann (1995), reviewing 26 other research studies, came to similar conclusions: Affirmative action and other federal compliance programs have had a modest impact, but it is difficult to assess, given larger economic changes such as recessions or the rapid increase in women in the paid labor force.

Reverse Discrimination

While researchers debated the merit of affirmative action, the general public—particularly Whites but also some affluent African Americans and Hispanics—questioned the wisdom of the program. Particularly strident were the charges of **reverse discrimination:** that government actions cause better-qualified White men to be bypassed in favor of women and minority men. *Reverse discrimination* is an emotional term because it conjures up the notion that somehow women and minorities will subject White men in the United States to the same treatment received by minorities during the last three centuries. Increasingly, critics of affirmative action call for color-blind policies that would end affirmative action and, they argue, allow all people to be judged fairly. Of major significance, often overlooked in public debates, is that a color-blind policy implies a very limited role for the state in addressing social inequality between racial and ethnic groups (Kahng 1978; Skrentny 1996; Winant 1994).

Is it possible to have color-blind policies in the United States as we move into the 21st century? Supporters of affirmative action contend that as long as businesses rely on informal social networks, personal recommendations, and family ties, White men will have a distinct advantage built on generations of being in positions of power. Furthermore, an end to affirmative action should also mean an end to the many programs that give advantages to certain businesses, homeowners, veterans, farmers, and others. Most of these preference holders are White (Kilson 1995; Mack 1996).

Consequently, by the 1990s, affirmative action had emerged as an increasingly important issue in state and national political campaigns. Generally, discussion focused on the use of quotas in hiring practices. Supporters of affirmative action argue that hiring goals establish "floors" for minority inclusion but do not exclude truly qualified candidates from any group. Opponents insist that these "targets" are, in fact, quotas that lead to reverse discrimination.

reverse discrimination
Actions that cause better qualified White men to be passed over for women and minority men.

MANAGEMENT'S IDEA OF PERFECT DIVERSITY

SIGNE
PHILADELPHIA DAILY NEWS
Philadelphia
USA

The state of California, in particular, was a battleground for this controversial issue. The California Civil Rights Initiative was placed on the ballot in 1996 as a referendum to amend the state constitution and prohibit any programs that give preference to women and minorities for college admission, employment, promotion, or government contracts. Overall, 54 percent of the voters backed the state proposition, with 61 percent of men in favor compared with only 48 percent of women. Whites, who represented 74 percent of the voters, voted in favor of the measure overwhelmingly, with 63 percent backing Proposition 209. This compares with 26 percent of African Americans, 24 percent of Hispanics, and 39 percent of Asian Americans favoring the end of affirmative action in state-operated institutions. Obviously, the voters—Whites and men—who perceived themselves as least likely to benefit from affirmative action overwhelmingly favored Proposition 209.

Legal challenges continue concerning Proposition 209, which is being implemented unevenly throughout the state. Much of the attention has focused on the impact that reducing racial preference programs will have in law and medical schools, in which competition for admission is very high. The courts have upheld the measures, and in 1998 voters in Washington state passed a similar anti–affirmative action measure (Dolan 2000).

The Glass Ceiling

We have been talking primarily about racial and ethnic groups as if they have uniformly failed to keep pace with Whites. Although that is accurate, there are tens of thousands of people of color who have matched and even exceeded Whites in terms of income. For example, in 2000, more than 815,000 Black households and more than 556,000 Hispanic households earned more than $100,000. What can we say about affluent members of subordinate groups in the United States (Bureau of the Census 2001e)?

glass ceiling
The barrier that blocks the promotion of a qualified worker because of gender or minority membership.

Prejudice does not necessarily end with wealth. Black newspaper columnist De Wayne Wickham (1993) wrote of the subtle racism he had experienced. He heard a White clerk in a supermarket ask a White customer whether she knew the price of an item the computer would not scan; when the problem occurred while the clerk was ringing up Wickham's groceries, she called for a price check. Affluent subordinate-group members routinely report being blocked as they move toward the first-class section aboard airplanes or seek service in upscale stores. Another journalist, Ellis Cose (1993), has called these insults the soul-destroying slights to affluent minorities that lead to the "rage of a privileged class."

Discrimination persists for even the educated and qualified from the best family backgrounds. As subordinate-group members are able to compete successfully, they sometimes encounter attitudinal or organizational bias that prevents them from reaching their full potential. They have confronted what has come to be called the **glass ceiling.** This refers to the barrier that blocks the promotion of a qualified worker because of gender or minority membership (Figure 3.3). Often, people entering nontraditional areas of employment become marginalized and are made to feel uncomfortable, much like the situation of immigrants who feel a part of two cultures, as we discussed in Chapter 1.

The reasons for glass ceilings are as many as the occurrences. It may be that one Black or one woman vice president is regarded as enough, so the second potential

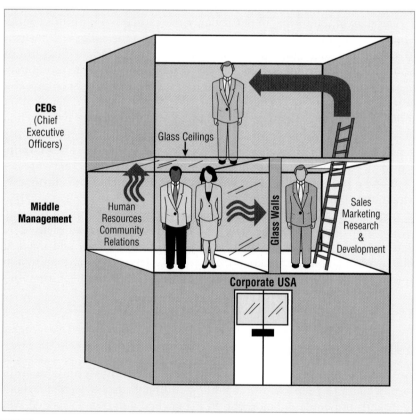

FIGURE 3.3 Glass Ceilings and Glass Walls
Women and minority men are moving up in corporations but encounter glass ceilings that block entry to top positions. In addition, they face glass walls that block lateral moves to areas from which executives are promoted.

candidate faces a block to movement up through management. Decision makers may be concerned that their clientele will not trust them if they have too many people of color or may worry that a talented woman could become overwhelmed with her duties as a mother and wife and thus perform poorly in the workplace.

Concern about women and minorities climbing a broken ladder led to the formation in 1991 of the Glass Ceiling Commission, with the U.S. Secretary of Labor chairing the 21-member group. Initially, it regarded some of the glass ceiling barriers as:

- Lack of management commitment to establishing systems, policies, and practices for achieving workplace diversity and upward mobility.
- Pay inequities for work of equal or comparable value.
- Sex-, race-, and ethnicity-based stereotyping and harassment.
- Unfair recruitment practices.
- Lack of family-friendly workplace policies.
- "Parent-track" policies that discourage parental leave policies.
- Limited opportunities for advancement to decision-making positions.

These barriers contribute to women not moving into the ultimate decision-making positions in the nation's corporate giants.

This significant underrepresentation of women and minority males in managerial positions results in large part from the presence of glass ceilings. Sociologist Max Weber wrote over a hundred years ago that the privileged class monopolizes the purchase of high-priced consumer goods and wields the power to grant or withhold opportunity from others. To grasp just how White and male the membership of this elite group is, consider the following: Eighty-two percent of the 11,500 people who serve on the boards of directors of *Fortune* 1,000 corporations are non-Hispanic White males. For every 82 White men on these boards, there are 2 Latinos, 2 Asian Americans, 3 African Americans, and 11 White women (Strauss 2002; Weber [1913–1922] 1947).

Glass ceilings are not the only barrier. There are also glass walls. Catalyst, a non-profit research organization, conducted interviews in 1992 and again in 2001 with senior and middle managers from larger corporations. The study found that even before glass ceilings are encountered, women and racial and ethnic minorities face **glass walls** that keep them from moving laterally. Specifically, the study found that women tend to be placed in staff or support positions in areas such as public relations and human resources and are often directed away from jobs in core areas such as marketing, production, and sales. Women are assigned to, and therefore trapped in, jobs that reflect their stereotypical helping nature and encounter glass walls that cut off access to jobs that might lead to broader experience and advancement (Catalyst 2001; Lopez 1992).

Researchers have documented a differential impact that the glass ceiling has on White males. It appears that men who enter traditionally female occupations are more likely to rise to the top. Male elementary teachers become principals and male nurses become supervisors. The **glass escalator** refers to the male advantage experienced in occupations dominated by women. While females may become tokens when they enter traditionally male occupations, men are more likely to be advantaged when they move out of sex-typical jobs. In summary, women and minority men confront a glass ceiling that limits upward mobility and glass walls reduce their ability to move into fast-track jobs that lead to the highest reaches of the corporate executive suite. Meanwhile men who do choose to enter female-dominated occupations are often rewarded with promotions and positions of responsibility coveted by their fellow female workers (Budig 2002 ; Cognard-Black 2004).

glass wall
A barrier to moving laterally in a business to positions that are more likely to lead to upward mobility.

glass escalator
The male advantage experienced in occupations dominated by women

Conclusion

Discrimination takes its toll, whether a person who is discriminated against is part of the informal economy or not. Even members of minority groups who are not today being overtly discriminated against continue to fall victim to past discrimination. We have also identified the costs of discrimination to members of the privileged group. The attitudes of Whites and even members of minority groups themselves are influenced by the images they have of racial and ethnic groups. These images come from what has been called statistical discrimination, which causes people to act based on stereotypes they hold and the actions of a few subordinate-group members.

From the conflict perspective, it is not surprising to find the widespread presence of the informal economy proposed by the dual labor market model and even an underclass. Derrick Bell (1994), an African American law professor, has made the sobering assertion that "racism is permanent." He contends that the attitudes of dominant Whites prevail, and society is willing to advance programs on behalf of subordinate groups only when they coincide with needs as perceived by those Whites.

The surveys presented in Chapter 2 show gradual acceptance of the earliest efforts to eliminate discrimination, but that support is failing, especially as it relates to affirmative action. Indeed, concerns about doing something about alleged reverse discrimination are as likely to be voiced as concerns about racial or gender discrimination or glass ceilings and glass walls.

Institutional discrimination remains a formidable challenge in the United States. Attempts to reduce discrimination by attacking institutional discrimination have met with staunch resistance. Partly as a result of this outcry from some of the public, especially White Americans, the federal government gradually deemphasized its affirmative action efforts in the 1980s and 1990s. As we turn to examine the various groups that make up the American people, through generations of immigration and religious diversity, look for the types of programs designed to reduce prejudice and discrimination that were discussed here. Most of the material in this chapter has been about racial groups, especially Black and White Americans. It would be easy to see intergroup hostility as a racial phenomenon, but that would be incorrect. Throughout the history of the United States, relations between some White groups have been characterized by resentment and violence. The next two chapters examine the nature and relations of White ethnic groups.

Key Terms

absolute deprivation 68
affirmative action 81
discrimination 67
double jeopardy 74
dual labor market 71
environmental justice 80
glass ceiling 86

glass escalator 87
glass wall 87
informal economy 70
institutional
    discrimination 69
irregular or underground
    economy 70

redlining 78
relative deprivation 67
reverse discrimination 84
states' rights 77
total discrimination 68

Review Questions

1. Why might people still feel disadvantaged, even though their incomes are rising and their housing circumstances have improved?
2. Why does institutional discrimination sometimes seem less objectionable than individual discrimination?
3. In what way does an industrial society operate on several economic levels?
4. Why are questions raised about affirmative action while inequality persists?
5. Distinguish between glass ceilings and glass walls. How do they differ from more obvious forms of discrimination in employment?

Critical Thinking

1. Discrimination can take many forms. Consider the college you attend. Select a case of discrimination that you think just about everyone would agree is wrong. Then describe another incident in which the alleged discrimination was of a more subtle form. Who is likely to condemn and who is likely to overlook such situations?
2. Resistance is a continuing theme of intergroup race relations. Discrimination implies the oppression of a group, but how can discrimination also unify the oppressed group to resist such unequal treatment? How can acceptance, or integration, for example, weaken the sense of solidarity within a group?
3. Voluntary associations such as the NAACP and government units such as the courts have been important vehicles for bringing about a measure of social justice. In what ways can the private sector—corporations and businesses—also work to bring about an end to discrimination?

Internet Connections—Research Navigator™

Follow the instructions found on page 31 of this text to access the features of Research Navigator™. Once at the Web site, enter your Login Name and Password. Then, to use the ContentSelect database, enter keywords such as "informal economy," "affirmative action," and "glass ceiling," and the research engine will supply relevant and recent scholarly and popular press publications. Use the *New York Times* Search-by-Subject Archive to find recent news articles related to sociology, and the Link Library feature to locate relevant Web links organized by the key terms associated with this chapter.

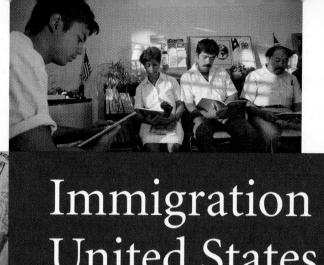

4

Immigration and the United States

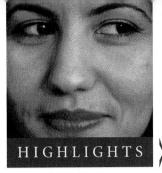

T HE DIVERSITY OF THE AMERICAN PEOPLE IS UNMISTAKABLE evidence of the variety of places from which immigrants have come. Yet each succeeding generation of immigrants found itself being reluctantly accepted, at best, by the descendants of earlier arrivals. The Chinese were the first immigrant group to be singled out for restriction, with the passage of the 1882 Exclusion Act. The initial Chinese immigrants became scapegoats for America's sagging economy in the last half of the 19th century. Growing fears that too many non-American types were immigrating motivated the creation of the national origin system and the quota acts of the 1920s. These acts gave preference to certain nationalities, until the passage of the Immigration and Naturalization Act in 1965 ended that practice. Many immigrants are transnationals who still maintain close ties to their country of origin, sending money back, keeping current with political events, and making frequent return trips. Concern about both illegal and legal immigration has continued through today with increased attention in the aftermath of the September 11, 2001, terrorist attacks. Restrictionist sentiment has grown, and debates rage over whether immigrants, even legal ones, should receive services such as education, government-subsidized health care, and welfare. Controversy also continues to surround the policy of the United States toward refugees.

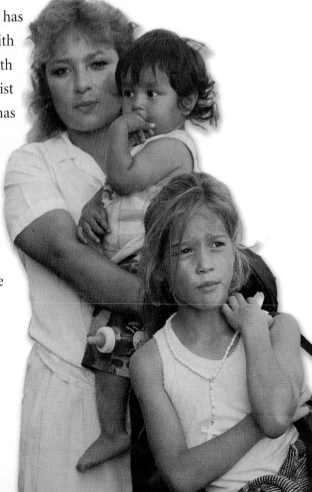

Two very different locales—a California car repair shop and voters' booths in a suburb of Washington, D.C.—point to the different lives of immigrants in the United States.

Eduardo Román García, age 29, works for $260 a week in a car body shop in southern California. His situation is both similar to and different from that of many new arrivals in the United States. The similarities lie in his desire for a better life. He works to send as much money as possible back to his wife and two children in Veracruz, Mexico. He hopes he can remain in the United States because he knows there is little chance to find employment back home. Even if he found a job, Mexican factory wages start at $2.90 a day. He found his job and a place to live through a network of Mexican Americans. Indeed, his place of employment is owned by a man who entered the United States illegally 20 years ago but later became a citizen and now operates a business with 10 employees. Román expected to work hard when he came. "Others told me it would be difficult in this country," he said, "but they said it was worth it [to come here] because you could live a little better" (Boyer 1996:B8).

Román's situation is different because his face was seen on national television in 1996. In April of that year, Román, along with 18 others, was being transported illegally by truck into the United States when it was stopped by police. News crews covered the long chase and videotaped the beating of two unarmed suspects. If it had not been for the national attention, Román and the others would soon have been deported, but instead they were granted temporary work permits while they waited to testify at the trials of the police deputies. Meanwhile, the Mexican government expressed outrage at their citizens' treatment here, just as the United States many times has condemned treatment of Americans abroad (Shuster 1996).

Meanwhile, across the continent, the officials of Takoma Park encourage voters to exercise their right to participate in city elections. What makes this arrangement unusual is that this Maryland suburb of Washington, D.C., calls all its residents 18 years of age and older to vote—whether they are citizens or legal residents or even illegal immigrants residing in the city. Takoma Park, a community of 17,000 people, is one of six Maryland towns that do not require citizenship to vote. Amidst calls throughout the nation for restricting immigration and English to be the official language, this welcoming action in this suburb, where a third of its residents are noncitizens, and similar voting policies in a few other communities show that attitudes to immigrants are extremely varied. In 2004, San Francisco is contemplating a similar move in its school board elections (Hennessey 2004).

These dramas being played out in California and Maryland illustrate the themes in immigration today. Immigrant labor is needed, but transition can be difficult, even if for immigrants individually it ultimately means a better life economically. Immigrants come to the United States trying to get ahead in places where they may be welcomed such as in Takoma Park. Many come legally, applying for immigrant visas, but others enter illegally. In the United States we may not like lawbreakers, but often we seek services and low-priced products made by people who come here illegally. How do we control this immigration without violating the principle of free movement within the nation? How do we decide who enters? And how do we treat those who come here either legally or illegally?

The diversity of ethnic and racial backgrounds of Americans today is the living legacy of immigration. Except for descendants of Native Americans or of Africans brought here enslaved, today's population is entirely the product of people who chose to leave familiar places to come to a new country.

The social forces that cause people to emigrate are complex. The most important have been economic: financial failure in the old country and expectations of higher incomes and standards of living in the new land. Other factors include dislike of new regimes in their native lands, racial or religious bigotry, and a desire to reunite families. All these factors push people from their homelands and pull them to other nations such as the United States. Immigration into the United States, in particular, has been facilitated by cheap ocean transportation and by other countries' removal of restrictions on emigration.

Patterns of Immigration

There have been three unmistakable patterns of immigration to the United States: The number of immigrants has fluctuated dramatically over time largely due to government policy changes, settlement has not been uniform across the country but centered in certain regions and cities, and the source of immigrants has changed over time. We will first look at the historical picture of immigrant numbers.

Vast numbers of immigrants have come to the United States. Figure 4.1 indicates the high but fluctuating number of immigrants who have arrived during every decade from the 1820s through the 1990s. The United States received the largest number of legal immigrants during the 1990s, but in the period from 1900 through 1910, the country was much smaller, so the numerical impact was even greater.

 CD-ROM *Activity 4.1*

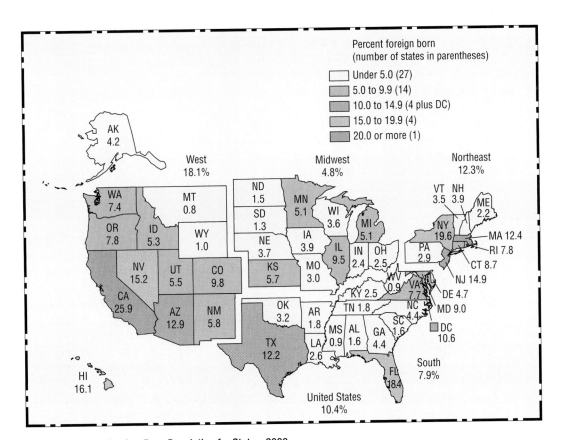

FIGURE 4.1 Foreign-Born Population for States, 2000

Source: Census Bureau data in Bureau of the Census 2001a:12.

The reception given to these immigrants in this country has not always been friendly. Open bloodshed, restrictive laws, and the eventual return of almost one-third of immigrants and their children to their home countries attest to the uneasy feeling toward strangers who want to settle here.

Opinion polls in the United States from 1965 through 2003 have never shown more than 17 percent of the public in favor of more immigration, and usually about 50 percent want less. Even a 2003 survey of Latinos found that only 24 percent wanted immigration increased, 35 percent wanted it left as is, and a sizable 36 percent advocated having immigration levels decreased. We want the door open until we get through, and then we want to close it (J. M. Jones 2003a).

Today's Foreign-Born Population

Before considering the sweep of past immigration policies, let's consider today's immigrant population. About 12 percent of the nation's people are <u>foreign born</u>; this proportion is between the high figure of 15 percent in 1890 and a low of 5 percent in 1970. By global comparisons, the foreign-born population in the United States is large but not unusual. While most industrial countries have a foreign population of around 5 percent, Canada's foreign population is 19 percent and Australia's is 25 percent.

CD-ROM *Activity 4.2*

As noted earlier, immigrants have not settled evenly across the nation. As shown in the map (Figure 4.2) six states—California, New York, Florida, Texas, New Jersey, and Illinois—account for 70 percent of the nation's total foreign-born population but less than 40 percent of the nation's total population.

Cities in these states are the focus of the <u>foreign-born population</u>. Almost half (43.3 percent) live in the central city of a metropolitan area, compared with about one-quarter (27.0 percent) of the nation's population. More than a third of residents

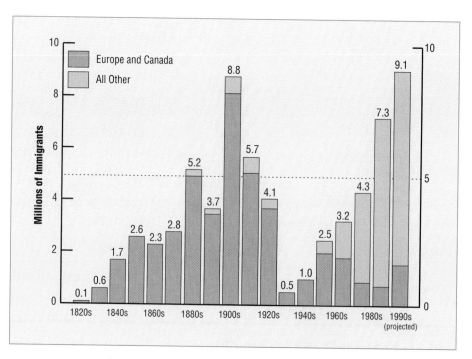

FIGURE 4.2 Legal Immigration in the United States, 1820s Through 1990s

Source: Bureau of the Census 2003a:11; Immigration and Naturalization Service 1999a, 1999b.

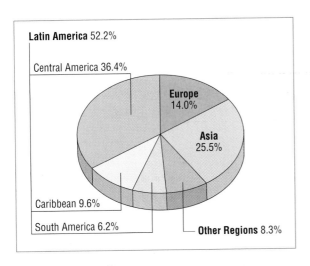

Latin America 52.2%

Central America 36.4%

Europe
14.0%

Asia
25.5%

Caribbean 9.6%

South America 6.2%

Other Regions 8.3%

FIGURE 4.3 Foreign Born by Region of Birth, 2002

Source: Schmidley 2003.

in the cities of Miami, Los Angeles, San Francisco, San Jose, and New York City are now foreign born (Singer 2004).

The third pattern of immigration is that the source of immigrants has changed. As shown in Figure 4.3, the majority of today's 32.5 million foreign-born people are from Latin America. Primarily they came from Central America—more specifically, Mexico. By contrast, Europeans, who dominated the early settlement of the United States, now account for less than one in six of the foreign born today.

Early Immigration

European explorers of North America were soon followed by settlers, the first immigrants to the Western Hemisphere. The Spanish founded St. Augustine, Florida, in 1565, and the English founded Jamestown, Virginia, in 1607. Protestants from England emerged from the colonial period as the dominant force numerically, politically, and socially. The English accounted for 60 percent of the 3 million White Americans in 1790. Although exact statistics are lacking for the early years of the United States, the English were soon outnumbered by other nationalities, as the numbers of Scots-Irish and Germans, in particular, swelled. However, the English colonists maintained their dominant position, as Chapter 5 will examine.

Throughout American history, immigration policy has been politically controversial. The policies of the English king, George III, were criticized in the U.S. Declaration of Independence for obstructing immigration to the colonies. Toward the end of the 19th century, the American republic itself was criticized for enacting immigration restrictions. In the beginning, however, the country encouraged immigration. At first, legislation fixed the residence requirement for naturalization at five years, although briefly, under the Alien Act of 1798, it was 14 years, and so-called dangerous people could be expelled. Despite this brief harshness, immigration was unregulated through most of the 1800s, and naturalization was easily available.

Besides holding the mistaken belief that concerns about immigration are something new, we also assume that immigrants to the United States rarely reconsider their decision to come to a new country. Analysis of available records beginning in the early 1900s suggests that about 35 percent of all immigrants to the United States eventually emigrated back to their home country. The proportion varies, with the figures for some countries being much higher, but the overall pattern is clear: About one in three immigrants to this nation eventually chooses to return home (Wyman 1993).

xenophobia
The fear or hatred of
strangers or foreigners.

nativism
Beliefs and policies favoring
native-born citizens over
immigrants.

The Anti-Catholic Crusade

The relative absence of federal legislation from 1790 to 1881 does not mean that all new arrivals were welcomed. **Xenophobia** (the fear or hatred of strangers or foreigners) led naturally to **nativism** (beliefs and policies favoring native-born citizens over immigrants). Roman Catholics in general and the Irish in particular were among the first Europeans to be ill treated. Anti-Catholic feeling originated in Europe and was brought by the early Protestant immigrants. The Catholics of colonial America, although few, were subject to limits of their civil and religious rights.

From independence until around 1820, little evidence appeared of the anti-Catholic sentiment of colonial days, but the cry against Roman Catholicism grew as Irish immigration increased. Prominent citizens encouraged hatred of these new arrivals. Samuel F. B. Morse, inventor of the telegraph and an accomplished painter, wrote a strongly worded anti-Catholic work in 1834 titled *A Foreign Conspiracy Against the Liberties of the United States*. Morse felt that the Irish were "shamefully illiterate and without opinions of their own" (1835:61). In the mind of the prejudiced people, the Irish were particularly unwelcome because they were Catholic. Many readily believed Morse's warning that the Pope planned to move the Vatican to the Mississippi River Valley (Silverman 2003).

This antagonism was not limited to harsh words. From 1834 to 1854, mob violence against Catholics across the country led to death, the burning of a Boston convent, the destruction of a Catholic church and the homes of Catholics, and the use of Marines and state militia to bring peace to American cities as far west as St. Louis.

A frequent pattern saw minorities striking out against each other rather than at the dominant class. Irish Americans opposed the Emancipation Proclamation and the freeing of the slaves because they feared Blacks would compete for the unskilled work open to them. This fear was confirmed when free Blacks were used to break a longshoremen's strike in New York. Therefore, much of the Irish violence during the 1863 riot was directed against Blacks, not against the Whites, who were most responsible for the conditions in which the immigrants found themselves (Duff 1971; Warner 1968).

In retrospect, the reception given to the Irish is not difficult to understand. Many immigrated after the 1845–1848 potato crop failure and famine in Ireland. They fled not so much to a better life as from almost certain death. The Irish Catholics brought with them a celibate clergy, who struck the New England aristocracy as strange and reawakened old religious hatreds. The Irish were worse than Blacks, according to the dominant Whites, because unlike the slaves and even the freed Blacks, who "knew their place," the Irish did not suffer their maltreatment in silence. Employers balanced minorities by judiciously mixing immigrant groups to prevent unified action by the laborers. For the most part, nativist efforts only led the foreign born to emphasize their ties to Europe.

By the 1850s, nativism became an open political movement pledged to vote only for "native" Americans, to fight Catholicism, and to demand a 21-year naturalization period. Party members were instructed to divulge nothing about their program and to say that they knew nothing about it. As a result, they came to be called the Know-Nothings. Although the Know-Nothings soon vanished, the antialien mentality survived and occasionally became formally organized into such societies as the Ku Klux Klan in the 1860s and the anti-Catholic American Protective Association in the 1890s. Revivals of anti-Catholicism continued well into the 20th century. However, the most dramatic outbreak of nativism in the 19th century was aimed at the Chinese. If there had been any doubt by the mid-1800s that the United States could harmoniously accommodate all, debate on the Chinese Exclusion Act would negatively settle the question once and for all (Gerber 1993; Wernick 1996).

The Anti-Chinese Movement

Before 1851, official records show that only 46 Chinese had immigrated to the United States. Over the next 30 years, more than 200,000 came to this country, lured by the discovery of gold and the opening of job opportunities in the West. Overcrowding, drought, and warfare in China also encouraged them to take a chance in the United States. Another important factor was improved oceanic transportation; it was actually cheaper to travel from Hong Kong to San Francisco than from Chicago to San Francisco. The frontier communities of the West, particularly in California, looked on the Chinese as a valuable resource to fill manual jobs. As early as 1854, so many Chinese wanted to emigrate that ships had difficulty handling the volume.

In the 1860s, railroad work provided the greatest demand for Chinese labor, until the Union Pacific and Central Pacific railroads were joined at Promontory, Utah, in 1869. The Union Pacific relied primarily on Irish laborers, but 90 percent of the Central Pacific labor force was Chinese because Whites generally refused the backbreaking work over the Western terrain. Despite the contribution of the Chinese, White workers physically prevented them from attending the driving of the golden spike to mark the joining of the two railroads.

With the dangerous railroad work largely completed, people began to rethink the wisdom of encouraging Chinese to immigrate to do the work no one else would do. Reflecting their xenophobia, White settlers found the Chinese immigrants and their customs and religion difficult to understand. Indeed, few people actually tried to understand these immigrants from Asia. Although they had had no firsthand contact with Chinese Americans, Easterners and legislators were soon on the anti-Chinese bandwagon as they read sensationalized accounts of the lifestyle of the new arrivals.

Even before the Chinese immigrated, stereotypes of them and their customs were prevalent. American traders returning from China, European diplomats, and Protestant missionaries consistently emphasized the exotic and sinister aspects of life in China. The **sinophobes,** people with a fear of anything associated with China, appealed to the racist theory developed during the slavery controversy that non-Europeans were subhuman. Similarly, Americans were beginning to be more conscious of biological inheritance and disease, so it was not hard to conjure up fears of alien genes and germs. The only real challenge the anti-Chinese movement had was to convince people that the negative consequences of unrestricted Chinese immigration outweighed any possible economic gain. Perhaps briefly, racial prejudice had

sinophobes
People with a fear of anything associated with China.

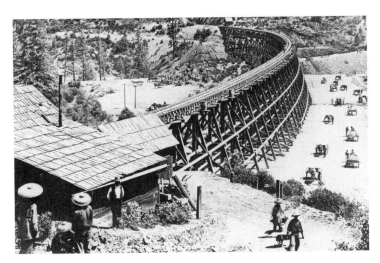

Chinese workers, such as these pictured in 1844, played a major role in building railroads in the West.

earlier been subordinated to industrial dependence on Chinese labor for the work that Whites shunned, but acceptance of Chinese was short-lived. The fear of the "yellow peril" overwhelmed any desire to know more about Asian people and their customs (Takaki 1989).

Another nativist fear of Chinese immigrants was based on the threat they posed as laborers. Californians, whose labor force felt the effects of the Chinese immigration first, found support throughout the nation as organized labor feared that the Chinese would be used as strikebreakers. By 1870, Chinese workers had been used for that purpose as far east as Massachusetts. When Chinese workers did unionize, they were not recognized by major labor organizations. Samuel Gompers, founder of the American Federation of Labor (AFL), consistently opposed any effort to assist Chinese workers and refused to consider having a union of Chinese restaurant employees admitted into the AFL. Gompers worked effectively to see future Chinese immigration ended and produced a pamphlet titled "Chinese Exclusion: Meat vs. Rice: American Manhood Against Asiatic Coolieism—Which Shall Survive?" (Gompers and Gustadt 1908; Hill 1967).

Employers were glad to pay the Chinese low wages, but laborers came to direct their resentment against the Chinese rather than against their compatriots' willingness to exploit the Chinese. Only a generation earlier, the same concerns had been felt about the Irish, but with the Chinese, the hostility reached new heights because of another factor.

Although many arguments were voiced, racial fears motivated the anti-Chinese movement. Race was the critical issue. The labor market fears were largely unfounded, and most advocates of restrictions at the time knew that. There was no possibility that Chinese would immigrate in numbers that would match those of Europeans at the time, so it is difficult to find an explanation other than racism for their fears (Winant 1994).

From the sociological perspective of conflict theory, we can explain how the Chinese immigrants were welcomed only when their labor was necessary to fuel growth in the United States. When that labor was no longer necessary, the welcome mat for the immigrants was withdrawn. Furthermore, as conflict theorists would point out, restrictions were not applied evenly: Americans focused on a specific nationality (the Chinese) to reduce the overall number of foreign workers in the nation. Because decision making at that time rested in the hands of the descendants of European immigrants, the steps to be taken were most likely to be directed against the least powerful: immigrants from China who, unlike Europeans seeking entry, had few allies among legislators and other policy makers.

In 1882 Congress enacted the Chinese Exclusion Act, which outlawed Chinese immigration for 10 years. It also explicitly denied naturalization rights to the Chinese in the United States; that is, they were not allowed to become citizens. There was little debate in Congress, and discussion concentrated on how suspension of Chinese immigration could best be handled. No allowance was made for spouses and children to be reunited with their husbands and fathers in the United States. Only brief visits of Chinese government officials, teachers, tourists, and merchants were exempted.

The rest of the 19th century saw the remaining loopholes allowing Chinese immigration closed. Beginning in 1884, Chinese laborers were not allowed to enter the United States from any foreign place, a ban that lasted 10 years. Two years later, the Statue of Liberty was dedicated, with a poem by Emma Lazarus inscribed on its base. To the Chinese, the poem welcoming the tired, the poor, and the huddled masses must have seemed a hollow mockery.

In 1892 Congress extended the Exclusion Act for another 10 years and added that Chinese laborers had to obtain certificates of residence within a year or face deportation. After the turn of the century, the Exclusion Act was extended again. Two decades later, the Chinese were not alone; the list of people restricted by immigration policy expanded many times.

Restrictionist Sentiment Increases

As Congress closed the door to Chinese immigration, the debate on restricting immigration turned in new directions. Prodded by growing anti-Japanese feelings, the United States entered into the so-called Gentlemen's Agreement, completed in 1908. Japan agreed to halt further immigration to the United States, and the United States agreed to end discrimination against the Japanese who had already arrived. The immigration ended, but anti-Japanese feelings continued. Americans were growing uneasy that the "new immigrants" would overwhelm the culture established by the "old immigrants." The earlier immigrants, if not Anglo-Saxon, were from similar groups such as the Scandinavians, the Swiss, and the French Huguenots. These people were more experienced in democratic political practices and had a greater affinity with the dominant Anglo-Saxon culture. By the end of the 19th century, however, more and more immigrants were neither English speaking nor Protestant and came from dramatically different cultures.

In 1917 Congress finally overrode President Wilson's veto and enacted an immigration bill that included the controversial literacy test. Critics of the bill, including Wilson, argued that illiteracy does not signify inherent incompetence but reflects lack of opportunity for instruction. Such arguments were not heeded, however. The act seemed innocent at first glance—it merely required immigrants to read 30 words in any language—but it was the first attempt to restrict immigration from Western Europe. The act also prohibited immigration from the South Sea islands and other parts of Asia not already excluded. Curiously, this law that closed the door on non-Anglo-Saxons permitted a waiver of the test if the immigrants came because of their home government's discrimination against their race (*New York Times* 1917a, 1917b).

The National Origin System

Beginning in 1921, a series of measures was enacted that marked a new era in American immigration policy. Whatever the legal language, the measures were drawn up to block the growing immigration from southern Europe, such as from Italy and Greece.

Anti-immigration sentiment, combined with the isolationism that followed World War I, caused Congress to severely restrict entry privileges not only of the Chinese and Japanese but of Europeans as well. The national origin system was begun in 1921 and remained the basis of immigration policy until 1965. This system used the country

Italian Americans aboard a ship arrive at Ellis Island.

of birth to determine whether a person could enter as a legal alien, and the number of previous immigrants and their descendants was used to set the group's annual immigration cap.

To understand the effect of the national origin system on immigration, it is necessary to clarify the quota system. The quotas were deliberately weighted in favor of immigration from northern Europe. Because of the ethnic composition of the country in 1920, the quotas placed severe restrictions on immigration from the rest of Europe and from other parts of the world. Immigration from the Western Hemisphere (i.e., Canada, Mexico, Central and South America, and the Caribbean) continued unrestricted. The quota for each nation was set at 3 percent of the number of people descended from each nationality recorded in the 1920 census. Once the statistical manipulations were completed, almost 70 percent of the quota for the Eastern Hemisphere went to just three countries: Great Britain, Ireland, and Germany.

The absurdities of the system soon became obvious, but it was nevertheless continued. British immigration had fallen sharply, so most of its quota of 65,000 went unfilled. However, the openings could not be transferred, even though countries such as Italy, with a quota of only 6,000, had 200,000 people who wanted to enter. However one rationalizes the purpose behind the act, the result was obvious: Any English person, regardless of skill and whether related to anyone already here, could enter the country more easily than, say, a Greek doctor whose children were American citizens. The quota for Greece was 305, with the backlog of people wanting to come reaching 100,000.

By the end of the 1920s, annual immigration had dropped to one-fourth of its pre-World War I level. The worldwide economic depression of the 1930s decreased immigration still further. A brief upsurge in immigration just before World War II reflected the flight of Europeans from the oppression of expanding Nazi Germany. The war virtually ended transatlantic immigration. The era of the great European migration to the United States had been legislated out of existence.

The 1965 Immigration and Naturalization Act

The national origin system was abandoned with the passage of the 1965 Immigration and Naturalization Act, signed into law by President Lyndon B. Johnson at the foot of the Statue of Liberty. The primary goals of the act were to reunite families and protect the American labor market. The act also initiated restrictions on immigration from Latin America. After the act, immigration increased by one-third, but the act's influence was primarily on the composition rather than the size of immigration. The sources of immigrants now included Italy, Greece, Portugal, Mexico, the Philippines, the West Indies, and South America. The effect is apparent when we compare the changing sources of immigration over the last 180 years, as shown in Figure 4.4. The most recent period shows that Asian and Latin American immigrants combined to account for 81 percent of the people who were permitted entry. This contrasts sharply with early immigration, which was dominated by arrivals from Europe.

As reflected in the title of this act, the law set down the rules for becoming a citizen. **Naturalization** is the conferring of citizenship on a person after birth. The general conditions for becoming naturalized in the United States are:

- 18 years of age
- Continuous residence for at least five years (three years for the spouses of U.S. citizens)
- Good moral character as determined by the absence of conviction of selected criminal offenses
- Ability to read, write, and speak and understand words of ordinary usage in the English language
- Ability to pass a test in U.S. government and history

naturalization
Conferring of citizenship on a person after birth.

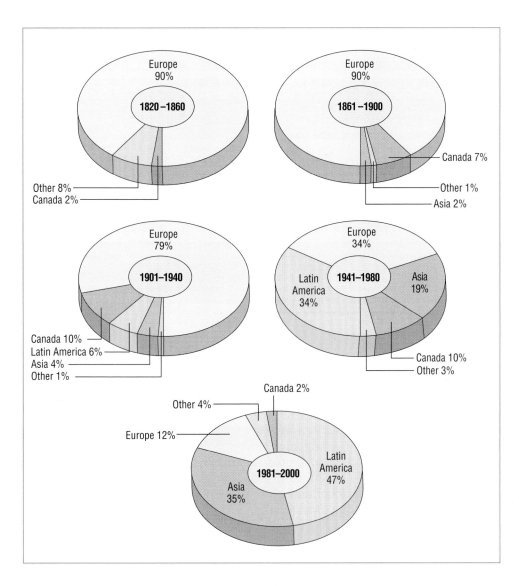

FIGURE 4.4 Legal Immigrants Admitted to the United States by Region of Last Residence, 1820–2000

Source: Bureau of the Census 2003a; Immigration and Naturalization Service 1999a, 1999b.

In Table 4.1 we offer a sample of the type of questions immigrants face on the citizenship test.

The nature of immigration laws is exceedingly complex and is subjected to frequent, often minor, adjustments. In 2001 and 2002, 1,060,000 people were legally admitted annually, for the following reasons:

Family unification	
Spouses of citizens	28%
Relatives of citizens	29
Relatives of legal residents	8
Employment-based	16
Refugees/people seeking political asylum	12
Other	7

Overall, half of the immigrants come to join their relatives, one seventh are admitted for their special skills, and one eighth enter because of special refugee status (Bureau of Citizenship and Immigration Services 2003a).

TABLE 4.1
So You Want to Be a Citizen?

Try these sample questions from the naturalization test (answers below).

1. What do the stripes on the flag represent?
2. How many changes, or amendments, are there to the Constitution?
3. Who is the chief justice of the Supreme Court?
4. What are some of the requirements to be eligible to become president?
5. In what year was the Constitution written?
6. What is the introduction to the Constitution called?
7. Name one right or freedom guaranteed by the first amendment.
8. What kind of government does the United States have?

Source: Bureau of Citizenship and Immigrant Services 2003b.

Answers:
1. The first 13 states;   2. 27;   3. William Rehnquist;   4. Candidates for President must be natural-born citizens, be at least 35 years old, and have lived in the United States for at least 14 years;   5. 1787;   6. The Preamble;   7. The rights are freedom of speech, of religion, of assembly, and to petition the government;   8. A republic

---

Contemporary Concerns

Although our current immigration policies are less restrictive than other nations' restrictions, they are the subject of great debate. In Table 4.2, we summarize the benefits and concerns regarding immigration to the United States. We will consider three continuing criticisms of our immigration policy: the brain drain, population growth, and illegal immigration. All three, but particularly illegal immigration, have provoked heated debates and continuing efforts to resolve them with new policies. We will then consider the economic impact of immigration, followed by the nation's policy toward refugees, a group distinct from immigrants.

The Brain Drain

How often have you identified your science or mathematics teacher or your physician as someone who was not born in the United States? This nation has clearly benefited from attracting human resources from throughout the world, but this phenomenon has had its price for the nations of origin.

TABLE 4.2
Immigration Benefits and Concerns

Potential Benefits	Areas of Concern
Provide needed skills	Drain needed resources from home country
Contribute to taxes	Send remittances (or migradollars) home
May come with substantial capital to start business	Less-skilled immigrants compete with those already disadvantaged
Diversify the population (intangible gain)	Population growth
Maintain ties with countries throughout the world	May complicate foreign policy by lobbying the government
	Illegal immigration

Even during times of strongest sentiment against immigration, provisions exist to allow legal entry to overseas technical workers who are in short supply in the United States.

The **brain drain** is the immigration to the United States of skilled workers, professionals, and technicians who are desperately needed by their home countries. In the mid-20th century, many scientists and other professionals from industrial nations, principally Germany and Great Britain, came to the United States. More recently, however, the brain drain has pulled emigrants from developing nations, including India, Pakistan, the Philippines, and several African nations. One out of four physicians in the United States are foreign born and play a critical role in serving areas with too few doctors. Thousands of skilled, educated Indians now seek to enter the United States, pulled by the economic opportunity. The pay differential is so great that by 2004, when foreign physicians were no longer favored with entry in the United States, physicians in the Philippines were retraining as nurses so that they could immigrate to the United States where, employed as nurses, they would make four times what they would as doctors in the Philippines (Paral 2004; Zarembo 2004).

The brain drain controversy was evident long before the passage of the 1965 Immigration Act. However, the 1965 act seemed to encourage such immigration by placing the professions in one of the categories of preference. Various corporations, including Motorola and Intel, now find that one-third of their high-tech jobs are held by people born abroad, although many received their advanced education in the United States. Furthermore, these immigrants have links to their old countries and are boosting U.S. exports to the fast-growing economic regions of Asia and Latin America (Bloch 1996).

Many foreign students say they plan to return home. Fortunately for the United States, many do not and make their talents available in the United States. One study showed that the majority of foreign students receiving their doctorates in the sciences and engineering are still here four years later. Yet critics note that this supply allows the country to overlook its minority scholars. Presently, for every two minority doctorates, there are five foreign citizens receiving this degree. In the physical sciences, for every doctorate issued to a minority citizen, 11 are received by foreign citizens. More attention needs to be given to encourage African Americans and Latinos to enter high-tech career paths (Hoffer et al. 2001; Wessel 2001).

Conflict theorists see the current brain drain as yet another symptom of the unequal distribution of world resources. In their view, it is ironic that the United States gives foreign aid to improve the technical resources of African and Asian countries

brain drain
Immigration to the United States of skilled workers, professionals, and technicians who are desperately needed by their home countries.

while maintaining an immigration policy that encourages professionals in such nations to migrate to our shores. These are the very countries that have unacceptable public health conditions and need native scientists, educators, technicians, and other professionals. In addition, by relying on foreign talent, the United States does not need to take the steps necessary to encourage native members of subordinate groups to enter these desirable fields of employment.

 ## Population Growth

The United States, like a few other industrial nations, continues to accept large numbers of permanent immigrants and refugees. Although such immigration has increased since the passage of the 1965 Immigration and Naturalization Act, the nation's birthrate has decreased. Consequently, the contribution of immigration to population growth has become more significant.

Legal immigration accounts for about 45 percent of the nation's growth in the first years in the 21st century. To some observers, the United States is already overpopulated. The respected environmentalist group Sierra Club debated for several years on taking an official position favoring restricting immigration, recognizing that more people put greater strain on the nation's natural resources. The majority of the members have indicated thus far a desire to keep a neutral position rather than enter the politically charged immigration debate (Barringer 2004).

The patterns of uneven settlement in the United States are expected to continue so that future immigrants' impact on population growth will be felt much more in certain areas: say, California and New York, rather than Iowa or Massachusetts. For example, California, which is the most extreme case, is expected to grow from 32 million people in 1995 to more than 49 million people by 2025. Of this increase of 17 million people, nearly half will be new immigrants to the United States, and a sizable proportion of the remaining will be the children of recent immigrants. Although immigration and population growth may be viewed as national concerns, their impact is localized in certain areas such as southern California and large urban centers nationwide (El Nasser 1996).

 ## Illegal Immigration

The most bitterly debated aspect of U.S. immigration policy has been the control of illegal or undocumented immigrants. These immigrants and their families come to the United States in search of higher-paying jobs than their home countries can provide. As we noted at the beginning of the chapter, people like Eduardo Román García, who left his home in Veracruz, Mexico, seek employment in the United States even if they are not able to enter legally.

In "Listen to Our Voices," journalist Dean Murphy ponders what the impact on citizens would be if all illegal immigrants were suddenly to disappear.

Since, by definition, illegal immigrants are in the country illegally, their exact number is subject to estimates and disputes. Based on the best available information, there are more than 8 million illegal immigrants in the United States. Although the federal government placed its official estimate at 7 million, the Census Bureau in 2000 counted 8.7 million illegal immigrants residing in the United States (FAIR US 2003).

Illegal immigrants, and even legal immigrants, have become tied by the public to almost every social problem in the nation. They become the scapegoats for unemployment; they are labeled as "drug runners" and, especially since September 11, 2001, "terrorists." Yet their vital economic and cultural contribution to the United States is generally overlooked, as it has been for more than a hundred years.

The cost of the federal government's attempt to police the nation's borders and locate illegal immigrants is sizable. There are significant costs for aliens, that is,

foreign-born noncitizens, and for other citizens as well. Civil rights advocates have expressed concern that the procedures used to apprehend and deport people are discriminatory and deprive many aliens of their legal rights. American citizens of Hispanic or Asian origin, some of whom were born in the United States, may be greeted with prejudice and distrust, as if their names automatically imply that they are illegal immigrants. Furthermore, these citizens and legal residents of the United States may be unable to find work because employers wrongly believe that their documents are forged.

In the context of this illegal immigration, Congress approved the Immigration Reform and Control Act of 1986 (IRCA) after debating it for nearly a decade. The act marked a historic change in immigration policy compared with earlier laws, as summarized in Table 4.3. Amnesty was granted to 1.7 million illegal immigrants who could document that they had established long-term residency in the United States. Under the IRCA, for the first time, hiring illegal aliens became illegal, so that employers are subject to fines and even prison sentences. It appears that the act has had mixed results in

TABLE 4.3
Major Immigration Policies

Policy	Target Group	Impact
Chinese Exclusion Act, 1882	Chinese	Effectively ended all Chinese immigration for more than 60 years
National origin system, 1921	Southern Europeans	Reduced overall immigration and significantly reduced likely immigration from Greece and Italy
Immigration and Naturalization Act, 1965	Western Hemisphere and the less skilled	Facilitated entry of skilled workers and relatives of U.S. residents
Immigration Reform and Control Act of 1986	Illegal immigration	Modest reduction of illegal immigration
Illegal Immigration Reform and Responsibility Act of 1996	Illegal immigration	Greater border surveillance and increased scrutiny of legal immigrants seeking benefits

Voices Listen to Our Voices Listen to Our

IMAGINING LIFE WITHOUT ILLEGAL IMMIGRANTS

Imagine America without illegal immigrants, the people who flip the burgers, clean the toilets, watch the kids, and send their children to public schools. Would the grass be greener?

The question got an answer of sorts last month in California, where about a third of the country's estimated 8 million to 10 million illegal immigrants live. Thousands of Latinos stayed home from school and work one Friday, protesting the repeal of a contentious new law that would have allowed illegal immigrants to obtain driver's licenses.

The boycott was not nearly the success its organizers had hoped for. Nonetheless, there were reports of fast-food counters closing and lawns going uncut. A few shops in cities with big immigrant populations, like Fresno, did not bother opening, and in Los Angeles, the second-largest school district in the country, the absentee rate nearly tripled from the Friday before. . . .

The Pew Hispanic Center estimated in 2001 that the unauthorized labor force in the

Dean E. Murphy

United States totaled 5.3 million workers, including 700,000 restaurant workers, 250,000 household employees, and 620,000 construction workers. In addition, about 1.2 million of the 2.5 million wage-earning farm workers live here illegally, according to a study by Philip L. Martin, a professor at the University of California at Davis who studies immigration and farm labor.

That is a whole lot of cheap labor.

Without it, fruit and vegetables would rot in fields. Toddlers in Manhattan would be without nannies. Towels at hotels in states like Florida, Texas, and California would go unlaundered. Commuters at airports from Miami to Newark would be stranded as taxi cabs sat driverless. Home improvement projects across the Sun Belt would grind to a halt. And bedpans and lunch trays at nursing homes in Chicago, New York, Houston, and Los Angeles would go uncollected. . . .

Immigrant advocacy groups dispute the notion that illegal immigration is a drag on America. Raul Yzaguirre, president of the

terms of illegal immigration. According to data compiled by the U.S. Border Patrol, arrests along the border declined substantially in the first three years after the law took effect. However, illegal immigration eventually returned to the levels of the early 1980s.

Many illegal immigrants continue to live in fear and hiding, subject to even more severe harassment and discrimination than before. From a conflict perspective, these immigrants, primarily poor and Hispanic or Asian, are being firmly lodged at the bottom of the nation's social and economic hierarchies. However, from a functionalist perspective, employers, by paying low wages, are able to produce goods and services that are profitable for industry and more affordable to consumers. Despite the poor working conditions often experienced by illegal immigrants here, they continue to come because it is still in their best economic interest to work here in disadvantaged positions rather than to seek wage labor unsuccessfully in their home countries.

In the 1996 presidential campaign, immigration became an issue in terms of both the number of immigrants to be allowed to enter and the benefits they should

National Council of La Raza, a Latino civil rights organization, said the economic impact of immigration plays out differently at the local and national levels.

While hospitals and clinics in Los Angeles County, for example, bear huge health care costs associated with uninsured illegal immigrants—one study put the total at $340 million in 2002—the federal government enjoys a "bonanza" from many of the same immigrants who pay federal taxes but receive no benefits in return, Mr. Yzaguirre said.

Mr. Yzaguirre suggested that Social Security would go broke without the payments of undocumented workers, many of whom, contrary to popular perception, do have regular payroll taxes deducted from their paychecks by employers. (In some instances, undocumented workers use false Social Security numbers, while others have valid numbers from when they had worked legitimately.)

Mr. Yzaguirre also rejected suggestions that Americans would maintain their standard of living without the low-wage contributions of those workers. He agreed with Professor Borjas that some Americans would enjoy fatter paychecks, but he said all Americans would be punished by having to pay more for everything from a McDonald's hamburger to a new house.

In a 2002 study conducted with the cooperation of immigrant rights organizations, researchers at the Center for Urban Economic Development at the University of Illinois at Chicago concluded that the 300,000 or so illegal immigrants in Chicago did not use government benefits at a substantial rate. The study also estimated that 70 percent of the undocumented workers paid payroll taxes, like Social Security and unemployment insurance. The researchers calculated other economic benefits, finding that consumer spending by illegal migrants generated more than 31,000 jobs and contributed $5.34 billion annually to the gross regional product in Chicago.

Which side to believe? The problem with gathering data about illegal immigrants, and the idea of an America without them, is that they tend to blend into the vast tapestry of legal immigrants. ■

Source: *The New York Times*, January 11, 2004. Copyright © 2004 by *The New York Times Co.* Reprinted with permission. Photo courtesy of The New York Times Company.

receive. Eventually a compromise passed, called the Illegal Immigration Reform and Immigrant Responsibility Act of 1996, which emphasized more effort to keep immigrants from entering the country illegally. Illegal immigrants will not have access to such benefit programs as Social Security and welfare. For now, legal immigrants will be entitled to such benefits, although social service agencies are required to verify their legal status. Another significant element was to increase border control and surveillance.

Policy makers continue to avoid the only real way to stop illegal immigration, and that is to discourage employment opportunities. The public often thinks in terms of greater surveillance at the border. After the terrorist attacks of September 11, 2001, greater control of border traffic took on a new sense of urgency, even though almost all the men who took over the planes had entered the United States legally. It is very difficult to secure the vast boundaries that mark the United States on land and sea.

TABLE 4.4
Transformation of Immigration Management

Following 9/11, management of immigration in the United States was reorganized, as of March 1, 2003, from INS in the Department of Justice to three new agencies in the new Department of Homeland Security.

Before	After
Located in Department of Justice	Located in Department of Homeland Security
Immigration and Naturalization Services (INS)	INS dissolved
Immigration services Naturalization (citizenship) Applications Visas	U.S. Citizen and Immigration Services (USCIS)
Border Patrol Inspections at border Deportations at border	U.S. Customs and Borders Protection (CBP)
Immigration enforcement-interior (includes removals and detentions)	U.S. Immigration and Customs Enforcement (ICE)

Reflecting the emphasis on heightened security, a potentially major shake-up recently took place. Since 1940, the Immigration and Naturalization Service has been in the Department of Justice, but in 2003 it was transferred to the newly formed Department of Homeland Security (see Table 4.4). The various functions of the INS were split into three agencies with a new Bureau of Citizenship and Immigration Services and two other units separately concerned with customs and border protection. For years, immigrant advocates had argued to separate border enforcement from immigration, but the placement of immigrant services in the office responsible for protecting the United States from terrorists sends a chilling message to immigrants.

Numerous civil rights groups and migrant advocacy organizations have expressed alarm over the large number of people now crossing into the United States illegally who perish in their attempt. Death occurs to some in deserts, in isolated canyons, and while concealed in containers or locked in trucks during smuggle attempts. Several hundred die annually in the Southwest, seeking more and more dangerous crossing points as border control has increased. However, this death toll has received little attention, causing one journalist to liken it to a jumbo jet crashing between Los Angles and Phoenix every year without anyone giving it much notice (del Olmo 2003; M. Martinez 2004).

The Economic Impact of Immigration

There is much public and scholarly debate about the economic effects of immigration, both legal and illegal. Varied, conflicting conclusions have resulted from research ranging from case studies of Korean immigrants' dominance among New York City greengrocers to mobility studies charting the progress of all immigrants and their children. The confusion results in part from the different methods of analysis. For example, the studies do not always include political refugees, who generally are less pre-

pared than other refugees to become assimilated. Sometimes the research focuses only on economic effects, such as whether people are employed or on welfare; in other cases it also considers cultural factors such as knowledge of English.

Perhaps the most significant factor is whether a study examines the national impact of immigration or only its effects on a local area. Overall, we can conclude from the research that immigrants adapt well and are an asset to the local economy. In some areas, heavy immigration may drain a community's resources. However, it can also revitalize a local economy. Marginally-employed workers, most of whom are either themselves immigrants or African Americans, often experience a negative impact by new arrivals. With or without immigration, competition for low-paying jobs in the United States is high, and those who gain the most from this competition are the employers and the consumers who want to keep prices down.

According to survey data, many people in the United States hold the stereotypical belief that immigrants often end up on welfare and thereby cause increases in taxes. Economist David Card (et al. 1998) studied the 1980 "Mariel" boatlift that brought 125,000 Cubans into Miami and found that even this substantial addition of mainly low-skilled workers had no measurable impact on the wages or unemployment rates of low-skilled White and African American workers in the Miami area.

About 70 percent of illegal immigrant workers pay taxes of one type or another. Many of them do not file to receive entitled refunds or benefits. For example, in 2003, the Social Security Administration identified thousands of unauthorized workers contributing to the fund about $6 billion that could not be credited properly (Mehta et al. 2002; *Migration News* 2003).

Social science studies generally contradict many of the negative stereotypes about the economic impact of immigration. A variety of recent studies found that immigrants are a net economic gain for the population. But despite national gains, in some areas and for some groups, immigration may be an economic burden or create unwanted competition for jobs (Fix et al. 2001; Moore 1998; Smith and Edmonston 1997).

remittances (or migradollars)
The monies that immigrants return to their country of origin.

In "Research Focus," we consider the most recent research on how immigrants are doing in the United States.

One economic aspect of immigration that has received increasing attention is the effort to measure remittances. **Remittances (or migradollars)** are the monies that immigrants return to their country of origin. The amounts are significant and measure in the tens of millions of dollars flowing from the United States to a number of countries where they are a very substantial source of support for families and even venture capital for new businesses. Although some observers express concern over this outflow of money, others counter that it probably represents a small price to pay for the human capital that the United States is able to use in the form of the immigrants themselves.

Focus Research Focus Research Focus

HOW WELL ARE IMMIGRANTS DOING?

In 2001, the respected Urban Institute released its comprehensive study of the progress immigrants are making in the United States. They acknowledged that there is great diversity in the immigrant experience between nationality groups. Furthermore, even within the most successful immigrating groups, people have to confront the challenge of adapting to a society that rewards assimilation and typically punishes those who want to maintain cultural practices different from those that dominate society.

Considering contemporary immigrants as a group, we can make some conclusions, which show a mix of some success and evidence that adaptation typically is very difficult.

LESS ENCOURAGING

- Although immigrants have lower divorce rates and are less likely to form single-parent households than natives, their rates equal or exceed these rates by the second generation.
- Children in immigrant families tend to be healthier than U.S.-born children, but the advantage declines.
- Immigrants are less likely to have health insurance.

- Immigrant children attend schools that are disproportionately attended by other poor children and students with limited English proficiency, so they are ethnically, economically, and linguistically isolated.

POSITIVE SIGNS

- Immigrant families, and, more broadly, noncitizen households, are more likely to be on public assistance, but their time on public assistance is less and they receive fewer benefits. This is even true when considering special restrictions that may apply to noncitizens.
- Second-generation immigrants (i.e., children of immigrants) are overall doing as well as or better than White non-Hispanic natives in educational attainment, labor force participation, wages, and household income.
- Immigrants overwhelmingly (65 percent) continue to see learning English as an ethical obligation of all immigrants.

These positive trends diverge between specific immigrant groups, with Asian immigrants doing better than European immigrants, who do better than Latino immigrants. ∎

Source: Capps et al. 2002; Farkas 2003; Fix et al. 2001.

One often overlooked consequence of immigration is that the foreign-born population has taken on growing importance in the labor-union movement in the United States. Immigrants and their children often enter occupations that are organized. As we noted in Chapter 2 with the New York service workers union, laborers are coming together in union meetings in cities from a variety of national backgrounds. As labor unions floundered through much of the 1980s, they are increasingly looking to immigrants to provide their growth (E. Porter 2004; T. Taylor 2004).

States have sought legal redress because the federal government has not seriously considered granting impact aid to heavily burdened states. In 1994, Florida joined California in suing the U.S. government to secure strict enforcement of immigration laws and reimbursement for services rendered to illegal immigrants. As frustration mounted, California voters approved a 1994 referendum (Proposition 187) banning illegal immigrants from public schools, public assistance programs, and all but emergency medical care. Although the proposal was later found not to be constitutional, voters heavily favored the referendum. Subsequently, California and other states have tried to enact measures that would partially reflect this view, such as prohibiting illegal immigrants from getting driver's licenses (D. Anderson 1998; V. Haynes 2003).

The concern about immigration in the 1990s is both understandable and perplexing. The nation has always been uneasy about new arrivals, especially those who are different from the more affluent and the policy makers. Yet the 1990s were marked by low unemployment, low inflation, and much-diminished anxiety about our economic future. This paradoxical situation—a strong economy and concerns about immigration framed in economic arguments—suggests that other concerns, such as ethnic and racial tension, are more important in explaining current attitudes toward immigration in the United States (Cornelius 1996).

The Global Economy and Immigration

Immigration exists because of political boundaries that bring the movement of peoples to the attention of national authorities. Within the United States, people may move their residence, but they are not immigrating. For residents in the member nations of the European Union, free movement of people within the union is also protected.

Yet increasingly people recognize the need to think beyond national borders and national identity. As was noted in Chapter 1, **globalization** is the worldwide integration of government policies, cultures, social movements, and financial markets through trade, movement of people, and the exchange of ideas. In this global framework, even immigrants are less likely to think of themselves as residents of only one country. For generations, immigrants have used foreign-language newspapers to keep in touch with events in their home country. Today, cable channels carry news and variety programs from their home country, and the Internet offers immediate access to the homeland and kinfolk thousands of miles away.

While bringing the world together, globalization has also sharpened the focus on the dramatic economic inequalities between nations. Today, people in North America, Europe, and Japan consume 32 times more resources than the billions of people in developing nations. Thanks to tourism, the media, and other aspects of globalization, the people of less-affluent countries know of this affluent lifestyle and, of course, often aspire to it (Diamond 2003).

globalization
Worldwide integration of government policies, cultures, social movements, and financial markets through trade, movements of people, and the exchange of ideas.

Remittances or migradollars are a significant source of income for many nations whose citizens immigrate to the United States. Pictured are Uruguayan citizens walking past a board showing the exchange rate of the Uruguayan Peso.

Transnationals are immigrants who sustain multiple social relationships linking their societies of origin and settlement. Immigrants from the Dominican Republic identify with Americans but also maintain very close ties to their Caribbean homeland. They return for visits, send remittances (migradollars), and host extended stays of relatives and friends. Back in the Dominican Republic, villages reflect these close ties, as shown in billboards promoting special long-distance services to the United States and by the presence of household appliances sent by relatives. The volume of remittances—perhaps $80 billion worldwide—is easily the most reliable source of foreign money going to poor countries, far outstripping foreign aid programs (Kapur and McHale 2003).

The growing number of transnationals, as well as immigration in general, directly reflects the world systems analysis we considered in Chapter 1. A global economic system that has such sharp contrasts between the industrial haves and the developing have-not nations only serves to encourage movement across borders. The industrial haves gain benefits from it even when they seem to discourage it. The movement back and forth only serves to increase globalization and the creation of informal social networks between people seeking a better life and those already enjoying increased prosperity.

Refugees

Refugees are people living outside their country of citizenship for fear of political or religious persecution. Enough refugees exist to populate an entire nation. There are approximately 13 million refugees worldwide. That makes the nation of refugees larger than Belgium, Sweden, or Cuba. The United States has touted itself as a haven for political refugees. However, as we shall see, the welcome to political refugees has not always been unqualified.

The United States makes the largest financial contribution of any nation to worldwide assistance programs. The United States resettles about 70,000 refugees annually and served as the host to a cumulative 1 million refugees between 1990 and 2003. The post-9/11 years have seen the procedures become much more cumbersome for foreigners to acquire refugee status and gain entry to the United States. Many other nations much smaller and much poorer than the United States have many more refugees than

transnationals
Immigrants who sustain multiple social relationships linking their societies of origin and settlement.

refugees
People living outside their country of citizenship for fear of political or religious persecution.

the U.S., with Jordan, Iran, and Pakistan hosting over a million refugees each (Immigration and Refugee Services of America 2004; U.S. Committee for Refugees 2003).

The United States, insulated by distance from wars and famines in Europe and Asia, has been able to be selective about which and how many refugees are welcomed. Since the arrival of refugees uprooted by World War II, the United States through the 1980s had allowed three groups of refugees to enter in numbers greater than regulations would ordinarily permit: Hungarians, Cubans, and Southeast Asians. Compared with the other two groups, the nearly 40,000 Hungarians who arrived after the unsuccessful revolt against the Soviet Union of November 1956 were few indeed. At the time, however, theirs was the fastest mass immigration to this country since before 1922. With little delay, the United States amended the laws so that the Hungarian refugees could enter. Because of their small numbers and their dispersion throughout this country, the Hungarians are in little evidence nearly 50 years later. The much larger and longer period of movement of Cuban and Southeast Asian refugees into the United States continues to have a profound social and economic impact.

Despite periodic public opposition, the U.S. government is officially committed to accepting refugees from other nations. According to the United Nations treaty on refugees, which our government ratified in 1968, countries are obliged to refrain from forcibly returning people to territories where their lives or liberty might be endangered. However, it is not always clear whether a person is fleeing for his or her personal safety or to escape poverty. Although people in the latter category may be of humanitarian interest, they do not meet the official definition of refugees and are subject to deportation.

Refugees are people who are granted the right to enter a country while still residing abroad. **Asylees** are foreigners who have already entered the United States and now seek protection because of persecution or a well-founded fear of persecution. This persecution may be based on the individual's race, religion, nationality, membership in a particular social group, or political opinion. Asylees are eligible to adjust to lawful permanent resident status after one year of continuous presence in the United States. The number of asylees is currently limited to 10,000 per year, but there is sharp debate over how asylum is granted.

Because asylees, by definition, are already here, the outcome is either to grant them legal entry or to return them. It is the practice of deporting people fleeing poverty that has been the subject of criticism. There is a long tradition in the United

asylees
Foreigners who have already entered the United States and now seek protection because of persecution or a well-founded fear of persecution.

Seen in this 1989 x-ray photo taken by Mexican authorities at the border are a wide shot, on top, and a close up version of human forms. New technology is used to scan passing trucks to detect human cargo as well as drugs and weapons.

States of facilitating the arrival of people leaving Communist nations, such as the Cubans. Mexicans who are refugees from poverty, Liberians fleeing civil war, and Haitians running from despotic rule are not similarly welcomed. The plight of Haitians has become one of particular concern.

Haitians began fleeing their country, often on small boats, in the 1980s. The U.S. Coast Guard intercepted many Haitians at sea, saving some of these boat people from death in their rickety and overcrowded wooden vessels. The Haitians said they feared detentions, torture, and execution if they remained in Haiti. Yet both Republican and Democratic administrations viewed most of the Haitian exiles as economic migrants rather than political refugees and opposed granting them asylum and permission to enter the United States. Once apprehended, the Haitians are returned. In 1993, the U.S. Supreme Court, by an 8–1 vote, upheld the government's right to intercept Haitian refugees at sea and return them to their homeland without asylum hearings.

African Americans and others denounce the Haitian refugee policy as racist. They contrast it to the "wet foot, dry foot" policy toward Cuban refugees. If the government intercepts Cubans at sea, they are returned; but if they escape detection and make it to the mainland, they may apply for asylum. About 75 percent of Cubans seeking asylum are granted refugee status, compared with only 22 percent of Haitians.

Even with only about a thousand Haitians successfully making it into the United States each year, there is an emerging Haitian American presence, especially in south Florida. An estimated 60,000 immigrants and their descendants live in the Little Haiti portion of Miami, where per capita income is a meager $5,700. Despite continuing obstacles, the community exhibits pride in those who have succeeded, from a Haitian American Florida state legislator to hip-hop musician Wyclef Jean (Dahlburg 2001; U.S. Committee for Refugees 2002).

Conclusion

For its first hundred years, the United States allowed all immigrants to enter and become permanent residents. However, the federal policy of welcome did not mean that immigrants would not encounter discrimination and prejudice. With the passage of the Chinese Exclusion Act, discrimination against one group of potential immigrants became law. The Chinese were soon joined by the Japanese as peoples forbidden by law to enter and prohibited from becoming naturalized citizens. The development of the national origin system in the 1920s created a hierarchy of nationalities, with people from northern Europe encouraged to enter, whereas other Europeans and Asians encountered long delays. The possibility of a melting pot, which had always been a fiction, was legislated out of existence.

In the 1960s and again in 1990, the policy was liberalized so that the importance of nationality was minimized, and a person's work skills and relationship to an American were emphasized. This liberalization came at a time when most Europeans no longer wanted to immigrate into the United States.

One out of 10 people in the United States is foreign born; many of them are technical, professional, and craft workers. Also, 34 percent are household workers, and 33 percent of our farm laborers are foreign born. The U.S. economy and society are built on immigrant labor from farm fields to science laboratories (Parker 2001).

Throughout the history of the United States, as we have seen, there has been intense debate over the nation's immigration and refugee policies. In a sense, this debate reflects the deep value conflicts in the U.S. culture and parallels the "American dilemma" identified by Swedish social economist Gunnar Myrdal (1944). One strand of our culture, epitomized by the words "Give us your tired, your poor, your huddled masses," has emphasized egalitarian principles and a desire to help people in their time of need. At the same time, however, hostility to potential immigrants and refugees, whether the Chinese in the 1880s, European Jews in the 1930s and 1940s, or Mexicans, Haitians, and Arabs today, reflects not only racial, ethnic, and religious prejudice but also a desire to maintain the dominant culture of the in-group by keeping out those viewed as outsiders. The conflict between these cultural values is central to the American dilemma of the 1990s.

At present the debate about immigration is highly charged and emotional. Some people see it in economic terms, whereas others see the new arrivals as a challenge to the very culture of our society. Clearly, the general per-

ception is that immigration presents a problem rather than a promise for the future.

Today's concern about immigrants follows generations of people coming to settle in the United States. This immigration in the past produced a very diverse country in terms of both nationality and religion, even before the immigration of the last 50 years. Therefore, the majority of Americans today are not descended from the English, and Protestants are just over half of all worshipers. This diversity of religious and ethnic groups is examined in Chapter 5.

Key Terms

asylees 113
brain drain 103
globalization 111
nativism 96

naturalization 100
refugees 112
remittances (or migradollars) 110

sinophobes 97
transnationals 112
xenophobia 96

Review Questions

1. What are the functions and dysfunctions of immigration?
2. What were the social and economic issues when public opinion mounted against Chinese immigration into the United States?
3. Ultimately, what do you think is the major concern people have about contemporary immigration to the United States: the numbers of immigrants or their nationality?
4. What principles appear to guide U.S. refugee policy?

Critical Thinking

1. What is the immigrant root story of your family? Consider how your ancestors arrived in the United States and also how your family's past has been shaped by other immigrant groups.
2. Can you find evidence of the brain drain in terms of the professionals with whom you come in contact? Do you regard this as a benefit? What groups in the United States may not have been encouraged to fill such positions by the availability of such professionals?

Internet Connections—Research Navigator™

Follow the instructions found on page 31 of this text to access the features of Research Navigator™. Once at the Web site, enter your Login Name and Password. Then, to use the ContentSelect database, enter keywords such as "remittances," "asylum," and "refugees," and the research engine will supply relevant and recent scholarly and popular press publications. Use the *New York Times* Search-by-Subject Archive to find recent news articles related to sociology, and the Link Library feature to locate relevant Web links organized by the key terms associated with this chapter.

5 Ethnicity and Religion

THE UNITED STATES INCLUDES A MULTITUDE OF ETHNIC and religious groups. Do they coexist in harmony or in conflict? How significant are they as sources of identity for their members? White is a race, so how this identity is socially constructed has received significant attention. Many White ethnic groups have transformed their ethnic status into Whiteness. In the 1960s and 1970s, there was a resurgence of interest in White ethnicity, partly in response to the renewed pride in the ethnicity of Blacks, Latinos, and Native Americans. We have an ethnicity paradox in which White ethnics seem to enjoy their heritage while at the same time seeking to assimilate into larger society. White ethnics are the victims of humor (or respectable bigotry) that some still consider socially acceptable, and they find themselves with little power in big business. Religious diversity continues and expands with immigration and the growth in the followings of non-Christian faiths. Religious minorities have experienced intolerance in the present as well as in the past. Constitutional issues such as school prayer, secessionist minorities, creationism, and public religious displays are regularly taken to the Supreme Court. Italian Americans and the Amish are presented as case studies of the experiences of specific ethnic and religious groups in the United States.

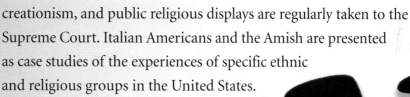

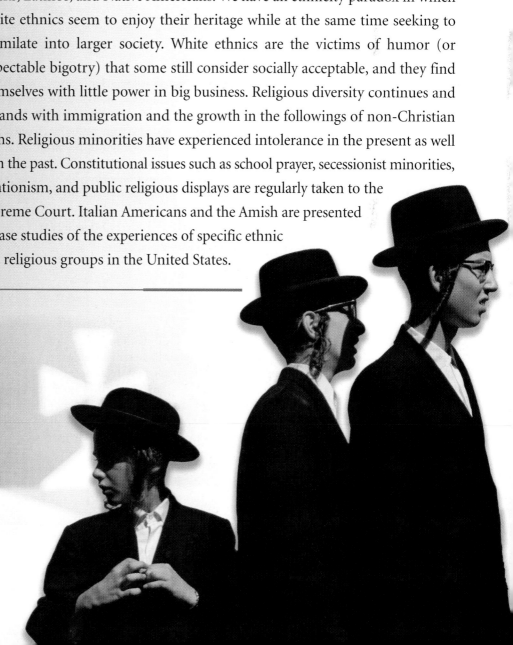

Betty O'Keefe is a 60-year-old Californian who is a fifth-generation Irish American, meaning that her grandmother's grandmother came to the United States from Ireland. Sociologist Mary Waters (1990:97) asked her what it was like growing up in the United States.

When I was in high school my maiden name was Tynan. This was 1940. I was dating some boys from school, and two different times when the parents found out I was an Irish Catholic, they told him he couldn't go out with me. The Protestants were like that. . . . One of his brothers later married someone named O'Flannery and I was so thrilled. I said I hope your mother is turning in her grave. So I am happy that my children have the name O'Keefe. So that people know right away what their background is. I think it is better. They would never be put in the position I was in.

Do you think something like that could happen now?

I don't think so openly. But I think it is definitely still there. You are not as bad (being an Irish Catholic) as a Black, but you are not Protestant. You are not Jewish either, which would be worse, but still you are not of their church.

Their names may be Badovich, Hoggarty, Jablonski, Reggio, or Williams. They may follow any one of thousands of faiths and gather at any of the 360,000 churches, mosques, synagogues, and temples. Our nation's motto is *E Pluribus Unum*, and although there may be doubt that we are truly united into one common culture following a single ideology, there is little doubt about our continuing diversity as a nation of peoples.

Indeed, the very complexity of relations between dominant and subordinate groups in the United States today is partly the result of its heterogeneous population. No one ethnic origin or religious faith encompasses all the inhabitants of the United States. Even though our largest period of sustained immigration is three generations past, an American today is surrounded by remnants of cultures and practitioners of religions whose origins are foreign to this country. Religion and ethnicity continue to be significant in defining a person's identity.

Ethnic Diversity

CD-ROM *Activity 9.3*

The ethnic diversity of the United States at the beginning of the 21st century is apparent to almost everyone. Passersby in New York City were undoubtedly surprised once when two street festivals met head-to-head. The procession of San Gennaro, the patron saint of Naples, marched through Little Italy, only to run directly into a Chinese festival originating in Chinatown. Teachers in many public schools often face students who speak only one language, and it is not English. Students in Chicago are taught in Spanish, Greek, Italian, Polish, German, Creole, Japanese, Cantonese, or the language of a Native American tribe. In the Detroit metropolitan area, classroom instruction is conveyed in 21 languages, including Arabic, Portuguese, Ukrainian, Latvian, Lithuanian, and Serbian. In many areas of the United States, you can refer to a special Yellow Pages and find a driving instructor who speaks Portuguese or a psychotherapist who will talk to you in Hebrew.

Germans are the largest ancestral group; the 2000 Census showed almost one-sixth of Americans saying they had at least some German ancestry. Although most German Americans are assimilated, it is possible to see the ethnic tradition in some areas, particularly in Milwaukee, whose population has 48 percent German ancestry. There, three Saturday schools teach German, and one can affiliate with 34 German American clubs and visit a German library that operates within the public library system. Just a bit to the south in River Forest, a Chicago suburb, *kinderwerksatt* meets weekly to help parents and children alike to maintain German culture (Carvajal 1996; D. Freedman 2004; Johnson 1992; Usdansky 1992).

Germany is one of 21 European nations from which at least 1 million people claim to have ancestry. The numbers are striking when one considers the size of some of the sending countries. For example, there are over 33 million Irish Americans, and the Republic of Ireland had a population of 3.7 million in 1998. Similarly, nearly 5 million people claim Swedish ancestry, and there are 8.9 million people living in Sweden today. Of course, many Irish and Swedish Americans are of mixed ancestry, but not everyone in Ireland is Irish, nor is everyone in Sweden Swedish.

Why Don't We Study Whiteness?

Race is socially constructed, as we learned in Chapter 1. Sometimes we come to define race in a clear-cut manner: A descendant of a Pilgrim is White, for example. But sometimes race is more ambiguous: People who are the children of an African American and Vietnamese American union are biracial or "mixed" or whatever they come to be seen as by others. Our recognition that race is socially constructed has sparked a renewed interest in what it means to be White in the United States. Two aspects of White as a race are useful to consider: the historical creation of whiteness and how contemporary White people reflect on their racial identity.

 CD-ROM *Activity 9.1*

 CD-ROM *Activity 9.2*

When the English immigrants established themselves as the political founders of the United States, they also came to define what it meant to be White. Other groups that today are regarded as White, such as Irish, Germans, Norwegians, or Swedes, were not always considered White in the eyes of the English. Differences in language and religious worship, as well as past allegiance to a king in Europe different from the English, all caused these groups to be seen not as Whites in the Western Hemisphere but more as nationals of their home country who happened to be residing in North America.

The old distrust in Europe, where, for example, the Irish were viewed by the English as socially and culturally inferior, continued on this side of the Atlantic Ocean. Karl Marx, writing from England, reported that the average English worker looked down on the Irish the way poor Whites in the American South looked down on Black people (Ignatiev 1994, 1995; Roediger 1994).

In "Listen to Our Voices," Diane Glancy, Macalester College professor of Native American literature and creative writing, draws on both insider and outsider perspectives on being White in the United States. As she describes, she is descended from Native Americans (American Indians) and from English and Germans. As this chapter continues, we will consider in a variety of ways what it means to be White in the United Sates at the beginning of the 21st century.

Whiteness

As European immigrants and their descendants assimilated to the English and distanced themselves from other oppressed groups such as American Indians and African Americans, they came to be viewed as White rather than as part of a particular culture. Writer Noel Ignatiev (1994:84), contrasting being White with being Polish, argues that "Whiteness is nothing but an expression of race privilege." This strong statement argues that being White, as opposed to being Black or Asian, is characterized by being a member of the dominant group.

Voices Listen to Our Voices Listen to

WHEN THE BOATS ARRIVED

Some of my ancestors came from Europe on boats. Others were already here when the boats arrived. I have done a lot of my writing examining the Indian part of my heritage, which came through my father. The white part didn't seem to need definition. It just was. Is. And shall be. But what does it mean to be part white? What does whiteness look like viewed from the other, especially when that other is also within oneself?

Diane Glancy

I can say whiteness is the dominant culture, for now anyway. Or I can say I was taught that whiteness gives definition instead of receiving it. It is the upright. The unblemished. The milk or new snow. It is the measure by which others are measured. There's nothing off center in it to make it aware of itself as outside or other. It doesn't need examination or explanation, but is the center around which others orbit. It is the plumb line. Other races/cultures/ethnicities are looked at in terms of their distance from whiteness.

Whiteness is a heritage I can almost enter, but I have unwhiteness in me. There is something that is not milk or new snow. I am a person of part color. I can feel my distance from whiteness. There is a dividing line into it I cannot cross. But neither can I cross fully into the Indian, because I am of mixed heritage.

When I look at my white heritage, it is as fragmented and hard to pinpoint as the native side. My mother's family came from England and Germany. They settled in Pennsylvania, then Virginia, and finally on the Missouri–Kansas border. What do I know of them any more than of my father's family? The European part of the family were practical, middle-of-the-road people. They got their work done. They didn't say a lot about it. They were fair-minded and tenacious. They were churchgoers and voters who migrated from the farm to the city in my parents' generation. They educated their children and died without much ceremony.

As for the white culture I saw in my mother's family— every Christmas Eve, they served Canadian bacon, which my father brought from the stockyards where he worked. I received an Easter basket on Easter. I got a sparkler on the Fourth of July. But that hardly defines culture.

I can look at the whiteness in my mother's family and say there was a determination, a punctuality, a dependability. There was a sense of Manifest Destiny, which was another tool for dominance. There was a need for maintenance and responsibility. A sense of a Judeo-Christian God. A holding to one's own. There was a need to be goal-oriented. To make use of resources.

There also was opportunity to do all these things.

Who can say what will happen to whiteness as the people of color become the majority in the new century? Who can say what will happen as the cultures of the minorities deepen, as the white is mixed with others and gets harder to define? Can the white culture continue to be defined by its lack of ceremonies, its Elvises and White Castles, its harbor of ideas? Will it continue to invent its inventiveness? Will it continue to thrive?

I guess I would define white American culture as industriousness without overwhelming tradition. It doesn't seem to have anchors, but slides past others into port. Into the port it created, after all. ■

Source: Diane Glancy. "When the Boats Arrived." First appeared in *The Hungry Mind Review*, Spring 1998.

Whites as people don't think of themselves as a race or have a conscious racial identity. The only occasion when a White racial identity emerges is momentarily when Whites fill out a form asking for self-designation of race or one of those occasions when they are culturally or socially surrounded by people who are not White.

Therefore, contemporary White Americans generally give little thought to "being White." Consequently, there is little interest in studying "Whiteness" or considering "being White" except that it is "not being Black." Unlike non-Whites, who are much more likely to interact with Whites, take orders from Whites, and see Whites as the leading figures in the mass media, Whites enjoy the privilege of not being reminded of their Whiteness.

Unlike racial minorities, Whites downplay the importance of their racial identity while being willing to receive the advantages that come from being White. This means that advocacy of a "color-blind" or "race-neutral" outlook permits the privilege of Whiteness to prevail (Bonilla-Silva 2002; Yancey 2003).

The new interest seeks to look at Whiteness, but not from the vantage point of a White supremacist. Rather, focusing on White people as a race or on what it means today to be White goes beyond any definition that implies superiority over non-Whites. Historian Noel Ignatiev observes that studying whiteness is a necessary stage to "abolition of whiteness"—just as, in Marxist analysis, class consciousness is a necessary stage to the abolition of class. By confronting Whiteness, society grasps the all-encompassing power that accompanies socially constructed race (Talbot 1997: 118).

White Privilege

Whiteness carries with it a sense of identity of being White as opposed to being, for example, Asian or African. For many people it may not be easy to establish a social identity of Whiteness, as in the case of biracial children. However, one can argue that the social identity of Whiteness exists if one enjoys the privilege of being White.

Scholar Peggy McIntosh of the Wellesley College Center for Research on Women looked at the privilege that comes from being White and the added privilege of being male. The other side of racial oppression is the privilege enjoyed by dominant groups. Being White or being successful in establishing a White identity carries with it distinct advantages. Among those that McIntosh (1988) identified were:

- Being considered financially reliable when using checks, credit cards, or cash
- Taking a job without having coworkers suspect it came because of one's race
- Never having to speak for all the people of one's race
- Watching television or reading a newspaper and seeing people of one's own race widely represented
- Speaking effectively in a large group without being called a credit to one's race
- Assuming that if legal or medical help is needed that one's race will not work against oneself

Whiteness does carry privileges, but most White people do not consciously think of them except on the rare occasions when they are questioned. We will return to the concepts of Whiteness and White privilege, but let us also consider the rich diversity of religion in the United States, which parallels the ethnic diversity of this nation.

A dramatic confirmation of White privilege came with a study published by sociologist Devah Pager in 2003. She sent four men out as trained "testers" to look for entry-level jobs in Milwaukee, Wisconsin, requiring no experience or special training. Each was a 23-year-old college student but they presented themselves as having a high school diploma with similar job histories.

White privilege as described by Peggy McIntosh includes holding a position in a company without co-workers suspecting it came because of one's race.

The job-seeking experiences with 350 different employers were vastly different among the four men. Why was that? Two of the testers where Black and two were White. Furthermore, one tester of each pair indicated in the job application that he had served 18 months of jail time for a felony conviction (possession of cocaine with intent to distribute). As you can see in Figure 5.1, applicants with a prison record received significantly fewer callbacks. But as dramatic a difference as a criminal record made, race was clearly more important. The differences were to the point that a White job applicant with a jail record actually received more callbacks for further consideration than a Black man with no criminal record. Whiteness has a privilege even when it comes to jail time (Pager 2003).

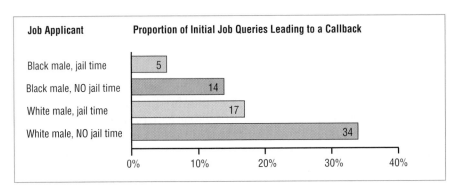

FIGURE 5.1   White Privilege in Job Seeking

Source: Pager 2003: 958.

The Rediscovery of Ethnicity

Robert Park (1950:205), a prominent early sociologist, wrote in 1913 that "a Pole, Lithuanian, or Norwegian cannot be distinguished, in the second generation, from an American, born of native parents." At one time, sociologists saw the end of ethnicity as nearly a foregone conclusion. W. Lloyd Warner and Leo Srole (1945) wrote in their often-cited Yankee City series that the future of ethnic groups seemed to be limited in the United States and that they would be quickly absorbed. Oscar Handlin's *Uprooted* (1951) told of the destruction of immigrant values and their replacement by American culture. Although Handlin was among the pioneers in investigating ethnicity, assimilation was the dominant theme in his work.

Many writers have shown almost a fervent hope that ethnicity would vanish. The persistence of ethnicity was for some time treated by sociologists as dysfunctional because it meant a continuation of old values that interfered with the allegedly superior new values. For example, to hold on to one's language delayed entry into the larger labor market and the upward social mobility it afforded. Ethnicity was expected to disappear not only because of assimilation but also because aspirations to higher social class and status demanded that it vanish. Somehow, it was assumed that one could not be ethnic and middle class, much less affluent.

The Third-Generation Principle

Historian Marcus Hansen's (1952) **principle of third-generation interest** was an early exception to the assimilationist approach to White ethnic groups. Simply stated, Hansen maintained that in the third generation—the grandchildren of the original immigrants—ethnic interest and awareness would actually increase. According to Hansen, "What the son wishes to forget the grandson wishes to remember."

Hansen's principle has been tested several times since it was first put forth. John Goering (1971), in interviewing Irish and Italian Catholics, found that ethnicity was more important to members of the third generation than it was to the immigrants themselves. Similarly, Mary Waters (1990), in her interviews of White ethnics living in suburban San Jose, California, and suburban Philadelphia, Pennsylvania, observed many grandchildren wanting to study their ancestors' language, even though it would be a foreign language to them. They also expressed interest in learning more of their ethnic group's history and a desire to visit the homeland.

Social scientists in the past were quick to minimize the ethnic awareness of blue-collar workers. In fact, ethnicity was viewed as merely another aspect of White ethnics' alleged racist nature, an allegation that will be examined later in this chapter. Curiously, the very same intellectuals and journalists who bent over backward to understand the growing solidarity of Blacks, Hispanics, and Native Americans refused to give White ethnics the academic attention they deserved (Wrong 1972).

The new assertiveness of Blacks and other non-Whites of their rights in the 1960s unquestionably presented White ethnics with the opportunity to reexamine their own position. "If solidarity and unapologetic self-consciousness might hasten Blacks' upward mobility, why not ours?" asked the White ethnics, who were often only a half step above Blacks in social status. The African American movement pushed other groups to reflect on their past. The increased consciousness of Blacks and their positive attitude toward African culture and the contributions worldwide of African Americans are embraced in what we called the Afrocentric perspective (Chapter 1). Therefore, the mood was set in the 1960s for the country to be receptive to ethnicity. By legitimizing Black cultural differences from White culture, along with those of Native Americans and Hispanics, the country's opinion leaders legitimized other types of cultural diversity.

principle of third-generation interest
Marcus Hansen's contention that ethnic interest and awareness increase in the third generation among the grandchildren of immigrants.

For many Irish American participants in a St. Patrick's Day Parade, this is their most visible expression of symbolic ethnicity during an entire year.

Symbolic Ethnicity

Observers comment both on the evidence of assimilation and on the signs of ethnic identity that seem to support a pluralistic view of society. How can both be possible?

First, there is the very visible evidence of **symbolic ethnicity**, which may lead us to exaggerate the persistence of ethnic ties among White Americans. According to sociologist Herbert Gans (1979), ethnicity today increasingly involves the symbols of ethnicity, such as eating ethnic food, acknowledging ceremonial holidays such as St. Patrick's Day, and supporting specific political issues or the issues confronting the old country. One example was the push in 1998 by Irish Americans to convince state legislatures to make it compulsory in public schools to teach about the Irish potato famine, which was a significant factor in immigration to the United States. This symbolic ethnicity may be more visible, but this type of ethnic heritage does not interfere with what people do, read, or say, or even whom they befriend or marry.

The ethnicity of the 21st century embraced by English-speaking Whites is largely symbolic. It does not include active involvement in ethnic activities or participation in ethnic-related organizations. In fact, sizable proportions of White ethnics have gained large-scale entry into almost all clubs, cliques, and fraternal groups. Such acceptance is a key indicator of assimilation. Ethnicity has become increasingly peripheral to the lives of the members of the ethnic group. Although they may not relinquish their ethnic identity, other identities become more important.

Second, the ethnicity that does exist may be more a result of living in the United States than actual importing of practices from the past or the old country. Many so-called ethnic foods or celebrations, for example, began in the United States. The persistence of ethnic consciousness, then, may not depend on foreign birth, a distinctive language, and a unique way of life. Instead, it may reflect the experiences in the United States of a unique group that developed a cultural tradition distinct from that of the mainstream. For example, in Poland the *szlachta*, or landed gentry, rarely mixed socially with the peasant class. In the United States, however, even with those associations still fresh, they interacted together in social organizations as they settled in concentrated communities segregated physically and socially from others (Glazer 1971; Glazer and Moynihan 1970; Lopata 1993).

Third, maintaining ethnicity can be a critical step toward successful assimilation. This **ethnicity paradox** facilitates full entry into the dominant culture. The ethnic community may give its members not only a useful financial boost but also the psy-

symbolic ethnicity
Herbert Gans's term that describes emphasis on ethnic food and ethnically associated political issues rather than deeper ties to one's heritage.

ethnicity paradox
The maintenance of one's ethnic ties in a way that can assist with assimilation in larger society.

chological strength and positive self-esteem that will allow them to compete effectively in larger society. Thus, we may witness people participating actively in their ethnic enclave while trying to cross the bridge into the wider community (Lal 1995).

Therefore, ethnicity gives continuity with the past in the form of an affective or emotional tie. The significance of this sense of belonging cannot be emphasized enough. Whether reinforced by distinctive behavior or by what Milton Gordon (1964) called a sense of "peoplehood," ethnicity is an effective, functional source of cohesion. Proximity to fellow ethnics is not necessary for a person to maintain social cohesion and in-group identity. Fraternal organizations or sports-related groups can preserve associations between ethnics who are separated geographically. Members of ethnic groups may even maintain their feelings of in-group solidarity after leaving ethnic communities in the central cities for the suburban fringe.

The Price Paid by White Ethnics

Many White ethnics shed their past and want only to be Americans, with no ancestral ties to another country. Some ethnics do not want to abandon their heritage, but to retain their past as a part of their present, they must pay a price because of prejudice and discrimination. Although the levels of present and past intolerance toward White ethnics are much less than those we saw in Chapters 2 and 3 toward African Americans, Latinos, Asian Americans, and Native Americans, this intolerance is a part of multicultural America.

Prejudice Toward White Ethnic Groups

Our examination of immigration to the United States in Chapter 4 pointed out the mixed feelings that have greeted European immigrants. They are apparently still not well received. In 1944, well after most immigration from Poland had ended, the Polish-American Congress, an umbrella organization of 40 Polish fraternities, was founded to defend the image of Polish Americans. Young Polish Americans are made to feel ashamed of their ethnic origin when teachers find their names unpronounceable and when they hear Polish jokes bandied about in a way that anti-Black or anti-Semitic humor is not. One survey found that half of second-generation Polish Americans encounter prejudice.

Curiously, it was socially proper to condemn the White working class as racist but improper to question the negative attitude of middle-class people toward White ethnics. Michael Lerner (1969) called this hostility toward White ethnics **respectable bigotry**. Polish jokes are acceptable, whereas anti-Black humor is considered to be in poor taste.

White ethnics in the early 1970s felt that the mass media unfairly ridiculed them and their culture while celebrating Black Power and African culture. For instance, Italian Americans remain concerned that their image is overwhelmed by stereotypes of organized crime, spaghetti, overweight mothers, and sexy women. Even television's Italian police seem to conform to the old stereotypes. In response to such stereotyping, the Columbian Coalition, founded in 1971, employs lawyers to handle cases of Italian Americans who claim they are victims of bigotry.

Even the broad group of White ethnics who still dominate Roman Catholicism have expressed feelings of being victimized. In 2000, a Roman Catholic was appointed chaplain of the U.S. House of Representatives for the first time. This led to angry sentiments against a Catholic being granted this symbolic position rather than keeping it in the hands of the Protestant clergy. About the same time, candidate George W. Bush appeared at the avowedly anti-Catholic Bob Jones University during the South Carolina primary campaign. The response to this appearance raised questions in some

respectable bigotry
Michael Lerner's term for the social acceptance of prejudice against White ethnics, when intolerance against non-White minorities is regarded as unacceptable.

quarters about lingering hostility toward Roman Catholics and the Roman Catholic Church. A national survey taken of Roman Catholics at that time found that the majority (56 percent) did not believe such a bias did exist, but one-third did perceive the presence of anti-Catholic bias in the country (Bendyna and Pearl 2000).

The Prejudice of Ethnics

In the 1960s, as the civil rights movement moved north, White ethnics replaced the southern White as the typical bigot portrayed in the mass media. The chanting of protestors resulted in ugly incidents that made White ethnics and bigots synonymous. This stereotype of the prejudiced White ethnic has rarely been questioned. The danger of this and any stereotype is that it becomes indistinguishable from fact. David Matza (1964:1) referred to these mental pictures, that "tend to remain beyond the reach of such intellectual correctives as argument, criticism and scrutiny. . . . Left unattended, they return to haunt us by shaping or bending theories that purport to explain major social phenomena." This 1964 picture of ethnics and the degree of truth behind it must be examined.

The first issue to resolve is whether White ethnic groups are more prejudiced than other Whites. Sociologist Andrew Greeley (1974a, 1977; Nie et al. 1974) examined attitudes toward race, social welfare, and American involvement in Vietnam. The evidence pointed to minimal differences between ethnics and others. Some of the differences actually showed greater tolerance and liberalism among White ethnics. For example, White ethnics were more in favor of welfare programs and more opposed to this country's participation in the Vietnam War.

Even when more sophisticated statistical analysis is introduced, the overall finding remains unchanged. No evidence supports the image of White ethnics as bigots. Greeley (1974a:202) concludes, "Our argument is not that ethnics are the last bastion of liberalism in America today, but rather that it is a misrepresentation of the facts to picture them as a vanguard of conservatism." However, working-class ethnic neighborhoods have undeniably been the scene of ugly racial confrontations. If ethnics are no more bigoted than others, how have such incidents come to occur, and how has this reputation developed? For that answer, the unique relationship between White ethnic groups and African Americans must be understood.

In retrospect, it should be no surprise that one group that has been antagonistic to African Americans is the White ethnics. For many citizens, including White ethnics, the United States they remembered from the 1950s seemed to change. When politicians told people in the 1960s, "We must fight poverty and discrimination," this translated to White ethnics as, "Share your job, share your neighborhood, but pay more taxes." Whites recalled how, in several generations, they had moved from membership in a poor immigrant group to becoming a prosperous part of the working class. Government assistance to the poor was almost nonexistent then, public education was more limited, and subsidized training programs were absent. Why was it different now? Many White ethnics found it difficult to understand why African Americans seemed to be singled out as a cause for concern in the 1960s when they perceived that they, too, had real needs (Glazer and Moynihan 1970; Novak 1996; Sanders and Morawska 1975; Tyler 1972).

White ethnics went so far as to turn their backs on federal aid offered them because they did not want to have their neighborhoods marked as "poverty pockets," nor did they want to be associated with Black-oriented programs. In Newark, New Jersey, Italians successfully prevented an antipoverty office from being established and thereby cut off the jobs its programs would have created (Barbaro 1974). This ethnic opposition to publicly sponsored programs was not new. James Wilson and Edward Banfield (1964) studied elections in seven major cities between 1956 and

1963 for referenda to build new hospitals, parks, and schools. The results indicated that the least support came from White ethnics, who would have paid the least and benefited the most.

White ethnics first learned that they are not considered part of the dominant group, but in time, through assimilation, they came to be redefined to enjoy most of the White privileges we identified earlier. The case about Italian Americans looks at how the ethnic experience can change over time.

Case Example: The Italian Americans

Although each European country's immigration to the United States has created its own social history, the case of Italians, though not typical of every nationality, offers insight into the White ethnic experience. Italians immigrated even during the colonial period, and they played prominent roles during the American Revolution and the early days of the republic. Mass immigration began in the 1880s, peaking in the first 20 years of the 20th century, when Italians accounted for one-fourth of European immigration.

Italian immigration was concentrated not only in time but also by geography. The majority of the immigrants were landless peasants from rural southern Italy, the *Mezzogiorno*. Although many people in the United States assume that Italians are a nationality with a single culture, this is not true either culturally or economically. The Italian people recognize multiple geographic divisions reflecting sharp cultural distinctions. These divisions were brought with the immigrants to the New World.

Many Italians, especially in the early years of mass immigration in the 19th century, received their jobs through an ethnic labor contractor, the *padrone*. Similar arrangements have been used by Asian, Hispanic, and Greek immigrants, where the labor contractors, most often immigrants, have mastered sufficient English to mediate for their compatriots. Exploitation was common within the *padrone* system through kickbacks, provision of inadequate housing, and withholding of wages. By World War I, 90 percent of Italian girls and 99 percent of Italian boys in New York City were leaving school at age 14 to work, but by that time Italian Americans were sufficiently fluent in English to seek out work on their own, and the *padrone* system had disappeared.

Along with manual labor, the Catholic Church was a very important part of Italian Americans' lives at this time. Yet they found little comfort in a Catholic church dominated by an earlier immigrant group: the Irish. The traditions were different; weekly

Italian Americans celebrate a religious festival in Cambridge, Massachusetts.

attendance for Italian Americans was overshadowed by the religious aspects of the *feste* (or festivals) held throughout the year in honor of saints (the Irish viewed the *feste* as practically a form of paganism). These initial adjustment problems were overcome with the establishment of ethnic parishes, a pattern repeated by other non-Irish immigrant groups. Thus, parishes would be staffed by Italian priests, sometimes imported for that purpose. Although the hierarchy of the church adjusted more slowly, Italian Americans were increasingly able to feel at home in their local parish church. Today, more than 70 percent of Italian Americans identify themselves as Roman Catholics (Luconi 2001).

As assimilation proceeded, Italian Americans began to construct a social identity as a nationality group, rather than viewing themselves in terms of their village or province. As shown in Figure 5.2, over time, Italian Americans shed old identities for a new one. As immigration from Italy declined, the descendants' ties became more nationalistic. This move from local or regional to national identity was followed by Irish and Greek Americans. The changing identity of Italian Americans reflected the treatment they received in the United States, where non-Italians did not make those regional distinctions. However, they were not treated well. For example, in turn-of-the-century New Orleans, Italian Americans established special ties to the Black community because both groups were marginalized in southern society. Gradually, Italian Americans became White and enjoyed all the privileges that come with it. Today it would be inconceivable to imagine that Italian Americans of New Orleans would reach out to the African American community as their natural allies on social and political issues (Guglielmo and Salerno 2003; Luconi 2001).

A controversial aspect of the Italian-American experience involves organized crime, as typified by Al Capone (1899–1947). Arriving in U.S. society in the bottom layers, Italians lived in decaying, crime-ridden neighborhoods that became known as Little Italies. For a small segment of these immigrants, crime was a significant means of upward social mobility. In effect, entering and leading criminal activity was one aspect of assimilation, though not a positive one. Complaints linking ethnicity and crime actually began in colonial times with talk about the criminally inclined Irish and Germans, and they continue with contemporary stereotyping about such groups as Colombian drug dealers and Vietnamese street gangs. Yet the image of Italians as criminals has persisted from Prohibition-era gangsters to the view of mob families today. As noted earlier, it is not at all surprising that groups such as the Columbian Coalition have been organized to counter such negative images.

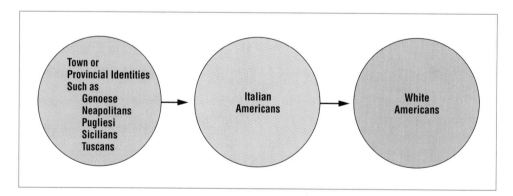

FIGURE 5.2   Constructing Social Identity Among Italian Immigrants
Over time Italian Americans moved from seeing themselves in terms of their provincial or village identity to their national identity, and then they successfully became indistinguishable from other Whites.

The fact that Italians often are characterized as criminal, even in the mass media, is another example of what we have called respectable bigotry toward White ethnics. The persistence of linking Italians, or any other minority group, with crime probably is attributable to attempts to explain a problem by citing a single cause: the presence of perceived undesirables. Many Italian Americans still see their image tied to old stereotypes. A 2001 survey of Italian American teenagers found that 39 percent felt the media presented their ethnic group as criminal or gang members and 34 percent as restaurant workers (National Italian American Foundation 2001).

The immigration of Italians was slowed by the national origin system, described in Chapter 4. As Italian Americans settled permanently, the mutual aid societies that had grown up in the 1920s to provide basic social services began to dissolve. More slowly, education came to be valued by Italian Americans as a means of upward mobility. Even becoming more educated did not ward off prejudice, however. In 1930, for example, President Herbert Hoover rebuked Fiorello La Guardia, then an Italian-American member of Congress from New York City, stating that "the Italians are predominantly our murderers and bootleggers" and recommending that La Guardia "go back to where you belong" because, "like a lot of other foreign spawn, you do not appreciate this country which supports you and tolerates you" (Baltzell 1964:30).

While U.S. troops, including 500,000 Italian Americans, battled Italy during World War II, some hatred and sporadic violence emerged against Italian Americans and their property. However, they were not limited to actions against individuals. Italian Americans were even confined by the federal government in specific areas of California by virtue of their ethnicity alone, and 10,000 were relocated from coastal areas. In addition, 1,800 Italian Americans who were citizens of Italy were placed in an internment camp in Montana. The internees were eventually freed on Columbus Day 1942 as President Roosevelt lobbied the Italian American community to gain full support for the impending land invasion of Italy (Department of Justice 2001a; Fox 1990).

In politics, Italian Americans have been more successful, at least at the local level, where family and community ties can be translated into votes. However, political success did not come easily because many Italian immigrants anticipated returning to their homeland and did not always take neighborhood politics seriously. It was even more difficult for Italian Americans to break into national politics: Not until 1962 was an Italian American named to a cabinet-level position. Geraldine Ferraro's nomination as the Democratic vice presidential candidate in 1984 was every bit as much an achievement for Italian Americans as it was for women (Cornacchia and Nelson 1992).

In 2000, the 15.9 million people of Italian ancestry accounted for about 6 percent of the population, although only a small fraction of them had actually been born in Italy. Italian Americans still remain the seventh-largest immigrant group. Just how ethnically conscious is the Italian-American community? Although the number is declining, 1 million Americans speak Italian at home; only six languages are spoken more frequently at home (Spanish, French, Chinese, Vietnamese, Tagalog (Philippines) and German). For another 14-plus million Italian Americans, however, the language tie to their culture is absent, and depending on their degree of assimilation, only traces of symbolic ethnicity may remain (Bureau of the Census 2003b).

Religious Pluralism

In popular speech, the term *pluralism* has often been used in the United States to refer explicitly to religion. Although certain faiths figure more prominently in the worship scene, there has been a history of greater religious tolerance in the United States than in most other nations. Today there are more than 1,500 religious bodies in the United

denomination
A large, organized religion not officially linked with the state or government.

States, ranging from the more than 66 million members of the Roman Catholic Church to sects with fewer than 1,000 adherents.

How do we view the United States in terms of religion? It is now more accurate to speak of the country as Judeo-Christian-Islamic or Abrahamic (referring to the historical religious leader common to the three faiths). There is an increasingly non-Christian presence in the United States. In 1900, an estimated 96 percent of the nation was Christian, just over 1 percent nonreligious, and about 3 percent all other faiths. In 2004, it is estimated that the nation is 86 percent Christian, nearly 7 percent nonreligious, and another 7 percent all other faiths. The United States has a long Jewish tradition, and Muslims number close to 5 million. A smaller but also growing number of people adhere to such Eastern faiths as Hinduism, Buddhism, Confucianism, and Taoism (Barrett and Johnson 2001; Gallup 2004).

The diversity of religious life in the United States is apparent from Figure 5.3, which shows the Christian faiths that dominate various areas of the country numerically. For many nations of the world, a map of religions would hardly be useful because one faith accounts for almost all religious followers in the country. The diversity of beliefs, rituals, and experiences that characterizes religious life in the United States reflects both the nation's immigrant heritage and the First Amendment prohibition against establishing a state religion.

Sociologists use the word **denomination** for a large, organized religion that is not linked officially with the state or government. By far the largest denomination in the United States is Catholicism, yet at least 23 other Christian religious denominations have 1 million or more members (Table 5.1).

There are also at least four non-Christian religious groups in the United States whose numbers are comparable to any of these large denominations. Jews, Muslims,

FIGURE 5.3 Predominant Christian Denominations by Counties, 2000

The diversity of Christian religious life in the United States is apparent in the figure. Many Christian denominations account for 25 percent or more of the church members in a county. Among non-Christian faiths, only Judaism figures so significantly—in New York County (Manhattan) of New York City and in Dade County, Florida (which includes Miami Beach).

Source: "Predominant Christian Denominations by Counties 2000" from *Churches and Church Membership in the United States, 2002* by D. Jones, et al. Reprinted with permission from Religious Congregations and Membership in the United States: 2000. (Nashville: Glenmary Research Center, 2002). © by Association of Statisticians of American Religious Bodies. All rights reserved.

TABLE 5.1
Churches with More Than a Million Members, 2003

Denomination Name	Inclusive Membership
The Roman Catholic Church	66,407,105
Southern Baptist Convention	16,247,736
The United Methodist Church	8,251,042
The Church of God in Christ	5,499,875
The Church of Jesus Christ of Latter-day Saints	5,410,544
Evangelical Lutheran Church in America	5,038,066
National Baptist Convention, USA, Inc.	5,000,000
National Baptist Convention of America, Inc.	3,500,000
Presbyterian Church (U.S.A.)	3,407,329
Assemblies of God	2,687,366
The Lutheran Church–Missouri Synod (LCMS)	2,512,714
Progressive National Baptist Convention, Inc.	2,500,000
African Methodist Episcopal Church	2,500,000
National Missionary Baptist Convention of America	2,500,000
Episcopal Church	2,333,628
Greek Orthodox Archdiocese of America	1,500,000
Pentecostal Assemblies of the World, Inc.	1,500,000
Churches of Christ	1,500,000
African Methodist Episcopal Zion Church	1,430,795
American Baptist Churches in the U.S.A.	1,484,291
United Church of Christ	1,330,985
Baptist Bible Fellowship International	1,200,000
Christian Churches and Churches of Christ	1,071,616
Jehovah's Witness	1,022,397

Source: Lindner 2004:11. "U.S. Membership Denominational Ranking: Largest 25 Churches" in *Yearbook of American and Canadian Churches 2004*, edited by Reverend Eileen W. Lindner, Ph.D. Copyright © 2004 by National Council of the Churches of Christ in the USA. Reprinted by permission [www.ncccusa.org].

Buddhists, and Hindus in the United States all number more than 1 million. Within each of these groups, there are branches or sects that distinguish themselves from each other. For example, in the United States and the rest of the world, some followers of Islam are Sunni Muslims and others are Shiites (refer to Chapter 11). There are further divisions within these groups, just as there are among Protestants and in turn among Baptists (Kosmin et al. 2001).

One notable characteristic of religious practice in the United States is its segregated nature at the local level. Even if religious faiths have broad representation, they tend to be fairly homogeneous at the local church level. This is especially ironic, given that many faiths have played critical roles in resisting racism and trying to bring together the nation in the name of racial and ethnic harmony (Orfield and Liebowitz 1999).

During the 1976 presidential campaign, attention was directed to the segregation practiced by churches in the United States. The church attended by Jimmy Carter in Plains, Georgia, captured headlines when it closed its doors to a Black civil rights activist seeking membership. The Plains church later opened its membership to African Americans at Carter's urging. Such formal racial restrictions are unusual, but today the church hour on Sunday mornings still fits the description "the most segregated hour of the week." A 2001 survey of Christian congregations found that 86 percent were either overwhelmingly White, Black, Latino, or Asian, with only 14 percent having a truly integrated congregation (Dudley and Roozen 2001: 16).

Broadly defined faiths show representation of a variety of ethnic and racial groups. In Figure 5.4, we consider the interaction of White, Black, and Hispanic race with religions. Muslims, Pentecostals, and Jehovah's Witnesses are much more diverse than Presbyterians or Lutherans. Religion plays an even more central role for Blacks and Latinos than Whites. A 2004 national survey indicated that 65 percent of African Americans and 51 percent of Latinos attend a religious service every week, compared to 44 percent of non-Hispanic Whites (Winseman 2004).

About two in three Americans (66 percent) are counted as church members, but it is difficult to assess the strength of their religious commitment. A persuasive case can be made that religious institutions continue to grow stronger through an influx of new members, despite mounting secularism in society. Some observers think that, after reaching a low in the 1960s, religion is becoming more important to people again. The past upheavals in American religious life are reflected on the covers of *Time* magazine, which have cried out variously, "Is God Dead?" (April 8, 1966), "Is God Coming Back to Life?" (December 26, 1969), and "The Jesus Revolution" (June 21, 1971). Much more recently, *Newsweek* proclaimed that "Science Finds God" (July 20, 1998). At present, there is little statistical support for the view that the influence of religion on society is diminishing (Moore 2002).

In "Research Focus" (see pp. 134–135), we consider how social scientists examine religious fervor in the United States and what recent studies have indicated.

It would also be incorrect to focus only on older religious organizations. Local churches that developed into national faiths in the 1990s, such as the Calvary Chapel, Vineyard, and Hope Chapel, have created a following among Pentecostal believers, who embrace a more charismatic form of worship devoid of many traditional ornaments, with pastors and congregations alike favoring informal attire. New faiths develop with increasing rapidity in what can only be called a very competitive market for individual religious faith. In addition, many people, with or without religious affiliation, become fascinated with spiritual concepts such as angels or become a part of loose-knit fellowships such as the Promise Keepers, an all-male movement of evangelical Christians founded in 1990. Religion in the United States is an ever-changing social phenomenon (Dudley and Roozen 2001; Miller and Schaefer 1998).

A significant part of this religious landscape has been non-Christian faiths. In Chapter 11, we consider the presence of followers of Islam and then, in Chapter 14, the history and contemporary experiences of Judaism in the United States. In looking at both these significant faiths, we will see that hostility to these religions has been a constant theme.

Ethnicity, Religion, and Social Class

Generally, several social factors influence a person's identity and life chances. Pioneer sociologist Max Weber described **life chances** as people's opportunities to provide themselves with material goods, positive living conditions, and favorable life experiences. Religion, ethnicity, or both may affect life chances.

Religion and ethnicity do not necessarily operate together. Sometimes, they have been studied as if they were synonymous. Groups have been described as Irish Catholic, Swedish Lutheran, Muslim Arabs, or Russian Jewish, as if religion and ethnicity had been merged into some type of national church. In the 1990s, the religion-ethnicity tie took on new meaning as Latin-American immigration invigorated the Roman Catholic Church nationwide, and West Indian immigration, particularly to New York City, brought new life to the Episcopal church.

In the 1960s, sociologists felt that religion was more important than ethnicity in explaining behavior. They based this conclusion not on data but on the apparently

life chances
People's opportunities to provide themselves with material goods, positive living conditions, and favorable life experiences.

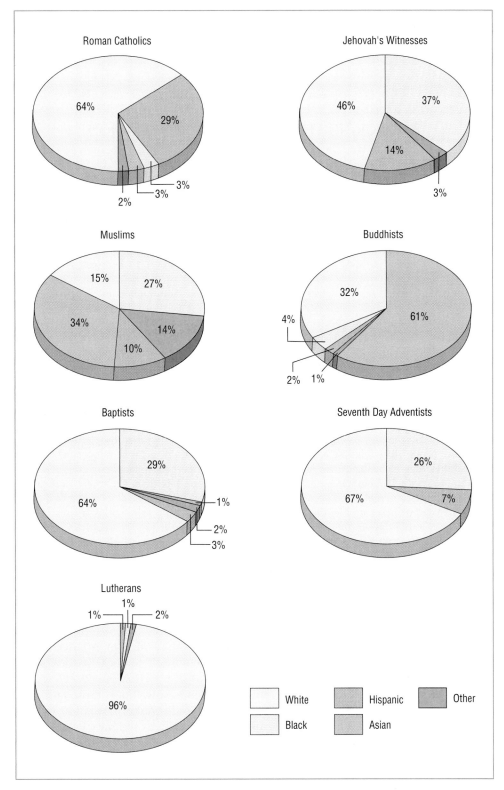

FIGURE 5.4   Racial and Ethnic Makeup of Selected Religions in the United States

Note: Totals do not always sum to 100 percent due to rounding.

Source: "Racial and Ethnic Make-Up of Selected Religions" in *American Religious Identification Survey, 2001* by Egon Mayer, et al., The Graduate Center of the City University of New York. Reprinted with permission.

Focus Research Focus Research Focus Res

MEASURING THE IMPORTANCE OF RELIGION

Social scientists and scholars of religious behavior have tried to measure the importance that religion has for people. Studies center on the holding of religious beliefs ("Do you believe in God?"), declarations of membership, contributions of money or time, and attendance at or participation in religious services.

We will focus on how people perceive the importance of religion to themselves and to others. This is a reasonable step because it does not make any assumptions about a specific religion, as if one were to ask people whether they read the Bible or attended church. In addition, we have reliable national data covering a long period of time with the same questions being asked using largely the same survey techniques.

In Figure 5.5 we see the responses for over the last 25 years to two questions: how important people feel religion is to them, and whether they feel religion is increasing its influence on the United States as a whole.

Two patterns emerge. First, somewhere between 53 and 61 percent of adults see religion as "very important" in their daily lives. Second, a much smaller proportion of peo-

ple, usually around 35 percent, see religion's influence increasing, but this has fluctuated more widely.

Of particular note across this time period is the dramatic increase in 2001. The events of September 11, 2001, had a pronounced impact on how people saw religion as influencing the nation. In February 2001, about 39 percent of the people felt religion was increasing its influence and 55 percent felt it was losing its hold on the nation—pretty typical responses for the 20-year period. Yet by December 7, 71 percent felt religion was increasing its influence and only 24 percent losing.

Will this dramatic shift in the perception of how the nation was influenced translate into people's own lives? Probably not. There was little lasting change in how people saw religion playing in their own lives: Fifty-seven percent saw it as "very important" in May 2001, 64 percent in late September after the attacks, and back down to 60 percent by December. Media accounts spoke of a possible reawakening as religious houses of worship were packed in the weeks after the September 11 terrorist attacks, but it appeared

higher visibility of religion in society. Using national survey data, Andrew Greeley came to different conclusions. He attempted to clarify the relative importance of religion and ethnicity by measuring personality characteristics, political participation, support for civil rights, and family structure.

The sample consisted of German and Irish Americans, both Protestant and Catholic. If religion was more significant than ethnicity, Protestants, whether of German or Irish ancestry, and Catholics, regardless of ethnicity, would have been similar in outlook. Conversely, if ethnicity was the key, then the similarities would be among the Germans of either faith or among the Irish as a distinct group.

On 17 of the 24 items that made up the four areas measured, the differences were greater between German Catholics and Irish Catholics than between German Catholics and Protestants or between Irish Catholics and Protestants. Ethnicity was a stronger predictor of attitudes and beliefs than religion. In one area—political party allegiance—religion was more important, but this was the exception rather than the rule.

Focus Research Focus Research Focus Research

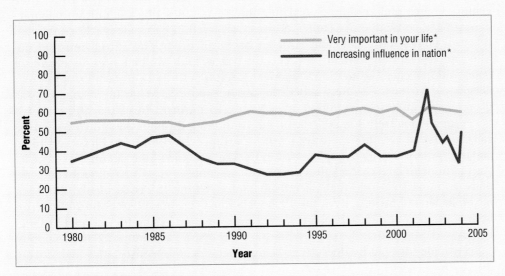

FIGURE 5.5   Religion's Importance and Influence

Note: Questions were "How important would you say religion is in your own life?" and "At the present time, do you think religion as a whole is increasing its influence on American life or losing its influence?"

Source: Gallup 2004. Copyright 2004. The Gallup Organization. Princeton, NJ. Reprinted with permission.

to be a short-term gathering out of a sense of grieving rather than a transformation.

These research data show the importance of not using a single measure to analyze something as complex as religion. They also show the importance of considering a broader historical perspective rather than attempting to reach a conclusion from a single snapshot. ◾

Sources: Gallup 2004; Goodstein 2001; Sherkat and Ellison 1999.

In sum, Greeley found ethnicity to be generally more important than religion in predicting behavior. In reality, it is very difficult to separate the influences of religion and ethnicity on any one individual, but Greeley's research cautions against discounting the influence of ethnicity in favor of religion (Glazer and Moynihan 1970; Greeley 1974a, 1974b; Herberg 1983).

In addition, as already noted several times, social class is yet another significant factor. Sociologist Milton Gordon (1978) developed the term **ethclass** (ethnicity and class) to denote the importance of both factors. All three factors—religion, ethnicity, and class—combine to form one's identity, determine one's social behavior, and limit one's life chances. For example, in certain ethnic communities, friendships are limited, to a degree, to people who share the same ethnic background and social class. In other words, neither race and ethnicity nor religion nor class alone places one socially. One must consider several elements together, as reflected in ethclass.

ethclass
The merged ethnicity and class in a person's status.

civil religion
The religious dimension in American life that merges the state with sacred beliefs.

Religion in the United States

Divisive conflicts along religious lines are muted in the United States compared with those in, say, Northern Ireland or the Middle East. Although not entirely absent, conflicts about religion in the United States seem to be overshadowed by civil religion. **Civil religion** is the religious dimension in American life that merges the state with sacred beliefs.

Sociologist Robert Bellah (1967) borrowed the phrase *civil religion* from 18th-century French philosopher Jean-Jacques Rousseau to describe a significant phenomenon in the contemporary United States. Civil religion exists alongside established religious faiths, and it embodies a belief system incorporating all religions but not associated specifically with any one. It is the type of faith to which presidents refer in inaugural speeches and to which American Legion posts and Girl Scout troops swear allegiance. In 1954, Congress added the phrase "under God" to the Pledge of Allegiance as a legislative recognition of religion's significance. Presidents of the United States, beginning with Ronald Reagan and continuing through George W. Bush, typically concluded even their most straightforward speeches with "God Bless the United States of America," which in effect evokes the civil religion of the nation.

Functionalists see civil religion as reinforcing central American values that may be more expressly patriotic than sacred in nature. Often, the mass media, following major societal upheavals, from the 1995 Oklahoma City bombing to the 2001 terrorist attacks, show church services with clergy praying and asking for national healing. Bellah sees no sign that the importance of civil religion has diminished in promoting collective identity, but he does acknowledge that it is more conservative than during the 1970s.

In the following section, we will explore the diversity among the major Christian groups in the United States, such as Roman Catholics and Protestants. However, as

Religion can provide a sense of cohesion for a people. Here overflow worshippers listen to mass on the steps of St. Matthew's Catholic Church in Washington, DC during services remembering the victims of September 11, 2001.

already noted, significant numbers of people in the United States now practice religions long established in other parts of the world, such as Islam, Hinduism, Judaism, and Buddhism. The greater visibility of religious diversity in the United States is primarily the result of immigrants bringing their religious faith with them and not assimilating to the dominant Christian rituals.

Diversity Among Roman Catholics

Social scientists have persistently tended to ignore the diversity within the Roman Catholic Church in the United States. Recent research has not sustained the conclusions that Roman Catholics are melding into a single group, following the traditions of the American Irish Catholic model, or even that parishioners are attending English-language churches. Religious behavior has been different for each ethnic group within the Roman Catholic Church. The Irish and the French Canadians left societies that were highly competitive both culturally and socially. Their religious involvement in the United States is more relaxed than it was in Ireland and Quebec. However, the influence of life in the United States has increased German and Polish involvement in the Roman Catholic Church, whereas Italians have remained largely inactive. Variations by ethnic background continue to emerge in studies of contemporary religious involvement in the Roman Catholic Church (Eckstrom 2001).

Since the mid-1970s, the Roman Catholic Church in America has received a significant number of new members from the Philippines, Southeast Asia, and particularly Latin America. Although these new members have been a stabilizing force offsetting the loss of White ethnics, they have also challenged a church that for generations was dominated by Irish, Italian, and Polish parishes. Perhaps the most prominent subgroup in the Roman Catholic Church is the Latinos, who now account for one-third of all Roman Catholic parishioners. In the new class of priests ordained in 2001, nearly one-third were foreign born. Some Los Angeles churches in or near Latino neighborhoods must schedule 14 masses each Sunday to accommodate the crowds of worshipers. According to one estimate, Latinos will constitute the majority of Roman Catholics nationwide by 2050 (Bonfante 1995; Eckstrom 2001).

The Roman Catholic Church, despite its ethnic diversity, has clearly been a powerful force in reducing the ethnic ties of its members, making it also a significant assimilating force. The irony in this role of Catholicism is that so many 19th-century Americans heaped abuse on Catholics in this country for allegedly being un-American and

The Roman Catholic church has experienced growth through immigration from Latin America but has had difficulty recruiting men into the priesthoood. Here we see ordination ceremony at the Holy Name Cathedral in Chicago, Illinois in 2003.

having a dual allegiance. The history of the Catholic Church in the United States may be portrayed as a struggle within the membership between the Americanizers and the anti-Americanizers, with the former ultimately winning. Unlike the various Protestant churches that accommodated immigrants of a single nationality, the Roman Catholic Church had to Americanize a variety of linguistic and ethnic groups. The Catholic Church may have been the most potent assimilating force after the public school system. Comparing the assimilationist goal of the Catholic Church and the present diversity in it leads us to the conclusion that ethnic diversity has continued in the Roman Catholic Church despite, not because of, this religious institution (Fishman et al. 1966; Greeley 1977).

Diversity Among Protestants

Protestantism, like Catholicism, often is portrayed as a monolithic entity. Little attention is given to the doctrinal and attitudinal differences that sharply divide the various denominations, in both laity and clergy. However, several studies document the diversity. Unfortunately, many opinion polls and surveys are content to learn whether a respondent is a Catholic, a Protestant, or a Jew. Stark and Glock (1968) found sharp differences in religious attitudes within Protestant churches. For example, 99 percent of Southern Baptists had no doubt that Jesus was the divine Son of God, as contrasted to only 40 percent of Congregationalists. We can identify four "generic theological camps":

1. Liberals: United Church of Christ (Congregationalists) and Episcopalians
2. Moderates: Disciples of Christ, Methodists, and Presbyterians
3. Conservatives: American Lutherans and American Baptists
4. Fundamentalists: Missouri Synod Lutherans, Southern Baptists, and Assembly of God

Roman Catholics generally hold religious beliefs similar to those of conservative Protestants, except on essentially Catholic issues such as papal infallibility (the authority of the spiritual role in all decisions regarding faith and morals). Whether or not there are four distinct camps is not important: The point is that the familiar practice of contrasting Roman Catholics and Protestants is clearly not productive. Some differences between Roman Catholics and Protestants are inconsequential compared with the differences between Protestant sects.

Religious faiths may be distinguished by secular criteria as well as doctrinal issues. Research has consistently shown that denominations can be arranged in a hierarchy based on social class. As Figure 5.6 reveals, members of certain faiths, such as Episcopalians, Jews, and Presbyterians, have a higher proportion of affluent members. Members of other faiths, including Baptists, tend to be poorer. Of course, all Protestant groups draw members from each social stratum. Nonetheless, the social significance of these class differences is that religion becomes a mechanism for signaling social mobility. A person who is moving up in wealth and power may seek out a faith associated with a higher social ranking. Similar contrasts are shown in formal schooling in Figure 5.7.

Protestant faiths have been diversifying, and many of their members have been leaving them for churches that follow strict codes of behavior or fundamental interpretations of Biblical teachings. This trend is reflected in the decline of the five mainline churches: Baptist, Episcopalian, Lutheran, Methodist, and Presbyterian. In 2001, these faiths accounted for about 33 percent of total membership, compared with 51 percent 30 years earlier. With a broader acceptance of new faiths and continuing immigration, it is unlikely that these mainline churches will regain their dominance (*Gallup Poll Monthly* 1995; Kosmin et al. 2001).

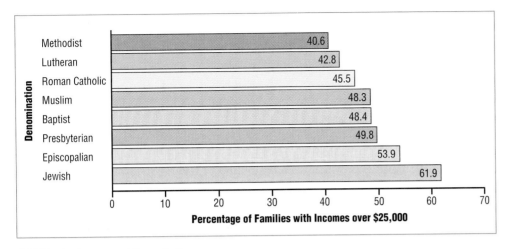

FIGURE 5.6 Income and Denominations

Denominations attract different income groups. All groups have both affluent and poor members, yet some have a higher proportion of members with high incomes, and others are comparatively poor.

Source: General social survey, 1993 through 2002. See J. Davis et al. 2003.

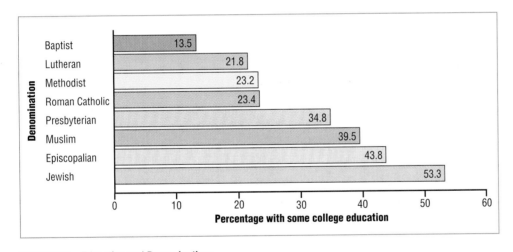

FIGURE 5.7 Education and Denominations

There are sharp differences in the proportion of those with some college education by denomination.

Source: General social survey, 1993 through 2002. See J. Davis et al. 2003.

Although Protestants may seem to define the civil religion and the accepted dominant orientation, some Christian faiths feel they, too, experience the discrimination usually associated with non-Christians such as Jews and Muslims. For example, the leadership of the military's chaplain corps is dominated by representatives of the liberal and moderate faiths, even though 41 percent of the military are conservatives and fundamentalists.

As another example of denominational discrimination, in 1998 the Southern Baptist Convention amended its basic theological statements of beliefs to include a strong statement on family life. However, the statement included a declaration that a woman should "submit herself graciously" to her husband's leadership. There were widespread attacks on this position, which many Baptists felt was inappropriate because they were offering guidance for their denomination's members. In some respects, Baptists felt this was a form of respectable bigotry. It was acceptable to attack them for their views on social issues even though such criticism would be much more muted for many more liberal faiths that seem free to tolerate abortion (Bowman 1998; Niebuhr 1998).

Women and Religion

Religious beliefs have often placed women in an exalted but protected position. As religions are practiced, this position has often meant being "protected" from becoming leaders. Perhaps the only major exception in the United States is the Christian Science church, in which the majority of practitioners and readers are women. Women may be evangelists, prophets, and even saints, but they find it difficult to enter the clergy within their own congregations.

Even today, the largest denomination in the United States, Roman Catholicism, does not permit women to be priests. A 1996 Gallup survey found that 65 percent of Roman Catholics in this country favor the ordination of women, compared with only 29 percent in 1974; but the church hierarchy has continued to maintain its long-standing requirement that priests be male (D. Briggs 1996).

The largest Protestant denomination, the Southern Baptist Convention, has voted against ordaining women (although some of its autonomous churches have women ministers). Other religious faiths that do not allow women clergy include the Lutheran Church–Missouri Synod, the Greek Orthodox Archdiocese of North and South America, the Orthodox Church in America, the Church of God in Christ, the Church of Jesus Christ of Latter-Day Saints, and Orthodox Judaism.

Women play a significant role as unpaid volunteers, but relatively few become members of the clergy with leadership responsibilities. Pictured is Barbara Harris as she was ordained the first female bishop in the Episcopalian Church in 1989.

Despite these restrictions, there has been a notable rise in female clergy in the last 20 years. The Bureau of the Census (2001j) shows that 6 percent of clergy were women in 1983, but that figure had increased to 14 percent in 2000. Increasingly, some branches of Protestantism and Judaism have been convinced that women have the right to become spiritual leaders. Yet a lingering question remains: Once ordained, are these female ministers and rabbis necessarily accepted by congregations? Will they advance in their calling as easily as their male counterparts, or will they face blatant or subtle discrimination in their efforts to secure desirable posts within their faiths?

It is too early to offer any definitive answers to these questions, but thus far, women clearly continue to face lingering sexism after ordination. Evidence to date indicates that women find it more difficult than men to secure jobs in larger, more prestigious congregations. Although they may be accepted as junior clergy or as copastors, women may fail to receive senior clergy appointments. In both Reform and Conservative Judaism, women rabbis are rarely hired by the largest and best-known congregations. Consequently, women clergy in many denominations are gathered at the low end of the pay scale and the hierarchy (Chang 1997; Religion Watch 1995b).

Religion and the U.S. Supreme Court

Religious pluralism owes its existence in the United States to the First Amendment declaration that "Congress shall make no law respecting an establishment of religion, or prohibiting the free exercise thereof." The U.S. Supreme Court has consistently interpreted this wording to mean not that government should ignore religion but that it should follow a policy of neutrality to maximize religious freedom. For example, the government may not help religion by financing a new church building, but it also may not obstruct religion by denying a church adequate police and fire protection. We will examine four issues that continue to require clarification: school prayer, secessionist minorities, creationism, and the public display of religious symbols.

Among the most controversial and continuing disputes has been whether prayer has a role in the schools. Many people were disturbed by the 1962 Supreme Court decision in *Engel v. Vitale* that disallowed a purportedly nondenominational prayer drafted for use in the New York public schools. The prayer was "Almighty God, we acknowledge our dependence upon Thee, and we beg Thy blessings upon us, our parents, our teachers, and our country." Subsequent decisions overturned state laws requiring Bible reading in public schools, laws requiring recitation of the Lord's Prayer, and laws permitting a daily one-minute period of silent meditation or prayer. Despite such judicial pronouncements, children in many public schools in the United States are led in regular prayer recitation or Bible reading.

What about prayers at public gatherings? In 1992, the Supreme Court ruled 5–4 in *Lee v. Weisman* that prayer at a junior high school graduation in Providence, Rhode Island, violated the U.S. Constitution's mandate of separation of church and state. A rabbi had given thanks to God in his invocation. The district court suggested that the invocation would have been acceptable without that reference. The Supreme Court did not agree with the school board that a prayer at a graduation was not coercive. The Court did say in its opinion that it was acceptable for a student speaker voluntarily to say a prayer at such a program (Marshall 2001).

Several religious groups have been in legal and social conflict with the rest of society. Some can be called **secessionist minorities**, in that they reject both assimilation and coexistence in some form of cultural pluralism. The Amish are one such group that comes into conflict with outside society because of their beliefs and way of life. The Old Order Amish shun most modern conveniences, and later in this chapter we will consider them as a case study of maintaining a lifestyle dramatically different from that of larger society.

secessionist minority
Groups, such as the Amish, that reject both assimilation and coexistence.

Are there limits to the free exercise of religious rituals by secessionist minorities? Today, tens of thousands of members of Native American religions believe that ingesting the powerful drug peyote is a sacrament and that those who partake of peyote will enter into direct contact with God. In 1990, the Supreme Court ruled that prosecuting people who use illegal drugs as part of a religious ritual is not a violation of the First Amendment guarantee of religious freedom. The case arose because Native Americans were dismissed from their jobs for the religious use of peyote and were then refused unemployment benefits by the State of Oregon's employment division. In 1991, however, Oregon enacted a new law permitting the sacramental use of peyote by Native Americans (*New York Times* 1991).

In another ruling on religious rituals, in 1993, the Supreme Court unanimously overturned a local ordinance in Florida that banned ritual animal sacrifice. The high court held that this law violated the free-exercise rights of adherents of the Santeria religion, in which the sacrifice of animals (including goats, chickens, and other birds) plays a central role. The same year Congress passed the Religious Freedom Restoration Act, which said the government may not enforce laws that "substantially burden" the exercise of religion. Presumably this action will give religious groups more flexibility in practicing their faith. However, many local and state officials are concerned that the law has led to unintended consequences, such as forcing states to accommodate prisoners' requests for questionable religious activities or to permit a church to expand into a historic district in defiance of local laws (Greenhouse 1996).

The third area of contention has been whether the biblical account of creation should be or must be presented in school curricula and whether this account should receive the same emphasis as scientific theories. In the famous "monkey trial" of 1925, Tennessee schoolteacher John Scopes was found guilty of teaching the scientific theory of evolution in public schools. Since then, however, Darwin's evolutionary theories have been presented in public schools with little reference to the biblical account in Genesis. People who support the literal interpretation of the Bible, commonly known as **creationists**, have formed various organizations to crusade for creationist treatment in American public schools and universities.

In a 1987 Louisiana case, *Edwards v. Aguillard,* the Supreme Court ruled that states may not require the teaching of creationism alongside evolution in public schools if the primary purpose of such legislation is to promote a religious viewpoint. Nevertheless, the teaching of evolution and creationism has remained a controversial issue in many communities across the United States (Applebome 1996).

The fourth area of contention has been a battle over public displays that depict symbols of or seem associated with a religion. Can manger scenes be erected on public property? Do people have a right to be protected from large displays such as a cross or a star atop a water tower overlooking an entire town? In a series of decisions in the 1980s through to 1995, the Supreme Court ruled that tax-supported religious displays on public government property may be successfully challenged but are not permissible if they are made more secular. Displays that combine a crèche, the Christmas manger scene depicting the birth of Jesus, or the Hanukkah menorah and also include Frosty the Snowman or even Christmas trees have been ruled secular. These decisions have been dubbed "the plastic reindeer rules." In 1995, the Court clarified the issue by stating that privately sponsored religious displays may be allowed on public property if other forms of expression are permitted in the same location. The final judicial word has not been heard, and all these rulings should be viewed as tentative because the Court cases have been decided by close votes, and changes in the Supreme Court composition may alter the outcome of future cases (Bork 1995; Hirsley 1991; Mauro 1995).

creationists
People who support a literal interpretation of the biblical book of Genesis on the origins of the universe and argue that evolution should not be presented as established scientific thought.

Limits of Religious Freedom: The Amish

The Amish began migrating to North America early in the 18th century and settled first in eastern Pennsylvania, where a large settlement is still found. Those who continued the characteristic lifestyle of the Amish are primarily members of the Old Order Amish Mennonite Church. By 2003, there were about 1,400 Old Order Amish settlements in the United States and Canada. Estimates place this faith at about 180,000, with approximately 75 percent living in three states: Ohio, Pennsylvania, and Indiana.

The Amish Way of Life

Amish practice self-segregation, living in settlements divided into church districts that are autonomous congregations composed of about 75 baptized members. If the district becomes much larger, it is again divided because the members meet in each other's homes. There are no church buildings. Amish homes are large, with the main floor often having removable walls so a household can take its periodic turn hosting the Sunday service.

Each Amish district has a bishop, two to four preachers, and an elder; but there are no general conferences, mission groups, or cooperative agencies. The Amish differ little from the Mennonites in formal religious doctrine. Holy Communion is celebrated twice each year, and both groups practice washing of feet. Adults are baptized when they are admitted to formal membership in the church at about age 17 to 20. Old Order Amish services are conducted in German with a mixture of English, commonly known as Pennsylvania Dutch (from *Deutsch,* the German word for "German").

The Amish are best known for their plain clothing and their nonconformist way of life. Sociologists sometimes use the term *secessionist minorities* to refer to groups such as the Amish, who reject assimilation and practice coexistence or pluralism with the rest of society primarily on their own terms. The practice of *Meidung,* or shunning, persists; and sociologists view it as central to the Amish system of social control. The social norms of this secessionist minority that have evolved over the years are known as the *Ordnung.* These "understandings" specify the color and style of clothing, color and style of buggies, the use of horses for fieldwork, the use of the Pennsylvania Dutch dialect, worship services in the homes, unison singing without instruments, and marriage within the church, to name a few.

The Amish shun telephones and electric lights, and they drive horses and buggies rather than automobiles. The *Ordnung* also prohibits filing a lawsuit, entering military service, divorce, using air transportation, and even using wall-to-wall carpeting. They are generally considered excellent farmers, but they often refuse to use modern farm machinery. Concessions have been made but do vary from one Amish settlement to another. Among common exceptions to the *Ordnung* is the use of chemical fertilizers, insecticides, and pesticides, the use of indoor bathroom facilities, and modern medical and dental practice.

The Amish and Larger Society

The Amish have made some concessions to the dominant society, but larger society has made concessions to the Amish to facilitate their lifestyle. For example, the 1972 U.S. Supreme Court, in *Yoder v. Wisconsin,* allowed Wisconsin Amish to escape prosecution from laws that required parents to send their children to school to age 18. Amish education ends at about age 13 because the community feels their members have received all the schooling necessary to prosper as Amish people. States waive for the Amish certification requirements for their teaching staff (who are other Amish people), minimum wage requirements for the teachers, and school building requirements.

The Amish today do not totally reject social change. For example, until the late 1960s, church members could be excommunicated for being employed in other than agricultural pursuits. Now their work is much more diversified. Although you will not find Amish computer programmers, there are Amish engaged as blacksmiths, harness makers, buggy repairers, and carpenters. Non-Amish often hire these craftspeople as well.

The Amish as shown in this group of young women on a farm in Kentucky have made relatively few accommodations with the larger culture— the culture of outsiders referred collectively to by the Amish as the "English."

The movement by the Amish into other occupations is sometimes a source of tension with larger society, or the "English," as the Amish refer to non-Amish people. Conflict theorists observe that as long as the Amish remained totally apart from dominant society in the United States, they experienced little hostility. As they entered the larger economic sector, however, intergroup tensions developed in the form of growing prejudice. The Amish today may underbid their competitors. The Amish entry into the commercial marketplace has also strained the church's traditional teaching on litigation and insurance, both of which are to be avoided. Mutual assistance has been the historical path taken, but that does not always mesh well with the modern businessperson. After legal action taken on their behalf, Amish businesses typically have been allowed to be exempt from paying Social Security and workers' compensation, another sore point with English competitors.

The Amish entrepreneur represents an interesting variation of the typical ethnic businessperson one might encounter in a Chinatown, for example. Research on ethnic businesses often cites discrimination against minorities and immigrants as a prime force prodding the development of minority enterprises. The Amish are a very different case because their own restrictions on education, factory work, and certain occupations have propelled them into becoming small business owners. However, stratification is largely absent among the Old Order Amish. The notion of ethclass would have no meaning, as the Amish truly regard one another as equal.

Children are not sent to high schools. This practice caused the Amish some difficulty because of compulsory school attendance laws, and some Amish parents have gone to jail rather than allow their children to go to high school. Eventually, as noted earlier, the Supreme Court, in *Yoder v. Wisconsin,* upheld a lower court's decision that a Wisconsin compulsory education law violated the Amish right to religious freedom. However, not all court rulings have been friendly to Amish efforts to avoid the practices and customs of the English. In another case, the effort by the Amish to avoid using the legally mandated orange triangles for marking slow-moving vehicles (such as their buggies) was rejected. If you travel through Amish areas, you can now see their horse-drawn buggies displaying this one symbol of modernity.

Living alongside this modernity, Amish youth often test their subculture's boundaries during a period of discovery called *rumspringe,* a term that means "running around." Amish young people attend barn dances where taboos like drinking, smoking, and driving cars are commonly broken. Parents often react by looking the other way, sometimes literally. For example, when they hear radio sounds from a barn or motorcycle entering their property in the middle of the night, they don't immediately investigate and punish their offspring. Instead, they pretend not to notice, secure in the comfort that their children almost always return to the traditions of the Amish lifestyle. In 2004, UPN aired the "Amish in the City" reality program featuring five Amish youths allegedly on *rumspringe* moving in with six citywise young adults in Los Angeles. Critics on behalf of the Amish community noted that this exploitation showed how vulnerable the Amish are, since no program was developed to try to show the conversion of Muslim or Orthodox Jewish youth.

A growing area of Amish-English legal clashes is over the custom of young Amish children working as laborers. Amish families in western and central Pennsylvania in 1998 protested the federal government's enforcement of labor laws that are intended to protect children from workplace hazards. The Amish are turning to new businesses, such as sawmills and wood shops, as their available farmland begins to disappear. That means more children on the shop floor. The Amish contend that their religious and cultural traditions hold that children should work, but the U.S. Labor Department had taken a different view. The Amish argued that letting children work alongside their fathers instills core values of hard work, diligence, cooperation, and responsibility, values that they say are central to their faith. English businesses see this underage employment as another form of unfair competition by the Amish. In 2004, Congress passed the law with the Amish in mind that exempted such child labor as long as machinery is not operated and adults are present.

The Old Order Amish have developed a pluralistic position that has become increasingly difficult to maintain as their numbers grow and as they enter the economy in competition with the English, or the non-Amish (Dart 1998; *The Economist* 2004a; Kraybill 2001, 2003; Kraybill and Nolt 1995; Public Broadcasting System 1998).

Conclusion

Considering ethnicity and religion reinforces our understanding of the patterns of intergroup relations first presented in Chapter 1. Figure 5.8 shows the rich variety of relationships as defined by people's ethnic and religious identity.

Any study of life in the United States, but especially one focusing on dominant and subordinate groups, cannot ignore religion and ethnicity. The two are closely related, as certain religious faiths predominate in certain nationalities. Both religious activity and interest by White ethnics in their heritage continue to be prominent features of the contemporary scene. People have been and continue to be ridiculed or deprived of opportunities solely because of their ethnic or religious affiliation. To get a true picture of people's place in society, we need to consider both ethnicity and social class (or what has been called ethclass) in association with their religious identification.

Religion is changing in the United States. As one commercial measure, Hallmark created its first greeting card in 2003 for the Muslim holiday Eid-al-fitr, which marks the end of the month-long feast of Ramadan. The issue of the persistence of ethnicity is an intriguing one. Some people may only casually exhibit their ethnicity and practice what has been called symbolic ethnicity. However, can people immerse themselves in their ethnic culture without society punishing them for their will to be different? The tendency to put down White ethnics through respectable bigotry continues. Despite this intolerance, ethnicity remains a viable source of identity for many citizens today. There is also the ethnicity paradox, which finds that practicing one's ethnic heritage often strengthens people and allows them to move successfully into the larger society.

The issue of religious expression in all its forms also raises a variety of intriguing ques-

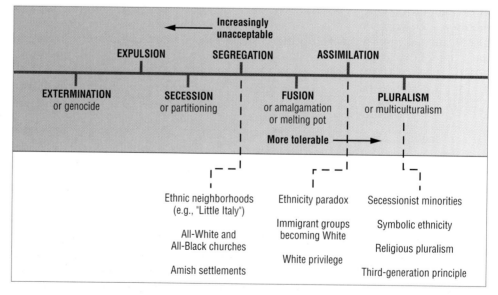

FIGURE 5.8 Intergroup Relations

tions. How can a country increasingly populated by diverse and often non-Christian faiths maintain religious tolerance? How might this change in decades ahead? How will the courts and society resolve the issues of religious freedom? This is a particularly important issue in such areas as school prayer, secessionist minorities, creationism, and public religious displays. Some examination of religious ties is fundamental to completing an accurate picture of a person's social identity.

Ethnicity and religion are a basic part of today's social reality and of each individual's identity. The emotions, disputes, and debate over religion and ethnicity in the United States are powerful indeed.

Key Terms

civil religion 136
creationists 143
denomination 130
ethclass 135

ethnicity paradox 124
life chances 132
principle of third-generation
   interest 123

respectable bigotry 125
secessionist minority 141
symbolic ethnicity 124

Review Questions

1. In what respect are the ethnic and the religious diversity of the United States related to each other?
2. Is assimilation automatic within any given ethnic group?
3. Can "blaming the victims" be applied to prejudice among White ethnic groups?
4. To what extent has a non-Christian tradition been developing in the United States?
5. How have court rulings affected religious expression?

Critical Thinking

1. When do you see ethnicity becoming more apparent? When does it appear to occur only in response to other people's advancing their own ethnicity? From these situations, how can ethnic identity be both positive and perhaps counterproductive or even destructive?
2. Why do you think we are so often reluctant to show our religion to others? Why might people of certain faiths be more hesitant than others?
3. How does religion reflect conservative and liberal positions on social issues? Consider services for the homeless, the need for child care, the acceptance or rejection of gay men and lesbians, and a woman's right to terminate a pregnancy versus the fetus's right to survive.

Internet Connections—Research Navigator™

Follow the instructions found on page 31 of this text to access the features of Research Navigator™. Once at the Web site, enter your Login Name and Password. Then, to use the ContentSelect database, enter keywords such as "Mormons," "Amish," and "whiteness studies," and the research engine will supply relevant and recent scholarly and popular press publications. Use the *New York Times* Search-by-Subject Archive to find recent news articles related to sociology, and the Link Library feature to locate relevant Web links organized by the key terms associated with this chapter.

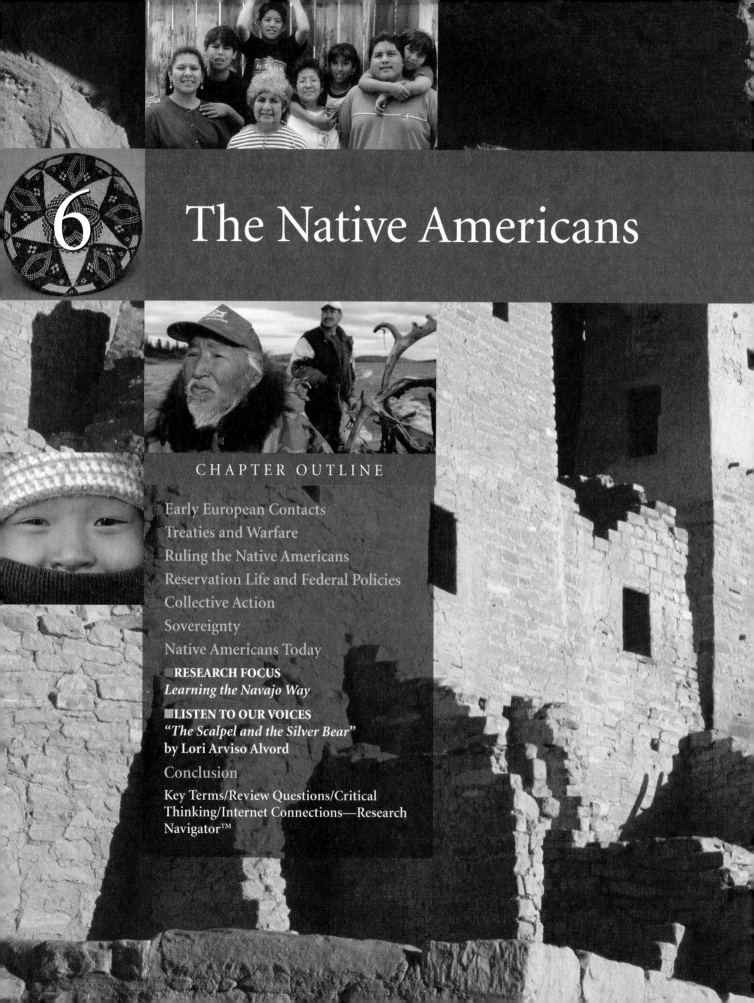

6 The Native Americans

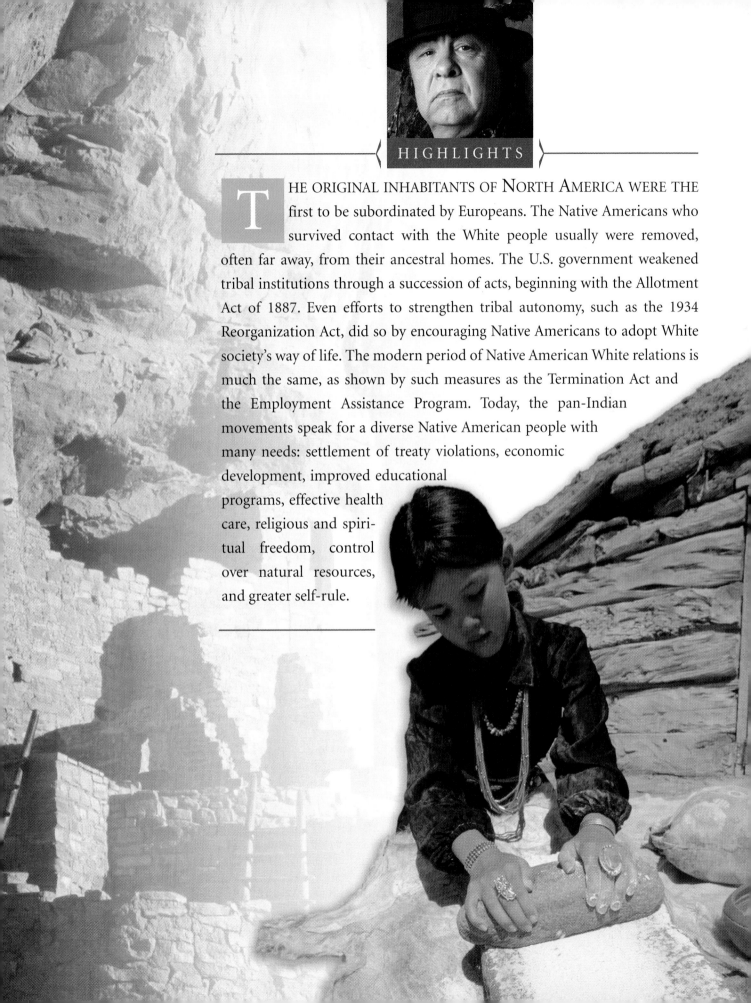

THE ORIGINAL INHABITANTS OF NORTH AMERICA WERE THE first to be subordinated by Europeans. The Native Americans who survived contact with the White people usually were removed, often far away, from their ancestral homes. The U.S. government weakened tribal institutions through a succession of acts, beginning with the Allotment Act of 1887. Even efforts to strengthen tribal autonomy, such as the 1934 Reorganization Act, did so by encouraging Native Americans to adopt White society's way of life. The modern period of Native American White relations is much the same, as shown by such measures as the Termination Act and the Employment Assistance Program. Today, the pan-Indian movements speak for a diverse Native American people with many needs: settlement of treaty violations, economic development, improved educational programs, effective health care, religious and spiritual freedom, control over natural resources, and greater self-rule.

The computer says "Zik" followed by "Cax sep." This is not the latest space adventure from the local arcade, but the words for "squirrel" and "eagle" as spoken by a Ho-chunk elder. Preschoolers gather around the computer at a Head Start program in Wisconsin, where Ho-chunk children learn the language of their tribe. The Ho-chunk, formerly known as the Winnebago tribe, are using modern technology to keep their language, and therefore their culture, alive. The challenge is immense, as Two Bears, an anthropologist who works at the tribe's cultural center, observes:

> There was a whole generation by the 1980s that didn't know a word. Turning that around will be a long process—we figure it'll take two years to advance our language curriculum up one grade level in the schools that Ho-chunk kids attend. (Salopek 1996:2)

It is critical to use schools to restore the Ho-Cak language of the Ho-Chunk people. Only 350 of the 6,200 tribal members speak their language fluently, and none of them have young children of their own (Kozlowicz 2001).

The concern of the Ho-chunk tribal elders is faced by most of the tribes in the United States. It is estimated that children are actively learning only 20 of the surviving 154 Native American languages. While much of the country debates the need for a larger percentage of new immigrants to master English, the first Americans' major concern is maintaining the tie to their linguistic past and making it a viable part of the present. In Chicago, adult students gather to learn the languages of their tribes, Kalota and Ojibwee, and in Window Rock, Arizona, the 1996 Super Bowl was broadcast in Navajo for the first time. All these efforts and many more are aimed at maintaining tribal identity within American society (Brooke 1998; Mitchel 1996; Reyhner 2001a).

Although our focus in this chapter is on the Native American experience in the United States, the pattern of land seizure, subjugation, assimilation, and resistance to domination has been repeated with indigenous people in nations throughout the world. Indeed, in Chapter 16, we will consider the experiences of the tribal people in Mexico and Canada. Another native people, Hawaiians, that fell under political, economic, and cultural control of the United States is considered in Chapter 12. Indigenous peoples on almost every continent are familiar with the patterns of subjugation and the pressure to assimilate. So widespread is this oppression that the United Nations (1997), and even its precursor organization, the League of Nations, have repeatedly considered this issue.

The common term *American Indians* tells us more about the Europeans who explored North America than it does about the native people. The label reflects the initial explorers' confusion in believing that they had arrived in "the Indies" of the Asian continent. However, reference to the diversity of tribal groups either by *American Indians* or *Native Americans* comes as a result of the forced subordination to the dominant group.

CD-ROM Activity 5.1

Census 2000 showed that there were 2,475,956 Native Americans in the United States. This represents an increase of 32 percent over the 1990s. In addition to the 2.5 million people who in 2000 listed American Indian or Alaskan Native as their sole racial identification, there were another 1.6 million people who listed multiple responses that included American Indian. As was shown in Figure 1.7, American Indian and White was the most common dual racial response given in Census 2000 (Grieco and Cassidy 2001; Ogunwole 2002).

Education on reservations stresses American Indian and tribal culture more than in the past. Pictured is a classroom on the Crow Reservation in Montana.

Early European Contacts

The Native Americans have been misunderstood and ill treated by their conquerors for several centuries. Assuming that he had reached the Indies, Christopher Columbus called them "people of India." The European immigrants who followed Columbus did not understand them any more than the Native Americans could have anticipated the destruction of their way of life. But the Europeans had superior weaponry, and the diseases they brought wiped out huge numbers of indigenous people throughout the Western Hemisphere.

The first explorers of the Western Hemisphere came long before Columbus and Leif Eriksson. The ancestors of today's Native Americans were hunters in search of wild game, including mammoths and long-horned bison. For thousands of years, these people spread through the Western Hemisphere, adapting to its many physical environments. Hundreds of cultures evolved, including the complex societies of the Maya, Inca, and Aztec (Deloria 1995, 2004).

It is beyond the scope of this chapter to describe the many tribal cultures of North America, let alone the ways of life of Native Americans in Central and South America and the islands of the Caribbean. We must appreciate that the term *Indian culture* is a convenient way to gloss over the diversity of cultures, languages, religions, kinship systems, and political organizations that existed—and in many instances, remain—among the peoples referred to collectively as Native Americans or American Indians. For example, in 1500, an estimated 700 distinct languages were spoken in the area north of Mexico. For simplicity's sake, we will refer to these many cultures as Native American, but we must be always mindful of the differences this term conceals. Similarly, we will refer to non-Native Americans as White people, although in this context this term encompasses many groups, including African Americans and Hispanics in some instances (J. Schwartz 1994; Swagerty 1983).

Columbus commented in his diary, "It appears to me that the people [of the New World] are ingenious and would be good servants. . . . These people are very unskilled in arms. . . . With fifty men they could all be subjected to do all that one wishes" (*Akwesasne Notes* 1972:22). The words of the first European explorer were prophetic. The period between initial European contact and the formation of the United States was characterized by cultural and physical conflict between Native Americans and Whites.

The number of Native Americans north of the Rio Grande, estimated at about 10 million in 1500, gradually decreased as their food sources disappeared and they

FIGURE 6.1   Eurocentric and Native American Views of Expansionism

Students typically are presented with a view that the United States gained its lands through settlement and from Mexico, Spain, France, and Great Britain. This depiction glosses over the land held by tribal groups.

Source: Maps from *Atlas of American History,* © 1993 by Rand McNally, R.L. #04-S-104. Reprinted by permission of Rand McNally.

fell victim to diseases such as measles, smallpox, and influenza. By 1800 the Native American population was about 600,000, and by 1900 it had been reduced to less than 250,000. This loss of human life can only be judged as catastrophic. The United States does not bear total responsibility. The pattern had been well established by the early Spaniards in the Southwest and by the French and English colonists who sought to gain control of the eastern seaboard. As Figure 6.1 (see page 152) reminds us, there were many tribal nations here for many centuries before European contact (Edmonds 1995).

Native Americans did have warfare between tribes, which presumably reduces the guilt for European-initiated warfare. However, their conflicts differed significantly from those of the conquerors. The Europeans launched large campaigns against the tribes, resulting in mass mortality. In contrast, in the Americas, the tribes limited warfare to specific campaigns designed for very specific purposes, such as recapturing some resource or avenging some loss.

Not all the initial contacts led to deliberate loss of life. Some missionaries traveled well in advance of settlement in efforts to Christianize the Native Americans before they came into contact with other less-tolerant Europeans. Fur trappers, vastly outnumbered by Native Americans, were forced to learn their customs, but these trappers established routes of commerce that more and more Whites were to follow (Snipp 1989; Swagerty 1983; Thornton 1991).

Gradually, the policies directed from Europe toward the indigenous peoples of North America resembled the approach described in the world systems theory. As introduced in Chapter 1, the **world systems theory** takes the view that the global economic system is divided between nations that control wealth and those that provide natural resources and labor. The indigenous peoples and, more important to the Europeans, the land they occupied were regarded as targets of exploitation by Spain, England, France, Portugal, and other nations with experience as colonizers in Africa and Asia (Chase-Dunn and Hall 1998).

Treaties and Warfare

The United States formulated a policy during the 19th century toward Native Americans that followed the precedents established during the colonial period. The government policy was not to antagonize the Native Americans unnecessarily. Yet if the needs of tribes interfered with the needs, or even the whims, of Whites, Whites were to have precedence. For example, the exploits of the Forty-Niners, the 19th-century gold miners in northern California, have been long glorified. However, 150,000 native people inhabited the areas they entered near Sacramento. Authorities offered bounties to the settlers for the heads of American Indians, and the state spent about $1 million to reimburse people for the bullets used to shoot them. Within 25 years, the native population had plummeted to about 30,000 (Ybarra 1996).

By this time, the tribes were viewed as separate nations, to be dealt with by treaties arrived at through negotiations with the federal government. Fair minded as that policy might seem, it was clear from the very beginning that the White people's government would deal harshly with the tribal groups that refused to agree to treaties. Federal relations with the Native Americans were the responsibility of the secretary of war. Consequently, when the Bureau of Indian Affairs was created in 1824 to coordinate the government's relations with the tribes, it was placed in the War Department. The government's primary emphasis was on maintaining peace and friendly relations along the frontier. Nevertheless, as settlers moved the frontier westward, they encroached more and more on land that Native Americans had inhabited for centuries.

world systems theory
A view of the global economic system as divided between nations that control wealth and those that provide natural resources and labor.

The Indian Removal Act, passed in 1830, called for the relocation of all Eastern tribes across the Mississippi River. The Removal Act was very popular with Whites because it opened more land to settlement through annexation of tribal land. Almost all Whites felt that the Native Americans had no right to block progress, defining progress as movement by White society. Among the largest groups relocated were the five tribes of the Creek, Choctaw, Chickasaw, Cherokee, and Seminole, who were resettled in what is now Oklahoma. The movement, lasting more than a decade, has been called the Trail of Tears because the tribes left their ancestral lands under the harshest conditions. Poor planning, corrupt officials, little attention to those ill from a variety of epidemics, and inadequate supplies characterized the forced migration (Remini 2001).

The Removal Act disrupted Native American culture but didn't move the tribes far enough or fast enough to stay out of the path of the ever-advancing White settlers. After the Civil War, settlers moved westward at an unprecedented pace. The federal government negotiated with the many tribes but primarily enacted legislation that affected them with minimal consultation. The government's first priority was almost always to allow the settlers to live and work regardless of Native American claims.

The Case of the Sioux

The 19th century was devastating for every Native American tribe in the areas claimed by the United States. No tribe was the same after federal policy touched it. The treatment of the Great Sioux Nation was especially cruel and remains fresh in the minds of tribal members even today.

In an effort to safeguard White settlers, the United States signed the Fort Laramie Treaty of 1868 with the Sioux, then under the leadership of Red Cloud. The government agreed to keep Whites from hunting or settling on the newly established Great Sioux Reservation, which included all of the land that is now South Dakota west of the Missouri River. In exchange, the Sioux relinquished most of the remaining land they occupied at that time. The first few years saw relative peace, except for some raids by warrior bands under the leadership of medicine man Sitting Bull. Red Cloud even made a much-publicized trip to Washington and New York in 1870.

A flood of White people eventually entered the Sioux territory, spurred on by Colonel George Custer's exaggerated 1874 reports of gold in the Black Hills. Hostilities followed, and bands of Native Americans were ordered to move during the winter, when travel was impossible. When the Sioux failed to move, Custer moved in to pacify them and the neighboring Cheyenne. Relying on Crow scouts, Custer underestimated the strength of the Sioux warriors under the leadership of Crazy Horse. The ensuing Battle of the Little Big Horn in 1876 was the last great Sioux victory. After the battle, the large encampment of warriors scattered throughout the plains into small bands,

By Jeff Kerr © 1999 *Indian Country Today*

In this famous Alexander Gardner photograph at the time of the 1868 Fort Laramie Treaty talks the military leaders are identified by name, shown sitting on chairs, and facing the camera. Reflecting the hierarchy of the situation, tribal leaders are not identified, seated on the ground and with their backs to the camera.

which were defeated one by one by a Congress and an Army more determined than ever to subdue the Sioux.

In 1876, the Sioux reluctantly sold the Black Hills and agreed to the reduction of the Great Sioux Reservation to five much smaller ones. The Sioux, unable to hunt game as they traditionally had, found life unbearable on the reservation. They sought escape through the supernatural: the Ghost Dance. The Ghost Dance was a religion that included dances and songs proclaiming the return of the buffalo and the resurrection of dead ancestors in a land free of White people. The religion soon became what social scientists call a **millenarian movement**, a movement founded on the belief that a cataclysmic upheaval would occur in the immediate future, followed by collective salvation. The movement originated among the Paiutes of Nevada and, ironically, spread northward to the Plains Indians via the cornerstone of the government's assimilationist policy: the schools. The English that Native Americans learned in the mission or government schools gave them the means to overcome the barriers of tribal languages and communicate with one another. By 1890, about 65 percent of the tribes in the West, according to sociologist Russell Thornton (1981), were involved in this movement.

From a functionalist perspective, this millenarian movement can be viewed as a means of coping with the domination of White intruders. Although the Ghost Dance was harmless to Whites, they feared that the new tribal solidarity encouraged by the movement would lead to renewed warfare. As a result, more troops were summoned to areas where the Ghost Dance had become popular.

In late December 1890, anticipating that a massive Ghost Dance would be staged, a cavalry division arrived at an encampment of Teton Sioux at Wounded Knee Creek on the Pine Ridge, South Dakota, reservation. When the soldiers began to disarm the warriors, a random shot was fired at the soldiers, touching off a close-range battle. The cavalry then turned its artillery on men, women, and children. Approximately 300 Sioux and 25 government soldiers were killed in the ensuing fighting, which is now called the Battle of Wounded Knee. One Sioux witness later recalled, "We tried to run, but they shot us like we were a buffalo. I know there are some good white people, but the soldiers must be mean to shoot children and women" (D. Brown 1971:417).

millenarian movements Movements, such as the Ghost Dance, that prophesy a cataclysm in the immediate future, to be followed by collective salvation.

For the federal government, what it considered the Indian problem remained. Despite the effects of disease and warfare, nearly 250,000 Indians still lived, according to the 1890 census. The reservation system constructed in the last decades of the 19th century to provide settlements for Native American peoples has formed the basis of the relationship of Native Americans to the government from then until the present.

Ruling the Native Americans

Along with the military defeat of the tribes, the federal government tried to limit the functions of tribal leaders. If tribal institutions were weakened, it was felt, the Native Americans would assimilate more rapidly. The government's intention to merge the various tribes into White society was unmistakably demonstrated in the 1887 Dawes, or General Allotment, Act. This failure to assist Native American people was followed by a somewhat more admirable effort: the Indian Reorganization Act of 1934. The Allotment Act and the Reorganization Act established the government's paternalistic approach.

The more significant federal actions that continue up to the present are summarized in Table 6.1.

These early policies also reflect the oppression of internal colonialism. As we presented in Chapter 1, **internal colonialism** is the treatment of subordinate groups like colonial subjects by those in power. Native Americans found themselves to be the subordinate group on land that once they occupied alone. Now they were being treated like a colonized people by the newly formed government, which itself had successfully broken from the colonial hold of Great Britain. Ironically, the former colony was practicing internal colonialism toward the indigenous people of the new land.

The Allotment Act

The Allotment Act bypassed tribal leaders and proposed to make individual landowners of tribal members. Each family was given up to 160 acres under the government's assumption that, with land, they would become more like the White homesteaders who were then flooding the not-yet-settled areas of the West.

internal colonialism
The treatment of subordinate peoples as colonial subjects by those in power.

TABLE 6.1
Major Federal Policies

Year	Policy	Central feature
1830	Removal Act	relocated Eastern tribes westward
1887	Allotment Act	tribal lands subdivided into individual household plots
1934	Reorganization Act	required tribes to develop election-based governments and leaders
1934	Johnson-O'Malley Act	aid to public school districts with Native American enrollments
1946	Indian Claims Commission	adjudicates litigation by tribes against the federal government
1952	Employment Assistance Program	relocates reservation people to urban areas for jobs
1953	Termination Act	closes reservations and their federal services
1971	Alaska Native Settlement Act	recognizes legally the lands of tribal people
1986	Indian Gaming Regulation Act	states can negotiate gaming rights to reservations
1990	Native American Graves and Repatriation Act	return of native remains to tribes with authentic claims
1990	Indian Arts and Crafts Act	monitors authenticity of crafts
1994	American Indian Religious Freedom Act	seeks to protect tribal spirituality including use of peyote

The effect of the Allotment Act on the Native Americans was disastrous. To guarantee that they would remain homesteaders, the act prohibited their selling the land for 25 years. Yet no effort was made to acquaint them with the skills necessary to make the land productive. Many tribes were not accustomed to cultivating land and, if anything, considered such labor undignified, and they received no assistance in adapting to homesteading.

Much of the land initially deeded under the Allotment Act eventually came into the possession of White landowners. The land could not be sold legally, but it could be leased and was subsequently transferred through fraudulent procedures. Whites even went so far as to arrange to become legal guardians of Native American youths who had received allotments. The Bureau of Indian Affairs (BIA) tried to close such loopholes, but unscrupulous Whites and their Native American allies inevitably discovered new ones. For Native Americans who managed to retain the land, the BIA required that, upon the death of the owner, the land be divided equally among all descendants, regardless of tribal inheritance customs. In documented cases, this division resulted in as many as 30 people trying to live off an 80-acre plot of worthless land. By 1934, Native Americans had lost approximately 90 million of the 138 million acres in their possession before the Allotment Act. The land left was generally considered worthless for farming and marginal even for ranching (Deloria and Lytle 1983; Hagan 1961; Holford 1975; Tyler 1973; M. Wax 1971; Witt 1970).

The Reorganization Act

The assumptions behind the Allotment Act and the missionary activities of the 19th century were that it was best for Native Americans to assimilate into the White society, and each individual was best considered apart from his or her tribal identity. Very gradually, in the 20th century, government officials have accepted the importance of tribal identity. The Indian Reorganization Act of 1934, known as the Wheeler-Howard Act, recognized the need to use, rather than ignore, tribal identity. But assimilation, rather than movement toward a pluralistic society, was still the goal.

Many provisions of the Reorganization Act, including revocation of the Allotment Act, benefited Native Americans. Still, given the legacy of broken treaties, many tribes at first distrusted the new policy. Under the Reorganization Act, tribes could

Tribal people have generally been supportive of a strong military. Fittingly, the first casualty of the War in Iraq was Lori Pestewa, shown on the right, a Hopi woman of Hispanic descent. On the left is her friend Jessica Lynch, whose capture and subsequent rescue made the headlines while Pestewa's death largely went unnoticed outside the Native American community.

adopt a written constitution and elect a tribal council with a head. This system imposed foreign values and structures. Under it, the elected tribal leader represented an entire reservation, which might include several tribes, some hostile to one another. Furthermore, the leader had to be elected by majority rule, a concept alien to many tribes. Many full-blooded Native Americans resented the provision that mixed-bloods were to have full voting rights. The Indian Reorganization Act did facilitate tribal dealings with government agencies, but the dictating to Native Americans of certain procedures common to White society and alien to the tribes was another sign of forced assimilation.

As had been true of earlier government reforms, the Reorganization Act sought to assimilate Native Americans into the dominant society on the dominant group's terms. In this case, the tribes were absorbed within the political and economic structure of the larger society. Apart from the provision about tribal chairmen who were to oversee reservations with several tribes, the Reorganization Act solidified tribal identity. Unlike the Allotment Act, it recognized the right of Native Americans to approve or reject some actions taken on their behalf. The act still maintained substantial non-Native American control over the reservations. As institutions, the tribal governments owed their existence not to their people but to the BIA. These tribal governments rested at the bottom of a large administrative hierarchy (Cornell 1984; Deloria 1971; McNickle 1973; Washburn 1984; Wax and Buchanan 1975).

In 2000, on the 175th anniversary of the BIA, its director, Kevin Guer, a Pawnee, declared that it was "no occasion for celebration as we express our profound sorrow for what the agency has done in the past." A formal apology followed (Stout 2000).

Reservation Life and Federal Policies

CD-ROM *Activity 5.2*

Today, over 530,000 Native Americans live on 557 reservations and trust lands in 33 states, which account for a bit more than 2 percent of the land throughout the United States. Even for those residing far away from the tribal lands, the reservations play a prominent role in the identity of the Native American peoples (Bureau of the Census 2004e) (Figure 6.2).

More than any other segment of the population, with the exception of the military, the reservation Native American finds his or her life determined by the federal government. From the condition of the roads to the level of fire protection to the quality of the schools, reservation life is effectively controlled by the federal government through such agencies as the BIA and the Public Health Service. Tribes and their leaders are now consulted more than in the past, but the ultimate decisions rest in Washington, D.C., to a degree that is not true for the rest of the civilian population.

As early as April 1954, an editorial in the *Washington Post* expressed approval of efforts of the federal government to "get out of the Indian business." Many of the policies instituted by the BIA in the 20th century have been designed with this purpose in mind. Most Native Americans and their organizations do not quarrel with this goal. They may only wish that the government and the White people had never gotten into Indian business in the first place. Disagreement between the BIA and the tribes and among Native Americans themselves has focused on how to reduce federal control and subsidies, not on whether they should be reduced. The government has taken three steps in this direction since World War II. Two of these measures have been the formation of the Indian Claims Commission and the passage of the Termination Act. The following section shows how the third step, the Employment Assistance Program, has created a new meeting place for Native Americans in cities, far from their native homelands and the reservations (Tyler 1973).

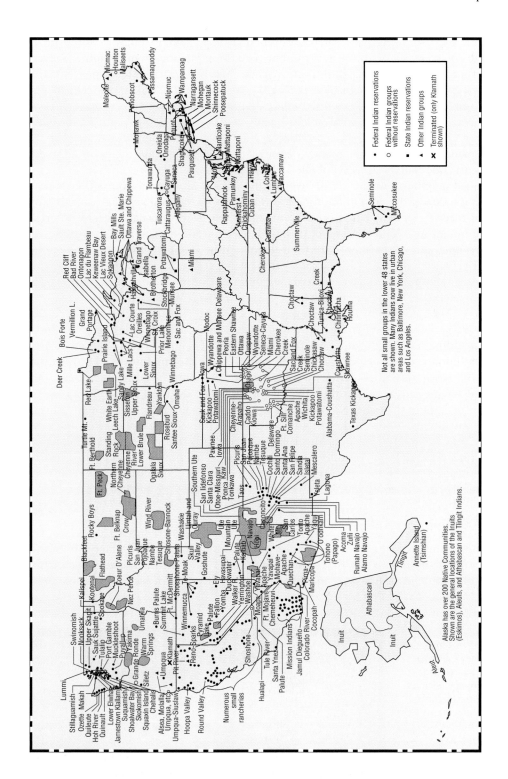

FIGURE 6.2   Native American Lands and Communities

Source: Bureau of Indian Affairs 1986:12–13.

Native American Legal Claims

Native Americans have had a unique relationship with the federal government. As might be expected, little provision was ever made for them as individuals or tribes to bring grievances against the government. From 1863 to 1946, Native Americans could bring no claim against the government without a special act of Congress, a policy that prevented most charges of treaty violations. Only 142 claims were heard during those

setoffs
Deductions from money due in U.S. government settlements with Native Americans, equal to the cost of federal services provided to the tribe.

83 years. In 1946, Congress created the Indian Claims Commission, with authority to hear all tribal cases against the government. The three-member commission was given a five-year deadline. During the first five years, however, nearly three times as many claims were filed as had been filed during the 83 years of the old system. Therefore, the commission's term was extended and extended again, and its size was expanded. The commission was disbanded in 1978, with its cases now being heard by the U.S. Court of Claims. As of 1997, the commission and Court, over a period of more than 50 years, paid claims totaling an average of $1,000 for each American Indian for all treaty violations and related claims (Drabelle 1997; Nagel 1996).

If legal judgments are made in favor of the Native Americans, courts then determine the value of the land at the time it was illegally seized. Native Americans usually do not receive payment based on present value, nor do they usually receive interest on the money due. Value at time of loss, perhaps a few pennies an acre, is considered "just compensation." Payments are then decreased by setoffs. **Setoffs** are deductions from the money due that are equal to the cost of federal services provided to the tribe. It is not unusual to have a case decided in favor of the tribe, only to have its settlement exceeded by the setoffs (Deloria 1971; Ellis 1972; Wilkinson 1966).

Native Americans increasingly express a desire to recover their land rather than accept financial settlements. After numerous legal decisions favoring the Sioux Indians, including a ruling of the U.S. Supreme Court, Congress finally agreed to pay $106 million for the land that was illegally seized in the aftermath of the Battle of the Little Big Horn, described earlier in this chapter. The Sioux rejected the money and lobbied for measures such as the 1987 Black Hills Sioux Nation Act in Congress, to return the land to the tribe. No positive action has yet been taken on these measures. In the meantime, however, the original settlement, the subsequent unaccepted payments, and the interest brought the 1991 total of funds being held for the Sioux to more than $330 million. Despite the desperate need for housing, food, health care, and education, the Sioux still would prefer to regain the land lost in the 1868 Fort Laramie Treaty and, as of 2002, have not accepted payment (Egan 2000).

The Termination Act

The most controversial government policy toward reservation Native Americans in the 20th century was initiated by the Termination Act of 1953. Like many such policies, the act originated in ideas that were meant to benefit Native Americans. The BIA commis-

Most reservations today have a measure of self-government through an elected tribal council. Pictured is the Apache tribal council at work.

sioner, John Collier, had expressed concern in the 1930s over extensive government control of tribal affairs. In 1947, congressional hearings were held to determine which tribes had the economic resources to be relieved of federal control and assistance. The policy proposed at that time was an admirable attempt to give Native Americans greater autonomy and at the same time to reduce federal expenditures, a goal popular among taxpayers.

The services the tribes received, such as subsidized medical care and college scholarships, should not have been viewed as special and deserving to be discontinued. These services were not the result of favoritism but merely fulfilled treaty obligations. The termination of the Native Americans' relationship to the government then came to be viewed by Native Americans as a threat to reduce services rather than a release from arbitrary authority. Native Americans might be gaining greater self-governance, but at a high price.

Unfortunately, the Termination Act as finally passed in 1953 emphasized reducing costs and ignored individual needs. Recommendations for a period of tax immunity were dropped. According to the act, federal services such as medical care, schools, and road equipment were supposed to be withdrawn gradually. Instead, when the Termination Act's provisions began to go into effect, federal services were stopped immediately, with minimal coordination between local government agencies and the tribes to determine whether the services could be continued by other means. The effect of the government orders on the Native Americans was disastrous, with major economic upheaval on the affected tribes, who were unable to establish some of the most basic services—such as road repair and fire protection—that the federal government had previously provided. The federal government resumed these services in 1975 with congressional action that signaled the end of another misguided policy intended to be good for tribal peoples (Deloria 1969; Fixico 1988; Tyler 1973; Wax and Buchanan 1975).

Employment Assistance Program

The depressed economic conditions of reservation life might lead one to expect government initiatives to attract business and industry to locate on or near reservations. The government could provide tax incentives that would eventually pay for themselves. However, such proposals have not been advanced. Rather than take jobs to the Native Americans, the federal government decided to lead the more highly motivated away from the reservation. This policy has further devastated the reservations' economic potential.

In 1952, the BIA began programs to relocate young Native Americans. One of these programs, after 1962, was called the Employment Assistance Program (EAP). Assistance centers were created in Chicago, Cleveland, Dallas, Denver, Los Angeles, Oakland, San Jose, Oklahoma City, Tulsa, and Seattle. In some cities, the Native American population increased as much as fivefold in the 1950s, primarily because of the EAP. By 1968, more than 100,000 people had participated in the program, and 200,000, or one-fourth of the Native American population, had moved to urban areas. They have tended not to spread throughout urban areas but to remain somewhat segregated. Though not as segregated as African Americans or Hispanics, Native Americans often experience moderate segregation, similar to that of European ethnic groups (Bohland 1982).

The EAP's primary provision was for relocation, individually or in families, at government expense, to urban areas where job opportunities were greater than those on the reservations. The BIA stressed that the EAP was voluntary, but as Howard Bahr (1972:408) correctly states, this voluntary aspect was "a fiction to the extent that the white man has structured the alternatives in such a way that economic pressures force

Powwows such as this one in California have become important social, cultural, and economic events that bring together members of many different tribes.

the Indian to relocate." The program was not a success for the many Native Americans who found the urban experience unsuitable or unbearable. By 1965, one-fourth to one-third of the people in the EAP had returned to their home reservation. So great was the rate of return that in 1959 the BIA stopped releasing data on the percentage of returnees, fearing that they would give too much ammunition to critics of the EAP.

The movement of Native Americans into urban areas has had many unintended consequences. It has further reduced the labor force on the reservation. Because those who leave tend to be better educated, it is the Native American version of the brain drain described in Chapter 4. Urbanization unquestionably contributed to the development of an intertribal network or pan-Indian movement, described later in this chapter. The city became the new meeting place of Native Americans, who learned of their common predicament both in the city and on the federally administered reservations. Government agencies also had to develop a policy of continued assistance to nonreservation Native Americans; despite such efforts, the problems of Native Americans in cities persist.

Programs have emerged to meet the needs of city-dwelling Native Americans. Founded in 1975, the Native American Education Service College in Chicago is an independent, accredited college trying to partially provide for the education of that city's 10,000 Native Americans, who represent 100 tribes. It offers college degrees, with specialized courses in Native American language and history. The college emphasizes small classes and individualized instruction. This institution is unusual not only in higher education but also in offering urban Native Americans a pluralistic solution to being an American Indian in White America (Lauerman 1993).

Collective Action

The growth of pan-Indian activism is an example of both panethnicity and social protest. As we noted in Chapter 1, the panethnic development of solidarity among ethnic subgroups has been reflected in terms such as *Hispanic, Latino,* and *Asian American.* **Pan-Indianism** refers to intertribal social movements in which several tribes, joined by political goals but not by kinship, unite in a common identity. Today, these pan-Indian efforts are most vividly seen in cultural efforts and political protests of government policies (Cornell 1996).

pan-Indianism
Intertribal social movements in which several tribes, joined by political goals but not by kinship, unite in a common identity.

Proponents of this movement see the tribes as captive nations or internal colonies. They generally see the enemy as the federal government. Until recently, pan-Indian efforts usually failed to overcome the cultural differences and distrust between tribal groups. However, some efforts to unite have succeeded. The Iroquois made up a six-tribe confederation dating back to the 17th century. The Ghost Dance briefly united the Plains tribes in the 1880s, some of which had earlier combined to resist the U.S. Army. But these were the exceptions. It took nearly a century and a half of BIA policies to accomplish a significant level of unification.

The National Congress of American Indians (NCAI), founded in 1944 in Denver, Colorado, was the first national organization representing Native Americans. The NCAI registered itself as a lobby in Washington, D.C., hoping to make the Native American perspective heard in the aftermath of the Reorganization Act described earlier. Concern about "White people's meddling" is reflected in the NCAI requirement that White members pay twice as much in dues. The NCAI has had its successes. Early in its history, it played an important role in creating the Indian Claims Commission, and it later pressured the BIA to abandon the practice of termination. It is still the most important civil rights organization for Native Americans and uses tactics similar to those of the NAACP, although the problems facing African Americans and Native Americans are legally and constitutionally different.

A later arrival was the more radical American Indian Movement (AIM), the most visible pan-Indian group. The AIM was founded in 1968 by Clyde Bellecourt (of the White Earth Chippewa) and Dennis Banks (of the Pine Ridge Oglala Sioux), both of whom then lived in Minneapolis. Initially, AIM created a patrol to monitor police actions and document charges of police brutality. Eventually, it promoted programs for alcohol rehabilitation and school reform. By 1972, AIM was nationally known not for its neighborhood-based reforms but for its aggressive confrontations with the BIA and law enforcement agencies.

Protest Efforts

Fish-ins began in 1964 to protest interference by Washington State officials with Native Americans who were fishing, as they argued, in accordance with the 1854 Treaty of Medicine Creek and were not subject to fine or imprisonment, even if they did violate White society's law. The fish-ins had protesters fishing en masse in restricted waterways. This protest was initially hampered by disunity and apathy, but several hundred Native Americans were convinced that civil disobedience was the only way to bring attention to their grievances with the government. Legal battles followed, and the U.S. Supreme Court confirmed the treaty rights in 1968. Other tribes continued to fight in the courts, but the fish-ins brought increased public awareness of the deprivations of Native Americans. One of the longest battles continues to the present: The Chippewas have rights to 50 percent of the fish, timber, and wildlife across the upper third of Wisconsin. In 1991, Wisconsin agreed with this long-standing treaty right, but Whites continue to demonstrate against what they feel is the unfair advantage extended to the Native Americans (Jolidon 1991; Steiner 1968).

The fish-ins were only the beginning. After the favorable Supreme Court decision in 1968, other events followed in quick succession. In 1969, members of the San Francisco Indian Center seized Alcatraz Island in San Francisco Bay. The 13-acre island was an abandoned maximum-security federal prison, and the federal government was undecided about how to use it. The Native Americans claimed "the excess property" in exchange for $24 in glass beads and cloth, following the precedent set in the sale of Manhattan more than three centuries earlier. With no federal response and the loss of public interest in the demonstration, the protesters left the island more than a year later. The activists' desire to transform it into a Native American

fish-ins
Tribes' protests over government interference with their traditional rights to fish as they like.

cultural center was ignored. Despite the outcome, the event gained international publicity for their cause. Red Power was born, and Native Americans who sympathized with the BIA were labeled "Uncle Tomahawks" or "apples" (red on the outside, white on the inside).

The federal government did not totally ignore calls for a new policy that involved Native Americans in its formulation. Nevertheless, no major breakthroughs came in the 1960s. One significant step was passage of the Alaska Native Settlement Act of 1971. Alaskan Native American people—the 100,000 Inuit Eskimo and other Aleuts—have maintained their claim to the land since Alaska was purchased from Russia in 1867. The federal government had allowed the natives to settle on about one-third of the land they claimed but had not even granted them title to that land. The discovery of huge oil reserves in 1969 made the issue more explosive as the state of Alaska auctioned off mineral rights, ignoring Inuit occupation of the land.

The Alaskan Federation of Natives (AFN), the major native Alaskan group, which had been organized in 1967, moved quickly to stop "the biggest land grab in the history of the U.S.," as the AFN called it. An AFN-sponsored bill was revised, and a compromise, the Native Claims Settlement Act, was passed in late 1971. The final act, which fell short of the requests by the AFN, granted control and ownership of 44 million acres to Alaska's 53,000 Inuits, Aleuts, and other peoples and gave them a cash settlement of nearly $1 billion. Given the enormous pressures from oil companies and conservationists, the Native Claims Settlement Act can be regarded as one of the more reasonable agreements reached between distinctive tribal groups of Native Americans and the government. Further reforms in 1988 helped to safeguard the original act, but as a major trade-off the Alaskan Native Americans surrendered future claims to all aboriginal lands (Cornell and Kalt 2003; Ogunwole 2002).

The most dramatic confrontation between Native Americans and the government came early the next year in the battle of Wounded Knee II. In January 1973, AIM leader Russell Means led an unsuccessful drive to impeach Richard Wilson as tribal chairman of the Oglala Sioux tribe on the Pine Ridge Reservation. In the next month, Means, accompanied by some 300 supporters, started a 70-day occupation of Wounded Knee, South Dakota, site of the infamous cavalry assault in 1890 and now part of the Pine Ridge Reservation. The occupation received tremendous press coverage.

However, the coverage did not affect the outcome. Negotiations between AIM and the federal government on the occupation itself brought no tangible results. Federal prosecutions were initiated against most participants. AIM leaders Russell Means and Dennis Banks eventually faced prosecution on a number of felony charges, and both men were imprisoned. AIM had less visibility as an organization then. Russell Means wryly remarked in 1984, "We're not chic now. We're just Indians, and we have to help ourselves" (Hentoff 1984:23; also see Nagel 1988, 1996; Smith and Warrior 1996; T. Johnson 1996).

The most visible recent AIM activity has been its efforts to gain clemency for one of its leaders, Leonard Peltier. Imprisoned since 1976, Peltier was given two life sentences for murdering two FBI agents the year before on the embattled Sioux reservation of Pine Ridge, South Dakota. Fellow AIM leaders such as Dennis Banks organized a 1994 Walk for Justice to bring attention in Washington, D.C., to the view that Peltier is innocent. This view was supported in two 1992 movie releases: the documentary *Incident at Oglala*, produced by Robert Redford, and the more entertaining, fictionalized *Thunderheart*. To date, clemency appeals to the president to lift the federal sentence have gone unheeded, but this issue remains the rallying point for today's remnants of AIM (Matthiessen 1991).

Pan-Indianism: An Overview

Pan-Indianism, an example of panethnicity, has created a greater solidarity among Native Americans as they seek solutions to common grievances with government agencies. Research shows that tribal people born since the collective action efforts of the 1960s are more likely to reject negative and stereotypic representations of American Indians than those born before the self-determination efforts. Whether through moderate groups such as the NCAI or the more activist AIM, these pan-Indian developments have awakened Whites to the real grievances of Native Americans and have garnered the begrudging acceptance of even the most conservative tribal members, who are more willing to cooperate with government action (Schulz 1998).

However, the results of pan-Indianism have not all been productive, even when viewed from a perspective sympathetic to Native American self-determination. The national organizations are dominated by Plains tribes, not only politically but culturally as well. Powwow styles of dancing, singing, and costuming derived from the Plains tradition are spreading nationwide as common cultural traits (see Figure 6.3 for the ten largest tribes).

The growing visibility of powwows is symbolic of Native Americans in the 1990s. The phrase *pau wau* referred to the medicine man or spiritual leader of the Algonquian tribes, but Europeans who watched medicine men dance thought that the word referred to entire events. Over the last hundred years, **powwows** have evolved into gatherings in which Native Americans of many tribes come to dance, sing, play music, and visit. More recently, they have become organized events featuring competitions and prizes at several thousand locations. The general public sees them as entertainment, but for Native Americans, they are a celebration of their culture (Eschbach and Applbaum 2000).

powwows
Native American gatherings of dancing, singing, music playing, and visiting, accompanied by competitions.

FIGURE 6.3 Ten Largest American Indian Tribal Groupings, 2000
Source: Ogunwole 2002:10.

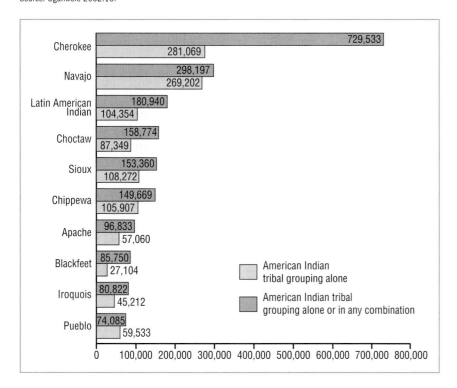

sovereignty
Refers in this context to tribal self-rule.

Sovereignty

While the collective gathering of tribes in pan-Indian efforts cannot be minimized, there continues to be a strong effort to maintain tribal sovereignty. Simply put, **sovereignty** refers in this context to tribal self-rule. Supported by every U.S. president since the 1960s, sovereignty is recognition for tribes to have vibrant economic and cultural lives. At the same time, numerous legal cases, including many at the level of the Supreme Court, continue to clarify to what extent a recognized tribe may rule itself and to what degree is it subject to state and federal laws. In 2004, the U.S. Supreme Court ruled 7–2 in *United States v. Lara* that a tribe has the inherent right to prosecute all American Indians, regardless of affiliation, for crimes that occur on the reservation. However, other cases in lower courts continue to chip away at tribal self-government (Indianz.com).

CD-ROM *Activity 5.3*

This legal relationship can be quite complex. For example, tribal members always pay federal income, Social Security, unemployment, and property taxes but do not pay state income if they live and work only on the reservation. Whether tribal members on reservations pay sales, gasoline, cigarette, or motor vehicle taxes has been negotiated on a reservation-by-reservation basis in many sites.

Focused on the tribal group, sovereignty remains linked to both the actions of the federal government and the actions of individual American Indians. The government ultimately determines which tribes are recognized, and while tribal groups may argue publicly for their recognition, self-declaration carries no legal recognition. This has always been an issue, but given the rise of casino gambling to be discussed shortly, the determination of who constitute a sovereign tribe and who do not may carry significant economic benefits.

The federal government takes this gate-keeping role of sovereignty very seriously—the irony of the conquering people determining who are "Indians" is not lost upon many tribal activists. In 1978, the Department of the Interior established what it called the acknowledgment process to decide whether any more tribes should have a government-to-government relationship. They must show that they were a distinct group and trace continuity since 1900. Through 2004, 294 groups have sought sovereignty, with just 16 acknowledged and another 9 receiving it though special congressional action.

Individual American Indians play a role as well. For most, their tribal affiliation is fairly clear, but for others it may be more problematic. Certainly if they are members of a group that has yet to receive federal recognition, a long and often costly legal battle is ahead for them to receive the recognition they already feel is their right. For those who have close descendants of more than one tribe, they usually can elect which tribe to belong to legally. While they may recognize the cultural heritage they have as belonging to more than one tribe, federal laws and most tribal governments require that they declare membership (sometimes also referred to as "enrollment" status) in one tribe (Kalt and Singer 2003; A. Wagner 2004).

Native Americans Today

The United States has taken most of the land originally occupied by or deeded to Native Americans; restricted their movement; unilaterally severed agreements; created a special legal status for them; and, after World War II, attempted to move them again. As a result of these efforts and generally poor economic conditions of most reservations, substantial numbers of Native Americans live in the nation's cities (Table 6.2).

TABLE 6.2
Urban Native Americans, 2000

According to Census 2000, there are seven cities with more than 10,000 Native Americans. By comparison, there are only four reservations with that many residents.

New York City	41,289
Los Angeles	29,412
Phoenix	26,696
Anchorage	18,941
Tulsa	18,551
Oklahoma City	17,743
Albuquerque	17,444
Tucson	11,038
Chicago	10,290

Source: Ogunwole 2002:8.

How are Native Americans being treated today? A very public insult is the continuing use of American Indian names as mascots for athletic teams of schools, including colleges and many professional sports teams in the United States. Almost all American Indian organizations, including AIM, have brought attention to the use of Native Americans as the mascots of sports teams, such as the Washington Redskins, and to such spectator practices as the "Tomahawk chop" associated with the Atlanta Braves baseball team.

Many sports fans and college alumni find it difficult to understand why Native Americans take offense at a name such as "Braves" or even "Redskins" if it is meant to represent a team about which they have positive feelings. For Native Americans, however, the use of such mascots trivializes their past and their presence today. In "Listen to Our Voices" in Chapter 2, journalist and Lakota Sioux tribe member Tim Giago, in a sharp editorial, expressed his disapproval of the use of American Indian names as mascots. In 2001, the U.S. Commission on Civil Rights called for an end to the use of Indian mascots at schools and universities. Although the statement attracted significant attention, it was not legally binding.

There is no easy answer for native peoples, who face a variety of challenges. Any discussion of Native American socioeconomic status today must begin with an emphasis on the diversity of the people. Besides the variety of tribal heritages already noted, the contemporary Native American population is split between those on and off reservations and those living in small towns and in central cities. Life in these contrasting social environments is quite different, but enough similarities exist to warrant some broad generalizations on the status of Native Americans in the United States today.

The sections that follow summarize the status of contemporary Native Americans in economic development, education, health care, religious and spiritual expression, and the environment.

Economic Development

Native Americans are an impoverished people. Even to the most casual observer of a reservation, the poverty is a living reality, not merely numbers and percentages. Some visitors seem unconcerned, arguing that because Native Americans are used to hardship and lived a simple life before the Europeans arrived, poverty is a familiar and traditional way of life. In an absolute sense of dollars earned or quality of housing, Native

Americans are no worse off now. But in a relative sense that compares their position with that of Whites, they are dismally behind on all standards of income and occupational status. A 1995 national survey showed that overall unemployment is more than 30 percent. Among those who do have jobs, a third earned less than $10,000.

In 1997, the federal government introduced a welfare program that limited how long people can receive public assistance. This clearly will have impact on many tribal reservations, where high proportions of people depend on public assistance because of the lack of training or job opportunities. For example, in South Dakota, American Indians make up 7 percent of the population but account for 53 percent of the welfare recipients. State officials declared they could give five tribes a one-time infusion of start-up money, but after that they would be on their own (Belluck 1997; Egan 1998).

Given the lower incomes and higher poverty rates, it is not surprising that the occupational distribution of Native Americans is similarly bleak. Those who are employed are less likely to be managers, professionals, technicians, salespeople, or administrators. This pattern of low-wage employment is typical of many of the racial and ethnic minorities in the United States, but Native Americans differ in three areas: their roles in tourism, casino gambling, and government employment.

Tourism   Tourism is an important source of employment for many reservation residents, who either serve the needs of visitors directly or sell souvenirs and craft items. Generally, such enterprises do not achieve the kind of success that improves the tribal economy significantly. Even if they did, sociologist Murray Wax (1971:69) argued, "It requires a special type of person to tolerate exposing himself and his family life to the gaze of tourists, who are often boorish and sometimes offensively condescending in their attitudes."

Tourism, in light of exploitation of tribal people, is a complex interaction of the outside with the Native American. Interviews with tourists visiting museums and reservations found that, regardless of the presentation, many visitors interpreted their brief experiences to be consistent with their previously held stereotypes of and prejudices toward Native Americans. Yet, at the other extreme, some contemporary tourists conscious of the historical context are uncomfortable taking in native foods and purchasing crafts at tribal settlements despite the large economic need many reservations have for such commerce (M. Padget 2004; J. Laxson 1991).

Craftwork rarely realizes the profits most Native Americans desire and need. The trading-post business has also taken its toll on Native American cultures. Many craft workers have been manipulated by other Native Americans and Whites to produce what the tourists want. Creativity and authenticity often are replaced by mechanical duplication of "genuine Indian" curios. There continues to be concern and controversy surrounding art such as paintings and pottery that may not be produced by real Native Americans. In 1935, the federal government had created the Indian Arts and Crafts Board to promote tribal arts. The influx of fraudulent crafts was so great that Congress added to its responsibilities the Indian Arts and Crafts Act, which severely punishes anyone who offers to sell an object as produced by a Native American artisan when it was not. The price of both economic and cultural survival is very high (R. McCoy 2004).

Casino Gambling   A more recent source of significant income and some employment has been the introduction of gambling on reservations. Forms of gambling, originally part of tribal ceremonies or celebrations, existed long before Europeans arrived in the Western Hemisphere. Today, however, commercial gambling is the only viable source of employment and revenue available to several tribes.

Sandia Pueblo reservation governor Alex Lujan visits the Pueblo's casino in New Mexico. Such economic ventures have been a major boon to the prosperity of some tribal groups.

Under the 1988 Indian Gaming Regulatory Act, states must negotiate gambling agreements with reservations and cannot prohibit any gambling already allowed under state law. By 2004, in 28 states, 224 tribal governments were operating a variety of gambling operations, including off-track betting, casino tables such as blackjack and roulette, lotteries, sports betting, video games of chance, telephone betting, slot machines, and high-stakes bingo. The gamblers, almost all non-Native Americans, sometimes travel long distances for the opportunity to wager money. The actual casinos are a form of tribal government enterprise as opposed to private business operations.

The economic impact on some reservations has been enormous, and nationwide receipts amounted to $15.9 billion in 2003 from reservation casino operations, compared to $65 billion for nontribal legal gambling operations. However, the wealth is uneven: About two-thirds of the recognized Indian tribes have no gambling ventures. A few successful casinos have led to staggering windfalls, such as the profits to the 820 members of the Connecticut Mashantucket Pequot Indians, whose Foxwoods Resort Casino, with gambling receipts annually well over $1.5 billion, provides generous benefits to anyone who can establish that he or she is at least one-sixteenth Pequot. Gaming money from the about 25 very successful operations not only supports tribal members but has been used to buy back tribal lands and even to help underwrite the cost of the Smithsonian Museum of the American Indian, which opened in 2004.

The more typical picture is of moderately successful gambling operations associated with tribes whose social and economic needs are overwhelming. Tribes that have opened casinos have experienced drops in unemployment and increases in household income not seen on non-gaming reservations. However, two important factors need to be considered. First, the impact of this revenue is limited. The tribes that make substantial revenue from gambling are a small fraction of all Native American people. Second, even on reservations that benefit from gambling enterprises, the levels of unemployment are substantially higher and the family income significantly lower than for the nation as a whole (Barlett and Steele 2002; National Indian Gaming Association 2004a; Sahagun 2004).

Criticism is not hard to find, even among Native Americans, some of whom oppose gambling both on moral grounds and because it is marketed in a form that is incompatible with Native American culture. Opponents are concerned about the appearance of compulsive gambling among some tribal members. The majority of the gamblers are not Native Americans, and almost all of the reservation casinos, though owned by the tribes, are operated by White-owned businesses. Some tribal members feel that the casinos trivialize and cheapen their heritage. The issue of who shares in gambling profits also has led to heated debates in some tribal communities about who is a member of the tribe. In addition, established White gaming interests lobby Congress to restrict the tribes, even though Native Americans generate only 21 percent of the nation's total of legal gambling revenue, including lotteries and racing (National Indian Gaming Association 2004b).

Although income from gambling has not dramatically changed the lifestyle of most Native Americans, it has been a magnet of criticism from outsiders. Critics question the special status being afforded to Native Americans and contend that there should be an even playing field. This view certainly would have been endorsed by tribal members, because most of what passed for government policies over the last 200 years placed tribes at a major disadvantage. Attention is drawn to some tribes that had made contributions to politicians involved in policies concerning gambling laws. Although some of these contributions may have been illegal, the national media attention was far more intense than was warranted in the messy area of campaign financing. It is another example of how the notion that Native Americans are now playing the White man's game of capitalism "too well" becomes big news (Glionna 2004).

Government Employment   Another major source of employment for Native Americans is the government, principally the BIA, but also other federal agencies, the military, and state and local governments. As recently as 1970, one of every four employed Native Americans worked for the federal government. More than half the BIA's employees have tribal ancestry. In fact, since 1854, the BIA has had a policy of giving employment preference to Native Americans over Whites. This policy has been questioned, but the U.S. Supreme Court (*Morton v. Mancari*) upheld it in 1974. Although this is a significant source of employment opportunity, other tribe members have leveled many criticisms at Native American government workers, especially federal employees.

These government employees form a subculture in Native American communities. They tend to be Christians, educated in BIA schools, and sometimes the third generation born into government service. Discrimination against Native Americans in private industry makes government work attractive, and once a person is employed and has seniority, he or she is virtually guaranteed security. Of course, this security may lead some people (whether Native Americans or Whites) to work inefficiently (Bureau of Indian Affairs 1970; Rachlin 1970).

We have examined the sources of economic development, such as tourism, government service, and legalized gambling, but the dominant feature of reservation life is, nevertheless, unemployment. A government report issued by the Full Employment Action Council opened with the statement that such words as *severe, massive,* and *horrendous* are appropriate to describe unemployment among Native Americans. Official unemployment figures for reservations range from 23 percent to 90 percent. It is little wonder that the 1990 Census showed that the poorest county in the nation was wholly on tribal lands: Shannon County, South Dakota, of the Pine Ridge Reservation, had a 63 percent poverty rate. Unemployment rates for urban-based Indians are also very high; Los Angeles reports more than 40 percent, and Minneapolis, 49 percent (Cornell and Kalt 1990; Kanamine 1992; Knudson 1987; Sullivan 1986).

The economic outlook for Native Americans need not be bleak. A single program is not the solution; the diversity of both Native Americans and their problems demands a multifaceted approach. The solutions need not be unduly expensive; indeed, because the Native American population is very small compared with the total population, programs with major influence may be financed without significant

Paul Moss is giving an Arapaho name to his newborn great-grandson, Raphael, who lies in his arms. The name he chose to give the infant is the one his own deceased son held, Himooko3onit, or Golden Eagle. At his feet are cloth goods and cash offerings given to the elder who has given the name.

federal expenditures. Murray Wax (1971) observed that reformers viewing the economically depressed position of Native Americans often seize on education as the key to success. As the next section shows, improving educational programs for Native Americans would be a good place to start.

Education

Government involvement in the education of Native Americans dates as far back as a 1794 treaty with the Oneida Indians. In the 1840s, the federal government and missionary groups combined to start the first school for American Indians. By 1860, the government was operating schools that were free of missionary involvement. Today, laws prohibit federal funds for Native American education from going to sectarian schools. Also, since the passage of the Johnson-O'Malley Act in 1934, the federal government has reimbursed public school districts that include Native American children.

Federal control of the education of Native American children has had mixed results from the beginning. Several tribes started their own school systems at the beginning of the 19th century, financing the schools themselves. The Cherokee tribe developed an extensive school system that taught both English and Cherokee, the latter using an alphabet developed by the famed leader Sequoyah. Literacy for the Cherokees was estimated by the mid-1800s at 90 percent, and they even published a bilingual newspaper. The Creek, Chickasaw, and Seminole also maintained school systems. But by the end of the 19th century, all these schools had been closed by federal order. Not until the 1930s did the federal government become committed to ensuring an education for Native American children. Despite the push for educational participation, by 1948 only a quarter of the children on the Navajo reservation, the nation's largest, were attending school (Pewewardy 1998).

Educational Attainment   A serious problem in Native American education has been the unusually low level of enrollment. Many children never attend school, or they leave while in elementary school and never return. Enrollment rates are as low as 30 percent for Alaska Eskimos (or Inupiats). This high dropout rate is at least 50 percent higher than that of Blacks or Hispanics and nearly three times that of Whites. The term *dropout* is misleading because many tribal American schoolchildren have found their educational experience so hostile that they had no choice but to leave (James et al. 1995).

Rosalie Wax (1967) conducted a detailed study of the education among the Sioux on the Pine Ridge Reservation of South Dakota. She concluded that terms such as **kickout or pushout** are more appropriate. The children are not so much hostile toward school as they are set apart from it; they are socialized by their parents to be independent and not to embarrass their peers, but teachers reward docile acceptance and expect schoolchildren to correct one another in public. Socialization is not all that separates home from school. Teachers often are happy to find parents not "interfering" with their job. Parents do not visit the school, and teachers avoid the homes, a pattern that only furthers the isolation of school from home. This lack of interaction results partly from the predominance of non-Native American teachers, many of whom do not recognize the learning styles of American Indian students, although the situation is improving (Hilberg and Tharp 2002).

Quality of Schooling   The quality of Native American education is more difficult to measure than is the quantity. How does one measure excellence? And excellence for what? White society? Tribal life? Both? Chapter 1 discussed the disagreement over measuring intellectual achievement (how much a person has learned) and the greater hazards in measuring intellectual aptitude (how much a person is able to learn). Studies of reservation children, using tests of intelligence that do not require a knowledge of English, consistently show scores at or above the levels of middle-class urban children. Yet in the upper grades, a **crossover effect** appears when tests used assume lifelong familiarity with English. Native American students drop behind their White peers and so would be classified by the dominant society as underachievers (Bureau of Indian Affairs 1988; Coleman et al. 1966; Fuchs and Havighurst 1972).

Preoccupation with such test results perhaps avoids the more important question: educational excellence for what? It would be a mistake to assume that the tribal peoples have reached a consensus. However, they do want to see a curriculum that, at the very least, considers the unique aspects of their heritage. Charles Silberman (1971:173) reported visiting a sixth-grade English class in a school on a Chippewa reservation where the students were all busily at work writing a composition for Thanksgiving: "Why We Are Happy the Pilgrims Came." A 1991 Department of Education report titled "Indian Nations at Risk" still found the curriculum presented from a European perspective. It is little wonder that a 1990 national survey found that at 48 percent of all schools Native American children attend, there is not a single Native American teacher.

Some positive changes are occurring in education. At the beginning of the chapter, we noted the example of the Ho-chunk preschoolers learning their native language. About 23 percent of the students in BIA-funded schools receive bilingual education, but as yet no coordinator exists in the BIA for this important activity. There is growing recognition of the need to move away from past policies that suppressed or ignored the native language and to acknowledge that educational results may be optimized when the native language is included. In "Research Focus: Learning the Navajo Way," we consider the importance of incorporating native teachings and culture (Bureau of Indian Affairs 1988; James et al. 1995; Reese 1996; Wells 1991).

kickouts or pushouts
Native American school dropouts who leave behind an unproductive academic environment.

crossover effect
An effect that appears when previously high-scoring Native American children score below average in intelligence when tests are given in English rather than their native languages.

Higher Education   The picture for Native Americans in higher education is decidedly mixed, with some progress and some promise. Enrollment in college increased steadily from the mid-1970s through the mid-1990s, but degree completion, especially the completion of professional degrees, may actually be declining. The economic and educational background of Native American students, especially reservation residents, makes considering entering a predominantly White college a very difficult decision. Native American students may soon feel isolated and discouraged, particularly if the college does not help them understand the alien world of American-style higher education. Even at campuses with large numbers of Native Americans in their student bodies, few Native American faculty or advisors are present to serve as role models. About 53 percent of the students leave at the end of their first year (Carnegie Foundation for the Advancement of Teaching 1990; Wells 1989).

Another encouraging development in higher education in recent years has been the creation of tribally controlled colleges, usually two-year community colleges. The

Focus Research Focus Research Focus

LEARNING THE NAVAJO WAY

What leads to academic success? Often the answer is a supportive family, but this has not always been said about Native Americans. Educators rooted in the European education traditions often argue that American Indian families whose children are faithful to the traditional culture cannot succeed in schools. This assimilationist view argues that to succeed in larger White-dominated society, it is important to begin to shed the "old ways" as soon as possible.

Interestingly, research done in the last 10 years questions the assimilationist view and concludes that American Indian students can improve their academic performance through educational programs that are less assimilationist and use curricula that build on what the Native American youth learn in their homes and communities.

Representative of this growing research is the study completed by sociologist Angela A. A. Willeto among her fellow Navajo tribal people. She studied a random sample of 451 Navajo high school students from eleven different Navajo Nation schools. She examined the impact of the students' orientation toward traditional Navajo culture on their performance. Willeto acknowledges that the prevailing view has been that all that is inherently Navajo in a child must be eliminated and replaced with mainstream White society beliefs and lifestyles.

The Navajo tradition was measured by a number of indicators, such as participating in Navajo dances, consulting a medicine man, entering a sweat bath to cleanse oneself spiritually, weaving rugs, living in a traditional hogan, and using the Navajo language. School performance was measured by grades, commitment to school, and aspirations to attend college. She found that the students who lived a more traditional life among the Navajo succeeded in school just as well and were just as committed to success in school and college as high schoolers leading a more assimilated life.

These results are important because many Native Americans themselves accept an assimilationist view. Even within the Navajo Nation, where Navajo language instruction has been mandated in all reservation schools since 1984, many Navajos still equate learning only with the mastery of White society's subject matter. ◼

Sources: Reyhner 2001b; Willeto 1999.

Navajo Community College (now called Diné College), the first such institution, was established in 1968, and by 1999 there were 31 nationwide in 12 states. Besides serving in some rural areas as the only educational institution for many miles, tribal colleges also provide services such as counseling and child care. Tribal colleges enable the students to maintain their cultural identity while training them to succeed outside the reservation (American Indian Higher Education Consortium 1999; Winik 1999).

At higher levels, Native Americans largely disappear from the educational scene. In 1998, of the 45,394 doctorates awarded to U.S. citizens, 187 went to Native Americans, compared with more than 11,000 that went to citizens of foreign countries (Bureau of the Census 2001j:175).

Summary   "Dine bizaad beeyashti!" Unfortunately, this declaration, "I speak Navajo!" is not commonly heard from educators. Gradually, schools have begun to encourage the preservation of native cultures. Until the 1960s, BIA and mission schools forbade speaking in the native languages, so it will take time to produce an educated teacher corps knowledgeable in and conversant with native cultures (Linthicum 1993).

As we have seen, there are many failures in our effort to educate, not just assimilate, the first Americans. The problems include:

- Underenrollment at all levels, from the primary grades through college
- The need to adjust to a school with values sometimes dramatically different from those of the home
- The need to make the curriculum more relevant
- The underfinancing of tribal community colleges
- The unique hardships encountered by reservation-born Native Americans who later live in and attend schools in large cities
- The language barrier faced by the many children who have little or no knowledge of English

Other problems include lack of educational innovation (the BIA had no kindergartens until 1967) and a failure to provide special education to children who need it.

Health Care

For Native Americans, "health care" is a misnomer, another broken promise in the array of unmet pledges the government has made. Native Americans are more likely to die before age 45 than any other racial or ethnic group. Even more frustrating, in 1994 they died of treatable diseases such as tuberculosis at rates 700 percent higher than those of White Americans. This dramatic difference is a result of their poverty and the lack of health services. There are only 96 doctors per 100,000 Native Americans, compared with 208 per 100,000 of the general population. Similarly, there are 251 nurses per 100,000 Native Americans compared with 672 per 100,000 for the nation as a whole. Even with efforts made to bring health professionals to reservations, the Indian Health Service showed vacancy rates for those positions approved for funding in 2004 at 11 percent for physicians and nurses and 24 percent for dentists (C. Grim 2004; Indian Health Service 1995; Kanamine 1992, 1994; McDonald et al 2002).

In 1955, the responsibility for health care for Native Americans was transferred from the BIA to the Public Health Service (PHS). Although their health has improved markedly since the mid-1960s, serious problems remain. As is true of industrial development and education, advances in health care are hampered by the poverty and geographic isolation of the reservations. Also, as in the educational and economic sectors, health policies, in effect, initiate a cultural war in which Native Americans must reject their traditions to secure better medical treatment (Kunitz 1996).

With the pressure to assimilate Native Americans in all aspects of their lives, there has been little willingness to recognize their traditions of healing and treating illnesses. Native treatments tend to be noninvasive, with the patient encouraged to contribute actively to the healing benefits and prevent future recurrence. In the 1990s, a pluralistic effort was slowly emerging to recognize alternative forms of medicine, including those practiced by Native Americans. In addition, reservation health care workers began to accommodate traditional belief systems as they administered the White culture's medicine (Angier 1993; Fox 1992; *Indian Country* 1999).

Some gifted health practitioners have been able to bridge the gap between the traditional Native American ways of healing and those developed out of the Western medical tradition. In "Listen to Our Voices," Dr. Lois Arviso Alvord, the first Navajo woman to become a surgeon, describes her effort to bridge the cultural gap. Dropping the impersonal clinical manner she had learned in medical school, Alvord reached out to her Navajo patients, acknowledging their faith in holistic healing practices.

It is not merely that Native Americans have more diseases and shorter life spans than the rest of the population; they also have acute problems in such areas as mental health, nutrition, diabetes, the needs of older adults, and alcoholism, which have been documented for generations but have only recently been addressed through innovative programs. Further improvement can be expected, but it will be some time before the gains make health care for Native Americans comparable to that of the general population (McDonald et al. 2002).

Contributing to the problems of health care and mortality on reservations are often high rates of reported crime. Poverty and few job opportunities offer an excellent environment for the growth of youth gang and drug trafficking. All the issues associated with crime can be found on the nation's reservations. There are 171 tribal enforcement agencies operating nearly 70 jails or detention facilities. As with other minority communities dealing with poverty, Native Americans strongly support law enforcement but at the same time sometimes contend their people are being abused by those very individuals selected to protect them. As with efforts for improving health care, the isolation and vastness of some of the reservations makes them uniquely vulnerable to crime (Hickman 2003; Major et al. 2004; Minton 2002).

Religious and Spiritual Expression

Like other aspects of Native American culture, the expression of religion is diverse, reflecting the variety of tribal traditions and the assimilationist pressure of the Europeans. Initially, missionaries and settlers expected Native Americans simply to forsake their traditions for European Christianity, and, as in the case of the repression of the Ghost Dance, sometimes force was used to do so. Today, many Protestant churches and Roman Catholic parishes with large tribal congregations incorporate customs such as the sacred pipe ceremony, native incenses, sweat lodges, ceremonies affirming care for the earth, and services and hymns in native languages.

Whether traditional in nature or reflecting the impact of Europeans, native people typically embrace a broad world of spirituality. While Christians, Jews, and Muslims adhere to a single deity and often confine spiritual expression to designated sites, traditional American Indian people see considerably more relevance in the whole of the world, including animals, water, and the wind.

After generations of formal and informal pressure to adopt Christian faiths and their rituals, in 1978 Congress enacted the American Indian Religious Freedom Act, which declares that it is the government's policy to "protect and preserve the inherent right of American Indians to believe, express, and practice their traditional religions." However, the act contains no penalties or enforcement mechanisms. For this reason,

Voices Listen to Our Voices Listen to

THE SCALPEL AND THE SILVER BEAR

I knew that Navajo people mistrusted Western medicine, and that Navajo customs and beliefs, even Navajo ways of interacting with others, often stood in direct opposition to the way I was trained at Stanford to deliver medical care. I wanted to make a difference in the lives of my people, not only by providing surgery to heal them but also by making it easier for them to understand, relate to, and accept Western medicine. By speaking some Navajo with them, by showing respect for their ways, and by being one of them, I could help them. I watched my patients. I listened to them. Slowly I began to develop better ways to heal them, ways that respected their culture and beliefs. I desired to incorporate these traditional beliefs and customs into my practice. . . .

Navajo patients simply didn't respond well to the brusque and distanced style of Western doctors. To them it is not acceptable to walk into a room, quickly open someone's shirt and listen to their heart with a stethoscope, or stick something in their mouth or ear. Nor is it acceptable to ask probing and personal questions. As I adapted my practice to my culture, my patients relaxed in situations that could otherwise have been highly stressful to them. As they became more comfortable and at ease, something even more remarkable—astonishing, even—happened.

Lori Arviso Alvord

When patients were trusting and accepting before surgery, their operations seemed to be more successful. If they were anxious, distrustful, and did not understand, or had resisted treatment, they seemed to have more operative or postoperative complications. Could this be happening? The more I watched, the more I saw it was indeed true. Incorporating Navajo philosophies of balance and symmetry, respect and connectedness into my practice, benefited my patients and allowed everything in my two worlds to make sense.

Navajos believe in *hózhó* or *hózhóni*—"Walking in Beauty"—a worldview in which everything in life is connected and influences everything else. A stone thrown into a pond can influence the life of a deer in the forest, a human voice and a spoken word can influence events around the world, and all things possess spirit and power. So Navajos make every effort to live in harmony and balance with everyone and everything else. Their belief system sees sickness as a result of things falling out of balance, of losing one's way on the path of beauty. In this belief system, religion and medicine are one and the same. ∎

Source: Alvord and Van Pelt 1999:13–14, 15. Excerpted from pp. 13, 14, 15 in *The Scalpel and the Silver Bear* by Lori Arviso Alvord, M.D. and Elizabeth Cohen Van Pelt. Copyright © 1999 by Lori Arviso Alvord and Elizabeth Cohen Van Pelt. Used by permission of Bantam Books, a division of Random House, Inc.

Hopi leader Vernon Masayesva (1994:93) calls it "the law with no teeth." Therefore, Native Americans are lobbying to strengthen this 1978 legislation. They are seeking protection for religious worship services for military personnel and incarcerated Native Americans, as well as better access to religious relics, such as eagle feathers, and better safeguards against the exploitation of sacred lands (Burgess 1992; Deloria 1992; Friends Committee on National Legislation 1993).

In recent years, significant publicity has been given to an old expression of religion: the ritual use of peyote, which dates back thousands of years. The sacramental use of peyote was first observed by Europeans in the 1640s. In 1918, the religious use of peyote, a plant that creates mild psychedelic effects, was organized as the Native American Church (NAC). At first a Southwest-based religion, the NAC has spread since World War II among northern tribes. The use of the substance is a small part of a long and moving ritual. The exact nature of NAC rituals varies widely. Clearly, the church maintains the tradition of ritual curing and the seeking of individual visions. However, practitioners also embrace elements of Christianity, representing a type of religious pluralism of Indian and European identities.

Peyote is a hallucinogen, however, and the government has been concerned about NAC use of it. Several states passed laws in the 1920s and 1930s prohibiting the use of peyote. In the 1980s, several court cases involved the prosecution of Native Americans who were using peyote for religious purposes. Finally, in 1994, Congress amended the American Indian Religious Freedom Act to allow Native Americans the right to use, transport, and possess peyote for religious purposes (J. Martin 2001).

Another area of spiritual concern is the stockpiling of Native American relics, including burial remains. Contemporary Native Americans are increasingly seeking the return of their ancestors' remains and artifacts, a demand that alarms museums and archeologists. The Native American Graves Protection and Repatriation Act of 1990 requires an inventory of such collections and provides for the return of materials if a claim can be substantiated. Many scholars believe the ancient bones and burial artifacts to be valuable clues to humanity's past. In part, however, this belief reflects a difference in cultural traditions. Western scientists have been dissecting cadavers for hundreds of years, but many tribes believe that disturbing the graves of ancestors will bring spiritual sickness to the living.

Today's Native Americans are asking that their traditions be recognized as an expression of pluralist rather than assimilationist coexistence. These traditions are also closely tied to religion. The sacred sites of Native Americans, as well as their religious practices, have been under attack. In the next section, we will focus on aspects of environmental disputes that are anchored in the spiritualism of Native Americans (Kinzer 2000; Mihesuah 2000).

Environment

Environmental issues bring together many of the concerns we have previously considered surrounding Native Americans: land rights, environmental justice, economic development, and spiritualism.

Efforts to keep sacred sites holy are difficult when they become popular tourist attractions, such as Devil's Tower National Monument in Wyoming.

First, we can find in some of today's environmental literature stereotypes of native peoples as the last defense against the encroachment of "civilization." This image tends to trivialize native cultures, making them into what one author called a "New Age savage" (Waller 1996).

Second, many environmental issues are rooted in continuing land disputes arising from treaties and agreements more than a century old. Reservations contain a wealth of natural resources and scenic beauty. In the past, Native Americans often lacked the technical knowledge to negotiate beneficial agreements with private corporations, and when they did have this ability, the federal government often stepped in and made the final agreements more beneficial to the non-Native Americans than to the residents of the reservations. The native peoples have always been rooted in their land. It was their land that became the first source of tension and conflict with the Europeans. At the beginning of the 21st century, it is not surprising that land and the natural resources it holds continue to be major concerns. In 1967, the Council of Energy Resource Tribes (CERT) was formed by the leaders of 25 of the West's largest tribes. This new council reasoned that by organizing together it could ensure more revenue from the tribes' vast mineral resources. CERT, which in 2004 represented 48 tribes in the United States and 4 in Canada, has provided numerous services to tribes. Working with consultants, CERT helps them develop their resources by marketing natural gas more effectively and dealing with deregulation of utilities (Archuleta 1998; CERT 2004).

Third, environmental issues reinforce the tendency to treat the first inhabitants of the Americas as inferior. This is manifested in **environmental justice**—a term introduced in Chapter 3 describing efforts to ensure that hazardous substances are controlled so that all communities receive protection regardless of race or socioeconomic circumstances. Reservation representatives often express concern about how their lands are used as dumping grounds. For example, the Navajo reservation is home to almost 1,100 abandoned uranium mines. After legal action, the federal government finally provided assistance in 2000 to Navajos who had worked in the mines and were showing ill effects from radiation exposure. Although compensation has been less than was felt necessary, the Navajos continue to monitor closely new proposals to use their land. Few reservations have escaped negative environmental impact, and some observers contend that Native American lands are targeted for nuclear waste storage. Critics see this as a de facto policy of nuclear colonialism, whereby reservations are forced to accept all the hazards of nuclear energy, but the Native American people have seen few of its benefits (B. Daitz 2003).

Fourth, environmental concerns by American Indians often are balanced against economic development needs, just as they are in the larger society. On some reservations, authorization by timber companies to access hardwood forests led to very conflicted feelings among American Indians. However, such arrangements often are the only realistic source of needed revenue, even if they mean entering into arrangements that more affluent people would never consider. The Skull Valley Goshote tribe of Utah has tried to attract a nuclear waste dump over state government objections. Even on the Navajo reservation, a proposed new uranium mine has its supporters, those who consider the promises of royalty payments coupled with alleged safety measures sufficient to offset the past half-century of radiation problems (Gorman 2002; Associated Press).

Fifth, spiritual needs must be balanced against demands on the environment. For example, numerous sacred sites lie in such public areas as the Grand Canyon, Zion, and Canyonlands National Parks that, though not publicized, are accessible to outsiders. Tribal groups have sought vainly to restrict entry to such sites. The San Carlos Apaches unsuccessfully tried to block the University of Arizona from erecting an observatory on their sacred Mt. Graham. Similarly, Plains Indians have sought to ban tourists from climbing Devil's Tower, long the site of religious visions, where prayer bundles of tobacco and sage were left behind by native peoples (Martin 2001).

environmental justice
Efforts to ensure that hazardous substances are controlled so that all communities receive protection regardless of race or socioeconomic circumstances.

Conclusion

Do Native Americans have to choose between assimilating to the dominant White culture and maintaining their identity? In Figure 6.4 we revisit the continuum of intergroup relations as it relates to Native Americans. Recently there is evidence of pluralism, but the desire to improve themselves economically usually drives them toward assimilation.

It is not easy to maintain one's tribal identity outside a reservation. One has to consciously seek out one's cultural heritage amid the pressure to assimilate. Even on a reservation, it is not easy to integrate being Native American with elements of contemporary society. The dominant society needs innovative approaches to facilitate pluralism.

The reservations are economically depressed, but they are also the home of the Native American people ideologically, if not always physically. Furthermore, the reservation's isolation means that the frustrations of reservation life and the violent outbursts against them do not alarm large numbers of Whites, as do disturbances in urban centers. Native Americans today, except in motion pictures, are out of sight and out of mind. Since the BIA was created in 1824, the federal government has had much greater control over Native Americans than over any other civilian group in the nation. For Native Americans, the federal government and White people are virtually synonymous. However, the typical White tends to be more sympathetic, if not paternalistic, toward Native Americans than toward African Americans.

Subordinate groups in the United States, including Native Americans, have made tremendous gains and will continue to do so in the years to come. But the rest of the population is not standing still. As Native American income rises, so does White income. As Native American children stay in school longer, so do White children. American Indian health care improves, but so does White health care. Advances have been made, but the gap remains between the descendants of the first Americans and those of later arrivals. Low

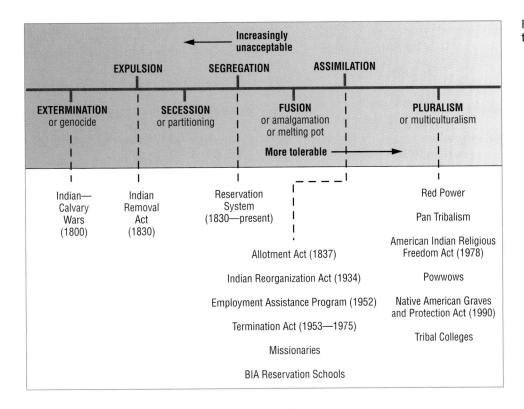

FIGURE 6.4 Intergroup Relations Continuum

incomes, inadequate education, and poor health care spurred relations between Native Americans and Whites to take a dramatic turn in the 1960s and 1970s, when Native Americans demanded a better life in America.

As Chapter 7 will show, African Americans have achieved a measure of recognition in Washington, D.C., that Native Americans have not. Only 5 percent as numerous as the Black population, Native Americans have a weaker collective voice. Only a handful of Native Americans have ever served in Congress, and many of the Whites representing states with large numbers of Native Americans have emerged as their biggest foes rather than their advocates.

The greatest challenge to and asset of the descendants of the first Americans is their land. Although it is only a small slice of what they once occupied, the land they still possess is an important asset. It is barren and largely unproductive agriculturally, but some of it is unspoiled and often rich in natural resources. No wonder many large businesses, land developers, environmentalists, and casino managers covet their land for their own purposes. For Native Americans, the land they still occupy, as well as much of that occupied by other Americans, represents their roots, their homeland.

One Thanksgiving Day, a scholar noted that, according to tradition, at the first Thanksgiving in 1621 the Pilgrims and the Wampanoag ate together. The descendants of these celebrants increasingly sit at distant tables with equally distant thoughts of equality. Today's Native Americans are the "most undernourished, most short-lived, least educated, least healthy." For them, "that long ago Thanksgiving was not a milestone, not a promise. It was the last full meal" (Dorris 1988: A23).

Key Terms

crossover effect 172	kickouts or pushouts 172	setoffs 160
environmental justice 178	millenarian movements 155	sovereignty 166
fish-ins 163	pan-Indianism 162	world systems theory 153
internal colonialism 156	powwows 165	

Review Questions

1. Why are sports team mascots such a burning issue for many Native Americans?

2. How have land rights been a continuing theme in White–Native American contact?

3. How much are Native Americans expected to shed their cultural heritage to become a part of contemporary society?

4. Do casinos and other gaming outlets represent a positive force for Native American tribes today?

5. What challenges are there to reservation residents receiving effective health care?

Critical Thinking

1. Consider Independence Day and Thanksgiving. How do these national holidays remind Native Americans today of their marginal status?

2. Chronicle how aspects of leisure time from schoolyard games to Halloween costumes to team mascots trivialize Native Americans. What experience have you had with such episodes or seen in the mass media?

3. Why do you think that many people in the United States hold more benevolent attitudes toward Native Americans than they do toward such other subordinate groups as African Americans and Latinos?

Internet Connections—Research Navigator™

 Follow the instructions found on page 31 of this text to access the features of Research Navigator™. Once at the Web site, enter your Login Name and Password. Then, to use the ContentSelect database, enter keywords such as "Trail of Tears," "Navajo," and "American Indian medicine," and the research engine will supply relevant and recent scholarly and popular press publications. Use the *New York Times* Search-by-Subject Archive to find recent news articles related to sociology, and the Link Library feature to locate relevant Web links organized by the key terms associated with this chapter.

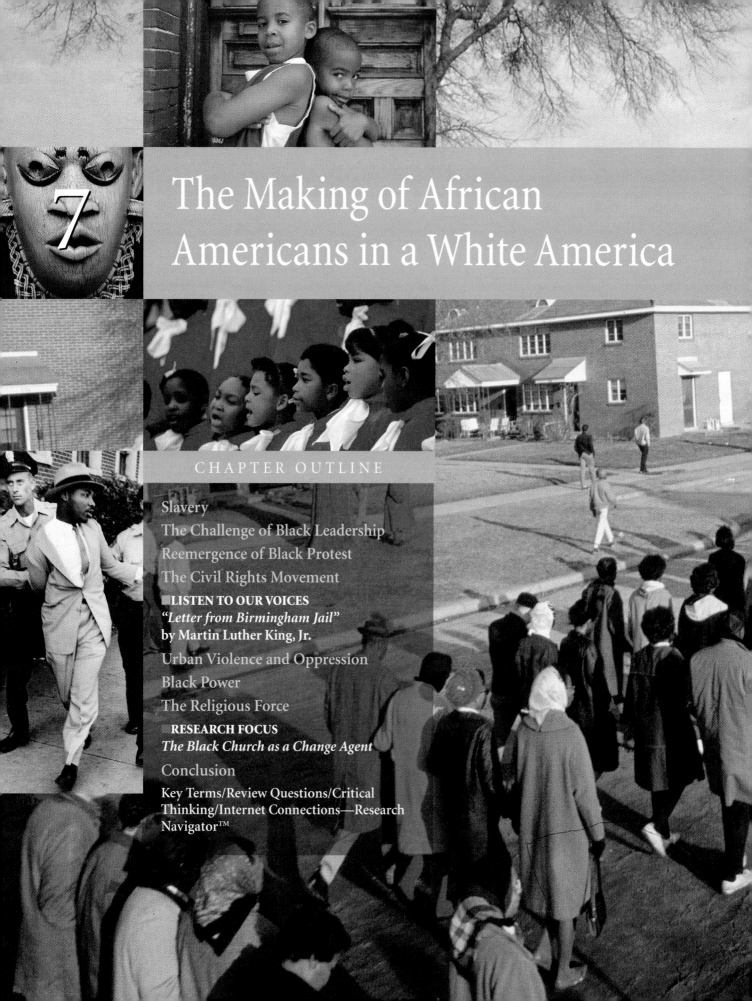

7 The Making of African Americans in a White America

THE AFRICAN PRESENCE IN THE UNITED STATES BEGAN almost simultaneously with permanent White settlement. Unlike most Europeans, however, the African people were brought involuntarily and in bondage. The end of slavery heralded new political rights during Reconstruction, but this was a short-lived era of dignity. Despite advocacy of nonviolence by leaders such as the Reverend Martin Luther King, Jr., the civil rights movement met violent resistance throughout the South. In the mid-1960s, the nation's attention was diverted to urban violence in the North and the West. Blacks responded to their relative deprivation and rising expectations by advocating Black Power, which in turn met with White resistance. While African Americans have made significant gains, the gap between Blacks and Whites remains remarkably unchanged in the last half century. Religion was and continues to be a major force in the African American community.

In 2003, the City Council of Zephyrhills, a community of 11,000 35 miles northeast of Tampa, Florida, voted to rename a street in honor of Martin Luther King, Jr. In taking this step they joined company with about 650 other cities in 41 states that have renamed streets in honor of the civil rights worker. While a few responded to the creation of Martin Luther King, Jr. Avenue with pleasure, the city council was unprepared for the strong protest that accompanied their decision. Protests became more vocal over the action, with critics saying they did not want to have to change their address. Observers noticed that all the townspeople who spoke against the policy were White, and most of the supporters were African American. In May, the council reversed itself and King Avenue became again Sixth Avenue. This is not the story of just one town, because this has occurred again. Efforts to recognize significant figures in African American history have often been controversial. The people of San Diego were so incensed about renaming a street after Martin Luther King Jr. that they successfully got the issue on the ballot in 1987 and had the old name restored. The people of Muncie, Indiana in 2003 defeated the idea of renaming a street after the slain civil rights leader, and similarly in Portsmouth, New Hampshire, the suggestion to name a city park after King did not succeed (S. Myers 2004).

Relationships between Whites and Blacks in the United States have been marked by many episodes like these, sometimes a step backward and occasionally a step forward.

CD-ROM *Activity 6.2*

The United States, with more than 38 million Blacks, has the eighth-largest Black population in the world; only Brazil, Congo, Ethiopia, Nigeria, South Africa, Sudan, and Tanzania have larger Black populations. Despite their large numbers, Blacks in this country have had almost no role in major national and political decisions and have been allowed only a peripheral role in many crucial decisions that influenced their own destiny.

The history of African Americans is, to a significant degree, the history of the United States. Black people accompanied the first explorers, and a Black man was among the first to die in the American Revolution. The enslavement of Africans was responsible for the South's wealth in the 19th century and led to the country's most violent domestic strife. After Blacks were freed from slavery, their continued subordination led to sporadic outbreaks of violence in the rural South and throughout urban America. This chapter concentrates on the history of African Americans into the 1990s. Their contemporary situation is the subject of Chapter 8.

As with European immigrants described in Chapter 4, Black Africans brought with them a variety of cultural traditions. As illustrated in Figure 7.1, although most of the people brought forcibly to North America from Africa came from a limited geographic area of the African continent, they represented diverse cultural experiences. Today, we rarely remember these tribal or ethnic variations among the descendants of the Africans in the way we customarily do among Europeans.

The Black experience in what came to be the United States began as something less than citizenship, yet slightly better than slavery. In 1619, 20 Africans arrived in Jamestown as indentured servants. Their children were born free people. These Blacks in the British colonies were not the first in the New World, however; some Blacks had accompanied European explorers, perhaps even Columbus. But all this is a historical footnote. By the 1660s, the British colonies had passed laws making Africans slaves for life, forbidding interracial marriages, and making children of slaves bear the status of their mother regardless of their father's race. Slavery had begun in North America; more than three centuries later we still live with its legacy.

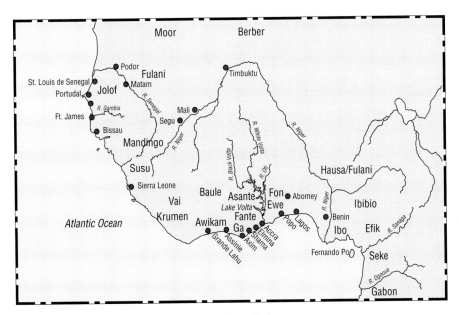

FIGURE 7.1   West African Tribal Groups During Slave Trade

Most Africans who were forcibly brought to the United States came from a limited area of Africa but brought with them a rich variety of cultural traditions, as reflected on this map.

Source: From *Historical and Cultural Atlas of African Americans* by Molefi K. Asante and Mark T. Mattson. Copyright © 1992 by Macmillan Library Reference. Reprinted by permission of The Gale Group.

Slavery

Slavery seems far removed from the debates over issues that divide Whites and Blacks today. However, both contemporary institutional and individual racism, which are central to today's conflicts, have their origins in the institution of slavery. Slavery was not merely a single aspect of American society for three centuries; it has been an essential part of our country's life. For nearly half of this country's history, slavery was not only tolerated but legally protected by the U.S. Constitution as interpreted by the U.S. Supreme Court.

In sharp contrast to the basic rights and privileges enjoyed by White Americans, Black people in bondage lived under a system of repression and terror. Nearly one out five people were Black and enslaved in the United States (see Table 7.1). Because the institution of slavery was so fundamental to our culture, it continues to influence Black-White relations as we begin the 21st century.

Slave Codes

Slavery in the United States rested on five central conditions: Slavery was for life, the status was inherited, slaves were considered mere property, slaves were denied rights, and coercion was used to maintain the system (Noel 1972). As slavery developed in colonial America and the United States, so did **slave codes**, laws that defined the low position of slaves in the United States. Although the rules varied from state to state and from time to time and were not always enforced, the more common features demonstrate how completely subjugated the Africans were:

1. A slave could not marry or even meet with a free Black.
2. Marriage between slaves was not legally recognized.

slave codes
Laws that defined the low position held by slaves in the United States.

3. A slave could not legally buy or sell anything except by special arrangement.

4. A slave could not possess weapons or liquor.

5. A slave could not quarrel with or use abusive language toward Whites.

6. A slave could not possess property (including money), except as allowed by his or her owner.

7. A slave could make no will, nor could he or she inherit anything.

8. A slave could not make a contract or hire himself or herself out.

9. A slave could not leave a plantation without a pass noting his or her destination and time of return.

10. No one, including Whites, was to teach a slave (and in some areas even a free Black) to read or write or to give a slave a book, including the Bible.

11. A slave could not gamble.

12. A slave had to obey established curfews.

13. A slave could not testify in court except against another slave.

Violations of these rules were dealt with in a variety of ways. Mutilation and branding were not unknown. Imprisonment was rare; most violators were whipped. An owner was largely immune from prosecution for any physical abuse of slaves. Because slaves could not testify in court, a White's actions toward enslaved African Americans were practically above the law (ACLU 1996b; Elkins 1959; Franklin and Moss 2000; Stampp 1956).

Slavery, as enforced through the slave codes, controlled and determined all facets of the lives of the enslaved Africans. The organization of family life and religious worship were no exceptions. Naturally, the Africans had brought to America their own cultural traditions. In Africa, people had been accustomed to a closely regulated family life and a rigidly enforced moral code. Slavery rendered it impossible for them to retain these family ties in the New World.

TABLE 7.1
Black Population, 1790–2050

Blacks accounted for a decreasing proportion of the total population until the 1940s, primarily because White immigration to the United States far outdistanced population growth by Blacks.

Census	Black Population (in thousands)	Black Percentage (of Total Population)
1790	757	19.3
1810	1,378	19.0
1830	2,329	18.1
1850	3,639	15.7
1870	4,880	12.7
1890	7,489	11.9
1910	9,828	10.7
1930	11,891	9.7
1950	15,042	10.0
1970	22,580	11.1
1990	29,986	12.1
2000	35,818	12.7
2050 (projection)	61,361	14.6

Source: Bureau of the Census 2002b, 2004b, 2004c.

The slave family had no standing in law. Marriages between slaves were not legally recognized, and masters rarely respected them in selling adults or children. Slave breeding—a deliberate effort to maximize the number of offspring—was practiced with little attention to the emotional needs of the slaves themselves. The slaveholder, not the parents, decided at what age children should begin working in the fields. The slave family could not offer its children shelter or security, rewards or punishments. The man's only recognized family role was that of siring offspring, being the sex partner of a woman. In fact, slave men often were identified as if they were the woman's possession, for example, as "Nancy's Tom." Southern law consistently ruled that "the father of a slave is unknown to our law." This does not imply that the male slave did not occupy an important economic role. Men held almost all the managerial positions open to slaves (Du Bois 1970; Stampp 1956).

Unlike the family structure, to which slavery dealt near-mortal blows, a strong religious tradition survived. In fact, a slaveholder wanting to do "God's work on Earth" would encourage the slave church, finding it functional in dominating the slaves. Of course, African religions were forbidden, and the White people's Christianity flourished, but Blacks still used West African concepts in the new way of life that slavery brought. The preacher maintained an intense relationship with the congregation, similar to the role played by the elder in West Africa. The Christianity to which the slaves were introduced stressed obeying their owner. Complete surrender to Whites meant salvation and eternal happiness in the hereafter. In contrast, to question God's will or to fight slavery caused everlasting damnation. Obviously, this twisted version of Christianity was intended to make slaves acquiesce to their holders' wishes in return for reward after death. To some degree, however, religion did keep the desire for freedom alive in slaves, and to some extent it formed the basis of their struggle for freedom: Nightly prayer meetings and singing gave them a sense of unity and common destiny necessary for that struggle. On a more personal level, religion made the slaves' daily lives more bearable (Frazier 1964; Rawick 1972; Stampp 1956).

African Americans and Africa

The importance of Africa to Black Americans can be seen in the aspects of African culture that became integral parts of Blacks' lives in the United States. This importance was recognized long before the emergence of the Afrocentric perspective in the 1990s. Black scholars W. E. B. Du Bois (1939) and Carter Woodson (1968) and respected White anthropologist Melville Herskovits (1930, 1941) have all argued persuasively for the continued influence of the African heritage.

Scholars debate to what degree African culture was able to persist despite efforts by slaveholders to replace any vestige of African tradition. The survival of African culture can be most easily documented in folklore, religion, language, and music. It is difficult to clarify the degree of survival, however, because Africans came from many different cultures. When we think of ethnic origins, our thoughts turn to European groups such as Poles or Greeks, but within Africa are the Ibos, Gas, and Yorubas, to name a few of the sources of slaves from Africa (see Figure 7.1). Thus, to speak of a single source of African culture ignores the complexity of social life on that continent. Furthermore, as the Afrocentric perspective argues, some aspects of African culture, such as certain art forms, have so permeated Western culture that we mistakenly believe their origins are European.

Africa has had and will always have an importance to Blacks that many Blacks and most Whites do not appreciate, and this importance is unlikely to be changed by the continued debate over which aspects of Black life today can be traced back to African culture. The significance of Africa to Black Americans is one of the most easily identifiable themes in the Black experience. During certain periods (the 1920s and the late

For many generations, Africans were treated by their White slave owners as property, with none of the rights extended to people. Pictured is a slave auction in Richmond, Virginia, in 1861.

1960s), the Black cultural tradition was the rallying point of many Blacks, especially those living in the cities. Studies continue to document the survival of African culture in North America.

Research has identified remnants of grammar and sentence construction in the speech patterns of low-income and rural Blacks. **Ebonics** is the distinctive dialect, with a complex language structure, that is found among Black Americans. Although the term *Ebonics* (*ebony* and *phonics*) was coined in the 1970s, there has long been a recognition of a distinctive language pattern, sometimes called "Black English," that includes some vocabulary and grammar rules that reflect the West African origins of Black Americans. In 1996, Ebonics became a national issue after the Oakland, California, school board's recognition of it as the primary language of schoolchildren who were then learning mainstream American English. This debate aside, there is consensus that, a century after slavery, remnants of African cultural traditions survive (Applebome 1997).

The Attack On Slavery

Although the slave was vulnerable to his or her owner's wishes, slavery as an institution was vulnerable to outside opinion. For a generation after the American Revolution, restrictions on slaves increased as Southerners accepted slavery as permanent. Slave revolts and antislavery propaganda only accelerated the intensity of oppression. This change led to the ironic situation that as slavery was attacked from within and without, its conditions became harsher and its defenders became more outspoken in asserting what they saw as its benefits.

Antislavery advocates, or **abolitionists**, included both Whites and free Blacks. Many Whites who opposed slavery, such as Abraham Lincoln, did not believe in racial equality. In their minds, even though slavery was a moral evil, racial equality was still unimaginable. This apparent inconsistency did not lessen the emotional fervor of the efforts to end slavery. Antislavery societies had been founded even before the American Revolution, but the Constitution dealt the antislavery movement a blow. To appease the South, the framers of the Constitution recognized and legitimized slavery's existence. The Constitution even allowed slavery to increase Southern political power. A slave was counted as three-fifths of a person in determining population representation in the House of Representatives.

Abolitionists, both Black and White, continued to speak out against slavery and the harm it was doing not only to the slaves but to the entire nation, which had become economically dependent on bondage. Frederick Douglass and Sojourner Truth, both

Ebonics
Distinctive dialect with a complex language structure found among many Black Americans.

abolitionists
Whites and free Blacks who favored the end of slavery.

freed slaves, became very visible in the fight against slavery through their eloquent speeches and publications. Harriet Tubman, along with other Blacks and sympathetic Whites, developed the Underground Railroad to convey escaping slaves to freedom in the North and Canada (Franklin and Moss 2000).

Another aspect of Black enslavement was the slaves' own resistance to servitude. Slaves did revolt, and between 40,000 and 100,000 actually escaped from the South and slavery. Yet fugitive slave acts provided for the return even of slaves who had reached free states. Enslaved Blacks who did not attempt escape, at least in part because failure often led to death, resisted slavery through such means as passive resistance. Slaves feigned clumsiness or illness; pretended not to understand, see, or hear; ridiculed Whites with a mocking, subtle humor that their owners did not comprehend; and destroyed farm implements and committed similar acts of sabotage (Bauer and Bauer 1942; L. Bennett 1966; Oakes 1993).

Slavery's Aftermath

On January 1, 1863, President Lincoln issued the Emancipation Proclamation. The document created hope in slaves in the South, but many Union soldiers resigned rather than participate in a struggle to free slaves. The proclamation freed slaves only in the Confederacy, over which the president had no control. Six months after the surrender of the Confederacy in 1865, abolition became law when the Thirteenth Amendment abolished slavery throughout the nation.

From 1867 to 1877, during the period called Reconstruction, Black-White relations in the South were unlike anything they had ever been. The Reconstruction Act of 1867 put each Southern state under a military governor until a new state constitution could be written, with Blacks participating fully in the process. Whites and Blacks married each other, went to public schools and state universities together, and rode side by side on trains and streetcars. The most conspicuous evidence of the new position of Blacks was their presence in elected office. In 1870, the Fifteenth Amendment was ratified, prohibiting the denial of the right to vote on grounds of race, color, or previous condition of servitude. Black men put their vote to good use; Blacks were elected as 6 lieutenant governors, 16 major state officials, 20 members of the House of Representatives, and 2 U.S. senators. Despite accusations that they were corrupt, Black officials and Black-dominated legislatures created new and progressive state constitutions. Black political organizations, such as the Union League and the Loyal League, rivaled the church as the focus of community organization (Berlin 1998; Berlin et al. 1998; Du Bois 1969b).

Reconstruction was ended as part of a political compromise in the election of 1876 and, consequently, segregation became entrenched in the South. Evidence of Jim Crow's reign was apparent by the close of the 19th century. The term **Jim Crow** appears to have its origin in a dance tune, but by the 1890s it was synonymous with segregation and referred to the statutes that kept African Americans in an inferior position. Segregation often preceded Jim Crow laws and in practice often went beyond their provisions. The institutionalization of segregation gave White supremacy its ultimate authority. In 1896, the U.S. Supreme Court ruled in *Plessy v. Ferguson* that state laws requiring "separate but equal" accommodations for Blacks were a "reasonable" use of state government power (L. Bennett 1966; C. Woodward 1974).

It was in the political sphere that Jim Crow exacted its price soonest. In 1898, the Court's decision in *Williams v. Mississippi* declared constitutional the use of poll taxes, literacy tests, and residential requirements to discourage Blacks from voting. In Louisiana that year, 130,000 Blacks were registered to vote. Eight years later only 1,342 were. Even all these measures did not deprive all African Americans of the vote, and so White supremacists erected a final obstacle: the **White primary**, which forbade Black voting in election primaries. By the turn of the century, the South had a

19th Cent.

Jim Crow
Southern laws passed in the late 19th century that kept Blacks in their subordinate position.

White primary
Legal provisions forbidding Black voting in election primaries, which in one-party areas of the South effectively denied Blacks their right to select elected officials.

slavery reparations
Act of making amends for the injustices of slavery.

one-party system, making the primary the significant contest and the general election a mere rubber stamp. Beginning with South Carolina in 1896 and spreading to 12 other states within 20 years, statewide Democratic party primaries were adopted. The party explicitly excluded Blacks from voting, an exclusion that was constitutional because the party was defined as a private organization that was free to define its own membership qualifications. The White primary brought an end to the political gains of Reconstruction (Lacy 1972; Lewinson 1965; C. Woodward 1974).

Reparations for Slavery

The legacy of slavery lives on more than 150 years after its end in the United States. We can see it in the nation's Capitol and the White House, which were built with slave labor, but we can also see it in the enduring poverty that grips a large proportion of the descendants of slavery.

For more than 30 years, there has been serious discussion about granting reparations for slavery. **Slavery reparations** refers to the act of making amends for the injustice of slavery. Few would argue that slavery was wrong and continues to be wrong where it is practiced in parts of the world even today. However, what form should the reparation take? Since 1989, Congressman John Conyers, a Black Democrat from Detroit, has annually introduced in Congress a bill to acknowledge the "fundamental injustice, cruelty, brutality, and inhumanity of slavery" and calls for the creation of a commission to examine the institution and to make recommendations on appropriate remedies. This bill has never made it out of committee, but the discussion continues outside the federal government.

There has not been an official government apology for slavery even though the U.S. government has apologized for injustices to the American Indians and to the Japanese Americans placed in internment camps during World War II. The absence of an official apology angers many African Americans today and those sympathetic to the reparation issue, but the true controversy surrounds what form a remedy should take. Should the government develop and fund some major program to assist the African American community? Should there be direct payments to all African Americans or

Source: By permission of Mike Luckovich and Creators Syndicate, Inc.

Within all racial and ethnic groups, celebrations emerge to reflect their distinctive experience. The annual Juneteenth celebration is spreading across the United States and marks the anniversary of the emancipation of the slaves in Texas on June 19, 1865.

These people could not afford this process.

only to people who can prove that they are descended from enslaved people? Each of these possibilities raises a variety of questions about fairness and equity, but many object in principle to giving any money to people who themselves were not enslaved.

Beginning in the late 1990s, legal researchers raised yet another issue as documentation emerged that private companies that still exist today benefited from slavery. Although it is not too difficult to see how much of the plantation economy of the South was built on enslaved people, the corporate profits from slavery go well beyond the cotton fields. The railroad industry depended heavily on slave labor for construction of railway systems still in use today. Insurance companies even in the North during slavery collected a substantial number of insurance premiums from slaveholders who insured their slaves, much as they would other forms of property. Proponents of slavery reparations argue that these companies owe payments to today's descendants similar to efforts to get payments from German companies that profited from the Jewish Holocaust during World War II.

Good point

Government policy makers, for the most part, have not been willing to endorse the concept of slave reparations in any way. A few cities and California have adopted resolutions to explore the issue, but the federal government has not acted. A national survey taken in 2002 showed that only a third of Whites and two-thirds of African Americans feel that corporations that benefited from slavery should even make an apology, although some, such as Aetna Insurance, have already done so. Attitudes are clearly divided along racial lines on government cash payments: only 6 percent of Whites and 55 percent of Black Americans endorse some kind of cash payment to the descendants of slaves. Although it may be futile to try to put a price on the cost of slavery, most African Americans and some other citizens are disappointed by the unwillingness to debate the issue in Washington, D.C. (Conley 2002; Cox 2002; Dawson and Popoff 2004; Salzberger and Turck 2004; Williams and Collins 2004).

The Challenge of Black Leadership

The institutionalization of White supremacy precipitated different responses from African Americans, just as slavery had. In the late 1800s and early 1900s, a number of articulate Blacks attempted to lead the first generation of freeborn Black Americans. Most prominent were Booker T. Washington and W. E. B. Du Bois. The personalities and ideas of these two men contrasted with one another. Washington was born a slave in 1856 on a Virginia plantation. He worked in coal mines after emancipation and attended elementary school. Through hard work and driving ambition, Washington became the head of an educational institute for Blacks in Tuskegee, Alabama. Within 15 years, his leadership brought the Tuskegee Institute national recognition and made him a national figure. Du Bois, on the other hand, was born in 1868 of a free family in Massachusetts. He attended Fisk University and the University of Berlin and became the first Black to receive a doctorate from Harvard. Washington died in 1915, and Du Bois died in self-imposed exile in Africa in 1963.

The Politics of Accommodation

Booker T. Washington's approach to White supremacy is called the politics of accommodation. He was willing to forgo social equality until White people saw Blacks as deserving of it. Perhaps his most famous speech was made in Atlanta on September 18, 1895, to an audience that was mostly White and mostly wealthy. Introduced by the governor of Georgia as "a representative of Negro enterprise and Negro civilization," Washington (1900:221) gave a five-minute speech in which he pledged the continued dedication of Blacks to Whites:

> *As we have proved our loyalty to you in the past, in nursing your children, watching by the sick-bed of your mothers and fathers, and often following them with tear-dimmed eyes to their graves, so in the future, in our humble way, we shall stand by you with a devotion that no foreigner can approach, ready to lay down our lives, if need be, in defense of yours.*

The speech catapulted Washington into the public forum, and he became the anointed spokesperson for Blacks for the next 20 years. President Grover Cleveland congratulated Washington for the "new hope" he gave Blacks. Washington's essential theme was compromise. Unlike Frederick Douglass, who had demanded the same rights for Blacks as for Whites, Washington asked that Blacks be educated because it would be a wise investment for Whites. He called racial hatred "the great and intricate problem which God has laid at the doors of the South." The Blacks' goal should be economic respectability. Washington's accommodating attitude ensured his popularity with Whites. His recognition by Whites contributed to his large following of Blacks, who were not used to seeing their leaders achieve fame among Whites (Hawkins 1962; R. Logan 1954; Pinkney 2000).

It is easy in retrospect to be critical of Washington and to write him off as simply a product of his times. Booker T. Washington entered the public arena when the more militant proposals of Douglass had been buried. Black politicians were losing political contests and influence. To become influential as a Black, Washington reasoned, required White acceptance. His image as an accommodator allowed him to fight discrimination covertly. He assisted Presidents Roosevelt and Taft in appointing Blacks to patronage positions. Washington's goal was for African Americans eventually to have the same rights and opportunities as Whites. Just as people disagree with leaders today, some Blacks disagreed over the means that Washington chose to reach that goal. No African American was more outspoken in his criticism of the politics of accommodation than W. E. B. Du Bois (Conyers 1996; Harlan 1972; Hawkins 1962; Meier and Rudwick 1966).

The Niagara Movement

The rivalry between Washington and Du Bois has been exaggerated. Actually, they enjoyed fairly cordial relations for some time. In 1900, Washington recommended Du Bois, at his request, for superintendent of Black schools in Washington, D.C. By 1905, however, relations between the two had cooled. Du Bois spoke critically of Washington's influence, arguing that his power was being used to stifle African Americans who spoke out against the politics of accommodation. He also charged that Washington

Pictured is a 1935 lynching in Ft. Lauderdale of Rubin Stacy, an African American who had been charged with "threatening and frightening" a White woman. Note the reaction of some of the onlookers. Over 3,000 Blacks were executed by lynching between 1889 and 1938.

had caused the transfer of funds from academic programs to vocational education. Du Bois's greatest objection to Washington's statements was that they encouraged Whites to place the burden of the Blacks' problems on the Blacks themselves (Du Bois 1961; Hawkins 1962).

As an alternative to Washington's program, Du Bois (1903) advocated the theory of the talented tenth, which reflected his atypical educational background. Unlike Washington, Du Bois was not at home with both intellectuals and sharecroppers. Although the very words *talented tenth* have an elitist ring to them, Du Bois argued that these privileged Blacks must serve the other nine-tenths. This argument was also Du Bois's way of criticizing Washington's emphasis on vocational education. He thought education for African Americans should emphasize academics, which would be more likely to improve their position. Drawing on the talented tenth, Du Bois invited 29 Blacks to participate in a strategy session near Niagara Falls in 1905. Out of a series of meetings came several demands that unmistakably placed the responsibility for the problems facing African Americans on the shoulders of Whites.

The Niagara Movement, as it came to be called, was closely monitored by Booker T. Washington. Du Bois encountered difficulty gaining financial support and recruiting prominent people, and Du Bois (1968:303) himself wrote, "My leadership was solely of ideas. I never was, nor ever will be, personally popular." The movement's legacy was the education of a new generation of African Americans in the politics of protest. After 1910, the Niagara Movement ceased to hold annual conventions. In 1909, however, the National Association for the Advancement of Colored People (NAACP), with White and Black members, was founded by the Niagara Movement leaders. It was through the work of the NAACP that the Niagara Movement accomplished most of the goals set forth in 1905. The NAACP also marked the merging of White liberalism and Black militancy, a coalition unknown since the end of the abolition movement and Reconstruction (L. Bennett 1966; Conyers 1996; Rudwick 1957).

CD-ROM *Activity 6.3*

In 1900, 90 percent of African Americans lived in the South. Blacks moved out of the South and into the West and North, especially the urban areas in those regions, during the post-Civil War period, and continued to migrate through the 1950s and 1960s. By the 1980s and 1990s, a migration to the South began as job opportunities grew in that part of the country and most vestiges of Jim Crow vanished in what had been the states of the Confederacy. By 2000, 55 percent of African Americans lived in the South, compared to 33 percent of the rest of the population (Figure 7.2).

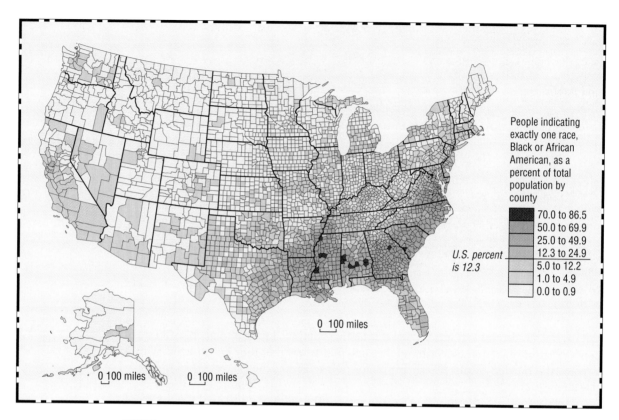

FIGURE 7.2   Black Population, 2000

Source: Bureau of the Census data map in C. Brewer and Suchan 2001.

The pattern of violence, with Blacks usually the victims, started in the South during Reconstruction and continued into the 20th century, when it also spread northward. In 1917, a riot in East St. Louis, Illinois, claimed the lives of 39 Blacks and nine Whites. The several days of violence resulted from White fear of social and economic gains made by Blacks. The summer of 1919 saw so much violence that it is commonly called the "red summer." Twenty-six riots broke out throughout the country as White soldiers who returned from World War I feared the new competition that Blacks represented. This period of violence against African Americans also saw a resurgence of the Ku Klux Klan, which at its height had nearly 9 million members (Grimshaw 1969; Schaefer 1971, 1980).

Reemergence of Black Protest

American involvement in World War II signaled improved economic conditions for both Whites and Blacks. Nearly a million African Americans served in the military in rigidly segregated units. Generally, more Blacks could participate in the armed services in World War II than in previous military engagements, but efforts by Blacks to contribute to the war effort at home were hampered by discriminatory practices in defense plants. A. Philip Randolph, president of the Brotherhood of Sleeping Car Porters, threatened to lead 100,000 Blacks in a march on Washington in 1941 to ensure their employment. Randolph's proposed tactic was nonviolent direct action, which he modeled on Mahatma Gandhi's practices in India. Randolph made it clear that he intended the march to be an all-Black event because he saw it as neither necessary nor desirable for Whites to lead Blacks to their own liberation. President Franklin Roosevelt responded to the pressure and agreed to issue an executive order prohibiting discrimination if Randolph would call off the march. Although the order and the Fair Employment Practices Commission (FEPC) it set up did not fulfill the original promises, a precedent had been established for federal intervention in job discrimination (Garfinkel 1959).

Racial turmoil during World War II was not limited to threatened marches. Racial disturbances occurred in cities throughout the country, the worst riot occurring in Detroit in June 1943. In that case, President Roosevelt sent in 6,000 soldiers to quell the violence, which left 25 Blacks and 9 Whites dead. The racial disorders were paralleled by a growth in civil disobedience as a means to achieve equality for Blacks. The Congress of Racial Equality (CORE) was founded in 1942 to fight discrimination with nonviolent direct action. This interracial group used sit-ins to open restaurants to Black patrons in Chicago, Baltimore, and Los Angeles. In 1947, CORE sent "freedom riders" to test a court ruling that prohibited segregation in interstate bus travel. In contrast to the red summer of 1919, the end of World War II was not followed by widespread racial violence, in part because the continued expansion of the postwar economy reduced competition between Whites and Blacks for employment (Grimshaw 1969; Meier and Rudwick 1966).

The war years and the postwar period saw several U.S. Supreme Court decisions that suggested the Court was moving away from tolerating racial inequities. The White primary elections endorsed in Jim Crow's formative period were finally challenged in the 1944 *Smith v. Allwright* decision. The effectiveness of the victory was limited; many states simply passed statutes that used new devices to frustrate African American voters.

A particularly repugnant legal device for relegating African Americans to second-class status was restrictive covenants. A **restrictive covenant** was a private contract entered into by neighborhood property owners stipulating that property could not be sold or rented to certain minority groups, thus ensuring that they could not live in the area. In 1948, the Supreme Court finally declared in *Shelley v. Kramer* that restrictive covenants were not constitutional, although it did not actually attack their discriminatory nature. The victory was in many ways less substantial than it was symbolic of the new willingness by the Supreme Court to uphold the rights of Black citizens.

restrictive covenants
Private contracts or agreements that discourage or prevent minority-group members from purchasing housing in a neighborhood.

In this classic Margaret Bourke-White photograph, a line of Black Americans awaits food handouts in 1937 in Louisville, Kentucky.

de jure segregation
Children assigned to schools specifically to maintain racially separated schools.

The Democratic administrations of the late 1940s and early 1950s made a number of promises to Black Americans. The party adopted a strong civil rights platform in 1948, but its provisions were not enacted. Once again, union president Randolph threatened Washington, D.C., with a march. This time he insisted that as long as Blacks were subjected to a peacetime draft, the military must be desegregated. President Truman responded by issuing an executive order on July 26, 1948, desegregating the armed forces. The U.S. Army abolished its quota system in 1950, and training camps for the Korean War were integrated. Desegregation was not complete, however, especially in the reserves and the National Guard, and even today charges of racial favoritism confront the armed forces. Whatever its shortcomings, the desegregation order offered African Americans an alternative to segregated civilian life (Moskos and Butler 1996).

The Civil Rights Movement

It is difficult to say exactly when a social movement begins or ends. Usually, a movement's ideas or tactics precede the actual mobilization of people and continue long after the movement's driving force has been replaced by new ideals and techniques. This description applies to the civil rights movement and its successor, the continuing struggle for African American freedom. Before 1954, there were some confrontations of White supremacy: the CORE sit-ins of 1942 and efforts to desegregate buses in Baton Rouge, Louisiana, in 1953. The civil rights movement gained momentum with a Supreme Court decision in 1954 that eventually desegregated the public schools, and it ended as a major force in Black America with the civil disorders of 1965 through 1968. However, beginning in 1954, toppling the traditional barriers to full rights for Blacks was the rule, not the exception.

Struggle to Desegregate the Schools

For the majority of Black children, public school education meant attending segregated schools. Southern school districts assigned children to school by race rather than by neighborhood, a practice that constituted de jure segregation. **De jure segregation** is segregation that results from children being assigned to schools specifically to maintain racially separate schools. It was this form of legal humiliation that was attacked in the landmark decree of *Linda Brown et al. v. Board of Education of Topeka, Kansas.*

The first Freedom Bus used to carry civil rights workers in Anniston, Alabama, on May 15, 1961, after Whites hurled incendiary bombs.

Seven-year-old Linda Brown was not permitted to enroll in the grade school four blocks from her home in Topeka, Kansas. Rather, school board policy dictated that she attend the Black school almost two miles away. This denial led the NAACP Legal Defense and Educational Fund to bring suit on behalf of Linda Brown and 12 other Black children. The NAACP argued that the Fourteenth Amendment was intended to rule out segregation in public schools. Chief Justice Earl Warren of the Supreme Court wrote the unanimous opinion that "in the field of public education the doctrine of 'separate but equal' has no place. Separate educational facilities are inherently unequal."

The freedom that African Americans saw in their grasp at the time of the *Brown* decision essentially amounted to a reaffirmation of American values. What Blacks sought was assimilation into White American society. The motivation for the Brown suit did not come merely because Black schools were inferior, although they were. Blacks were assigned to poorly ventilated and dilapidated buildings, with overcrowded classrooms and unqualified teachers. Less money was spent on Black schools than on White schools throughout the South in both rural and metropolitan areas. The issue was not such tangible factors, however, but the intangible effect of not being allowed to go to school with Whites. All-Black schools could not be equal to all-White schools. Even in this victory, Blacks were reaffirming White society and the importance of an integrated educational experience.

Although *Brown* marked the beginning of the civil rights movement, the reaction to it showed just how deeply prejudice was held in the South. Resistance to court-ordered desegregation took many forms: Some people called for impeachment of all the Supreme Court justices; others petitioned Congress to declare the Fourteenth Amendment unconstitutional; cities closed schools rather than comply; and the governor of Arkansas used the state's National Guard to block Black students from entering a previously all-White high school in Little Rock (Figure 7.3).

FIGURE 7.3   Major Events of the Civil Rights Movement

1963: March on Washington "I Have a Dream"

1960: Sit-in movement begins, spreads to Nashville and Atlanta

1954: Supreme Court rules on *Brown v. Board of Education;* public school segregation unconstitutional

1968: April King Assassination

1961: Freedom Ride to Mississippi meets with violence in Anniston and Montgomery

1957: Eisenhower sends federal troops to integrate Central High School

1963: SCLC demonstrates; "Letter from Birmingham Jail"

1962: James Meredith integrates University of Mississippi

1962: Martin Luther King and SCLC fail in desegregation attempt

1963: Medgar Evers assassinated

1964: Volunteers arrive for Freedom Summer

1955–56: Boycott of bus system

1965: "Bloody Sunday" and march to Montgomery

Washington, D.C. · Topeka · Nashville · Greensboro · Little Rock · Memphis · Oxford · Anniston · Atlanta · Birmingham · Jackson · Selma · Montgomery · Albany

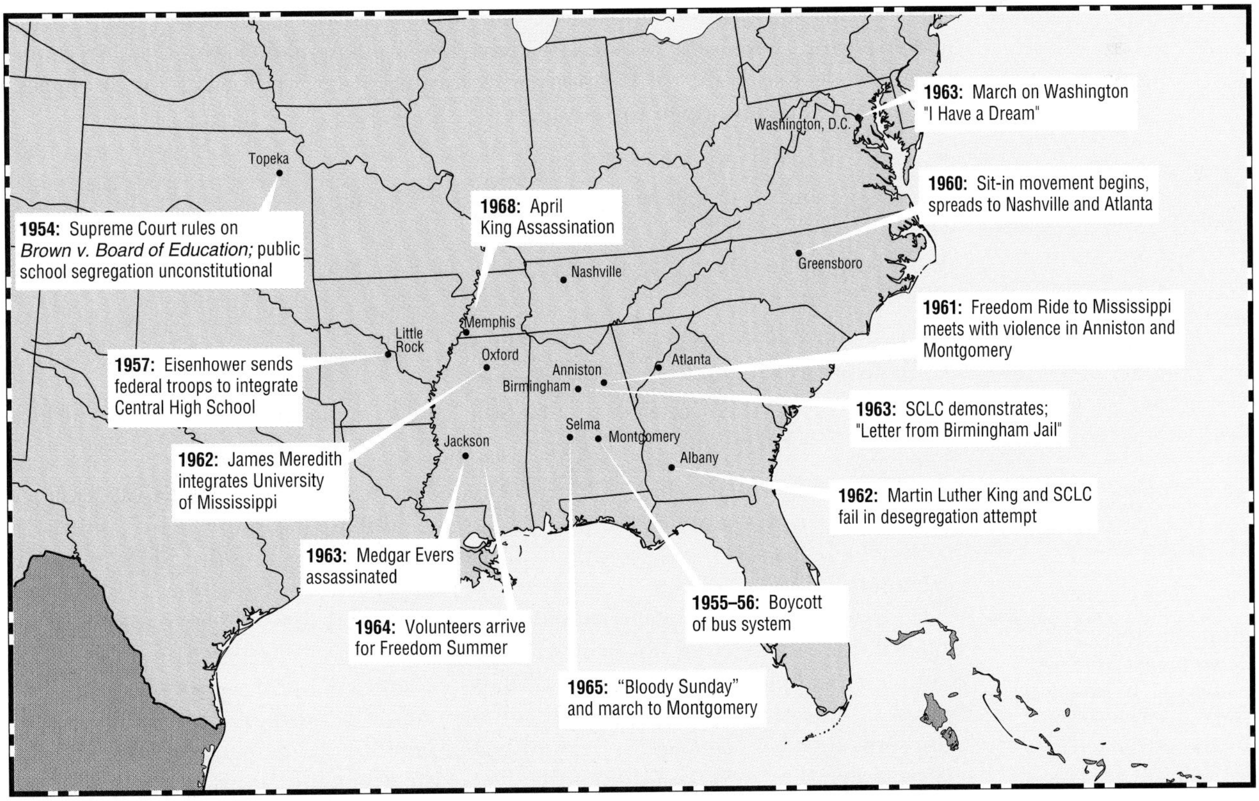

The issue of school desegregation was extended to higher education, and Mississippi state troopers and the state's National Guard confronted each other over the 1962 admission of James Meredith, the first African American accepted by the University of Mississippi. Scores were injured, and two were killed in this clash between segregationists and the law. A similar defiant stand was taken a year later by Governor George Wallace, who "stood in the schoolhouse door" to block two Blacks from enrolling in the University of Alabama. President Kennedy federalized the Alabama National Guard to guarantee admission of the students. *Brown* did not resolve the school controversy, and many questions remain unanswered. More recently, the issue of school segregation resulting from neighborhood segregation has been debated. In Chapter 8, another form of segregation, called de facto segregation, is examined more closely (Butler 1996).

Civil Disobedience

The success of a year-long boycott of city buses in Montgomery, Alabama, dealt Jim Crow another setback. On December 1, 1955, Rosa Parks defied the law and refused to give her seat on a crowded bus to a White man. Her defiance led to the organization of the Montgomery Improvement Association, headed by 26-year-old Martin Luther King, Jr., a Baptist minister with a Ph.D. from Boston University. The bus boycott was the first of many instances in which Blacks used nonviolent direct action to obtain the rights that Whites already enjoyed. The boycott eventually demanded the end of segregated seating. The *Brown* decision woke up all of America to racial injustice, but the Montgomery boycott marked a significant shift away from the historical reliance on NAACP court battles (Killian 1975).

Civil disobedience is based on the belief that people have the right to disobey the law under certain circumstances. This tactic was not new; it had been used before in India and also by Blacks in the United States. Under King's leadership, however, civil disobedience became a widely used technique and even gained a measure of acceptability among some prominent Whites. King distinguished clearly between the laws to be obeyed and those to be disobeyed: "A just law is a man-made law of God. An unjust law is a code that is out of harmony with the moral law" (1963:82). In disobeying unjust laws, King developed this strategy:

- Active nonviolent resistance to evil
- Not seeking to defeat or humiliate opponents but to win their friendship and understanding
- Attacking the forces of evil rather than the people who happen to be doing the evil
- Willingness to accept suffering without retaliating
- Refusing to hate the opponent
- Acting with the conviction that the universe is on the side of justice (1958:101–107)

King, like other Blacks before him and since, made it clear that passive acceptance of injustice was intolerable. He hoped that by emphasizing nonviolence, southern Blacks would display their hostility to racism in a way that would undercut violent reaction by Whites.

The pattern had now been established and a method devised to confront racism. But civil disobedience did not work quickly. The struggle to desegregate buses in the South, for example, took seven years. Civil disobedience was also not spontaneous. The success of the civil rights movement rested on a dense network of local efforts. People were spontaneously attracted to the efforts, but organized tactics and targets were crucial to dismantling racist institutions that had existed for generations (Payne 1995).

civil disobedience
A tactic promoted by Martin Luther King, Jr., based on the belief that people have the right to disobey unjust laws under certain circumstances.

Beginning in April 1963, the Southern Christian Leadership Conference (SCLC), founded by King, began a series of marches in Birmingham to demand fair employment opportunities, desegregation of public facilities, and the release of 3,000 people arrested for participating in the marches. King, himself arrested, tells in "Listen to Our Voices" why civil disobedience and the confrontations that followed were necessary. In May, the Birmingham police used dogs and water from high-pressure hoses on the marchers, who included many schoolchildren.

Congress had still failed to enact any sweeping federal barrier to discrimination. Following the example of A. Philip Randolph in 1941, Blacks organized the March on Washington for Jobs and Freedom on August 28, 1963. With more than 200,000

Voices Listen to Our Voices Listen to

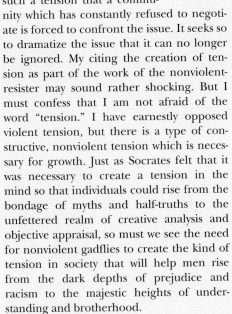

LETTER FROM BIRMINGHAM JAIL

You may well ask: "Why direct action? Why sit-ins, marches and so forth? Isn't negotiation a better path?" You are quite right in calling for negotiation. Indeed, this is the very purpose of direct action. Nonviolent direct action seeks to create such a crisis and foster such a tension that a community which has constantly refused to negotiate is forced to confront the issue. It seeks so to dramatize the issue that it can no longer be ignored. My citing the creation of tension as part of the work of the nonviolent-resister may sound rather shocking. But I must confess that I am not afraid of the word "tension." I have earnestly opposed violent tension, but there is a type of constructive, nonviolent tension which is necessary for growth. Just as Socrates felt that it was necessary to create a tension in the mind so that individuals could rise from the bondage of myths and half-truths to the unfettered realm of creative analysis and objective appraisal, so must we see the need for nonviolent gadflies to create the kind of tension in society that will help men rise from the dark depths of prejudice and racism to the majestic heights of understanding and brotherhood.

Martin Luther King, Jr.

The purpose of our direct-action program is to create a situation so crisis-packed that it will inevitably open the door to negotiation. I therefore concur with you in your call for negotiation. Too long has our beloved Southland been bogged down in a tragic effort to live in monologue rather than dialogue. . . .

You express a great deal of anxiety over our willingness to break laws. This is certainly a legitimate concern. Since we so diligently urge people to obey the Supreme Court's decision of 1954 outlawing segregation in the public schools, at first glance it may seem rather paradoxical for us consciously to break laws. One may well ask: "How can you advocate breaking some laws and obeying others?" The answer lies in the fact that there are two types of laws: just and unjust. I would be the first to advocate obeying just laws. One has not only a legal but a moral responsibility to obey just laws. Conversely, one has a moral responsibility to disobey unjust laws. I would agree with St. Augustine that "an unjust law is no law at all." ∎

Source: "Letter from Birmingham Jail," in *Why We Can't Wait,* by Martin Luther King, Jr. Copyright © 1963 by Martin Luther King, Jr. Renewed 1991 by Coretta Scott King. Reprinted by arrangement with The Estate of Martin Luther King, Jr., c/o Writer's House as agents for the proprietor.

people participating, the march was the high point of the civil rights movement. The mass of people, middle-class Whites and Blacks looking to the federal government for support, symbolized the struggle. However, a public opinion poll conducted shortly before the march documented the continuing resentment of the majority of Whites: Sixty-three percent were opposed to the rally (G. Gallup 1972).

King (1971:351) delivered his famous "I Have a Dream" speech before the large crowd; he looked forward to a time when all Americans "will be able to join hands and sing in the words of the old Negro spiritual, 'Free at last! free at last! Thank God almighty, we are free at last!'" Just 18 days later, a bomb exploded in a Black church in Birmingham, killing 4 little girls and injuring 20 others.

Despair only increased as the November 1963 elections saw segregationists successful in their bids for office. Most distressing was the assassination of President Kennedy on November 22. As president, Kennedy had appealed to Blacks despite his previously mediocre legislative record in the U.S. Senate. His death left doubt as to the direction and pace of future actions on civil rights by the executive branch under President Lyndon Baines Johnson. Two months later, the Twenty-Fourth Amendment was ratified, outlawing the poll tax that had long prevented Blacks from voting. The enactment of the Civil Rights Act on July 2, 1964, was hailed as a major victory and provided at least for a while what historian John Hope Franklin called "the illusion of equality" (Franklin and Moss 2000).

In the months that followed the passage of the act, the pace of the movement to end racial injustice slowed. The violence continued, however, from the Bedford-Stuyvesant section of Brooklyn to Selma, Alabama. Southern state courts still found White murderers of Blacks innocent, and they had to be tried and convicted in federal civil, rather than criminal, court on the charge that by killing a person one violates that person's civil rights. Government records, which did not become public until 1973, revealed a systematic campaign by the FBI to infiltrate civil rights groups in an effort to discredit them, in the belief that such activist groups were subversive. It was in such an atmosphere that the Voting Rights Act was passed in August 1965, but this significant, positive event was somewhat overshadowed by violence in the Watts section of Los Angeles in the same week (Blackstock 1976).

Urban Violence and Oppression

Riots involving Whites and Blacks did not begin in the 1960s. As we saw earlier in this chapter, urban violence occurred after World War I and even during World War II, and violence against Blacks in the United States is nearly 350 years old. But the urban riots of the 1960s influenced Blacks and Whites in the United States and throughout the world so extensively that they deserve special attention. However, we must remember that most violence between Whites and Blacks has not been large-scale collective action but has involved only a small number of people.

The summers of 1963 and 1964 were a prelude to riots that gripped the country's attention. Although most people knew of the civil rights efforts in the South and legislative victories in Washington, everyone realized that the racial problem was national after several cities outside the South experienced violent disorders. In April 1968, after the assassination of Martin Luther King, more cities exploded than had in all of 1967. Even before the summer of 1968 began, there were 369 civil disorders. Communities of all sizes were hit (Oberschall 1968).

As the violence continued and embraced many ghettos, a popular explanation was that riot participants were mostly unemployed youths who had criminal records, often involving narcotics, and who were vastly outnumbered by the African Americans who repudiated the looting and arson. This explanation was called the **riff-raff theory** or the rotten-apple theory because it discredited the rioters and left the barrel of apples, White society, untouched. On the contrary, research shows that the Black community expressed sympathetic understanding toward the rioters and that the rioters were not merely the poor and uneducated but included middle-class, working-class, and educated residents (Sears and McConahay 1969, 1973; Tomlinson 1969; R. Turner 1994).

Several alternatives to the riff-raff theory explain why Black violent protest increased in the United States at a time when the nation was seemingly committed to civil rights for all. Two explanations stand out. One ascribes the problem to Black frustration with rising expectations in the face of continued deprivation relative to Whites.

The standard of living of African Americans improved remarkably after World War II, and it continued to do so during the civil rights movement. However, White income and occupation levels also improved, so the gap between the groups remained. Chapter 3 showed that feelings of relative deprivation often are the basis for perceived discrimination. **Relative deprivation** is the conscious feeling of a negative discrepancy between legitimate expectations and present actualities (W. Wilson 1973).

It is of little comfort to African Americans that their earning power matches that of Whites 10 or more years earlier. As shown in Figure 7.4, Black family income has increased significantly, but so has that of White families, leaving the gap between the two largely unchanged. Relative to Whites, most Blacks made no tangible gains in housing, education, jobs, or economic security. African Americans were doing better in absolute numbers, but not relative to Whites.

At the same time that African Americans were feeling relative deprivation, they were also experiencing growing discontent. **Rising expectations** refers to the increasing sense of frustration that legitimate needs are being blocked. Blacks felt that they

riff-raff theory
Also called the rotten-apple theory; the belief that the riots of the 1960s were caused by discontented youths rather than by social and economic problems facing all African Americans.

relative deprivation
The conscious experience of a negative discrepancy between legitimate expectations and present actualities.

rising expectations
The increasing sense of frustration that legitimate needs are being blocked.

Since the riots of the 1960s, inner city neighborhoods such as South Central Los Angeles (renamed South Los Angles in 2003 to try to symbolically erase the stigma) have undergone only modest redevelopment and much less than originally anticipated by the residents. Santa Ana Pines development, pictured here, is one of the few examples of economic investment in the community.

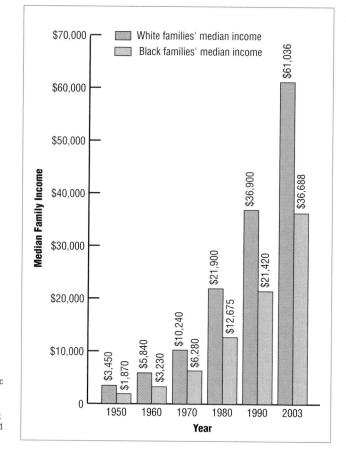

FIGURE 7.4 **Black-White Income Gap**

For the 50 years of available data, median Black family income has been only about half that of White family income.

Note: 2003 data are for White, non-Hispanic households. The comparable figure for all White households is $54,067.

Sources: Bureau of the Census 1975:297; 2002c; DeNavas-Walt et al. 2004. FINC-01 (Parts 4, 5)

had legitimate aspirations to equality, and the civil rights movement reaffirmed that discrimination had blocked upward mobility. As the horizons of African Americans broadened, they were more likely to make comparisons with Whites and feel discontented. The civil rights movement gave higher aspirations to Black America, yet for the majority, life remained basically unchanged. Not only were their lives unchanged, but the feeling was widespread that the existing social structure held no prospect for improvement (Garner 1996; Sears and McConahay 1970; Thomas and Thomas 1984).

Black Power

The riots in the northern ghettos captured the attention of Whites, and Black Power was what they heard. Appropriately enough, Black Power was born not of Black but of White violence. On June 6, 1966, James Meredith was carrying out a one-person march from Memphis to Jackson, Mississippi, to encourage fellow African Americans to overcome their own fears and vote after the passage of the Voting Rights Act. During that march, an unidentified assailant shot and wounded Meredith. Blacks from throughout the country immediately continued the march. During the march, Stokely Carmichael of the Student Nonviolent Coordinating Committee (SNCC) proclaimed to a cheering Black crowd, "What we need is Black Power." King and others later urged "Freedom Now" as the slogan for the march. A compromise dictated that no slogan would be used, but the mood of Black America said otherwise (King 1967; Lomax 1971).

In retrospect, it may be puzzling that the phrase *Black Power* frightened Whites and offended so many Blacks. It was not really new. The National Advisory Commission on Civil Disorders (1968:234–235) correctly identified it as old wine in new bottles: Black consciousness was not new, even if the phrase was.

By advocating Black Power, Carmichael was distancing himself from the assimilationism of King. Carmichael rejected the goal of assimilation into White middle-class society. Instead, he said, Blacks must create new institutions. To succeed in this endeavor, Carmichael argued that Blacks must follow the same path as the Italians, Irish, and other White ethnic groups. "Before a group can enter the open society, it must first close ranks. . . . Group solidarity is necessary before a group can operate effectively from a bargaining position of strength in a pluralistic society" (Ture and Hamilton 1992:44). Prominent Black leaders opposed the concept; many feared that Whites would retaliate even more violently. King (1967) saw Black Power as a "cry of disappointment" but acknowledged that it had a "positive meaning."

Eventually Black Power gained wide acceptance among Blacks and even many Whites. Although it came to be defined differently by nearly every new proponent, support of Black Power generally implied endorsing Black control of the political, economic, and social institutions in Black communities. One reason for its popularity among African Americans was that it gave them a viable option for surviving in a segregated society. The civil rights movement strove to end segregation, but the White response showed how committed White society was to maintaining it. Black Power presented restructuring society as the priority item on the Black agenda (Ladner 1967; Pinkney 2000).

One aspect of Black Power clearly operated outside the conventional system. The Black Panther party was organized in October 1966 in Oakland, California, by Huey Newton, age 24, and Bobby Seale, age 30, to represent urban Blacks in a political climate that the Panthers felt was unresponsive. The Panthers were controversial from the beginning, charging police brutality and corruption among government officials. They engaged in violent confrontations with law enforcement officers. From 1969 to 1972, internal weaknesses, a long series of trials involving most of the leaders, intraparty strife, and several shoot-outs with police combined to bring the organization to a standstill. Although they were often portrayed as the most separatist of the Black militant movements, the Panthers were willing to form alliances with non-Black organizations, including Students for a Democratic Society (SDS), the Peace and Freedom Party, the Young Lords, the Young Patriots, and the Communist party of the United States. Despite, or perhaps because of, such coalitions, the Panthers were not a prominent force in shaping contemporary Black America. Newton himself admitted in 1973 that the party had alienated Blacks and had become "too radical" to be accepted by the Black community (Abron 1986; Cleaver 1982; C. Woodward 1974).

The militant Black Panthers encountered severe difficulties in the 1970s and fell victim to both internal political problems and external surveillance. Finally, their formerly outspoken leaders moved in new directions. Eldridge Cleaver became a bornagain Christian and confined himself to lecturing on the virtues of his evangelical faith. Cofounder Bobby Seale ran unsuccessfully for mayor of Oakland, California, in the kind of traditional campaign he had formerly denounced as unproductive. After that unsuccessful bid, Seale became an organizer of moderate community groups. Former Panther defense minister Bobby Rush became deputy chairman of the Illinois State Democratic party, was elected to the U.S. Congress in 1992, and has been reelected to five more terms. The role of spokesperson for a minority group in the United States is exhausting, and people who have assumed that role for a time often turn to more conventional, less personally demanding roles, especially if public support for their programs wanes.

The Religious Force

It is not possible to overstate the role religion has played, good and bad, in the social history of African Americans. Historically, Black leaders have emerged from the pulpits to seek out rights on behalf of all Blacks. Churches have served as the basis for community organization in neighborhoods abandoned by businesses and even government. Religion has been a source of antagonism as well. In "Research Focus," we consider how the Black church continues to be socially involved in the community.

Focus Research Focus Research Focus

THE BLACK CHURCH AS A CHANGE AGENT

The church is one of the few social organizations that was tolerated during slavery. White slaveowners often viewed the Christian church experience as a part of their role in "helping" the enslaved Africans and their descendants. As the years passed after slavery, African Americans continued to find the church a focal point of community activities. Unwelcome in White churches, religious Blacks had little choice, and even those with modest religious fervor found the church the place where one could gather with friends and family free of White dominance. For generations, the profession of the ministry was the only one that Blacks could enter free of restriction.

Sociologist Mary Pattillo-McCoy conducted fieldwork or ethnographic research in the mid-1990s in a middle-class Black neighborhood in Chicago. She found the power of church rituals as a means to facilitate local organizing and activism among African Americans. It is not so much religious belief itself, although most in the neighborhood believed in God and Jesus, but the gathering together and interacting in a spiritual setting that caused churches to be a powerful organizing tool. Although the church is sometimes viewed by some as leading people to escape their daily lives and problems, the Black church is significantly more likely than a White church to participate in local activities and address the problems of the needy in the immediate area.

How does the church serve as a social change agent in the neighborhood? Churches organize members and interest others to identify challenges to the neighborhood. The outreach committee of one church organized a community meeting attended by 100 residents who decided that closing down three identified drug houses was a priority. Related to this initiative was a church-sponsored "March Against Drugs." Church representatives regularly meet with police officials on what action is being taken. Church leadership is courted by local politicians, who seek to have their approval. Once received, ministerial approval is widely publicized as a stamp of approval from a progressive segment of the neighborhood. Community meetings totally apart from church organizations reflect religious feelings of African Americans: Meetings open with prayers, choruses of "Amens" punctuate positive statements, and spontaneous singing of hymns is evident. The line between the secular and spiritual efforts to bring about positive change is very fuzzy.

Generally when people think of Black religious faith and social activism, they think of national figures such as Martin Luther King, Jr., Malcolm X, and Jesse Jackson. McCoy's research reminds us that in many Black communities, in much more subtle ways, the church is not only the anchor of the community but also prods society to move in desired directions. ■

Sources: Marable 2000; Pattillo-McCoy 1998, 1999.

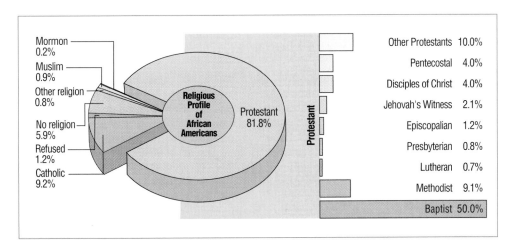

FIGURE 7.5 Religious Profile of African Americans

Based on a 1990 national sample, most African Americans are Baptist, Roman Catholic, or Methodist.

Source: From *One Nation Under God* by Seymour P. Lachman and Barry A. Kosmin. Copyright © 1993 by Seymour P. Lachman and Barry A. Kosmin. Reprinted by permission of Harmony Books, a division of Random House Inc.

As we saw earlier in this chapter, because the Africans who were brought involuntarily to the Western Hemisphere were non-Christian, they were seen as heathens and barbarians. To "civilize" the slaves in the period before the Civil War, Southern slaveholders encouraged and often required their slaves to attend church and embrace Christianity. The Christian churches to which Blacks were introduced in the United States encouraged them to accept the inferior status enforced by Whites, and the religious teaching that the slaves received equated whiteness with salvation, presenting whiteness as an acceptable, if not preferred, object of reverence.

Despite being imposed in the past by Whites, the Christian faiths are embraced by most African Americans today. As shown in Figure 7.5, African Americans are overwhelmingly Protestant, with half being Baptist. Methodists and Roman Catholics account for another 9 percent each. Therefore, almost 7 out of 10 African Americans are members of these three faiths, compared with less than half of Whites.

However, a variety of non-Christian groups have exerted a much greater influence on African Americans than the reported numbers of their followers suggest. The Nation of Islam, for example, which became known as the Black Muslims, has attracted a large number of followers and received the most attention. We will look at this group in grater detail in Chapter 11 when we consider the large Muslim community in the United States.

Especially in urban centers, recent immigrants from Africa have begun to provide a new diversity to the Black community in the United States. Here a Senegalese restaurateur is shown in front of her Philadelphia restaurant.

Conclusion

The dramatic events affecting African Americans today have their roots in the forcible bringing of their ancestors to the United States as slaves. In the South, whether as slaves or later as victims of Jim Crow, Blacks were not a real threat to any but the poorest Whites, although even affluent Whites feared the perceived potential threat that Blacks posed. During their entire history here, Blacks have been criticized when they rebelled and praised when they went along with the system. During the time of slavery, revolts were met with increased suppression; after emancipation, leaders calling for accommodation were applauded.

The Black migration to the urban North helped to define a new social order. Whites found it more difficult to ignore Blacks as residents of the ghetto than as sharecroppers in the rural South. No longer excluded by the White primary as in the South, the Black urban voter had potential power. The federal government and city halls slowly began to acknowledge the presence of Blacks. From the Black community came voices that spoke of pride and self-help: Douglass, Tubman, Washington, Du Bois, King, and Malcolm X.

Most people today look back at the civil rights movement and accept the significance of its legacy but, like so many things in society, Black and White perceptions differ. A national survey found that 46 percent of Whites compared to 75 percent felt the movement was extremely important. Half of Whites felt that most of the goals of the civil rights movement have been achieved, while only 30 percent of African Americans were similarly convinced (Ludwig 2004).

Blacks, in their efforts to bring about change, have understandably differed in their willingness to form coalitions with Whites. Resisting African Americans, in the days of either slavery or the Civil Rights movement, would have concurred with Du Bois's (1903:3–4) comment that a Black person "simply wishes to make it possible to be both a Negro and an American, without being cursed and spit upon by his fellows, without having the door of opportunity closed roughly in his face." The object of Black protest seems simple enough, but for many people, including presidents, the point was lost.

How much progress has been made? When covering several hundred years, beginning with slavery and ending with rights recognized constitutionally, it is easy to be impressed. Yet let us consider Topeka, Kansas, the site of the 1954 *Brown v. Board of Education* case. Linda Brown, one of the original plaintiffs, was recently touched by another segregation case. In 1992, the courts held that Oliver Brown, her grandchild, was being victimized because the Topeka schools were still segregated, now for reasons of residential segregation. The remedy to separate schools in this Kansas city is still unresolved (Hays 1994).

Chapter 8 assesses the status of African Americans today. Recall the events chronicled in this chapter as you consider the advances that have been made. These events are a reminder that any progress has followed years—indeed, generations—of struggle by African Americans, enlisting the support of Whites seeking to end second-class status for African Americans in the United States.

Key Terms

abolitionists 188
civil disobedience 198
de jure segregation 196
Ebonics 188

Jim Crow 189
relative deprivation 201
restrictive covenants 197
riff-raff theory 201

rising expectations 201
slave codes 185
slavery reparations 190
White primary 189

Review Questions

1. In what ways were slaves defined as property?
2. How did slavery provide a foundation for both White and Black America today?
3. If civil disobedience is nonviolent, why is so much violence associated with it?
4. How did observers of the urban riots tend to dismiss any social importance to the outbreaks?
5. Why has religion proved to be a force for both unity and disunity among African Americans?

Critical Thinking

1. How much time do you recall spending in school thus far learning about the history of Europe? How about Africa? What do you think this says about the way education is delivered or what we choose to learn?
2. What would you consider the three most important achievements in civil rights for African Americans since 1900? What roles did Whites and Blacks play in making these events happen?
3. Growing numbers of Blacks are immigrating to the United States (especially to the eastern United States) from the Caribbean. What impact may this have on what it means to be Black or African American in the United States? What would the social construction of race say about this development?

Internet Connections—Research Navigator™

 Follow the instructions found on page 31 of this text to access the features of Research Navigator™. Once at the Web site, enter your Login Name and Password. Then, to use the ContentSelect database, enter keywords such as "slavery," "reparations," and "civil disobedience," and the research engine will supply relevant and recent scholarly and popular press publications. Use the *New York Times* Search-by-Subject Archive to find recent news articles related to sociology, and the Link Library feature to locate relevant Web links organized by the key terms associated with this chapter.

8

African Americans Today

CHAPTER OUTLINE

AFRICAN AMERICANS HAVE MADE SIGNIFICANT PROGRESS IN many areas, but they have not kept pace with White Americans in any sectors. African Americans have advanced in formal schooling to a remarkable degree, although in most areas residential patterns have left many public schools predominantly Black or White. Higher education also reflects the legacy of a nation that has operated two schooling systems: one for Blacks and another for Whites. Gains in earning power have barely kept pace with inflation, and the gap between Whites and Blacks has remained largely unchanged. African American families are susceptible to the problems associated with a low-income group that also faces discrimination and prejudice.

Housing in many areas remains segregated, despite growing numbers of Blacks in suburban areas. African Americans are more likely to be victims of crimes and to be arrested for violent crimes. The subordination of Blacks is also apparent in health care delivery. African Americans have made substantial gains in elective office but still are underrepresented compared with their numbers in the general population.

John and Glenn are alike in almost every way: about the same age, Big Ten college graduates, similar jobs, and active sports enthusiasts. But they find that they have very dissimilar experiences in such everyday activities as walking into a shopping mall to buy shoes or look over the latest CDs. John typically receives instant attention when he walks even near the shoe department, but the same salesperson fails to acknowledge Glenn even though he has been waiting five minutes. A little later John casually picks up some CDs in a record store. At the very same time, Glenn is engaged in exactly the same behavior in the same store, but he is closely shadowed by a store employee, who observes Glenn's every move.

John is White and Glenn is Black, which makes all the difference even in this everyday shopping behavior. They were part of an experiment conducted by the television newsmagazine *Primetime Live* in St. Louis to assess the impact of race on the day-to-day lives of average African Americans and Whites. Over a period of three weeks, the program closely monitored the two researchers, who had been trained to present themselves in an identical manner in a variety of situations.

In a televised report on this experiment, *Primetime Live* host Diane Sawyer acknowledged that, at times, the two men were treated equally. However, Sawyer added that not once or twice but "every single day," there were instances of differential treatment. At an employment agency, Glenn was lectured on laziness and told that he would be monitored "real close." John, by contrast, was encouraged to pursue job leads, and staff members made it clear that he could expect to find a suitable position (ABC News 1992).

Despite the publicity given to obvious discrimination that has persisted well into the present, a superficial sense of complacency about the position of African Americans in the United States is evident as the 21st century begins. Uninformed casual observers see that more African Americans are inside city halls and Congress rather than marching outside, and conclude that equality has been achieved. From time to time, however, this sense that everything was going well has been interrupted. For example, the 1992 Los Angeles riots led to short-lived expressions of concern over police brutality and insufficient government policies. By 1995, however, complacency had returned. Plans to address inner-city problems were low on the nation's list of priorities. Instead, the dismantling of affirmative action emerged as the major race issue of the 1996 elections.

CD-ROM *Activity 6.1* As you read this chapter, try to keep in perspective the profile of African Americans in the United States today. This chapter will assess education, the economy, family life, housing, criminal justice, health care, and politics among the nation's African Americans. Progress has occurred, and some of the advances are nothing short of remarkable. The deprivation of the African American people relative to Whites remains, however, even if absolute deprivation has been softened. A significant gap remains between African Americans and the dominant group, and to this gap a price is assigned: the price of being African Americans in the United States.

Education

The African American population in the United States has placed special importance on acquiring education, beginning with its emphasis in the home of the slave family and continuing through the creation of separate schools for Black children because the public schools were closed to them by custom or law. Today, long after the old civil rights coalition has disbanded, education remains a controversial issue. Because racial and ethnic groups realize that formal schooling is the key to social mobility, they want to maximize this opportunity for upward mobility and therefore want better schooling. White Americans also appreciate the value of formal schooling and do not want to do anything that they perceive will jeopardize their own position.

Quality and Quantity Of Education

Several measures document the inadequate education received by African Americans, starting with the quantity of formal education. The gap in educational attainment between Blacks as a group and Whites as a group has always been present. Despite programs directed at the poor, such as Head Start, White children are still more likely to have formal prekindergarten education than are African American children. Later, Black children generally drop out of school sooner and therefore are less likely to receive high school diplomas, let alone college degrees. Table 8.1 shows the gap in the amount of schooling African Americans receive compared to Whites. It also illustrates progress in reducing this gap in recent years. Despite this progress, however, the gap remains substantial, with nearly twice the proportion of Whites holding a college degree as Blacks in 2003.

A second aspect of inadequate schooling, many educators argue, is that many students would not drop out of school were it not for the combined inadequacies of their education. Among the deficiencies noted have been:

- Insensitive teachers
- Poor counseling
- Unresponsive administrators
- Overcrowded classes
- Irrelevant curricula
- Dilapidated school facilities

CD-ROM *Activity 3.2*

(handwritten margin notes: Less likely to have formal pre-Kindergarten. Drops out of School more sooner. less to go to college)

TABLE 8.1
Years of School Completed (Percentages of People 25 Years Old and Over)

	1960	1980	2003
COMPLETING HIGH SCHOOL			
BLACK			
Male	18.2%	50.8%	79.6%
Female	21.8	51.5	80.3
WHITE			
Male	41.6	69.6	89.0
Female	44.7	68.1	89.7
COMPLETING COLLEGE			
BLACK			
Male	2.8	8.4	16.7
Female	3.3	8.3	19.5
WHITE			
Male	10.3	21.3	32.3
Female	6.0	13.3	27.9

Note: Data for Whites are for non-Hispanic Whites.

Source: Bureau of the Census 2003a: 153; Stoops 2004.Detailed Table 10.

Although several of these problems can be addressed with more adequate funding, some are stalemated by disagreements over what changes would lead to the best outcome. For example, there is significant debate among educators and African Americans in general over the content of curriculum that is best for minority students. Some schools have developed academic programs that take an Afrocentric perspective and immerse students in African American history and culture. Yet a few of these programs have been targeted as ignoring fundamentals, as in the debate in Oakland, California, noted in Chapter 7, over recognizing Ebonics as a language in the classroom. On other occasions, the Afrocentric curriculum has even been viewed as racist against Whites. The debates over a few controversial programs attract a lot of attention, clouding the widespread need to reassess the curriculum for racial and ethnic minorities.

Middle- and upper-class children occasionally face these barriers to a high-quality education, but they are more likely than the poor to have a home environment that is favorable to learning. Even African American schoolchildren who stay in school are not guaranteed equal opportunities in life. Many high schools do not prepare students who are interested in college for advanced schooling. The problem is that schools are failing to meet the needs of students, not that students are failing in school. Therefore, the problems with schooling were properly noted as a part of the past discrimination component of total discrimination illustrated in Figure 3.1.

School Segregation

It has been more than 40 years since the U.S. Supreme Court issued its unanimous ruling in *Brown v. Board of Education of Topeka, Kansas*, that separate educational facilities are inherently unequal. What has been the legacy of that decision? Initially, the courts, with the support of the federal government, ordered Southern school districts to end racial separation. But as attention turned to larger school districts, especially in the North, the challenge was to have integrated schools even though the neighborhoods were segregated. In addition, some city school districts were predominantly African American and Hispanic, surrounded by suburban school districts that were predominantly White. This type of school segregation, which results from residential patterns, is called **de facto segregation**.

Initially, courts sought to overcome de facto segregation just as they had with the de jure school segregation dealt with in the *Brown* case. Typically, students were bused within a school district to achieve racial balance, but in a few cases Black students were bused to predominantly White suburban schools and White children were bused into the city. In 1974, however, the Supreme Court ruled in *Millikin v. Bradley* that it was improper to order Detroit and the suburbs to have a joint metropolitan busing solution. These and other Supreme Court decisions have effectively ended initiatives to overcome residential segregation, once again creating racial isolation in the schools. Indeed, even in Topeka, one-third of the schools are segregated today (Orfield et al. 1996).

Racial diversity in individual schools was still largely absent in schools in 2000. White students typically attend public schools that on the average are 80 percent White. Trend data since the 1960s indicates that public schools are increasingly becoming all-White or all-Black or all-Hispanic.

So enduring has been school segregation, the term **apartheid schools** has been coined to refer to schools that are all-Black. An analysis released in 2003 by the Civil Rights Project of Harvard University documented that one of six of the nation's Black students attend apartheid schools, and this proportion rose to one out of four in the Northeast and Midwest. If there has been any trend, it is that the typical African American student was less likely to have White classmates in 2000 than in 1970 (Frankenberg, Lee and Orfield 2003).

de facto segregation
Segregation that is the result of residential patterns.

apartheid schools
Refers to schools that are all-Black.

Although studies have shown positive effects of integration, a diverse student population does not guarantee an integrated, equal schooling environment. For example, tracking in schools, especially middle and high schools, intensifies segregation at the classroom level. **Tracking** is the practice of placing students in specific curriculum groups on the basis of test scores and other criteria. It also has the effect of decreasing White-Black classroom interaction as African American children are disproportionately assigned to general classes, and more White children are placed in college preparatory classes. It is estimated that about 60 percent of elementary schools in the United States and about 80 percent of secondary schools use some form of tracking. Studies indicate that African American students are more likely than White students to be classified as learning disabled or emotionally disturbed. Although there are successes in public education, integration clearly is not one of them (Eitle 2002; Hallinan 2003; Sadker and Sadker 2003).

tracking
The practice of placing students in specific curriculum groups on the basis of test scores and other criteria.

Higher Education

Higher education for Blacks reflects the same pattern: The overall picture of African American higher education is not promising. Although strides were made in the period after the civil rights movement, a plateau was reached in the mid-1970s. African Americans are more likely than Whites to be part-time students and to need financial aid, which began to be severely cut in the 1980s. They are also finding the social climate on predominantly White campuses less than positive. As a result, the historically Black colleges and universities (HBCUs) are once again playing a significant role in educating African Americans. For a century, they were the only real source of college

Black colleges

Historically, Black universities such as Howard University, founded in 1867 in Washington, D.C., continue to serve as pivotal institutions in the education of African Americans.

degrees for Blacks. Then, in the 1970s, predominantly White colleges began to recruit African Americans. As of 2002, however, the 105 HBCUs still accounted for about one-quarter of all Black college graduates (Fletcher 2002).

As shown in Table 8.1, although African Americans are more likely today to be college graduates, the upward trend has declined. Several factors account for this reversal in progress:

1. A reduction in financial aid and more reliance on loans than on grants-in-aid, coupled with rising costs, have tended to discourage students who would be the first members of their families to attend college.

2. Pushing for higher standards in educational achievement without providing remedial courses has locked out many minority students.

3. Employment opportunities, though slight for African Americans without some college, have continued to lure young people who must contribute to their family's income and who otherwise might have gone to college.

4. Negative publicity about affirmative action may have discouraged some African Americans from even considering college.

5. Attention to what appears to be a growing number of racial incidents on predominantly White college campuses has also been a discouraging factor.

Colleges and universities seem uneasy about these problems; publicly, the schools appear committed to addressing them.

There is little question that special challenges face the African American student at a college with an overwhelmingly White student body, faculty, advisors, coaches, and administrators. The campus culture may be neutral at best, and it is often hostile to members of racial minorities. The high attrition rate of African American students on predominantly White college campuses confirms the need for a positive environment.

Because fewer African Americans complete their higher education, fewer are available to fill faculty and administrative positions. This means that despite increases in the numbers of Blacks who enter college, there are no more, and perhaps fewer, role models in college classrooms for students from subordinate groups to see.

The disparity in schooling becomes even more pronounced at the highest levels, and the gap is not closing. Only 4.9 percent of all doctorates awarded in 2001 were to African Americans; that proportion was about the same (i.e., 3.9 percent) in 1981 (Bureau of the Census 2003a:191).

In summary, the picture of education for Black Americans is uneven—marked progress in absolute terms (much better educated than a generation ago), but relative to Whites the gap in educational attainment remains at all levels. Fifty years ago, the major issue appeared to be school desegregation, but at the heart it was to improve the quality of education received by Black schoolchildren. Today the concerns of African American parents and most educators are similar—quality education. W. E. B. Du Bois advanced the same point in 1935—that what Black students need "is neither segregated schools nor mixed schools. What he needs is Education." (Du Bois 1935:335).

The Economic Picture

The general economic picture for African Americans has been gradual improvement over the last 40 years, but this improvement is modest compared with that of Whites, whose standard of living has also increased. Therefore, in terms of absolute deprivation, African Americans are much better off today but have experienced much less significant improvement with respect to their relative deprivation to Whites on almost all economic indicators. We will consider income and wealth, employment, and African American-owned businesses.

Few but growing in number, African Americans are entering positions that few people, of any color, reach. Ayana Howard, with an Electrical Engineering Ph.D., sits beside SmartNarv, a prototype for an autonomous Mars rover, on a set of the planet at NASA's Jet Propulsion Laboratory in California.

Income and Wealth

There are two useful measures of the overall economic situation of an individual or household: income and wealth. **Income** refers to salaries, wages, and other money received; **wealth** is a more inclusive term encompassing all of a person's material assets, including land and other types of property.

There is a significant gap between the incomes of Black and White households in the United States. As we saw in Figure 7.4, Black income has been increasing steadily, but so has that of Whites. In 2003, the median income of Black households was $29,681, compared with $45,631 for White non-Hispanic households. Another way to consider the gap is that Black income resembles that of Whites more than 10 years ago. This lag has been present since World War II. In Figure 8.1, we look at the overall distribution of Black and White income.

The underside of the income picture is people trapped in poverty. In 2003, 24.3 percent of Black people lived below the poverty level, compared with 8.2 percent of non-Hispanic Whites. Low incomes are counterbalanced to some extent by Medicare, Medicaid, public assistance, and food stamps. However, that an African American family is three times more likely to be poor shows that social inequality is staggering (DeNavas-Walt et al. 2004: 4, 42).

Wealth is more difficult to measure because it takes more effort to determine accurately how much people own and owe, as opposed to how much they earn in a given year. Yet wealth is very important in that it protects one against financial hardship and may offer a way to pass money or property to future generations, giving them a good start. On the other hand, the lack of wealth or even the presence of debt can place young people at a severe disadvantage as they seek to become independent.

The wealth picture in the United States shows even greater disparity between Whites and Blacks than does income. Sociologists Melvin Oliver and Thomas Shapiro (1995) drew on data from more than 12,000 households and conducted in-depth interviews with a range of Black and White families. There is clearly a significant difference in wealth patterns because generations of social inequality have left African Americans, as a group, unable to accumulate the kind of wealth that Whites, as a group, have. This is particularly true in the ability to own a home, most people's biggest asset. The inability of many Blacks to own a home and develop this asset results not only from lower incomes but also from discriminatory lending practices, which we consider later in this chapter. Of course, there are poor Whites and very rich Blacks,

income
Salaries, wages, and other money received.

wealth
An inclusive term encompassing all of a person's material assets, including land and other types of property.

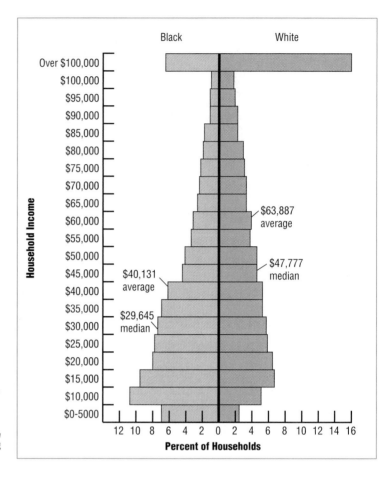

FIGURE 8.1 Income Distribution: Black Versus White

Note: Income data for 2003 were reported in 2004, and these data are for White non-Hispanics.

Sources: DeNavas et al. 2004. U.S. Census Bureau, Current Population Reports, p 60–226, *Income, Poverty and Health Insurance Coverage in the United States:* 2003, U.S. Government Printing Office, Washington, D.C.

but the group differences that the researchers documented are unmistakable. The most striking differences are seen when we compare Blacks and Whites in their 30s and when we compare the most educated Blacks with the most educated Whites. Both the young adults and the more educated African Americans would have benefited the most from efforts to reduce inequality, but the gap remains (Shapiro 2004).

As shown in Figure 8.2, most Whites are not in debt in terms of assets, and 30 percent have a net worth over $100,000. In contrast, more than 40 percent of African Americans have a net worth of less than $1,000, with only 8 percent showing assets worth more than $100,000. Assets are valuable as a means to protect people from falling into poverty if all sources of income are interrupted. About 57 percent of all Whites can stay out of poverty for at least six months if all income ends, but only 17 percent of African Americans are in a similar situation.

Assets are important both to insulate households against short-term crisis and to help other family members, whether for furthering their education, paying insurance premiums, buying the latest computer, or even starting to furnish their first home.

Employment

This precarious situation for African Americans—the lack of dependable assets—is particularly relevant as we consider their employment picture. Higher unemployment rates for Blacks have persisted since the 1940s, when they were first documented. Since 1990, the national unemployment rate for Whites has ranged from 3 percent to 6 percent, whereas for Blacks it has ranged from 7 percent to 11 percent. This means that, even in the best economic times, the Black unemployment rate is still significantly

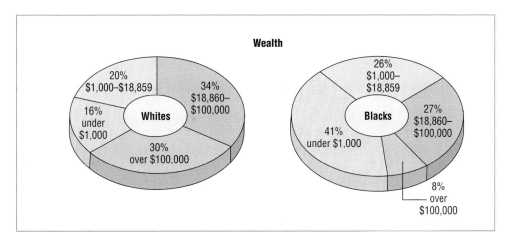

FIGURE 8.2   Comparing Wealth

Note: The wealth data for 1988 were reported in 1996.

Sources: Melvin Oliver and Thomas Shapiro, *Black Wealth/White Wealth: A New Perspective on Racial Equality.* Copyright © 1996. Reproduced by permission of Routledge/ Taylor & Francis Books, Inc.

higher than it is for Whites during recessions. Obviously, when there is a national economic downturn, the results for the African American community are disastrous. Recessions take a heavy toll on African Americans (Bureau of the Census 2003a).

The employment picture is especially grim for African American workers aged 16 to 24. Many live in the central cities and fall victim to the unrecorded, irregular—perhaps illegal—economy outlined in Chapter 3. Many factors have been cited by social scientists to explain why official unemployment rates for young African Americans exceed 30 percent:

■ Many African Americans live in the depressed economy of the central cities.

■ Immigrants and illegal aliens present increased competition.

■ White middle-class women have entered the labor force.

■ Illegal activities at which youths find they can make more money have become more prevalent.

None of these factors is likely to change soon, so depression-like levels of unemployment probably will persist.

The picture grows even more somber when we realize that we are considering only official unemployment. The federal government's Bureau of Labor Statistics counts as unemployed only people who are actively seeking employment. Therefore, to be counted as unemployed, a person must not hold a full-time job, must be registered with a government employment agency, and must be engaged in writing job applications and seeking interviews.

Quite simply, the official unemployment rate leaves out millions of Americans, Black and White, who are effectively unemployed. It does not count people so discouraged that they have temporarily given up looking for employment. The problem of unemployment is further compounded by underemployment. The term **underemployment** refers to working at a job for which one is overqualified, involuntarily working part-time, or being employed only intermittently.

The official unemployment rate for African American teenagers in a central city is about 40 to 45 percent, well above the 25 percent jobless rate for the nation as a whole during the Depression of the 1930s. Again, such official statistics do not include youths who have dropped out of the system: those who are not at school, not at work, and not looking for a legitimate job. If we add to the official figures the discouraged job seeker, the rate of unemployment and underemployment of African American teenagers in central-city areas climbs to 90 percent. As discouraging as these data are, the picture becomes even grimmer as we consider studies showing that underemployment remains high for young African Americans.

underemployment
Work at a job for which the worker is overqualified, involuntary part-time instead of full-time employment, or intermittent employment.

Although few African Americans have crashed through the glass ceiling and made it into the top echelons of business or government, more have entered a wider variety of jobs. The taboo against putting them in jobs in which they would supervise Whites has weakened, and the percentage of African Americans in professional and managerial occupations rose from 4 percent in 1949 to 8.2 percent in 2000, a remarkable improvement. However, most of this advancement came before 1980. Little advancement has occurred since then.

As shown in Table 8.2, African Americans, who constitute 13 percent of the population, are underrepresented in high-status, high-paying occupations. Less than 6 percent of lawyers, judges, physicians, financial managers, public relations specialists, architects, pharmacists, and dentists are African American. On the other hand, they account for more than 15 percent of cooks, health aides, hospital orderlies, maids, janitors, and stock handlers.

Even when they enter highly paid, prestigious positions, Black men typically earn less than their White male colleagues in similar positions. For example, Black lawyers make 79 cents to the "White dollar," 80 cents compared to White physicians. This is not to say they don't do well. African American physicians enjoy high wages—$134,000 annually in 2001—but this compares to $166,890 among White male physicians. Although they have high prestige, such professionals must build a client base, and a White professional is at an advantage as he seeks to gain the respect of high-paying, largely White potential clients (Grodsky and Pager 2001; Tran 2001).

African American Businesses

Many people aspire to run their own businesses, but this possibility is more attractive to subordinate groups, including African Americans. Frustrated by the difficulty of moving up in conventional businesses, members of minority groups often seek to begin their own businesses. Going into business themselves offers the opportunity to make it into the middle class. It is also a way to avoid some of the racism in business: the glass ceilings that block the promotion of a qualified worker and the tensions of a multiracial work environment.

TABLE 8.2
African American Employees in Selected Occupations, 1972 and 2000

Occupation	1972	2002
PROFESSIONAL WORKERS	6%	9%
Engineers	2	5
Lawyers and judges	2	5
Physicians	3	5
Registered nurses	6	10
College teachers	4	5
Other teachers	8	10
Social workers	16	23
Managers	3	8
Sales workers	3	9
Service workers	17	18
Cleaners and servants	64	14
Firefighters	4	10
Police and detectives	8	17

Source: Bureau of the Census 2003a:399–401.

Historically, the first Black-owned businesses developed behind the wall of segregation. African Americans provided other African Americans with services that Whites would not provide, such as insurance, hairdressing, legal assistance, and medical help. Although this is less true today, African American entrepreneurs usually cater first to the market demand in their own community in such areas as music and mass media. However, if these new ventures become profitable, the entrepreneur usually faces stiff competition from outside the African American community. A very visible example is the rhythm-and-blues music industry and more recently the rap music business, which began as small Black-owned businesses, but, as they became profitable, were often taken into larger White-owned corporations.

The future for Black-owned businesses is uncertain. Among the factors creating new obstacles are the following:

- Continuing backlash against affirmative action programs
- Difficulty in obtaining loans and other capital
- A changing definition of *minority* that allows women, veterans, and people with disabilities to qualify for special small business assistance programs
- A reduction in the number and scope of set-aside programs

The last item warrants further explanation. **Set-asides** are stipulations that government contracts must be awarded in a minimum proportion, usually 10 to 30 percent, to minority-owned businesses. However, in 1989 the U.S. Supreme Court determined that the city of Richmond, Virginia, had acted illegally in its set-aside programs (see Table 3.2). Since *City of Richmond v. Croson*, cities and government have abandoned programs with specific quotas for minority-owned enterprises, thus jeopardizing already fragile African American businesses. Then, in 1995, amid criticism of affirmative action, set-aside programs at the federal level also came under attack (Savage 1995).

Even if programs that stress increasing the number of African American businesses succeeded, most ghetto Blacks would still be left poor. Writing in 1940, W. E. B. Du Bois mentioned this potentially negative effect of Black capitalism. Encouraging a few African Americans to move up the capitalistic ladder, he said, "will have inserted into the ranks of the Negro race a new cause of division, a new attempt to subject the masses of the race to an exploiting capitalist class of their own people" (1968:208). Du Bois's alternative was a program that would substantially improve the economic conditions of all African Americans, not just a few.

In summary, the economic differences between Whites and Blacks remain striking. The same generalizations made before the civil rights movement are still accurate as the 21st century begins. African Americans still have lower incomes, significantly fewer assets, a higher unemployment rate, lower-paying jobs, and a greater rate of business failures than Whites. As might be expected, this weak economic picture takes a toll on family life.

Family Life

In its role as a social institution providing for the socialization of children, the family is crucial to its members' life satisfaction. The family also reflects the influence, positive or negative, of income, housing, education, and other social factors. For African Americans, the family reflects both amazing stability and the legacy of racism and low income across many generations.

---

set-asides
Programs stipulating that a minimum proportion of government contracts must be awarded to minority-owned businesses.

Challenges to Family Stability

It is the conventional view that a female heads the typical African American family. Most children are still in two-parent households. About 52 percent of African American households had both a father and a mother present in 2002 (see Figure 8.3). Although single-parent African American families are common, they are not universal. In comparison, such single-parent arrangements were also present among about one in five White families in 2002.

It is as inaccurate to assume that a single-parent family is necessarily deprived as it is to assume that a two-parent family is always secure and happy. Nevertheless, life in a single-parent family can be extremely stressful for all single parents and their children, and not just those who are members of subordinate groups. Because the absent parent is most often the father, lack of the male presence almost always means the lack of a male income. This monetary impact of a single-parent household cannot be overstated (A. Hacker 1995; Tucker and Mitchell-Kernan 1995).

Looming behind the issue of woman-headed families is the plight of the African American man. Simply stated, the economic status of Black men has been deteriorating for several generations. Despite the negative outlook, leaders within the Black community continue to call upon men to assume responsibility for the family. In 1995, Nation of Islam Minister Louis Farrakhan organized the Million Man March in Washington, D.C., to assert the role of Black men in their family and in their community. More recently, entertainer Bill Cosby in the Rainbow/PUSH Coalition's annual meeting criticized African American youth for not taking on more responsibility (Hams and Farhi 2004; Loury 1996).

Historically, female-headed families have not always been a significant economic problem. Despite the absence of legal protection for the slave family, African Americans were nevertheless able to establish significant kinship relationships with the sharing of economic resources, meager as they might be. After emancipation, men preferred that their wives remain at home because a working woman was considered a mark of slavery. But it was hard for many Black men to find work as anything other than strikebreakers, so women were the more important source of wages anyway.

For many single African American women living in poverty, having a child is an added burden. However, the tradition of extended family among African Americans eases this burden somewhat. The absence of a husband does not mean that no one shares in child care: Out-of-wedlock children born to Black teenage mothers live with their grandparents and form three-generation households.

FIGURE 8.3 Children's Living Arrangements

Source: Fields 2003:5.

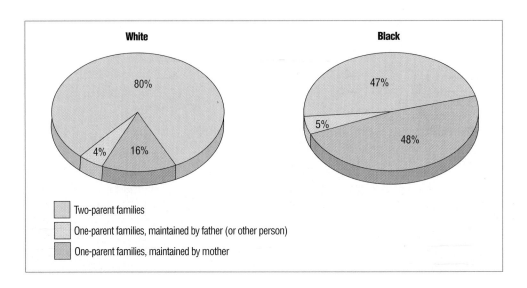

- Two-parent families
- One-parent families, maintained by father (or other person)
- One-parent families, maintained by mother

No one explanation accounts for the rise in single-parent households. Sociologists attribute the rapid expansion in the number of such households primarily to shifts in the economy that have kept Black men, especially in urban areas, out of work. The phenomenon certainly is not limited to African Americans. Increasingly, both unmarried White and Black women bear children. More and more parents, both White and Black, divorce; so even children born into a two-parent family end up living with only one parent.

Strengths of African American Families

In the midst of ever-increasing single parenting, another picture of African American family life becomes visible: success despite discrimination and economic hardship. Robert Hill (1999), of the National Urban League and Morgan State University, listed five strengths of African American families that allow them to function effectively in a hostile (racist) society.

1. Strong kinship bonds. Blacks are more likely than Whites to care for children and the elderly in an extended family network.
2. A strong work orientation. Poor Blacks are more likely to be working, and poor Black families often include more than one wage earner.
3. Adaptability of family roles. In two-parent families, the egalitarian pattern of decision making is the most common. The self-reliance of Black women who are the primary wage earners best illustrates this adaptability.
4. Strong achievement orientation. Working-class Blacks indicate a greater desire for their children to attend college than do working-class Whites. Even a majority of low-income African Americans want to attend college.
5. A strong religious orientation. Since the time of slavery, Black churches have been the impetus behind many significant grass-roots organizations.

Social workers and sociologists have confirmed through social research the strengths that Hill noted first in 1972. In the African American community, these are the sources of family strength (Hudgins 1992).

Increasingly, social scientists are learning to look at both the weaknesses and the strengths of African American family life. Expressions of alarm about instability date

Family reunions are important annual events for many African Americans.

back to 1965, when the Department of Labor issued the report *The Negro Family: The Case for National Action*. The document, commonly known as the Moynihan Report, after its principal author, sociologist Daniel Patrick Moynihan, outlined a "tangle of pathology" with the Black family at its core. More recently, two studies, the Stable Black Families Project and the National Survey of Black Americans, sought to learn how Black families encounter problems and resolve them successfully with internal resources such as those that Hill outlined in his highly regarded work (Department of Labor 1965; Gary et al. 1983).

The most consistently documented strength of African American families is the presence of an extended family household. The most common feature is having grandparents residing in the home. Extended living arrangements are much more common among Black households than among White ones. These arrangements are recognized as having the important economic benefit of pooling limited economic resources. Because of the generally lower earnings of African American heads-of-household, income from second, third, and even fourth wage earners is needed to achieve a desired standard of living or, in all too many cases, simply to meet daily needs (Bryson and Casper 1999).

The African American Middle Class

Many characterizations of African American family life have been attacked because they overemphasize the poorest segment of the African American community. An opposite error is the exaggeration of the success African Americans have achieved. Social scientists face the challenge of avoiding a selective, one-sided picture of Black society. The problem is similar to viewing a partially filled glass of water. Does one describe it as half-empty and emphasize the need for assistance? Or does one describe the glass as half-full to give attention to what has been accomplished? The most complete description would acknowledge both perspectives (Gouldner 1970).

A clearly defined African American middle class has emerged. In 2000, nearly one-third of African Americans earned more than the median income for Whites. At least 29 percent of Blacks, then, are middle class or higher. Many have debated the character of this middle class. E. Franklin Frazier (1957), a Black sociologist, wrote an often critical study of the African American middle class in which he identified its overriding goal as achieving petty social values and becoming acceptable to White society (DeNavas et al. 2001:HINC-07).

African Americans are still aware of their racial subordination even when they have achieved economic equality. The Black middle class may not be militant, but its newest members do not forget their roots. They are more likely than Whites to be first-generation middle class, dependent on two or more sources of income, and precariously close to the lower class both financially and residentially. Yet with their relative success has come a desire to live in better surroundings. The migration of middle-class African Americans out of the ghetto in the 1970s and 1980s has left a vacuum. They may still care about the problems of the Black poor, but they are no longer present as role models (Durant and Louden 1986; Landry 1987; Lemann 1986a, 1986b).

Members of the African American middle class do not automatically accept all aspects of the White middle class. For years, for example, Whites have relied on books and magazines on infant and child care; such materials treated African American children as if they did not exist. To counter this neglect, James Comer and Alvin Poussaint wrote *Raising Black Children* (1992), in which the authors advise parents on how to deal with questions such as "What is Black?", a child's first encounter with prejudice, and a teenage girl being watched by store security.

Directing attention to the Black middle class also requires that we consider the relative importance of the two components in ethclass, Milton Gordon's concept introduced in Chapter 5. The degree to which affluent Blacks identify themselves in class terms or racial terms is an important ideological question. W. E. B. Du Bois (1952) argued that when racism decreases, class issues become more important. As Du Bois saw it, exploitation would remain, and many of the same people would continue to be subordinate. Black elites might become economically successful, either as entrepreneurs (Black capitalists) or professionals (Black white-collar workers), but they would continue to identify with and serve the dominant group's interest.

Social scientists have long recognized the importance of class. **Class** is a term that was used by sociologist Max Weber to refer to people who share a similar level of wealth and income. The significance of class in people's lives is apparent to all. In the United States today, roughly half the lower-class population suffers from chronic health conditions that limit their activity, compared with only 1 in 11 among the affluent. The poor are more likely to become victims of crime, and they are only about half as likely as the affluent to send their children to colleges or vocational schools. When considering class difference, one finds remarkable similarities in childrearing practices between Black and White households (Lareau 2002).

The complexity of the relative influence of race and class was apparent in the controversy surrounding the publication of sociologist William J. Wilson's *The Declining Significance of Race* (1980). Pointing to the increasing affluence of African Americans, Wilson concluded that "class has become more important than race in determining black life-chances in the modern world" (p. 150). The policy implications of his conclusion are that programs must be developed to confront class subordination rather than ethnic and racial discrimination. Wilson did not deny the legacy of discrimination reflected in the disproportionate number of African Americans who are poor, less educated, and living in inadequate and overcrowded housing. However, he pointed to "compelling evidence" that young Blacks were competing successfully with young Whites.

Critics of Wilson comment that focusing attention on this small educated elite ignores vast numbers of African Americans relegated to the lower class (Pinkney 1984; Willie 1978, 1979). Wilson himself was not guilty of such an oversimplification and indeed expressed concern over lower-class, inner-city African Americans' seemingly falling even further behind, like those who become a part of the irregular economy discussed in

class
As defined by Max Weber, people who share similar levels of wealth.

Black parents have a special challenge in raising a child to deal with racism.

Voices Listen to Our Voices Listen to Our

OF RACE AND RISK

Several years ago, at a moment when I was particularly tired of the unstable lifestyle that academic careers sometimes require, I surprised myself and bought a real house. Because the house was in a state other than the one where I was living at the time, I obtained my mortgage by telephone. I am a prudent little squirrel when it comes to things financial, always tucking away stores of nuts for the winter, and so I meet the criteria of a quite good credit risk. My loan was approved almost immediately.

Patricia J. Williams

A little while later, the contract came in the mail. Among the papers the bank forwarded were forms documenting compliance with the Fair Housing Act, which outlaws racial discrimination in the housing market. The act monitors lending practices to prevent banks from redlining—redlining being the phenomenon whereby banks circle certain neighborhoods on the map and refuse to lend in those areas. It is a practice for which the bank with which I was dealing, unbeknownst to me, had been cited previously—as well as since. In any event, the act tracks the race of all banking customers to prevent such discrimination. Unfortunately, and with the creative variability of all illegali-

ty, some banks also use the racial information disclosed on the fair housing forms to engage in precisely the discrimination the law seeks to prevent.

I should repeat that to this point my entire mortgage transaction had been conducted by telephone. I should also note that I speak a Received Standard English, regionally marked as Northeastern perhaps, but not easily identifiable as black. With my credit history, my job as a law professor and, no doubt, with my accent, I am not only middle class but apparently match the cultural stereotype of a good white person. It is thus, perhaps, that the loan officer of the bank, whom I had never met, had checked off the box on the fair housing form indicating that I was white.

Race shouldn't matter, I suppose, but it seemed to in this case, so I took a deep breath, crossed out "white" and sent the contract back. That will teach them to presume too much, I thought. A done deal, I assumed. But suddenly the transaction came to a screeching halt. The bank wanted more money, more points, and a higher rate of interest. Suddenly I found myself facing great resistance and much more debt. To make a long story short, I threatened to sue

Chapter 3. He pointed out that the poor are socially isolated and have shrinking economic opportunities (1988, 1996). However, it is easy to conclude superficially that because educated Blacks are entering the middle class, race has ceased to be of concern.

As many African Americans have learned, prejudice and discrimination do not end with professional status and scholarship. Glenn encountered discrimination, as described in the chapter-opening example, that could be experienced by any Black person. In "Listen to Our Voices," respected law professor Patricia J. Williams, an African American, describes her inability to secure a mortgage despite initial approval after an analysis of her financial status but before the bank realized she was Black. Her recent experience is not unusual and helps to explain the housing patterns still found in the United States that we consider next.

ces Listen to Our Voices Listen to Our Voices

under the act in question, the bank quickly backed down, and I procured the loan on the original terms. What was interesting about all this was that the reason the bank gave for its new-found recalcitrance was not race, heaven forbid. No, it was all about economics and increased risk: The reason they gave was that property values in that neighborhood were suddenly falling. They wanted more money to buffer themselves against the snappy winds of projected misfortune.

Initially, I was surprised, confused. The house was in a neighborhood that was extremely stable. I am an extremely careful shopper; I had uncovered absolutely nothing to indicate that prices were falling. It took my realtor to make me see the light. "Don't you get it," he sighed. "This is what always happens." And even though I suppose it was a little thick of me, I really hadn't gotten it: For of course, I was the reason the prices were in peril. . . .

In retrospect, what has remained so fascinating to me about this experience was the way it so exemplified the problems of the new rhetoric of racism. For starters, the new rhetoric of race never mentions race. It wasn't race but risk with which the bank was so concerned. . . .

By this measure of mortgage-worthiness, the ingredient of blackness is cast not just as a social toll but as an actual tax. A fee, an extra contribution at the door, an admission charge for the high costs of handling my dangerous propensities, my inherently unsavory properties. I was not judged based on my independent attributes or financial worth; not even was I judged by statistical profiles of what my group actually does. (For in fact, anxiety-stricken, middle-class black people make good cake-baking neighbors when not made to feel defensive by the unfortunate historical strategies of bombs, burnings or abandonment.) Rather, I was being evaluated based on what an abstraction of White Society writ large thinks we—or I—do, and that imagined "doing" was treated and thus established as a self-fulfilling prophecy. It is a dispiriting message: that some in society apparently not only devalue black people but devalue themselves and their homes just for having us as part of their landscape.

"I bet you'll keep your mouth shut the next time they plug you into the computer as white," laughed a friend when he heard my story. It took me aback, this postmodern pressure to "pass," even as it highlighted the intolerable logic of it all. For by these "rational" economic measures, an investment in my property suggests the selling of myself. ■

Source: "Of Race and Risk" by Patricia J. Williams. Reprinted with permission from the December, 29 issue of *The Nation.* For subscription information, call 1-800-333-8536. Portions of each week's Nation magazine can be accessed at http: //www.thenation.com.

Housing

Housing plays a major role in determining the quality of a person's life. For African Americans, as for Whites, housing is the result of personal preferences and income. However, African Americans differ from Whites in that their housing has been restricted through discrimination in a manner that it has not for Whites. Although Black housing has improved, as indicated by statistics on home ownership, new construction, density of living units, and quality as measured by plumbing facilities, African Americans remain behind Whites on all these standards. The quality of Black housing is inferior to that of Whites at all income levels, yet Blacks pay a larger proportion of their income for shelter.

Housing was the last major area to be covered by civil rights legislation. The delay was not caused by its insignificance; quite the contrary, it was precisely because housing touches so many parts of the American economy and relates to private property rights that legislators were slow to act. After an executive order by President Kennedy, the government required nondiscrimination in federally assisted housing, but this ruling included only 7 percent of the housing market. In 1968, the Federal Fair Housing Law (Title VIII of the 1968 Civil Rights Act) and the U.S. Supreme Court decision in *Jones v. Mayer* combined to outlaw all racial discrimination in housing. Enforcement has remained weak, however, and many aspects of housing, real estate customs, and lending practices remain untouched.

Residential Segregation

Typically in the United States, as noted, White children attend predominantly White schools, Black children attend predominantly Black schools, and Hispanic children attend predominantly Hispanic schools. This school segregation is not only the result of the failure to accept busing but also the effect of residential segregation. In their studies on segregation, Douglas Massey and Nancy Denton (1993:8) concluded that racial separation "continues to exist because white America has not had the political will or desire to dismantle it." In Chapter 1, we noted the persuasiveness of residential segregation as reflected in Census 2000 (refer back to Figure 1.4). This racial isolation in neighborhoods has not improved since the beginnings of the civil rights movement in the 1950s.

What factors create residential segregation in the United States? Among the primary factors are the following:

- Because of private prejudice and discrimination, people refuse to sell or rent to people of the "wrong" race, ethnicity, or religion.
- The prejudicial policies of real estate companies steer people to the "correct" neighborhoods.
- Government policies enforce antibias legislation ineffectively.
- Public housing policies today, as well as past construction patterns, reinforce housing for the poor in inner-city neighborhoods.
- Policies of banks and other lenders create barriers based on race to financing home purchasing.

This last issue of racial-basis financing deserves further explanation. In the 1990s, new attention was given to the persistence of **redlining**, the practice of discrimination against people trying to buy homes in minority and racially changing neighborhoods. As we noticed in our "Research Focus" in Chapter 3, this practice persists in the United States in a more subtle fashion.

It is important to recall the implications of this discrimination in home financing for the African American community. Earlier in the chapter, we noted the great disparity between Black and White family wealth and the implications this had for both the present and future generations. The key factor in this inequality was the failure of African Americans to accumulate wealth through home buying. Now we see that discrimination plays a documented role in this barrier to what is possible; in 2002, 47 percent of Blacks were homeowners, compared with 75 percent of non-Hispanic Whites (Bureau of the Census 2004h).

Although the African American concentration in the central cities has increased, a small but growing number of Blacks have moved into suburban areas. By 2000, 35 percent of the nation's metropolitan African Americans lived in suburban areas. Yet the most significant growth in the percentage of suburban African Americans has come from movement into suburbs that are predominantly Black or are adjacent to predominantly Black areas. In many instances, therefore, it represents further ghettoization

redlining
The pattern of discrimination against people trying to buy homes in minority and racially changing neighborhoods.

and spillover from city slums; it is not necessarily a sign of two cars and a backyard pool. In many instances, the suburbs with large Black populations are isolated from surrounding White communities and have less satisfactory housing and municipal services but, ironically, pay higher taxes (Bureau of the Census 2001b:Table 21).

A dual housing market is part of today's reality, although attacks continue against the remaining legal barriers to fair housing. In theory, **zoning laws** are enacted to ensure that specific standards of housing construction will be satisfied. These regulations can also separate industrial and commercial enterprises from residential areas. However, some zoning laws in suburbs have seemed to curb the development of low- and moderate-income housing that would attract African Americans who want to move out of the central cities.

For years, the construction of low-income public housing in the ghetto has furthered racial segregation. The courts have not ruled consistently in this matter in recent years so, as with affirmative action, public officials lack clear guidance. Even if court decisions continue to dismantle exclusionary housing practices, the rapid growth of integrated neighborhoods is unlikely. In the future, African American housing probably will continue to improve and remain primarily in all-Black neighborhoods. This gap is greater than can be explained by differences in social class.

zoning laws
Legal provisions stipulating land use and the architectural design of housing, often used to keep racial minorities and low-income people out of suburban areas.

Criminal Justice ✓

A complex, sensitive topic affecting African Americans is their role in criminal justice. It was reported in 2002 that Blacks constitute 4.7 percent of judges and lawyers, 15.5 percent of police and detectives, and 28.1 percent of correction institution officers but 41 percent of jail inmates (Bureau of the Census 2003a: 219, 399–401).

Data collected annually in the FBI's Uniform Crime Report show that Blacks account for 27 percent of arrests, even though they represent only about 13 percent of the nation's population. Conflict theorists point out that the higher arrest rate is not surprising for a group that is disproportionately poor and therefore much less able to afford private attorneys, who might be able to prevent formal arrests from taking place. Even more significantly, the Uniform Crime Report focuses on index crimes (mainly property crimes), which are the type of crimes most often committed by low-income people (Department of Justice 2003a:252).

Most (actually 70 percent) of all the violent crimes against Whites are perpetrated by Whites, according to the FBI. In contrast to popular misconceptions about crime,

Despite concerns about police brutality and racial profiling, African Americans are strongly in favor of efforts to reduce crime in their neighborhoods. Black police officers play an important but challenging role in crime control.

victimization surveys
Annual attempts to measure crime rates by interviewing ordinary citizens who may or may not have been crime victims.

differential justice
Whites being dealt with more leniently than Blacks, whether at time of arrest, indictment, conviction, sentencing, or parole.

victim discounting
Tendency to view crime as less socially significant if the victim is viewed as less worthy.

African Americans and the poor are especially likely to be the victims of serious crimes. This fact is documented in **victimization surveys**, which are systematic interviews of ordinary people carried out annually to reveal how much crime occurs. These Department of Justice statistics show that African Americans are 22 percent more likely to be victims of violent crimes than are Whites (Rennison and Rand 2003).

Central to the concern that minorities often express about the criminal justice system is **differential justice**; that is, Whites are dealt with more leniently than are Blacks, whether at the time of investigation, arrest, indictment, conviction, sentencing, incarceration, or parole. Studies demonstrate that police often deal with African American youths more harshly than with White youngsters (Engen et al. 2002; E. Lotke 2004).

The "Research Focus" considers the application of differential justice to the harshest judgment that can be made in the legal system—the death penalty.

There is also a reluctant acceptance that the government cannot be counted on to address inner-city problems. When a schoolchild walks into a cafeteria or schoolyard with automatic weapons and kills a dozen children and teachers, it becomes a case of

Focus Research Focus *Research Focus*

THE ULTIMATE PENALTY: EXECUTION

The death penalty in the United States is enormously controversial partly because many states do not even permit it, and because increasingly the United States is marginalized as more of the world's nations have ceased to rely on it as a method of punishment. But given that the death penalty continues to be used in the United States—65 executions in 2003—what role does being African American play in its use?

While Blacks and Whites are relatively equal numbers of homicide perpetrators, a U.S. Department of Justice study indicated that Blacks were the defendant in 72 percent of the cases where attorney generals approved the death penalty. As disturbing as this finding is alone, it also points to the clearest and most consistent research finding—the race of the victim is the best indicator of whether an execution will occur. If the victim is White, the defendant is more likely to be tried under the death penalty and later be executed than if the victim is Black.

This reflects the broader concern that the Black-on-Black crime was not being dealt with as seriously as when Whites were victimized. Researchers on crime have come to call

this **victim discounting**: that is, society's tendency to view crimes as less socially significant if the victim is viewed as less worthy.

Clearly the use of the death penalty is the most extreme form of victim discounting. Numerous studies show that homicide defendants are more likely to be sentenced to death if their victims were White rather than Black. So even in a murder case, a Black death counts less. About 83 percent of the victims in death penalty cases are White, even though only 50 percent of all murder victims are White.

There is also some evidence that Black defendants, who constituted 45 percent of all death row inmates in 2004, are more likely to face execution than Whites in the same legal circumstances. There is even evidence that capital case clients receive poor legal services because of racist attitudes of their own defense counsel. Although racism in the criminal justice system is never acceptable, it is particularly devastating when the process results in an execution. ■

Sources: Cole 1999; Death Penalty Information Center 20004; Swarns 2004.

national alarm as with Columbine; but when children kill each other in drive-by shootings, it is viewed as a local concern reflecting the need to clean up a dysfunctional neighborhood. Many African Americans note that the main difference between these two situations is not the death toll but who is being killed: middle class Whites in the schoolyard shootings and Black ghetto youth in the drive-bys.

Health Care ꜱꜰₐₜ

The price of being an African American took on new importance with the release in 1996 of a shocking study in a prestigious medical journal that revealed that two-thirds of boys in Harlem, a predominantly Black neighborhood in New York City, can expect to die in young or mid-adulthood—that is, before they reach age 65. In fact, they have less chance to survive even to 45 than their White counterparts nationwide have of reaching 65. The medical researchers noted that it is not the stereotyped images of AIDS and violence that explain the staggering difference. Black men are much more likely to fall victim to unrelenting stress, heart disease, and cancer (Fing et al. 1996).

The morbidity and mortality rates for African Americans as a group, and not just Harlem men, are equally distressing. Compared with Whites, Blacks have higher death rates from diseases of the heart, pneumonia, diabetes, and cancer. The death rate from strokes was twice as high among African Americans as it was among Whites. Such epidemiologic findings reflect in part the higher proportion of Blacks found among the nation's lower classes. White Americans can expect to live 75.0 years if male and 80.2 years among females. By contrast, life expectancy for African Americans is only 68.6 years for males and 75.5 years for females (Arias et al. 2003).

Drawing on the conflict perspective, sociologist Howard Waitzkin (1986) suggests that racial tensions contribute to the medical problems of African Americans. In his view, the stress resulting from racial prejudice and discrimination helps to explain the higher rates of hypertension found among African Americans (and Hispanics) than among Whites. Death due to hypertension is twice as common in Blacks as in Whites; it is believed to be a critical factor in Blacks' high mortality rates from heart disease, kidney disease, and stroke. Although medical experts disagree, some argue that the stress resulting from racism and suppressed hostility exacerbates hypertension among African Americans (Cooper et al. 1999).

The previous section noted that African Americans are underrepresented among lawyers in the criminal justice system. A similar phenomenon is visible in health care. Blacks represent less than 5 percent of practicing physicians. This is especially significant given that communities with a high proportion of African American residents are four times more likely to have a physician shortage than are White neighborhoods. There is little reason to expect this to improve soon. Applications by Blacks to medical schools and subsequent acceptances declined beginning in 1997. Among the students entering medical school in Fall of 2003, only 8.6 percent of the women and 4.4 percent of the men were African American. There is also evidence of a declining presence of minorities among medical school faculty members, reflecting disenchantment with rolling back of affirmative action in many professional schools (Association of American Medical Colleges 2004; Bureau of the Census 2003a).

Related to the health care dilemma is the problem of environmental justice, which was introduced in Chapter 3 and again in Chapter 6 with reference to Native Americans. Problems associated with toxic pollution and hazardous garbage dumps are more likely to be faced by low-income Black communities than their affluent counterparts. This disproportionate exposure to environmental hazards can be viewed as part of the complex cycle of discrimination faced by African Americans and other subordinate groups in the United States (Pinderhughes 1996).

Here in the White House in 1997, after receiving an official apology from then President Bill Clinton, is Herman Shaw, age 94, one of the last known survivors of the infamous Tuskegee Syphilis study. This Federal government study knowingly infected Black men with Syphilis to observe the progression of the disease. Despite discovery of treatments, the men were never given medical assistance until the program was revealed decades later. Such events cause contemporary African Americans to be particularly leery of the medical establishment.

Just how significant is the impact of poorer health on the lives of the nation's less educated people, less affluent classes, and subordinate groups? Drawing on a variety of research studies, population specialist Evelyn Kitagawa (1972) estimated the "excess mortality rate" to be 20 percent. In other words, 20 percent more people were dying than otherwise might have because of poor health linked to race and class. Using Kitagawa's model, we can calculate that if every African American in the United States were White and had at least one year of college education, some 56,000 fewer Blacks would have died in 2003 and in each succeeding year (Bureau of the Census 2003a).

Politics

African Americans have never received an equal share of the political pie. After Reconstruction, it was not until 1928 that a Black was again elected to Congress. Now, more than 70 years and several civil rights acts later, there are still only 38 African American congressional representatives. Recent years have brought some improvement. In fact, between 1970 and 2001, the number of Black elected officials has increased by more than fivefold (Table 8.3).

Yet there are major problems in the continued success by African American politicians. Locally elected Black officials find it difficult to make the jump to statewide office. Voters, particularly non-Black voters, have difficulty in seeing Black politicians as anything other than a representative of the Black community and express concern that the view of Whites and other non-Blacks will not be represented by an African American.

The political gains by African Americans, as well as Hispanics, had been placed in jeopardy by legal actions that questioned race-based districts. Boundaries for elective office, ranging from city council positions to the U. S House of Representatives, have been drawn in such a way to group enough members of a racial or ethnic group to create a "safe majority" to make it likely a member of that group will get elected.

TABLE 8.3
Black Elected Officials, 1972–2000

Although the rate of increase has leveled off, the number of Black elected officials has continued to increase.

Year	Number	Percentage Change in Preceding Four years	Percentage Increase Since 1972
1972	2,264	—	—
1976	3,979	76	76
1980	4,912	23	117
1984	5,700	16	152
1988	6,829	20	202
1992	7,552	11	234
1996	8,579	14	279
2000	9,040	5	299

Note: There were 9,101 elected officials in 2001 (Bositis 2003).

Source: From *Black Elected Officials: A Statistical Summary 2000* by David Bositis. Reprinted by permission of the Joint Center for Political and Economic Studies.

The creation of these minority districts redrawn in this manner raised cries of **gerrymandering**. A practice dating from 1810, gerrymandering is the bizarre outlining of districts to create politically advantageous outcomes. While creating race-based districts may seem discriminatory, boundaries have routinely been drawn based on a commonality of interests, such as rural versus urban interests, or even to maximize the likelihood of electing a representative from a certain political party. For over a decade, the legality of these actions has been debated, and finally in 2003, the Supreme Court ruled 5-4 that a state may consider overall minority influence in the political process (A. Clymer 2003).

In the wake of the very close 2000 presidential election between George W. Bush and Al Gore, another long-standing legal issue came to the forefront nationally. In 13 states, ex-felons are barred from voting for life after leaving prison. Prisoners are barred from voting in all states except Maine and Vermont. In the 2000 election, 3.9 million people were ineligible to vote because of felony convictions. Because states with such policies tend to be in the South, it is not surprising that 36 percent of these potential voters are African Americans. Given that Blacks tend to vote overwhelmingly for Democrats, many supporters of Al Gore observed that their candidate would have won decisively if such citizens had been permitted to vote. There is little movement to repeal these voting prohibitions where they do exist for ex-felons (King and Mauer 2004; Mauer 2004).

The changing racial and ethnic landscape can be expected to have an impact on future strategies to elect African Americans to office, especially in urban areas. However, now that the number of Hispanics exceeds the number of Blacks nationwide, observers wonder how this might play out in the political world. A growing number of major cities, including Los Angeles and Chicago, are witnessing dramatic growth in the Hispanic population. Latinos often settle near Black neighborhoods or even displace Blacks who move out into suburbs, making it more difficult to develop safe African American districts. For example, South Central Los Angeles, the site of rioting in 1992 described in the previous chapter, is now largely a Latino neighborhood. The full impact has not been felt yet because the Latino population tends to be younger, with many not reaching voting age yet; and, even more significantly, many Latino adults have not obtained their citizenship yet. As the Hispanic population becomes eligible to vote, the impact is going to be particularly felt by African Americans, who have just begun to enjoy success in local elections (Schodolski 2002).

gerrymandering
Redrawing districts bizarrely to create politically advantageous outcomes.

Conclusion

Black and White Americans have dealt with the continued disparity between the two groups by endorsing several ideologies, as shown in Figure 8.4. Assimilation was the driving force behind the civil rights movement, which sought to integrate Whites and Blacks into one society. People who rejected contact with the other group endorsed separatism. As Chapter 2 showed, both Whites and Blacks generally lent little support to separatism. In the late 1960s, the government and various Black organizations began to recognize cultural pluralism as a goal, at least paying lip service to the desire of many African Americans to exercise cultural and economic autonomy. Perhaps on no other issue is this desire for control more evident than in the schools.

As the future of African American people in the United States unfolds, one element of the population generally unnoticed thus far may move into prominence. An ever-growing proportion of the Black population consists of people of foreign birth. In the 1980 census, 816,000 foreign-born Blacks were counted, or 3.1 percent of the Black population, the highest level ever recorded. By 2000, the number had tripled to 2,100,000, which constituted

8.6 percent of the Black population. In cities such as New York City, Miami, Ft. Lauderdale, and Boston, the foreign-born population of the Black community is at least 25 percent. The immigration numbers are expected to increase, as is the proportion of the African American population that is foreign born. Diversity exists to a significant degree in the Black community today (Bureau of the Census 2003a:44; El Nasser 2003).

Twice in this nation's history, African Americans have received significant attention from the federal government and, to some degree, from the larger White society. The first period extended from the Civil War to the end of Reconstruction. The second period was during the civil rights movement of the 1960s. In both periods, the government acknowledged that race was a major issue, and society made commitments to eliminate inequality (Farley 1993). As noted in Chapter 7, Reconstruction was followed by decades of neglect, and on several measures the position of Blacks deteriorated in the United States. Although the 1980s and 1990s were not without their successes, race is clearly not a major issue on today's national agenda. Even inner city violence only diverts

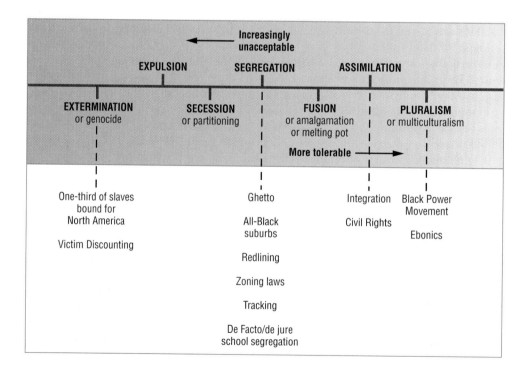

FIGURE 8.4   Intergroup
Relations Continuum

much of the nation's attention for a few fleeting moments, while attacks on school integration and affirmative action persist.

The gains that have been made are substantial, but will the momentum continue? Improvement has occurred in a generation inspired and spurred on to bring about change. If the resolve to continue toward that goal lessens in the United States, the picture may become bleaker, and the rate of positive change may decline further.

Key Terms

apartheid schools   212

class   223

de facto segregation   212

differential justice   228

gerrymandering   231

income   215

redlining   226

set-asides   219

tracking   213

underemployment   217

victim discounting   228

victimization surveys   228

wealth   215

zoning laws   227

Review Questions

1. To what degree have the civil rights movement initiatives in education been realized, or do they remain unmet?
2. What challenges face the African American middle class?
3. What are the biggest assets and problems facing African American families?
4. How are differential justice and victim discounting related?
5. How is race-based gerrymandering related to affirmative action?

Critical Thinking

1. Without the comparison to John, Glenn might have taken the shoe salesman to be merely incompetent at his job rather than purposefully avoiding selling to African Americans. Drawing on the case of John and Glenn, what are other types of situations in which people may be victims of discrimination but be unaware of it?
2. What has been the ethnic and racial composition of the neighborhoods you have lived in and the schools you have attended? Consider how the composition of one may have influenced the other. What steps would have been necessary to ensure more diversity?
3. How are the problems in crime, housing, and health interrelated?

Internet Connections—Research Navigator™

Follow the instructions found on page 31 of this text to access the features of Research Navigator™. Once at the Web site, enter your Login Name and Password. Then, to use the ContentSelect database, enter keywords such as "race and health," "Black elected officals," and "environmental justice," and the research engine will supply relevant and recent scholarly and popular press publications. Use the *New York Times* Search-by-Subject Archive to find recent news articles related to sociology, and the Link Library feature to locate relevant Web links organized by the key terms associated with this chapter.

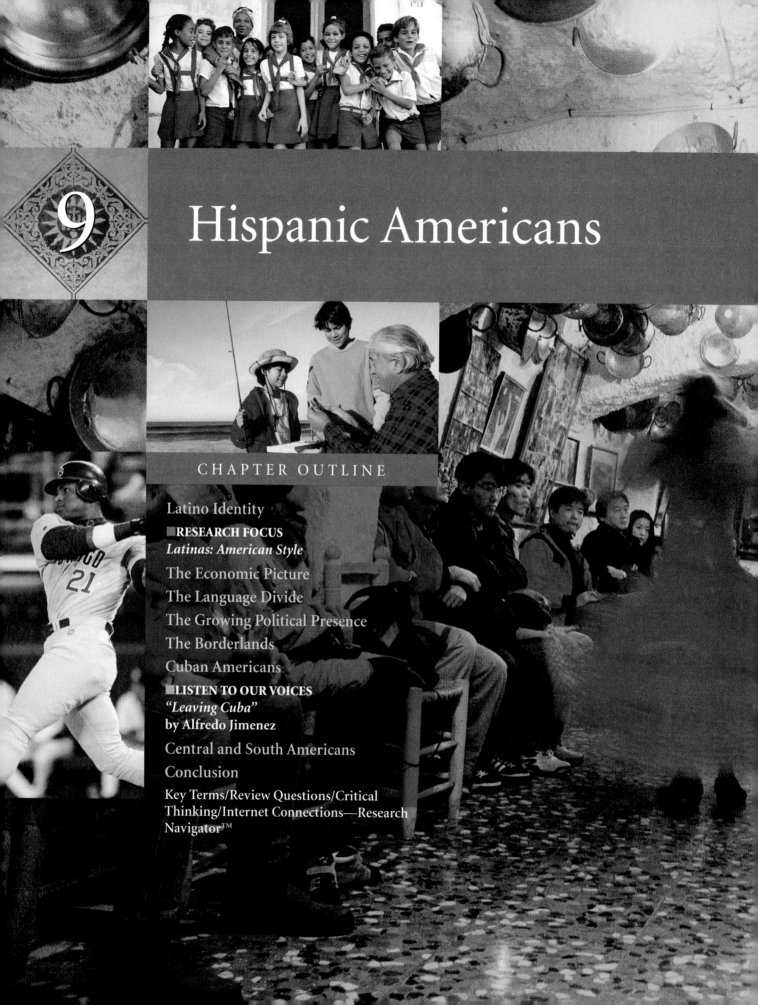

9

Hispanic Americans

CHAPTER OUTLINE

THE GROUP LABEL *HISPANIC* OR *LATINO AMERICAN* LINKS A diverse population that shares a common language heritage but otherwise has many significant differences. The language barrier in an assimilation-oriented society has been of major significance to Hispanics. For generations, schools made it difficult for Spanish-speaking children to succeed. The United States has only recently recognized its bilingual, bicultural heritage and allowed those whose native language is not English to use it as an asset rather than a liability. The strength of resistance, even to elements of pluralism, has been exhibited by the language purity movement. Latinos include several major groups, of which Mexican Americans, Puerto Ricans, and Cubans are the largest in the United States. Cuban Americans constitute a significant presence in southern Florida. Increasingly, immigrants and refugees from Central and South America have also established communities throughout the United States.

The Los Angeles Coliseum is rocking with a crowd of 92,000. Is it the USC Trojan football team playing at home? Britney Spears in a sold-out concert? No, it is Mexico and Argentina playing futbol (soccer) to a crowd with partisan fans cheering on Mexico. While it took until 2003, AOL now offers customer support in Spanish; now Latinos are expected to account for $1 trillion in online purchases by 2007. Consequently, Microsoft MSN launched a Spanish-language personal site and Yahoo en Español publishes news from *La opinión*, the nation's largest Spanish-language newspaper, and Notimex, Mexico's leading wire service.

As recently as 1997, American Airlines was roundly criticized for the contents of its manual for pilots flying between the United States and Latin America. A section called "Surviving in Latin America" included guidelines concerning mountainous areas near some local airports, but also declared that Latin American fliers like to drink alcohol before a flight, and "Unruly and/or intoxicated passengers are not infrequent" (O'Connor 1999; Swartz 2003; UPI 1997).

More than one in eight people in the U.S. population are of Spanish or Latin American origin. Collectively this group is called Hispanics or Latinos, two terms that we use interchangeably in this book. The Census Bureau estimates that by the year 2100, Hispanics will constitute about one-third of the U.S. population (refer back to Figure 1.1 on p. 6).

CD-ROM *Activity 7.1 & 7.2*

Already by 2003, population data showed 37.4 million Latinos, outnumbering the 34.7 million African Americans. The Latino population is very diverse. Today, 25 million, or two-thirds of Hispanics in the United States, are Mexican Americans, or Chicanos. The diversity of Latinos and their geographical distribution in the United States is shown in Figures 9.1 and 9.2 (Bureau of the Census 2004c; Ramirez and de la Cruz 2003).

The Latino influence is everywhere. Motion pictures such as *La Bamba, Born in East L.A., Stand and Deliver, Salsa, The Mambo Kings, Frida*, and *My Family/Mi Familia* did not cater only to Hispanic audiences. MTV offers a channel, MTV Ritmo, featuring all-Latin music. The number-one radio stations in Los Angeles and Miami broadcast in Spanish. In their speeches, politicians address the needs and desires of Latino Americans.

FIGURE 9.1 Hispanic Population of the United States by Origin, 2002

Source: Ramirez and de la Cruz 2003.

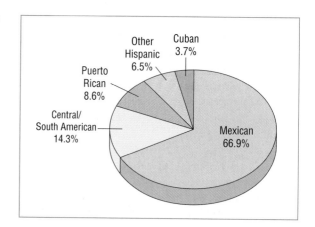

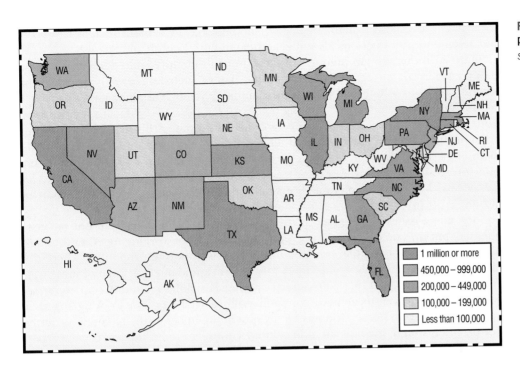

FIGURE 9.2   **Where Most Hispanic Americans Lived, 2002**
Source: Bureau of the Census 2003h.

Some prevailing images of Hispanic settlements in the United States are no longer accurate. Latinos do not live in rural areas. They are generally urban dwellers: 91 percent live in metropolitan areas, in contrast to 78 percent of non-Hispanic Whites. In addition, some Hispanics have moved away from their traditional areas of settlement. Many Mexican Americans have left the Southwest, and many Puerto Ricans have left New York City. In 1940, 88 percent of Puerto Ricans residing in the United States lived in New York City, but by the 2000 Census the proportion had dropped to less than a third (J. Logan 2001; Ramirez and de la Cruz 2003).

Latino Identity

Is there a common identity among Latinos? Is a panethnic identity emerging? **Panethnicity** is the development of solidarity between ethnic subgroups. We noted in Chapter 1 that ethnic identity is not self-evident in the United States and may lead to heated debates even among those who share the same ethnic heritage. Non-Hispanics often give a single label to the diverse group of native-born Latino Americans and immigrants. This labeling by the out-group is similar to the dominant group's way of viewing "American Indians" or "Asian Americans" as one collective group. For example, sociologist Clara Rodríguez has noted that Puerto Ricans, who are American citizens, are often mistakenly viewed as an immigrant group and lumped with all Latinos or Hispanics. She observes that, to most Anglos, "All Hispanics look alike. It's the tendency to see all Latinos as the same. It's an unfortunate lack of attention to U.S. history" (Rodríguez 1994:32).

Are Hispanics or Latinos themselves developing a common identity? Indicators vary. The collective term itself is subject to debate with regional variations; for example, *Latino* is more common in the West, and *Hispanic* is used more often in the East and is the term employed by the federal government. Whatever the term, the actions of the dominant group have an impact to some degree in defining cultural identity. Latinos

panethnicity
The development of solidarity between ethnic subgroups, as reflected in the terms *Hispanic* or *Asian American*.

ethclass
The merged ethnicity and class in a person's status.

are brought together through language, national cable TV stations such as Univision and Telemundo, and periodicals aimed at them in both English and Spanish.

Sharp divisions remain among Hispanics on the identity issue. Only a minority, about 24 percent, prefers to use panethnic names such as *Hispanic* or *Latino*. In Miami, one can see bumper stickers proclaiming "No soy Hispano, soy Cubano": "I am not Hispanic, I am Cuban." Among U.S.-born Latinos, there is clearly a move away from using the native country as a means of identity. Among this segment of the Latino population, 46 percent say they either first use or only use "American" to describe themselves, and 29 percent use their parents' country of origin. This contrasts sharply with foreign-born Latinos, a group in which only 21 percent use American and 54 percent use Mexican or Colombian or similar national terms of reference (Brodie et al 2002).

Such name issues or language battles, as they have been called, are not inconsequential, but they do distract these groups' attention from working together for common concerns. For example, bridging differences is important in politics, where the diverse Latino or Hispanic groups meet to support candidates or legislative initiatives. When specifically asked in a 2003 survey whether Hispanics from different countries are working together to achieve common political goals or not working together politically, their own perception was evenly split between believing in panethnic terms or not. Interestingly, income and education do not seem to influence Hispanics' perceptions, but the younger generation does seem to be thinking more in panethnic terms (Brodie et al. 2002). The identity issue for Latinos in the United States is complicated by class. In Chapter 5, we introduced the term **ethclass,** which describes the merging of ethnicity and class in a person's status. For Latino households that have achieved a measure of economic security—and there is a significant and growing middle class—the issue of identity is complicated as they move economically and perhaps socially further from their roots. In "Research Focus," we examine the special challenges that face many immigrant Latinas in the United States.

A very fluid issue is how successive generations of Latinos will identify themselves. Will they continue to see themselves in terms of their nationality background such as Nicaraguan or will they begin to converge toward a more panethnic identity?

LATINAS: AMERICAN STYLE

Being an adolescent in the United States is difficult—so many demands and changes in one's own desires that are difficult to manage. Add to this mix being an immigrant and the challenges escalate dramatically.

For adolescent Hispanics, it is particularly challenging because of the close-knit family ties. For example, a 2002 national survey of Latinos documented the emphasis on maintaining the household with a more traditional view. For example, 78 percent said it was better to have children continue to live with their parents until they get married, compared to less than half of Whites and African Americans. The feelings are even stronger among foreign-born Latinos, with 91 percent wanting their unmarried children at home.

To get a more personal perspective of what is happening in the lives of young Latins, Hispanic girls, a group of researchers interviewed at length Spanish-speaking Latinas at an urban midwestern school. They found that the Latinas are subject to harsher control both within the family and from the conformist school culture, which marks them as outsiders.

The Latinas are expected to help their family succeed through child care and housekeeping chores. These demands are much greater in the United States than they would have experienced in their home country, because here virtually all the adult family members have to work and often do so at odd hours. This expectation for the young Latinas of being at home when not at school effectively prevents them from working for wages like so many teenage girls, and that makes them seem different to their school peers. Without money from jobs, they are less able to "look American." The Latinas talk about how they wear inexpensive supermarket-brand tennis shoes, which stigmatizes them not only from other high school girls but even from their brothers, who manage to acquire more respectable footwear through their jobs. Indeed, they commented that even Mexican Americans snubbed them. Added to their household responsibilities is the greater supervision that young Latinas receive from their elders whenever they are not at home and especially at nonschool-related events.

Meanwhile their brothers are encouraged to work outside the home, which gives them greater freedom from the family and also gives them greater opportunities to practice English language skills with coworkers and customers. This in turn may lead to networking for future employment. Participation in high school sports is also encouraged for the Latino boys, and this furthers their acceptance within the culture of the high school. The gender structure of the family diminishes opportunities available to Latinas outside the family.

The Latinas described are typical of many teenage girls concerned with how they fit in. They want to belong, but family expectations of their role as girls keep them more removed from the very culture in which they want to assimilate. This research and survey data remind us of the special challenges faced by many immigrant girls, and especially those who do not speak English, a situation that, at least initially, serves to isolate them from others. They struggle to overcome being stigmatized as different. One Latina said that her classmates think Latinas "travel on burros" and that "we are called Maria." At the same time that they are trying to acquire skills in school, they are also faced with moving between identifying with the culture of their family and that of the society at large. ■

Sources: Brodie et al 2002; L. Williams 2002.

The Economic Picture

CD-ROM *Activity 7.3* There are many indicators of how well a group is doing economically in the United States, but probably income is the best one. As we can see in Figure 9.3, the median household income of Latinos has gradually increased over the last 20 years, with some fluctuations. However, relative to non-Hispanic Whites, the income gap has remained. Generally over the recent years, the Latino household can expect to earn 70 cents on the dollar received by its White counterpart.

The trend in poverty rate reflects that of the pattern in income. In 2002, 21.8 percent of Latinos were below the poverty level, compared to 8.1 percent of non-Hispanic Whites. This meant that one out of five Latinos in 2002 were in households of two adults and two children, for example, who received less than $18,244. Typically over the last twenty years, the proportion of Latinos in poverty has been two or three times that of non-Hispanic Whites (See Figure 9.4).

Looking at income trends of Latino households shows how much, but also how little, has been accomplished to reduce social inequality between ethnic and racial groups. While the income of Latinos has gradually increased over the last 30 years so has White income. The gap between the two groups in both income and poverty level has remained relatively constant. Indeed, the income of the typical Latino household in the 21st century has yet to match that of non-Hispanic Whites of 1979.

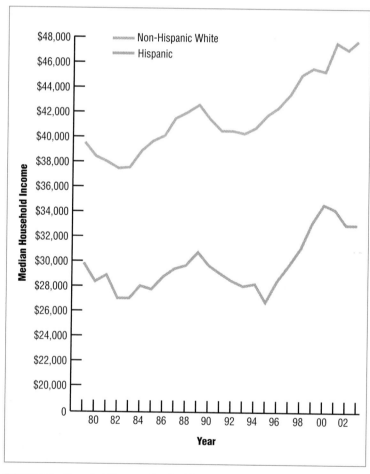

FIGURE 9.3   Household Income Trends, 1979–2003
Source: Bureau of the Census data in DeNavas-Walt et al. 2004

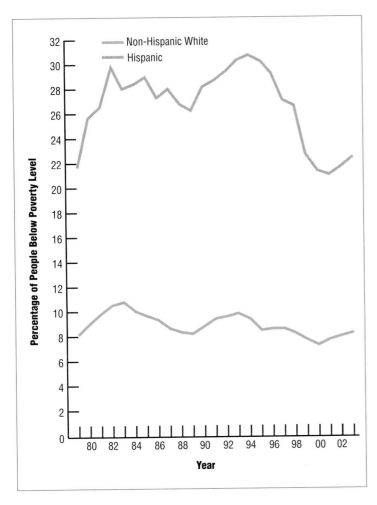

FIGURE 9.4   People in Poverty Trends, 1979–2003

Source: Bureau of the Census data in DeNavas-Walt et al. 2004.

The Language Divide

Hispanics, wherever they reside in the United States, share the heritage of the Spanish language. They do not all speak Spanish all the time; some, despite their heritage, do not know the language at all. The level of Spanish use relates to some degree to their area of origin and is certainly affected by length of time in the United States and whether or not they were born here.

As of 2002, about 23 percent of Mexican Americans are English dominant, 26 percent are bilingual, and 51 percent are Spanish dominant. Puerto Ricans in the United States tend to be more English-language oriented, with 39 percent English-dominant, 40 percent bilingual, and 21 percent Spanish dominant. At the other extreme, Salvadorans, Dominicans, Colombians, and other Central and South Americans tend to be more Spanish dominant, and they are also more likely to be more recent immigrants. Nationally, about 70 percent of Latino schoolchildren report speaking Spanish at home (Brodie et al. 2002; Bureau of the Census 2003a:158)

The myth of Anglo superiority has rested in part on language differences. (The term *Anglo* in the following text is used to mean all non-Hispanics, but primarily Whites.) First, the criteria for economic and social achievement usually include proficiency in English. By such standards, Spanish-speaking pupils are judged less able to compete until they learn English. Second, many Anglos believe that Spanish is not an asset occupationally. Only recently, as government agencies have belatedly begun to serve Latino people and as businesses recognize the growing Latino consumer market, have Anglos recognized that knowing Spanish is not only useful but also necessary to carry out certain tasks. However, as we see in education, voting, and language practices, many people in the United States are concerned and suspicious about the public use of any language other than English.

Bilingual Education

Until the last 20 or 30 years, there was a conscious effort to devalue the Spanish language and to discourage Hispanics from using it in schools. This practice was built on a pattern of segregating Hispanic schoolchildren from Anglos. In the recent past in the Southwest, Mexican Americans were assigned to Mexican schools to keep Anglo schools all White. These Mexican schools, created through de jure school segregation, were substantially underfunded compared with the regular public schools. Legal action against such schools dates back to 1945, but it was not until 1970 that the U.S. Supreme Court ruled, in *Cisneros v. Corpus Christi Independent School District,* that the de jure segregation of Mexican Americans was unconstitutional. Appeals delayed implementation of that decision, and not until September 1975 was the de jure plan forcibly overturned in Corpus Christi, Texas (Commission on Civil Rights 1976).

Even in integrated schools, Latino children were given separate, unequal treatment. "No Spanish" was a rule enforced throughout the Southwest, Florida, and New York City by school boards in the 1960s. Children speaking Spanish on school grounds, even on the playground, might be punished with detention after school, fines, physical reprimands, and even expulsion for repeated violations. From 1855 to as recently as 1968, teaching in any language other than English was illegal in California. Such laws existed despite a provision in the 1848 Treaty of Guadalupe Hidalgo between the United States and Mexico that guaranteed the right of Mexicans to maintain their culture. All official publications were to be bilingual, but "English only" became the social norm.

Is it essential that English be the sole language of instruction in schools in the United States? **Bilingualism** is the use of two or more languages in places of work or educational facilities, according each language equal legitimacy. Thus, a program of **bilingual education** may instruct children in their native language (such as Spanish) while gradually introducing them to the language of the dominant society (English). If such a program is also bicultural, it will teach children about the culture of both linguistic groups. Bilingual education allows students to learn academic material in their own language while they are learning a second language. Proponents believe that, ideally, bilingual education programs should also allow English-speaking pupils to be bilingual, but generally they are directed only at making non-English speakers proficient in more than one language.

Programs to teach English as a second language (ESL) have been the cornerstones of bilingual education, but they are limited in approach. For example, ESL programs tend to emphasize bilingual but not bicultural education. As a result, the method can unintentionally contribute to ethnocentric attitudes, especially if it seems to imply that a minority group is not really worthy of attention. As conflict theorists are quick to note, the interests of the less powerful—in this case, millions of non-English-speaking children—are those least likely to be recognized and respected. One alternative to the ESL approach, viewed with much less favor by advocates of bilingualism, is **English immersion**, in which students are taught primarily in English, using their native languages only when they do not understand their lessons. In practice, such instruction usually becomes an English-only "crash program" (Hechinger 1987).

bilingualism
The use of two or more languages in places of work or education and the treatment of each language as legitimate.

bilingual education
A program designed to allow students to learn academic concepts in their native language while they learn a second language.

English immersion
Teaching in English by teachers who know the students' native language but use it only when students do not understand the lessons.

Since its introduction into U.S. schools, bilingual education has been beset by problems. Its early supporters were disillusioned by the small number of English-speaking children participating and by the absence of a bicultural component in most programs. However, the frustration has been most clearly visible in the lack of consensus among educators on how best to implement bilingual programs. Even when a school district decides what methods it prefers, superintendents find it difficult to hire qualified instructors, although this varies depending on the language and the part of the country. The problem is further complicated by the presence of children speaking languages other than the predominant second language, so superintendents may want to mount bilingual programs in many languages.

Do bilingual programs help children to learn English? It is difficult to reach firm conclusions on the effectiveness of the bilingual programs in general because they vary so widely in their approach to non-English-speaking children. The programs differ in the length of the transition to English and how long they allow students to remain in bilingual classrooms. A major study released in 2004 analyzed more than three decades of research, combining 17 different studies, and found that bilingual education programs produce higher levels of student achievement in reading. The most successful are paired bilingual programs—those offering ongoing instruction in a naive language and English at different times of day (Slavin and Cheung 2003).

Drawing on the perspective of conflict theory, we can understand some of the attacks on bilingual programs. The criticisms do not necessarily result from careful educational research. Rather, they stem from the effort to assimilate children and to deprive them of language pluralism. This view, that any deviation from the majority is bad, is expressed by those who want to stamp out foreigners, especially in our schools. Research findings have little influence on those who, holding such ethnocentric views, try to persuade policy makers to follow their thinking. This perspective does not take into account that success in bilingual education may begin to address the problem of high school dropouts and the paucity of Hispanics in colleges and universities.

As one might expect, Latinos tend to be very supportive of bilingual programs. A 2003 national survey found that 72 percent of Hispanics (and a similar proportion of African Americans) favor school districts offering such programs compared to 53 percent of non-Hispanic Whites. Nonetheless, opposition to bilingualism can be quite strong among some Hispanics. A few are very active in organized efforts to stop such programs, and some Latino parents pressure schools to keep their children out of classrooms where Spanish may be spoken out of the misguided notion that English-only education, even for the youngest children, is the key to success (S. Freedman 2004; H. Mason 2003).

Official Language Movement

Attacks on bilingualism both in voting and in education have taken several forms and have even broadened to question the appropriateness of U.S. residents using any language other than English. Federal policy has become more restrictive. Local schools have been given more authority to determine appropriate methods of instruction; they have also been forced to provide more of their own funding for bilingual education.

Challenges to bilingualism continue. In 1997, California voters supported Proposition 227, calling for the end of bilingual education in its public schools. Implementation has been uneven, with some districts taking advantage of a provision for parents to keep their children out of English-immersion classes if they fill out a form declaring they have an "educational need" to remain in bilingual classes (Puente and Morello 1998).

Proposition 227, passed by California voters in 1997, called for an end to bilingual education in public schools.

Source: Philadelphia Business Journal/ John Spencer

Attacks on bilingualism have come on a number of fronts, but most seek to declare English a state's official language. By 2004, 27 states, by law or constitutional amendment, had established English as the official language. The measures range from simple declarations to actually preventing state business from being conducted in any language other than English. However, generally such measures are mostly symbolic, having little impact on bilingual publications, for example. On the national level, measures have been introduced in Congress for a constitutional amendment, most recently in 2001. The Declaration of Official Language Act would have repealed the Bilingual Education Act and repealed all bilingual ballot requirements (ProEnglish Language Association 2002a, 2002b; U.S English 2004).

McDonald's touts its "hamburguesas," and Anheuser-Busch insists that "Budweiser es para usted" ("is for you"). Perhaps at some time in the future, teachers and poll watchers will more often offer the greeting "Se habla inglés y español" ("English and Spanish spoken"). But for now, all too often, *bilingual* in reality means "Learn English."

The Growing Political Presence

In the last 30 years, the major political parties have begun to acknowledge that Latinos form a force in the election process. This recognition has come primarily by the growth of the Hispanic population but also through policies that have facilitated non-English voters.

In 1975, Congress moved toward recognizing the multilingual background of the U.S. population. Federal law now requires bilingual or even multilingual ballots in voting districts where at least 5 percent of the voting-age population or 10,000 of the population do not speak English. Even before Congress acted, the federal courts had been ordering cities such as Chicago, Miami, and New York City to provide bilingual ballots where necessary. In the November 2002 elections, some 296 counties and municipalities in 30 states issued multilingual ballots (Migration News 2002b).

Latino political involvement is often frustrated by old time politics that favor those long in power. Here Texas state senator Gonzala Basrietos holds a proposed redistricting map for defining boundaries to elect state representatives that many felt would not reflect the growing presence of Hispanics in his state.

These voting reforms did not have the impact that many of their advocates had hoped for. The turnout was poor, not because Hispanics were not interested in voting, but because many were ineligible under the U.S. Constitution because they were noncitizens. At the time of the 2000 presidential election, 39 percent of Hispanics of voting age were noncitizens compared with only 22 percent of White non-Hispanics (Jamieson et al. 2002).

The potential for a greater Latino political presence is strong. Anticipating the greater turnout, political parties are advancing more Hispanic candidates. Generally, the Democrats have been more successful in garnering the Hispanic vote: Al Gore garnered 62 percent of the Hispanic vote in 2000, compared with 35 percent for George W. Bush. However, observers agree that this is not as much a pro-Democrat vote as a stand against the Republicans, who favor reducing legal immigration, limiting welfare benefits to legal immigrants, and eliminating bilingual education. In fact, Latinos as a group are not nearly as pro-Democrat as, for example, African Americans.

Unlike the Black voter, the major political parties are more likely to see the Latino vote still in play. The 2004 Bush-Cheney ticket heavily promoted the "agenda del Presidente," while Kerry-Edwards encouraged "contribuya al Partido Democrático." Indeed, evidence shows that younger Hispanics are becoming more conservative and more likely to consider Republican candidates. All these factors among Hispanics— rapidly growing population, higher proportions of voter registration, higher participation in elections, less commitment to a single political party—will increase efforts by politicians to elicit their support (Keen and Benedetto 2001).

Like African Americans, many Latinos resent the fact that every four years political movers and shakers rediscover they exist. In between major elections, little effort is made to court their interest except by Latino elected officials.

borderlands
The area of a common culture along the border between Mexico and the United States.

The Borderlands

"The border is not where the U.S. stops and Mexico begins," says Laredo, Texas, mayor Betty Flores. "It's where the U.S. blends into Mexico" (Gibbs 2001:42). The term **borderlands** here refers to the area of a common culture along the border between Mexico and the United States. Though particularly relevant to Mexicans and Mexican Americans, the growing Mexican influence is relevant to the other Latino groups that we will discuss.

Maquiladoras are foreign-owned manufacturers located in Mexico along the U.S. border. Workers assemble components for export to the U.S. at a plant in Nueva Laredo, Mexico.

maquiladoras
Foreign-owned companies on the Mexican side of the border with the United States.

remittances (or migradollars)
The monies that immigrants return to their country of origin.

hometown clubs
Nonprofit organizations that maintain close ties to immigrants' hometowns in Mexico and other Latin American countries.

Legal and illegal emigration from Mexico to the United States, day laborers crossing the border regularly to go to jobs in the United States, the implementation of the North American Free Trade Agreement (NAFTA), and the exchange of media across the border all make the notion of separate Mexican and U.S. cultures obsolete in the borderlands.

The economic position of the borderlands is complex in terms of both businesses and workers. Very visible is the presence of **maquiladoras** on the Mexican side (Figure 9.5). These are foreign-owned companies that establish operations in Mexico yet are exempt from Mexican taxes and are not required to provide insurance or benefits for their workers. Pay at $2.00 to $2.50 an hour is considered very good by prevailing wage standards in Mexico. However, this one example of international trade soon became trumped by another aspect of globalization. As low as these hourly wages seem to people in industrial countries, multinational corporations soon found even lower wages in China. Over 40 percent of the 700,000 new maguiladora jobs created in the 1990s were eliminated by 2003 (*Migration News* 2002c, 2004).

Immigrant workers have a significant economic impact on their home country while employed in the United States. Many Mexicans, as well as other Hispanic groups we will be discussing, send some part of their earnings back across the border to family members remaining in their native country. This substantial flow of money, sometimes called **remittances** (or **migradollars**), is estimated at a minimum of $14.5 billion in 2003. Most of the money is spent to pay for food, clothing, and housing; but increasingly a growing proportion is being invested to create small businesses (G. Thompson 2003).

The closeness culturally and economically of the home country found in the borderlands is applicable to other Latino groups. We will see the continuing prominent role that the events, economic and political, have on the immigrants and their children, and even grandchildren, in the United States.

Inland from the border, hometown clubs have sprung up well into northern cities with large settlements of Mexicans. **Hometown clubs** typically are nonprofit organizations that maintain close ties to immigrants' hometowns in Mexico and other Latin

FIGURE 9.5   The Borderlands

In search of higher wages, undocumented Mexicans often attempt to cross the border illegally, risking their lives in the process. Maquiladoras located just south of the U.S.-Mexican border employ Mexican workers at wages far lower than those earned by U.S. workers. The Mexican workers and Mexican Americans send large amounts of money, called remittances, to assist kinfolk and communities in Mexico.
Source: Prepared by the author based on Ellingwood 2001 and Thompson 2001.

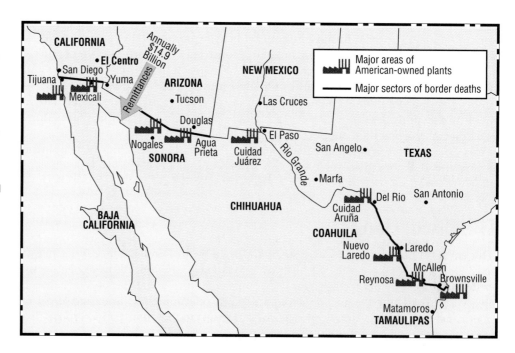

American countries. Hometown clubs collect money for improvements in hospitals and schools that are beyond the means of the local people back home. The impact of hometown clubs has become so noticeable that some states in Mexico have begun programs whereby they will match funds from hometown clubs to encourage such public-spirited efforts. The work of over 1,500 hometown clubs in the United States or Mexican communities alone reflects the blurring of border distinctions within the Latino community (Korecki 2003; *Migration News* 2000).

As we have noted, the Latino or Hispanic community is made up of several nationalities. The Mexican Americans, the people of the borderlands and beyond, and the Puerto Ricans are by far the two largest and are considered separately in Chapter 10. We will continue in this chapter by considering the other Latino groups.

Cuban Americans

Third in numbers only to Mexican Americans and Puerto Ricans, Cuban Americans are a significant ethnic Hispanic minority in the United States. Their presence in this country is a long one, with Cuban settlements in Florida dating back to as early as 1831. These settlements tended to be small, close-knit communities organized around a single enterprise, such as a cigar-manufacturing firm.

Until recently, however, the number of Cuban Americans was very modest. The 1960 Census showed that 79,000 people who had been born in Cuba lived in the United States. By 2000, more than 1.4 million people of Cuban birth or descent lived in the United States. This tremendous increase followed Fidel Castro's assumption of power after the 1959 Cuban Revolution.

Immigration

Cuban immigration to the United States since the 1959 revolution has been continuous, but there have been three significant influxes of large numbers of immigrants through the 1980s. First, the initial exodus of about 200,000 Cubans after Castro's assumption of power lasted about three years. Regular commercial air traffic continued despite the United States' severing of diplomatic relations with Cuba. This first wave stopped with the missile crisis of October 1962, when all legal movement between the two nations was halted.

An agreement between the United States and Cuba in 1965 produced the second wave through a program of freedom flights: specially arranged charter flights from Havana to Miami. Through these, more than 340,000 refugees arrived between 1965 and 1973. Despite efforts to encourage these arrivals to disperse into other parts of the United States, most settled in the Miami area (M. Abrahamson 1996).

The third major migration, the 1980 Mariel boatlift, has been the most controversial. In 1980, more than 124,000 refugees fled Cuba in the "freedom flotilla." In May of that year, a few boats from Cuba began to arrive in Key West, Florida, with people seeking asylum in the United States. President Carter, reflecting the nation's hostility toward Cuba's communist government, told the new arrivals and anyone else who might be listening in Cuba that they were welcome "with open arms and an open heart." As the number of arrivals escalated, it became apparent that Castro had used the invitation as an opportunity to send prison inmates, patients from mental hospitals, and addicts. However, the majority of the refugees were neither marginal to the Cuban economy nor social deviants.

Other Cubans soon began to call the refugees of this migration **Marielitos**. The word, which implies that these refugees were undesirable, refers to Mariel, the fishing port west of Havana from which the boats departed, where Cuban authorities herded

Marielitos
People who arrived from Cuba in the third wave of Cuban immigration, most specifically those forcibly deported by way of Mariel Harbor. The term is generally reserved for refugees seen as especially undesirable.

people into boats. The term *Marielitos* remains a stigma in the media and in Florida. Because of their negative reception by longer-established Cuban immigrants, as well as the group's modest skills and lack of formal education, this group had a great deal of difficulty in adjusting to their new life in the United States.

Now a Chicago real estate broker, Alfredo Jimenez tells in "Listen to Our Voices" of his experience he had as a young child being taken by his family and leaving everything behind in Cuba to go to the United States.

The difficult transition for many members of this freedom flotilla is linked with other factors as well. Unlike the earlier waves, they grew up in a country bombarded with anti-American images. Despite these problems, their eventual acceptance by the Hispanic community has been impressive, and many members of this third significant wave have found employment. Most have applied for permanent resident status. Gov-

 Voices **Listen to Our Voices** Listen to

LEAVING CUBA

At the age of eight I first realized my family was planning on leaving Cuba when my mother went to my second grade school in Havana to inform the principal that my brother and I would not be returning. I remember my teacher was not surprised that we were leaving but was surprised that we were *gusanos,* literally meaning worms or political dissidents. I returned home as my family waited to receive word that we were allowed to leave.

We waited about a week when a policeman knocked at our door in the middle of the night on May 17, 1980, and handed my father a document granting permission to leave Cuba. Within hours we had to get to the processing center, so my parents woke us up and prepared my grandmother who was in a wheelchair. At the center, the Cuban government confiscated our passports, searched us keeping all valuables including my parents' wedding rings. From there it was to Mariel Port three hours away by a special bus.

The trip on the bus was tough for an eight year old as people along the entire

Alfredo Jimenez

route beat on our bus with bats, sticks, stones, eggs, and tomatoes. Once at the Port, my brother and I managed to get away from the adults to play with other children at the beach where I remember playing with small crabs in the sand. My parents got very upset when our pant legs got wet. They had written on the inside of our pant legs the names, addresses, and phone numbers of friends and family in the United States and Spain.

Days of waiting and we were finally able to board an overcrowded boat headed for Florida. Already filled to the brim, the boat in the middle of the night rescued 12 people from another boat that was sinking. After twelve hours, we arrived in Key West to be greeted by waving American flags. Soon we headed on to Tampa to live with an aunt and her family—she had come to America soon after Fidel Castro assumed power.

The entire trip was an experience that my family values very much to this day. As young as my brother and I were, we didn't appreciate how difficult it was for my parents to leave everything behind. ■

ernment assistance to these immigrants was limited, but help from some groups of Cuban Americans in the Miami area was substantial. However, for a small core group, adjustment was impossible. The legal status of a few of these detainees (i.e., arrivals who were held by the government pending clarification of their refugee or immigrant status) was ambiguous because of alleged offenses committed in Cuba or the United States (Peréz 2001).

The Cuban refugee situation continues to be caught up in the strong anti-Castro, anticommunist feelings of most Cuban Americans and many others in the United States. Cuban refugees have a special advantage over other refugees in terms of public opinion. The issue of refugee rights came to an emotional and headline-grabbing climax with the decision to return six-year-old Elián Gonzalez to Cuba in 2000. His mother had drowned as she sought to bring him to the United States. After months of vehement protests by the Cuban American community to allow the boy to remain in the United States with some cousins, the federal government returned the boy to his father, with the full understanding that the boy would be returned to Cuba. In 2004, the Bush administration launched a series of steps including restricting travel to Cuba and remittances as a means to punish the Castro regime. Although refugee/immigrant issues often are driven by economics, the issue of communist governments still overshadows many people's attitudes about our relationship with Cuba (Dahlburg 2004b; Warren 2000).

The Present Picture

Compared with other recent immigrant groups and with Latinos as a whole, Cuban Americans are doing well. As shown in Table 9.1, Cuban Americans have college completion rates twice those of other Latinos. In this and all other social measures, the pattern is similar. Cuban Americans in 2000 compared favorably with other Hispanics, although recent arrivals as a group trail behind White Americans.

The presence of Cubans has been felt in urban centers throughout the United States, but most notably in the Miami, Florida, area. Throughout their various immigration phases, Cubans have been encouraged to move out of southern Florida, but many have returned to Dade County (metropolitan Miami), with its warm climate and proximity to other Cubans and Cuba itself. As of 2000, 55 percent of all Cuban Americans lived in the Miami area; another 15 percent lived elsewhere in Florida. Metropolitan Miami itself now has a Hispanic majority of 57 percent of the total population, compared with a Hispanic presence of only 4 percent in 1950 (J. Logan 2001).

TABLE 9.1
Selected Social and Economic Characteristics of Cubans and South Americans, 2000

	Total Non-Hispanic White	Total Hispanic	Cuban	Central and South American
Percentage completing college, 25 years and over	28.1	10.6	23.0	17.4
Percentage unemployed	3.4	6.8	5.8	5.1
Percentage of families with a single parent	17.4	32.1	22.9	35.0
Percentage living below poverty level	7.7	22.8	17.3	16.7
Median family income	$54,906	$33,077	$39,432	$34,806

Source: Therrien and Ramirez 2001:Tables 1, 4.1, 7.1, 9.2, 14.1.

Probably no ethnic group has had more influence on the fortunes of a city in a short period of time than have the Cubans on Miami. Most consider the Cubans' economic influence positive. The Cuban and other Latin American immigrants have transformed Miami from a quiet resort to a boomtown. To a large degree, they have re-created the Cuba they left behind. Today, the population of metropolitan Miami is more than 35 percent foreign born—more than any other city. Residents like to joke that one of the reasons they like living in Miami is that it is close to the United States (Clary 1997b).

The relations between Miami's Cuban Americans and other groups have not been perfect. For example, Miami's other Hispanics, including Venezuelans, Ecuadorians, and Colombians, resent being mistaken for Cubans and feel that their own distinctive nationalities are being submerged. Cubans now find in Miami's Little Havana area that storefronts advertise Salvordoran corn pancakes and waitresses hail from El Salvador. Cuban Miamians are also slowly adjusting to sharing their influence with the growing diversity of Hispanics. One obvious symbol is the investment of the park district in building more and more soccer fields—Cubans traditionally play baseball (Dahlburg 2004a).

All Cuban immigrants have had much to adjust to, and they have not been able to immediately establish the kind of life they sought. Although some of those who fled Cuba were forced to give up their life's savings, the early immigrants of the first wave were generally well educated, had professional or managerial backgrounds, and therefore met with greater economic success than later immigrants. However, regardless of the occupations the immigrants were able to enter, there was tremendous adjustment for the family. Women who typically did not work outside the home often had to seek employment. Immigrant parents found their children being exposed to a foreign culture. All the challenges typically faced by immigrant households were complicated by uncertainty surrounding those they left behind in Cuba.

The primary adjustment among south Florida's Cuban Americans is more to each other than to Whites, African Americans, or other Latinos. The prolonged immigration now stretching across two generations has led to differences between Cuban Americans in terms of ties to Cuba, social class, and age. There is not a single Cuban American lifestyle (Navarro 1999).

The long-range prospects for Cubans in the United States depend on several factors. Of obvious importance are events in Cuba, for many Cuban refugees publicly proclaim their desire to return if the communist government is overturned. A powerful force in politics in Miami is the Cuban-American National Foundation, which takes a strong anti-Castro position. They have actively opposed any proposals that the United States develop a more flexible policy toward Cuba. More moderate voices in the Cuban exile community have not been encouraged to speak out. Indeed, sporadic violence has even occurred within the community over U.S.–Cuban relations. In addition, artists or speakers who come from Cuba receive a cold reception in Miami unless they are outspoken critics of Fidel Castro (L. Martin 1996).

Cuban Americans have selectively accepted Anglo culture. But Cuban culture has been tenacious; the Cuban immigrants do not feel that they need to forget Spanish while establishing fluency in English, the way other immigrant children have shunned their linguistic past. Still, a split between the original exiles and their children is evident. Young people are more concerned about the Miami Dolphins football team than they are about what is happening in Havana. They are more open to reestablishing relations with a Castro-led Cuba. However, the more recent wave of immigrants, the *recién llegados* (recently arrived), have again introduced more openly anti-Castro feelings, as evidenced in the battles over Elián Gonzalez in 2000 and travel restrictions in 2004.

Central and South Americans

The immigrants who have come from Central and South America are a diverse population that has not been closely studied. Indeed, most government statistics treat its members collectively as "other" and rarely differentiate between them by nationality. Yet people from Chile and Costa Rica have little in common other than their hemisphere of origin and the Spanish language, if that. Not all Central and South Americans have Spanish as their native tongue; for example, immigrants from Brazil speak Portuguese, immigrants from French Guyana speak French, and those from Suriname speak Dutch.

Many of the nations of Central and South America have a complex system of placing people into myriad racial groups. African slaves were brought to almost all of these countries, and these people of African descent, in varying degrees, have intermarried with each other or with indigenous peoples, as well as with the European colonists. Rather than placing people in two or three distinct racial groupings, these societies describe skin color in a continuum from light to dark in what is called a color gradient. A **color gradient** is the placement of people along a continuum from light to dark skin color rather than in distinct racial groupings by skin color. The presence of color gradients is yet another reminder of the social construction of race. Terms such as *mestizo Hondurans*, *mulatto Colombians*, or *African Panamanians* reflect this continuum of a color gradient.

Added to language diversity and the color gradient are social class distinctions, religious differences, urban-versus-rural backgrounds, and differences in dialect even among those speaking the same language. We can understand historians Ann Orlov and Reed Ueda's (1980:212) conclusion that "social relations among Central and South American ethnic groups in the United States defy generalization." Central and South Americans do not form, nor should they be expected to form, a cohesive group, nor do they naturally form coalitions with Cuban Americans, Mexican Americans, or Puerto Ricans.

color gradient
The placement of people on a continuum from light to dark skin color rather than in distinct racial groupings by skin color.

The civil unrest that has occurred in some Latin American countries, such as El Salvador, spurred immigration to the United States in the 1980s and 1990s.

Immigration

Immigration from the various Central and South American nations has been sporadic, influenced by both our immigration laws and social forces operating in the home country. Perceived economic opportunities escalated the northward movement in the 1960s. By 1970, Panamanians and Hondurans represented the largest national groupings, most of them being identified in the census as "nonwhite."

Since the mid-1970s, increasing numbers of Central and South Americans have fled unrest. Although Latinos as a whole are a fast-growing minority, Central and South Americans increased in numbers even faster than Mexicans or any other group in the 1980s. In particular, from about 1978, war and economic chaos in El Salvador, Nicaragua, and Guatemala prompted many to seek refuge in the United States. Not at all a homogeneous group, they range from Guatemalan Indian peasants to wealthy Nicaraguan exiles. These latest arrivals probably had some economic motivation for migration, but this concern was overshadowed or at least matched by their fear of being killed or hurt if they remained in their home country (Camarillo 1993).

The immigrants who fled violence and poverty often have difficulty in adjusting initially because they received little preparation for their movement to a foreign culture. Mario fled to the United States from Nicaragua when he was 16. As he writes, the initial years were trying:

> *At first it was difficult to adjust. People are very materialistic in the U.S. I was starting from zero. I had nothing. They made fun of my clothes. They treated me differently. They pushed me out of their circle. Luckily, I met a friend from school back home who had been in the U.S. eight years. He took care of me. (Cerar 1995:57)*

Eventually Mario felt comfortable enough to help immigrants and to serve as a tutor at the local community college. His experience has been played out before in the United States and undoubtedly will be again many times.

The Present Picture

Two issues have clouded the recent settlement of Central and South Americans. First, many of the arrivals are illegal immigrants. Among those uncovered as undocumented workers, citizens from El Salvador, Guatemala, and Colombia are outnumbered only by Mexican nationals. Second, significant numbers of highly trained and skilled people have left these countries, which are in great need of professional workers. We noted in Chapter 4 how often immigration produces a **brain drain**: immigration to the United States of skilled workers, professionals, and technicians.

As a group, Central and South Americans experience high unemployment levels compared with whites, yet are better educated than most Hispanics, as shown in Table 9.1. This reflects the plight that often faces recent immigrants. Upon relocating to a new country, they initially experience downward mobility in terms of occupational status.

The challenges to immigrants from Latin America are reflected in the experience of Colombians, numbering close to a half million in the United States. The initial arrivals from this South American nation after World War I were educated middle-class people who quickly assimilated to life in the United States. Rural unrest in Colombia in the 1980s triggered large-scale movement to the United States, where the Colombian immigrants had to adapt to a new culture and to urban life. The adaptation of this later group has been much more difficult. Some have found success through catering to other Colombians. For example, enterprising immigrants have opened *bodegas* (grocery stores) to supply traditional, familiar foodstuffs. Similarly,

brain drain
Immigration to the United States of skilled workers, professionals, and technicians who are desperately needed by their home countries.

Latinos rarely appear on television in central roles, much less on successful television programs. While animated, Dora the Explorer on Nickelodeon is an exception to this rule.

Colombians have established restaurants, travel agencies, and real estate firms that serve other Colombians. However, many find themselves obliged to take menial jobs and to combine the income of several family members to meet the high cost of urban life. Colombians of mixed African descent face racial as well as ethnic and language barriers (Guzmán 2001).

What is likely to be the future of Central and South Americans in the United States? Although much will depend on future immigration, they could assimilate over the course of generations. One alternative is that they will become trapped with Mexican Americans as a segment of the dual labor market of the urban areas where they have taken residence. A more encouraging possibility is that they will retain an independent identity, like the Cubans, while also establishing an economic base. For example, nearly 600,000 Dominicans (from the Dominican Republic) settled in the New York City area, where they make up a significant 7 percent of the population. In some neighborhoods, such as Washington Heights, one can easily engage in business, converse, and eat just as if one were in the Dominican Republic. People continue to remain attentive to events in Dominican politics, which often commands greater attention than events in the United States. However, within their local neighborhoods, Dominicans here are focused on improving employment opportunities and public safety (J. Logan 2001a; Pessar 1995; Suro 1998).

Conclusion

The signals are mixed. Many movies and television programs and much music have a Hispanic flavor. Candidates for political office seek Latino votes and sometimes even speak Spanish to do so. Yet the poverty rate of Latino families reported in 2000 was more than 22 percent, compared with less than 8 percent for White Americans.

This mixture of positive and negative trends is visible in other areas. Ballots are printed in Spanish and other languages. Bilingual education at taxpayer expense is available throughout the United States. Yet more and more states are declaring English their official language, and even Congress from time to time considers a constitutional amendment to that effect. Many Latinos feel that to be bilingual is not to be less a part of the United States. Espousing pluralism rather than assimilation is not un-American.

The contrast of images and substance will be evident again in Chapter 10. "In World War II, more Latinos won Medals of Honor than any other ethnic group," said Democratic Representative Matthew Martinez, a former U.S. Marine who represented part of Los Angeles. "How much blood do you have to spill before you prove you are a part of something?" (Whitman 1987:49). Yet a contrasting image is offered by the refrain "Si usted no habla inglés puede quedarse rezagado" ("If you don't speak English, you might be left behind").

Key Terms

bilingual education 242
bilingualism 242
borderlands 245
brain drain 252
color gradient 251

English immersion 242
ethclass 238
hometown clubs 246
maquiladoras 246

Marielitos 247
panethnicity 237
remittances (or migradollars) 246

Review Questions

1. What different factors seem to unite and to divide the Latino community in the United States?

2. How do Hispanics view themselves as a group? How are they viewed by others?

3. Why have language and bilingualism become almost ideological issues in the United States?

4. To what extent has the Cuban migration been positive, and to what degree do significant challenges remain?

5. How have Central and South Americans contributed to the diversity of the Hispanic peoples in the United States?

Critical Thinking

1. Language and culture are almost inseparable. How do you imagine your life would change if you were not permitted to speak your native language? Or how has it been affected if you have been expected to speak some other language?

2. How have you witnessed the presence of a different culture in the United States? At what times have you found it to be interesting and intriguing? Are there times you felt threatened by it or felt its presence to be unfair?

3. Why do you think the borderlands of the U.S.-Mexico border region have been the subject of such close scrutiny, whereas there is little attention to similar areas along the U.S.-Canada border?

Internet Connections—Research Navigator™

Follow the instructions found on page 31 of this text to access the features of Research Navigator™. Once at the Web site, enter your Login Name and Password. Then, to use the ContentSelect database, enter keywords such as "bilingualism," "remittances," "maquiladoras," and "Little Havana," and the research engine will supply relevant and recent scholarly and popular press publications. Use the *New York Times* Search-by-Subject Archive to find recent news articles related to sociology, and the Link Library feature to locate relevant Web links organized by the key terms associated with this chapter.

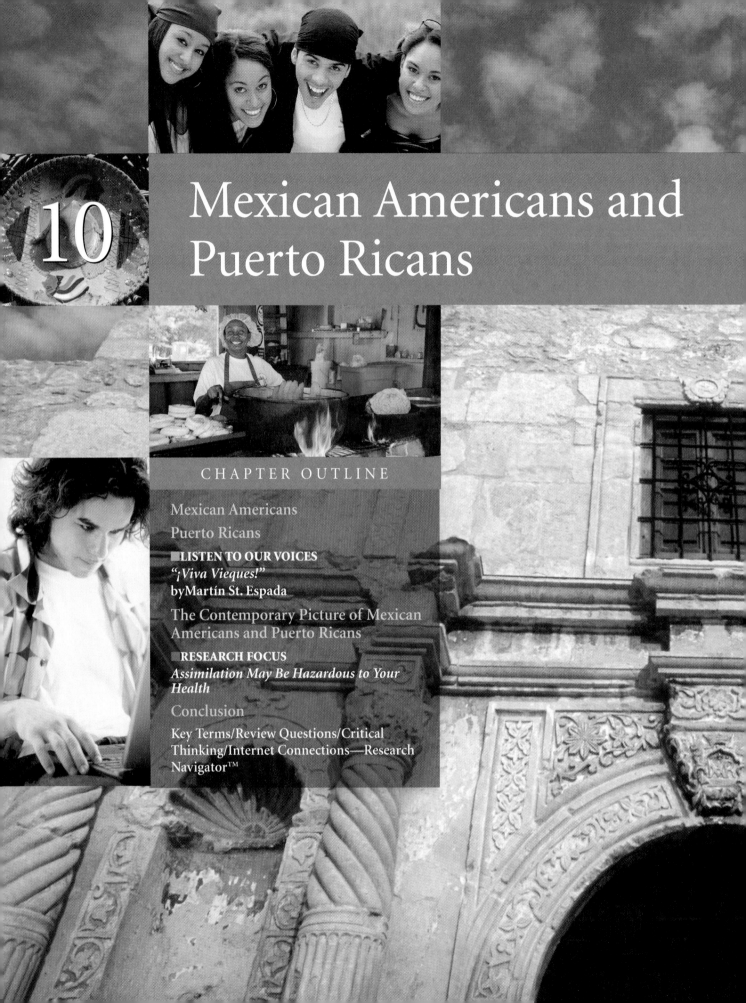

10 Mexican Americans and Puerto Ricans

THE HISTORY OF MEXICAN AMERICANS IS CLOSELY TIED TO immigration, which has been encouraged (the *bracero* program) when Mexican labor is in demand or discouraged (repatriation and Operation Wetback) when Mexican workers are unwanted. The Puerto Rican people are divided between those who live in the island commonwealth and those who live on the mainland. Puerto Ricans who migrate to the mainland most often come in search of better jobs and housing. Both Mexican Americans and Puerto Ricans, as groups, have lower incomes, less formal education, and greater health problems than White Americans. Both the family and religion are sources of strength for the typical Puerto Rican or Mexican American.

Citizenship is the basic requirement for receiving one's legal rights and privileges in the United States. However, for both Mexican Americans and Puerto Ricans, citizenship has been an ambiguous concept at best. Mexican Americans (or Chicanos) have a long history in the United States, stretching back before the nation was even formed, to the early days of European exploration. Santa Fe, New Mexico, was founded more than a decade before the Pilgrims landed at Plymouth. The Mexican American people trace their ancestry to the merging of Spanish settlers with the Native Americans of Central America and Mexico. This ancestry reaches back to the brilliant Mayan and Aztec civilizations, which attained their height about A.D. 700 and 1500, respectively. However, roots in the land do not guarantee a group dominance over it. Over several centuries, the Spaniards conquered the land and merged with the Native Americans to form the Mexican people. In 1821, Mexico obtained its independence, but this independence was short lived, for domination from the north began less than a generation later (Meier and Rivera 1972).

Today, Mexican Americans are creating their own destiny in the United States while functioning in a society that is often concerned about immigration, legal and illegal. In the eyes of some, including a few in positions of authority, to be Mexican American is to be suspected of being in the country illegally or, at least, of knowingly harboring illegal aliens.

For no other minority group in the United States is citizenship so ambiguous as it is for Puerto Ricans. Even Native Americans, who are subject to some unique laws and are exempt from others because of past treaties, have a future firmly dominated by the United States. This description does not necessarily fit Puerto Ricans. Their island home is the last major U.S. colonial territory and, for that matter, one of the few colonial areas remaining in the world. Besides assessing the situation of Puerto Ricans on the mainland, we will also need to consider the relationship of the United States to Puerto Rico.

Mexican Americans

Wars play a prominent part in any nation's history. The United States was created as a result of the colonies' war with England to win their independence. In the 1800s, the United States acquired significant neighboring territory in two different wars. The legacy of these wars and the annexation that resulted was to create the two largest Hispanic minorities in the United States: Mexican Americans and Puerto Ricans.

A large number of Mexicans became aliens in the United States without ever crossing any border. These people first became Mexican Americans with the conclusion of the Mexican–American War. This two-year war culminated with U.S. occupation of 11 months. Today Mexicans visit the Museum of Interventions in Mexico City, which outlines the war and Mexico's permanently giving up half its country. The war is still spoken of today as "the Mutilation" (T. Weiner 2004).

In the war-ending Treaty of Guadalupe Hidalgo, signed February 2, 1848, Mexico acknowledged the annexation of Texas by the United States and ceded California and most of Arizona and New Mexico to the United States for $15 million. In exchange, the United States granted citizenship to the 75,000 Mexican nationals who remained

The Roman Catholic Church has a long history among Mexicans and Mexican Americans. The Mission San Xavier del Bac in Arizona was founded in 1700.

on the annexed land after one year. With citizenship, the United States was to guarantee religious freedom, property rights, and cultural integrity—that is, the right to continue Mexican and Spanish cultural traditions and to use the Spanish language.

The beginnings of the Mexican experience in the United States were as varied as the people themselves. Some Mexican Americans were affluent, with large land holdings. Others were poor peasants barely able to survive. Along such rivers as the Rio Grande, commercial towns grew up around the increasing river traffic. In New Mexico and Arizona, many Mexican American people welcomed the protection that the U.S. government offered against several Native American tribes. In California, life was quickly dominated by the gold miners, and Anglos controlled the newfound wealth. One generalization can be made about the many segments of the Mexican American population in the 19th century: They were regarded as a conquered people. In fact, even before the war, many Whites who traveled into the West were already prejudiced against people of mixed blood (in this instance, against Mexicans). Whenever Mexican American and Anglo interests conflicted, Anglo interests won (Servin 1974).

A pattern of second-class treatment for Mexican Americans emerged well before the 20th century. Gradually, the Anglo system of property ownership replaced the Native American and Hispanic systems. Mexican Americans who inherited land proved no match for Anglo lawyers. Court battles provided no protection for poor Spanish-speaking landowners. Unscrupulous lawyers occasionally defended Mexican Americans successfully, only to demand half the land as their fee. Anglo cattle ranchers gradually pushed out Mexican American ranchers. By 1892, the federal government was granting grazing privileges on public grasslands and forests to anyone except Mexican Americans. Effectively, the now Mexican *Americans* had become outsiders in their own homeland. The ground was laid for the social structure of the Southwest in the 20th century, an area of growing productivity in which minority groups have increased in size but remain largely subordinate (Moquin and Van Doren 1971:251).

The Immigrant Experience

Nowhere else in the world do two countries with such different standards of living and wage scales share such an open border. Immigration from Mexico is unique in several respects. First, it has been a continuous large-scale movement for most of this century.

The United States did not restrict immigration from Mexico through legislation until 1965. Second, the proximity of Mexico encourages past immigrants to maintain strong cultural and language ties with the homeland through friends and relatives. Return visits to the old country are only 1- or 2-day bus rides for Mexican Americans, not once-in-a-lifetime voyages, as they were for most European immigrants. The third point of uniqueness is the aura of illegality that has surrounded Mexican migrants. Throughout the 20th century, the suspicion in which Anglos have held Mexican Americans has contributed to mutual distrust between the two groups.

The years before World War I brought large numbers of Mexicans into the expanding agricultural industry of the Southwest. The Mexican revolution of 1909–1922 thrust refugees into the United States, and World War I curtailed the flow of people from Europe, leaving the labor market open to the Mexican Americans. After the war, continued political turmoil in Mexico and more prosperity in the Southwest brought still more Mexicans across the border.

Simultaneously, corporations in the United States, led by agribusiness, invested in Mexico in such a way as to maximize their profits but minimize the amount of money remaining in Mexico to provide needed employment. Conflict theorists view this investment as part of the continuing process in which American businesses, with the support and cooperation of affluent Mexicans, have used Mexican people when it has been in corporate leaders' best interests. The Mexican workers are used either as cheap laborers in their own country by their fellow Mexicans and by Americans or as undocumented workers here who are dismissed when they are no longer judged to be useful (Guerin-Gonzales 1994).

Beginning in the 1930s, the United States embarked on a series of measures aimed specifically at Mexicans. The Depression brought pressure on local governments to care for the growing number of unemployed and impoverished. Government officials developed a quick way to reduce welfare rolls and eliminate people seeking jobs: Ship Mexicans back to Mexico. This program of deporting Mexicans in the 1930s was called **repatriation**. As officially stated, the program was constitutional because only illegal aliens were to be repatriated. Actually, it was much more complex. Border records were incomplete because, before 1930, the United States had shown little interest in whether Mexicans entered with all the proper credentials. Also, many Mexicans who could be classified as illegal aliens had resided in the United States for decades. Because they had children who were citizens by birth, they could not legally be deported. The legal process of fighting a deportation order was overwhelming, however, especially for a poor Spanish-speaking family. The Anglo community largely ignored this outrage against the civil rights of those deported and did not show interest in helping repatriates to ease the transition (Meier and Rivera 1972).

When the Depression ended, Mexican laborers again became attractive to industry. In 1942, when World War II was depleting the labor pool, the United States and Mexico agreed to a program allowing migration across the border by contracted laborers, or *braceros*. Within a year of the initiation of the **bracero** program, more than 80,000 Mexican nationals had been brought in; they made up one-eleventh of the farm workers on the Pacific Coast. The program continued with some interruptions until 1964. It was devised to recruit labor from poor Mexican areas for U.S. farms. In a program that was supposed to be supervised jointly by Mexico and the United States, minimum standards were to be maintained for the transportation, housing, wages, and health care of the *braceros*. Ironically, these safeguards placed the *braceros* in a better economic situation than Mexican Americans, who often worked alongside the protected Mexican nationals. The Mexicans were still regarded as a positive presence by Anglos only when useful, and the Mexican American people were merely tolerated (Galarza 1964; Stoddard 1973).

repatriation
The program during the 1930s of deporting Mexicans.

bracero
Contracted Mexican laborers brought to the United States during World War II.

Another crackdown on illegal aliens was to be the third step in dealing with the perceived Mexican problem. Alternately called Operation Wetback and Special Force Operation, it was fully inaugurated by 1954. The term *wetbacks,* or **mojados**, the derisive slang for Mexicans who enter illegally, refers to those who secretly swim across the Rio Grande. Like other roundups, this effort failed to stop the illegal flow of workers. For several years, some Mexicans were brought in under the *bracero* program while other Mexicans were being deported. With the end of the *bracero* program in 1964 and stricter immigration quotas for Mexicans, illegal border crossings increased because legal crossings became more difficult (W. Gordon 1975; Stoddard 1973, 1976a, 1976b).

More dramatic than the negative influence that continued immigration has had on employment conditions in the Southwest is the effect on the Mexican and Mexican American people themselves. Routinely, the rights of Mexicans, even the rights to which they are entitled as illegal aliens, are ignored. Of the illegal immigrants deported, few have been expelled through formal proceedings. The Mexican American Legal Defense and Education Fund (MALDEF) has repeatedly expressed concern over the government's handling of illegal aliens.

Against this backdrop of legal maneuvers is the tie that the Mexican people have to the land both in today's Mexico and in the parts of the United States that formerly belonged to Mexico. *Assimilation* may be the key word in the history of many immigrant groups, but for Mexican Americans the key term is **La Raza**. *La Raza* literally means "the people," but among contemporary Mexican Americans the term connotes pride in a pluralistic Spanish, Native American, and Mexican heritage. Mexican Americans cherish their legacy and, as we shall see, strive to regain some of the economic and social glory that once was theirs.

Despite passage of various measures designed to prevent illegal immigration, neither the immigration nor the apprehension of illegal aliens is likely to end. Mexican Americans will continue to be more closely scrutinized by law enforcement officials because their Mexican descent makes them more suspect as potential illegal aliens. The Mexican American community is another group subject to racial profiling that renders, in the eyes of many, their presence in the United States suspect (A. Aguirre Jr. 2004).

In the United States, Mexican Americans have mixed feelings toward the illegal Mexican immigrants. Many are their kin, and Mexican Americans realize that entry

mojados
"Wetbacks;" derisive slang for Mexicans who enter illegally, supposedly by swimming the Rio Grande.

La Raza
"The People," a term referring to the rich heritage of Mexican Americans and therefore used to denote a sense of pride among Mexican Americans today.

Mexican migrants harvest strawberries in California.

culture of poverty
A way of life that involves no future planning, no enduring commitment to marriage, and no work ethic; this culture follows the poor even when they move out of the slums or the barrio.

into the United States brings Mexicans better economic opportunities. However, numerous deportations only perpetuate the Anglo stereotype of Mexican and Mexican American alike as surplus labor. Mexican Americans, largely the product of past immigration, find that the continued controversy over illegal immigration places them in the ambivalent role of citizen and relative. Mexican American organizations opposing illegal immigration must confront people to whom they are closely linked by culture and kinship, and they must cooperate with government agencies they deeply distrust (W. Graham 1996).

The Economic Picture

As shown in Table 10.1, both Mexican Americans and Puerto Ricans have higher unemployment rates, higher rates of poverty, and significantly lower incomes than White Americans. In 2002, 6 percent of all managerial and professional positions were held by Latinos. When considering their economic situation, two topics deserve special attention: the debate over what has been called the culture of poverty and the effort to improve the status of migrant workers (Bureau of the Census 2003a:399).

The Culture of Poverty   Like the African American families described in Chapter 8, Mexican American families are labeled as having traits that, in fact, describe poor families rather than specifically Mexican American families. Indeed, as long ago as 1980, a report of the Commission on Civil Rights (1980:8) stated that the two most prevalent stereotypical themes appearing in works on Hispanics showed them as exclusively poor and prone to commit violence.

Social scientists have also relied excessively on the traits of the poor to describe an entire subordinate group such as Mexican Americans. Anthropologist Oscar Lewis (1959, 1965, 1966), in several publications based on research conducted among Mexicans and Puerto Ricans, identified the "culture of poverty." According to its theorists, the **culture of poverty** embraces a deviant way of life that involves no future planning, no enduring commitment to marriage, and absence of the work ethic. This culture supposedly follows the poor, even when they move out of the slums or the barrio.

The culture-of-poverty view is another way of blaming the victim: The affluent are not responsible for social inequality, nor are the policy makers; it is the poor who are to blame for their own problems. This stance allows government and society to attrib-

> **TABLE 10.1**
> **Selected Social and Economic Characteristics of Mexican Americans and Puerto Ricans, 2000**
>
> | | Total Non-Hispanic White | Total Hispanic | Mexican Americans | Puerto Ricans |
> |---|---|---|---|---|
> | Percentage completing college, 25 years and over | 28.1 | 10.6 | 6.9 | 13.0 |
> | Percentage unemployed | 3.4 | 6.8 | 7.0 | 8.1 |
> | Percentage of families with a single parent | 17.4 | 32.1 | 30.0 | 43.2 |
> | Percentage living below poverty level | 7.7 | 22.8 | 24.1 | 25.8 |
> | Median family income | $54,906 | $33,077 | $32,345 | $31,312 |
>
> *Source:* Therrien and Ramirez 2001:Tables 1, 4.1, 7.1, 9.2, 14.1.

ute the failure of antipoverty and welfare programs to Mexican Americans and other poor people, rather than to the programs themselves. These are programs designed and too often staffed by middle-class, English-speaking Anglo professionals. Conflict theorists, noting a similar misuse of the more recent term *underclass,* argue that it is unfair to blame the poor for their lack of money, low education, poor health, and low-paying jobs (Ryan 1976).

Lewis's hypothesis about the culture of poverty came to be used indiscriminately to explain continued poverty. Critics argue that Lewis sought out exotic, pathological behavior, ignoring the fact that even among the poor, most people live fairly conventionally and strive to achieve goals similar to those of the middle class. A second criticism challenges the use of the term *culture of poverty* to describe an entire ethnic group. Because Lewis's data were on poor people, social scientists have increasingly stressed that his conclusions may be correct as far as the data permit, but the data cannot be generalized to all Latinos. His sample was not a representative cross-section drawn from different economic and educational levels (Gans 1995; Valentine 1968).

More recent social science research, unlike Lewis's, does sample Mexican American families across a broad range of socioeconomic levels. This research shows that when Anglo and Mexican American families of the same social class are compared, they differ little in family organization and attitudes toward childrearing. In addition, comparisons of work ethics find no significant differences between Mexican Americans and Anglos. Poverty is present among Mexican Americans; there is no doubt about that. However, that does not mean there is a culture of poverty or a permanent underclass. Institutions such as the family and the church seem viable, but the schools are in despair, and the picture on businesses is mixed. However, to question the label *culture of poverty* does not deny the poor life chances facing many Mexican Americans (Aponte 1991; Moore and Pinderhughes 1993; Winkler 1990).

Chávez and the Farm Laborers   The best-known Hispanic labor leader for economic empowerment was César Chávez, the Mexican American who crusaded to organize migrant farm workers. Efforts to organize agricultural laborers date back to the turn of the century, but Chávez was the first to enjoy any success. These laborers had never won collective bargaining rights, partly because their mobility made it difficult for them to organize into a unified group.

In 1962, Chávez, then 35 years old, formed the National Farm Workers Association, later to become the United Farm Workers (UFW). Organizing migrant farm workers was not easy, for they had no savings to pay for organizing or to live on while striking. Growers could rely on an almost limitless supply of Mexican laborers to replace the Mexican Americans and Filipinos who struck for higher wages and better working conditions.

Chávez's first success was the grape boycott launched in 1965, which carried the struggle into the kitchens of families throughout the country. The UFW launched the boycott with the aim of damaging growers economically until they accepted the union and improved working conditions. It took five years for the grape growers to sign three-year contracts with Chávez's union, which had affiliated with the AFL-CIO. This victory signaled a new era in labor relations and made Chávez a national folk hero (Levy 1975).

Despite their success, Chávez and the UFW were plagued with continual opposition by agribusiness and many lawmakers. This was about the time the UFW was also trying to heighten public consciousness of the pesticides used in the fields. Research into the long-term effects of pesticides had only begun. Although Chávez's 1988 fast to bring attention to this issue was widely publicized, his efforts did not gain the support he had hoped for.

César Chávez

Chávez had difficulty fulfilling his objectives. By 1993, union membership had dwindled from a high of 80,000 in 1970 to 21,000. Nevertheless, what he and the UFW accomplished was significant. First, they succeeded in making federal and state governments more aware of the exploitation of migrant laborers. Second, the migrant workers, or at least those organized in California, developed a sense of their own power and worth that will make it extremely difficult for growers to abuse them in the future as they had in the past. Third, working conditions improved. California agricultural workers were paid an average of less than $2 an hour in the mid-1960s. By 1987, they were being paid an average of about $5.85 an hour (Mandelbaum 2000; Sanchez 1998).

Migrant workers still face a very harsh life. An ongoing study of agricultural workers found they are much more likely to suffer from high blood pressure, dental disease, anemia, and poor nutrition, which is ironic because they are harvesting the nation's food. About 70 percent of the workers lack health insurance, and most make less than $10,000 a year, which makes obtaining health care very difficult. Women have far better access to medical treatment because of special maternal and child health services, but a third of the men surveyed said they had never been to a physician or a clinic (Rainey 2000).

César Chávez died in 1993. Although his legacy is clear, many young people, when they hear mention of Chávez, are more likely to think of professional boxer Julio Cesar Chavez. By the beginning of the 21st century, the primary challenge came from efforts to permit more foreign workers, primarily from Mexico and Central America, to enter the United States temporarily at even lower wages. The problems of migrant farm workers are inextricably tied to the lives of both Latinos and Latin Americans (S. Greenhouse 2001).

Political Organizations

As noted in Chapter 9, Latinos are becoming more involved in party politics in the United States. Though tending to support Democratic candidates (with the exception of Cuban Americans, who typically back Republicans), Latinos are showing a willingness to be more independent voters. As one might expect, given their growing numbers and greater voting power, more Latinos are successfully seeking elective office. This has not always been the case. Politically oriented Mexican Americans such as

FARM WORKERS' SANITATION FACILITIES...

Recently, farm workers have protested their working conditions and the pesticide use that may threaten their lives.

Source: © Gary Huck/UE, Huck/Konopacki Labor Cartoons

Rodolpho "Corky" Gonzales in Denver turned to grassroots community organizing. Frustrated by the lack of responsiveness of established politicians, Mexican Americans for a brief period created their own independent party in Texas. La Raza Unida (LRU) was a third party supporting candidates who offered alternatives to the Democratic and Republican parties (Hero 1995; Rosales 1996).

The social protests that characterized much of the political activity in the United States of the mid-1960s touched the Mexican American community as well. In southern California in 1966, young Chicanos in college were attracted to the ideology of **Chicanismo** (or *Chicanozaje*) and joined what is popularly called the Chicano movement. Like Black Power, Chicanismo has taken on a variety of meanings, but all definitions stress a positive self-image and place little reliance on conventional forms of political activity. Followers of Chicanismo, unlike the more assimilation-oriented older generations, have been less likely to accept the standard claim that the United States is equally just to all.

Besides a positive self-image, Chicanismo and the movement of La Raza include renewed awareness of the plight of Chicanos at the hands of Anglos. Mexican Americans are a colonial minority, as Joan Moore (1970) wrote, because their relationship with Anglos was originally involuntary. Mexican culture in the United States has been either transformed or destroyed by Anglos, and the Mexican American people themselves have been victims of racism. The colonial model points out the ways in which societal institutions have failed Mexican Americans and perpetuated their problems. Militant Mexican Americans refer to assimilationists, who they say would sell out to the White people, as *vendidos,* or traitors. The ultimate insult is the term *Malinche,* the name of the Mexican American woman who became the mistress of Spanish conqueror Cortés. Many in the Chicano movement believe that if one does not work actively in the struggle, one is working against it (Rosales 1996; see also Barrera et al. 1972; Moore and Pachon 1985).

Perhaps as well as any recent Mexican American, Reies Lopéz Tijerina captures the spirit of Chicanismo. Born in a cotton field worked by migrant farmers, Tijerina

Chicanismo
An ideology emphasizing pride and positive identity among Mexican Americans.

became a Pentecostal preacher and in the late 1950s took an interest in old Spanish land grants. From research in Mexico, Spain, and the Southwest, he concluded that the Mexican Americans—and, more specifically, the Hispanos—had lost significant tracts of land through quasi-legal and other questionable practices. In 1963, he formed the Atlanza Federal de Mercedes (Federal Alliance of Land Grants), whose purpose is to recover the lost land. To publicize his purpose when few Anglos would pay attention, he seized part of the Kit Carson National Forest in New Mexico. Tijerina spent the next few years either in jail or awaiting trial. Tijerina's quest for restoration of land rights has been accompanied by violence, even though he advocates civil disobedience. However, the violence led him to be criticized by some Hispanics as well as Anglos (Nabokov 1970; Rosales 1996).

Thirty years later, Tijerina's arguments, which had seemed outrageous to most, were beginning to be endorsed by politicians. In 1997, Republican members of Congress introduced the Guadalupe-Hidalgo Treaty Claims Act to review Latino land claims especially as they relate to government-held forestland. Clearly, the Republicans are trying to garner support from Hispanic voters, but most important, this action shows that the goals of Tijerina and his followers are finally being considered seriously (Brooke 1998).

Organized in 1967, the Mexican American Legal Defense and Education Fund (MALDEF) has emerged as a potent force to protect Mexican Americans' constitutional rights. Although it does not endorse candidates, it has made itself felt in the political arena, much as the NAACP has for African Americans. On the education side, it has addressed segregation, biased testing, inequities in school financing, and failure to promote bilingualism. MALDEF has been involved in litigation concerning employment practices, immigration reform, and voting rights. It has emerged as the primary civil rights group for Mexican Americans and other Latinos (Vigil 1990).

The late 1990s saw the Mexican community in the United States faced with a new political challenge. Beginning in 1998, Mexicans in the United States could acquire rights as Mexican nationals under Mexico's new dual nationality law. Their children, even if U.S. born, are also eligible for Mexican nationality. The United States does not prohibit dual nationality, and it is estimated that anywhere from 5 to 10 million Mexican Americans are eligible for such dual nationality. Although many dual-nationality people will not be allowed to vote in Mexico's elections, this measure is likely to further their interest in political life south of the border. As we will now see with Puerto Rico, Latinos in the United States find political issues of importance outside the 50 states (*Migration News* 1998).

Puerto Ricans

Puerto Ricans' current association with the United States, like that of the Mexican people, began as the result of the outcome of a war. The island of Borinquén, subsequently called Puerto Rico, was claimed by Spain in 1493. The native inhabitants, the Taino Indians, were significantly reduced in number by conquest, slavery, and genocide. While for generations the legacy of the Taíno was largely thought to be archaeological in nature, recent DNA tests revealed that more than 60 percent of Puerto Ricans today have a Taíno ancestor (Cockburn 2003:41).

After Puerto Rico had been ruled by Spain for four centuries, the island was seized by the United States in 1898 during the Spanish-American War. Spain relinquished control of it in the Treaty of Paris. The value of Puerto Rico for the United States, as it had been for Spain, was mainly its strategic location, which was advantageous for maritime trade (Figure 10.1).

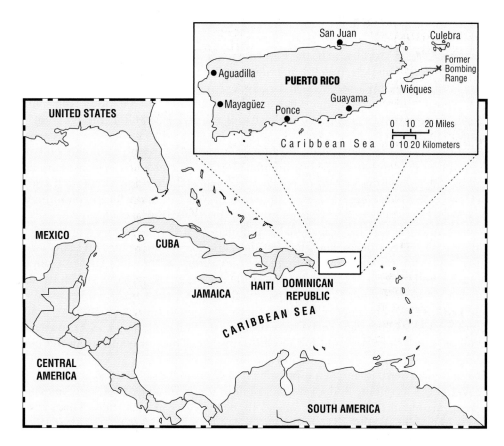

FIGURE 10.1   Puerto Rico

The beginnings of rule by the United States quickly destroyed any hope that Puerto Ricans—or Boricua, as Puerto Ricans call themselves—had for self-rule. All power was given to officials appointed by the president, and any act of the island's legislature could be overruled by Congress. Even the spelling was changed briefly to Porto Rico to suit North American pronunciation. English, previously unknown on the island, became the only language permitted in the school systems. The people were colonized—first politically, then culturally, and finally economically (Aran et al. 1973; Christopulos 1974).

Citizenship was extended to Puerto Ricans by the Jones Act of 1917, but Puerto Rico remained a colony. This political dependence altered in 1948, when Puerto Rico elected its own governor and became a commonwealth. This status, officially Estado Libre Asociado, or Associated Free State, extends to Puerto Rico and its people privileges and rights different from those of people on the mainland. Although Puerto Ricans are U.S. citizens and elect their own governor, they may not vote in presidential elections and have no voting representation in Congress. They are subject to military service, Selective Service registration, and all federal laws. Puerto Ricans have a homeland that is and at the same time is not a part of the United States.

The Bridge Between the Island and the Mainland

Despite their citizenship, Puerto Ricans are occasionally challenged by immigration officials. Because other Latin Americans attempt to enter the country posing as Puerto Ricans, Puerto Ricans find their papers scrutinized more closely than do other U.S. citizens.

Puerto Ricans came to the mainland in small numbers in the first half of the century, often encouraged by farm labor contracts similar to those extended to Mexican braceros. During World War II, the government recruited hundreds of Puerto Ricans to work on the railroads, in food manufacturing plants, and in copper mines on the mainland. But migration has been largely a post–World War II phenomenon. The 1940 census showed fewer than 70,000 on the mainland. In 2002, there were more than 3.2 million Puerto Ricans on the mainland and 3.8 million residents on the island.

Among the factors that have contributed to migration are the economic pull away from the underdeveloped and overpopulated island, the absence of legal restrictions against travel, and the growth of cheap air transportation. As the migration continues, the mainland offers the added attraction of a large Puerto Rican community in New York City, which makes adjustment easier for new arrivals.

New York City still has a formidable population of Puerto Ricans, but significant changes have taken place. First, Puerto Ricans no longer dominate the Latino scene in New York City, making up a little more than a third of the city's Hispanic population. Second, Puerto Ricans are now more dispersed throughout the mainland's cities, with sizable numbers in New Jersey, Illinois, Florida, California, Pennsylvania, and Connecticut. The Puerto Ricans who have moved out of the large ethnic communities in cities such as New York City, Chicago, and Philadelphia are as a group more familiar with U.S. culture and the English language. This movement from the major settlements also has been hastened by the loss of manufacturing jobs in these cities, a loss that hits Puerto Rican men especially hard (Logan 2001a; Navarro 2000).

As the U.S. economy underwent recession in the 1970s and 1980s, unemployment among mainland Puerto Ricans, always high, increased dramatically. This increase shows in migration. In the 1950s, half of the Latino arrivals were Puerto Rican. By the 1970s, they accounted for only 3 percent. Indeed, in some years of the 1980s, more Puerto Ricans went from mainland to the island than the other way around.

Puerto Ricans returning to the island have become a significant force. Indeed, they have come to be given the name **Neoricans** (or Nuyoricans), a term the islanders also use for Puerto Ricans in New York. Longtime islanders direct a modest amount of hostility toward these Neoricans. They usually return from the mainland with more formal schooling, more money, and a better command of English than native Puerto Ricans have. Not too surprisingly, Neoricans compete very well with islanders for jobs and land.

The ethnic mix of the nation's largest city has gotten even more complex over the last 10 years as Mexican and Mexican American arrivals in New York City have far outpaced any growth among Puerto Ricans. New York City is now following the pattern of other cities such as Miami, where the Latino identity is not defined by a single group (Kugel 2004; Muschkin 1993).

The Island of Puerto Rico

Puerto Rico, located about a thousand miles from Miami, has never been the same since Columbus discovered it in 1493. The original inhabitants of the island were wiped out in a couple of generations by disease, tribal warfare, hard labor, unsuccessful rebellions against the Spanish, and fusion with their conquerors. These social processes are highlighted in the Intergroup Relations Continuum that summarizes the experience of Latinos in the United States (Figure 10.2).

Among the institutions imported to Puerto Rico by Spain was slavery. Although slavery in Puerto Rico was not as harsh as in the southern United States, the legacy of the transfer of Africans is present in the appearance of Puerto Ricans today, many of whom are seen by people on the mainland as Black.

Neoricans
Puerto Ricans who return to the island to settle after living on the mainland of the United States (also Nuyoricans).

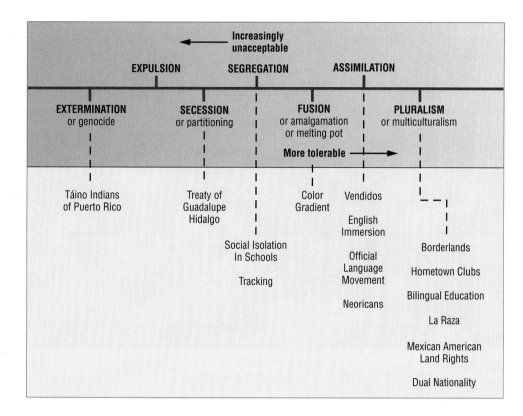

FIGURE 10.2 Intergroup Relations Continuum

The commonwealth period that began in 1948 has been a significant one for Puerto Rico. Change has been dramatic, although whether it has all been progress is debatable. On the positive side, Spanish has been reintroduced as the language of classroom instruction, but the study of English is also required. The popularity in the 1980s of music groups such as Menudo shows that Puerto Rican young people want to maintain ties with their ethnicity. Such success is a challenge because Puerto Rican music is almost never aired on non-Hispanic radio stations. The Puerto Rican people have had a vibrant and distinctive cultural tradition, as seen clearly in their folk heroes, holidays, sports, and contemporary literature and drama. Dominance by the culture of the United States makes it difficult to maintain their culture on the mainland and even on the island itself.

Puerto Rico and its people reflect a phenomenon called **neocolonialism**, which refers to continuing dependence of former colonies on foreign countries. Initially, this term was introduced to refer to African nations that, even after gaining their political independence from Great Britain, France, and other European nations, continued to find their destiny in the hands of the former colonial powers. Although most Puerto Ricans today are staunchly proud of their American citizenship, they also want to have their own national identity, independent of the United States. This has not been and continues not to be easy.

From 1902, English was the official language of the island, but Spanish was the language of the people, reaffirming the island's cultural identity independent of the United States. In 1992, however, Puerto Rico also established Spanish as an official language.

In reality, the language issue is related more to ideology than to substance. Although English is once again required in primary and secondary schools, textbooks may be written in English while the classes are conducted in Spanish. Indeed, Spanish

neocolonialism
Continuing dependence of former colonies on foreign countries.

Puerto Ricans generally maintain dual identity proudly, celebrating Puerto Rican Day each June by observing independence of the island from Spain.

remains the language of the island; only 8 percent of the islanders speak only English, and among Spanish-speaking adults about one-third speak it "well" or "very well" (Bureau of the Census 2004p).

Issues of Statehood and Self-Rule   Puerto Ricans have periodically argued and fought for independence for most of the 500 years since Columbus landed. They continued to do so in the 1990s. The contemporary commonwealth arrangement is popular with many Puerto Ricans, but others prefer statehood, whereas some call for complete independence from the United States.

The arguments for continuation of commonwealth status include both the serious and the trivial. Among some island residents, the idea of statehood invokes the fear of higher taxes and an erosion of their cultural heritage. Some even fear the end of separate Puerto Rican participation in the Olympics and the Miss Universe pageant. On the other hand, although independence may be attractive, commonwealth supporters argue that it includes too many unknown costs, so they embrace the status quo. Others view statehood as a key to increased economic development and expansion for tourism.

for Commonwealth

Proponents of independence have a long, vocal history of insisting on the need for Puerto Rico to regain its cultural and political autonomy. Some of the supporters of independence have even been militant. In 1950, nationalists attempted to assassinate President Truman, killing a White House guard in the process. Four years later, another band of nationalists opened fire in the gallery of the U.S. House of Representatives, wounding five members of Congress. Beginning in 1974, a group calling itself the Armed Forces of National Liberation (FALN, for Fuerzas Armadas de Liberación Nacional) took responsibility for more than 100 explosions that continued through 1987. The FALN is not alone; at least four other militant groups advocating independence were identified as having been at work in the 1980s. The island itself is occasionally beset by violent demonstrations, often reacting to U.S. military installations there—a symbol of U.S. control (Squitieri 1999).

for Independence

The possible use of Vieques as a military bombing site is strongly opposed by most Puerto Ricans both in Puerto Rico and on the Mainland.

Source: Steve Benson. Reprinted by permission of United Feature Syndicate, Inc.

The use for more than 60 years of a portion of Puerto Rico as a bombing target by the military had been to many an obvious example of colonial oppression. Protests for years focused on the bombing practice runs over Vieques (see Figure 10.1). The federal government ended the bombing in 2003. In "Listen to Our Voices," poet and professor Martín St. Espada questioned the continued bombing and called on people on the mainland to join Puerto Ricans on the island in calling for an immediate halt to the military exercises (Canedy 2003).

The issue of Puerto Rico's political destiny is in part ideological. Independence is the easiest way for the island to retain and strengthen its cultural and political identity. Some nationalists express the desire that an autonomous Puerto Rico develop close political ties with communist Cuba. The crucial arguments for and against independence probably are economic. An independent Puerto Rico would no longer be required to use U.S. shipping lines, which are more expensive than those of foreign competitors. However, an independent Puerto Rico might be faced by a tariff wall when trading with its largest current customer, the mainland United States. Also, Puerto Rican migration to the mainland could be restricted.

Puerto Rico's future status most recently faced a vote in 1998. In the latest nonbinding referendum, 50 percent favored continuing commonwealth status, and 47 percent backed statehood. Less than 3 percent favored independence. Interestingly, a 1998 survey of people on the mainland found the population evenly split, with a third favoring each option. Given the lack of overwhelming feelings for statehood on the island, it is unlikely that there will be sufficient support in Congress to move toward statehood. Yet with half the island population expressing a preference for a change, it is clear that discontent with the current arrangement prevails and remains a "colonial dilemma" (Saad 1998; Navarro 1998).

The Social Construction of Race   The most significant difference between the meaning of race in Puerto Rico and on the mainland is that Puerto Rico, like so many other Caribbean societies, has a color gradient. The phrase **color gradient** describes

color gradient
The placement of people on a continuum from light to dark skin color rather than in distinct racial groupings by skin color.

Voices Listen to Our Voices Listen to

¡VIVA VIEQUES!

Martín St. Espada

More than eighty years ago, Puerto Rican poet and political leader Jose de Diego wrote, "Puerto Ricans do not know how to say no." And yet, he pointed out, "the no of the oppressed has been the word, the genesis, of the liberation of peoples." De Diego warned: "We must learn to say no."

Today, the people of Puerto Rico say no; the people of Vieques say no; the Puerto Rican community in the U.S. says no. We say no to the Navy, no to the bombing of Vieques. The admirals and apologists of the Navy say they cannot find anywhere else in the world to play their war games. Still we say no. They say they will use dummy bombs. Still we say no. They promise a referendum some day. Still we say no. The word no is the same in English and Spanish. Since translation is not the problem, we must assume they cannot hear us. So we must say it louder: *No.*

Vieques is an offshore island municipality of Puerto Rico. It is controlled, like the rest of Puerto Rico, by the United States. More than 9,300 people live in Viéques. Yet since 1941, the U.S. Navy has occupied two-thirds of this inhabited island for war games and live-ammunition target practice. According to

journalist Juan Gonzalez, "Practice at the range goes on for as many as 200 days a year. Combat planes bomb and strafe the island. Destroyers bomb it from the sea. . . . Maneuvers have included, on occasion, practice with depleted uranium shells, napalm, and cluster bombs."

Federal tax dollars go directly to the military budget, and thus to support the Navy presence in Vieques. We share a responsibility to the people of Viéques to protest the injustice our dollars make possible. Keep in mind, too, that Puerto Rico lacks a voting representative in Congress. Given the absence of democratic representation for the people of Puerto Rico, the people of the United States must speak for them.

We Puerto Ricans must keep saying no. And by saying no, we say yes. As Eduardo Galeano has written, "By saying no to the devastating empire of greed whose center lies in North America, we are saying yes to another possible America. . . . In saying no to a peace without dignity, we are saying yes to the sacred right of rebellion against injustice." ■

Source: "¡Viva Vieques!" by Martín St. Espada, *The Progressive*, July 2000, vol. 64, pp. 27–29. Copyright © 2000 by *The Progressive*. Reprinted by permission of *The Progressive*, 409 E. Main Street, Madison, WI 53703. www.progressive.org.

distinctions based on skin color made on a continuum rather than by sharp categorical separations. The presence of a color gradient reflects past fusion between different groups (see Figure 10.2). Rather than being either "black" or "white," people are judged in such societies as "lighter" or "darker" than others. Rather than seeing people as either black or white in skin color, Puerto Ricans perceive people as ranging from pale white to very black. Puerto Ricans are more sensitive to degrees of difference and make less effort to pigeonhole a person into one of two categories.

The presence of a color gradient rather than two or three racial categories does not necessarily mean that prejudice is less. Generally, however, societies with a color gradient permit more flexibility and therefore are less likely to impose specific sanctions against a group of people based on skin color alone. Puerto Rico has not suffered interracial conflict or violence; its people are conscious of different racial heritages. Studies disagree on the amount of prejudice in Puerto Rico, but all concur that race is not as clear-cut an issue on the island as it is on the mainland.

Racial identification in Puerto Rico depends a great deal on the attitude of the individual making the judgment. If one thinks highly of a person, he or she may be seen as a member of a more acceptable racial group. A variety of terms are used in the color gradient to describe people racially: *Blanco* (white), *trigueño* (bronze- or wheat-colored), *moreno* (dark-skinned), and *negro* (black) are a few of these. Factors such as social class and social position determine race, but on the mainland race is more likely to determine social class. This situation may puzzle people from the mainland, but racial etiquette on the mainland may be just as difficult for Puerto Ricans to comprehend and accept. Puerto Ricans arriving in the United States may find a new identity thrust on them by the dominant society (Aranda and Rebollo-Gil 2004; Landale and Oropesa 2002; Rodríguez 1997, 2000).

The Island Economy

The United States' role in Puerto Rico has produced an overall economy that, though strong by Caribbean standards, remains well below that of the poorest areas of the United States. For many years, the federal government exempted U.S. industries locating in Puerto Rico from taxes on profits for at least 10 years. In addition, the federal government's program of enterprise zones, which grants tax incentives to promote private investment in inner cities, has been extended to Puerto Rico. Unquestionably, Puerto Rico has become attractive to mainland-based corporations. Skeptics point out that, as a result, the island's agriculture has been largely ignored. Furthermore, the economic benefits to the island are limited. Businesses have spent the profits gained on Puerto Rico back on the mainland.

Puerto Rico's economy is in severe trouble compared with that of the mainland. Its unemployment rate has been about three times that of the mainland. In addition, the per capita income is less than half that of Mississippi, the poorest state. Efforts to raise the wages of Puerto Rican workers only make the island less attractive to labor-intensive businesses, that is, those employing larger numbers of unskilled people. Capital-intensive companies, such as the petrochemical industries, have found Puerto Rico attractive, but they have not created jobs for the semiskilled. A growing problem is that Puerto Rico is emerging as a major gateway to the United States for illegal drugs from South America, which has led the island to experience waves of violence and the social ills associated with the drug trade (Castañeda 1996; Hemlock 1996; Navarro 1995).

Puerto Rico is an example of the world systems theory initially presented in Chapter 1. **World systems theory** is the view of the global economic system as divided between certain industrialized nations that control wealth and developing countries that are controlled and exploited. Although Puerto Rico may be well off compared with many other Caribbean nations, it clearly is at the mercy of economic forces in the United States and, to a much lesser extent, other industrial nations. Puerto Rico continues to struggle with the advantages of citizenship and the detriment of playing a peripheral role in the economy of the United States.

Another major factor in Puerto Rico's economy is tourism. Government subsidies have encouraged the construction of luxury hotels. After U.S. citizens' travel to Cuba was cut off in 1962, tourists discovered Puerto Rico's beaches and warm climate. Critics complain that the major economic beneficiaries of tourism are not local but are primarily investors from the mainland, and that high prices prevent the less affluent from visiting, thus unnecessarily restricting tourism. As has been true of other aspects

Homeland

world systems theory
A view of the global economic system as divided between nations that control wealth and those that provide natural resources and labor.

In many cities, Mexican Americans create large ethnic enclaves that also serve to attract Anglos to stores and restaurants. This heavily Mexican area of Los Angeles augments the usual businesses with street festivals that feature the clothing, music, and food of Mexico.

of the island's economic development, the tourist boom has had little positive effect on most Puerto Ricans.

Puerto Rico continues to face new challenges. First, with congressional approval in 1994 of the North American Free Trade Agreement (NAFTA), Mexico, Canada, and the United States became integrated into a single economic market. The reduction of trade barriers with Mexico, coupled with that nation's lower wages, may combine to undercut Puerto Rico's commonwealth advantage. Second, many more island nations now offer sun-seeking tourists from the mainland alternatives to Puerto Rico. In addition, cruise ships present another attractive option for tourists. Given the economic problems of the island, it is not surprising that many Puerto Ricans migrate to the mainland (Rivera-Batiz and Santiago 1996; Rohter 1993).

For years, migration to the mainland has served as a safety valve for Puerto Rico's population, which has grown annually at a rate 50 percent faster than that of the rest of the United States. Typically, migrants from Puerto Rico represent a broad range of occupations. There are seasonal fluctuations as Puerto Rican farm workers leave the island in search of seasonal employment. Puerto Ricans, particularly agricultural workers, earn higher wages on the mainland; yet a significant proportion returns despite the higher wages (Meléndez 1994).

The Contemporary Picture of Mexican Americans and Puerto Ricans

We will now consider the major social institutions of education, the family, health care, and religion, noting the similarities in their organization between Puerto Ricans and Mexican Americans.

Education

Both Mexican Americans and Puerto Ricans, as groups, have experienced gains in formal schooling but still lag behind White Americans in many standards of educational attainment. As is apparent in Table 10.1, Mexican Americans and Puerto Ricans lag well behind other Latinos and even further behind Anglos. Although bilingual education is still endorsed in the United States, the implementation of effective, high-quality programs has been difficult, as Chapter 9 showed. In addition, attacks on the funding of bilingual education has continued into the present.

Latinos, including Mexican Americans and Puerto Ricans, have become increasingly isolated from non-Latinos. In 1968, 55 percent of all Hispanics attended predominantly minority schools: that is, schools where at least half of the students were members of minorities. Just a little over three decades later, this had increased to 76 percent. During the 2000–2001 school year, the typical Latino student was in a school that was 54 percent Hispanic. Over a third of Latinos were in schools that were at least 90 percent non-White. Furthermore, as we noted in Chapter 1, the separation continues, with the highest patterns of residential segregation occurring in the cities with the largest number of Hispanics (Frankenburg et al. 2003; Orfield 2002).

Three factors explain this increasing social isolation of Mexican Americans and Puerto Ricans from other students in school. First, Latinos are increasingly concentrated in the largest cities, where minorities dominate. Second, the numbers of Latinos have increased dramatically since the 1970s, when efforts to desegregate schools began to lose momentum. Third, schools once desegregated have become resegregated as the numbers of school-aged Mexican Americans in an area have increased and as the determination to maintain balances in schools has lessened.

Even where Anglos and Latinos live in the same school district, the problem of social isolation in the classroom is often furthered through tracking. **Tracking** is the practice of placing students in specific classes or curriculum groups on the basis of test scores and other criteria. Tracking begins very early in the classroom, often in reading groups during first grade. These tracks may reinforce the disadvantages of Hispanic children from less affluent families and non-English-speaking households that have not been exposed to English reading materials in their homes during early childhood (Rodríguez 1989; Schaefer 2005).

Students see few teachers and administrators like themselves because few Latino university students have been prepared to serve as teachers and administrators. In 2000, only 51 percent of Mexican Americans and 64 percent of Puerto Ricans aged 25 or over had completed high school, compared with 88 percent of non-Hispanic Whites. Mexican Americans and Puerto Ricans who do choose to continue their education beyond high school are more likely to select a technical school or community college to acquire work-related skills (Therrien and Ramirez 2001).

Mexican Americans and Puerto Ricans are underrepresented in higher education in all roles. Recent reports have documented the absence of Hispanics among college teachers and administrators: Less than 6 percent of all college teachers were Latino in 2002. The situation is similar in this respect to that of Blacks; however, there are no Latino counterparts to historic Black colleges, such as Tuskegee Institute, to provide a source of leaders (Bureau of the Census 2003a:399).

Motivation does not appear to be the barrier to school achievement, at least among Mexican immigrants. A Harvard University study of the attitudes of Mexican immigrant adolescents showed that 84 percent felt that school was the most important thing, compared with 40 percent of White teenagers. Again, 68 percent of immigrant children felt that doing their homework was more important than helping a friend, compared with only 20 percent of White adolescents who held the same priorities. However, there is evidence that as these children assimilate, they begin to take on the prevailing White views. The same survey showed second-generation Mexican Americans still giving education a higher priority, but not as high as their immigrant counterparts. We will consider shortly how assimilation has a similar effect on health (Woo 1996).

With respect to higher education, Latinos face challenges similar to those that Black students meet on predominantly White campuses. Given the social isolation of Latino high schools, Mexican Americans are likely to have to adjust for the first time

tracking
The practice of placing students in specific curriculum groups on the basis of test scores and other criteria.

to an educational environment almost totally populated by Anglos. They may experience racism for the first time, just as they are trying to adjust to a heavier academic load.

Family Life

The most important organization or social institution among Latinos, or for that matter any group, is the family. The structure of the Mexican American family differs little from that of all families in the United States, a statement remarkable in itself, given the impoverishment of a significant number of Mexican Americans.

Latino households are described as laudably more familistic than others in the United States. **Familism** means pride and closeness in the family, which results in family obligation and loyalty coming before individual needs. The family is the primary source of both social interaction and caregiving.

Familism has been viewed as both a positive and a negative influence on individual Mexican Americans and Puerto Ricans. It may have the negative effect of discouraging youths with a bright future from taking advantage of opportunities that would separate them from their family. Familism is generally regarded as good, however, because an extended family provides emotional strength in times of crisis. Close family ties maintain the mental and social well-being of the elderly. Most Latinos therefore see the intact, extended family as a norm and as a nurturing unit that provides support throughout a person's lifetime. The many significant aspects of familism include the importance of *campadrazgo* (the godparent-godchild relationship), the benefits of the financial dependency of kin, the availability of relatives as a source of advice, and the active involvement of the elderly in the family.

This traditional value of familism, whether judged good or bad, is expected to decline in importance with urbanization, industrialization, and the acquisition of middle-class status. It will also mean taking on some practices more common in the United States, such as divorce. Characteristics that marked differences between Latino and Anglo family life were sharper in the past. Even among past generations, the differences were of degree, not of kind; that is, Hispanic families tended to exhibit some traits more than Anglos, not different traits altogether. A comparison between similar Anglo and Mexican American families in San Diego found no significant differences in family life between the two groups. In short, the Mexican American and Puerto Rican families display all the variety of American families in general, while also suffering higher levels of poverty (Alárcon 1995; Kanellos 1994; Landale and Ogena 1995; Vega et al. 1986; Zambrana 1995).

Health Care

Earlier, in Chapter 5, we introduced the concept of **life chances**, which are people's opportunities to provide themselves with material goods, positive living conditions, and favorable life experiences. We have consistently seen Latino groups as having more limited life chances. Perhaps in no other area does this apply so much as in the health care system.

Hispanics as a group are locked out of the health care system more often than any other racial or ethnic group. A third had no health insurance (or other coverage such as Medicaid) for all of 2002, compared with 10.7 percent of White non-Hispanics and 19.9 percent of Blacks. Predictably, the uninsured are less likely to have a regular source of medical care. This means that they wait for a crisis before seeking care. Fewer are immunized, and rates of preventable diseases such as lead poisoning are higher. Noncoverage is increasing, a circumstance that may reflect a further breakdown in health care delivery or may be a result of continuing immigration (Mills and Brandari 2003).

familism
Pride and closeness in the family that result in placing family obligation and loyalty before individual needs.

life chances
People's opportunities to provide themselves with material goods, positive living conditions, and favorable life experiences.

The health care problem facing Mexican Americans and other Hispanic groups is complicated by the lack of Hispanic health professionals. In 2002, Hispanics account-ed for 5 percent or less of dentists and physicians, yet they are about 14 percent of the population. Obviously, one does not need to be administered health care by someone in one's own ethnic group, but the paucity of Hispanic professionals increases the likelihood that the group will be underserved (Bureau of the Census 2003a:399).

Given the high proportion of uninsured people and the low number of Latino health care personnel, it is not surprising to learn of the poor status of Latinos' health care as a group. Interestingly, once they settle in the United States, immigrants from Latin America may well experience a decline in their health care. The "Research Focus" considers the impact that immigration may have on a family's health.

Some Mexican Americans and many other Latinos have cultural beliefs that make them less likely to use the medical system. They may interpret their illnesses accord-ing to folk practices or **curanderismo**: Latino folk medicine, a form of holistic health care and healing. This orientation influences how one approaches health care and even how one defines illness. Most Hispanics probably use folk healers, or *curanderos,* infrequently, but perhaps 20 percent rely on home remedies. Although these are not necessarily without value, especially if a dual system of folk and establishment medi-cine is followed, reliance on natural beliefs may be counterproductive. Another

curanderismo
Hispanic folk medicine.

Focus **Research Focus** *Research Focus*

ASSIMILATION MAY BE HAZARDOUS TO YOUR HEALTH

Immigrants come to the United States seeking a better life, but the transition can be very difficult. We are familiar with the problems new arrivals experience in finding good jobs, but we may be less aware of how pervasive the challenges are.

Researchers continuously show that immi-grants often encounter health problems as they leave behind old health networks and confront the private pay system of medical care in the United States. The outcome is that the health of immigrants often deteriorates. Interestingly, this occurs with Puerto Ricans, who are citizens upon arrival and obviously do not experience as much culture shock as other new arrivals. Scholars Nancy Landale, R. S. Orapesa, and Bridget Gorman looked at the implications for infant mortality of migra-tion from Puerto Rico to the United States. Their analysis showed that children of migrants have lower rates of infant mortality than do children of mainland-born Puerto Rican women. This means that babies of Puer-to Rican mothers who are born in the United States are more likely to die than those of mothers who migrated from Puerto Rico.

Why does this happen? Immigrants gen-erally are still under the protection of their fellow travelers. They are still networked with other immigrants, who assist them in adapting to life in the United States. How-ever, as life in a new country continues, these important social networks break down as people learn to navigate the new social system—in this example, the health care system. The researchers do note that Puerto Ricans in the United States, regardless of recency of arrival, still experience better health than those in Puerto Rico. Of course, this finding only further indicates the colo-nial relationship of Puerto Rico to the United States. ∎

Source: Landale et al. 2000.

aspect of folk beliefs is the identification of folk-defined illnesses such as *susto* (or fright sickness) and *atague* (or fighting attack). Although these complaints, alien by these names to Anglos, often have biological bases, they must be dealt with carefully by sensitive medical professionals who can diagnose and treat illnesses accurately (Council on Scientific Affairs 1991; Keilman 2002; Rivera 1988).

Religion

The most important formal organization in the Hispanic community is the church. Most Puerto Ricans and Mexican Americans express a religious preference for the Catholic Church. In 1994, about 70 percent of Hispanics were Catholic, as shown in Figure 10.3.

The Roman Catholic Church took an assimilationist role in the past, whether with Hispanic Catholics or with other minority Catholics. The church has only sporadically involved itself in the Chicano movement, and rarely in the past did the upper levels of the church hierarchy support Chicanismo. For example, only with some prodding did the Roman Catholic Church support the United Farm Workers, a group whose membership was predominantly Catholic.

FIGURE 10.3 Religious Preferences

Using national data, we see that the majority of both Mexican Americans and Puerto Ricans expressed a preference for the Roman Catholic Church.

Source: One Nation Under God by Barry A. Kosmin and Seymour P. Lachman. Copyright © 1993 by Barry A. Kosmin and Seymour P. Lachman. Used by permission of Harmony Books, a division of Random House, Inc.

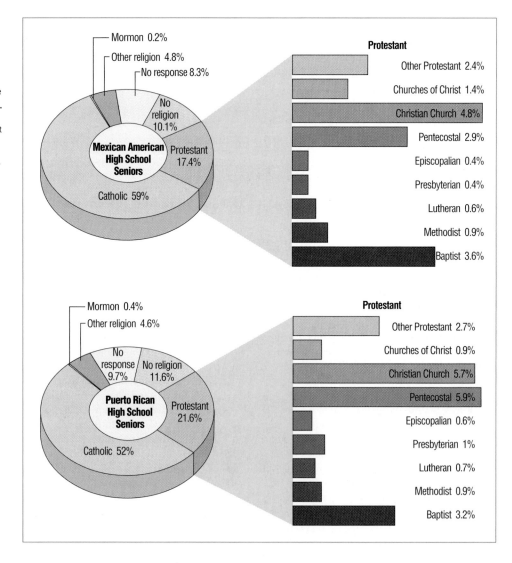

Recently the Roman Catholic Church has become more community oriented, seeking to identify Latino, or at least Spanish-speaking, clergy and staff to serve Latino parishes. The lack of Spanish-speaking priests has been complicated by a smaller proportion of a declining number training for the priesthood who speak Spanish (Ramirez 2000; Rosales 1996).

Not only is the Catholic Church important to Hispanics, but Hispanics also play a significant role for the church. The population growth of Mexican Americans and other Hispanics has been responsible for the Catholic Church's continued growth in recent years, whereas mainstream Protestant faiths have declined in size. Hispanics account for more than a third of Catholics in the United States. The church is trying to adjust to Hispanics' more expressive manifestation of religious faith, with frequent reliance on their own patron saints and the presence of special altars in their homes. Catholic churches in some parts of the United States are even starting to accommodate observances of the Mexican Día de los Muertos, or Day of the Dead. Such practices are a tradition from rural Mexico, where religion was followed without trained clergy. Yet even today in the United States, Hispanics continue to be underrepresented among priests, with only 4.4 percent nationwide being Hispanic (O'Connor 1998).

Although Latinos are predominantly Catholic, their membership in Protestant and other Christian faiths is growing. First-generation Latinos are 74 percent Catholic, but by the third generation only 59 percent are Catholic (Lobdell 2001).

Pentecostalism, a type of evangelical Christianity, is growing in Latin America and is clearly making a significant impact on Latinos in the United States. Adherents to Pentecostal faiths hold beliefs similar to those of the evangelicals, but also believe in the infusion of the Holy Spirit into services and in religious experiences such as faith healing. Pentecostalism and similar faiths are attractive to many because they offer followers the opportunity to express their religious fervor openly. Furthermore, many of the churches are small and therefore offer a sense of community, often with Spanish-speaking leadership. Gradually, the more established faiths are recognizing the desirability of offering Latino parishioners a greater sense of belonging (Hunt 1999).

Pentecostalism
A religion similar in many respects to evangelical faiths that believes in the infusion of the Holy Spirit into services and in religious experiences such as faith healing.

Conclusion

David Gomez (1971) described Mexican Americans as "strangers in their own land." Puerto Ricans, on the other hand, are still debating what should be the political destiny of their island nation. All of this makes nationality a very real part of the destiny of Mexican Americans and Puerto Ricans. Can they also preserve their culture along with a sense of national fervor, or will these be a casualty of assimilation?

As we have seen, even when we concentrate on just Mexican Americans or Puerto Ricans out of the larger collective group of Hispanics or Latinos, diversity remains. As shown in Table 10.2, large concentrations of Latinos live in a number of our largest cities.

Mexican Americans are divided among the Hispanos and the descendants of earlier Mex-

ican immigrants and the more recent arrivals from Mexico. Puerto Ricans can be divided by virtue of residency and the extent to which they identify with the island culture. For many Puerto Ricans, the identity dilemma is never truly resolved: "No soy de aquí ni de allá," "I am not from here nor from there" (Comas-Díaz et al. 1998).

Economic change is also apparent. Poverty and unemployment rates are high, and new arrivals from Mexico and Puerto Rico are particularly likely to enter the lower class, or working class at best, upon arrival. However, there is a growing middle class within the Hispanic community.

Mexican culture is alive and well in the Mexican American community. Some cultural practices that have become more popular

TABLE 10.2
Cities with the Largest Latino Concentrations, 2000

City	Number of Latinos	Proportion of City's Population
New York City	2,160,554	27.0%
Los Angeles	1,719,073	46.5
Chicago	753,644	26.0
Houston	730,868	37.4
San Antonio	671,394	58.7
Phoenix	449,972	34.1
El Paso	431,875	76.6
Dallas	422,587	35.6
San Diego	310,752	25.4
San Jose	269,989	30.2
Santa Ana	257,097	76.1
Miami	238,351	65.8

Note: San Juan, Puerto Rico, reported 413,328 Latinos for 98 percent of its population.

Source: Bureau of the Census 2001h.

here than in Mexico are being imported back to Mexico, with their distinctive Mexican American flavor. All this is occurring in the midst of a reluctance to expand bilingual education and a popular move to make English the official language. In 1998, Puerto Rico observed its 500th anniversary as a colony: four centuries under Spain and another century under the United States. Its dual status as a colony and as a developing nation has been the defining issue for Puerto Ricans, even those who have migrated to the mainland (Perusse 1990).

Key Terms

bracero 260	familism 276	Neoricans 268
Chicanismo 265	*La Raza* 261	Pentecostalism 279
color gradient 271	life chances 276	repatriation 260
culture of poverty 262	*mojados* 261	tracking 275
curanderismo 277	neocolonialism 269	world systems theory 273

Review Questions

1. In what respects has Mexico been viewed as a source of workers and a place to leave unwanted laborers?
2. In what respects are Hispanic families similar to and different from Anglo households?
3. How does *Chicanismo* relate to the issue of Hispanic identity?
4. How does the case of Puerto Rico support the notion of race as a social concept?
5. What role does religion play in the Latino community?

Critical Thinking

1. Consider what it means to be patriotic and loyal in terms of being a citizen of the United States. How do the concerns that Puerto Ricans have for the island's future and the Mexican concept of dual nationality affect those notions of patriotism and loyalty?

2. The phrase *territorial minorities* has been used to apply to subordinate groups who have special ties to their land, such as Native American tribes. How would you apply this to Mexican Americans?

3. The family is often regarded by observers as a real strength in the Latino community. How can this strength be harnessed to address some of the challenges that Mexican Americans and Puerto Ricans face in the United States?

4. Evaluate the statement, "The United States is the last great colonial power and does not even realize it." How might your response change if we substitute the term *neocolonial* for *colonial?*

Internet Connections—Research Navigator™

 Follow the instructions found on page 31 of this text to access the features of Research Navigator™. Once at the Web site, enter your Login Name and Password. Then, to use the ContentSelect database, enter keywords such as "César Chávez," "curanderismo," "Puerto Rico," and "neocolonialism," and the research engine will supply relevant and recent scholarly and popular press publications. Use the *New York Times* Search-by-Subject Archive to find recent news articles related to sociology, and the Link Library feature to locate relevant Web links organized by the key terms associated with this chapter.

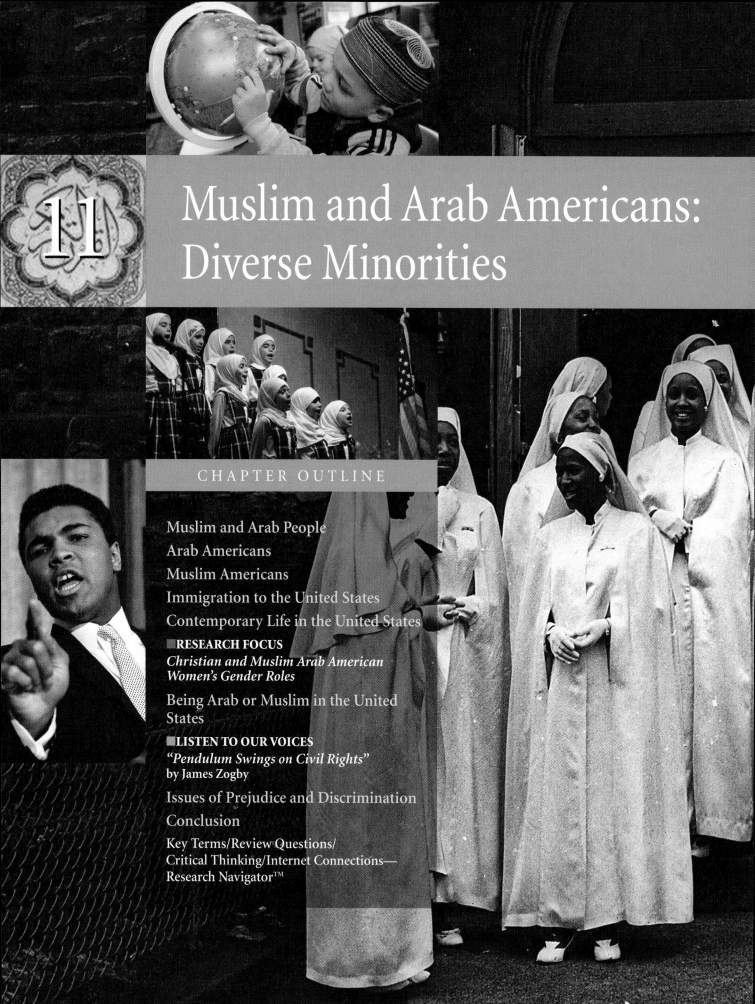

11

Muslim and Arab Americans: Diverse Minorities

MUSLIM AND ARAB AMERICANS ARE DIFFERENT GROUPS IN the United States; although they overlap with some Muslim Americans being of Arab ancestry, they are distinct from each other. Most Arab Americans are not Muslim and most Muslim Americans are not of Arab background. Within each group is a significant diversity that can be seen by differences in forms of religious expression, ancestral background, and recentness of arrival in the United States. Both groups have been seen and stereotyped in the West through the lens of Orientalism. This stigmatizing of people grew more all-encompassing with the outbreak of terrorism and specifically the events of September 11, 2001. Even without these violent events, it is a challenge for Muslim and Arab Americans to sort out their identity, but nonetheless both function in strong and growing communities in the United States.

In downtown Chicago, Jahan Ghaemi stops the taxi he operates and briefly changes roles to become an outreach worker for the Sabeel Food Pantry, the nation's first Muslim-run pantry. The Iranian immigrant takes time from his job to give food to an obviously needy man on the street who is most likely neither Muslim nor Arab. Speaking of his action, he observes, "It doesn't matter what religion you are. It's everyone's responsibility to help others."

Meanwhile in Seattle, Iraqi-born Jawad al-Gheezi has lately come to tell people when they ask that he is from Mesopotamia, especially since one of his "buddies" on his construction crew spray painted his car "Go Home Terrorist."

In contrast, Rebecca Khoury of Cleveland directly tells people she is Arab American rather then perhaps the safer answer of Lebanese. She is the fourth generation descendant of Joseph Khouy, who at age 12 left a southern Lebanese port city and stowed away on a boat to the United States, where he became a coal miner. Rebecca cannot speak Arabic, and most of her family members no longer remember the meanings behind the script that adorns the Maronite Church they attend, a Christian faith with roots in the 4th century.

At a political rally in Houston, Texas, during the 2004 presidential campaign, Black Muslims and Muslim immigrants joined together in a get-out-the-vote campaign because many issues, such as U.S. foreign policy and racial profiling, are ones in which they have a common interest (Basu 2004; Brachear 2002; Clemetson 2004; Rosin 2002).

There are two objectives for considering Arab and Muslim Americans together in this chapter. One is to clarify the distinctions between two groups often incorrectly referred to as the same population. Second is to overcome the prism of Orientalism through which many contemporary Americans view the Arab and Muslim world. **Orientalism** is the simplistic view of the people and history of the Orient, with no recognition of change over time or the diversity within its many cultures. Palestinian American literary scholar Edward Said (1978) stressed how so many in North America and Europe came to define, categorize, and study the Orient, and therefore create a static stereotype of hundreds of millions of people stretched around the globe.

The diversity of Arabs and Muslims is thereby discounted, which allows the outsider to come up with simplistic descriptions and often simplistic policies. Orientalism has led people to see a sweeping unity in both Arab and Muslim societies. It is also an unchanging and clearly a nonmodern image. One must focus on smaller culturally consistent groups or countries rather than surrender to the temptation of a single broad generalization.

Muslim and Arab People

Orientalism
The simplistic view of the people and history of the Orient with no recognition of change over time or the diversity within its many cultures.

The Arab American and Muslim American communities are among the most rapidly growing subordinate groups in the United States. Westerners often confuse the two groups. Actually, Arabs are an ethnic group, and Muslims are a religious group. Typically, Islam is the faith (like Christianity), and a Muslim is a believer of that religion (like a Christian). Worldwide, many Arabs (12 million) are not Muslims, and most (85 percent) Muslims are not Arabs (David and Ayouby 2005).

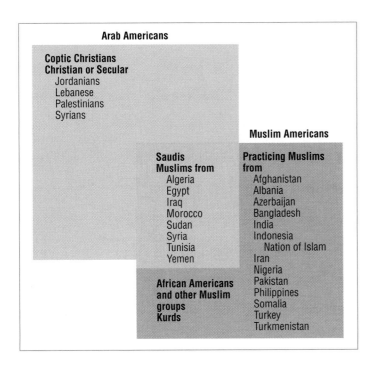

FIGURE 11.1   Relationship Between Muslim and Arab Americans

Many Arab Americans are not Muslims, and most Muslim Americans are not Arabs.

Source: Reproduced from PH © 2005 *Race and Ethnicity in the US.*

This relationship between religion and an ethnic group that crosses many nationalities is illustrated in Figure 11.1. As we can see, one cannot accurately identify the Muslim faithful by nationality alone, and clearly being Arab does not define one as being a follower of Islam.

Arab Americans

The name Arab Americans refers to the immigrants and their descendants from the countries that now comprise the Arab world (see Figure 11.2). These are the 22 nations, as defined by the membership of the League of Arab States, of North Africa and what is popularly called the Middle East, including Morocco, Syria, Iraq, Saudi Arabia, and Somalia. Not all people living in these countries are necessarily Arab (e.g., the Kurds of Iraq), and some Arab Americans may have immigrated from non-Arab countries such as Great Britain or France, where their families have lived for generations.

The Arabic language is the single most-unifying force among Arabs, although not all Arabs and certainly not all Arab Americans can read and speak Arabic. As the language has evolved over the centuries, people in different parts of the Arab world speak with a different dialect using their own choices of vocabulary and pronunciation. Although most Arab Americans are not Muslim, the fact that the Qur'an was originally in Arabic 1,400 years ago gives the knowledge of Arabic special importance. This is similar to many Jews' reading of the Torah in Hebrew, but unlike Christians, who almost always read the Bible in a translation to their native tongue.

Estimates of the size of the Arab American community differ widely. Despite efforts of the Census Bureau to enlist the assistance of experts, census results are often regarded as severely undercounting the Arab American community. The government only counts those individuals who have identified their ancestry from the countries of the Arab world and, therefore, would not include those descended from other large

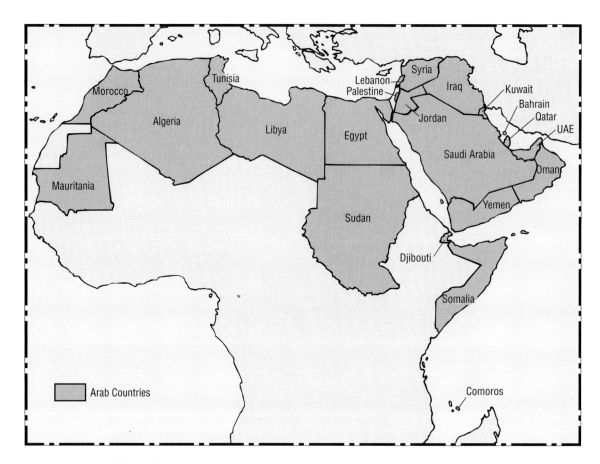

FIGURE 11.2 Arab Countries

overseas Arab communities. The Arab American community doubled in size during the 1990s, and even by the official census count, would be equivalent to that of Greek Americans.

By some estimates, there are up to 3 million people with Arab ancestry in the United States. Among those identifying themselves as Arab American, the largest single source of ancestry was Lebanon, followed by Syria, Egypt, and Palestine. These four groups account for two-thirds of Arab Americans in 2000. As with other racial and ethnic groups, Arab Americans, as shown in Figure 11.3, are not uniformly distributed throughout the United States. This rising population has led to the development of Arab retail centers in several cities, including Dearborn and Detroit, Michigan; Los Angeles; Chicago; New York City; and Washington, D.C. (Wertsman 2001).

Diversity underlies virtually everything about Arab Americans. First, there are variations in time of arrival. Many Arab Americans have lived for several generations in the United States, while others are foreign born. A second aspect of diversity is point of origin, ranging from urban Cairo, Egypt to rural Morocco. Third, there is a rich variety of religious tradition that can include Christian or Muslim, practicing or nonpracticing, and so forth. It becomes impossible to characterize Arab Americans having *a* family type or *a* gender role or *an* occupational pattern (David 2004).

As with any ethnic or immigrant community, divisions arise over who can truly be counted as a member of the community. Sociologist Gary David (2002, 2003) devel-

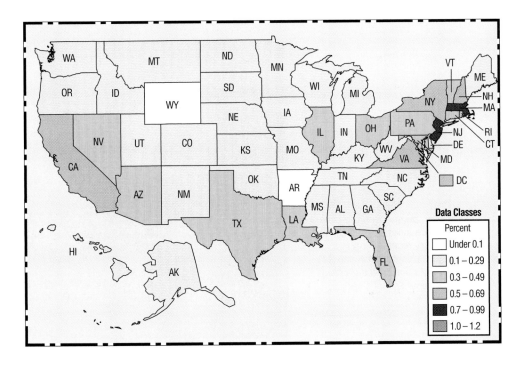

FIGURE 11.3 Arab American Population, 2000

Source: U.S Census Bureau data reported in de la Cruz and Brittingham 2003.

oped the concept of the **deficit model of ethnic identity**. This states that one's identity is viewed by others as a factor of subtracting away characteristics corresponding to some ideal ethnic type. Each factor encompassing a perfect ethnic identity missing from a person's background or identity leads to be the person viewed by others as more assimilated and less ethnic. In the case of Arab Americans, if they are unable to speak Arabic, that makes them less Arab to some; if they are married to non-Arabs, less ethnic; if they have never been to the home country, less ethnic. Depending upon one's perspective, an Arab American can come to regard another Arab American as either "too American" or "too Arab." Arab American organizations, magazines, and associations may seek to cater to the entire Arab American community, but, more likely, cater to certain segments based on nationality, religion, or degree of assimilation, groups that gravitate to one or the other depending upon the perception of what it means to be an Arab American.

Muslim Americans

Islam, with approximately 1.3 billion followers worldwide, is second to Christianity among the world's religions. Although news events and a worldview of Orientalism suggest an inherent conflict between Christians and Muslims, the two faiths are similar in many ways. Both are monotheistic (i.e., based on a single deity) and indeed worship the same God. Allah is the Arabic word for God and refers to the God of Moses, Jesus, and Muhammad. Both Christianity and Islam include a belief in prophets, an afterlife, and a judgment day. In fact, Islam recognizes Jesus as a prophet, though not the son of God. Islam reveres both the Old and New Testaments as integral parts of its tradition. Both faiths impose a moral code on believers, which varies from fairly rigid proscriptions for fundamentalists to relatively relaxed guidelines for liberals.

Although they have some beliefs in common with Christians, Islam is guided by the teachings of the Qur'an (or Koran), which Muslims believe was revealed to the Prophet Muhammad, the collected sayings or hadeeth, and deeds of the seventh-

deficit model of ethnic identity
One's ethnicity is viewed by others as a factor of subtracting away the characteristics corresponding to some ideal ethnic type.

While the Muslim presence in the United States has only been recognized by the general public very recently, it has a long history. Yarrow Marnout, an African Muslim and former slave, was painted in this portrait by famed artist Charles Wilson Peele in 1819.

Source: Charles Wilson Peale, "Yarrow Mamout." Courtesy of The Historical Society of Pennsylvania Collection, Atwater Kent Museum of Philadelphia.

century Prophet Muhammad, called Sunnah or the way of the Prophet. He grew up an orphan and became a respected businessman who rejected the widespread polytheism of his day and turned to the one God (Allah) as worshipped by the region's Christians and Jews. Islam says that he was visited by the angel Gabriel, who began reciting the Word of Allah, the Qur'an. Muslims see Muhammad as the last in a long line of prophets, preceded by Abraham, Moses, and Jesus. Islam is more communal, encompassing all aspects of one's life. Consequently, in countries that are predominantly Muslim, the separation of religion and the state is not considered necessary or even desirable. In fact, governments in Muslim countries often reinforce Islamic practices through their laws. Muslims do vary in their interpretation of several traditions, some of which—such as the requirement for women to wear face veils—are disputed.

Like other religious systems, certain rituals characterize Islam. Muslims fast during the month of Ramadan, which marks the revelation of the Qur'an to the Prophet Muhammad; pray to Allah facing Mecca five times a day; make charitable donations; and say, where possible, Friday afternoon prayers within their community. They also undertake the **hajj**, the pilgrimage, at least once in their lifetime, to Mecca. This city in contemporary Saudi Arabia is home of the House of Allah, or Ka'aba, built by Abraham and his son Ismael. Muslims perform the hajj in accordance with the Qur'an and in the manner prescribed by the Prophet Muhammed in his Sunnah.

Islamic believers are divided into a variety of faiths and sects, such as Sunnis and Shi'is (or Shiites). These divisions sometimes result in antagonisms between the members, just as there are religious rivalries between Christian denominations. The large majority of Muslims in the United States are Sunni Muslims—literally those who follow the *Sunnah*, the way of the Prophet. Compared to other Muslims, they tend to be more moderate in their religious orthodoxy. The Shi'ia (primarily from Iraq, Iran, and southern Lebanon) are the second largest group. The two groups differ on who should have been the Caliph, or ruler, after the death of the Prophet Muhammad. This disagreement resulted in different understandings of beliefs and practices, con-

hajj
A Muslim pilgrimage, undertaken at least once in a lifetime, to Mecca.

cluding in the Sunni and Shi'ia worshipping separately from each other. They worship separately even if it means crossing national and linguistic lines to do so—provided there are sufficient numbers of Shi'ia to support their own mosque or masjid.

There are many other expressions of Islamic faith and even divisions among Sunnis and Shi'is, so to speak of Muslims as Sunni or Shi'i would be akin to speaking of Christians as Roman Catholic or Baptist, forgetting that there are other denominations as well as sharp divisions within the Roman Catholic and Baptist faiths. Furthermore, there are Muslim groups unique to the United States; later we will focus on the largest one—Islam among African Americans.

Verses in the Qur'an prescribe to Muslims **jihad** or struggle against the enemies of Allah. Typically, this is taken by Muslims to refer to their internal struggle for spiritual purity. Today, a very visible minority of Muslims in the world see this as a pretext to carry out an armed struggle against what they view as the enemies of the Palestinians such as Israel and the United States. Such interpretations, even if held by a few, cannot be dismissed because Islam is a faith without an established hierarchy; there is no Muslim pope to deliver the one true interpretation, and there is no provision for excommunication. Individual imams who serve as the clergy for a mosque can offer guidance and scholarship, but Islam's authority rests with the scripture and the teachings of the Prophet (Belt 2002).

It is even more difficult to estimate the number of Muslim Americans in the United States than the number of Arab Americans. There are no census data from which to work, and Islamic institutions such as mosques operate rather independently. Therefore, even considering the most scientific analyses brings wide variation in estimates. Based on the most recent studies, there are at least 2 million and perhaps as many as 5.7 million Muslims in the United States. About two-thirds are U.S.-born and citizens. In terms of ethnic and racial background, the more acceptable estimates still vary widely. Estimates range as follows:

- 20–42 percent African American
- 24–33 percent South Asian (Afghan, Bangladeshi, Indian and Pakistani)
- 12–32 percent Arab
- 10–22 percent "other" (Bosnian, Iranian, Turk, and White and Hispanic converts)

jihad
Struggle against the enemies of Allah, usually taken to mean one's own internal struggle.

Celebrating Edi al-Adha, a three-day feast of charity commemorating Abraham's willingness to sacrifice his son, Muslim worshippers come to the Los Angeles Convention Hall.

blended identity
Self-image and worldview that is a combination of religious faith and cultural background based on nationality and current residency.

There appears to be total agreement that the Muslim population in the United States is growing rapidly through immigration and conversion (Ba-Yunus and Kone 2004; Institute for Social Policy and Understanding 2004; P. King 2004b; Paik 2001; T. Smith 2001).

Reflecting the growth of the Muslim population in the United States, the number of mosques has grown to more than 1,700. Mosques (or more properly referred to as masjids) do not maintain identifiable membership roles as do churches, but scholars have observed that mosques and the imam, the leader or spiritual guide of a mosque, are today taking some of the characteristics of a congregation. In order to maintain their tax-exempt status, mosques are forced to incorporate boards and bylaws. Imams in the United States are more likely to take on a pastoral role relating to nonreligious functions, such as helping immigrants adjust, and representing the Muslim community to other nonprofit groups serving the larger community.

However more common mosques are in the United States, these symbols of faith and houses of worship still attract a different kind of attention than a steeple atop a Lutheran church. For many people in the United States, the mosque does not represent religious freedom and diversity or even a curiosity but a foreign threat in yet another example of Orientalism. Muslim groups have found some communities blocking their efforts to build religious centers. Local authorities may require that the building be stripped of cultural symbols and even to forgo the traditional dome.

Existing mosques have also experienced city councils' blocking their efforts to publicly broadcast their call to prayer over loudspeakers even when neighboring churches just as loudly ring bells to signal the start of worship. Even after accepting some community-driven changes, mosques or Islamic centers often are victims of vandalism. However, there are also signs of acceptance. College campuses experiencing growing numbers of Muslims are adjusting by hiring part-time imams to minister to their needs, dedicating space for Muslims' prayer to be said five times a day, and providing for the dietary restrictions of the Muslim diet (Ba-Yunus and Kone 2004; Leinwand 2004; Leonard 2003; S. Simon 2004; Wilgoren 2001).

In summary, Muslim Americans reflect a blended identity. **Blended identity** is the self-image and worldview that is a combination of religious faith, cultural background based on nationality, and the status of being a resident of the United States. As shown in Figure 11.4, Muslims often find their daily activities defined by their

FIGURE 11.4   Blended Identity of Muslim Americans

Muslim Americans, as shown in this illustration of a Pakistani Muslim living in the United States, form their identity by bringing together three different identities: their faith, their homeland, and the United States.

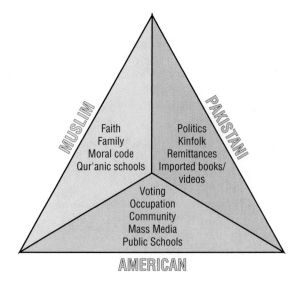

faith, their nationality, and their status as American, however defined in terms of citizenship. Younger Muslims especially can move freely among the different identities. In Chicago, Muslim college students perform hip hop in Arabic with lyrics like "La ilaha ila Allah" (There is no God but Allah). In Fremont, California, high school Muslim girls and some of their non-Muslim girlfriends hold an alternative prom decked out in silken gowns, dancing to both 50 Cent and Arabic music, dining on lasagna, but pausing at sunset to face toward Mecca and pray (Abdo 2004a; P. Brown 2003).

There is one remaining but basic question: What, if anything, is different about being Muslim in the United States as opposed to an Islam country? In the United States, we have a Muslim population that numbers in the millions but reflects the diversity of the worldwide Islamic faith, and practices their rituals and beliefs in a nation where the expression of Christianity dominates culturally. Some scholars of Islam argue that the experience of democracy and the history of religious diversity and free expression have facilitated a stronger and even more correct Islamic practice—uninhibited by the more totalitarian regimes many find in their homelands. Certainly there is disagreement over what is correct, but there is little pressure outside the Muslim community in the United States about how to precisely follow the teachings of the Prophet Muhammad.

Other scholars contend that what makes the American Muslim experience unique is that followers must place an even stronger focus on Islam in order to survive in a culture that is so permissive and, indeed, encourages so much behavior that is prohibited by either Islamic law or their cultural traditions. For many Muslims in the United States, pop culture looks like old-fashioned paganism, a cult that celebrates money and sex. In the United States, many Muslims experience both the freedom to be Muslim and the pressure to be Muslim (Belt 2002; G, Schmidt 2004:4).

Black Muslims

African Americans who embrace Islam form a significant segment within the Muslim American community. Islam is also a significant expression of religious beliefs among Black Americans. They number around 1.6 to 1.7 million or about 5 percent of all African Americans, yet they are estimated to account for 90 percent of all converts to Islam in the United States.

The history of Black American Islam begins in the 17th century, when members of some Muslim tribes were forcibly brought to the American colonies. It is estimated that 10 percent of African slaves were Muslim. As was typical of slave spiritual beliefs, slave owners discouraged anything that linked them culturally to Africa. Furthermore, many in the South saw making slaves Christians as part of their mission in civilizing the enslaved people. Enslaved Muslims in the colonies and elsewhere often resisted the pressure to assimilate to the dominant group's faith and maintained their dedication to Islam (Ba-Yunus and Kone 2004; Leonard 2003; McCloud 1995).

It was exceedingly difficult, if not impossible, for a collective Muslim community to survive slavery. Organized Muslim groups within the African American community grew and dispersed in the late 19th century and the first half of the 20th century. Resurgence of Islam among Black Americans often centered around the leadership of charismatic people such as West Indian born Edward Wilnot Blyden and North Carolinian Noble Drew Ali, who founded the Moorish Science Temple. Typically, followers of the movements dispersed at the death of the central leader, but with each movement, the core of converts to Islam grew within the African American community (Ansari 2004; R. Turner 2003).

Like other Muslims, generally African Americans who follow Islam are not tightly organized into a single religious fellowship. However, most today trace their roots either to the teachings of W. Fard Muhammad or, just as significantly, to those who responded against his version of the faith. Little is known of the early years of Arab immigrant W. Fard Muhammad, who arrived in Detroit around 1930, introducing the teaching of Islam to poor African Americans. He spoke strongly against adultery and alcohol consumption (which are forbidden by Islamic tradition) and smoking and dancing (which are prohibited among some Muslims). However, he also spoke of the natural superiority of Black people that would cause them to win out in the inevitable struggle between Blacks and Whites, but only if they adopted their "natural religion" and reclaimed their identity as Muslims (Lincoln 1994; R. Turner 2003).

Under the leadership of Elijah Muhammad, Fard's most trusted follower and his successor, the Nation of Islam became a well-known and controversial organization. This Muslim group preached racial hatred and experienced internal dissension, but they also gradually built a financial empire not unlike many of the large Christian denominations in the United States. The group also maintained very strong feelings toward Africa specifically and Arabs in general, even if its more unorthodox beliefs left it alienated from Muslim immigrants to the United States. Despite the controversies, many members of White society respected the Nation of Islam for its impressive use of capitalism to the organization's advantage and for the strict moral code its members followed. Warith Deen Muhammad, successor and son of Elijah Muhammad, aligned his followers in 1975 with the practices of the Sunni Muslim faith and to people of all races, although he acknowledged that the American Society of Muslims (ASM), as it is called today, is basically an African American organization (Abdo 2004b; Ansari 2004).

Malcolm X, originally a member of the Nation of Islam, became the most powerful and brilliant voice of Black self-determination in the 1960s. He was an authentic folk hero to his sympathizers and to many people today, more than a generation after his death. Besides his own followers, he commanded an international audience and is still referred to in a manner befitting a prophet. Indeed, Spike Lee's 1993 movie, based on the *Autobiography of Malcolm X*, reintroduced him to another generation. Malcolm X was highly critical of the civil rights movement in general and of Martin Luther King, Jr., in particular.

Malcolm X is remembered for his sharp attacks on other Black leaders, for his break with the Nation of Islam, and for his apparent shift to support the formation of

Malcolm X, reflecting his conversion to Islam, made a pilgrimage to the Muslim holy city of Mecca. On this trip in 1964, the year before his assassination in New York City, he also met with area leaders such as Prince Faisal al-Saud of Saudi Arabia.

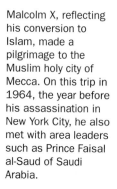

coalitions with progressive Whites. He is especially remembered for teaching Blacks lessons that came to concern the champions of nonviolent direct action, among them that Blacks must resist violence "by any means necessary." By the last year of his life, Malcolm X (by then known as Malik El-Shabazz) had taken on a very different orientation. He created the secular Organization of Afro-American Unity, which was meant to internationalize the civil rights movement. Malcolm X's life was ended by three assassins in 1964. "His philosophy can be summarized as pride in Blackness, the necessity of knowing Black history, Black autonomy, Black unity, and self-determination for the Black community" (Pinkney 1975:213; see also Dyson 1995; Kieh 1995).

In recent years, Minister Louis Farrakhan, despite leading a small proportion of Black Muslims, has been the most visible spokesperson among the various Muslim groups in the African American community. Farrakhan broke with W. Deen Muhammad in 1977 and named his group Nation of Islam, adopting, along with the name used by the earlier group, the more unorthodox-to-Islam ideas of Elijah Muhammad, such as Black moral superiority. Farrakhan jumped into the limelight, although his public statements about Jews and Israel gave an anti-Semitic taint to his teachings. W. Deen Muhammad resigned as leader of the ASM in 2003. Although Mohammed remains its spiritual guide, ASM mosques now tend to operate more independently of each other. The split between Farrakhan and Muhammad is not new to the Black followers of Islam, as Malcolm X's life indicates (Abodo 2004; Henry 1994; Lincoln 1994).

Although Farrakhan's statements against Whites—Jews in particular—and his anti-Israel foreign policy have attracted the media's attention, many of his speeches and writings reflect the basic early tenets of the Nation of Islam. Abortion, drugs, and homosexuality are condemned. Self-help, bootstrap capitalism, and strict punishment are endorsed. Farrakhan is not pessimistic about the future of race relations in the United States. As leader of the 1995 Million Man March, he encouraged those present and African Americans nationwide to register to vote and work for positive change (Bositis 1996; Loury 1996).

Compared to most faiths, an unusual source of converts to Islam has been in the nation's prisons. One estimate released in 2002 states that 32 percent of all incarcerated African Americans in the New York State prison system have embraced Islam. The Muslim prayer, a different diet, and commitment to a highly moral lifestyle help the inmates create an alternative social space within the prison (Dannin 2002).

Traditionally, there has been little contact, at best, and actually some friction between the African American Muslim community, particularly those who adhere to the Nation of Islam, and immigrant Muslims and their descendants. Black Muslims may feel that the larger Islamic community does not speak to what they feel is the unique oppression faced by people who are Black and Muslim in the Untied States. Meanwhile, other Muslims often assume incorrectly that all African American Muslims embrace the Black superiority view and do not follow orthodox Muslim traditions. It is likely that a single dominating voice of Islam will not emerge among African Americans. That is not surprising because a pluralistic interpretation of faith is common to Muslims worldwide just as it is to Christians and Jews (Abodo 2004; McCloud 2004).

Immigration to the United States

The history of both Muslims and Arabs in the United States is a long one, but their visibility as a true immigrant presence is more of a 20th century phenomenon. As has already been noted, a significant proportion of African slaves were followers of Islam. Even earlier, Spanish Muslims accompanied explorers and *conquistadores* to the

New media outlets, such as *Azizah* magazine, have developed to serve the Muslim American community.

Americas. In the 19th century, contingents of Arabs made dramatic impressions at a series of world's fairs held in Philadelphia, St. Louis, and Chicago, where millions of fair goers had certainly their first contact and probably their first awareness of Arab culture. Although often viewed through the lens of Orientalism, fair goers came away with an awareness of cultures previously unknown to them. Positive reports of the reception of these delegations began to encourage Arabs, particularly from Syria and Lebanon, to immigrate to the United States. At about the same time, other Arabs immigrated as the result of encouragement from U.S.-funded missionary programs in the Middle East.

Just as immigration of Arabs and, to a lesser extent, practicing Muslims began to annually number in the thousands in the early 20th century, World War I intervened and then the restrictive National Origins System (see Chapter 4), with its pro-Western and Northern Europe bias, slowed the movement to the Untied States. As with so many other immigrant groups, the pattern was for immigration to be disproportionately male and the destination to be cities of the east coast. Pressure to assimilate caused many newcomers to try to reduce the differences between themselves and the host country. So, for example, many women ceased to cover their head—a practice common to both Christian Arab and Muslim women.

The growth and continuing vibrancy of an Arab presence in the Dearborn, Michigan, area is a unique development in the history of Arab immigration. A few Lebanese immigrants of the late 19th century were soon to be joined by fellow countrymen and women, as well as immigrants from Lebanon who were largely Christian, and from Yemen, typically Sunni Muslims. With the expansion of the automobile industry during the 1910s, Arabs came to work in the area's many factories. Pleased by their treatment and wages, more immigrants joined them. By 1919, the first mosque was established and a variety of service agencies began to serve the needs of the immigrant community.

As of 2003, there were 33 mosques in the metropolitan Detroit area, serving an estimated 200,000 Muslims. With at least 40 percent of this area's population of Arab ancestry today, it is hard for a visitor not to see the evidence of this century-long immigration. Business establishments will often feature greetings for Christmas, Ramadan, New Year's, and the two Islamic holidays called "Eids" in both English and Arabic. Today, it is by far the largest concentration of Arab Americans as well as Muslims. Indeed, this is probably the largest Arab community outside of the Arab world (Abraham and Shryock 2000; Bagby 2004; David and Ayouby 2004; S. Gold 2001).

In the wake of professional-preference clauses within the 1965 Immigration and Naturalization Act, immigration increased among both Muslims and Arabs. This movement of skilled workers greatly benefited the United States, as the law intended, but obviously contributed to the brain drain experienced throughout the Arab and Muslim worlds. With the Arab defeat in the 1967 Arab-Israeli War, there was a noticeable rise in immigration, with many Arab and Muslim Americans seeking to bring family members to join them from throughout the Middle East (Naff 1980).

Contemporary Life in the United States

As has already been noted, Arab Americans tended to immigrate to urban areas. There they have filled a variety of occupational roles, and immigrants, since the 1965 Immigration and Naturalization Act, have been filling skilled and professional roles in the United States. Another area in which Arab Americans often find opportunities for upward mobility is to become self-employed merchants or entrepreneurs. They typically are financially unable to buy into prosperous businesses or high-end retail stores. Rather, they have tended to become involved in precisely those businesses that privileged Whites have long since left behind or avoided altogether. To some degree, Arabs follow a pattern of Jewish and Korean immigrant entrepreneurs, operating stores in low-income areas of central cities that major retailers ignore. Opportunities for success are great, but it also means that the Arab American merchant faces the challenges of serving a low-income population with few consumer choices and a history of being exploited by outsiders (Cainkar 2005).

For many people in the United States, such as this couple in Los Angeles, their primary interaction with the Arab community is by dining at Middle Eastern restaurants.

Family Life and Gender

The family, as with any people, plays a central role in the lives of Muslim and Arab Americans. Given the diversity within both groups, it is impossible to generalize about typical patterns. Traditionally, Islam permitted men to have multiple wives—a maximum

Arab entrepreneurs are present in a broad spectrum of activities. Here in Hollywood, California, an Arab American took over a long-term store called Mugsy Malone, leading to the culturally confusing sign embracing Arabic letters and a shamrock.

of four. The Qur'an admonished Muslim men to do justice economically and emotionally to their wives, and if they could not, then they should have only one wife. In some non-Islamic countries, this practice of multiple marriages is legal but is exceedingly rare for Muslim households in countries where the law is not supportive.

In the United States, for those who are recent immigrants or the children of immigrants, family patterns are more likely to be affected by the traditions of their homeland than by the fact that they are Muslim or Arab. Certainly, the role of women receives a great deal of attention because their outer clothing is a conspicuous symbol that to some seems to represent repression of women in society. There is a full range of views of women among Muslims and Arabs, just as there is among Christians and other ethnicities. However, Islam does stress that women need to be protected and should present themselves modestly in public. This code is operationalized very differently among countries where Muslims dominate and varies within Muslim populations in the United States (Haeri 2004).

Dress codes particularly have been the focus of attention both within and outside the Muslim community. Individually, all Muslims, men and women alike, must cover themselves and avoid revealing clothes designed to accentuate contours of the body and emphasize its physical beauty. According to the Qur'an, more revealing garments can be worn in private with one's family or before members of the same sex, so in some Muslim countries some beaches and public pools are designated for use by men or by women.

While the Qur'an dictates that women should wear a headcovering that also covers their upper chest and neck, the Prophet Muhammad did clarify in his Sunnah that the female body should be covered except the face, hands, and feet. Hence, traditional Muslim women should wear head coverings. The **hijab** refers to a variety of garments that allow women to follow the guidelines of modest dress. It may include head coverings or a face veil and can take the form of a headscarf rather than something that actually covers the face; the latter would be dictated by a cultural tradition, not Islam. U.S. Muslims select from an array of traditional garments from Muslim countries. These garments include long, loose overgarments which are tailored coats, or a loose black overgarment along with a scarf and perhaps a face veil. U.S. Muslim women are just as apt to wear long skirts or loose pants and overblouses that they may buy at any local retail outlet (Haeri 2004).

When it comes to the hijab, or outer garments, research has identified three perspectives among Muslim women in the United States and other settlements outside Islamic countries. Younger, better-educated women who support wearing the hijab in public draw upon Western ideas of individual rights, arguing in favor of veiling as a form of personal expression. In contrast, older, less-educated women who also support the wearing of hijab tend to make their arguments without any reference to Western ideology. They cannot see why veiling should be an issue in the first place. A third group of women, of all ages and educational backgrounds, oppose the hijab. Some countries, notably France, have come under fire for taking official positions banning the hijab or headscarf in public schools. Generally this has not been an issue in the United States; however, one 11-year-old had to go to federal court to be able to attend school in Muskogee, Oklahoma, wearing a headscarf. Interestingly, the Department of Justice supported the girl in her lawsuit (C. Killian 2003; Religious Diversity News 2004).

In "Research Focus," sociologist Jen'nan Ghazal Read reports on research showing how Christian and Muslim Arab American women view gender roles.

Gender role differences among Muslims are not limited to the home and the family. There are differences in the role of women within the faith and in the mosque or masjid. In part, this reflects the differences in Islamic practices worldwide. For example, in Pakistan and Bangladesh, women are rarely allowed to enter most mosques.

hijab
Refers to a variety of garments that allow women to follow the guidelines of modest dress.

Focus Research Focus Research Focus

CHRISTIAN AND MUSLIM ARAB AMERICAN WOMEN'S GENDER ROLES

Few issues concerning Islam and Arabs spark more discussion than the role of women. Images of both groups tend to assume women's role is very limited and that any deviation from that role is heavily sanctioned. Sociologist Jen'nan Ghazal Read conducted a national survey of Arab American women in 2000. She was able to compare attitudes on gender roles between Christian and Muslim Arab Americans. The gender role questions highlighted such issues as attitudes on marital roles (who should make the decision), parenting (mothers with preschool children working full-time), and nontraditional public roles such as leading religious services.

Read found that Muslim women were more gender traditional than their non-Muslim peers in the Arab American community. However, she also noted the Muslim respondents were more likely to be immi-grants, have an Arab spouse, and tended to be more conservative in their faith com-pared to Christian Arab women. Once she considered these differences, being Muslim seemed to have no impact on how the women viewed gender roles. For example, both the Bible and Qur'an encourage women to be more domestic and less public. Hence, she found that devout Christians and devout Muslim women were conservative in their gender attitudes compared to those of both faiths who were less inclined to accept their holy scripture literally.

Research into the views of Arab and Muslim Americans is just beginning, and Read's research underscores the importance of considering immigrant status and commit-ment to one's faith. The next step is to col-lect such data but also include a comparable non-Muslim, non-Arab sample. ■

However, in Mecca and Medina, Saudi Arabia, the most holy mosques in Islam, women pray apart from the men but not in separate areas or behind curtains. In the United States, it is not unusual for women to be members of the boards of mosques, and it is also common for women worshippers to be relegated to praying in rooms outside the mosques. In many mosques, the explanation for segregating the sexes is the lack of space necessary to maintain modesty while kneeling for prayer, and it is true that many mosques are little more than small storefronts. However, even newly built mosques do not necessarily accommodate women worshippers in the same way they do men. In mosques that attract more U.S.-born Muslims, these issues remain points of contention and anxiety within the Muslim community (Goodstein 2004).

Education

Muslim Americans recognize the importance of education, and many of the recent immigrants have high levels of formal education and have benefited by the immigration policy that gave preference to those having job skills needed to enter the United States. Muslims also value formal instruction in their faith, and there are several hundred elementary and secondary schools, the majority attached to mosques, that offer what is been referred to in other religious contexts as a parochial school education.

While many Muslim children attend public schools in the United States, others attend private or parochial schools. A teacher at the American Islamic Academy in Dearborn, Michigan, reminds her young students to be quiet when walking through school hallways.

Schools are specific to particular expressions of Islam and specific nationalities, and some schools serve principally Black Muslims. Qur-anic or Sunday schools also coexist, offering specifically religious instruction either to those attending mosque schools or as a supplement for children enrolled in public schools. A major growth industry has emerged in North America, providing curriculum materials and software to serve these schools, which range from preschool and continue through college, including graduate education (K. Leonard 2003).

Children attending public schools encounter the type of adjustment experienced by those of a religious faith different from the dominant one of society. Although public schools are intended to be secular, it is difficult to escape the orientation of many activities to Christmas and Easter or dietary practices that may not conform to the cultural tradition of the children's families. In some school districts with larger Muslim student populations, strides have been made to recognize the religious diversity. A few have granted Eid-al-Fitr, the day marking the end of Ramadan, as an official school holiday for all students (Avila 2003).

Politics

Muslim and Arab Americans are politically aware and often active. For those who identify with their homeland, politics may take the form of closely monitoring international events as they affect their home country and perhaps their kinfolk who still live there. Admittedly, since U.S. foreign policy often is tilted against some areas such as Palestine, the concerns that Arab Americans may have about events abroad may not be reduced by statements and actions taken by government officials in the United States. On a different level, Muslims and Arab Americans are increasingly involved in politics in the United States. Certainly the most visible Arab American in politics has been consumer advocate Ralph Nader, who has tried to open up presidential politics to consider a true alternative to the two-party system.

Muslims in the United States often express the view that their faith encourages political participation. They note that as Prophet Muhammad lay on his deathbed, he explicitly refused to name a successor to his rule, preferring that the people choose their own leaders. Individual Arabs and Muslims have sought elective office and have been appointed to high-level positions. As voters, they are eagerly sought out by the major parties because they are concentrated in states such as Michigan, Pennsylvania, Ohio, and Florida that often play a critical role in close presidential elections.

There is a clear distancing that one can observe between the major parties and Muslims and Arab Americans. Although there are frequent official welcoming statements of support, close identification as might be shown in routine dinners and convention appearances are rare. This represents a contrast to how politicians cater to African Americans and Latinos to gain votes and more closely resembles the arm's-length relationship to gay and lesbian voters. As charges have escalated in the last decade that some organizations and charities in the Arab and Muslim community were financially assisting overseas groups unfriendly to Israel or even supportive of terrorist objectives, U.S. politicians began to take the safe position of refusing campaign money from virtually any group linked to the Muslim or Arab community. Needless to say, this did not make U.S. citizens who also happen to be of Arab decent or followers of Islam feel very welcomed in the political process (Clemetson 2003; Hassaballa 2004).

Being Arab or Muslim in the United States

News events have fueled anti-Arab, anti-Muslim feeling. Activities carried out by Arabs or Muslims, including the 1972 terrorist raid at the Munich Olympics and the 1998 bombings of the U.S. embassies in Kenya and Tanzania, contributed to the negative image. The attack of September 11, 2001, engineered by Arab Muslim extremists, caused many Americans to associate Arab and Muslim Americans with America's enemy in the war against terrorism. As the economy softened and taxpayers paid for increased security, Arab and Muslim Americans became the scapegoat in many people's minds. Vandalism of mosques, attacks on Arab-appearance people, and calls for widespread dragnets based on ethnicity or religion were common. Terrorism, even domestic terrorism, often is the product of homegrown troublemakers, as evidenced by hundreds of attacks on abortion clinics and the 1995 bombing of the federal building in Oklahoma City, Oklahoma.

Following the 1972 Munich Olympics attack, President Richard Nixon initiated Operation Boulder, which allowed for coordinated intelligence activities by the CIA, FBI, and other agencies to spy on and harass any Arab Americans engaging in political activity. With the objective to block support for the Palestinian cause, the three-year effort was to be directed against anyone of Arabic background (David and Ayouby 2004).

The immediate aftermath of the 1995 bombing of the federal building in Oklahoma City showed the willingness of the public to accept stereotypes. Many television news reports indicated that Islamic fundamentalists or Arab terrorists were the prime suspects. A Jordanian American who lives in Oklahoma City was arrested in London but cleared of any involvement in the terrorist attack. Nevertheless, in the first three days after the bombing, there were at least 222 attacks against Muslims in the United States. In the end, two White American men were convicted in the bombing, but this hardly erased the pain felt by many Arab Americans and Muslim Americans about the way in which they were scapegoated (Brooke 1995; Zogby 1998).

The events of September 11, 2001, catapulted the United States to focus on segments of the population with a scrutiny that had not been witnessed since the attack on Pearl Harbor 60 years earlier. President George W. Bush (2001) assured the nation, speaking from the Washington, D.C. Islamic Center within days of the hijacking of four airliners, that "the face of terror is not the true faith of Islam. . . . Islam is peace" and that "Muslims make an incredibly valuable contribution to our country." However, much harm had already been done. Follow-up remarks in the days to come were made by the president and other administrative officials in front of mosques or in the presence of representatives of the Muslim and Arab American community. Even the USA PATRIOT Act passed in October 2001, which has been sharply criticized for contributing to fear within the Arab and Muslim communities, has specific provisions condemning discrimination against Arab and Muslim Americans. Although these were positive symbols of reaching out, the further stigmatization of Muslim and Arab Americans was unstoppable.

In light of these suspicions, some citizens have found themselves under special surveillance because of racial profiling at airports and border checkpoints. As noted earlier in Chapter 2, racial profiling is any arbitrary police-initiated action based on race, ethnicity, or national origin rather than a person's behavior. Profiling of Arabs and Muslims became especially intense after September 11, 2001. The profiling has moved into everyday life. Muslim women who choose to don hair scarves, in keeping with their tradition to dress modestly, encounter harassment from strangers in the street and find many employers insisting that they shed the covering if they want to get a job or expect to be promoted. These citizens find it difficult to understand these attitudes in a nation of immigrants that is grounded in religious freedom.

In those weeks after 9/11, surveys showed that both Muslim and Arab Americans supported the president's policy of going after terrorists. At the same time, they were fearful that continued military action would hurt how the United States is viewed. In the wake of 9/11, expressions and proof of loyalty were forced on Arab and Muslim Americans. Based on interviews with Muslim American college students in New York City, analysis of the responses showed that many felt the same sense of frustration and anger from the terrorist attacks. However, they also expressed an obligation to show their sorrow to others and, if true, indicate that they were born in the United States and actively supported the war on terrorism. In a national survey of Muslim Americans, completed in November 2001, 41 percent reported being more patriotic toward the United States, and only 5 percent less patriotic despite the majority having experienced anti-Muslim discrimination in the weeks following 9/11 (Muslims in the American Public Square 2001; P. King 2004a; L. Peek 2002; J. Zogby 2001).

In an effort to locate domestic terrorists, the U.S. Department of Justice required that all foreign-born Muslim men report to the Bureau of Citizenship and Immigration Services to be photographed, fingerprinted, and interviewed. Some questions were mundane: Where did they work? Where they married? Did they have children? Some were more pointed: Had they been asked by any Arabs or Muslims to teach them to fly airplanes? With very little public notice, 144,513 Muslim men from 25 countries reported during a five-month period ending in 2003. Of those who reported, about 13,000 faced deportation because of visa violations such as overstaying their visas, and 11 remained in custody because they were suspected terrorists.

The registration deepened fear and disillusionment among the many law-abiding Muslims in the United States. Many of the over 144,000 men interviewed were embarrassed to even be questioned, since their code of behavior (no drinking or illegal drugs) meant they were less likely to have faced routine encounters with law enforcement officials. Immigration advocates argued that the government was selectively enforcing immigration laws, but the courts have upheld the process and the right of the government to keep names of those deported or detained secret (P. King 2004c; N. Lewis 2003; *Migration News* 2003b).

In "Listen to Our Voices," opinion pollster and founder of the Arab American Institute, James Zogby, raises his concerns about how government policies within the United States have created problems for Arab Americans, but remains optimistic that these policies will be revisited and changed.

Consider the particular case of some 100,000 Afghan Americans, typically Muslim but, like the people of Afghanistan, not considered Arabs. After September 11,

Voices **Listen to Our Voices** Listen to

PENDULUM SWINGS ON CIVIL RIGHTS

There is growing concern that the Department of Justice (DOJ) has over-reached in the post 9/11 period, implementing several programs that have caused harm to Arab and Muslim immigrants and visitors to the United States.

Of particular concern have been: the large number of detentions and deportations that took place right after the 2001 terrorist attacks; the so-called "voluntary call-in" of 8,000 young Arab and Muslim immigrants; and the special registration program that has targeted visitors from twenty-five Arab and Muslim countries. . . .

These programs created suspicion as well. Some Americans came to feel that if the DOJ was targeting tens of thousands of Arabs and Muslims, based on their religion and ethnicity, then maybe there was reason to suspect these individuals. So even while President Bush was urging Americans not to discriminate against Arabs and Muslims, a different message was being send by those DOJ initiatives. . . .

As a frequent traveler to the Arab world, I am aware of yet another negative impact of these DOJ initiatives. They have damaged the U.S. image and harmed our credibility and our relationship with the people of the region.

Because the effect of these DOJ programs have been well publicized in the Arab world there is a growing perception that Arab immigrants and visitors are not welcome in the United States. As a result many fewer Arabs are coming to the United States for medical treatment, tourism, study or business.

The good news is that there is a growing political coalition committed to challenging these practices, and they are having an impact. Broad coalitions of immigrant rights advocates have formed to demand an end to profiling, the registration program and other violations of civil liberties. Similarly,

James Zogby

affected institutions like universities, hospitals and major businesses have mobilized to pressure for changes in the restrictive visa procedures that have made the United States appear to be less open to visitors and immigrants. And major studies have been done both by reputable independent institutions and official government oversight bodies that have called into question the legality of some of these practices and their effectiveness.

Last year, for example, the Justice Department's own Inspector General issued a report that vindicated our concerns. The IG found that the Justice Department classified 762 of the detainees as "September 11 detainees." The IG concluded that none of these detainees were charged with terrorist-related offenses, and that the decision to detain them was "extremely attenuated" from the 9/11 investigation. The IG concluded that the Justice Department's designation of detainees of interest to the 9/11 investigation was "indiscriminate and haphazard." and did not adequately distinguish between terrorism suspects and other immigration detainees. . . .

Last week I testified before a Senate Judiciary Committee hearing on "America after 9/11: Freedom Preserved or Freedom Lost?"

There was strong support for change. Many Senators expressed their concern with the behavior of the DOJ and there are now a number of bills in the House and Senate that seek to correct the post 9/11 abuses. In fact, the American public wants civil liberties to be protected, wants the United States to remain open and welcoming to Arab visitors, students and immigrants....

Two years after the United States was traumatized by terror, the pendulum now appears to be swinging back. ■

Source: "Pendulum Swings on Civil Rights" by James Zogby as posted on www.aaiusa.org/wwatch/112303.htm (November 23, 2003.

Afghan Americans found themselves specially targeted for prejudice and were understandably concerned when the United States bombed Afghanistan in search of terrorist groups. Some Afghan Americans talk of leaving for Afghanistan, generally out of a desire to reestablish family ties. Like other Muslim immigrants, they came to the United States seeking better education, improved housing, and a higher standard of living in a country they perceived as tolerant of religious diversity. Most came in the 1970s and now have children who are more American than Afghan. Increasingly, their family ties, not just the economic ones, are in the United States (Ritter and Squiteri 2002).

Issues of Prejudice and Discrimination

Al tikrar bialllem il hmar

(By repetition even the donkey learns)

Media scholar Jack Shaheen (2003:171) uses this Arab proverb to underscore how the media has reinforced the negative image of Arabs and Muslims. Motion pictures such as *The Sheik* (1921), *The Mummy* (1932), *True Lies* (1994), and *The Mummy Returns* (2001) uniformly show Arabs and Muslims as savages and untrustworthy. Even Disney's 1995 animated film *Aladdin* referred to Arabs as "barbaric" and depicted, contrary to Islamic law, a guard threatening to cut off a young girl's hand for stealing food. In what ways do prejudice and discrimination manifest themselves with respect to Muslim and Arab Americans? In form and magnitude, they are much like what is shown toward other subordinate groups. Regrettably, the situation appears to have gone beyond Orientalism in which one sees people as "the other" and somewhat frightening. What makes current expressions of hostility strikingly different are that the events of the 21st century have been given a decidedly patriotic fervor; that is, for many who overtly express their anti-Muslim or anti-Arab feeling, they are also being pro-American.

Perhaps even more troubling to many Arab and Muslim Americans are the portrayals and images in the news and general information programming on television. To some, there is an overemphasis on the extreme representations, such as the wearing of opaque face veils by women, with little social context offered. Furthermore, the interests of the United States are depicted either as leaning against the Arabs and Muslims, as in the Israel-Palestinian violence, or presented as hopelessly dependent on them, in the case of our reliance on foreign oil production (Saeed 2004).

Not surprisingly, analysis of surveys done in the months after 9/11 found growing willingness to view Arabs and Muslims generally as a dangerous people and to require that Muslim and Arab Americans carry special identification cards. Nevertheless, there seemed little interest in repeating the internment camp experience of Japanese Americans following the attack on Pearl Harbor. One survey found that 65 percent were opposed to the federal government's holding Arabs who were U.S. citizens in camps until it could be determined whether they had links to terrorist organizations (Parmelee 2002).

Evidence of hate crimes and harassment toward Arab and Muslim Americans rose sharply after 9/11, compared to studies done in the mid-1990s. It continued to remain high through 2004, according to more recent studies. Incidents have ranged from beatings to vandalism of mosques. Evidence of a backlash also includes Muslim Americans' getting unwarranted eviction notices (Institute for Social Policy and Understanding 2004; J. Stewart 2002; Watanabe 2004).

A national survey released in October 2004 found that one in four people believe a number of anti-Muslim stereotypes, such as the idea that Islam teaches violence and

There is no question that 9/11 has brought unwanted attention to the many patriotic and law-abiding Arab and Muslim Americans.

hatred. Negative images are 16 times more prevalent than positive ones. However, large numbers do hold positive views. More than half of the survey respondents view Muslims as family oriented and disagree with the statement that "Muslims are dishonest" (Council on American-Islamic Relations 2004).

Arab Americans and Muslim Americans, like other subordinate groups, have not responded passively to their treatment. Organizations have been created in their communities to counter negative stereotypes and to offer schools material responding to the labeling that has occurred. Even before 2001, Arab Americans and Muslim Americans were beginning to become active in both major political parties in the United States. However, during the 2000 campaign, candidates already were distancing themselves from campaign contributions from Muslim and Arab organizations. As with other groups that have been disadvantaged and do not have clear access to the top levels of decision making in the public and private sectors, nonprofit organizations, such as the Council of American-Islamic Relations, the American Muslim Alliance, and the American Arab Anti-Discrimination Committee, have developed to represent their interests and to promote understanding as well as to bring attention to discrimination and expressions of prejudice in public life and the mass media.

Conclusion

We have seen the diversity within the Native American tribal community and among Latinos. Prejudice, discrimination, and responses of resistance have typified these groups and African Americans' long history in the United States. Now we can see in a special way that Arab Americans and Muslim Americans share in this experience. Not very numerous in absolute terms until the latter part of the 20th century, both Arabs and Muslims have built upon a fragmented history that in the United States literally goes back 200 years. When Muslims were less numerous, it was difficult to maintain any sense of communal identity, but as their numbers increased, identifiable groups emerged.

Diversity has marked both Arab Americans and Muslim Americans in the United States. For the descendants of earlier Arab settlers, their identity as Arab may be discounted by recent Arab immigrants through a process of the deficit model of ethnic identity. For the

Muslim community, the divisions within the faith overseas are reproduced in the United States, with the added significant presence of African Americans who have embraced Islam.

The world and domestic events of recent years, and especially in the early years of the 21st century, have created some new challenges. In some respects, the continuing conflict in Israel and Palestine has served to create an Arab identity that was largely missing a few generations ago, when more strictly nationalistic agendas prevailed. Similarly, the agenda of fundamentalist and militant Muslims has created an us-them mentality found both in international organizations and on street corners of the United States. This lack of truly understanding one another is not totally new, but is built upon the Orientalism that has its roots in the initial contacts between Europeans and the people of the Middle East and South Asia.

To Chicago's Jahan Ghaemi, Seattle's Jawad al-Gheezi, and Cleveland's Rebecca Khoury—all mentioned at the beginning of this chapter—this is all ancient history. They, like other U.S. citizens, are seeking to define themselves and move ahead in their society. The challenges for them to do this seem measurably greater than they were just a few years ago, but their efforts to create bridges are also significant.

Key Terms

blended identity 290	hijab 296	jihad 289
deficit model of ethnic identity 287	hajj 288	Orientalism 284

Review Questions

1. What are the dimensions of diversity among Arab Americans and among Muslims?

2. What distinguishes African American Muslims from other practicing Muslims in the United States?

3. How has the immigration of Muslims and Arabs been influenced by the governmental policies of the United States?

4. What would you identify as the four most important differences between being a Christian in the United States and being a Muslim in this country?

Critical Thinking

1. Besides Arab Americans and Muslim Americans, identify other groups recently subjected to prejudice, perhaps in your own community.

2. Apply the deficit model of ethnic identity to another group besides Arab Americans.

3. What are some characteristics associated with Muslim and Arab Americans that come to be viewed as negatives, but when practiced by Christian Whites are seen as positives?

4. How does the press coverage and mass media that you have seen perpetuate Orientalism?

Internet Connections—Research Navigator™

 Follow the instructions found on page 31 of this text to access the features of Research Navigator™. Once at the Web site, enter your Login Name and Password. Then, to use the ContentSelect database, enter keywords such as "Qu'ran" and "Orientalism," and the research engine will supply relevant and recent scholarly and popular press publications. Use the *New York Times* Search-by-Subject Archive to find recent news articles related to sociology and the Link Library feature to find relevant Web links organized by the key terms associated with this chapter.

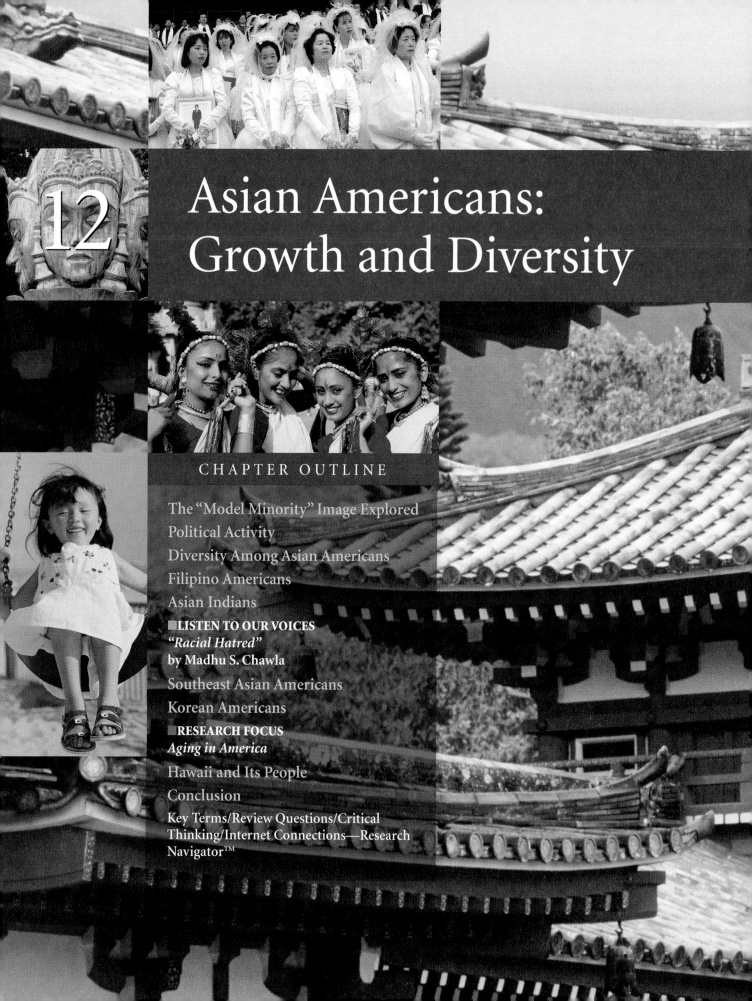

12

Asian Americans: Growth and Diversity

ASIAN AMERICANS AND PACIFIC ISLANDERS ARE A DIVERSE group that is one of the fastest-growing segments of the U.S. population. Asian Americans often are viewed as a model minority that has successfully overcome discrimination. This inaccurate image disguises lingering maltreatment and anti–Asian American violence. Furthermore, it denies Asian Americans the assistance afforded other racial minorities. Immigration is the primary source of growth among Filipinos, Asian Indians, Southeast Asians, and Koreans. All Asian groups, along with Blacks and Whites (or Haoles, as they are known) coexist in Hawaii.

When she talks, people listen. Even though she is only 27, Alpana Singh is a well-regarded authority on cuisine and fine dining, whether on television or in the upscale Chicago restaurant Everest. Singh's story is remarkable but not uncommon among many people in the United States of Asian descent. At age 21, she became the youngest woman to pass the exacting Court of Master Sommelier advanced examination for wine experts. This is all the more incredible because she grew up in a Hindu home where wine was not consumed, yet she gathered an appreciation for the fine points of food from her immigrant parents, who ran an Indian grocery in California. Now nationally known and respected, she speaks proudly of heritage and her fluency in Hindi, English, and Spanish. Reflecting on her fellow South Asians, she remarks, "We have this amazing ability to adapt to the surroundings. We became doctors and golfers, but we never forget where we came from" (Kantrowitz and Scelfo 2003:53).

Alpana Singh could be speaking for all Asian Americans who are often aware of the country from which they or their grandparents came and their position in the United States. An up-and-coming food expert reminds us that the legacy of immigration to the United States is not merely quaint turn-of-the-century black-and-white photos posed at Ellis Island. It is not merely a thickly accented elderly person telling of the "old country." Immigration, race, and ethnicity are being lived out among people of all ages, and for no collective group is this truer than for Asian Americans who live throughout the United States (Figure 12.1).

Asian Americans include groups such as Chinese Americans and Filipinos, nationality groups that include different linguistic groups and identifiable ethnic groups

FIGURE 12.1 Where Most Asian Pacific Islanders Live

Source: Barnes and Bennett 2002; Grieco 2001.

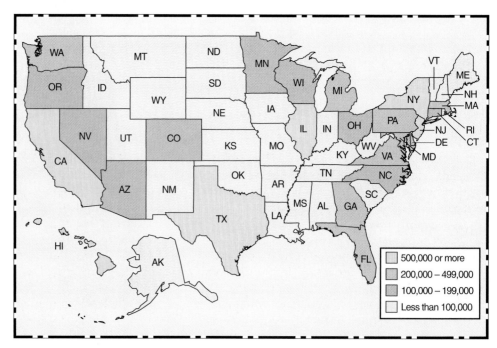

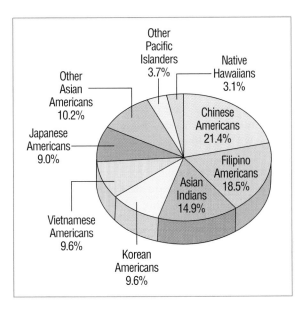

FIGURE 12.2 Asian Pacific Islanders

Note: Based on 12.8 million who identified Asian or Pacific Islander alone or in combination with another race. If only one race alone were used, the major difference would be to decrease slightly the proportion of Asian Pacific Islanders who were Japanese, Hawaiian, and Filipino.

Source: Barnes and Bennett 2002; Grieco 2001.

(Figure 12.2). Also, Asian Americans include ethnic groups such as the Hmong that do not correspond to any one nation. Finally, the U.S. population also includes Pacific Islanders, which include Hawaiians, Samoans, Tongans, and many smaller groups. Collectively, Asian Pacific Islanders in 2002 numbered 12.5 million—an 87 percent increase over 1990, compared with an overall population increase of only 16 percent (Bureau of the Census 2003a: 21, 47; Reeves and Bennett 2003).

To comprehend better the collective picture of Asian Americans, we will first consider a powerful image that many people have of Asian Americans: that they constitute some kind of perfect, model minority. We will then turn our attention to the role they play politically in the United States.

  CD-ROM *Activity 8.2*

We will then consider four of the larger groups—Filipinos, Asian Indians, Southeast Asians, and Koreans—in greater depth. The chapter concludes by examining the coexistence of a uniquely mixed group of peoples—Hawaiians—among whom Asian Americans form the numerical majority. Chapter 13 concentrates on the Chinese and the Japanese, the two Asian groups with the longest historical tradition in the United States.

The "Model Minority" Image Explored

"Asian Americans are a success! They achieve! They succeed! There are no protests, no demands. They just do it!" This is the general image that people in the United States so often hold of Asian Americans as a group. They constitute a **model or ideal minority** because, although they have experienced prejudice and discrimination, they seem to have succeeded economically, socially, and educationally without resorting to political or violent confrontations with Whites. Some observers point to the existence of a model minority as a reaffirmation that anyone can get ahead in the United States. Proponents of the model minority view declare that because Asian Americans have achieved success, they have ceased to be subordinate and are no longer disadvantaged. This is only a variation of blaming the victim; with Asian Americans, it is "praising the victim." An examination of aspects of their socioeconomic status will allow a more thorough exploration of this view (Fong 2002; Hurh and Kim 1989; Thrupkaew 2002).

model or ideal minority
A group that, despite past prejudice and discrimination, succeeds economically, socially, and educationally without resorting to political or violent confrontations with Whites.

Education and the Economy

Asian Americans as a group have impressive school enrollment rates in comparison to the total population. In 2002, 57 percent of Asian Americans 25 years or older held bachelor's degrees, compared with 32 percent of the White population (Table 12.1). These rates vary between Asian American groups, with Asian Indians, Chinese Americans, and Japanese Americans having higher levels of educational achievement.

CD-ROM *Activity 8.3*

This encouraging picture does have some qualifications, however, which call into question the optimistic model minority view. According to a study of California's state university system, while Asian Americans often are viewed as successful overachievers, they have unrecognized and overlooked needs and experience discomfort and harassment on campus. As a group, they also lack Asian faculty and staff members to whom they can turn for support. They confront many identity issues and have to do a "cultural balancing act" along with all the usual pressures faced by college students. The report noted that an "alarming number" of Asian American students appear to be experiencing intense stress and alienation, problems that have often been "exacerbated by racial harassment" (Ohnuma 1991; Zhou 2004).

Even the positive stereotype of Asian American students as "academic stars" or "whiz kids" can be burdensome to people so labeled. Asian Americans who do only modestly well in school may face criticism from their parents or teachers for their failure to conform to the "whiz kid" image. Some Asian American youths disengage from school when faced with these expectations or receive little support for their interest in vocational pursuits or athletics (Kibria 2002).

That Asian Americans as a group work in the same occupations as Whites suggests that they have been successful, and many have. However, the pattern shows some differences. Asian immigrants, like other minorities and immigrants before them, are found disproportionately in the low-paying service occupations. At the same time, they are also concentrated at the top in professional and managerial positions. Yet as we will see, they rarely reach the very top. They hit the glass ceiling (as described in Chapter 3) or, as some others say, try to "climb a broken ladder," before they reach management. In 2002, only 2 percent of 11,500 people who serve on the boards of the nation's 1,000 largest corporations were Asian American (G. Strauss 2002).

The absence of Asian Americans as top executives also indicates that their success is not complete. Asian Americans have done well in small businesses and modest agricultural ventures. While self-employed and managing their own businesses, Asian

---

TABLE 12.1
Selected Social and Economic Characteristics of Asian Americans

	Non-Hispanic White	Asian Americans
Percentage completing college, 25 years and over	31.7%	56.9%
Percentage unemployed	5.1%	5.7%
Percentage of families with a single parent	17.7%	21.2%
Percentage living below poverty level	8.2%	11.8%
HOUSEHOLD INCOME		
-below $10,000	7.1%	10.7%
-over $50,000	17.3%	23.4%

Note: Income and poverty data for 2003; other data for 2002.

Source: Reeves and Bennett 2003: p. 1, Detailed Tables 4, 10, 14, 16; DeNavas-Walt et al. 2004: 10, 29, 31.

Americans have had very modest-sized operations. Because of the long hours, the income from such a business may be below prevailing wage standards, so even when they are business owners, they may still constitute cheap labor, although they also get the profits. Chinese restaurants, Korean American cleaning businesses and fruit and vegetable stores, and motels, gasoline stations, and newspaper vending businesses operated by Asian Indians fall into this category.

Asian Americans therefore are typical of what sociologists call **middlemen minorities**, groups that occupy middle positions rather than positions at the bottom of the social scale, where many racial and ethnic minorities typically are located, at least in the early years of residence here. Asian Americans involved in small businesses tend to maintain closer ties with other Asian Americans than do people who join larger corporations. These ethnic owners generally hire other ethnics, who are paid low wages in exchange for paternalistic benefits such as on-the-job training or even assistance in creating their own middleman businesses. However, the present high proportion of Asian Americans as middlemen often is the result of exclusion from other work, not of success. Furthermore, serving as shopkeepers, for example, often contributes to their outsider status because they are resented by both the economic movers of a community and the customers they serve (Bonacich 1988; Bonacich and Modell 1981; Kim and Kim 1998).

Another misleading sign of the apparent success of Asian Americans is their high incomes as a group. Like other elements of the image, however, this deserves closer inspection. Asian American family income approaches parity with that of Whites because of their greater achievement than Whites in formal schooling. If we look at specific educational levels, Whites earn more than their Asian counterparts of the same age. Asian Americans' average earnings increased by at least $2,300 for each additional year of schooling, whereas Whites gained almost $3,000. As we see in Table 12.1, Asian Americans as a group have significantly more formal schooling but actually have lower median family income (F. Wu 2002; Zhou and Kamo 1994).

There are striking contrasts among Asian Americans. Nevertheless, for every Asian American family with an annual income of $75,000 or more, another earns less than $10,000 a year. In New York City's Chinatown neighborhood, about one-quarter of all

middlemen minorities
Groups such as Japanese Americans that typically occupy middle positions in the social and occupational stratification system.

Asian Americans are subject to stereotypes, one of which, "straight-A student," reflects the model minority image.

Source: © 2001 Oliver Chin. Reprinted by permission of Oliver Chin.

families live below the poverty level. In San Diego, dropout rates were close to 60 percent among Southeast Asians in 1997. Even successful Asian Americans continue to face obstacles because of their racial heritage. According to a study of three major public hospitals in Los Angeles, Asian Americans account for 34 percent of all physicians and nurses but fill only 11 percent of management positions at these hospitals (Dunn 1994; Reeves and Bennett 2003; Sengupta 1997).

At first, one might be puzzled to see criticism of a positive generalization such as "model minority." Why should the stereotype of adjusting without problems be a disservice to Asian Americans? The answer is that this incorrect view helps to exclude Asian Americans from social programs and conceals unemployment and other social ills. For example, Asian American participation has been questioned in **set-aside** programs that stipulate government contracts must be awarded to a minimum proportion of minority-owned business. More and more local governments are eliminating Asian Americans from the definition of minority in their set-aside programs, essentially buying into the model minority myth (Committee of 100 2001; S. Cho 2004).

The Door Half Open

Despite the widespread belief that they constitute a model minority, Asian Americans are victims of both prejudice and violence. Reports released annually by the National Asian Pacific American Legal Consortium (2002) chronicle incidents of suspected and proven anti–Asian American incidents that occur. After the terrorist attacks of September 11, 2001, anti-Asian violence increased dramatically for several months in the United States. The first fatality was an Indian American who was shot and killed by a gunman in Mesa, Arizona, shouting, "I stand for America all the way."

This anti–Asian American feeling is built on a long cultural tradition. The term *yellow peril* dates back to the view of Asian immigration, particularly from China, as unwelcome. **Yellow peril** came to refer to the generalized prejudice toward Asian people and their customs. The immigrants were characterized as heathen, morally inferior, drug addicted, savage, or lustful. Although the term was first used around the turn of the 20th century, this anti-Asian sentiment is very much alive today. Many contemporary Asian Americans find this intolerance very unsettling given their conscientious efforts to extend their education, seek employment, and conform to the norms of society (Hurh 1994).

What explains the increase in violence against Asian Americans? Prejudice against Asian Americans is fueled by how they are represented in the media. The Asian American Journalists Association (2000) annually conducts a "media watch" to identify how mainstream news media use ethnic slurs and stereotypes, demonstrate insensitivity, and otherwise exhibit bias in reporting. We can identify several ways in which this occurs—some subtle, some more overt:

■ *Inappropriate use of clichés.* News reports use the term "Asian invasion" even when referring to a small number of Asian Americans. For example, a 1994 *Sports Illustrated* article about Asians trying out for major league baseball teams was billed "Orient Express" and "Asian Invasion," yet the story noted only two Asians as examples.

■ *Mistaken identity.* Not only are Asians identified by the wrong nationality, but American citizens of Asian descent are presented as if they were foreigners.

■ *Overgeneralization.* Inappropriate assumptions are made and too widely applied. For example, a newspaper article discussing the growth of Chinatown was headlined "There Goes the Neighborhood," implying that any increase in the number of Chinese Americans was undesirable.

set-asides
Programs stipulating that a minimum proportion of government contracts must be awarded to minority-owned businesses.

yellow peril
A term denoting a generalized prejudice toward Asian people and their customs.

Generally, Asian Americans only reach the top rungs of the corporate ladder when it is their own business. Jerry Yang, born in Taiwan and raised in San Jose, California, co-founded Jerry and David's guide to the World Wide Web in 1993. Today we know it as Yahoo.

- *Ethnic slurs.* Although the print media generally take great pains to avoid racially derogatory terms, radio talk shows offer frequent examples of racism.

- *Inflammatory reporting.* Unbalanced coverage of such events as World War II or Asian investment in the United States can needlessly contribute to ill feelings.

- *Japan bashing.* News accounts may unfairly blame Asian nations for economic problems in the United States. For example, as Japan-based automakers gained a foothold in the United States, much of the coverage failed to note that U.S. carmakers had not maintained their own competitive advantage.

- *Media invisibility.* News reports may ignore Asian Americans and rarely seek their views on issues related to Asia.

- *Model minority.* This positive portrayal can also have a negative effect.

In its own way, each of these biases contributes to the unbalanced view we have developed of the large, diverse Asian American population.

The resentment against Asian Americans is not limited to overt incidents of violence. Like other subordinate groups, Asian Americans are subject to institutional discrimination. For example, some Asian American groups have large families and find themselves subject to zoning laws stipulating the number of people per room, which make it difficult to live together. Kinfolk are unable to take in family members legally. Whereas we may regard these family members as distant relatives, many Asian cultures view cousins, uncles, and aunts as relatives to whom they have a great deal of familial responsibility.

The marginal status of Asian Pacific Islanders leaves them vulnerable to both selective and collective oppression. In 1999, news stories implicated Wen Ho Lee, a

racial profiling
Any arbitrary police-initiated action based on race, ethnicity, or natural origin rather than a person's behavior.

nuclear physicist at Los Alamos National Laboratory in New Mexico, as a spy for China. Subsequent investigation, during which Lee was imprisoned under very harsh conditions, concluded that the naturalized citizen scientist had indeed downloaded secret files to an unsecured computer, but there was no evidence that the information ever went further.

In the aftermath of the Wen Ho Lee incident, a new form of racial profiling emerged. We introduced **racial profiling** in Chapter 2 as any police-initiated action that relies on race, ethnicity, or national origin rather than a person's behavior. Despite Lee's being found not guilty, Asian Americans were viewed as security risks. A survey found that 32 percent of the people in the United States felt that Chinese Americans are more loyal to China than to the United States. In fact, the same survey showed that 46 percent were concerned about Chinese Americans passing secrets to China. Subsequent studies found that Asian Americans were avoiding top-secret science labs for employment because they became subject to racial profiling at higher security levels (Committee of 100 2001; Department of Energy 2000; Glanz 2000; F. Wu 2002).

For young Asian Americans, life in the United States often is a struggle for one's identity when their heritage is so devalued by those in positions of influence. Sometimes identity means finding a role in White America; other times, it involves finding a place among Asian Americans collectively and then locating oneself within one's own racial or ethnic community.

Political Activity

Against this backdrop of prejudice, discrimination, and searching for one's identity, it would not be surprising to see Asian Americans seeking to recognize themselves. Historically, Asian Americans have followed the pattern of other immigrant groups: They bring organizations from the homeland and later develop groups to respond to the special needs identified in the United States. Recently, during the expressions of anti-immigrant sentiment that began in the late 1990s and that were given a boost by anti-alien feelings after 9/11, Asian Americans staged demonstrations in several cities, seeking to persuade people to become citizens and register to vote.

These efforts, similar to the recent steps taken by Hispanic groups discussed in previous chapters, have also met with mixed success. Asians and Pacific Islanders' political clout is still developing; many still are not citizens. At the time of the 2002 election, 37.6 percent were not citizens and were therefore ineligible to vote, compared with 38 percent of Hispanics and 2 percent of non-Hispanic Whites (Day and Holder 2004).

For newly arrived Asians, grassroots organization and political parties are a new concept. With the exception of Asian Indians, the immigrants come from nations where political participation was unheard of or looked upon with skepticism and sometimes fear. Using the sizable Chinese American community as an example, we can see why Asian Americans have been slow to achieve political mobilization. At least six factors have been identified that explain why Chinese Americans—and, to a large extent, Asian Americans in general—have not been more active in politics:

1. To become a candidate means to take risks, invite criticism, be assertive, and be willing to extol one's virtues. These traits are alien to Chinese culture.
2. Older people remember when discrimination was blatant, and they tell others to be quiet and not attract attention.
3. As noted earlier, many recent immigrants have no experience with democracy and arrive with a general distrust of government.

Compared to the other groups discussed in this book, the national political agenda has paid almost no attention to issues particular to Asian Americans.

4. Like many new immigrant groups, Chinese Americans have concentrated on getting ahead economically and educating their children, rather than thinking in terms of the larger community.

5. The careers that the brightest students pursue tend to be in business and science rather than law or public administration, and therefore do not provide preparation for politics.

6. Chinatowns notwithstanding, Chinese and other Asian American groups are dispersed and cannot control the election even of local candidates.

On the other hand, Asian Americans are increasingly being regarded by both Democrats and Republicans as a future political force in the United States (Gross 1989; Holmes 1996).

Many political observers expect Asian Americans to favor Democratic candidates, as most Latinos and especially African Americans do. Indeed, in the 2000 elections, the majority of Asian Americans favored Democratic candidates, compared with 43 percent of Whites. However, the Republicans, nationally and locally, continue to try to cut into this Democratic preference among these voters. In local politics, it is much easier to see Asian Americans getting involved in city council and school board elections, where they can more readily see the immediate impact of the democratic process on their lives (L. Romney 2004).

Diversity Among Asian Americans

The political activity of Asian Pacific Islanders occurs within a complex segment of the population: Asian Americans who reflect the diversity of their native lands. Asia is a vast region, holding more than half the world's population. The successive waves of immigrants to the United States from that continent have been composed of a large number of nationalities and cultures. In addition to the seven groups listed in Figure 12.2, the Census Bureau enumerates 47 groups, as shown in Table 12.2. Given this variety among Asian Pacific Islanders, we can apply to Asian Americans several generalizations made earlier about Native Americans. Both groups are a collection of diverse peoples with distinct linguistic, social, and geographic backgrounds.

Asian Americans, like Native Americans, are not evenly distributed across the United States. To lump these people together ignores the sharp differences between them. Any examination of Asian Americans quickly reveals their diversity, which will be apparent as we focus on individual Asian American groups, beginning with Filipinos.

 CD-ROM *Activity 8.1*

TABLE 12.2
Asian Pacific Islander Groups in the United States

Asian	Pacific Islander
Asian Indian	Polynesian
Bangladeshi	Native Hawaiian
Bhutanese	Samoan
Burmese	Tongan
Cambodian	Tahitian
Chinese	Tokelauan
Filipino	Micronesian
Hmong	Guamanian or Chamorro
Indo Chinese	Mariana Islander
Indonesian	Saipanese
Iwo Jiman	Palauan
Japanese	Carolinian
Korean	Kosraean
Laotian	Pohnpeian
Malaysian	Chuukese
Maldivian	Yapese
Nepalese	Marshallese
Okinawan	I-Kiribati
Pakistani	Melanesian
Singaporean	Fijian
Sri Lankan	Papua New Guinean
Taiwanese	Solomon Islander
Thai	Ni-Varnualu
Vietnamese	

Note: Groups as enumerated separately in the Census 2000.

Source: Barnes and Bennett 2002; Grieco 2001.

Filipino Americans

Little has been written about the Filipinos (or Philipinos), although they are the second-largest Asian American group in the United States, with 1.8 million people now living here. Social science literature considers them Asians for geographic reasons, but physically and culturally, they also reflect centuries of Spanish colonial rule and the more recent colonial and occupation governments of the United States.

Immigration Patterns

Immigration from the Philippines is documented during the 18th and 19th centuries; it was relatively small but significant enough to create a "Manila Village" along the Louisiana coast in the 1890s. Increasing numbers of Filipino immigrants came as American nationals when, in 1899, the United States gained possession of the Philippine Islands at the conclusion of the Spanish-American War. In 1934, the islands gained commonwealth status. The Philippines gained their independence in 1948 and with it lost their unrestricted immigration rights. Despite the close ties that remained, immigration was sharply restricted to only 50 to 100 people annually until the 1965 Immigration Act lifted these quotas. Before the restrictions were removed, pineapple growers in Hawaii lobbied successfully to import Filipino workers to the islands.

Besides serving as colonial subjects of the United States, Filipinos played another role in this country. The U.S. military accepted Filipinos in selected positions. In particular, the Navy put Filipino citizens to work in kitchens. Filipino veterans of World War II believed that their U.S. citizenship would be expedited. This proved untrue; the problem was only partially resolved by a 1994 federal court ruling. However, many of these veterans felt they were welcomed not as former Navy employees but as unwanted immigrants (Espiritu 1996; Posadas 1999).

Filipino immigration can be divided into four distinct periods:

1. The first generation, immigrating in the 1920s, was mostly male and employed in agricultural labor.
2. A second group, also arriving in the early 20th century, immigrated into Hawaii to serve as contract workers on Hawaii's sugar plantations.
3. The post–World War II arrivals included many war veterans and wives of U.S. soldiers.
4. The newest immigrants, who include many professionals (physicians, nurses, and others), arrived under the 1965 Immigration Act (Min 1995; Posadas 1999).

As in other Asian groups, the people are diverse. Besides these stages of immigration, the Filipinos can also be defined by various states of immigration (different languages, regions of origin, and religions), distinctions that sharply separate people in their homeland as well. In the Philippines and among Filipino immigrants to the United States, eight distinct languages with 200 dialects are spoken. Yet assimilation is under way; a 1995 survey showed that 47 percent of younger Filipino Americans speak only English and do not speak Tagalog, the primary language of the Philippine people (Kang 1996; Pido 1986).

The Present Picture

The Filipino population increased dramatically when restrictions on immigration were eased in 1965. More than two-thirds of the new arrivals qualified for entry as professional and technical workers, but like Koreans, they have often worked at jobs ranked below those they left in the Philippines. Surprisingly, U.S.-born Filipinos often have less formal schooling and lower job status than the newer arrivals. They come from poorer families that are unable to afford higher education, and they have been

Filipino American World War II veterans protest in 1997 for full veteran's benefits for Filipinos who served in World War II.

relegated to unskilled work, including migrant farm work. Their poor economic background means that they have little start-up capital for businesses. Therefore, unlike other Asian American groups, Filipinos have not developed small business bases such as retail or service outlets that capitalize on their ethnic culture.

Yet there is a significant segment of the immigration from the Philippines that constitutes a more professional educated class in the area of health professionals. This is apparent when we consider areas in the United States that reflect Filipino settlement in the last 40 years. For example, in metropolitan Chicago, Filipino Americans have household incomes 30 percent higher then the general population, and higher than that of Asian Indians. When the United States ceased giving preference to physicians from abroad, doctors in the Philippines began to enter the United States retrained as nurses, which dramatically illustrates the incredible income differences between the United States and the Philippines (Espiritu and Wolf 2001; Kim 2005; Lau 2005; Zarembo 2004).

urban settlement

Despite their numbers, no significant single national Filipino social organization has formed, for several reasons. First, Filipinos' strong loyalty to family (*sa pamilya*) and church, particularly Roman Catholicism, works against time-consuming efforts to create organizations that include a broad spectrum of the Filipino community. Second, their diversity makes forming ties here problematic. Divisions along regional, religious, and linguistic lines present in the Philippines persist in the United States. Third, although Filipinos have organized many groups, they tend to be clublike or fraternal. They do not seek to represent the general Filipino population and therefore remain largely invisible to Anglos. Fourth, although Filipinos initially stayed close to events in their homeland, they show every sign of seeking involvement in broader non-Filipino organizations and avoiding group exclusiveness. The two terms of Filipino American Benjamin Cayetano as governor of Hawaii from 1994 to 2002 are an example of such involvement in mainstream political organizations (Bonus 2000; Espiritu 1996; Kang 1996; Posadas 1999).

Asian Indians

Among the four largest Asian American groups are the immigrants from India and their descendants. Sometimes the immigrants from Pakistan, Bangladesh, and Sri Lanka are also included in this group.

Immigration

Indochinese

Like several other Asian immigrant groups, Asian Indians (or East Indians) are recent immigrants. Only 17,000 total came from 1820 to 1965, with the majority of those arriving before 1917. These pioneers were subjected to some of the same anti-Asian measures passed to restrict Chinese immigration. In the 10 years after the Immigration and Naturalization Act, which eliminated national quotas, more than 110,000 arrived (Takaki 1989).

Immigration law, while dropping nationality preferences, gave priority to the skilled, so the Asian Indians arriving in the 1960s through the 1980s tended to be urban, educated, and English-speaking. Three times the proportion of Asian Indians aged 25 and over had a college degree, compared with the general population. These families experienced a smooth transition from life in India to life in the United States. They usually settled here in urban areas or located near universities or medical centers. Initially, they flocked to the Northeast, but by 1990, California had edged out New York as the state with the largest concentration of Asian Indians. The growth of Silicon Valley information technology furthered the increase of Asian Indian professionals in northern California (Boxall 2001; Mogelonsky 1995).

Interestingly,

More recent immigrants, sponsored by earlier immigrant relatives, are displaying less facility with English, and the training they have tends to be less easily adapted to the U.S. workplace. They are more likely to work in service industries, usually with members of their extended families. They are often in positions that many Americans reject because of the long hours, the seven-day workweek, and vulnerability to crime. Consequently, Asian Indians are as likely to be cab drivers or managers of motels or convenience stores as they are to be physicians or college teachers. Asian Indians see the service industries as transitional jobs to acclimatize them to the United States and to give them the money they need to become more economically self-reliant (Kalita 2003; Levitt 2004; Varadarajan 1999).

The Present Picture

It is difficult to generalize about Asian Indians because, like all other Asian Americans, they reflect a diverse population. With more than 1 billion people in 2000, India is soon to be the most populous nation in the world. Diversity governs every area. The Indian government recognizes 18 official languages, each with its own cultural heritage. Some can be written in more than one type of script. Hindus are the majority in India and among the immigrants to the United States, but significant religious minorities include Sikhs, Muslims, Jains, and Zoroastrians.

Religion among Asian Indians presents an interesting picture. Among initial immigrants, religious orthodoxy often is stronger than it is in India. Immigrants try to practice the Hindu and Muslim faiths true to their practices in India rather than joining the Caribbean versions of these major faiths already established in the United States by other immigrant groups. While other Indian traditions are maintained, older immigrants see challenges not only from U.S. culture but also from pop culture from India, which is imported through motion pictures and magazines. It is a very dynamic situation as the Asian Indian population moves into the 21st century (Lessinger 1995; Rangaswamy 2005).

Maintaining traditions within the family household is a major challenge for Indian immigrants to the United States. These ties remain strong, and many Indians see themselves more connected to their relatives 10,000 miles away than Americans are to their kinfolk less than a hundred miles away. Parents are concerned about the erosion of traditional family authority among the desi. **Desi** (pronounced "DAY-see") is a colloquial name for people who trace their ancestry to South Asia, especially India.

desi
colloquial name for people who trace their ancestry to South Asia, especially India and Pakistan.

Reflecting the growth of the Indian American population, the landscape is changing. A Hindu priest makes his way toward the entrance to the largest Hindu temple in the United States, which is located outside Chicago.

Indian children, dressed like their peers, go to fast-food restaurants and eat hamburgers while out on their own, yet both Hindus and Muslims are vegetarian by practice. Sons do not feel the responsibility to the family that tradition dictates. Daughters, whose occupation and marriage could, in India, be closely controlled by the family, assert their right to choose work and select a husband or, in an even more dramatic break from tradition, remain single (Asian American Journalists Association 2000; Kalita 2003; Rudrappa 2004).

Arranged marriage is a custom at variance with U.S. customs. Marriages arranged by one's parents and other relatives are the subject of endless discussion among second-generation Indian immigrants. One study showed that at least one-third of Asian Indian young people in California still seemed to accept the custom, but the balance rejected it in varying degrees. Sometimes feeling pressure, a young person may allow his parents to introduce him to eligible mates, but the event may be simply tolerated rather than regarded as a step toward marriage. Many people may find it

Voices Listen to Our Voices Listen to

RACIAL HATRED

Madhu S. Chawla

We don't speak well. They don't like us because of our culture. We get things because we're educated. Some of them are not educated and they would say, "How come you're educated and we aren't?" They're jealous. But we're really not that educated. My dad went up to tenth grade and my mother went through college. I don't really like it in school when they say, "Hindu, you ugly Hindu. You're gross. I'm not your friend because you're Hindu." So I really don't talk to anybody in my class, and I tell my teacher I want to sit in the back row, so she makes me sit in the back of the class. In the front they say, "Don't touch me. You're disgusting. You eat roaches." They're serious when they say things like that. They are not kidding around. My school only goes up to the fifth grade. I'm in the fourth grade. There are only about ten to fifteen blacks in the whole building. The rest are Puerto Rican, Filipino and American. There are only four Indians. When I try to go down this block, some of the older black boys put their feet up so that I will trip and fall. It makes my head bleed. Once this girl smacked me really hard, and I smacked her back. They were chasing me, so I had to run

to my aunt's house because it was closer than the school.

I like black people but the only thing is, they don't like us because the Indian people like to dress their own way. Old ladies wear saris. They put this red stuff on their head. They put a dot on their forehead, and that's what they don't like.

My uncle was doing an interview for an Indian program on a local station, and this man said on TV, "I don't like Indian people because they own all the stores, but I don't even have one. I wanted to buy this store but an Indian came along and bought it, and the Indians have the stores I want to buy. I cannot own a store, so I don't like Indian people. They are coming to America and taking our stuff and keeping us out of it. I don't even like talking on this dirty Hindu microphone." I don't like it when people say such things. Why do they have to say them?

What is Asian? I guess I consider myself both Indian and American because if I say I consider myself American, my parents will ask me why I don't like India. ■

Source: Madhu S. Chawla, "Racial Hatred," pp. 116–117 in Joann Faung Lee (ed.), *Asian Americans.* New York: The New Press, Copyright 1992.

difficult to understand how a young man or woman growing up in the United States, attending high school dances and joining a sorority or fraternity in college, could accept an arranged or even a semiarranged marriage. However, Asian Indian young people see the involvement of their parents as a possible improvement over potential rejection or failure and the sexual pressure that is integral to the contemporary dating scene. However, it would be incorrect to assume that arranged marriages, like other family customs, are not changing significantly because of the practices of the host society (Leonard 1997; Lessinger 1995).

In "Listen to Our Voices," 11-year-old Madhu Chawla speaks of her own experiences as a victim of racial hatred. Her experiences, though less dramatic than violent hate crimes, are typical of the intolerance people feel from both the dominant group and other subordinate groups. We can see that she is ambivalent about her marginal identity: she was born in the United States of parents who emigrated from India and practices a religious faith, Hinduism, different from the norm in the United States. So what impact does prejudice from Whites, Puerto Ricans, Filipinos, and African Americans have on her? Although it obviously makes the young woman unhappy, we can also see that it causes her to reassert her pride in being Indian.

Southeast Asian Americans

Indochinese

The people of Southeast Asia—Vietnamese, Cambodians, and Laotians—were part of the former French Indochinese Union. *Southeast Asian* is an umbrella term used for convenience; the peoples of these areas are ethnically and linguistically diverse. Ethnic Laotians constitute only half of the Laotian people, for example; a significant number of Mon-Khmer, Yao, and Hmong form minorities. Numbering more than 2 million in 2000, Vietnamese Americans are the largest group, with 1,222,528 members, or 11.2 percent of the total Asian American population (Barnes and Bennett 2002).

The Refugees

The problem of U.S. involvement in Indochina did not end when all U.S. personnel were withdrawn from South Vietnam in 1975. The final tragedy was the reluctant welcome given to the refugees from Vietnam, Cambodia, and Laos by Americans and people of other nations. One week after the evacuation of Vietnam in April 1975, a Gallup poll reported that 54 percent of Americans were against giving sanctuary to the Asian refugees, with 36 percent in favor and 11 percent undecided. The primary objection to Vietnamese immigration was that it would further increase unemployment (Schaefer and Schaefer 1975).

Many Americans offered to house refugees in their homes, but others declared that the United States had too many Asians already and was in danger of losing its "national character." This attitude toward the Indochinese has been characteristic of the feeling that Harvard sociologist David Riesman called the **gook syndrome**. *Gook* is a derogatory term for an Asian, and the syndrome refers to the tendency to stereotype these people in the worst possible light. Riesman believed that the American news media created an unflattering image of the South Vietnamese and their government, leading the American people to believe they were not worth saving (Luce 1975).

The initial 135,000 Vietnamese refugees who fled in 1975 were joined by more than a million running from the later fighting and religious persecution that plagued Indochina. The United States accepted about half of the refugees, some of them the so-called boat people, primarily Vietnamese of ethnic Chinese background, who took to the ocean in overcrowded vessels, hoping that some ship would pick them up and offer sanctuary. Hundreds of thousands were placed in other nations or remain in overcrowded refugee camps administered by the United Nations.

gook syndrome
David Riesman's phrase describing Americans' tendency to stereotype Asians and to regard them as all alike and undesirable.

The Present Picture

Like other immigrants, the refugees from Vietnam, Laos, and Cambodia face a difficult adjustment. Few expect to return to their homeland for visits, and fewer expect to return there permanently. Therefore, many look to the United States as their permanent home and the home of their children. However, the adult immigrants still accept jobs well below their occupational positions in Southeast Asia; geographic mobility has been accompanied by downward social mobility. For example, only a small fraction of refugees employed as managers in Vietnam have been employed in similar positions in the United States.

Language is also a factor in adjustment by the refugees; a person trained as a manager cannot hold that position in the United States until he or she is fairly fluent in English. The available data indicate that refugees from Vietnam have increased their earnings rapidly, often by working long hours. Partly because Southeast Asians comprise significantly different subgroups, assimilation and acceptance are not likely to occur at the same rate for all.

Although most refugee children spoke no English upon their arrival here, they have done extremely well in school. Studies indicate that immigrant parents place great emphasis on education and are pleased by the prospect of their children going to college—something very rare in their homelands. The children do very well with this encouragement, which is not unlike that offered by Mexican immigrants to their children, as we discussed in Chapter 10. It remains to be seen whether this motivation will decline as the next young generation looks more to their American peers as role models.

The picture for young Southeast Asians in the United States is not completely pleasant. Crime is present in almost all ethnic groups, but some fear that in this case it has two very ugly aspects. Some of this crime may represent reprisals for the war: anti-Communists and communist sympathizers who continue their conflicts here. At the same time, gangs are emerging as young people seek the support of close-knit groups even if they engage in illegal and violent activities. Of course, this pattern is very similar to that followed by all groups in the United States. Indeed, defiance of authority can be regarded as a sign of assimilation. Another unpleasant but well-documented aspect of the present picture is the series of violent episodes directed at Southeast Asians by Whites and others expressing resentment over their employment or even their mere presence (Alvord 2000; Zhou and Bankston 1998).

In contrast to its inaction concerning earlier immigrant groups, the federal government involved itself conspicuously in locating homes for the refugees from Vietnam, Cambodia, and Laos. Pressured by many communities afraid of being overwhelmed by immigrants, government agencies attempted to disperse the refugees throughout the nation. Such efforts failed, mostly because the refugees, like European immigrants before them, sought out their compatriots. As a result, Southeast Asian communities and neighborhoods have become visible, especially in California and Texas. In such areas, where immigrants from Asia have reestablished some cultural practices from their homeland, a more pluralistic solution to their adjustment seems a possible alternative to complete assimilation. Also, Southeast Asians living outside metropolitan areas may make frequent trips to major urban areas, where they can stock up on food, books, and even videotapes in their native language (Aguillar-San Juan 1998; Mui 2001).

In 1995, the United States initiated normal diplomatic relations with Vietnam, which is leading to more movement between the nations. Gradually, Vietnamese Americans are returning to visit but generally not to take up permanent residence. **Viet Kieu**, Vietnamese living abroad, are making the return—some 270,000 in 1996 compared with only 80,000 four years earlier. Generational issues are also merging as time passes. In Vietnamese communities from California to Virginia, splits emerge over a powerful symbol—under what flag to unite a nationality. Merchants, home residents, and college Vietnamese student organizations take a stand by whether they

Viet Kieu
Vietnamese living abroad such as in the United States.

Vietnamese Americans are sometimes divided over their loyalty to their "home country." Some Vietnamese in the United States make a point of displaying the "heritage flag" on the left that was last used by South Vietnam. They regard those who display the flag on the right, the flag of Vietnam and formerly North Vietnam, as embracing the past injustices committed under communism.

decide to display the yellow with red bars flag of the now-defunct South Vietnam, sometimes called the "heritage flag," or the red with yellow star flag of the current (and communist) Vietnam (Avila 2004; Lamb 1997).

Case Study: A Hmong Community

Wausau (population 38,000) is a community in rural Wisconsin, best known, perhaps, for the insurance company bearing its name. To sociologists, it is distinctive for its sizable Hmong (pronounced "Mong") population. Wausau finds itself with the greatest percentage of Hmong of any city in Wisconsin. Hmong and a few other Southeast Asians account for 12 percent of the city's population and 25 percent of its public school students (T. Jones 2003).

The Hmong, who now number 186,000, immigrated to the United States from Laos and Vietnam after the April 1975 end of the U.S. involvement in Vietnam. Like other refugees at the time, the first Hmong came to Wausau invited by religious groups. Others followed as they found the surrounding agricultural lands were places they could find work. Coming from a very rural peasant society, the immigrants faced dramatic adjustment upon arrival in the United States (Hein 2000; T. Jones 2003).

Wausau school officials believed that progress in teaching the Hmong English was stymied because the newcomers continued to associate with each other and spoke only their native tongue. In the fall of 1993, the Wausau school board decided to distribute the Hmong and other poor students more evenly by restructuring its elementary schools in a scheme that required two-way busing.

Recalls of elected officials are rare in the United States, but in December 1993, opponents of the busing plan organized a special election that led to the removal of the five board members. This left the Wausau board with a majority who opposed the busing plan that had integrated Asian American youngsters into mostly White elementary schools. By 2002, neighborhood schools ruled in Wausau so that one elementary school had no Hmong children, several were more than 40 percent Hmong, and one was 55 percent Hmong (Seibert 2002; Wausau School District 2001).

How events will unfold in Wausau are unclear. However, positive signs are identifiable in Wausau and other centers of Hmong life in the United States. Immigrants and their children are moving into nonagriculture occupations. Enrollment in citizenship classes is growing. The Wausau Area Hmong Mutual Association, funded by a federal grant and the local United Way, offers housing assistance. Although many struggle to

Despite objections by the Hmong and sympathetic White citizens, a Wisconsin county with a large presence of Hmong made English the official language—a move with little practical significance but one that spoke loudly in terms of symbolism.

make a go of it economically, large numbers are able to move off public assistance. Language barriers and lack of formal schooling still are barriers encountered by older Hmong residents, but the younger generation is emerging to face some of the same identity and assimilation questions experienced by other Asian American groups (Peckham 2002).

The challenges facing the Hmong extend well beyond Wausau, Wisconsin. In other cities with concentrations of Hmong immigrants, disputes break out over contemporary U.S. policies. Hmong were recruited by the U.S. military intelligence in the Vietnam War to gather information about communists. To this day, occasional violence occurs in the Hmong community over whether the United States might lift trade barriers with the communist-run government of Laos. Finally in 2004, the United States, recognizing the special role that the Hmong people played in the Vietnam conflict era, agreed to accept thousands of Hmong people that had been in overseas refugee camps for 30 years (Aglionby 2004; Torriero 2004).

Korean Americans

The population of Korean Americans, with more than 1 million in 2000 (see Table 1.1), is now the fifth largest Asian American group, yet Korean Americans often are overlooked in studies in favor of groups such as Chinese Americans and Japanese Americans, who have a longer historical tradition.

Historical Background

Today's Korean American community is the result of three waves of immigration. The initial wave of a little more than 7,000 immigrants came to the United States between 1903 and 1910, when laborers migrated to Hawaii. Under Japanese colonial rule (1910–1945), Korean migration was halted except for a few hundred "picture brides" allowed to join their prospective husbands.

The second wave took place during and after the Korean War, accounting for about 14,000 immigrants from 1951 through 1964. Most of these immigrants were war orphans and wives of American servicemen. Little research has been done on these first two periods of immigration.

The third wave was initiated by the passage of the 1965 Immigration Act, which made it much easier for Koreans to immigrate. In the four years before passage of the act, Koreans accounted for only 7 of every 1,000 immigrants. In the first four years after the act's passage, 38 of every 1,000 immigrants to the United States were Korean. This third wave, which continues today, reflects the admission priorities set up in the 1965 immigration law. These immigrants have been well educated and have arrived in the United States with professional skills (Min 1995).

However, many of the most recent immigrants must at least initially settle for positions of lower responsibility than those they held in Korea and must pass through a period of "exigency" or disenchantment, as described in Chapter 2. The problems documented reflect the pain of adjustment: stress, loneliness, alcoholism, family strife, and mental disorders. Korean American immigrants who accompanied their parents to the United States when young now occupy a middle, marginal position between the cultures of Korea and the United States. They have also been called the **ilchomose**, or "1.5 generation": Today, they are middle-aged, remain bilingual and bicultural, and tend to form the professional class in the Korean American community (Hurh 1998; Kim 2005).

The Present Picture

Today's young Korean Americans face many of the cultural conflicts common to any initial generation born in a new country. The parents may speak the native tongue, but the signs on the road to opportunity are in the English language, and the road itself runs through U.S. culture. It is very difficult to maintain a sense of Korean culture in the United States; the host society is not particularly helpful. Although the United States fought a war there and U.S. troops remain in South Korea, Korean culture is very foreign to contemporary Americans. In the few studies of attitudes toward Koreans, White Americans respond with vague, negative attitudes or simply lump Korean Americans with other Asian groups.

Studies by social scientists indicate that Korean Americans face many problems typical for immigrants, such as difficulties with language. In Los Angeles, home to the largest concentration, more than 100 churches have only Korean-language services, and local television stations feature several hours of Korean programs. The Korean immigrants' high level of education should help them cope with the challenge. Although Korean Americans stress conventional Western schooling as a means to success, Korean schools have also been established in major cities. Typically operated on Saturday afternoons, they offer classes in Korean history, customs, music, and language to help students maintain their cultural identity (Abelmann and Lie 1995; Hurh and Kim 1982, 1984; D. Lee 1992).

Korean American women commonly participate in the labor force, as do many other Asian American women. About 60 percent of U.S.-born Korean American women and half the women born abroad work in the labor force. These figures may not seem striking compared with the data for White women, but the cultural differences make the figures more significant. Korean women come here from a family system with established, well-defined marital roles: The woman is expected to serve as homemaker and mother only. Although these roles are carried over to the United States, because of their husbands' struggles to establish themselves, women are pressed to help support their families financially as well.

One characteristic associated with Korean and other Asian Americans is respect for one's elder relatives. In "Research Focus," we consider whether this filial piety is persisting in the United States.

Many Korean American men begin small service or retail businesses and gradually involve their wives in the business. Wages do not matter as the household mobilizes to make a profitable enterprise out of a marginal business. Under economic pressure, Korean American women must move away from traditional cultural roles. However, the move is only partial; studies show that despite the high rate of participation in the labor force by Korean immigrant wives, first-generation immigrant couples continue in sharply divided gender roles in other aspects of daily living.

ilchomose
The 1.5 generation of Korean Americans—those who immigrated into the United States as children.

Focus Research Focus Research Focus Research Focus

AGING IN AMERICA

The traditional values of many Asian cultures include the strong feeling that adult children are responsible for the care of aging parents. Filial obligation is assumed and not viewed as going beyond the norm. Failing to take care of one's parents is seen as a very negative trait. There are differences in the source of this obligation historically. For the Chinese, Confucianism has a core of filial piety, and this obligation is unconditional. Theoretically, the adult child is obligated to provide his or her elderly parent with emotional and financial support at any cost. For example, it would be inappropriate for an adult child to move away for a great job opportunity if the move had any negative impact on his or her aging parents.

Masako Ishii-Kuntz focused on 628 Korean, Chinese, and Japanese adult children and their parents residing in California. The scholar notes that filial piety is present as Asians immigrate to the United States. The question is whether this dedication persists in a culture that is prepared to leave the responsibility to nonfamily caregivers and expects people to plan financially for their old age.

Ishii-Kuntz found some striking differences between the three Asian American groups, which, in part, reflected recency of immigration. On average, Korean American adult children provide more services for their elderly parents than their Chinese and Japanese counterparts. When controlling for generation, there were no differences; that is, second-generation Korean Americans were no more or less responsible for their parents than Chinese and Japanese Americans.

With the passing of generations, filial responsibility declines and begins to resemble levels of care typical of non-Asian Americans. This does not mean that it is not somewhat different. For example, the move away from filial responsibility has created a demand for Asian American assisted-living communities and nursing homes, a type of service that would have been unthinkable just 30 years ago. Nonetheless, aging in America for Asians, across generations, becomes more American and less Asian. ■

Source: Ishii-Kuntz 1997; Kershaw 2003; Kong 2002; Thorson 1995.

Korean American businesses are seldom major operations; most are small. They do benefit from a special form of development capital (or cash) used to subsidize businesses, called a **kye** (pronounced "kay"). Korean Americans pool their money through the kye, an association that grants members money on a rotating basis to allow them to gain access to additional capital. Kyes depend on trust and are not protected by laws or insurance, as bank loans are. Kyes work as follows. Say, for example, that 12 people agree to contribute $500 a year. Then, once a year, one of these individuals receives $6,000. Few records are kept because the entire system is built on trust and friendship. Rotating credit associations are not unique to Korean Americans; they have been used in the United States by West Indians and Ethiopians, for example. Not all Korean business entrepreneurs use the kye, but it does represent a significant source of capital. A 1984 Chicago survey revealed that 34 percent of Korean merchants relied on a kye.

In the early 1990s, nationwide attention was given to the friction between Korean Americans and other subordinate groups, primarily African Americans but also Hispanics. In New York City, Los Angeles, and Chicago, Korean American merchants confronted African Americans who were allegedly robbing them. The African American

kye
Rotating credit system used by Korean Americans to subsidize the start of businesses.

neighborhood sometimes responded with hostility to what they perceived as the disrespect and arrogance of the Korean American entrepreneurs toward their Black customers. Such friction is not new; earlier generations of Jewish, Italian, and Arab merchants encountered similar hostility from what to outsiders seems an unlikely source, another oppressed subordinate group. The contemporary conflict was dramatized in Spike Lee's 1989 movie *Do the Right Thing*, in which African Americans and Korean Americans clashed. The situation arose because Korean Americans are the latest immigrant group prepared to cater to the needs of the inner city that has been abandoned by those who have moved up the economic ladder (Hurh 1998; Kang and Richardson 2002).

The tension that can arise between subordinate groups gained national attention during the 1992 riots in south central Los Angeles. In that city's poor areas, the only shops in which to buy groceries, liquor, or gasoline are owned by Korean immigrants. They have largely replaced the White business owners who left the ghetto area after the 1965 Watts riot. African Americans were well aware of the dominant role Korean Americans played in their local retail market. Some Blacks' resentment of the Koreans had previously been fueled by the 1991 fatal shooting of a 15-year-old Black girl by a Korean grocer in a dispute over a payment for orange juice. The resentment grew when the grocer, convicted of manslaughter, had her prison sentence waived by a judge in favor of a five-year probation period.

The 1992 riots focused in part on retailers in south central Los Angeles and therefore on Korean Americans. During the unrest, 2,000 Korean businesses valued at $400 million were destroyed. Desire to succeed had led Korean Americans to the inner city, where they did not face competition from Whites. But it also meant that they had to deal on a daily basis with the frustration of another minority group. As a direct outgrowth of the violence and tension, numerous cross-ethnic groups have been organized in Los Angeles and other cities, such as Chicago and New York City, to improve relations between Korean Americans and other subordinate groups (Kang and Richardson 2002).

Among Korean Americans, the church is the most visible organization holding the group together. Half the immigrants were affiliated with Christian churches before immigrating. One study of Koreans in Chicago and Los Angeles found that 70 percent were affiliated with Korean ethnic churches, mostly Presbyterian, with small numbers of Catholics and Methodists. Korean ethnic churches are the fastest-growing segment of the Presbyterian and Methodist faiths. The church performs an important function, apart from its religious one, in giving Korean Americans a sense of attachment and a practical way to meet other Korean Americans. The churches are much more than simply sites for religious services; they assume multiple secular roles for the Korean community. As the second generation seeks a church with which to affiliate as adults, they may find the ethnic church and its Korean-language services less attractive, but for now, the fellowship in which Korean Americans participate is both spiritual and ethnic (Kwon et al. 2001).

Hawaii and Its People

The entire state of Hawaii (or Hawai'i) appears to be the complete embodiment of cultural diversity. Nevertheless, despite a dramatic blending of different races living together, prejudice, discrimination, and pressure to assimilate are very much present in Hawaii. As we will see, life on the island is much closer to that in the rest of the country than to the ideal of a pluralistic society. Hawaii's population is unquestionably diverse, as shown in Figure 12.3. To grasp contemporary social relationships, we must first understand the historical circumstances that brought races together on the islands: the various Asian peoples and the **Haoles** (pronounced "hah-oh-lehs"), the term often used to refer to Whites in Hawaii.

Haoles
Hawaiian term for Caucasians.

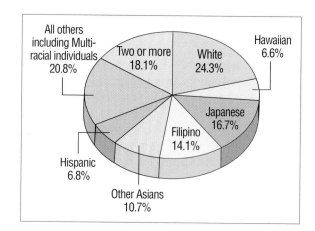

FIGURE 12.3   Hawaii: Racial Composition, 2000

Source: Lind 1969:47; State of Hawaii 2001: Tables 27, 29, 31.

Historical Background

Geographically remote, Hawaii was initially populated by Polynesian people who had their first contact with Europeans in 1778, when English explorer Captain James Cook arrived. The Hawaiians (who killed Cook) tolerated the subsequent arrival of plantation operators and missionaries. Fortunately, the Hawaiian people were united under a monarchy and received respect from the European immigrants, a respect that developed into a spirit of goodwill. Slavery was never introduced, even during the colonial period, as it was in so many areas of the Western Hemisphere. Nevertheless, the effect of the White arrival on the Hawaiians themselves was disastrous. Civil warfare and disease had reduced the number of full-blooded natives to fewer than 30,000 by 1900, and the number is probably well under 10,000 now. Meanwhile, large sugarcane plantations imported laborers from China, Portugal, Japan, and, in the early 1900s, the Philippines, Korea, and Puerto Rico.

In 1893, a revolution encouraged by foreign commercial interests overthrew the monarchy. During the revolution, the United States landed troops, and five years later, Hawaii was annexed as a territory to the United States. The 1900 Organic Act guaranteed racial equality, but foreign rule dealt a devastating psychological blow to the proud Hawaiian people. American rule had mixed effects on relations between the races. Citizenship laws granted civil rights to all those born on the islands, not just the wealthy Haoles. However, the anti-Asian laws still applied, excluding the Chinese and Japanese from political participation.

The 20th century witnessed Hawaii's transition from a plantation frontier to the 50th state and an integral part of the national economy. During that transition, Hawaii became a strategic military outpost, although that role has had only a limited effect on race relations. Even the attack on Pearl Harbor had little influence on Japanese Americans in Hawaii.

The Present Picture

Hawaii has achieved some fame for its good race relations. Tourists, who are predominantly White, have come from the mainland and have seen and generally accepted the racial harmony. Admittedly, Waikiki Beach, where large numbers of tourists congregate, is atypical of the islands, but even there tourists cannot ignore the differences in intergroup relations.

One clear indication of the multicultural nature of the islands is the degree of exogamy: marrying outside one's own group. The out-group marriage rate varies annually but seems to be stabilizing; about 45 percent of all marriages performed in the state involving residents are exogamous. The rate varies by group, from a low of 41 percent among Haoles to 62 percent among Chinese Americans (Hawaii Department of Health 2001:Table 80).

A closer look shows that equality between the people is not absolute, let alone between the races as groups. The pineapple and sugarcane plantation legacy persists. As recently as 1972, an estimate placed 97 percent of Hawaiian workers in the employ of 40 landholders. One estate alone owned nearly one-tenth of the state's territory. Native Hawaiians tend to be least well off, working land they do not own. Japanese Americans and Haoles dominate the economy. The **AJAs** (Americans of Japanese ancestry, as they are called in Hawaii) are especially important in education, where they account for nearly 58 percent of teachers, and in politics, where they dominate. The political activity of the AJAs certainly contrasts to that of mainland Japanese Americans. The majority of the state legislators are AJAs. Chinese Americans have been successful in business in Hawaii, but almost all top positions are filled by Haoles. Recent immigrants from Asia and, more significantly, even long-term residents of Filipino and Hawaiian descent, showed little evidence of sharing in Hawaii's overall picture of affluence (Kaser 1977; W. Turner 1972; Wright and Gardner 1983).

Prejudice and discrimination are not alien to Hawaii. Attitudinal surveys show definite racial preferences and sensitivity to color differences. Housing surveys taken before the passage of civil rights legislation showed that many people were committed to nondiscrimination, but racial preferences were still present. Certain groups sometimes dominate residential neighborhoods, but there are no racial ghettos. The various racial groups are not distributed uniformly among the islands, but they are clustered rather than sharply segregated.

Discrimination by exclusive social clubs exists but is diminishing. Groups such as the Rotary and Lions' clubs opened their doors to Asians in Hawaii before they did on the mainland. Undoubtedly, Hawaii has gradually absorbed the mainland's racial consciousness, but a contrast between the islands and the rest of the nation remains. Evidence of racial harmony is much more abundant. Hawaii has never known forced school segregation, Jim Crow laws, slavery, or laws prohibiting racial intermarriage.

The multiracial character of the islands will not change quickly, but the identity of the native Hawaiians has already been overwhelmed. Though rich in cultural heritage, they tend to be very poor and often view the U.S. occupation as the beginning of their cultural and economic downfall. The organization Ka Lahui Hawaii, or Hawaiian Nation, is seeking to have Hawaiian native people receive federal recognition similar to that accorded mainland tribes; to date, that recognition has not occurred.

The **sovereignty movement** is the effort by the indigenous people of Hawaii to secure a measure of self-government and restoration of their lands. Its roots and significance to the people are very similar to the sovereignty efforts by tribal people on the continental United States. The growing sovereignty movement has also sought restoration of the native Hawaiian land that has been lost to Anglos over the last century, or compensation for it. Sometimes, the native Hawaiians successfully form alliances with environmental groups that want to halt further commercial development on the islands. In 1996, a native Hawaiian vote was held seeking a response to the question, "Shall the Hawaiian people elect delegates to propose a native Hawaiian government?" The results indicated that 73 percent voting were in favor of such a government structure. Since then, the state Office of Hawaiian Affairs has sought to create a registry of Hawaiians that is only about halfway to having all the estimated 200,000 people of significant Hawaiian descent on the islands to come forward (Cart 2001; Staton 2004; Ward 1996).

In an absolute sense, Hawaii is not a racial paradise. Certain occupations and even social classes tend to be dominated by a single racial group. Hawaii is not immune to intolerance, and it is expected that the people will not totally resist prejudice as the

AJAs
Americans of Japanese ancestry in Hawaii.

sovereignty movement
Effort by the indigenous people of Hawaii to secure a measure of self-government and restoration of their lands.

A 2001 march of 1,500 people through downtown Honolulu protesting that insufficient progress has been made in the Hawaiian Sovereignty movement. Note they are flying the Hawaiian State flag upside down.

island's isolation is reduced. On the other hand, newcomers to the islands do set aside some of their old stereotypes and prejudices. The future of race relations in Hawaii is uncertain, but relative to the mainland and much of the world, Hawaii's race relations are characterized more by harmony than by discord.

Conclusion

Despite the diversity among groups of Asian Americans or Asian Pacific Islanders, they have spent generations being treated as a monolithic group. Out of similar experiences have come panethnic identities in which people share a self-image, as do African Americans or Whites of European descent. As we noted in Chapter 1, **panethnicity** is the development of solidarity between ethnic subgroups. Are Asian Americans finding a panethnic identity? It is true that, in the United States, extremely different Asian nationalities have been lumped together in past discrimination and present stereotyping. Asian Americans now see the need to unify their diverse subgroups. After centuries of animosity between ethnic groups in Asia, any feelings of community among Asian Americans must develop anew here; they bring none with them.

Asian Americans are a rapidly growing group, with well over 10 million now living in the United States. Despite striking differences between them, they are often viewed as if they arrived all at once and from one culture. Also, they are often characterized as a successful or model minority. However, individual cases of success and some impressive group data do not imply that the diverse group of peoples who make up the Asian American community are uniformly successful. Indeed, despite high levels of formal schooling, Asian Americans earn far less than Whites with comparable education and continue to be victims of discriminatory employment practices (F. Wu 2002).

The diversity within the Asian American community belies the similarity suggested by the panethnic label *Asian American*. Chinese and Japanese Americans share a history of several generations in the United States. Filipinos are veterans of a half-century of direct U.S. colonization and a cooperative role with the military. In contrast, Vietnamese, Koreans, and Japanese are associated in a negative way with three wars. Korean Americans come from a nation that still has a major U.S. military presence and a persisting "cold war" mentality. Korean Americans and Chinese Americans have taken on middleman roles, whereas Filipinos, Asian Indians, and Japanese Americans tend to avoid the ethnic enclave pattern.

panethnicity
The development of solidarity between ethnic subgroups, as reflected in the terms *Hispanic* or *Asian American*.

Who are the Asian Americans? This chapter has begun to answer that question by focusing on four of the larger groups: Filipino Americans, Asian Indians, Southeast Asian Americans, and Korean Americans. Hawaii is a useful model because its harmonious social relationships cross racial lines. Although it is not an interracial paradise, Hawaii does illustrate that, given proper historical and economic conditions, continuing conflict is not inevitable. Chinese and Japanese Americans, the subjects of Chapter 13, have experienced problems in American society despite striving to achieve economic and social equality with the dominant culture.

Key Terms

AJAs   329
desi   319
gook syndrome   321
Haoles   327
ilchomose   325

kye   326
middlemen minorities   311
model or ideal minority   309
panethnicity   330
racial profiling   314

set-asides   312
sovereignty movement   329
Viet Kieu   322
yellow peril   312

Review Questions

1. In what respects has the mass media image of Asian Americans been both undifferentiated and negative?

2. How is the model minority image a disservice to both Asian Americans and other subordinate racial and ethnic groups?

3. How has the tendency of many Korean Americans to help each other been an asset but also been viewed with suspicion by those outside their community?

4. What critical events or legislative acts increased each Asian American group's immigration into the United States?

5. To what degree do race relations in Hawaii offer both promise and a chilling dose of reality to the future of race and ethnicity on the mainland?

Critical Thinking

1. How is the model minority image reinforced by images in the media?

2. Coming of age is difficult for anyone, given the ambiguities of adolescence in the United States. How is it doubly difficult for the children of immigrants? How do you think the immigrants themselves, such as those from Asia, view this process?

3. *American Indians, Hispanics,* and *Asian Americans* are all convenient terms to refer to diverse groups of people. Do you see these broad umbrella terms as being more appropriate for one group than for the others?

Internet Connections—Research Navigator™

Follow the instructions found on page 31 of this text to access the features of Research Navigator™. Once at the Web site, enter your Login Name and Password. Then, to use the ContentSelect database, enter keywords such as "race and health," "Black elected officals," and "environmental justice," and the search engine will supply relevant and recent scholarly and popular press publications. Use the *New York Times* Search-by-Subject Archive to find recent news articles related to sociology, and the Link Library feature to locate relevant Web links organized by the key terms associated with this chapter.

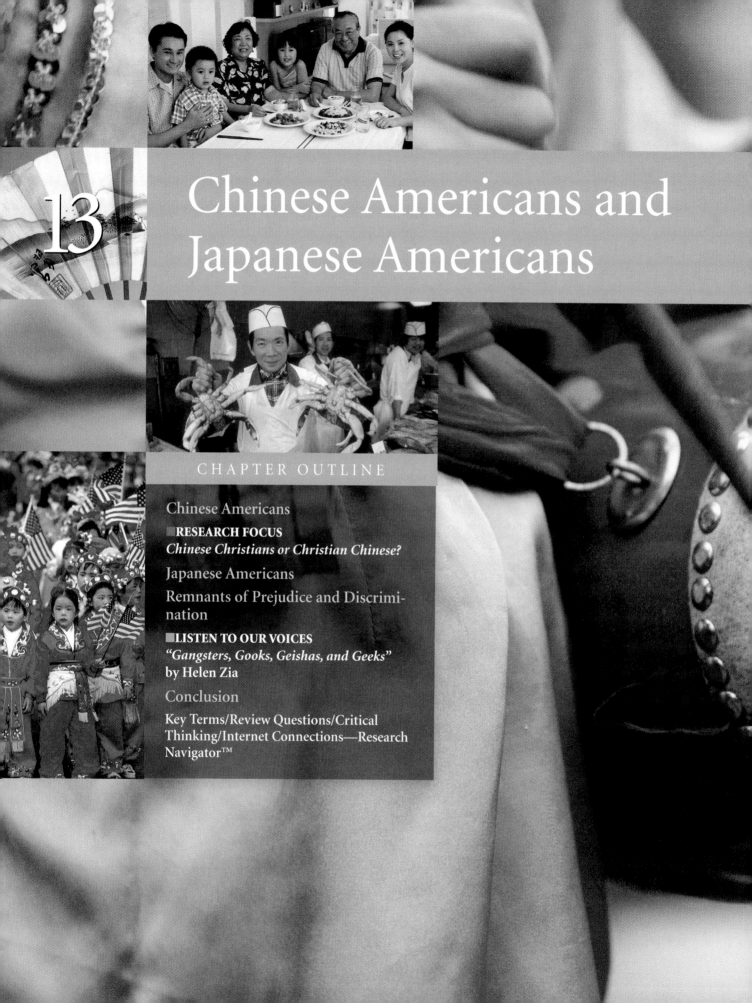

13 Chinese Americans and Japanese Americans

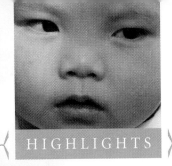

P RESENT-DAY CHINESE AMERICANS ARE DESCENDANTS OF both pre-Exclusion Act immigrants and those who immigrated after World War II. Although Chinese Americans are associated with Chinatown and its glitter of tourism, this facade hides the poverty of the newly arrived Chinese and the discontent of the U.S.-born Chinese Americans. Japanese Americans encountered discrimination and ill treatment in the early 20th century. The involuntary wartime internment of 113,000 Japanese Americans was the result of sentencing without charge or trial. During wartime, merely to be of Japanese ancestry was reason enough to be suspected of treason. A little more than a generation later, Japanese Americans did very well, with high educational and occupational attainment. Today, Chinese Americans and Japanese Americans experience both prejudice and discrimination despite a measure of economic success.

The Los Angeles Japanese American festival was in full swing in mid-July 2004 when, during the opening ceremonies a South Pasadena 24-year-old grabbed a heavy mallet and took a swing at a drum as she had practiced for months. Nicole Miyako Cherry, the daughter of a Japanese American mother and a White American father, had had little interest in her Japanese roots except for wearing a kimono for Halloween as a youngster. Yet in the last couple of years, she has begun to take interest in all things Japanese, including a visit to Japan. Looking to her future as a social work therapist, she says she would like her own children to learn Japanese, go to Japanese festivals, play in Japanese sports leagues, and have a Japanese first name, (M. Navarro 2004).

Nicole's experience is certainly a case of the principle of third-generation interest—that ethnic awareness may increase among the grandchildren. But Nicole is of mixed ancestral background, so she is obviously making a choice to maintain her Japanese American identity as an important part of her future. But for many other Asian Americans, particularly recent immigrants, they are just trying to survive and to accumulate savings for their family here and kinfolk in the old country.

Many people in the United States find it difficult to distinguish between Japanese Americans and Chinese Americans physically, culturally, and historically. As we will see in this chapter, the two groups differ in some ways but also share similar patterns in their experiences in the United States.

Chinese Americans

China, the most populous country in the world, has been a source of immigrants for centuries. Many nations have a sizable Chinese population whose history there may be traced back more than five generations. The United States is such a nation. Even before the great migration from Europe began in the 1880s, more than 100,000 Chinese already lived in the United States. Today, Chinese Americans number more than 2.3 million (Table 13.1).

From the beginning of Chinese immigration, Americans have held conflicting views about it. In one sense, Chinese immigration was welcome because it brought to these shores needed hard-working laborers. At the same time, it was unwelcome because the Chinese brought with them an alien culture that the European settlers were unwilling to tolerate. There was also a perception of economic competition by people in the western United States, and the Chinese newcomers proved to be very convenient and powerless scapegoats. As detailed in Chapter 4, the anti-Chinese mood led to the passage of the Exclusion Act in 1882, which was not repealed until 1943. Even then, the group that lobbied for repeal, the Citizens' Committee to Repeal Chinese Exclusion, encountered the old racist arguments against Chinese immigration.

Very gradually, the Chinese were permitted to enter the United States after 1943. Initially, the annual limit was 105, then several thousand wives of servicemen were admitted, and later, college students were allowed to remain after finishing their education. Not until after the 1965 Immigration Act did Chinese immigrants arrive again in large numbers, almost doubling the Chinese American community. Immigration

TABLE 13.1
Chinese American and Japanese American Population, 1860–2000

Year	Chinese Americans	Japanese Americans
1860	34,933	–
1880	105,465	148
1900	89,863	24,326
1930	74,954	138,834
1950	117,629	141,768
1960	237,292	464,332
1970	435,062	591,290
1980	806,027	700,747
1990	1,640,000	847,562
2000	2,314,533	796,700

Note: Data beginning with 1960 include Alaska and Hawaii. Data are for responses of one race. In 2000, 2,734,841 reported Chinese American and another race, and 1,148,932 reported Japanese American and another race.

Source: Barnes and Bennett 2002; S. Lee 1998:15; Ng 1991.

continues to exert a major influence on the growth of the Chinese American population. It has approached 100,000 annually. The influx was so great in the 1990s that the number of new arrivals in the 1990s exceeded the total number of Chinese Americans present in 1980.

The underside of immigration, illegal immigration, is also functioning in the Chinese American community. The lure of perceived better jobs and a better life lead overseas Chinese to seek alternative routes to immigration if legal procedures are unavailable to them. The impact of illegal entry in some areas of the country can be significant. For example, every month in 2002, 340 illegal Chinese immigrants were apprehended at Chicago's O'Hare Airport and taken to a rural jail (Starks 2002).

It is also important to appreciate that even *Chinese Americans* is a collective term. There is diversity within this group represented by nationality (China versus Taiwan for example), language, and region of origin. It is not unusual for a church serving a Chinese American community to have five separate services, each in a different dialect. These divisions can be quite sharply expressed. For example, near the traditional Chinatown of New York City, a small neighborhood has emerged serving Chinese from the Fujian Province of China. In this area, job postings include annotation in Chinese that translates as "no north," meaning people from the provinces north of Fujian are not welcomed. Throughout the United States, Chinese Americans often divide along pro-China and pro-Taiwan allegiances (K. Guest 2003; Lau 2005b; Louie 2004; Sachs 2001).

Occupational Profile of Chinese Americans

The background of the contemporary Chinese American labor force lies in Chinatown. For generations, Chinese Americans were largely barred from working elsewhere. The Chinese Exclusion Act was only one example of discriminatory legislation. Many laws were passed that made it difficult or more expensive for Chinese Americans to enter certain occupations. Whites did not object to Chinese in domestic service occupations or in the laundry trade because most White men were uninterested in such menial, low-paying work. When given the chance to enter better jobs, as they were in wartime, Chinese Americans jumped at the opportunities. Without those

With the growth of the Chinese American population in the United States, businesses developed to cater to their needs. Bo Bo Poultry Market, located in upstate New York, produces Buddhist-style chicken— referring to birds sold with their heads and feet still attached and killed and prepared to precise specifications.
Source: John Sotomayor/ *The New York Times*

opportunities, however, many Chinese Americans sought the relative safety of China-town. The tourist industry and the restaurants dependent on it grew out of the need to employ the growing numbers of idle workers in Chinatown.

Chinatowns Today

Chinatowns represent a paradox. The casual observer or tourist sees them as thriving areas of business and amusement, bright in color and lights, exotic in sounds and sights. Behind this facade, however, they have large poor populations and face the problems associated with all slums. Most Chinatowns are in older, deteriorating sections of cities. There are exceptions, such as Monterey Park outside Los Angeles, where Chinese Americans dominate the economy. However, in the older enclaves, the problems of Chinatowns include the entire range of the social ills that affect low-income areas but with even greater difficulties because the glitter sometimes conceals the problems from outsiders and even social planners. A unique characteristic of Chinatowns, one that distinguishes them from other ethnic enclaves, is the variety of social organizations they encompass.

Organizational Life   The Chinese in this country have a rich history of organizational membership, much of it carried over from China. Chief among such associations are the clans, or *tsu;* the benevolent associations, or *hui kuan;* and the secret societies, or *tongs.*

The clans, or **tsu**, that operate in Chinatown have their origins in the Chinese practice in which families with common ancestors unite. At first, immigrant Chinese continued to affiliate themselves with those sharing a family name, even if a blood relationship was absent. Social scientists agree that the influence of clans is declining as young Chinese become increasingly acculturated. The clans in the past provided mutual assistance, a function increasingly taken on by government agencies. The strength of the clans, although diminished today, still points to the extended family's important role for Chinese Americans. Social scientists have found parent-child relationships stronger and more harmonious than those among non-Chinese Americans. Just as the clans have become less significant, however, so has the family structure changed. The differences between family life in Chinese

tsu
Clans established along family lines that form a basis for social organization by Chinese Americans.

and non-Chinese homes are narrowing with each new generation (Li 1976; Lyman 1986; Sung 1967).

The benevolent associations, or **hui kuan** (or *huiguan*), help their members adjust to a new life. Rather than being organized along kinship ties like the clans, *hui kuan* membership is based on the person's district of origin in China. Besides extending help with adjustment, the *hui kuan* lend money to and settle disputes between their members. They have thereby exercised wide control over their members. The various *hui kuan* are traditionally, in turn, part of an unofficial government in each city called the Chinese Six Companies, later changed to the Chinese Consolidated Benevolent Association (CCBA). The president of the CCBA is sometimes called the mayor of a Chinatown. The CCBA often protects newly arrived immigrants from the effects of racism. The organization works actively to promote political involvement among Chinese Americans and to support the democracy movement within the People's Republic of China. Some members of the Chinese community have resented, and still resent, the CCBA's authoritarian ways and its attempt to speak as the sole voice of Chinatown.

The Chinese have also organized in **tongs**, or secret societies. The secret societies' membership is determined not by family or locale but by interest. Some have been political, attempting to resolve the dispute over which China (the People's Republic of China or the Taiwan) is the legitimate government, and others have protested the exploitation of Chinese workers. Other *tongs* provide illegal goods and services, such as drugs, gambling, and prostitution. Because they are secret, it is difficult to determine accurately the power of *tongs* today. Most observers concur that their influence has dwindled over the last 50 years and that their functions, even the illegal ones, have been taken over by elements less closely tied to Chinatown.

Some conclusions can be reached about these various social organizations. First, all have followed patterns created in traditional China. Even the secret societies had antecedents, organizationally and historically, in China. Second, all three types have performed similar functions, providing mutual assistance and representing their members' interests to a sometimes hostile dominant group. Third, because all these groups have had similar purposes and have operated in the same locale, conflict between them has been inevitable. Such conflicts were very violent in the 19th century, but in the 20th century they tended to be political. Fourth, the old associations have declined in significance, notably since the mid-1970s, as new arrivals from Asian

hui kuan
Chinese American benevolent associations organized on the basis of the district of the immigrant's origin in China.

tongs
Chinese American secret associations.

Chinatown, despite its tourist image, offers limited job opportunities for young people.

metropolises bring little respect for the old rural ways to which such organizations were important. Fifth, when communicating with the dominant society, all these groups have downplayed the problems that afflict Chinatowns. Only recently has the magnitude of social problems become known (Lyman 1974, 1986; Soo 1999; Tong 2000; Wei 1993; Zhao 2002).

Social Problems   It is a myth that Chinese Americans and Chinatowns have no problems. This false impression grows out of our tendency to stereotype groups as being all one way or the other, as well as the Chinese people's tendency to keep their problems within their community. The false image is also reinforced by the desire to maintain tourism. The tourist industry is a double-edged sword. It does provide needed jobs, even if some pay substandard wages. But it also forces Chinatown to keep its problems quiet and not seek outside assistance, lest tourists hear of social problems and stop coming. Slums do not attract tourists. This parallel between Chinese Americans and Native Americans finds both groups depending on the tourist industry even at the cost of hiding problems (Light et al. 1994).

In the late 1960s, White society became aware that all was not right in the Chinatowns. This awareness grew not because living conditions suddenly deteriorated in Chinese American settlements but because the various community organizations could no longer maintain the facade that hid Chinatowns' social ills. Despite Chinese Americans' remarkable achievements as a group, the inhabitants suffered by most socioeconomic measures. Poor health, high suicide rates, run-down housing, rising crime rates, poor working conditions, inadequate care for the elderly, and the weak union representation of laborers were a few of the documented problems.

These problems have grown more critical as Chinese immigration has increased. For example, the population density of San Francisco's Chinatown in the late 1980s was 10 times that of the city as a whole. The problems faced by elderly Chinese are also exacerbated by the immigration wave because the proportion of older Chinese immigrants is more than twice that of older people among immigrants in general. The economic gap between Chinatown residents and outsiders is growing. As Chinese Americans become more affluent, they move out of Chinatowns. Census data showed the household income for Chinese Americans in New York City's Chinatown was 26 percent lower than those who lived outside the ethnic enclave (Logan et al. 2002; Wong 1995).

Life in Chinatown may seem lively to an outsider, but beyond the neon, the picture can be quite different. Chinatown in New York City remained a prime site of sweatshops in the 1990s. Dozens of women labor over sewing machines, often above restaurants. These small businesses, often in the garment industry, consist of workers sewing 12 hours a day, six or seven days a week, and earning about $200 weekly—well below minimum wage. The workers, most of whom are women, can be victimized because they are either illegal immigrants who may owe labor to the smugglers who brought them into the United States or legal residents unable to find better employment (Finder 1995; Kwong 1994).

The attacks on the World Trade Center in 2001 made the marginal economy of New York's Chinatown even shakier. Though not located by the World Trade Center, it was close enough to feel the drop in customary tourism and a significant decline in shipments to the garment industry. Initially, emergency relief groups ruled out assistance to Chinatown, but within a couple of months, agencies opened up offices in Chinatown. Within two months, 42,000 people had received relief as 60 percent of businesses cut staff. Like many other minority neighborhoods, New York City's Chinatown may be economically viable, but it always is susceptible to severe economic setbacks that most other areas could withstand much more easily (J. Lee 2001; S. Swanson 2004).

Increasingly, Chinese neither live nor work in Chinatowns; most have escaped them or never experienced their social ills. Chinatown remains important for many of those who now live outside its borders, although it is less important than in the past. For many Chinese, movement out of Chinatown is a sign of success. Upon moving out, however, they soon encounter discriminatory real estate practices and White parents' fears about their children playing with Chinese American youths.

The movement of Chinese Americans out of Chinatowns parallels the movement of White ethnics out of similar enclaves. It signals the upward mobility of Chinese Americans, coupled with their growing acceptance by the rest of the population. This mobility and acceptance are especially evident in their presence in managerial and professional occupations.

However, with their problems and constant influx of new arrivals, we should not forget that, first and foremost, Chinatowns are communities of people. Originally, in the 19th century, they emerged because the Chinese arriving in the United States had no other area in which they were allowed to settle. Today, Chinatowns represent cultural decompression chambers for new arrivals and an important symbolic focus for long-term residents. Even among many younger Chinese Americans, these ethnic enclaves serve as a source of identity.

Family and Religious Life

Family life and religious worship are major forces shaping all immigrant groups' experience in the United States. Generally, with assimilation, cultural behavior becomes less distinctive. Family life and religious practices are no exceptions. For Chinese Americans, the latest immigration wave has helped preserve some of the old ways, but traditional cultural patterns have undergone change even in the People's Republic of China, so the situation is very fluid.

In the People's Republic of China, organized religion barely exists, with state policy sharply discouraging it and prohibiting foreign mission activity. In "Research Focus," we consider religion in the Chinese American community.

The contemporary Chinese American family often is indistinguishable from its White counterpart except that it is victimized by prejudice and discrimination. Older Chinese Americans and new arrivals often are dismayed by the more American behavior patterns of Chinese American youths. Change in family life is one of the most difficult cultural changes to accept. Children's questioning parental

The extended family is an important part of the Chinese American community.

Focus Research Focus Research Focus

CHINESE CHRISTIANS OR CHRISTIAN CHINESE?

Religion plays an important role in most immigrant communities, but the Chinese are an unusual case because they come from a country where organized religion has been strongly discouraged for three generations. Many festivals are celebrated in the Chinese American community, such as Chingming or Tomb-Sweeping Day, but such observances have lost their religious significance and have become largely social occasions.

What about organized religion within the Chinese American community? A 1997 survey of Chinese Americans in southern California found that a large proportion have no ties to organized religion. Asked, "What religion—if any—do you currently consider yourself?" Forty-four percent said none, and 32 percent identified themselves as Christian, and 20 percent as Buddhists. This is at least twice as a high a proportion of no religious affiliation as the general population.

Most Christian Chinese are Protestant: about one in five Chinese Americans, compared with 1 in 20 who are Roman Catholic. What kind of Christianity is pursued by the Chinese Americans? On one level, it typically embraces what one would normally expect to be practices in a church, but on a second level, Chinese Americans often bring into the faith the moral virtues and filial piety (discussed in Chapter 11) that are taught by Buddhism.

Protestant churches attended by Chinese Americans often were initially sponsored by a major denomination such as the Methodists, Presbyterians, or United Church of Christ to serve an ethnic Chinese community. Services often are bilingual, making prolonged sermons a bit laborious to worshippers.

As in nonethnic churches, social events play a prominent role in the church calendar. However, there is little to distinguish these events in a Protestant Chinese church, except that the food served is typically Chinese, with some non-Chinese options for the young people. Distinctive touches do exist, such as celebration of the Chinese (or Lunar) New Year and the use of Chinese calligraphy or the playing of the lantern puzzle at get-togethers.

Although each Chinese American church has its own manner of approaching religious faith, one tends to find that the links to the larger Chinese American community, including non-Christian Chinese, tends to be stronger than the links to congregations of the same faith that are not of Chinese ancestry. This is not to say that religion is not important, but ethnicity ties the congregation together. Consequently, the Chinese American community of Christian worshippers probably is best seen as Christian Chinese, where *Chinese* is the operative identifier rather than *Christian*. ■

Source: J. Dart 1997; Ng 1999, 2003.

authority, which Americans grudgingly accept, is a painful experience for tradition-oriented Chinese.

Where acculturation has taken hold less strongly among Chinese Americans, the legacy of China remains. Parental authority, especially the father's, is more absolute, and the extended family is more important than is typical in White middle-class families. Divorce is rare, and attitudes about sexual behavior tend to be strict because the Chinese generally frown on public expressions of emotion. We noted earlier that Chinese immigrant women in Chinatown survive a harsh existence. A related problem beginning to surface is domestic violence. Although the available data do not indicate that Asian American men are any more abusive than men in other groups, their wives, as a rule, are less willing to talk about their plight and to seek help. The nation's first shelter for Asian women was established in Los Angeles in 1981, but increasingly, the problem is being recognized in more cities (Banerjee 2000; Tong 2000).

Another problem for Chinese Americans is the rise in gang activity since the mid-1970s. Battles between opposing gangs have taken their toll, including the lives of some innocent bystanders. Some trace the gangs to the *tongs* and thus consider them an aspect, admittedly destructive, of the cultural traditions some groups are trying to maintain. However, a more realistic interpretation is that Chinese American youths from the lower classes are not part of the model minority. Upward mobility is not in their future. Alienated, angry, and with prospects of low-wage work in restaurants and laundries, they turn to gangs such as the Ghost Shadows and Flying Dragons and force Chinese American shopkeepers to give them extortion money. Asked why he became involved in crime, one gang member replied, "To keep from being a waiter all my life" (Takaki 1989:451; see also Chin 1996).

Japanese Americans

The 19th century was a period of sweeping social change for Japan: It brought the end of feudalism and the beginning of rapid urbanization and industrialization. Only a few pioneering Japanese came to the United States before 1885 because Japan prohibited emigration. After 1885, the numbers remained small relative to the great immigration from Europe at the time.

With little consideration of the specific situation, the American government began to apply to Japan the same prohibitions it applied to China. The early feelings of yellow peril were directed at the Japanese as well. The Japanese who immigrated into the United States in the 1890s took jobs as laborers at low wages under poor working conditions. Their industriousness in such circumstances made them popular with employers but unpopular with unions and other employees.

Japanese Americans distinguish sharply between themselves according to the number of generations a person's family has been in the United States. Generally, each succeeding generation is more acculturated, and each is successively less likely to know Japanese. The **Issei** (pronounced "EE-say") are the first generation, the immigrants born in Japan. Their children, the **Nisei** ("NEE-say"), are American-born. The third generation, the **Sansei** ("SAHN-say"), must go back to their grandparents to reach their roots in Japan. The **Yonsei** ("YAWN-say") are the fourth generation. Because Japanese immigration is recent, these four terms describe almost the entire contemporary Japanese American population. Some *Nisei* are sent by their parents to Japan for schooling and to have marriages arranged, after which they return to the United States. Japanese Americans expect such people, called **Kibei** ("KEE-boy"), to be less acculturated than other Nisei. These terms sometimes are used loosely, and occasionally *Nisei* is used to describe all Japanese Americans. However, we will use them as they were intended, to differentiate the four generational groups.

The Japanese arrived just as bigotry toward the Chinese had been legislated in the harsh Chinese Exclusion Act of 1882. For a time after the act, powerful business interests on the West Coast welcomed the Issei. They replaced the dwindling number of Chinese laborers in some industries, especially agriculture. In time, however, anti-Japanese feeling grew out of the anti-Chinese movement. The same Whites who disliked the Chinese made the same charges about the new yellow peril. Eventually, a stereotype developed of Japanese Americans as lazy, dishonest, and untrustworthy.

The attack on Japanese Americans concentrated on limiting their ability to earn a living. In 1913, California enacted the Alien Land Act, which 1920 amendments made

Issei
First-generation immigrants from Japan to the United States.

Nisei
Children born of immigrants from Japan.

Sansei
The children of the *Nisei*, that is, the grandchildren of the original immigrants from Japan.

Yonsei
The fourth generation of Japanese Americans in the United States, the children of the *Sansei*.

Kibei
Japanese Americans of the *Nisei* generation sent back to Japan for schooling and to have marriages arranged.

still stricter. The act prohibited anyone who was ineligible for citizenship from owning land and limited leases to three years. The anti-Japanese laws permanently influenced the form that Japanese American business enterprise was to take. In California, the land laws drove the *Issei* into cities. In the cities, however, government and union restrictions prevented large numbers from obtaining the available jobs, leaving self-employment as the only option. Japanese, more than other groups, ran hotels, grocery stores, and other medium-sized businesses. Although this specialty limited their opportunities to advance, it did give urban Japanese Americans a marginal position in the expanding economy of the cities (Bonacich 1972; Light 1973; Lyman 1986).

The Wartime Evacuation

Japan's attack on Pearl Harbor on December 7, 1941, brought the United States into World War II and marked a painful tragedy for the *Issei* and *Nisei*. Almost immediately, public pressure mounted to "do something" about the Japanese Americans living on the West Coast. Many feared that if Japan attacked the mainland, Japanese Americans would fight on behalf of Japan, making a successful invasion a real possibility. Pearl Harbor was followed by successful Japanese invasions of one Pacific island after another. A Japanese submarine actually attacked a California oil tank complex early in 1943.

Rumors mixed with racism rather than facts explain the events that followed. Japanese Americans in Hawaii were alleged to have cooperated in the attack on Pearl Harbor by using signaling devices to assist the pilots from Japan. Front-page attention was given to pronouncements by the Secretary of the Navy that Japanese Americans had the greatest responsibility for Pearl Harbor. Newspapers covered in detail FBI arrests of Japanese Americans allegedly engaging in sabotage to assist the attackers. They were accused of poisoning drinking water, cutting patterns in sugarcane fields to form arrows directing enemy pilots to targets, and blocking traffic along highways to the harbor. None of these charges was substantiated, despite thorough investigations. It made no difference. In the 1940s, the treachery of the Japanese Americans was a foregone conclusion regardless of evidence to the contrary (Kimura 1988; Lind 1946; ten Brock et al. 1954).

Executive Order 9066   On February 13, 1942, President Franklin Roosevelt signed Executive Order 9066. It defined strategic military areas in the United States and authorized the removal from those areas of any people considered threats to national security. The events that followed were tragically simple. All people on the West Coast of at least one-eighth Japanese ancestry were taken to assembly centers for transfer to evacuation camps. These camps are identified in Figure 13.1. This order covered 90 percent of the 126,000 Japanese Americans on the mainland. Of those evacuated, two-thirds were citizens, and three-fourths were under age 25. Ultimately, 120,000 Japanese Americans were in the camps. Of mainland Japanese Americans, 113,000 were evacuated, but to those were added 1,118 evacuated from Hawaii, 219 voluntary residents (Caucasian spouses, typically), and, most poignantly of all, the 5,981 who were born in the camps (Weglyn 1976).

The evacuation order did not arise from any court action. No trials took place. No indictments were issued. Merely having a Japanese great-grandparent was enough to mark a person for involuntary confinement. The evacuation was carried out with little difficulty. For Japanese Americans to have fled or militantly defied the order would only have confirmed the suspicions of their fellow Americans. There was little visible objection initially from the Japanese Americans. The Japanese American Citizens League (JACL), which had been founded by the *Nisei* as a self-help organization in 1924, even decided not to arrange a court test of the evacuation order. The JACL felt that cooperating with the military might lead to sympathetic consideration later when tensions subsided.

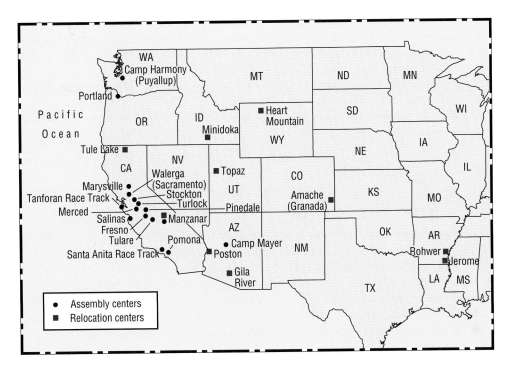

FIGURE 13.1 Evacuation Camps
Japanese Americans were first ordered to report to "assembly centers," from which, after a few weeks or months, they were resettled in "relocation centers."

Source: Map "Evacuation Camps" from Michi Nishura Weglyn, *Years of Infamy: The Untold Story of America's Concentration Camps,* John Hawkins & Associates, Inc., 1976.

Even before reaching the camps, the **evacuees**, as Japanese Americans being forced to resettle came to be called officially, paid a price for their ancestry. They were instructed to carry only personal items. No provision was made for shipping their household goods. The federal government took a few steps to safeguard the belongings they left behind, but the evacuees assumed all risks and agreed to turn over their property for an indeterminate length of time. These Japanese Americans were destroyed economically. Merchants, farmers, and business owners had to sell all their property at any price they could get. Precise figures of the loss in dollars are difficult to obtain, but after the war, the Federal Reserve Bank estimated it to be $400 million. To place this amount in perspective, one estimate stated that, in 1995 dollars, the economic damages sustained, excluding personal income, would be more than $3.7 billion (Bureau of the Census 1996:483; Commission on Wartime Relocation and Internment of Civilians 1982a, 1982b; Hosokawa 1969; Thomas and Nishimoto 1946).

The Camps   Ten camps were established in seven states. Were they actually concentration camps? Obviously, they were not concentration camps constructed for the murderous purposes of those in Nazi Germany, but such a positive comparison is no compliment to the United States. To refer to them by their official designation, relocation centers, ignores these facts: The Japanese Americans did not go there voluntarily, they had been charged with no crime, and they could not leave without official approval.

Japanese Americans were able to work at wage labor in the camps. The maximum wage was set at $19 a month, which meant that camp work could not possibly recoup the losses incurred by evacuation. The evacuees had to depend on the government for food and shelter, a situation they had not experienced in prewar civilian life. More devastating than the economic damage of camp life was the psychological damage. Guilty of no crime, the Japanese Americans moved through a monotonous daily routine with no chance of changing the situation. Forced community life, with such shared activities as eating in mess halls, weakened the strong family ties that Japanese Americans, especially the *Issei,* took so seriously (Kitsuse and Broom 1956).

evacuees

Japanese Americans interned in camps for the duration of World War II.

Amid the economic and psychological devastation, the camps began to take on some resemblance to U.S. cities of a similar size. High schools were established, complete with cheerleaders and yearbooks. Ironically, Fourth of July parades were held, with camp-organized Boy Scout and Girl Scout troops marching past proud parents. But the barbed wire remained, and the Japanese Americans were asked to prove their loyalty.

A loyalty test was administered in 1943 on a form all had to fill out, the "Application for Leave Clearance." Many of the Japanese Americans were undecided how to respond to two questions:

No. 27. Are you willing to serve in the armed forces of the United States on combat duty, wherever ordered?

No. 28. Will you swear to abide by the laws of the United States and to take no action which would in any way interfere with the war effort of the United States? (Daniels 1972:113)

The ambiguity of the questions left many confused about how to respond. For example, if *Issei* said yes to the second question, would they then lose their Japanese citizenship and be left stateless? The *Issei* would be ending allegiance to Japan but were unable, at the time, to gain U.S. citizenship. Similarly, would *Nisei* who responded yes be suggesting that they had been supporters of Japan? For whatever reasons, 6,700 *Issei* and *Nisei,* many because of their unacceptable responses to these questions, were transferred to the high-security camp at Tule Lake for the duration of the war (Bigelow 1992).

Overwhelmingly, Japanese Americans showed loyalty to the government that had created the camps. In general, security in the camps was not a problem. The U.S. Army, which had overseen the removal of the Japanese Americans, recognized the value of the Japanese Americans as translators in the war ahead. About 6,000 *Nisei* were recruited to work as interpreters and translators, and by 1943, a special combat unit of 23,000 *Nisei* volunteers had been created to fight in Europe. The predominantly *Nisei* unit was unmatched, and it concluded the war as the most decorated of all American units.

Japanese American behavior in the concentration camps can be seen only as reaffirming their loyalty. True, some refused to sign an oath, but that was hardly a treasonous act. More typical were the tens of thousands of evacuees who contributed to the U.S. war effort.

A few Japanese Americans resisted the evacuation and internment. Several cases arising out of the evacuation and detention reached the U.S. Supreme Court during the war. Amazingly, the Court upheld lower court decisions on Japanese Americans without even raising the issue of the whole plan's constitutionality. Essentially, the Court upheld the idea of the collective guilt of an entire race. Finally, after hearing *Mitsuye Endo v. United States,* the Supreme Court ruled, on December 18, 1944, that the detainment was unconstitutional and consequently the defendant (and presumably all evacuees) must be granted freedom. Two weeks later, Japanese Americans were allowed to return to their homes for the first time in three years, and the camps were finally closed in 1946 (ten Brock et al. 1954).

The immediate postwar climate was not pro-Japanese American. Whites terrorized returning evacuees in attacks similar to those against Blacks a generation earlier. Labor unions called for work stoppages when Japanese Americans reported for work. Fortunately, the most blatant expression of anti-Japanese feeling disappeared rather quickly. Japan stopped being a threat as the atomic bomb blasts destroyed Nagasaki and Hiroshima. For the many evacuees who lost relatives and friends in the bombings, however, it must have been a high price to pay for marginal acceptance (Maykovich 1972a, 1972b; Petersen 1971).

8

The Evacuation: What Does It Mean?   The social significance of the wartime evacuation has often been treated as a historical exercise, but in the wake of the stigmatizing of Arab and Muslim Americans after 9/11, singling out people of Japanese descent some 60 years ago takes on new meaning. Japanese American playwright Chay Yew reflected recently, "You think you can walk away from history and it takes you on the back" (M. Boehm 2004: E2). We will not know the consequences of the current focus on identifying potential disloyal Americans, but we do have some perspective on stigmatizing Japanese Americans during and after World War II.

The evacuation policy cost the U.S. taxpayers a quarter of a billion dollars in construction, transportation, and military expenses. Japanese Americans, as already noted, effectively lost at least several billion dollars. These are only the tangible costs to the nation. The relocation was not justifiable on any security grounds. No verified act of espionage or sabotage by a Japanese American was recorded. How could it happen?

Racism cannot be ignored as an explanation. Japanese Americans were placed in camps, but German Americans and Italian Americans were largely ignored. Many of those whose decisions brought about the evacuation were of German and Italian ancestry. The fact was that the Japanese were expendable. Placing them in camps posed no hardship for the rest of society, and, in fact, some profited by their misfortune. That Japanese Americans were evacuated because they were seen as expendable is evident from the decision not to evacuate Hawaii's Japanese. In Hawaii, the Japanese were an integral part of the society; removing them would have destroyed the islands economically (Hosokawa 1969; Kimura 1988; Miyamoto 1973).

Some argue that Japanese lack of resistance made internment possible. This seems a weak effort to transfer guilt—to blame the victim. In the 1960s, some *Sansei* and *Yonsei* were concerned about the alleged timidity of their parents and grandparents when faced with evacuation orders. However, many evacuees, if not most, probably did not really believe what was happening. "It just cannot be that bad," they may have thought. At worst, the evacuees can be accused of being naive. But even if they did see clearly how devastating the order would be, what alternatives were open? None (Haak 1970; Kitano 1976; Takezawa 1991).

The Commission on Wartime Relocation and Internment of Civilians in 1981 held hearings on whether additional reparations should be paid to evacuees or their heirs. The final commission recommendation in 1983 was that the government formally apologize and give $20,000 tax-free to each of the approximately 82,000 surviving

Mournful Japanese Americans during World War II, as depicted in this present day mural in Los Angeles.

internees. Congress began hearings in 1986 on the bill authorizing these steps, and President Ronald Reagan signed the Civil Liberties Act of 1988, which authorized the payments. The payments, however, were slow in coming because other federal expenditures had higher priority. Meanwhile, the aging internees were dying at a rate of 200 a month. In 1990, the first checks were finally issued, accompanied by President Bush's letter of apology. Many Japanese Americans were disappointed by and critical of the begrudging nature of the compensation and the length of time it had taken to receive it (Commission on Wartime Relocation and Internment of Civilians 1982a, 1982b; Department of Justice 2000).

Perhaps actor George Takei, of *Star Trek* fame, sums up best the wartime legacy of the evacuation of Japanese Americans. As a child, he had lived with his parents in the Tule Lake, California, camp. In 1996, on the 50th anniversary of the camp's closing and five years before 9/11 would turn the nation's attention elsewhere, he reflected on his arrival at the camp. "America betrayed American ideals at this camp. We must not have national amnesia; we must remember this" (S. Lin 1996:10).

The Economic Picture

The socioeconomic status of Japanese Americans as a group is very different from that of Chinese Americans. Many of the latter are recent immigrants and refugees, who have fewer of the skills that lead to employment in higher-paying positions. In contrast, the Japanese American community is more settled and less affected by new arrivals from the home country, yet it continues to operate in a society in which tensions remain with Japan. We will first consider the Japanese American economic situation, which, on balance, has been very positive.

The camps left a legacy with economic implications; the Japanese American community of the 1950s was very different from that of the 1930s. Japanese Americans were more widely scattered. In 1940, 89 percent lived on the West Coast. By 1950, only 58 percent of the population had returned to the West Coast. Another difference was that a smaller proportion than before was *Issei*. The *Nisei* and even later generations accounted for 63 percent of the Japanese population. By moving beyond the West Coast, the Japanese Americans seemed less of a threat than if they had remained concentrated. Furthermore, by dispersing, Japanese American businesspeople had to develop ties to the larger economy rather than do business mostly with other Japanese Americans. Although ethnic businesses can be valuable initially, those who limit their dealings to those from the same country may limit their economic potential (Oliver and Shapiro 1995:46).

After the war, some Japanese Americans continued to experience hardship. Some remained on the West Coast and farmed as sharecroppers in a role similar to that of the freed slaves after the Civil War. Sharecropping involved working the land of others, who provided shelter, seeds, and equipment and who also shared any profits at the time of harvest. The Japanese Americans used the practice to gradually get back into farming after being stripped of their land during World War II (Parrish 1995).

However, perhaps the most dramatic development has been the upward mobility that Japanese Americans collectively and individually have accomplished. By occupational and academic standards, two indicators of success, Japanese Americans are doing very well. The educational attainment of Japanese Americans as a group, as well as their family earnings, is higher than that of Whites, but caution should be used in interpreting such group data. Obviously, large numbers of Asian Americans, as well as Whites, have little formal schooling and are employed in poor jobs. Furthermore, Japanese Americans are concentrated in areas of the United States such as Hawaii, California, Washington, New York, and Illinois, where both wages and the cost of living are far above the national average. Also, the proportion of Japanese American families with multiple wage earners is higher than that of White families. Nevertheless, the overall picture for Japanese Americans is remarkable, especially for a racial minority that had been discriminated against so openly and so recently (Inoue 1989; Kitano 1980; Nishi 1995; Woodrum 1981).

The Japanese American story does not end with another account of oppression and hardship. Today, Japanese Americans have achieved success by almost any standard. However, we must qualify the progress that *Newsweek* (1971) once billed as their "Success Story: Outwhiting the Whites." First, it is easy to forget that several generations of Japanese Americans achieved what they did by overcoming barriers that U.S. society had created, not because they had been welcomed. However, many, if not most, have become acculturated. Nevertheless, successful Japanese Americans still are not wholeheartedly accepted into the dominant group's inner circle of social clubs and fraternal organizations. Second, Japanese Americans today may represent a stronger indictment of society than economically oppressed African Americans, Native Americans, and Hispanics. There are few excuses apart from racism that Whites can use to explain why they continue to look on Japanese Americans as different, as "them."

Family and Religious Life

The contradictory pulls of tradition and rapid change that are characteristic of Chinese Americans are very strong among Japanese Americans today. Surviving *Issei* see their grandchildren as very nontraditional. Change in family life is one of the most difficult cultural changes for any immigrant to accept in the younger generations.

As cultural traditions fade, the contemporary Japanese American family seems to continue the success story. The divorce rate has been low, although it is probably rising. Similar conclusions apply to crime, delinquency, and reported mental illness. Data on all types of social disorganization show that Japanese Americans have a lower incidence of such behavior than all other minorities; it is also lower than that of Whites. Japanese Americans find it possible to be good Japanese and good Americans simultaneously. Japanese culture demands high in-group unity, politeness, respect for authority, and duty to community, all traits highly acceptable to middle-class Americans. Basically, psychological research has concluded that Japanese Americans share the high-achievement orientation held by many middle-class White Americans. However, one might expect that as Japanese Americans continue to acculturate, the breakdown in traditional Japanese behavior will be accompanied by a rise in social deviance (Nishi 1995).

As is true of the family and other social organizations, religious life in these groups has its antecedents in Asia, but there is no single Japanese faith. In Japan, religious beliefs tend to be much more accommodating than Christian beliefs are: One can be Shinto but also Buddhist at the same time. Consequently, when they came to the United States, immigrants found it easy to accept Christianity, even though doing so ultimately meant rejecting their old faiths. In the United States, a Christian cannot also be a Shintoist or a Buddhist. As a result, with each generation, Japanese Christians depart from traditional ways.

Although traditional temples are maintained in most places where there are large numbers of Japanese Americans, many exist only as museums, and few are places of worship with growing memberships. Religion is still a source of community attachment, but it is in the Protestant Chinese church, not in the temple. At the same time, some Eastern religions, such as Buddhism, are growing in the United States; but, overwhelmingly, the new adherents are Whites who are attracted to what they perceive as a more enriching value system. This has led to friction between more traditional Buddhist centers and those associated with the more Americanized Zen Buddhism (Kosmin and Lachman 1993).

Remnants of Prejudice and Discrimination

The Fu Manchu image may be gone, but its replacement is not much better. In popular television series, Asian Americans, if they are present, usually are either karate experts or technical specialists involved in their work. Chinese Americans are ignored or misrepresented in history books. Even past mistakes are repeated. When the transcontinental railroad was completed in Utah in 1869, Chinese workers were barred from attending the ceremony. Their contribution is now well known, one of the stories of true heroism in the West. However, in 1969, when Secretary of Transportation John Volpe made a speech marking the hundredth anniversary of the event, he neglected to mention the Chinese contribution. He exclaimed, "Who else but Americans could drill tunnels in mountains 30 feet deep in snow? Who else but Americans could chisel through miles of solid granite? Who else but Americans could have laid 10 miles of track in 12 hours?" (Yee 1973:100). The Chinese contribution was once again forgotten.

Today, young Japanese Americans and Chinese Americans are very ambivalent about their cultural heritage. The pull to be American is intense, but so are the reminders that, in the eyes of many others, Asian Americans are "they," not "we." Journalist Helen Zia comments in "Listen to Our Voices" about how immigrant parents grapple with the decision whether to teach their children their language or push them to become American as fast as possible.

Voices Listen to Our Voices Listen to Our

GANGSTERS, GOOKS, GEISHAS, AND GEEKS

Ah so. No tickee, no washee. So sorry, so sollee. Chinkee, Chink. Jap, Nip, zero, kamikaze. Dothead, flat face, flat nose, slant eye, slope. Slit, mamasan, dragon lady. Gook, VC, Flip, Hindoo.

By the time I was ten, I'd heard such words so many times I could feel them coming before they parted lips. I knew they were meant in the unkindest way. Still, we didn't talk about these incidents at home, we just accepted them as part of being in America, something to learn to rise above.

The most common taunting didn't even utilize words but a string of unintelligible gobbledygook that kids—and adults—would

Helen Zia

spew as they pretended to speak Chinese or some other Asian language. It was a mockery of how they imagined my parents talked to me.

Truth was that Mom and Dad rarely spoke to us in Chinese, except to scold or call us to dinner. Worried that we might develop an accent, my father insisted that we speak English at home. This, he explained, would lessen the hardships we might encounter and make us more acceptable as Americans.

I'll never know if my father's language decision was right. On the one hand, I, like most Asian Americans, have been complimented countless times on my spoken English by people who assumed I was a for-

Chinese Americans and Japanese Americans believe that prejudice and discrimination have decreased in the United States, but subtle reminders remain. Third-generation Japanese Americans feel insulted when they are told, "You speak English so well." Adopting new tactics, Asian Americans are now trying to fight racist and exclusionary practices (Lem 1976).

Marriage statistics also illustrate the effects of assimilation. At one time, 29 states prohibited or severely regulated marriages between Asians and non-Asians. Today, intermarriage, though not typical, is legal and certainly more common, and more than one-fourth of Chinese Americans under 24 marry someone who is not Chinese. The degree of intermarriage is even higher among Japanese Americans: 1990 census data showed that two-thirds of all children born to a Japanese American had a parent of a different race.

The increased intermarriage indicates that Whites are increasingly accepting of Chinese Americans. It also suggests that Chinese and Japanese ties to their native cultures are weakening. As happened with the ways of life of European immigrants, the traditional norms are being cast aside for those of the host society. In one sense, these changes make Chinese Americans and Japanese Americans more acceptable and less alien to Whites. But this points to all the changes in Asian Americans rather than any recognition of diversity in the United States. As illustrated in Figure 13.2, intermarriage patterns reflect the fusion of different racial groups; but, compared with examples of assimilation and pluralism, they are a limited social process at present (S. Fong 1965, 1973; Kibria 2002; Onishi 1995).

s Listen to Our Voices Listen to Our Voices Listen

eigner. "My, you speak such good English," they'd cluck. "No kidding, I ought to," I would think to myself, then wonder: should I thank them for assuming that English isn't my native language? Or should I correct them on the proper usage of "well" and "good"?

More often than feeling grateful for my American accent, I've wished that I could jump into a heated exchange of rapid-fire Chinese, volume high and spit flying. But with a vocabulary limited to "*Ni hao?*" (How are you?) and "*Ting bu dong*" (I hear but don't understand), meaningful exchanges are woefully impossible. I find myself smiling and nodding like a dashboard ornament. I'm envious of the many people I know who grew up speaking an Asian language yet converse in English beautifully.

Armed with standard English and my flat New Jersey "a," I still couldn't escape the name-calling. I became all too familiar with other names and faces that supposedly matched mine—Fu Manchu, Suzie Wong, Hop Sing, Madame Butterfly, Charlie Chan, Ming the Merciless—the "Asians" produced for mass consumption. Their faces filled me with shame whenever I saw them on TV or in the movies. They defined my face to the rest of the world: a sinister Fu, Suzie the whore, subservient Hop Sing, pathetic Butterfly, cunning Chan, and warlike Ming. Inscrutable Orientals all, real Americans none. ■

Source: Excerpt from pp. 109–110 in *Asian-American Dreams* by Helen Zia. Copyright © 2000 by Helen Zia. Reprinted by permission of Farrar, Straus and Giroux, LLC.

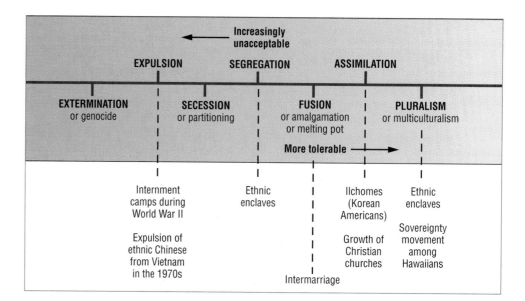

FIGURE 13.2 Intergroup Relations Continuum

The Japanese American community struggles to maintain its cultural identity while also paying homage to those who were interned during World War II. Paradoxically, as many see parallels between the collective guilt forced on people of Japanese ancestry during the 1940s and profiling of Arab and Muslim Americans, a few are seeking to justify the internment. Books and even a public middle school named after an internee in Washington state have been criticized; critics feel that when internment was taught it was too bias and that arguments for internment being the correct action should be included. For many Japanese Americans, the more things change, the more they stay the same (Malkin 2004; Tizor 2004).

It would be incorrect to interpret assimilation as an absence of protest. Because a sizable segment of the college youth of the 1960s and early 1970s held militant attitudes and because the *Sansei* are more heterogeneous than their *Nisei* and *Issei* relatives, it was to be expected that some Japanese Americans, especially the *Sansei*, would

News media treat Asian Americans, such as Olympic figure skater Michelle Kwan, a Chinese American, as if they are foreigners. The news network MSNBC, an affiliate of the NBC network, covered the 1996 Olympics when Tara Lipinski defeated Kwan and then proclaimed "American Beats out Kwan."

be politically active. For example, Japanese and other Asian Americans have emerged as activists for environmental concerns ranging from contaminated fish to toxic working conditions, and the targets of Japanese Americans' anger have included the apparent rise in hate crimes in the United States against Asian Americans in the 1990s. They also lobbied for passage of the Civil Rights Restoration Act, extending reparations to the evacuees. They have expressed further activism through Hiroshima Day ceremonies, marking the anniversary of the detonation in World War II of the first atomic bomb over a major Japanese city. Also, each February, a group of Japanese American youths makes a pilgrimage to the site of the Tule Lake evacuation camp in a "lest we forget" observance. Such protests are modest, but they are a militant departure from the almost passive role played by the *Nisei* (Shaffer 1994; Takezawa 1991; Wei 1993).

Is pluralism developing? Japanese Americans show little evidence of wanting to maintain a distinctive way of life. The Japanese values that have endured are attitudes, beliefs, and goals shared by and rewarded by the White middle class in America. All Asian Americans, not only Japanese Americans, are caught in the middle. Any Asian American is culturally a part of a society that is dominated by a group that excludes him or her because of racial distinctions.

Conclusion

The presence of Asian and Pacific Islanders is unmistakable throughout much of the United States. As shown in Table 13.2, urban centers from coast to coast are homes of significant numbers of immigrants from Asia and their descendants.

Most White adults are confident that they can distinguish Asians from Europeans. Unfortunately, though, White Americans often cannot tell Asians apart from their physical appearance and are not disturbed about their confusion.

However, there are definite differences in the experience of the Chinese and the Japanese, as we have seen, in the United States. One obvious difference is in the degree of assimilation. The Chinese Americans have maintained their ethnic enclaves more than the Japanese Americans have. Chinatowns live on, both as welcomed halfway points for new arrivals and as enclaves where many make very low wages. However, Little Tokyos are few because of the differences in the cultures of China and Japan. China was almost

TABLE 13.2 Cities with the Largest Asian Pacific Islander Concentrations, 2000		
City	Number of Asian Pacific Islanders	Proportion of City's Population
New York City	792,477	9.9%
Los Angeles	375,167	10.2
San Jose	243,959	27.3
San Francisco	243,409	31.3
Honolulu	233,045	62.7
San Diego	172,821	14.1
Chicago	127,762	4.4
Houston	104,876	5.4
Fremont, California	75,984	37.4
Seattle	75,769	13.4

Source: Barnes and Bennett 2002; Grieco 2001.

untouched by European influence, but even by the early 1900s, Japan had already been influenced by the West. Therefore, the Japanese arrived somewhat more assimilated than their Chinese counterparts. The continued migration of Chinese in recent years has also meant that Chinese Americans as a group have been less assimilated than Japanese Americans.

Both groups have achieved some success, but this success has not extended to all members. For Chinese Americans, a notable exception to success can be found in Chinatowns, which, behind the tourist front, are much like other poverty-stricken areas in American cities. Neither Chinese Americans nor Japanese Americans have figured prominently in the executive offices of the nation's large corporations and financial institutions. Compared with other racial and ethnic groups, Asian Americans have shown little interest in political activity on their own behalf.

However, the success of Asian Americans, especially that of the Japanese Americans, belongs to them, not to U.S. society. First, Asian Americans have been considered successful only because they conform to the dominant society's expectations. Their acceptance as a group does not indicate growing pluralism in the United States.

Second, the ability of the *Nisei*, in particular, to recover from the camp experience cannot be taken as a precedent for other racial minorities. The Japanese Americans left the camps a skilled group, ambitious to overcome their adversity and placing a cultural empha-

sis on formal education. They entered a booming economy in which Whites and others could not afford to discriminate even if they wanted to. African Americans after slavery and Hispanic immigrants have entered the economy without skills at a time when the demand for manual labor has been limited. Many of them have been forced to remain in a marginal economy, whether that of the ghetto, the barrio, or subsistence agriculture. For Japanese Americans, the post-World War II period marked the fortunate coincidence of their having assets and ambition when they could be used to full advantage.

Third, some Whites use the success of the Asian Americans to prop up their own prejudice. Bigoted people twist Asian American success to show that racism cannot possibly play a part in another group's subordination. If the Japanese or Chinese can do it, why cannot African Americans, the illogical reasoning goes. More directly, Japanese Americans' success may serve as a scapegoat for another's failure ("They advanced at my expense") or as a sign that they are clannish or too ambitious. Regardless of what a group does, a prejudiced eye will always view it as wrong.

As for other racial and ethnic minorities, assimilation seems to be the path most likely to lead to tolerance but not necessarily to acceptance. However, assimilation has a price that is well captured in the Chinese phrase *Zhancao zhugen*: "To eliminate the weeds, one must pull out their roots." To work for acceptance means to uproot all traces of one's cultural heritage and former identity (Wang 1991).

Key Terms

evacuees 343	Kibei 341	tongs 337
hui kuan 337	Nisei 341	tsu 336
Issei 341	Sansei 341	Yonsei 341

Review Questions

1. What has been the legacy of the "yellow peril"?
2. What made the placement of Japanese Americans in internment camps unique?
3. In what respects does diversity characterize Chinatowns?
4. How has Japanese American assimilation been blocked in the United States?
5. What are the most significant similarities between the Chinese American and Japanese American experience? What are the differences?

Critical Thinking

1. Considering the past as well as the present, are the moves made to restrict or exclude Chinese and Japanese Americans based on economic or racist motives?
2. What events can you imagine that could cause the United States to again identify an ethnic group for confinement in some type of internment camps?
3. What stereotypical images of Chinese Americans and Japanese Americans can you identify in the contemporary media?

Internet Connections—Research Navigator™

Follow the instructions found on page 31 of this text to access the features of Research Navigator™. Once at the Web site, enter your Login Name and Password. Then, to use the ContentSelect database, enter keywords such as "Chinatowns," "model minority," and "Tule Lake," and the research engine will supply relevant and recent scholarly and popular press publications. Use the *New York Times* Search-by-Subject Archive to find recent news articles related to sociology and the Link Library feature to locate relevant Web links organized by the key terms associated with this chapter.

14 Jewish Americans: Quest to Maintain Identity

CHAPTER OUTLINE

THE JEWISH PEOPLE ARE AN ETHNIC GROUP. THEIR IDENTITY rests not on the presence of physical traits or religious beliefs but on a sense of belonging that is tied to Jewish ancestry. The history of anti-Semitism is as ancient as the Jewish people themselves. Today, evidence suggests that this intolerance persists today in both thought and action. Jews in the United States may have experienced less discrimination than did earlier generations in Europe, but some opportunities are still denied them. Contemporary Jews figure prominently in the professions and as a group exhibit a strong commitment to education. Many Jews share a concern about either the lack of religious devotion of some members or the division within American Judaism over the degree of orthodoxy. Jews in the United States practice their faith as Orthodox, Conservative, or Reform. Paradoxically, the acceptance of Jews by Gentiles has made the previously strong identity of Jews weaker with each succeeding generation.

Two events reflect the complexity of Jewish life in the United States; one began with a lawsuit and the other with violence.

On December 21, 2001, the Second Court of Appeals upheld earlier court decisions that ruled in favor of Yale University and against the "Yale Five." The case began in 1997 when three Orthodox Jews felt that the Yale housing policy that requires unmarried freshmen and sophomores under age 21 to live on campus was discriminatory. The freshmen felt it would force Orthodox Jews to violate their faith's call for modesty in living by expecting them to live in co-ed residence halls. Even a compromise offered by Yale to place them in rooms with bathrooms on single-sex floors was rejected. The students contended that the dormitory atmosphere of sexual promiscuity is irreconcilable with their deeply held religious beliefs. Two sophomores, who had paid for university housing the year before while living off-campus, soon joined their lawsuit. Many supported the Yale Five, but even other Orthodox Jewish students at Yale expressed anger over the lawsuit, feeling that they could be respectful to their faith and still conform to the housing standards of the university (Itano 1997; Muller 2001).

Billings, Montana, does not have a large Jewish population, but it does have an established community of Jews. Billings had no history of visible anti-Jewish hostility. However, beginning in 1992, swastikas appeared outside a Jewish temple, tombstones in a Jewish cemetery were toppled, and bomb threats were made to a synagogue. Then, in the fall of 1993, rocks and bottles were thrown through the windows of homes of prominent members of the Jewish community in Billings. Police advised one of the victim households to remove the "Happy Hanukkah" pictures from their front windows. In light of this tension, local Christian ministers encouraged their members to place menorahs in their windows. Stores instantly sold out of them, and local newspapers printed color pictures of them for people to hang in their windows. As Christmas Day came in this overwhelmingly Christian community, home after home displayed symbols of Judaism, defying those who had attacked the Jews. The culprits were never identified, but they had succeeded in bringing a city together (Cohon 1995).

The United States has the largest Jewish population in the world. This nation's approximately 6 million Jews account for 46 percent of the world's Jewish population. Jewish Americans not only represent a significant group in the United States but also play a prominent role in the worldwide Jewish community. The nation with the second-largest Jewish population, Israel, is the only one in which Jews are in the majority, accounting for 81 percent of the population, compared with just over 2 percent in the United States. Figure 14.1 depicts the worldwide distribution of Jews.

The Jewish people form a contrast to the other subordinate groups we have studied. At least 1,500 years had passed since Jews were the dominant group in any nation until Israel was created in 1948. Even there, Jews are in competition for power. American Jews superficially resemble Asian Americans in that both are largely free from poverty, compared to Chicanos or Puerto Ricans. Unlike those groups, however, the Jewish cultural heritage is not nationalistic in origin. Perhaps the most striking difference is that the history of anti-Jewish prejudice and discrimination (usually called **anti-Semitism**) is nearly as old as relations between Jews and Gentiles (non-Jews).

anti-Semitism
Anti-Jewish prejudice or discrimination.

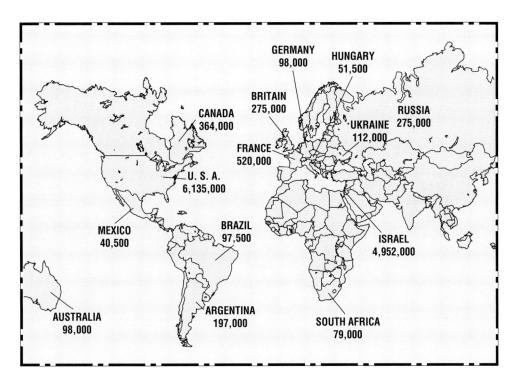

FIGURE 14.1   Worldwide Distribution of Jews, 2001

Note: Data include all nations with at least 40,000 Jews.

Source: Sergio Dellapergola, "World Jewish Population 2001," *American Jewish Yearbook,* ed. David Singer and Lawrence Grossman, American Jewish Committee, 2001.

The most distinctive aspect of the Jewish population is its concentration in urban areas and in the Northeast. The most recent estimates place more than 45 percent of the Jewish population in the Northeast (Figure 14.2). Jews are concentrated especially in the metropolitan areas of New York City, Los Angeles, and Miami, where altogether they account for half of the nation's Jewish population.

The Jewish People: Race, Religion, or Ethnic Group?

Jews are a subordinate group. They fulfill the criteria set forth in Chapter 1:

- Jewish Americans experience unequal treatment from non-Jews in the form of prejudice, discrimination, and segregation.
- Jews share a cultural history that distinguishes them from the dominant group.
- Jews do not choose to be Jewish, in the same way that Whites do not choose to be White or Mexican Americans to be Mexican American.
- Jews have a strong sense of group solidarity.
- Jewish men and women tend to marry one another rather than marrying outside the group.

What are the distinguishing traits for Jewish Americans? Are they physical features, thus making Jews a racial group? Are these characteristics matters of faith, suggesting that Jews are best regarded as a religious minority? Or are they cultural and social, making Jews an ethnic group? To answer these questions, we must address the ancient and perennial question: What is a Jew?

The issue of what makes a Jew is not only a scholarly question; in Israel, it figures in policy matters. The Israel Law of Return defines who is a Jew and extends Israeli citizenship to all Jews. Currently, the law recognizes all converts to the faith, but pressure

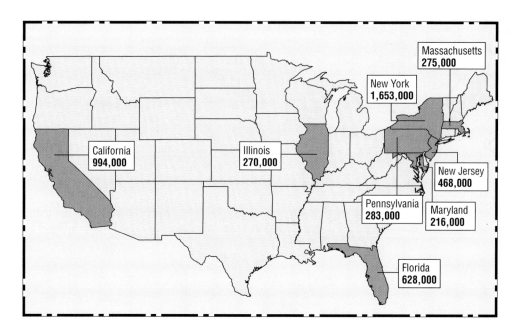

FIGURE 14.2 Jewish Population Distribution in the United States, 2001

Note: States highlighted have largest Jewish populations.

Source: Jim Schwartz and Jeffrey Scheckner, "Jewish Population in the United States, 2001." *American Jewish Yearbook,* ed. David Singer and Lawrence Grossman, American Jewish Committee, 2001.

has grown recently to limit citizenship to those whose conversions were performed by Orthodox rabbis. Although the change would have little practical impact, symbolically this pressure shows the tension and lack of consensus even among Jews over who is a Jew (Watson 1988).

The definition of race used here is fairly explicit. The Jewish people are not physically differentiated from non-Jews. True, many people believe they can tell a Jew from a non-Jew, but actual distinguishing physical traits are absent. Jews today come from all areas of the world and carry a variety of physical features. Most Jewish Americans are descended from northern and eastern Europeans and have the appearance of Nordic and Alpine people. Many others carry Mediterranean traits that make them indistinguishable from Spanish or Italian Catholics. Many Jews reside in North Africa, and although they are not significantly represented in the United States, many people would view them only as a racial minority, Black. The wide range of variation among Jews makes it inaccurate to speak of a Jewish race in a physical sense (Gittler 1981; Montagu 1972).

To define Jews by religion seems the obvious answer because there are Judaic religious beliefs, holidays, and rituals. But these beliefs and practices do not distinguish all Jews from non-Jews. To be a Jewish American does not mean that one is affiliated with one of the three religious groups: the Orthodox, the Reform, and the Conservative. A large segment of adult Jewish Americans, more than a third, do not participate in religious services or even belong, however tenuously, to a temple or synagogue. They have not converted to Christianity, nor have they ceased to think of themselves as Jews. Nevertheless, Jewish religious beliefs and the history of religious practices remain significant legacies for all Jews today, however secularized their everyday behavior. In a 1998 survey, half of all Jews felt that a "shared history or culture" much more so than religion defined what it means to be Jewish (*Los Angeles Times* Poll 1998).

Judaization
The lessening importance of Judaism as a religion and the substitution of cultural traditions as the tie that binds Jews.

The trend for some time, especially in the United States, has been toward a condition called **Judaization**, the lessening importance of Judaism as a religion and the substitution of cultural traditions as the ties that bind Jews. Depending on one's definition, Judaization has caused some Jews to become so assimilated in the United States that very traditional Jews no longer consider them acceptable spouses (Gans 1956).

Jewish identity is ethnic. Jews share cultural traits, not physical features or uniform religious beliefs. The level of this cultural identity differs for the individual Jew. Just as some Apaches may be more acculturated than others, the degree of assimilation varies between Jewish people. Judaization may base identity on such things as eating traditional Jewish foods, telling Jewish jokes, and wearing the Star of David. For others, this cultural identity may be the sense of a common history of centuries of persecution. For still others, it may be an unimportant identification. They say, "I am a Jew," just as they say, "I am a resident of California."

The question of what constitutes Jewish identity is not easily resolved. The most appropriate explanation of Jewish identity may be the simplest. A Jew in contemporary America is a person who thinks of himself or herself as a Jew. That also means that being a Jew is a choice and, as we will return to later in the chapter, many Jews may not be making that choice (Abrahamson and Pasternak 1998; Himmelfarb 1982).

Immigration of Jews to the United States

As every schoolchild knows, 1492 was the year in which Christopher Columbus reached the western hemisphere, exploring on behalf of Spain. That year also marked the expulsion of all Jews from Spain. The resulting exodus was not the first migration of Jews, nor was it the last. This is but one illustration of several of the social processes in the intergroup relations continuum illustrated in Figure 14.3. Other examples will be presented throughout this chapter.

One of the most significant movements among Jews is the one that created history's largest concentration of Jews: the immigration to the United States. The first Jews arrived in 1654 and were of Sephardic origin, meaning that they were originally from Spain and Portugal. These immigrants sought refuge after they had been expelled from other European countries.

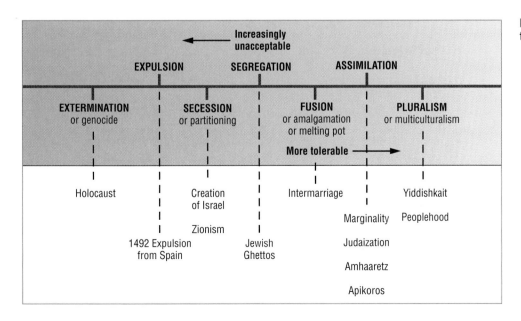

FIGURE 14.3   Intergroup Relations Continuum

When the United States gained its independence from Great Britain, only 2,500 Jews lived here. By 1870 the Jewish population had climbed to about 200,000, supplemented mostly by Jews of German origin. They did not immediately merge into the older Jewish American settlements any more than the German Catholics fused immediately with native Catholics. Years passed before the two groups' common identity as Jews overcame nationality differences (Dinnerstein 1994; Jaher 1994).

The greatest migration of Jews to the United States occurred around the end of the 19th century and was simultaneous with the great European migration described in Chapter 4. Because they arrived at the same time does not mean that the movement of Gentiles and of Jews was identical in all respects. One significant difference was that Jews were much more likely to stay in the United States; few returned to Europe. Although between 1908 and 1937, one-third of all European immigrants returned, only 5 percent of Jewish immigrants did. The legal status of Jews in Europe at the turn of the century had improved since medieval times, but their rights were still revoked from time to time (Sherman 1974).

Despite the legacy of anti-Semitism in Europe, past and present, most of the Jews who migrated to the United States up to the early 20th century came voluntarily. These immigrants tended to be less pious and less observant of Judaic religious customs than those who remained in Europe. As late as 1917, there were only five small day schools, as Jewish parochial schools were called, in the entire nation. Nevertheless, although the earliest Jewish immigration was not a direct response to fear, the United States had special meaning for the Jewish arrivals. This nation had no history of anti-Semitism like that of Europe. Many Jews must have felt a new sense of freedom, and many clearly demonstrated their commitment to their new nation by becoming citizens at a rate unparalleled in other ethnic groups (Herberg 1983; Sklare 1971).

The immigration acts of the 1920s sharply reduced the influx of Jews, as they did for other European groups. Beginning in about 1933, the Jews arriving in the United States were not merely immigrants; they were also refugees. The tyranny of the Third Reich began to take its toll well before World War II. German and Austrian Jews fled Europe as the impending doom became more evident. Many of the refugees from Nazism in Poland, Hungary, and the Ukraine tended to be more religiously orthodox and adapted slowly to the ways of the earlier Jewish immigrants, if they adapted at all. As Hitler's decline and fall came to pass, the concentration camps, the speeches of Hitler, the atrocities, the war trials, and the capture of Nazi leaders undoubtedly made all American Jews—natives and refugees, the secular and the orthodox—acutely aware of their Jewishness and the price one may be required to pay for ethnicity alone.

Because the U.S. Citizenship and Immigration Services do not identify an immigrant's religion, precise data are lacking for the number of people of Jewish background migrating recently to the United States. Estimates of 500,000 have been given for the number of Jews who made the United States their home in the 1960s and 1970s. The majority came from Israel, but 75,000 came from the Soviet Union and another 20,000 from Iran, escaping persecution in those two nations. As the treatment of Jews in the Soviet Union improved in the late 1980s, U.S. immigration officials began to scrutinize requests for entry to see whether refugee status was still merited. Although some Soviet Jews had difficulty demonstrating that they had a "well-founded fear of persecution," the United States admitted more than 13,600 in 1988 (through the processing center in Rome alone). The situation grew more complicated with the collapse of the Soviet Union in 1991. Throughout the period, the immigrants' arrival brought about a growth in the Jewish community in the United States.

Jewish Hostility

Anti-Semitism: Past and Present

fringe-of-values theory
Behavior that is on the border of conduct that a society regards as proper and is often carried out by subordinate groups, subjecting those groups to negative sanctions.

The history of the Jewish people is a history of struggle to overcome centuries of hatred. Several religious observances, such as Passover, Hanukkah, and Purim, commemorate the past sacrifices or conflicts Jews have experienced. Anti-Jewish hostility, or anti-Semitism, has followed the struggle of the Jewish people since before the beginning of the Christian faith to the present.

Origins

Many anti-Semites justify their beliefs by pointing to the role of some Jews in the crucifixion of Jesus Christ, although he was also a Jew. For nearly 2,000 years various Christians have argued that all Jews share in the responsibility of the Jewish elders who condemned Jesus Christ to death. Much anti-Semitism over the ages bears little direct relationship to the crucifixion, however, and has more to do with the persisting stereotype that sees Jews as behaving treacherously to members of the larger society in which they live.

A 2004 survey found that 26 percent of Americans felt Jews were "responsible for Christ's death"—a significant increase over a similar survey nine years earlier. At the time of the survey, many Jews felt that Mel Gibson's *The Passion of the Christ* reinforces such a view. Indeed the same survey shows that among those who had seen the film, 36 percent held Jews responsible for the crucifixion (Pew Research Center 2004).

What truth is there in such stereotypes? Even prominent political leaders have publicly expressed stereotyped opinions about Jews. In 1974, the chairman of the Joint Chiefs of Staff of the U.S. armed forces declared that Jews "own, you know, the banks in this country" (*Time* 1974:16). Yet the facts show that Jewish Americans are dramatically underrepresented in management positions in the nation's leading banks. Even in New York City, where Jews account for half the college graduates, Jewish Americans represent only 4 percent of that city's senior banking officials. Similarly, a 1998 national survey found that 8 percent of Jews were business owners, compared with 9 percent of the total U.S. population (Getlin 1998; Slavin and Pradt 1979, 1982).

If the stereotype that Jews are obsessed with money is false, how did it originate? Social psychologist Gordon Allport (1979), among others, advanced the **fringe-of-values theory**. Throughout history, Jews have occupied positions economically

Jewish shoppers, many immigrants, crowd Orchard Street in New York City in 1923.

in-group virtues
Proper behavior by one's own group (in-group virtues) becomes unacceptable when practiced by outsiders (out-group vices).

out-group vices
Proper behavior by one's own group (in-group virtues) becomes unacceptable when practiced by outsiders (out-group vices).

different from those of Gentiles, often because laws forbade them to farm or practice trades. For centuries, the Christian church prohibited the taking of interest in the repayment of loans, calling it the sin of usury. Consequently, in the minds of Europeans, the sinful practice of money lending was equated with the Jew. In reality, most Jews were not moneylenders, and most of those who were did not charge interest. In fact, many usurers were Christians, but because they worked in secret, it was only the reputation of the Jews that was damaged. To make matters worse, the nobles of some European countries used Jews to collect taxes, which only increased the ill feeling. To the Gentile, such business practices by the Jews constituted behavior on the fringes of proper conduct. Therefore, this theory about the perpetuation of anti-Semitism is called the fringe of values theory (American Jewish Committee 1965, 1966a, 1966b; *Time* 1974).

A similar explanation is given for other stereotypes, such as the assertion that Jews are clannish, staying among themselves and not associating with others. In the ancient world, Jews in the Near East area often were under attack by neighboring peoples. Throughout history, Jews have also at times been required to live in closed areas, or ghettos. This experience naturally led them to unify and rely on themselves rather than others. More recently, the stereotype of clannishness has gained support because Jews have been more likely to interact with Jews than with Gentiles. But this behavior is reciprocal because Gentiles have tended to stay among their own kind, too.

Being critical of others for traits for which you praise members of your own group is an example of **in-group virtues** becoming **out-group vices**. Sociologist Robert Merton (1968) described how proper behavior by one's own group becomes unacceptable when practiced by outsiders. For Christians to take their faith seriously is commendable; for Jews to withstand secularization is a sign of backwardness. For Gentiles to prefer Gentiles as friends is understandable; for Jews to choose other Jews as friends suggests clannishness. The assertion that Jews are clannish is an exaggeration and also ignores the fact that the dominant group shares the same tendency. It also fails to consider to what extent anti-Semitism has logically encouraged— and indeed, forced—Jews to seek out other Jews as friends and fellow workers (Allport 1979).

This only begins to explore the alleged Jewish traits, their origin, and the limited value of such stereotypes in accurately describing several million Jewish people. Stereotypes are only one aspect of anti-Semitism; another has been discrimination against Jews. In A.D. 313, Christianity became the official religion of Rome. Within another two centuries, Jews were forbidden to marry Christians or to try to convert them. Because Christians shared with Jews both the Old Testament and the origin of Jesus, they felt ambivalent toward the Jewish people. Gentiles attempted to purge themselves of their doubts about the Jews by projecting exaggerated hostility onto the Jews. The expulsion of the Jews from Spain in 1492 is only one example. Spain was merely one of many countries, including England and France, from which the Jews were expelled. In the mid-14th century, the bubonic plague wiped out a third of Europe's population. Because of their social conditions and some of their religious prohibitions, Jews were less likely to die from the plague. Anti-Semites pointed to this as evidence that the Jews were in league with the devil and had poisoned the wells of non-Jews. Consequently, from 1348 to 1349, 350 Jewish communities were exterminated, not by the plague but by Gentiles.

The Holocaust

The injustices to the Jewish people continued for centuries. However, it would be a mistake to say that all Gentiles were anti-Semitic. History, drama, and other literature record daily, presumably friendly interaction between Jews and Gentiles. At particular times and places, anti-Semitism was an official government policy. In other situations, it was the product of a few bigoted individuals and sporadically became very widespread. Regardless of the scope, anti-Semitism was a part of Jewish life, something that Jews were forced to contend with. By 1870, most legal restrictions aimed at Jews had been abolished in Western Europe. Since then, however, Jews have again been used as scapegoats by opportunists who blame them for a nation's problems.

The most tragic example of such an opportunist was Adolf Hitler, whose "final solution" to Germany's problems led to the Holocaust. The **Holocaust** is the state-sponsored systematic persecution and annihilation of European Jewry by Nazi Germany and its collaborators. The move to eliminate Jews from the European continent started slowly, with Germany gradually restricting the rights of Jews: preventing them from voting, living outside the Jewish ghetto, and owning businesses. Much of the anti-Semitic cruelty was evident before the beginning of the war. If there was any doubt, "Night of Broken Glass," or *Kristallnacht,* in Berlin on November 9, 1938, ended any doubt. Ninety Berlin Jews were murdered, hundreds of homes and synagogues were set on fire or ransacked, and thousands of Jewish store windows were broken.

Despite the obvious intolerance, Jews desiring to immigrate were turned back by government officials in the United States and elsewhere. Just a few months after *Kristallnacht,* 907 Jewish refugees aboard the liner *St. Louis* were denied entry to Cuba. Efforts to gain entry in the United States, including special appeals to Congress and President Roosevelt, were useless. Ultimately the ship returned, with many of the Jews later dying in the death camps. Between 1933 and 1945, two-thirds of Europe's total Jewish population were killed; in Poland, Germany, and Austria, 90 percent were murdered. Even today, there are still 17 percent fewer Jews than in 1940.

Many eyewitnesses to the events of the Holocaust remind us of the human tragedy involved. Among the most eloquent are the writings and speeches of Nobel Peace Prize winner Elie Wiesel. In "Listen to Our Voices," he recalls the moments before he and other Jews were freed from the Buchenwald concentration camp.

Despite the enormity of the tragedy, a small but vocal proportion of the world community are **Holocaust revisionists** who claim that the Holocaust did not happen. Debates also continue between those who contend that this part of modern history must be remembered and others, in the United States and Europe, who feel that it is time to put the Holocaust behind us and go on. However, the poignant statements by Holocaust survivors such as Elie Wiesel and the release of such films as *Schindler's List* (1993) and *Life Is Beautiful* (1998) keep the tragedy of the Holocaust in our minds (Cooper and Brackman 2001; Stern 2001).

Anti-Semitism is definitely not just a historical social phenomenon in Europe. After the attacks on the United States on September 11, 2001, fresh outbreaks occurred throughout the continent. Newspapers reported Jewish worshippers being subjected to rocks and insults as they walked to services. A growing Arab and Muslim population in Europe is also serving to offer an audience for Christian-generated anti-Semitism, especially after the U.S. occupation of Iraq beginning in 2003 and the continued uncertainty of Palestine's future (J. Fleishman 2004).

U.S. Anti-Semitism: Past

Compared with the brutalities of Europe from the time of the early Christian church to the rule of Hitler, the United States cannot be described as a nation with a history of severe anti-Semitism. Nevertheless, the United States has also had its outbreaks of anti-Semitism, though none have begun to approach the scope of western Europe's. An examination of the status of Jewish Americans today indicates the extent of remaining discrimination against Jews. However, contemporary anti-Semitism must be seen in relation to past injustices.

Holocaust
The state-sponsored systematic persecution and annihilation of European Jewry by Nazi Germany and its collaborators.

Holocaust revisionists
People who deny the Nazi effort to exterminate the Jews or who minimize the numbers killed.

Voices **Listen to Our Voices** Listen to

NIGHT

On April tenth, there were still about twenty thousand of us in the camp, including several hundred children. They decided to evacuate us all at once, right on until the evening. Afterward, they were going to blow up the camp.

So we were massed in the huge assembly square, in rows of five, waiting to see the gate open. Suddenly, the sirens began to wail. An alert! We went back to the blocks. It was too late to evacuate us that evening. The evacuation was postponed again to the following day.

We were tormented with hunger. We had eaten nothing for six days, except a bit of grass or some potato peelings found near the kitchens.

At ten o'clock in the morning the SS scattered through the camp, moving the last victims toward the assembly place.

Then the resistance movement decided to act. Armed men suddenly rose up everywhere. Bursts of firing. Grenades exploding. We children stayed flat on the ground in the block.

The battle did not last long. Toward noon everything was quiet again. The SS had fled and the resistance had taken charge of the running of the camp.

Elie Wiesel

At about six o'clock in the evening, the first American tank stood at the gates of Buchenwald.

Our first act as free men was to throw ourselves onto the provisions. We thought only of that. Not of revenge, not of our families. Nothing but bread.

And even when we were no longer hungry, there was still no one who thought of revenge. On the following day, some of the young men went to Weimar to get some potatoes and clothes—and to sleep with the girls. But of revenge, not a sign.

Three days after the liberation of Buchenwald I became very ill with food poisoning. I was transferred to the hospital and spent two weeks between life and death.

One day I was able to get up, after gathering all my strength. I wanted to see myself in the mirror hanging on the opposite wall. I had not seen myself since the ghetto.

From the depths of the mirror, a corpse gazed back at me.

The look in his eyes, as they stared into mine, has never left me. ■

Source: Excerpt from *Night* by Elie Wiesel, translated by Stella Rodway. Copyright © 1960 by MacGibbon & Kee. Copyright renewed 1988 by The Collins Publishing Group. Reprinted by permission of Hill & Wang, a division of Farrar, Straus & Giroux, LLC.

In 1654, the year Jews arrived in colonial America, Peter Stuyvesant, governor of New Amsterdam (the Dutch city later named New York), attempted to expel them from the city. Stuyvesant's efforts failed, but they were the beginning of an unending effort to separate Jews from the rest of the population. Because the pre-1880 immigration of Jews was small, anti-Semitism was little noticed except, of course, by Jews. Most 19th-century movements against minorities were targeted at Catholics and Blacks and ignored Jews. In fact, Jews occasionally joined in such movements. By the 1870s, however, signs of a pattern of social discrimination against Jews had appeared. Colleges limited the number of Jewish students or excluded Jews altogether. The first Jewish fraternity was founded in 1898 to compensate for the barring of Jews from campus social organizations. As Jews began to compete for white-collar jobs early in the 20th century, job discrimination became the rule rather than the exception (Higham 1966; Selzer 1972).

The 1920s and the 1930s were periods of the most virulent and overt anti-Semitism. In these decades, the myth of an internationally organized Jewry took shape. According to a forged document titled *Protocols of the Elders of Zion,* Jews throughout the world planned to conquer all governments, and the major vehicle for this rise to power was communism, said by anti-Semites to be a Jewish movement. Absurd though this argument was, some respected Americans accepted the thesis of an international Jewish conspiracy and believed in the authenticity of the *Protocols.*

Henry Ford, founder of the automobile company that bears his name, was responsible for the publication of the *Protocols.* The *Dearborn Independent,* a weekly newspaper owned by Ford, published anti-Semitic material for seven years. Finally in 1927, faced with several million dollars' worth of civil suits for slandering well-known Jewish Americans, he published a halfhearted apology. In his later years, Ford expressed regret for his espousal of anti-Semitic causes, but the damage had been done; he had lent an air of respectability to the most exaggerated charges against Jewish people.

It is not clear why Henry Ford, even for a short period of his life, so willingly accepted anti-Semitism. But Ford was not alone. Groups such as the Ku Klux Klan and the German American Bund, as well as radio personalities preached about the Jewish conspiracy as if it were fact. By the 1930s, these sentiments expressed a fondness for Hitler. Even famed aviator Charles Lindbergh made speeches to gatherings claiming that Jews were forcing the United States into a war so that Jewish people could profit by wartime production. When the barbarous treatment of the Jews by Nazi Germany was exposed, most Americans were horrified by such events, and people such as Lindbergh were as puzzled as anyone about how some Americans could have been so swept up by the pre-World War II wave of anti-Semitism (N. Baldwin 2001; Meyers 1943; Selzer 1972). Historical anti-Semitism is never far below the surface. As Israeli-Arab tensions increased, the discredited *Protocols* resurfaced in the mass media from Egypt to France in 2002.

The next section examines anti-Semitic feelings in contemporary America. Several crucial differences between anti-Semitism in Europe and in the United States must be considered. First, and most important, the U.S. government has never promoted anti-Semitism. Unlike its European counterparts, the U.S. government has never embarked on an anti-Semitic program of expulsion or extermination. Second, because anti-Semitism was never institutionalized in the United States as it sometimes has been in Europe, American Jews have not needed to develop a defensive ideology to ensure the survival of their people. A Jewish American can make a largely personal decision about how much to assimilate or how secular to become.

Contemporary Anti-Semitism

Next to social research on anti-Black attitudes and behavior of Whites, anti-Semitism has been the major focus of studies of prejudice by sociologists and psychologists. Most of the conclusions described in Chapter 2 apply equally to the data collected on anti-Semitism. Little concern was expressed by Jews in the United States about anti-Semitism immediately after World War II. From the late 1960s through the 1990s, however, anti-Semitism has again appeared to be a threat in many parts of the world. A 2003 national survey found that 9 percent felt anti-Semitism was a "very serious problem" and 48 percent "somewhat of a problem" in the United States (J. Jones 2003b).

The Anti-Defamation League (ADL) of B'nai B'rith, founded in 1913, makes an annual survey of reported anti-Semitic incidents. Although the number has fluctuated, the 1994 tabulation reached the highest level in the 22 years during which the

ADL has been recording such incidents. It dropped slightly over the next seven years only to rise again in 2002. Figure 14.4 shows the rise of harassment, threats, and assaults, which, adding episodes of vandalism, brings the total to 1,559 incidents for 2002. Some incidents were inspired and carried out by neo-Nazis or skinheads, groups of young people who champion racist and anti-Semitic ideologies. In our mapping of racist fringe groups (see Figure 14.4), we see the widespread presence of such groups.

Particularly disturbing has been the number of reported anti-Semitic incidents on college campuses. Incidents continue to be reported. Anti-Jewish graffiti, anti-Semitic speakers, and swastikas affixed to predominantly Jewish fraternities were among the documented incidents. Another manifestation of it appears in editorial-style advertisements in college newspapers that argue that the Holocaust never occurred. A chilling development is the Internet as a growing vehicle for anti-Semitism, either delivering such messages or serving as a means of reaching Web sites that spread intolerance (Anti-Defamation League 2004).

Acts of anti-Semitic violence in the United States, along with the continuing conflict in the Middle East and the expression of anti-Semitic themes by some African Americans, have prompted renewed national attention to anti-Semitism.

American Jews and Israel   When the Middle East became a major hot spot in international affairs in the 1960s, a revival of 1930s anti-Semitism occurred. Many Jewish Americans expressed concern that because Jews are freer in the United States than they have been in perhaps any other country in their history, they would ignore the struggle of other Jews. Israel's precarious status has proven to be a strong source of identity for Jewish Americans. Major wars in the Middle East in 1967, 1973, and 1991 reminded the world of Israel's vulnerability. Palestinian uprisings in the Occupied Territories and international recognition of the Palestine Liberation Organization

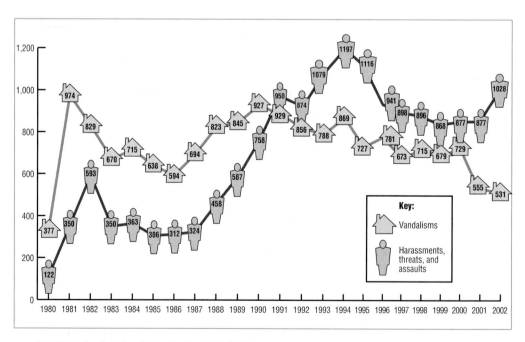

FIGURE 14.4   Anti-Semitic Incidents, 1980–2002

Source: Reprinted with permission of the Anti-Defamation League, www.adl.org.

This anti-Semitic graffiti was painted on the outside walls of Pacadah, Kentucky's Temple Israel in 2004.

(PLO) in 1988 and 2002 eroded the strong pro-Israeli front among the Western powers. Some Jewish Americans have shown their commitment to the Israeli cause by immigrating to Israel.

Jewish American support is not uniform. Although not all American Jews agree with Israel's actions, many Jews express support for Israel's struggles by contributing money and trying to influence American opinion and policy to be more favorable to Israel. A survey taken in 2001 (after the September 11 attack and the heightened violence in the Middle East) showed that 29 percent of Jewish Americans feel "very close" to Israel and another 43 percent feel "fairly close." But that still leaves more than a quarter (28 percent) who feel distant from Israel. A similar proportion disagree that caring about Israel is an important part of being a Jew (American Jewish Committee 2002).

In the year after the oil embargo (1974), the United Nations General Assembly ignored American and Israeli objections and passed a resolution declaring that "Zionism is a form of racism and racial discrimination." **Zionism**, which initially referred to the old Jewish religious yearning to return to the biblical homeland, has been expressed in the twentieth century in the movement to create a Jewish state in Palestine. Ever since the **Diaspora**, the exile of Jews from Palestine several centuries before Christianity, many Jews have seen the destiny of their people only as the establishment of a Jewish state in the Holy Land.

The Zionism resolution, finally repealed by the UN in 1991, had no lasting influence and did not change any nation's foreign policy. However, it did increase Jewish fears of reawakened anti-Semitism thinly disguised as attacks on Zionist beliefs. Even the development of agreements between Israel and its Arab neighbors and the international recognition of Palestinian autonomy in Israel did not end the concern of Jewish Americans that continuing anti-Israeli feeling reflected anti-Semitism.

American Jews and African Americans   The contemporary anti-Semitism of African Americans is of special concern to Jewish Americans. There is no reason why anti-Semites should be exclusively White, but Jews have been especially troubled by Blacks expressing ethnic prejudices, given their own history of oppression. Jewish Americans have been active in civil rights causes and have contributed generously to legal

Zionism
Traditional Jewish religious yearning to return to the biblical homeland, now used to refer to support for the state of Israel.

Diaspora
The exile of Jews from Palestine.

defense funds. Jewish neighborhoods and employers have also been quicker than their Gentile counterparts to accept African Americans. Therefore, there is a positive Black-Jewish alliance with a long history. For these reasons, some Jews find it especially difficult to understand why another group experiencing prejudice and discrimination should express anti-Semitic sentiments.

Beginning in the 1960s, some African American activists and the Black Panther party supported the Arabs in the Middle East conflict and called on Israel to surrender. Black-Jewish relations were again inflamed in 1984 by the Reverend Jesse Jackson during his campaign for the Democratic party's nomination for the presidency. His off-the-record reference to Jews as "Hymies" and the publicly broadcast anti-Semitic remarks by one of his supporters, Nation of Islam minister Louis Farrakhan, gave rise to new tensions between Blacks and Jews. During the 1988 campaign, Jackson distanced himself from anti-Semitic rhetoric, stating, "The sons and the daughters of the Holocaust and the sons and the daughters of slavery must find common ground again" (Schmidt 1988:14).

In the 1990s, unrelated events again seemed to draw attention to the relationship between Jews and African Americans. On several college campuses, invited African American speakers made anti-Israeli statements, inflaming the Jewish students in attendance. In a 1991 New York City incident, a Hasidic Jew ran a red light, killing an African American child, and the ambulance that regularly serves the Hasidic community did not pick up the child. In the emotional climate that resulted, an Australian Jewish researcher was stabbed to death, and several days of rioting in the Brooklyn, New York, neighborhood of Crown Heights followed (Morris and Rubin 1993).

In response to these and other events, many Jewish and African American leaders perceived a crisis in intergroup relations, and calls for unity became very public. For example, in 1994, the Reverend Jesse Jackson sought to distance himself from the statements of Khalid Abdul Muhammad, an aide of Farrakhan, calling him "racist, anti-Semitic, divisive, untrue, and chilling" (Finder 1994:21).

African American resentment, in many situations attracting notoriety, has rarely been anti-Jewish as such but rather has been opposed to White institutions. As author James Baldwin (1967:114) said, Blacks "are anti-Semitic because they're anti-White." That racial prejudice is deep in the United States is shown by the fact that two groups suffering discrimination, groups that might unite in opposition to the dominant society, fight each other instead.

An old Yiddish saying, "Schwer zu sein a Yid," means "It is tough to be a Jew." Anti-Semitism past and present are related. The old hostilities seem never to die. The atrocities of Nazi Germany have not been forgotten, nor should they be. Racial and ethnic hostility, against whatever group, unifies the group against its attackers, and Jewish Americans are no exception. The Jewish people of the United States have come together, regardless of nationality, to form a minority group with a high degree of group identity.

Position of Jewish Americans

Jewish Americans have an important role in contemporary America. They are active participants in the fight for civil rights and work on behalf of Israel. These efforts are important but only begin to describe their role in the United States. For a better perspective on Jewish people in the United States, the following summarizes their present situation with respect to employment and income, education, organizational activity, and political activity.

Employment and Income

Discrimination conditions all facets of a subordinate group's life. Jews have experienced, and to a limited extent still experience, differential treatment in the American job market. A 1956 survey of employers in San Francisco showed that one out of four acknowledged that it either barred Jews altogether or limited their employment to a predetermined level. Civil rights acts and U.S. Supreme Court decisions have made it illegal to discriminate in employment. The results of a 1998 national survey showed that 71 percent of Jews viewed anti-Semitism as a problem in the United States, although not necessarily in hiring practices. As shown in Table 14.1, through perseverance and emphasis on education, Jewish Americans as a group have overcome barriers to full employment and now enjoy high incomes (*Los Angeles Times* Poll 1998).

Using a variety of techniques, social science studies have documented declining discrimination against Jews in the business world. Sociologist Samuel Klausner interviewed business school graduates, comparing Jews with Protestants and Catholics who graduated from the same university in the same year. Klausner (1988:33) concludes, "(1) Jewish MBAs are winning positions in the same industries as their Catholic and Protestant classmates; (2) they are rising more rapidly in corporate hierarchies than their Catholic and Protestant colleagues; (3) they are achieving higher salaries than their Catholic and Protestant colleagues." Klausner adds that researchers tested seven indicators of discrimination and in each case failed to find evidence of

TABLE 14.1 Profile of Jews in the United States		
	Jewish Americans	**All U.S.**
INCOME		
Less than $40,000	28%	52%
$40,000–$59,999	18	21
$60,000 or more	38	20
Don't know/refused	16	7
OCCUPATION		
Professional	40	15
Manager	24	20
White collar	19	19
Business owner	8	9
Unskilled blue collar	5	16
Skilled blue collar	3	19
IDEOLOGY		
Liberal	46	24
Moderate	28	31
Conservative	23	40
POLITICAL PARTY		
Democrat	45	32
Independent	29	31
Republican	12	23
EDUCATION		
High school or less	13	59
Some college	27	21
College graduate	24	10
Graduate school	35	9

Source: Los Angeles Times Poll 1998.

discrimination against Jewish executives. Interestingly, however, this same study detected substantial discrimination against African Americans and women.

The economic success of the Jewish people as a group obscures the poverty of many individual Jewish families. We reached a similar conclusion in Chapter 12 from income data on Asian Americans and their image as a model minority. Sociologists largely agree that Jews in 1930 were as likely to be poverty stricken and to be living in slums as any minority group today. Most have escaped poverty, but what Ann Wolfe (1972) calls "the invisible Jewish poor" remains invisible to the rest of society. Like Chinese Americans, the Jewish poor were not well served by the Economic Opportunity Act and other federal experiments to eradicate poverty in the 1960s and 1970s. Although the proportion of the poor among the Jews is not as substantial as among Blacks or Hispanics, it does remind us that not all Jewish families have affluent lifestyles (Gold 1965; Lavender 1977; Levine and Hochbaum 1974).

✓ Education

Jews place great emphasis on education (see Table 14.1). This desire for formal schooling stems, it is argued, from the Judaic religion, which places the rabbi, or teacher, at the center of religious life.

In the United States today, all Jewish congregations emphasize religious instruction more than Protestants typically do. A 2000 estimate stated that there were 7,000 day schools with 200,000 pupils. Day schools are, in effect, private elementary schools with a substantial proportion of the curriculum given to Judaic studies and the learning of Hebrew. The less religiously committed may attend instruction on Sundays or on weekday afternoons after attending public schools. Seventy-six percent of Jews have received some form of formal Jewish education before they reach 30 years of age. The Jewish-sponsored component of higher education is not limited to strict religious instruction such as that found in rabbinical schools. Beginning in 1947, Jews founded graduate schools of medicine, education, social work, and mathematics, along with Brandeis University, which offers both undergraduate and graduate degrees. These institutions are nonsectarian (i.e., admission is not limited to Jews) and are conceived of as a Jewish-sponsored contribution to higher education (Abrahamson 1997; *Los Angeles Times* Poll 1998; *Religion Watch* 2000).

The religiously based tradition of lifelong study has left as a legacy a value system that stresses education. The poverty of Jewish immigrants kept them from devoting years to secular schooling, but they were determined that their children would do better. Despite their high levels of educational attainment, some members of the Jewish community express concern about Jewish education. They are disappointed with its highly secularized nature, not only because religious teaching has been limited but also because the Jewish sociocultural experience has been avoided altogether. It may even contribute to Judaization, the lessening of Judaism.

✓ Organizational Activity

The American Jewish community has encompassed a variety of organizations since its beginnings. These groups serve many purposes: Some are religious, and others are charitable, political, or educational. No organization, secular or religious, represents all American Jews, but there are more than 300 nationwide organizations.

Among the most significant are the United Jewish Appeal (UJA), the American Jewish Committee, the American Jewish Congress, and B'nai B'rith. The UJA was founded in 1939 and serves as a fund-raising organization for humanitarian causes. Recently, Israel has received the largest share of the funds collected. The American Jewish Committee (founded in 1906) and Congress (1918) work toward the similar purpose of improving Jewish-Gentile relations. B'nai B'rith (Sons of the Covenant) was founded in 1843 and claims 500,000 members in 40 nations. It promotes cultural and social programs and, through its Anti-Defamation League, monitors and fights anti-Semitism and hate crimes directed at other groups.

Besides the national groups, many community-based organizations are active. Some local organizations, such as social and business clubs, were founded because the existing groups barred Jews from membership. The U.S. Supreme Court has consistently ruled that private social organizations such as country clubs and business clubs may discriminate against Jews or any other ethnic or racial group. Jewish community centers are also prominent local organizations. To Gentiles, the synagogue is the most visible symbol of the Jewish presence at the community level. However, the Jewish community center is an important focus of local activity. In many Jewish neighborhoods throughout the United States, it is the center of secular activity. Hospitals, nurseries, homes for the elderly, and child care agencies are only a few of the community-level activities sponsored by Jewish Americans (Rabinove 1970; Sklare 1971).

Political Activity ✓

American Jews play a prominent role in politics as both voters and elected officials. Jews as a group are not typical in that they are more likely than the general population to label themselves liberal (refer back to Table 14.1). Although upper-middle-class voters tend to vote Republican, Jewish voters in that category have been steadfastly Democratic. Although Democratic presidential candidate Al Gore was unsuccessful in his election bid to defeat George W. Bush in 2000, he received 79 percent of Jewish American support. Despite renewed efforts by the Republicans to attract Jewish voters, they remained firmly Democratic in 2004 (*Religion Weekly* 2004).

Jews have long been successful in being elected to office, but it was not until 1988 that an Orthodox Jew from Connecticut was elected to the U.S. Senate. Joseph Lieberman refrained from campaigning on the Sabbath each week; his religious views were not an issue. He went on to be named as the vice presidential running mate of Al Gore. Even during the campaign, he honored the Sabbath and did not actively campaign, even avoiding dialing a telephone to potential supporters. Many view the positive response to his campaign as a sign of openness to devout Jews as political candidates (Issacson and Foltin 2001; Pew Charitable Trust 2000).

As in all subordinate groups, the political activity of Jewish Americans has not been limited to conventional electoral politics. Radical Jewish politics has been dominated by college students. At the height of their involvement in the late 1960s, Jewish youths

Parents and their daughter study a temple's Torah.

were active with Gentiles in the New Left movement and in working alone for causes unique to Jews, such as the support of Israel. Into the 1980s and 1990s, some Jews backed the more extreme responses to the friction between Israel and its Arab neighbors. A few even settled in Israel and, though small in number, were often vocal backers of resistance to any accommodation to the Arab nations or the Palestinian Authority.

Religious Life

Jewish identity and participation in the Jewish religion are not the same. Many Americans consider themselves Jewish and are considered Jewish by others even though they have never participated in Jewish religious life. The available data indicate that 44 percent of American Jews are affiliated with a synagogue or temple, but only one-quarter attend services monthly. Even in Israel, only 30 percent of Jews are religiously observant. Nevertheless, the presence of a religious tradition is an important tie among Jews, even secular Jews (S. Cohen 1991).

The Judaic faith embraces a number of factions or denominations that are similar in their roots but marked by sharp distinctions. No precise data reveal the relative numbers of the three major groups. Part of the problem is the difficulty of placing individuals in the proper group. For example, it is common for a Jew to be a member of an Orthodox congregation but consider himself or herself Conservative. The following levels of affiliation are based on a December 2001 national survey of Jewish Americans (American Jewish Committee 2001):

- Orthodox: 7 percent
- Conservative: 29 percent
- Reconstructionist: 2 percent
- Reform: 29 percent
- Just Jewish: 33 percent

We will focus on two forms of Judaism at either end of the continuum: the Orthodox, which attempts to uphold a very traditional practice of Judaism, and the Reform faith, which accommodates itself to the secular world.

The Orthodox Tradition

The unitary Jewish tradition developed in the United States into three sects, beginning in the mid-19th century. The differences between Orthodox, Conservative, and Reform Judaism are based on their varying acceptance of traditional rituals. All three sects embrace a philosophy based on the Torah, the first five books of the Old Testament. The differences developed because some Jews wanted to be less distinguishable from other Americans. Another significant factor in explaining the development of different groups is the absence of a religious elite and bureaucratic hierarchy. This facilitated the breakdown in traditional practices.

Orthodox Jewish life is very demanding, especially in a basically Christian society such as the United States. Almost all conduct is defined by rituals that require an Orthodox Jew to reaffirm his or her religious conviction constantly. Most Americans are familiar with **kashrut**, the laws pertaining to permissible and forbidden foods. When strictly adhered to, kashrut governs not only what foods may be eaten (kosher) but also how the food is prepared, served, and eaten. Besides day-to-day practices, Orthodox Jews have weekly and annual observances.

Even Orthodox Jews differ in their level of adherence to traditional practices. Among the ultraorthodox are the Hasidic Jews, or Hasidim, who reside chiefly in sev-

kashrut
Laws pertaining to permissible (kosher) and forbidden foods and their preparation.

eral neighborhoods in Brooklyn. To the Hasidim, following the multitude of mitzvahs, or commandments of behavior, is as important today as it was in the time of Moses. They wear no garments that mix linen and wool. Men wear a yarmulke, or skullcap, constantly, even while sleeping. Attending a secular college is frowned on. Instead, the men undertake a lifetime of study of the Torah and the accompanying rabbinical literature of the Talmud. Women's education consists of instruction on how to run the home in keeping with Orthodox tradition (M. Abrahamson 1996).

Orthodox children attend special schools in order to meet minimal New York State educational requirements. The devotion to religious study is reflected in this comment by a Hasidic Jew: "Look at Freud, Marx, Einstein—all Jews who made their mark on the non-Jewish world. To me, however, they would have been much better off studying in a yeshivah [a Jewish school]. What a waste of three fine Talmudic minds" (H. Arden 1975:294). Although devoted to their religion, the Hasidim participate in local elections and politics and are employed in outside occupations. All such activities are influenced by their orthodoxy and a self-reliance rarely duplicated elsewhere in the United States.

The Reform Tradition ✓

Reform Jews, though deeply committed to the religious faith, have altered many of the rituals. Women and men sit together in Reform congregations, and both participate in the reading of the Torah at services. A few Reform congregations have even experimented with observing the Sabbath on Sunday. Circumcision for males is not mandatory. Civil divorce decrees are sufficient and recognized so that a divorce granted by a three-man rabbinical court is not required before remarriage. Reform Jews recognize the children of Jewish men and non-Jewish women as Jews with no need to convert. All these practices would be unacceptable to the Orthodox Jew.

Conservative Judaism is a compromise between the rigidity of the Orthodox and the extreme modification of the Reform. Because of the middle position, the national organization of Conservatives, the United Synagogue of America, strives to create its own identity and seeks to view its traditions as an appropriate, authentic approach to the faith.   *Conservative*

Table 14.2 displays some results of a national survey on Jewish identification. The three sects here include both members and nonmembers of local congregations. Reform Jews are the least likely of the three religious groups to participate in religious events, to be involved in the Jewish community, or to participate in predominantly   *Reform*

A rabbi blesses a 13-year-old at her Bat Mitzvah in the temple.

TABLE 14.2
Jewish Identification by Group

Indices	Orthodox	Conservative	Reform	"Just Jewish"
Ethnic pride	86%	79%	73%	65%
Closeness to Jews	90	83	71	54
Observance of Jewish holidays	73	42	28	18
Observance of Christian holidays	6	6	17	28
Pro-Israel	78	71	56	50

Source: S. Cohen 1991:58, 63, 74.

Jewish organizations. Yet in Reform temples, there has been an effort to observe religious occasions such as Rosh Hashanah (*Religion Watch* 1995; Wertheimer 1996).

The one exception in Reform Jews' lower levels of participation is on issues concerning world Jewry, such as Israel or the treatment of Jews in such nations as the former Soviet Union and Iran. For the Orthodox Jew, these issues are less important than those strictly related to the observance of the faith. Although no nationwide organized movement advocates this, in recent years Reform Jews seem to have reclaimed traditions they once rejected.

Unlike people of other faiths in the United States, Jews historically have not embarked on recruitment or evangelistic programs to attract new members. Beginning in the late 1970s, Jews, especially Reform Jews, debated the possibility of outreach programs. Least objectionable to Jewish congregations were efforts begun in 1978 aimed at non-Jewish partners and children in mixed marriages. In 1981, the program was broadened to invite conversions by Americans who had no religious connection, but these modest recruitment drives are still far from resembling those that have been carried out by Protestant denominations for decades (K. Briggs 1978; *New York Times* 1982).

Like Protestant denominations, Jewish denominations are associated with class, nationality, and other social differences. The Reform Jews are the wealthiest and have the best formal education of the group, the Orthodox are the poorest and least educated in years of formal secular schooling, and the Conservatives occupy a position between the two. A fourth branch of American Judaism, Reconstructionism, an offshoot of the Conservative movement, has only recently developed an autonomous institutional structure with ritual practices similar to those of Reform Jews. Religious identification is associated with generation: immigrants and older Jews are more likely to be Orthodox, and their grandchildren are more likely to be Reform (*Los Angeles Times* Poll 1998).

✓ Jewish Identity

Ethnic and racial identification can be positive or negative. Awareness of ethnic identity can contribute to a person's self-esteem and give that person a sense of group solidarity with similar people. When a person experiences an identity only as a basis for discrimination or insults, he or she may want to shed that identity in favor of one more acceptable to society. Unfavorable differential treatment can also encourage closer ties between members of the community being discriminated against, as it has for Jews.

Most would judge the diminishing of out-group hostility and the ability of Jews to leave the ghetto as a positive development (G. Friedman 1967). However, the improvement in Jewish-Gentile relations also creates a new problem in Jewish social

Young people gather at a Jewish school in Manhattan.

identity. It has become possible for Jews to shed their "Jewishness," or **Yiddishkait**. Many retain their *Yiddishkait* even in suburbia, but it is more difficult there than in the ghetto. In the end, however, Jews cannot lose their identity entirely. Jews are still denied total assimilation in the United States no matter how much the individual ceases to think of himself or herself as Jewish. Social clubs may still refuse membership, and prospective non-Jewish in-laws may try to interfere with plans to marry.

Events in the world also remind the most assimilated Jew of the heritage left behind. A few such reminders in the past generation include Nazi Germany, the founding of Israel in 1948, the Six-Day War of 1967, Soviet interference with Jewish life and migration, the terrorist attack at the 1972 Munich Olympics, the Yom Kippur War of 1973, the 1973 oil embargo, the UN's 1974 anti-Zionism vote, and the Scud missile attacks during the 1991 Gulf War.

A unique identity issue presents itself to Jewish women, whose religious tradition has placed them in a subordinate position. For example, it was not until 1972 that the first female rabbi was ordained. Jewish feminism has its roots in the women's movement of the 1960s and 1970s, several of whose leaders were Jewish. There have been some changes in **halakha** (Jewish law covering obligations and duties), but it is still difficult for a woman to get a divorce recognized by the Orthodox Jewish tradition. Sima Rabinowicz of upstate New York has been hailed as the Jewish Rosa Parks for her recent bus battle. Rabinowicz refused to give up her seat in the women's section of a Hasidic-owned, publicly subsidized bus to Orthodox men who wanted to pray in private, segregated from women as required by *halakha*. The courts defended her right to ride as she wished, just as an earlier court had ruled with Rosa Parks in the Birmingham bus boycott. Jewish women contend that they should not be forced to make a choice between their identity as a woman and as a Jew (Baum 1998; Frankel 1995).

We will now examine three factors that influence the ethnic identity of Jews in the United States: family, religion, and cultural heritage.

Role of the Family

In general, the family works to socialize children, but for religious Jews it also fulfills a religious commandment. In the past, this compulsion was so strong that the *shadchan* (the marriage broker or matchmaker) fulfilled an important function in the Jewish community by ensuring marriage for all eligible people. The emergence of romantic love in modern society made the *shadchan* less acceptable to young Jews, but recent statistics show Jews more likely to marry than any other group.

Yiddishkait
Jewishness.

halakha
Jewish laws covering obligations and duties.

Jews have traditionally remained in extended families, intensifying the transmission of Jewish identity. Numerous observers have argued that the Jewish family today no longer maintains its role in identity transmission and that the family is consequently contributing to assimilation. The American Jewish Committee released a report in 1976 identifying 10 problems that are endangering "the family as the main transmission agent of Jewish values, identity, and continuity" (Conver 1976:A2). The following issues are still relevant to Jews nearly two decades later:

- More Jews marry later than members of other groups.
- Most organizations of single Jews no longer operate solely for the purpose of matching. These groups are now supportive of singles and the single way of life.
- The divorce rate is rising; there is no presumption of the permanence of marriage and no stigma attached to its failure.
- The birthrate is falling, and childlessness has become socially acceptable.
- Financial success has taken precedence over child raising in importance and for many has become the major goal of the family.
- The intensity of family interaction has decreased, although it continues to be higher than in most other religious and ethnic groups.
- There is less socializing across generation lines, partly as a result of geographic mobility.
- The sense of responsibility of family members to other family members has declined.
- The role of Jewishness is no longer central to the lives of Jews.
- Intermarriage has lessened the involvement of the Jewish partner in Jewish life and the emphasis on Jewish aspects of family life.

Data and sample surveys have verified these trends. Nevertheless, to use a term introduced in Chapter 10 in connection with the Latino family, Jewish Americans still have a higher than typical degree of familism. Jews are more likely than other ethnic or religious groups to be members of a household that interacts regularly with kinfolk. Nonetheless, the trend is away from familism, a trend that could further erode Jewish identity.

Without question, of the 10 problems cited by the American Jewish Committee, intermarriage has received the greatest attention from Jewish leaders. Therefore, it has been the subject of significant social research and not just idle speculation. This topic is the subject of our "Research Focus."

Several trends come together to lead to a stabilization or decline in the number of active Jews in the United States. As shown in Figure 14.5, the continuation of a Jewish tradition varies dramatically by denomination. Conservative and Orthodox Jews have larger families, encourage formal Jewish instruction, and are much less likely to witness intermarriage than Reform or unaffiliated ("just Jewish") Jewish Americans. Analysts of these data are concerned that Jews, especially if they are not Orthodox, cannot take it for granted that they will have grandchildren with whom to share Seders, Sabbath, and other Jewish moments.

Role of Religion

Devotion to Judaism appears to be the clear way to preserve ethnic identity. Yet Jews are divided about how to practice their faith. Many of the Orthodox see Reform Jews as little better than nonbelievers. Even among the Orthodox, some sects such as the Lubavitchers try to awaken less-observant Orthodox Jews to their spiritual obligation. Added to these developments is the continuing rise in Jewish out-marriages previously noted. Many Jewish religious rituals are centered in the home rather than in the syna-

Focus Research Focus Research Focus

INTERMARRIAGE: THE FINAL STEP TO ASSIMILATION?

"Sex and the City's" Charlotte York, the quintessential WASP character, descends again into a Jewish ritual bath marking her conversion to Judaism. While this fictional portrayal was welcomed by Jewish viewers, is it representative of what happens when Jews take a spouse today?

Since Christianity's influence has grown in Europe and North America, a persistent fear among Jews had been that their children or grandchildren would grow up ignorant of the Torah. Equally bad, a descendant might become *apikoros*, an unbeliever who engages in intellectual speculation about the relevance of Judaism. These concerns are growing as Jewish Americans' resistance to intermarriage declines.

Why does intermarriage emerge as a social issue rather than a personal dilemma? Intermarriage makes a decrease in the size of the Jewish community in the United States more likely. In marriages that occurred in the 1970s, more than 70 percent of Jews mar-

ried Jews or people who converted to Judaism. In marriages since 1996, that proportion has dropped to 53 percent. This trend means that American Jews today are just as likely to marry a Gentile as a Jew. Two-thirds of the children of these Jewish-Gentile marriages are not raised as Jews.

Many Jewish Americans respond that intermarriage is inevitable and the Jewish community must build on whatever links the intermarried couple may still have with a Jewish ethnic culture. There are many programs throughout the United States to help Gentile spouses of Jews feel welcome so that the faith will not lose them both. Yet other Jews feel that such efforts may be sending a dangerous signal that intermarriage is inevitable. Therefore, it is not surprising to see that probably more than any other ethnic or religious group, organizations within the Jewish community commission research on the trends in intermarriage. ■

Source: Freedman 2003; United Jewish Communities 2003.

gogue, from lighting Sabbath candles to observing dietary laws. Therefore, Jews are far more likely to feel that children cannot be brought up in the faith without that family support.

The religious question facing Jews is not so much one of ideology as of observing the commandments of traditional Jewish law. The religious variations among the nearly 6 million Jewish Americans are a product of attempts to accommodate traditional rituals and precepts to life in the dominant society. It is in adhering to such rituals that Jews are most likely to be at odds with the Christian theme advanced in public schools, even if it appears only in holiday parties. In Chapter 1, we introduced the term **marginality** to describe the status of living in two distinct cultures simultaneously. Jews who give some credence to the secular aspects of Christmas celebrations exemplify individuals' accommodating themselves to two cultures. For all but the most Orthodox, this acceptance means disobeying commandments or even accepting non-Jewish traditions by singing Christmas carols or exchanging greeting cards.

Is there a widespread pattern among Jewish Americans of reviving the old ways? Some Jews, especially those secure in their position, have taken up renewed orthodoxy.

marginality
The status of being between two cultures at the same time, such as the status of Jewish immigrants in the United States.

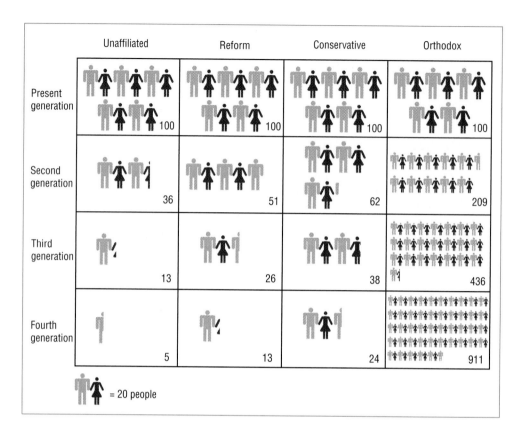

FIGURE 14.5 Generational Patterns by Denomination

Source: Gordon and Horowitz 1997. Based on the 1990 National Population Survey and the 1991 NY Jewish Population Study.

It is difficult to say whether the sporadic rise of traditionalism among Jews is a significant force or a fringe movement. Novelist Tom Ross at age 67 retook his birth name, Tom Rosenberg. Shortly after coming to the United States, his parents voluntarily Anglicized their name. Now Tom wanted to take another step in reclaiming his roots. Still, at the beginning of the 21st century, Jewish leaders in North America and Europe are much more likely to express concern about the increase in the number of secularized Jews than to find reasons to applaud an increase in *Yiddishkait* (Rosenberg 2000).

Role of Cultural Heritage

For many Jews, religious observance is a very small aspect of their Jewishness. They express their identity instead in a variety of political, cultural, and social activities. For them, acts of worship, fasting, eating permitted foods, and the study of the Torah and the Talmud are irrelevant to being Jewish. Of course, religious Jews find such a position impossible to accept (Liebman 1973).

Many Gentiles mistakenly suppose that a measure of Jewishness is the ability to speak Yiddish. Few people have spoken as many languages as the Jews through their long history. Yiddish is only one, and it developed in Jewish communities in eastern Europe between the 10th and 12th centuries. Fluency in Yiddish in the United States has been associated with the immigrant generation and the Orthodox. Sidney Goldstein and Calvin Goldscheider (1968) reported that evidence overwhelmingly supports the conclusion that linguistic assimilation among Jews is almost complete by the third generation. However, the 1960s and 1970s brought a slight increase in the use of Hebrew. This change probably resulted from increased pride in Israel and a greater interaction between that nation and the United States.

Hillel Houses, such as this one at the University of Southern California, are both social and spiritual gathering places for Jewish students on college campuses.

Overall, the differences between Jews and Gentiles have declined in the United States. To a large extent, this reduction is a product of generational changes typical of all ethnic groups. The first-generation Mexican American in Los Angeles contrasts sharply with the middle-class White living in suburban Boston. The convergence in culture and identity is much greater between the fourth-generation Mexican American and his or her White counterpart. A similar convergence is occurring among Jews. This change does not signal the eventual demise of the Jewish identity. Moreover, Jewish identity is not a single identity, as we can see from the heterogeneity in religious observance, dedication to Jewish and Israeli causes, and participation in Jewish organizations.

Being Jewish comes from the family, the faith, and the culture, but it does not require any one criterion. Jewishness transcends nation, religion, or culture. A sense of peoplehood is present that neither anti-Semitic bigotry nor even an ideal state of fellowship among all religions would destroy. American life may have drastically modified Jewish life in the direction of dominant society values, but it has not eliminated it. Milton Gordon (1964) refers to **peoplehood** as a group with a shared feeling. For Jews, this sense of identity originates from a variety of sources, past and present, both within and without (Goldscheider 2003).

Conclusion

Jewish Americans are the product of three waves of immigration originating from three different Jewish communities: the Sephardic, the western European, and the eastern European. They brought different languages and, to some extent, different levels of religious orthodoxy. Today, they have assimilated to form an ethnic group that transcends the initial differences in nationality.

Jews are not a homogeneous group. Among them are the Reform, the Conservative, and Orthodox denominations, listed in ascending order of adherence to traditional rituals. Non-religious Jews make up another group, probably as large as any one segment, and still see themselves as Jewish.

Jewish identity is reaffirmed from within and outside the Jewish community; however, both sources of affirmation are weaker today. Identity is strengthened by the family, religion, and the vast network of national and community-based organizations. Anti-Semitism

peoplehood
Milton Gordon's term for a group with a shared feeling.

outside the Jewish community strengthens the in-group feeling and the perception that survival as a people is threatened.

Today, American Jews face a new challenge: They must maintain their identity in an overwhelmingly Christian society in which discrimination is fading and outbreaks of prejudice are sporadic. *Yiddishkait* may not so much have decreased as changed. Elements of the Jewish tradition have been shed in part because of modernization and social change. Some of this social change—a decline in anti-Semitic violence and restrictions—is certainly welcome. Although *kashrut* observance has declined, most Jews care deeply about Israel, and many engage in pro-Israel activities. Commitment has changed with the times, but it has not disappeared (S. Cohen 1988).

Some members of the Jewish community view the apparent assimilation with alarm and warn against the grave likelihood of the total disappearance of a sizable and identifiable Jewish community in the United States. Others see the changes not as erosion but as an accommodation to a pluralistic, multicultural environment. We are witness to a progressive change in the substance and style of Jewish life. According to this view, Jewish identity, the Orthodox and Conservative traditions

notwithstanding, has shed some of its traditional characteristics and has acquired others. The strength of this view comes with the knowledge that doomsayers have been present in the American Jewish community for at least two generations. Only the passage of time will reveal the future of Jewish life in the United States (Finestein 1988; Glazer 1990).

Despite their successes, Jews experience discrimination and prejudice, as does any subordinate group. Michael Lerner (1993:33), editor of the liberal Jewish journal *Tikkun*, declares that "Jews can only be deemed 'white' if there is massive amnesia on the part of non-Jews about the monumental history of anti-Semitism." As we noted earlier, reported episodes of anti-Semitism are on the increase in Europe and North America, even on the college campuses in the United States.

Although discrimination against Jews has gone on for centuries, far more ancient than anti-Semitism and the experience of the Diaspora is the subordinate role of women. Women were perhaps the first to be relegated to an inferior role and may be the last to work collectively to struggle for equal rights. Studying women as a subordinate group will reaffirm the themes in our study of racial and ethnic groups.

Key Terms

anti-Semitism   356
Diaspora   367
fringe-of-values theory   361
halakha   375
Holocaust   363

Holocaust revisionists   363
in-group virtues   362
Judaization   358
kashrut   372
marginality   377

out-group vices   362
peoplehood   379
Yiddishkait   375
Zionism   367

Review Questions

1. Why are the Jewish people most accurately characterized as an ethnic group?
2. How have the patterns of anti-Semitism changed or remained the same?
3. Why do African American–Jewish American relationships receive special scrutiny?
4. Why is maintaining Jewish identity so difficult in the United States?
5. Why does the family play such a critical role in Jewish identity?

Critical Thinking

1. Most minority groups regard acceptance as a positive outcome. Why do some Jewish Americans seem threatened by being accepted in contemporary Gentile society?

2. Using the Jewish experience as a basis for comparison, how has fusion functioned or not functioned for any other subordinate group when compared with Jews in the United States?

3. In Chapter 5, we presented Marcus Hansen's principle of third-generation interest. How does that apply or not apply to the generational differences displayed by denomination in Figure 14.5?

4. How different and similar have the experiences of women in organized religion been, compared with those of women in the Jewish faith?

Internet Connections—Research Navigator™

Follow the instructions found on page 31 of this text to access the features of Research Navigator™. Once at the Web site, enter your Login Name and Password. Then, to use the ContentSelect database, enter keywords such as "anti-Semitism," "bar mitzvah," "genocide," and "Holocaust," and the research engine will supply relevant and recent scholarly and popular press publications. Use the *New York Times* Search-by-Subject Archive to find recent news articles related to sociology and the Link Library feature to locate relevant Web links organized by the key terms associated with this chapter.

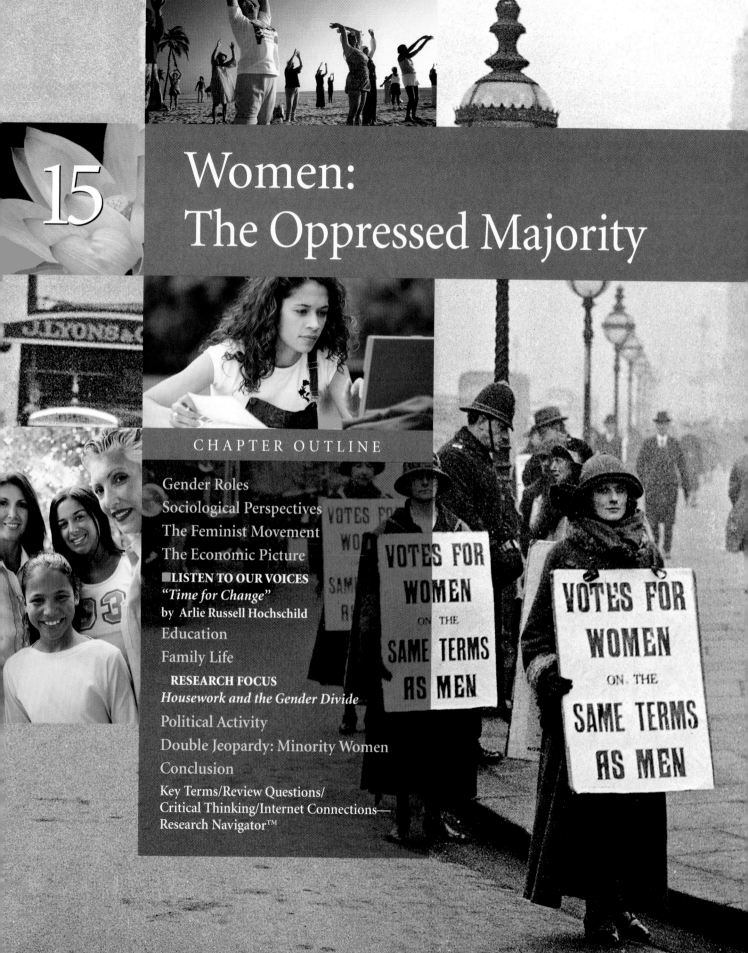

15

Women:
The Oppressed Majority

CHAPTER OUTLINE

S UBORDINATE STATUS MEANS CONFINEMENT TO SUBORDINATE roles not justified by a person's abilities. Society is increasingly aware that women are a subordinate group. There are biological differences between males and females; however, one must separate differences of gender from those produced by sexism, distinctions that result from social-ization. The feminist movement did not begin with the women's movement of the 1960s but has a long history and, like protest efforts by other subordinate groups, has not been warmly received by society. A comparison of the socioe-conomic position of men and women leaves little doubt that they have unequal opportunities in employment and political power. While men are taking on greater responsibilities with child care and housework, these are still dispropor-tionately the responsibilities of women. Minority women occupy an espe-cially difficult position in that they experience subordinate sta-tus by virtue of their race or eth-nicity as well as their gender.

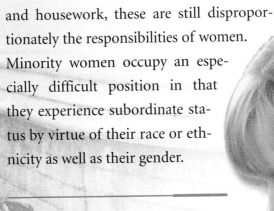

Women are an oppressed group even though they form the numerical majority. They are a social minority in the United States and throughout Western society. Men dominate in influence, prestige, and wealth. Women do occupy positions of power, but those who do are the exceptions, as evidenced by newspaper accounts that declare, "She is the first woman" or "the only woman" to be in a particular position.

CD-ROM *Activity 10.1*

Many people, men and women, find it difficult to conceptualize women as a subordinate group. After all, not all women live in ghettos. They no longer have to attend inferior schools. They freely interact and live with their alleged oppressors, men. How, then, are they a subordinate group? Let us reexamine the five properties of a subordinate or minority group introduced in Chapter 1:

1. Women do experience unequal treatment. Although they are not segregated by residence, they are victims of prejudice and discrimination.

2. Women have physical and cultural characteristics that distinguish them from the dominant group (men).

3. Membership in the subordinate group is involuntary.

4. Through the rise of contemporary feminism, women have become increasingly aware of their subordinate status and have developed a greater sense of group solidarity.

5. Women are not forced to marry, yet many women feel that their subordinate status is most irrevocably defined within marriage.

In this chapter, the similarities between women and racial and ethnic groups will become apparent.

The most common analogy about minorities used in the social sciences is the similarity between the status of African Americans and that of women. Blacks are considered a minority group, but, one asks, how can women of all groups be so similar in condition? We recognize some similarities in recent history; for example, an entire generation has observed and participated in both the civil rights movement and the women's movement. A background of suffrage campaigns, demonstrations, sit-ins, lengthy court battles, and self-help groups is common to the movements for equal rights for both women and African Americans. But similarities were recognized long before the recent protests against inequality. In *An American Dilemma* (1944), the famous study of race described in Chapter 1, Gunnar Myrdal observed that a parallel to the Blacks' role in society was found among women. Others, such as Helen Mayer Hacker (1951, 1974), later elaborated on the similarities.

What do these groups have in common besides recent protest movements? The negative stereotypes directed at the two groups are quite similar: Both groups have been considered emotional, irresponsible, weak, or inferior. Both are thought to fight subtly against the system: Women allegedly try to outwit men by feminine wiles, as historically Blacks allegedly outwitted Whites by pretending to be deferential or respectful. To these stereotypes must be added another similarity: Neither women nor African Americans are accepting a subordinate role in society any longer.

Nearly all Whites give lip service, even if they do not wholeheartedly believe it, to the contention that African Americans are innately equal to Whites. They are inherently the same. But men and women are not the same, and they vary most dramatically in their roles in reproduction. Biological differences have contributed to sexism. **Sexism** is the ideology that one sex is superior to the other. Quite different is the view that there are few differences between the sexes. Such an idea is expressed in the concept of **androgyny**. An androgynous model of behavior permits people to see that humans can be both aggressive and expressive, depending on the requirements of the situation. People do not have to be locked into the behavior that accompanies the labels *masculine* and *feminine*. In the United States, people disagree widely as to what implications, if any, the biological differences between the sexes have for social roles. We will begin our discussion of women as a subordinate group with this topic.

Gender Roles

A college man, done with afternoon classes, heads off to get a pedicure and, while the nail polish is drying, sits on a nearby park bench finishing some needlepoint he started. Meanwhile, a college woman walks through the park chewing tobacco and spitting along the path. What is wrong with this picture? We are witnessing the open violation of how men and women are expected to act. So unlikely are these episodes that I have taken them from sociology teachers who specifically ask their students to go out, violate gender expectations, and record how they feel and how people react to their behavior (Nielsen et al. 2000:287).

Gender roles are society's expectations of the proper behavior, attitudes, and activities of males and females. Toughness has traditionally been seen in the United States as masculine, desirable only in men, whereas tenderness has been viewed as feminine. A society may require that one sex or the other take the primary responsibility for the socialization of the children, economic support of the family, or religious leadership.

Without question, socialization has a powerful impact on the development of females and males in the United States. Indeed, the gender roles first encountered in early childhood often are a factor in defining a child's popularity. Sociologists Patricia Adler and her colleagues (1992, 1998) observed elementary school children and found that boys typically achieved high status on the basis of their athletic ability, coolness, toughness, social skills, and success in relationships with girls. By contrast, girls gained popularity based on their parents' economic background and their own physical appearance, social skills, and academic success.

sexism
The ideology that one sex is superior to the other.

androgyny
The state of being both masculine and feminine, aggressive and gentle.

gender roles
Expectations regarding the proper behavior, attitudes, and activities of males and females.

Women's roles have changed significantly since the early 1960s, when they were generally depicted in the media solely as wives and mothers, as shown in the popular television series of that time, *Leave It to Beaver.*

It may be obvious that males and females are conditioned to assume certain roles, but the origin of gender roles as we know them is less clear. Many studies have been done on laboratory animals, such as injecting monkeys and rats with male and female hormones. Primates in their natural surroundings have been closely observed for the presence and nature of gender roles. Animal studies do not point to instinctual gender differences similar to what humans are familiar with as masculinity and femininity. Historically, women's work came to be defined as a consequence of the birth process. Men, free of child-care responsibilities, generally became the hunters and foragers for food. Even though women must bear children, men could have cared for the young. Exactly why women were assigned that role in societies is not known.

Women's role varies across different cultures. Furthermore, we know that acceptable behavior for men and women changes over time in a society. For example, the men in the royal courts of Europe in the late 1700s fulfilled present-day stereotypes of feminine appearance in their display of ornamental dress and personal vanity rather than resembling the men of a century later, although they still engaged in duels and other forms of aggression. The social roles of the sexes have no constants in time or space (Doyle and Paludi 1998).

Sociological Perspectives

Sociologist Estelle Disch (1997) points out that gender differences are maintained in our culture through the systematic socialization of babies and infants, children, adolescents, and adults. Even though different subcultures and even different families vary in childrearing, we teach our children to be boys and girls, even though men and women are more alike than they are different. But she noted that gender socialization is not something that stops with youth. "From the time we are born until we die, gender socialization is a constant part of our lives" (p. 74). Gender training persists, and the larger institutional structures reinforce it.

We are bombarded with expectations for behavior as men and women from many sources simultaneously. Many individual women hold positions involving high levels of responsibility and competence but may not be accorded the same respect as men. Similarly, individual men find the time to get involved with their children's lives only to meet with disbelief and occasional surprise from health care and educational systems accustomed to dealing only with mothers. Even when individuals are motivated to stretch the social boundaries of gender, social structure and institutions often impede them. Gender differentiation in our culture is embedded in social institutions: the family, of course, but also education, religion, politics, the economy, medicine, and the mass media.

Through this lifelong socialization, people are labeled by virtue of their sex. Certain activities and behaviors are associated with men and others with women. Besides the labeling perspective, we can also use functionalist and conflict perspectives to grasp more firmly how gender roles develop.

Functionalists maintain that sex differentiation has contributed to overall social stability. Sociologists Talcott Parsons and Robert Bales (1955) argued that, to function most efficiently, the family needs adults who will specialize in particular roles. They believed that the arrangement of gender roles with which they were familiar had arisen because marital partners needed a division of labor.

The functionalist view is initially persuasive in explaining the way in which women and men are typically brought up in U.S. society. However, it would lead us to expect even girls and women with no interest in children to still become babysitters and mothers. Similarly, males with a caring feeling for children may be "programmed" into careers in the business world. Clearly, such a differentiation between the sexes can have harmful consequences for the person who does not fit into specific roles, while depriving society of the optimal use of many talented people who are confined by sexual labeling. Consequently, the conflict perspective is increasingly convincing in its analysis of the development of gender roles.

Conflict theorists do not deny the presence of a differentiation by sex. In fact, they contend that the relationship between females and males has been one of unequal power, with men being dominant over women. Men may have become powerful in preindustrial times because their size, physical strength, and freedom from childbearing duties allowed them to dominate women physically. In contemporary societies, such considerations are not as important, yet cultural beliefs about the sexes are now long established.

Both functionalists and conflict theorists acknowledge that it is not possible to change gender roles drastically without dramatic revisions in a culture's social structure. Functionalists see potential social disorder, or at least unknown social consequences, if all aspects of traditional sex differentiation are disturbed. Yet for conflict theorists, no social structure is ultimately desirable if it has to be maintained through the oppression of its citizens.

The Feminist Movement

Women's struggle for equality, like the struggles of other subordinate groups, has been long and multifaceted. From the very beginning, women activists and sympathetic men who spoke of equal rights were ridiculed and scorned.

In a formal sense, the American feminist movement was born in upstate New York in a town called Seneca Falls in the summer of 1848. On July 19, the first women's rights convention began, attended by Elizabeth Cady Stanton, Lucretia Mott, and other pioneers in the struggle for women's rights. This first wave of feminists, as they are currently known, battled ridicule and scorn as they fought for legal and political equality for women, but they were not afraid to risk controversy on behalf of their cause. In 1872, for example, Susan B. Anthony was arrested for attempting to vote in that year's presidential election.

Suffragists struggled for many years to convince Congress and the states to pass the Nineteenth Amendment to the Constitution, extending to women the right to vote, beginning in 1920.

All social movements—and feminism is no exception—have been marked by factionalism and personality conflicts. The civil rights movement and pan-Indianism have been hurt repeatedly by conflicts over what tactics to use and which reforms to push for first, as well as personality conflicts. Despite similar divisiveness, the women's movement struggled on toward its major goal: to gain the right to vote.

The Suffrage Movement

The **suffragists** worked for years to get women the right to vote. From the beginning, this reform was judged to be crucial. If women voted, it was felt, other reforms would quickly follow. The struggle took so long that many of the initial advocates of women's suffrage died before victory was reached. In 1879, an amendment to the Constitution was introduced that would have given women the right to vote. Not until 1919 was it finally passed, and not until the next year was it ratified as the Nineteenth Amendment to the Constitution.

The opposition to giving women the vote came from all directions. Liquor interests and brewers correctly feared that women would assist in passing laws restricting or prohibiting the sale of their products. The South feared the influence that more Black voters (i.e., Black women) might have. Southerners had also not forgotten the pivotal role women had played in the abolitionist movement. Despite the opposition, the suffrage movement succeeded in gaining women the right to vote, a truly remarkable achievement because it had to rely on male legislators to do so.

The Nineteenth Amendment did not automatically lead to other feminist reforms. Women did not vote as a bloc and have not been elected to office in proportion to their numbers. The single-minded goal of suffrage was harmful to the cause of feminism in many respects. Many suffragists thought that any changes more drastic than granting the vote would destroy the home. They rarely questioned the subordinate role assigned to women. For the most part, agitation for equal rights ended when suffrage was gained. In the 1920s and 1930s, large numbers of college-educated women entered professions, but these individual achievements did little to enhance the rights of women as a group. The feminist movement as an organized effort that gained national attention faded, to regain prominence only in the 1960s (Freeman 1975; O'Neill 1969; Rossi 1964).

Nevertheless, the women's movement did not die out completely in the first half of the century. Many women carried on the struggle in new areas. Margaret Sanger fought for legalized birth control. She opened birth control clinics because the medical profession refused to distribute birth control information. Sanger and Katherine Houghton Hepburn (mother of actress Katharine Hepburn) lobbied Congress for reform throughout the 1920s and 1930s. The police closed Sanger's early clinics. Not until 1937 were nationwide restrictions on birth control devices lifted, and some state bans remained in force until 1965.

The Women's Liberation Movement

Ideologically, the women's movement of the 1960s had its roots in the continuing informal feminist movement that began with the first subordination of women in Western society. Psychologically, it grew in America's kitchens, as women felt unfulfilled and did not know why, and in the labor force, as women were made to feel guilty because they were not at home with families. Demographically, by the 1960s, women had attained greater control about when and whether to become pregnant if they used contraception and hence had greater control over the size of the population (Heer and Grossbard-Shectman 1981).

Sociologically, several events delayed progress in the mid-1960s. The civil rights movement and the antiwar movement were slow to embrace women's rights. The New

suffragists
Women and men who worked successfully to gain women the right to vote.

Left seemed as sexist as the rest of society in practice, despite its talk of equality. Groups protesting the draft and demonstrating on college campuses generally rejected women as leaders and assigned them traditional duties like preparing refreshments and publishing organization newsletters. The core of early feminists often knew each other from participating in other protest or reform groups that had initially been unwilling to accept women's rights as a legitimate goal. Beginning in about 1967, as Chapter 7 showed, the movement for Black equality was no longer as willing to accept help from sympathetic Whites. White men moved on to protest the draft, a cause not as crucial to women's lives. While somewhat involved in the antiwar movement, many White women began to struggle for their own rights, although at first they had to fight alone. Eventually, civil rights groups, the New Left, and most established women's groups endorsed the feminist movement with the zeal of new converts, but initially they resisted the concerns of feminists (Freeman 1973, 1983).

The movement has also brought about a reexamination of men's roles. Supporters of "male liberation" wanted to free men from the constraints of the masculine value system. The masculine mystique is as real as the feminine one. Boys are socialized to think that they should be invulnerable, fearless, decisive, and even emotionless in some situations. Men are expected to achieve physically and occupationally at some risk to their own values, not to mention those of others. Failure to take up these roles and attitudes can mean that a man will be considered less than a man. Male liberation is the logical counterpart of female liberation. If women are to redefine their gender role successfully, men must redefine theirs as workers, husbands, and fathers (Messner 1997; National Organization for Men Against Sexism 2003).

Amid the many changing concerns since the mid-1960s, the feminist movement too has undergone significant change. Betty Friedan, a founder of the National Organization for Women (NOW), argued in the early 1960s that women had to understand the **feminine mystique**, recognizing that society saw them only as their children's mother and their husband's wife. Later, in the 1980s, though not denying that women deserved to have the same options in life as men, she called for restructuring the "institution of home and wife." Friedan and others now recognize that many young women are frustrated when time does not permit them to do it all: career, marriage, and motherhood. Difficult issues remain, and feminists continue to discuss and debate concerns such as the limits businesses put on careers of women with children, domestic violence, and male bias in medical research (Ferree and Hess 1994; Friedan 1963, 1981, 1991; Somners 1994).

Where are women's rights at the close of the 20th century? In "Listen to Our Voices," sociologist Arlie Russell Hochschild sees the women's movement as a stalled revolution in which women may have more opportunities in the workplace but now are forced to do everything.

A sign of progress? Changing images of gender roles has meant the gradual emergence of the depiction of women, such as Laura Croft, as aggressive and violent characters in video games.

The Economic Picture

He works. She works. They are both physicians—a high status occupation with financial rewards. He makes $140,000. She makes $88,000. Those are the results of a detailed study of occupations by the U.S. Census Bureau in 2004. They looked at the earnings of 821 occupations ranging from chief executives to dishwashers, considering one's age, education, and work experience. The unmistakable conclusion was there is a substantial gap in median earnings between full-time male and female workers in the same occupation. He's an air traffic controller and makes $67,000. She earns $56,000. He's a housekeeper and makes $19,000. She earns $15,000. He's a teacher's assistant and makes $20,000. She earns $15,000.

 CD-ROM *Activity 10.5*

feminine mystique
Society's view of a woman as only her children's mother and her husband's wife.

Voices Listen to Our Voices *Listen to*

TIME FOR CHANGE

Nationwide, work absorbs more of a parent's time than it did 25 years ago. Women go back to work earlier after childbirth—in the 1960s, one in eight women returned to work less than a year after childbirth; in 1996, it was approximately one in two. Once back, more mothers now work full-time, year-round. Studies on hours vary, but one national study conducted by Families and Work Institute found that, of workers with children age 12 and under, only 4 percent of men and 13 percent of women worked less than 40 hours a week.

Arlie Russell Hochschild

This is part of a larger pattern I refer to as "stalled revolution." In the last 25 years, women have changed, but everything else has not changed as fast or as much. Thus, tens of millions of women go out to work in offices and plants that demand long hours and inflexible schedules, live in a world without widespread quality child care, and come home to mates who don't share the domestic load. The family has become the shock absorber for the strains between faster-changing women and slower-changing men and workplaces. This was already true for some families in the 1950s and 1960s, but now it's true for most. And we've come to think of the family under these strained conditions as the "normal" family. Then we wonder why young people are scared to death to become working parents and why our divorce rate is one of the world's highest.

Thoughtful public discussion about this state of affairs has been oddly silenced by two opposing parties, both of which divert our attention from the project of transforming the workplace. First, there are what I call the "accusatory traditionals," who have an eagle eye out for the problems of working mothers. If working mothers are tired, have troubled kids or tense marriages, the traditionals admonish women to junk their careers and stay home. Men, they don't touch.

Responding to these scolding traditionals are the "sunshine moderns," who get cornered into saying, "Two-, three-, and four-year-olds in nine- and ten-hour child care? Fine." "Middle-school children home alone after school? Let's call it 'self-care.'" The sunshiners' motto is "Don't bring me any bad news." Or at least no news that isn't strictly about the external world. Anything internal—like the idea that we can become complicit in the very cultural pressures that end up hurting us—is too dangerous, because if you admit such a thing, you're playing into the hands of the scolding traditionals and you're back to square one. . . .

Other societies—Sweden, Norway, Canada—have led the way. And a number of organizations, inspired by the women's movement, are fighting the good fight here. The Women's Legal Defense Fund, for example, is trying to expand the 1993 Family and Medical Leave Act to cover more working people and more family needs, such as minor illnesses. It is also trying to make these leaves paid for low-wage workers. We can begin to think about a broader movement pressing for a shorter work-week and work-sharing as an alternative to layoffs. And we need men to join us in taking pressure off kids and putting it on the workplace. These are all ways we can unstall the feminist revolution in the next 25 years. ■

Men do not always earn more. The Census Bureau found two occupations out of 821 in which women typically earn about 1 percent more—hazardous materials recovery workers and telecommunications line installers (D. Weinberg 2004).

Another aspect of women's subordinate status is that, more than any other group, they are confined to certain occupations. Some sex-typed jobs for women pay well above the minimum wage and carry moderate prestige, such as nursing and teaching. Nevertheless, they are far lower in pay and prestige than such stereotyped male positions as physician, college president, or university professor. When they do enter nontraditional positions, as we have seen, women as a group receive lower wages or salary.

The data in Table 15.1 present an overall view of the male dominance of high-paying occupations. Among the representative occupations chosen, men unquestionably dominate in those that pay well. Women dominate as secretaries, seamstresses, health care workers, and domestic workers. Trends show the proportions of women increasing slightly in the professions, indicating that some women have advanced into better-paying positions, but these gains have not significantly changed the overall picture.

How pervasive is segregation by gender in the workforce? To what degree are women and men concentrated in different occupations? Bureau of Labor Statistics researchers have compiled a segregation index to estimate the percentage of women who would have to change their jobs to make the distribution of men and women in each occupation mirror the relative percentage of each sex in the adult working population. This study showed that 54 percent of women and men workers would need to switch jobs to create a labor force without sex segregation. There has been a steady decline in such segregation, but the decrease was not as great in the 1990s as in earlier decades (Wooton 1997).

Although occupational segregation by gender continues, women have increased their participation in the labor force. A greater proportion of women seek and obtain paid employment than ever before in U.S. history. In 1870, less than 15 percent of all workers were women, compared with 46 percent in 2002. The most dramatic rise in

TABLE 15.1
Women as a Percentage of All Workers in Selected Occupations, 1950, 1980, and 2002

Occupation	1950	1980	2002
PROFESSIONAL WORKERS			
Accountants	14.9%	36.2%	59.4%
Engineers	1.2	4.0	10.8
Lawyers and Judges	4.1	12.8	29.3
Physicians	6.5	12.9	30.6
Registered nurses	97.8	96.5	92.9
College professors	22.8	33.9	42.7
School teachers	74.5	70.8	75.0
OTHER OCCUPATIONS			
Carpenters	0.4	1.5	1.8
Protective services (firefighters, police, guards)	2.0	9.5	19.9
Sales clerks, retail	48.9	71.1	62.7
Cashiers	81.7	86.6	76.7
Bookkeepers	77.7	90.5	92.7
Food service	61.6	66.9	55.8
Private household	94.9	97.5	99.7

Sources: Bureau of the Census 1981, 2003a: 399–401; Department of Labor 1980.

the female workforce has been among married women and mothers. Among new mothers, 56 percent return to the labor force within a year of giving birth. As recently as 1975, only 29 percent went back to work (Bureau of the Census 1975:129, 133; 2003a: 387, 390, 391).

It is logical to assume that these percentages would be even higher if day care in the United States received more support. A number of European nations, including France, the Netherlands, Sweden, and the former Soviet Union, provide preschool care at minimal or no cost, although such benefits are underwritten through higher taxes. However, in the United States, these costs are borne entirely by the working parent. Recently, some employers have recognized the benefits of offering care and have begun to provide or subsidize this care, but they are the exception, not the rule (Schaefer 2005).

A primary goal of many feminists is to eliminate sex discrimination in the labor force and to equalize job opportunities for women. Without question, women earn less than men. As we noted earlier, in Table 3.1 and Figure 3.2, women earn less than men even when race and education are held constant; that is, college-educated women working full time make less than comparably educated men. Even when additional controls are introduced, such as previous work experience, a substantial earnings gap remains. A detailed analysis of the wage gap, considering schooling, employment history, time with the current employer, and medical leaves of absence, found that all these factors can explain less than 42 percent of the wage differences between men and women (Wellington 1994; also see Tomaskovic-Devey 1993).

Sources of Discrimination

If we return to the definition of *discrimination* cited earlier, are not men better able to perform some tasks than women, and vice versa? If ability means performance, there certainly are differences. The typical woman can sew better than the typical man, but the latter can toss a ball farther than the former. These are group differences. Certain-

Many occupations such as engineering have relatively few women. Engineer Joyce Engebretsen is speaking in 2001 to a group of structural engineers on how to construct buildings to resist an attack from a car bomb.

ly many women outthrow many men, and many men outsew many women, but society expects women to excel at sewing and men to excel at throwing. The differences in those abilities result from cultural conditioning. Women usually are taught to sew, and men are less likely to learn such a skill. Men are encouraged to participate in sports requiring the ability to throw a ball much more than are women. True, as a group, males have greater potential for the muscular development needed to throw a ball, but U.S. society encourages men to realize their potential in this area more than it encourages women to pursue athletic skills.

Today's labor market involves much more than throwing a ball and using a needle and thread, but the analogy to these two skills is repeated time and again. Such examples are used to support sexist practices in all aspects of the workplace. Just as African Americans can suffer from both individual acts of racism and institutional discrimination, women are vulnerable to both sexism and institutional discrimination. Women are subject to direct sexism such as sexist remarks and also to differential treatment because of institutional policies.

Removing barriers to equal opportunity would eventually eliminate institutional discrimination. Theoretically, men and women would sew and throw a ball equally well. We say "theoretically" because cultural conditioning would take generations to change. In some formerly male jobs, such as gas station clerk and attendant, society seems quite willing to accept women. In other occupations, such as president, it will take longer; and many years may pass before full acceptance can be expected in other fields, such as professional contact sports.

Many efforts have been made to eliminate institutional discrimination as it applies to women. The 1964 Civil Rights Act and its enforcement arm, the Equal Employment Opportunity Commission, address cases of sex discrimination. As we saw in Chapter 3, the inclusion of sex bias along with prejudice based on race, color, creed, and national origin was an unexpected last-minute change in the provisions of the landmark 1964 act. Federal legislation has not removed all discrimination against women in employment. The same explanations presented in Chapter 3 for the lag between the laws and reality in race discrimination apply to sex discrimination: lack of money, weak enforcement powers, occasionally weak commitment to using the laws available, and, most important, institutional and structural forces that perpetuate inequality.

What should be done to close the gap between the earnings of women and men? As shown in Figure 15.1, women earn more annually with more formal schooling, just like their male counterparts. However, as women continue their education, the wage gap does not narrow and even shows signs of growing.

In the 1980s, pay equity, or comparable worth, was a controversial solution presented to alleviate the second-class status of working women. It directly attempted to secure equal pay when occupational segregation by gender was particularly pervasive. **Pay equity** calls for equal pay for different types of work that are judged to be comparable by measuring such factors as employee knowledge, skills, effort, responsibility, and working conditions.

This doctrine sounds straightforward, but it is not so simple to put into operation. How exactly does one determine the comparability of jobs to identify comparable worth? Should a zookeeper be paid more than a child-care worker? Does our society pay zookeepers more because we value caretaking for children less than caretaking for animals? Or do zookeepers earn more than child-care workers because the former tend to be male and the latter are generally female?

Despite some local initiatives, pay equity has not received much support in the United States except from the feminist movement. From a policy perspective, pay equity would have to broaden the 30-year-old Equal Pay Act and be initiated at the

pay equity
The same wages for different types of work that are judged to be comparable by such measures as employee knowledge, skills, effort, responsibility, and working conditions; also called comparable worth.

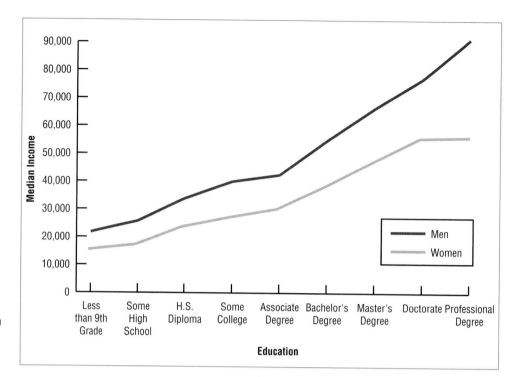

FIGURE 15.1 Financial Return on Education for Women and Men

Note: See Table 3.1.

Source: Bureau of the Census 2001g: Tables 76, 141.

federal level. Proposed legislation such as the Paycheck Fairness Act and the Fair Pay Act has failed to mobilize much support. With the government backing away from affirmative action, it is unlikely to launch an initiative on pay equity (Business and Professional Women 2002; Sorensen 1994).

What about women aspiring to crack the glass ceiling? The phrase **glass ceiling**, as noted in Chapter 3 and illustrated in Figure 3.3, refers to the invisible barrier blocking the promotion of a qualified worker because of gender or minority membership. Despite continuing debate over affirmative action, the consensus is that there is little room at the top for women and minorities. The glass ceiling operates so that all applicants may be welcomed by a firm, but when it comes to the powerful or more visible positions, there are limits—generally unstated—on the number of women and nonwhites welcomed or even tolerated (Table 15.2). Women are doing better in top-management positions than minorities, but they still lag well behind men, according to a study that showed that only 15 percent of the director seats of Fortune 1000's largest corporations were held by women. As for CEOs of the Fortune 500, there are so few—six as of 2003—that the corporations can be named: Avon, Golden West Financial, Hewlett-Packard, Lucent, Mirant, Xerox (D. Jones 2003; G. Strauss 2002).

Women are still viewed differently in the world of management. In making hiring decisions, executives may assume that women are not serious about their commitment to the job and will be "distracted" by family and home. They assume that women are on a **mommy track**, an unofficial career track that firms use for women who want to divide their attention between work and family. This assumption would be false if applied to all women. It also implies that corporate men are not interested in maintaining a balance between work and family. Even competitive, upwardly mobile women are not always taken seriously in the workplace (F. Schwartz 1989; Schwartz and Zimmerman 1992).

glass ceiling
The barrier that blocks the promotion of a qualified worker because of gender or minority membership.

mommy track
An unofficial corporate career track for women who want to divide their attention between work and family.

TABLE 15.2
Major Barriers to Women's Executive Advancement

- Initial placement and clustering in dead-end staff jobs or highly technical professional jobs
- Lack of mentoring
- Lack of management training
- Lack of opportunities for career development
- Lack of opportunities for training tailored to the individual
- Lack of rotation to line positions or job assignments that produce revenue
- Little or no access to critical developmental assignments, including service on highly visible task forces and committees
- Different standards for performance evaluation
- Biased rating and testing systems
- Little or no access to informal communication networks
- Counterproductive behavior and harassment by colleagues

Source: Glass Ceiling Commission, cited in Department of Labor 1995:7–8.

Sexual Harassment

Under evolving legal standards, **sexual harassment** is recognized as any unwanted and unwelcome sexual advances that interfere with a person's ability to perform a job and enjoy the benefits of a job. Increased national attention was given to harassment in the 1990s and into the present through allegations made against elected officials and high-ranking military officers.

The most obvious example of sexual harassment is the boss who tells an employee, "Put out or get out!" However, the unwelcome advances that constitute sexual harassment may take the form of subtle pressures regarding sexual activity, inappropriate touching, attempted kissing, or sexual assault. Indeed, in the computer age, there is growing concern that sexually harassing messages are being sent anonymously over computer networks through e-mail and picture phones.

In 1986, in a unanimous decision (*Meritor Savings Bank v. Vinson*), the Supreme Court declared that sexual harassment by a supervisor violates the federal law against sex discrimination in the workplace as outlined in the 1964 Civil Rights Act. If sufficiently severe, harassment is a violation even if the unwelcome sexual demands are not linked to concrete employment benefits such as a raise or promotion. Women's groups hailed the court's decisiveness in identifying harassment as a form of discrimination. A federal judge subsequently ruled that the public display of photographs of nude and partly nude women at a workplace constitutes sexual harassment. Despite these rulings, it is very difficult legally and emotionally for a person to bring forward a case of sexual harassment (Domino 1995).

Sexual harassment must be understood in the context of continuing prejudice and discrimination against women. Whether it occurs in the federal bureaucracy, the military, the corporate world, or universities, sexual harassment generally takes place where the hierarchy of authority finds White men at the top and in which women's work is valued less than men's. One survey of the private sector found that African American women were three times more likely than White women to experience sexual harassment. From a conflict perspective, it is not surprising that women, especially women of color, are most likely to become victims of sexual harassment. These groups typically are an organization's most vulnerable employees in terms of job security (J. Jones 1988).

sexual harassment
Any unwanted and unwelcome sexual advances that interfere with a person's ability to perform a job and enjoy the benefits of a job.

Feminization of Poverty

Since World War II, an increasing proportion of the poor in the United States have been female, many of them divorced or never-married mothers. This alarming trend has come to be known as the **feminization of poverty**. In 2003, 10.8 percent of all families in the United States lived in poverty, but 30 percent of families headed by single mothers did so (De-Navas-Walt et al. 2004:40).

CD-ROM *Activity 10.2*

Poor women share many social characteristics with poor men: low educational attainment, lack of market-relevant job skills, and residence in economically deteriorating areas. However, conflict theorists believe that the higher rates of poverty among women can be traced to two distinct causes: Sex discrimination and sexual harassment on the job place women at a clear disadvantage when seeking vertical social mobility.

The burden of supporting a family is especially difficult for single mothers, not only because of low salaries but also because of inadequate child support. The average child-support payment in 1999 for the 45 percent who receive the full award was a mere $93 per week. This level of support is clearly insufficient for rearing a child in the early 21st century. In light of these data, federal and state officials have intensified efforts to track down delinquent spouses and ensure the payment of child support: More than 16 million cases were under investigation in 2002 (Bureau of the Census 2003a: 373).

According to a study based on census data by the advocacy group Women Work, families headed by single mothers and displaced homemakers are four times as likely to live in poverty as other households in the United States. **Displaced homemakers** were defined as women whose primary occupation had been homemaking but who did not find full-time employment after being divorced, separated, or widowed. Gilda Nardone, president of Women Work, noted that single mothers and displaced homemakers tend to work in service jobs, which offer low wages, few benefits, part-time work, and little job security. Moreover, single mothers and displaced homemakers are also more likely to have an unstable housing situation, including frequent changes of residence (Women Work 1998).

Many feminists feel that the continuing dominance of the political system by men contributes to government indifference to the problem of poor women. As more and more women fall below the official poverty line, policy makers will face growing pressure to combat the feminization of poverty.

Education

The experience of women in education has been similar to their experience in the labor force: a long history of contribution, but in traditionally defined terms. In 1833, Oberlin College became the first institution of higher learning to admit women, two centuries after the first men's college began in this country. In 1837, Wellesley became the first women's college. But it would be a mistake to believe that these early experiments brought about equality for women in education: At Oberlin, the women were forbidden to speak in public. Furthermore,

> *Washing the men's clothes, caring for their rooms, serving them at table, listening to their orations, but themselves remaining respectfully silent in public assemblages, the Oberlin "coeds" were being prepared for intelligent motherhood and a properly subservient wifehood. (Flexner 1959:30)*

The early graduates of these schools, despite the emphasis in the curriculum on traditional roles, became the founders of the feminist movement.

feminization of poverty
The trend since 1970 that has women accounting for a growing proportion of those below the poverty line.

displaced homemakers
Women whose primary occupation had been homemaking but who did not find full-time employment after being divorced, separated, or widowed.

Today, research confirms that boys and girls are treated differently in school: Teachers give boys more attention. In teaching students the values and customs of the larger society, schools in the United States have treated children as if men's education were more important than that of women. Professors of education Myra and David Sadker (2003) documented this persistence of classroom sexism: The researchers noted that boys receive more teacher attention than girls, mainly because they call out in class eight times more often. Teachers praise boys more than girls and offer boys more academic assistance. Interestingly, they found that this differential treatment was present with both male and female teachers.

Despite these challenges, in many communities across the nation, girls seem to outdo boys in high school, grabbing a disproportionate share of the leadership positions, from valedictorian to class president to yearbook editor—everything, in short, except captain of the boys' athletic teams. Their advantage numerically seems to be continuing after high school. In the 1980s, girls in the United States became more likely than boys to go to college. By 2001, women accounted for over 57 percent of college students nationwide. And in 2002, for the first time, more women than men in the United States earned doctoral degrees (Bureau of the Census 2003a: tables 176, 183; Conlin 2003; Smallwood 2003).

At all levels of schooling, significant changes also occurred with congressional amendments to the Education Act of 1972 and the Department of Health, Education, and Welfare guidelines developed in 1974 and 1975. Collectively called Title IX provisions, the regulations are designed to eliminate sexist practices from almost all school systems. Schools must make these changes or risk the loss of all federal assistance:

1. Schools must eliminate all sex-segregated classes and extracurricular activities. This means an end to all-girl home economics and all-boy shop classes, although single-sex hygiene and physical education classes are permitted.

2. Schools cannot discriminate by sex in admissions or financial aid and cannot inquire into whether an applicant is married, pregnant, or a parent. Single-sex schools are exempted.

3. Schools must end sexist hiring and promotion practices among faculty members.

4. Although women do not have to be permitted to play on all-men's athletic teams, schools must provide more opportunities for women's sports, intramural and extramural (*Federal Register,* June 4, 1975).

The impact of Title IX over the last thirty years has been particularly apparent as more opportunities have emerged for women to participate in sports both in high school and in college.

Title IX became one of the more controversial steps ever taken by the federal government to promote and ensure equality.

Efforts to bring gender equity to sports have been attacked as excessive. The consequences have not fully been intended: For example, colleges have often cut men's sports rather than build up women's sports. Also, most of the sports with generous college scholarships added for women over the last 30 years are in athletic fields that have not been traditionally attractive to minority women (Suggs 2002).

Family Life

CD-ROM *Activity 10.3*

CD-ROM *Activity 10.4*

Our society generally equates work with wages and holds unpaid work in low esteem. Women who do household chores and volunteer work are given little status in our society. Typically this unrecognized labor is done on top of wage labor in the formal economy. These demands traditionally placed on a mother and homemaker are so extensive that simultaneously pursuing a career is extremely difficult. For women, the family is, according to sociologists Lewis Coser and Rose Laub Coser (1974) a "greedy institution." More recently, other social scientists have also observed the overwhelming burden of the multiple social roles associated with being a mother and working outside the home.

Child Care and Housework

A man can act as a homemaker and caretaker for children, but in the United States, these roles are customarily performed by women. Studies indicate that men do not even think about their children as much as women do. Sociologist Susan Walzer (1996) was interested in whether there are gender differences in the amount of time that parents spend thinking about the care of their children. Drawing on interviews, Walzer found that mothers are much more involved than fathers in the invisible men-

Source: Kirk Anderson, www.kirktoons.com

tal labor associated with taking care of a baby. For example, while involved in work out-side the home, mothers are more likely to think about their babies and to feel guilty later if they become so consumed with the demands of their jobs that they fail to think about their babies.

Is the gender gap closing in housework? In "Research Focus," we consider the lat-est scientific evidence in answer to this question.

Women are much more preoccupied than men in both thought and action with child care and housework, but it does not end there. Another challenge women dis-proportionately face is caring for aging parents. According to a Department of Labor (1998) study, 72 percent of caregivers are women, typically spending around 18 hours per week caring for a parent.

Given the stresses of performing most housework and caregiving, why do mar-ried women accept this arrangement? Psychologist Mary Clare Lennon and sociol-ogist Sarah Rosenfield (1994) studied this issue using interviews of adults from a national sample. When questioned in that survey, almost 61 percent of the women and more than 67 percent of the men suggested that this uneven distribution of housework is fair to both spouses. According to the researchers, married women with the fewest alternatives and financial prospects outside marriage are most likely to accept unequal household arrangements as fair. Apparently, the more eco-nomically dependent a particular wife is, the more she will do (and justify) to pre-serve the marital relationship. In a striking finding, Lennon and Rosenfield report-ed that women who view unequal housework as unjust experience more symptoms of depression.

Sociologist Arlie Hochschild has used the term **second shift** to describe the dou-ble burden—work outside the home followed by child care and housework—that many women face and that few men share equitably. As shown in Figure 15.3, this issue has become increasingly important as greater proportions of mothers work outside the home. On the basis of interviews with and observations of 52 couples over an eight-year period, Hochschild reports that the wives (and not their hus-bands) plan domestic schedules and play dates for children while driving home from the office and then begin their second shift (Hochschild and Machung 1989; Hochschild 1990).

Hochschild found that the married couples she studied were fraying at the edges psychologically and so were their careers and their marriages. The women she spoke with hardly resembled the beautiful young businesswomen pictured in magazine advertisements, dressed in power suits but with frilled blouses, holding briefcases in one hand and happy young children in the other. Instead, many of Hochschild's female subjects talked about being overtired and emotionally drained by the demands of their multiple roles. They were much more intensely torn by the conflict-ing demands of work outside the home and family life than were their husbands. Hochschild (1990) concludes that "if we as a culture come to see the urgent need of meeting the new problems posed by the second shift, and if society and government begin to shape new policies that allow working parents more flexibility, then we will be making some progress toward happier times at home and at work" (p. 73). Many feminists share this view.

There is an economic cost to this second shift. Households do benefit from the free labor of women, but women pay what has been called the **mommy tax**: the lower salaries women receive over their lifetime because they have children. Moth-ers earn less than men and other women over their lifetime because having chil-dren causes them to lose job experience, trade off higher wages for following the mommy track, and be discriminated against by employers. How high is this mommy tax? Estimates range from 5 to 13 percent of lifetime wages for the first

second shift
The double burden—work outside the home followed by child care and housework—that is faced by many women and that few men share equi-tably.

mommy tax
Lower salaries women receive over their lifetime because they have children.

 Focus Research Focus Research Focus

HOUSEWORK AND THE GENDER DIVIDE

It is a commonly held notion that in dual-income households men and women share the housework, but this is not supported by the research. Study after study leads to the same conclusion: Men are gradually doing more housework, typically, but women do far more even when they work full-time.

The latest study, released in 2004 by the Bureau of Labor Statistics, interviewed 21,000 men and women about their activities during a 24-hour period. In Figure 15.2, we can see the results of a typical day's amount of time spent by married men and women ages 25 to 54. This age group is used because it generally includes people who have completed going to school full-time but excludes retired people.

We can see that men generally spend about an hour more a day in paid labor but married women spend twice as much time than mar-

ried men doing unpaid household work and caregiving, whether it be for their children or elderly parents and other relations.

But we have seen almost as many women as men hold jobs as men. Yet the time-use study showed that two-thirds of all women said they prepared meals and did housework on an average day, compared with only 19 percent of men who said they did any housework, and 34 percent who said they gave any assistance with meals or cleanup.

There are two ways that one can interpret gender roles and housework during the last 40 years. Men are gradually doing more housework, but women still account for the vast majority of all time a couple devotes to housework. ■

Source: Bureau of Labor Statistics 2004; Institute for Social Research 2002; Kaufman and Uhlenberg 2000.

FIGURE 15.2 Division of Labor

Source: Bureau of Labor Statistics 2004.

Division of Labor

Amount of time spent on various activities by married men and women ages 25 to 54, with children, who work full time.

Average hours per day spent:

Activity	Men	Women
Sleeping	7.43	7.43
Leisure and sports	2.62	2.18

Men ▪
Women □

Work

Activity	Men	Women
Paid labor	8.87	7.74
Caring for and helping family members	0.83	1.55
Housework, cooking and other chores	0.73	1.44
Work: total	10.43	10.73

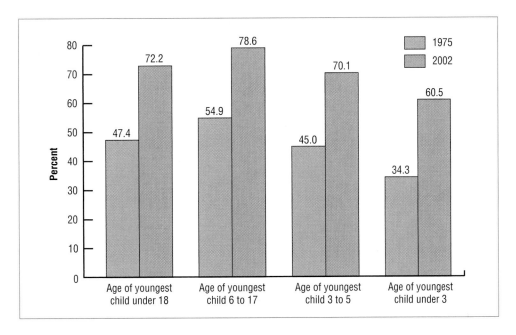

FIGURE 15.3   Labor Force Participation Rates Among Mothers

Source: Department of Labor 2001; 2004:18–19; and author's estimate for 2002 (6 to 17-year-olds).

child alone. Having two children lowers earnings 10 to 19 percent. There is no denying that motherhood and the labor market are intertwined (Budig and England 2001; Szegedy-Maszak 2001).

Abortion

A particularly controversial subject affecting family life in the United States has been the call for women to have greater control over their bodies, especially their reproductive lives, through contraceptive devices and the increased availability of abortions. Abortion law reform was one of the demands NOW made in 1967, and the controversy continues despite many court rulings and the passage of laws at every level of government.

On January 22, 1973, the feminist movement received unexpected assistance from the U.S. Supreme Court decision in *Roe v. Wade.* By a 7–2 margin, the justices held that the "right to privacy . . . founded in the Fourteenth Amendment's concept of personal liberty . . . is broad enough to encompass a woman's decision whether or not to terminate a pregnancy." However, the Court did set certain limits on a woman's right to abortion. During the last three months of pregnancy, the fetus was ruled capable of life outside the womb. Therefore, states were granted the right to prohibit all abortions in the third trimester except those needed to preserve the life, physical health, or mental health of the mother.

The Court's decision in *Roe v. Wade,* though generally applauded by prochoice groups, which support the right to legal abortions, was bitterly condemned by those opposed to abortion. For people who call themselves "prolife," abortion is a moral and often a religious issue. In their view, human life actually begins at the moment of conception rather than when the fetus could stay alive outside the womb. On the basis of this belief, the fetus is a human, not merely a potential life. Termination of this human's life, even before it has left the womb, is viewed as an act of murder. Consequently, antiabortion activists are alarmed by the more than 1 million legal abortions carried out each year in the United States (Luker 1984).

The early 1990s brought an escalation of violent antiabortion protests. Finally, a 1994 federal law made it a crime to use force or threats or to obstruct, injure, or interfere

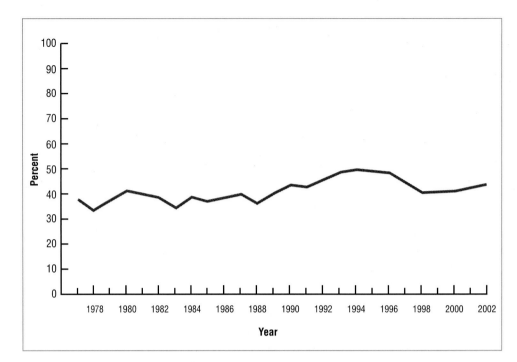

FIGURE 15.4   Public Opinion on Abortion, 1977–2002

Percentage of adults surveyed nationally who think it should be possible for a pregnant woman to obtain a legal abortion if she wants it for any reason.

Source: General Social Survey in Davis et al. 2003.

with anyone providing or receiving abortions and other reproductive health services. In a 6–3 decision, the Supreme Court's majority upheld the constitutionality of a 36-foot buffer zone that keeps antiabortion protesters away from a clinic's entrance and parking lot. Abortion remains a disputed issue both in society and in the courts. The law has apparently had some impact, but acts of violence, including deaths of clinic workers and physicians, continue.

In terms of social class, the first major restriction on the legal right to terminate a pregnancy affected poor people. In 1976, Congress passed the Hyde Amendment, which banned the use of Medicaid and other federal funds for abortions. The Supreme Court upheld this legislation in 1980. State laws also restrict the use of public funds for abortions. Another obstacle facing the poor is access to abortion providers: In the face of vocal prolife public sentiment, fewer and fewer hospitals throughout the world are allowing their physicians to perform abortions, except in extreme cases. As of 2004, only about 3 percent of nonmetropolitan counties in the United States had even one provider able and willing to perform abortions (Guttmacher Institute 2004).

Although courts restrict abortions, and sporadic violence near clinics continues, public opinion has remained remarkably stable over the last 25 years. As shown in Figure 15.4, public opinion has remained fairly constant, with about 40 percent supporting abortion for any reason and larger proportions supporting abortion in cases where a woman's health is endangered or where the woman has been raped.

Political Activity

CD-ROM *Activity 10.6*

Women in the United States constitute 53 percent of the voting population and 49 percent of the labor force but only 8 percent of those holding high government positions. In 2005, Congress included only 60 women (out of 435 members) in the House of Representatives and only 14 women (out of 100 members) in the Senate. As shown in

TABLE 15.3 Women in Elected Office					
	1969	**1975**	**1981**	**1987**	**2005**
House	10	19	21	23	60
Senate	1	0	2	2	14
Governors	0	1	1	2	9
State legislatures	301	604	908	1,170	1,653

Source: Reprinted by permission of the Center for American Women and Politics, Eagleton Institute of Politics, Rutgers University.

Table 15.3, although the number of women in state legislatures in 2005 was more than five times as large as it was in 1969, state legislatures are still 77.4 percent male. Only eight states—Arizona, Delaware, Hawaii, Kansas, Louisiana, Michigan, Montana, Connecticut, and Utah—had a woman governor as of 2005.

The low number of women office holders until recently has not resulted from women's inactivity in politics. About the same proportion of eligible women and men vote in presidential elections. The League of Women Voters, founded in 1920, performs a valuable function in educating the electorate of both sexes, publishing newsletters describing candidates' positions, and holding debates among candidates. Perhaps women's most visible role in politics until recently has been as unpaid campaign workers for male candidates: doorbell ringers, telephone callers, newsletter printers, and petition carriers. Runs for elective office in the 1990s showed women overcoming one of their last barriers to electoral office: attracting campaign funds. Running for office is very expensive, and women candidates have begun to convince backers to invest in their political future. Their success as fundraisers will also contribute to women's acceptance as serious candidates in the future (S. Carroll 2004).

Women have worked actively in both political parties, but women office holders are more likely to be Democrats by a slight margin. A recent effective force is the National Women's Political Caucus (NWPC), which works to get more women elected. The NWPC was founded in 1971 by Betty Friedan, Gloria Steinem (founder of *Ms.* magazine), Bella Abzug, and Shirley Chisholm (the last two have been congresswomen from New York City). The NWPC oversees state caucuses that rally support for women's issues. It is difficult to represent all politically active women in the caucus because women's views encompass a whole range of ideologies, including women who are unmistakably antifeminists. (NWPC 2002).

Double Jeopardy: Minority Women

We have seen the historical oppression of women that limits them by tradition and law to specific roles. Many women experience differential treatment not only because of their gender but also because of race and ethnicity. These citizens face a **double jeopardy**: that of subordinate status twice defined. A disproportionate share of this low-status group also is poor, so the double jeopardy becomes a triple jeopardy. The litany of social ills continues for many as we add old age, ill health, disabilities, and the like.

Feminists have addressed themselves to the needs of minority women, but the oppression of these women because of their sex is overshadowed by the subordinate status that both White men and White women impose on them because of their race or ethnicity. The question for the Latina (Hispanic woman), African American

double jeopardy
The subordinate status twice defined, as experienced by women of color.

woman, Asian American woman, Native American woman, and so on appears to be whether she should unify with her brothers against racism or challenge them for their sexism. The answer is that society cannot afford to let up on the effort to eradicate both sexism and racism (Epstein 1999).

The discussion of gender roles among African Americans has always provoked controversy. Advocates of Black nationalism contend that feminism only distracts women from full participation in the African American struggle. The existence of feminist groups among Blacks, in their view, simply divides the Black community and thereby serves the dominant White society. By contrast, Black feminists such as bell hooks (1994) argue that little is to be gained by accepting the gender role divisions of the dominant society that place women in a separate, subservient position. African American journalist Patricia Raybon (1989) has noted that the media commonly portray Black women in a negative light: as illiterate, as welfare mothers, as prostitutes, and so forth. Black feminists emphasize that it is not solely Whites and White-dominated media that focus on these negative images; Black men (most recently, Black male rap artists) have also been criticized for the way they portray African American women.

Native Americans stand out as a historical exception to the North American patriarchal tradition. At the time of the arrival of the European settlers, gender roles varied greatly from tribe to tribe. Southern tribes, for reasons unclear to today's scholars, usually were matriarchal and traced descent through the mother. European missionaries sought to make the native peoples more like the Europeans, and this aim included transforming women's role. Some Native American women, like members of other groups, have resisted gender stereotypes (Pleck 1993).

The plight of Latinas usually is considered part of either the Hispanic or feminist movements, and the distinctive experience of Latinas is ignored. In the past, they have been excluded from decision making in the two social institutions that most affect their daily lives: the family and the church. The Hispanic family, especially in the lower class, feels the pervasive tradition of male domination. The Catholic Church relegates women to supportive roles while reserving for men the leadership positions (Browne 2001; De Andra 2004).

Conclusion

Women and men are expected to perform, or at least to prefer to perform, specific tasks in society. The appropriateness to one gender of all but a very few of these tasks cannot be justified by the biological differences between females and males any more than differential treatment based on race can be justified. Psychologists Sandra Bem and Daryl Bem (1970) make the following analogy.

Suppose that a White male college student decided to room with a Black male friend. The typical White student would not blithely assume that his roommate was better suited to handle all domestic chores. Nor should his conscience allow him to do so even in the unlikely event that his roommate said, "No, that's okay. I like doing housework. I'd be happy to do it." We would suspect that the White student would still feel uncomfortable about taking advantage of the fact that his roommate has simply been socialized to be "happy with such an arrangement." But change this hypothetical Black roommate to a female marriage partner, and the student's conscience goes to sleep (p. 99).

The feminist movement has awakened women and men to assumptions based on sex and gender. New opportunities for the sexes require the same commitment from individuals and the government as they make to achieve equality between racial and ethnic groups.

Women are systematically disadvantaged in both employment and the family. Gender inequality is a serious problem, just as racial inequality continues to be a significant social challenge. Separate, socially defined roles for men and women are not limited to the United States. Chapter 16 concentrates on the inequality of racial and ethnic groups in societies other than the United States. Just as sexism is not unique to this nation, neither is racism nor religious intolerance.

Key Terms

androgyny   385
displaced homemakers   396
double jeopardy   403
feminine mystique   389
feminization of poverty   396

gender roles   385
glass ceiling   394
mommy tax   399
mommy track   394
pay equity   393

second shift   399
sexism   385
sexual harassment   395
suffragists   388

Review Questions

1. How is women's subordinate position different from that of oppressed racial and ethnic groups? How is it similar?
2. How has the focus of the feminist movement changed from the suffragist movement to the present?
3. How do the patterns of women in the workplace differ from those of men?
4. How has the changing role of women in the United States affected the family?
5. What are the special challenges facing women of subordinate racial and ethnic groups?

Critical Thinking

1. Women have many characteristics similar to those of minority groups, but what are some differences? For example, they are not segregated from men residentially.
2. Earlier in the 1990s, the phrase *angry white men* was used by some men who viewed themselves as victims. In what respect may men see themselves as victims of reverse discrimination? Do you think these views are justified?
3. How are men's and women's roles defined differently when it comes to such concepts as the mommy track, second shift, and the displaced homemaker?

Internet Connections—Research Navigator™

Follow the instructions found on page 31 of this text to access the features of Research Navigator™. Once at the Web site, enter your Login Name and Password. Then, to use the ContentSelect database, enter keywords such as "adrogyny," "suffrage movement," and "Title VIX," and the research engine will supply relevant and recent scholarly and popular press publications. Use the *New York Times* Search-by-Subject Archive to find recent news articles related to sociology and the Link Library feature to locate relevant Web links organized by the key terms associated with this chapter.

16

Beyond the United States:
The Comparative Perspective

SUBORDINATING PEOPLE BECAUSE OF RACE, NATIONALITY, OR religion is not a phenomenon unique to the United States; it occurs throughout the world. In Mexico, women and the descendants of the Mayans are given second-class status. Despite its being viewed as a homogeneous nation by some, Canada faces racial, linguistic, and tribal issues. Northern Ireland is a modern nation torn by religious strife. In Israel, Jews and Palestinians struggle over territory and the definition of each other's autonomy. In the Republic of South Africa, the legacy of apartheid dominates the present and the future.

Ironically, by bringing more and more diverse groups of people into contact, modernization has increased the opportunities for confrontation, both peaceful and violent, between culturally and physically different people. The decline in colonialism by European powers in the 1960s and the end of communist domination in Eastern Europe in the 1990s have also allowed interethnic rivalries to resume. Confrontations along racial or ethnic or religious lines, as Chapter 1 showed, can lead to extermination, expulsion, secession, segregation, fusion, assimilation, or pluralism. At the conclusion of this chapter, we will review how these processes have been illustrated in this chapter as we look beyond the United States.

Confrontations between racial and ethnic groups have escalated in frequency and intensity in the 20th century. In surveying these conflicts, we can see two themes emerge: the previously considered world systems theory and ethnonational conflict. **World systems theory** considers the global economic system as divided between nations that control wealth and those that provide natural resources and labor. Historically, the nations we will be considering reflect this competition between "haves" and "have nots." Whether the laborers are poor Catholics in Ireland or Black Africans, their contribution to the prosperity of the dominant group created the social inequality that people are trying to address today (I. Wallerstein 1974; 2004).

Ethnonational conflict refers to conflicts between ethnic, racial, religious, and linguistic groups within nations. In some areas of the world, ethnonational conflicts are more significant than tension between nations as the source of refugees and even death. As you can see in Figure 16.1, countries in all parts of the world, including the most populous nations, have significant diversity within their borders. These conflicts remind us that the processes operating in the United States to deny racial and ethnic groups rights and opportunities are at work throughout the world (Connor 1994; Olzak 1998).

The sociological perspective on relations between dominant and subordinate groups treats race and ethnicity as social categories. As social concepts, they can be understood only in the context of the shared meanings attached to them by societies and their members. Although relationships between dominant and subordinate groups vary greatly, there are similarities across societies. Racial and ethnic hostilities arise out of economic needs and demands. These needs and demands may not always be realistic; that is, a group may seek out enemies where none exist or where victory will yield no rewards. Racial and ethnic conflicts are both the results and the precipitators of change in the economic and political sectors (Barclay et al. 1976; Coser 1956).

Relations between dominant and subordinate groups differ from society to society, as this chapter will show. Intergroup relations in Mexico, Canada, Northern Ireland, Israel, and South Africa are striking in their similarities and contrasts. As shown in Figure 16.2, each society, in its own way, illustrates the processes of intergroup relations first introduced in Chapter 1. The examples range from the Holocaust, which precipitated the emergence of Israel, to the efforts to create a multiracial government in South Africa. A study of these five societies, coupled with knowledge of subordinate groups in the United States, will provide the background from which to draw some conclusions about patterns of race and ethnic relations in the world today.

Mexico

Usually in the discussions of race relations, Mexico is considered only as a source of immigrants to the United States. In questions of economic development, Mexico again typically enters the discussion only as it affects our own economy. However, Mexico, a nation of 106 million people (in the Western Hemisphere, only Brazil and the United States are larger) is an exceedingly complex nation (see Table 16.1). It is therefore appropriate that we understand Mexico and its issues of inequality better. This understanding will also shed light on the relationship of its people to the United States.

In the 1520s, Spain overthrew the Aztec Indian tribe that ruled Mexico. Mexico remained a Spanish colony until the 1820s. In 1836, Texas declared its independence

CD-ROM *Activity 12.2*

CD-ROM *Activity 12.1*

world systems theory
A view of the global economic system as divided between nations that control wealth and those that provide natural resources and labor.

ethnonational conflict
Conflicts between ethnic, racial, religious, and linguistic groups within nations replacing conflicts between nations.

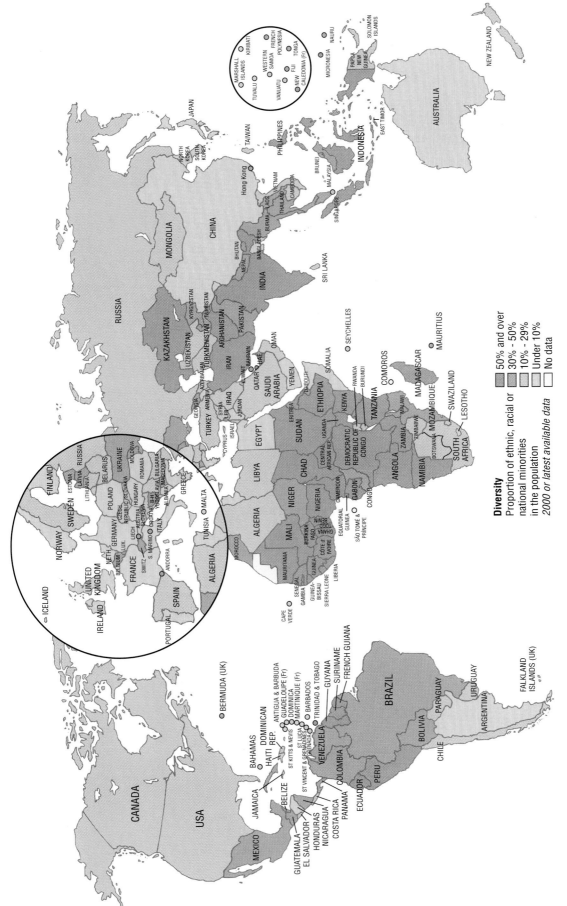

FIGURE 16.1 Ethnic Diversity Worldwide

Source: "Diversity," from *The Penguin State of the World Atlas* by Dan Smith, copyright © 2003 by Dan Smith. Illustration © 2003 by Myriad Editions Ltd. Used by permission of Penguin, a division of Penguin Group (USA) Inc.

Diversity
Proportion of ethnic, racial or national minorities in the population
2000 or latest available data

- 50% and over
- 30% - 50%
- 10% - 29%
- Under 10%
- No data

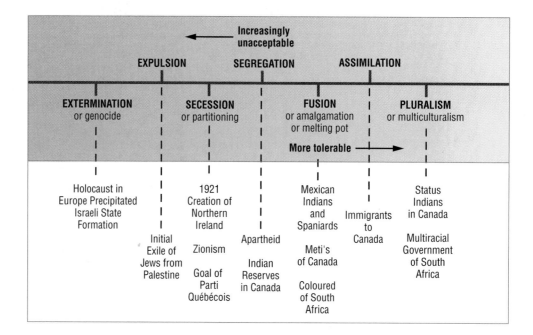

FIGURE 16.2 Intergroup Relations Continuum

Population	GNI/per capita (in millions)	Groups (USA = $36,610)	Current Nation's Represented	Formation
TABLE 16.1 Five-Nation Comparison, 2004				
Mexico	106.2	$8,800	Mexican Indians, 9%	1823: Republic of Mexico declared independent from Spain
Canada	31.9	$28,930	French speaking, 24% Aboriginal people, 3–6% "Visible" minorities, 13%	1857: Dominion of Canada formed independent of England
Northern Ireland	1.6	Not available	Protestants, 54% Catholics, 43%	1921: Created from Ireland and becomes part of the United Kingdom
Israel	6.1	$19,000	Jews, 80%	1948: Independence from British mandate under United Nations
Israel Occupied Territories	3.8	$4,247	Others (citizens), 1% Muslims, Christians, Palestinians (noncitizens), 19%	
South Africa	46.9	$9,810	Black Africans, 76% Whites, 13% Coloureds, 9% Asians, 3%	1948: Independence from Great Britain

Sources: Author estimates based on Canak and Swanson 1998; Dahlburg 1998; Haub 2004; Lynch 2000; Statistics Canada 2001, 2003a.

from Mexico, and by 1846 Mexico was at war with the United States. As we described in Chapter 9, the Mexican-American War forced Mexico to surrender more than half of its territory. In the 1860s, France sought to turn Mexico into an empire under Austrian prince Maximilian but ultimately withdrew after bitter resistance led by a Mexican Indian, Benito Juárez, who later served as the nation's president.

The Mexican Indian People and the Color Gradient

In contemporary Mexico, a major need has been to reassess the relations between the indigenous peoples—the Mexican Indians, many descended from the Mayas, and the government of Mexico. In 1900, the majority of the Mexican population still spoke Indian languages and lived in closed, semi-isolated villages or tribal communities according to ancestral customs. Many of these people were not a part of the growing industrialization in Mexico and were not truly represented in the national legislature. Perhaps the major change for them in this century was that many intermarried with the descendants of the Europeans, forming a *mestizo* class of people of mixed ancestry. These *mestizos* have become increasingly identified with Mexico's growing middle class. Initially the subject of derision, the *mestizos* have developed their own distinct culture and, as the descendants of the European settlers are reduced in number and influence, have become the true bearers of the national Mexican sentiment.

Meanwhile, however, these social changes have left the Mexican Indian people even further behind the rest of the population economically. Indian cultures have been stereotyped as backward, resistant to progress and modern ways of living. Indeed, the existence of the many (at least 56) Indian cultures has been seen in this century as an impediment to the development of a national culture in Mexico. In an effort to bring the indigenous people into the mainstream economy, in the late 1930s the Mexican government embarked on a government policy known as *indigenismo* or national integration. The Mexican Indians were given land rights to make them economically self-sufficient. This program was not unlike the U.S. policy in the 1880s with respect to the Native Americans (American Indians). However, *indigenismo* did not take place; the native people did not fade away culturally.

As noted in Chapter 9, a **color gradient** is the placement of people on a continuum from light to dark skin color rather than in distinct racial groupings by skin color. This is another example of the social construction of race in which social class is linked to the social reality (or at least the appearance) of racial purity. At the top of this gradient or hierarchy are the *criollos,* the 10 percent of the population who are typically White, well-educated members of the business and intellectual elites with familial roots in Spain. In the middle is the large impoverished *mestizo* majority, most of whom have brown skin and a mixed racial lineage as a result of intermarriage. At the bottom of the color gradient are the destitute Mexican Indians and a small number of Blacks, some the descendants of 200,000 African slaves brought to Mexico. Ironically, although this color gradient is an important part of day-to-day life—enough so that some Mexicans use hair dyes, skin lighteners, and blue or green contact lenses to appear more European—nearly all Mexicans are considered part Mexican Indian because of centuries of intermarriage (Castañeda 1995; DePalma 1995).

On January 1, 1994, rebels from an armed insurgent group called the Zapatista National Liberation Army seized four towns in the state of Chiapas in southern Mexico. The rebels—who named their organization after Emiliano Zapata, a farmer and leader of the 1910 revolution against a corrupt dictatorship—were backed by 2,000 lightly armed Mayan Indians and peasants. Zapatista leaders declared that they had turned to armed insurrection to protest economic injustices and discrimination against the region's Indian population. The Mexican government mobilized the army to crush the revolt but was forced to retreat as news organizations broadcast pictures of the

color gradient
The placement of people on a continuum from light to dark skin color rather than in distinct racial groupings by skin color.

confrontation around the world. A cease-fire was declared after only 12 days of fighting, but 196 people had already died. Negotiations collapsed between the Mexican government and the Zapatista National Liberation Army, with sporadic violence ever since.

In response to the crisis, the Mexican legislature enacted the Law on Indian Rights and Culture, which went into effect in 2001. The act allows 62 recognized Indian groups to apply their own customs in resolving conflicts and electing leaders. Unfortunately, state legislatures must give final approval to these arrangements, a requirement that severely limits the rights of large Indian groups whose territories span several states. Tired of waiting for state approval, many indigenous communities in Chiapas have declared self-rule without obtaining official recognition (Bourdreaux 2002; J. Smith 2001).

While many factors contributed to the Zapatista revolt, the subordinate status of Mexico's Indian citizens, who account for an estimated 14 percent of the nation's population, was surely important. More than 90 percent of the indigenous population live in houses without access to sewers, compared with 21 percent of the population as a whole. And whereas just 10 percent of Mexican adults are illiterate, the proportion for Mexican Indians is 44 percent (Bourdreaux 2002; *The Economist* 2004c; Thompson 2001).

The Status of Women

Often in the United States we consider our own problems to be so significant that we fail to recognize that many of these social issues exist elsewhere. Gender stratification is an example of an issue we share with almost all other countries, and Mexico is no exception. In 1975, Mexico City was the site of the first United Nations conference on the status of women. Much of the focus was on the situation of women in developing countries; in that regard, Mexico remains typical.

Women in Mexico did not receive the right to vote until 1953. They have made significant progress in that short period in being elected into office, but they have a long way to go. As of 2004, women accounted for 23 percent of Mexico's national assembly, ranking Mexico 29th (the United States is 59th) among 136 nations worldwide in representation of women (Inter-Parliamentary Union 2004).

Even when Mexican women work outside the home, they are often denied recognition as active and productive household members, and men are typically viewed as heads of the household in every respect. As one consequence, women find it difficult to obtain credit and technical assistance in many parts of Mexico and to inherit land in rural areas.

The poverty of Mexican Indians is well documented and in some instances has led to violent protests for social change.

In the larger economy in Mexico, women often are viewed as the "ideal workers." This appears to be particularly true of the foreign-owned factories or *maquiladoras* of the borderlands (discussed in Chapter 9) that rely heavily on women. For example, in a Tijuana electronics plant, women receive elementary training and work in the least-skilled and least-automated jobs because there is little expectation of advancement, organizing for better working conditions, or developing unions.

Men are preferred over women in the more skilled jobs, and women lose out entirely as factories, even in developing nations such as Mexico, require more complex skills. In 2000, only 42 percent of women were in the paid labor force, compared with about 70 percent in Canada and 72 percent in the United States (Bureau of the Census 2003a:859).

In recent decades, Mexican women have begun to address an array of economic, political, and health issues. Often this organizing occurs at the grassroots level, outside traditional government forums. Because women continue to serve as household managers for their families, even when they work outside the home, they have been aware of the consequences of the inadequate public services in low-income urban neighborhoods. As far back as 1973, women in Monterrey, the nation's third-largest city, began protesting the continuing disruptions of the city's water supply. At first, individual women made complaints to city officials and the water authority, but subsequently, groups of female activists emerged. They sent delegations to confront politicians, organized protest rallies, and blocked traffic as a means of getting media attention. As a result of their efforts, there have been improvements in Monterrey's water service, although the issue of reliable and safe water remains a concern in Mexico and many developing countries (V. Bennett 1995).

Canada

Multiculturalism is a fairly recent term in the United States; it is used to refer to diversity. In Canada, it has been adopted as a state policy for more than two decades. Still, many people in the United States, when they think of Canada, see it as a homogeneous nation with a smattering of Arctic-type people—merely a cross between the northern mainland United States and Alaska. This is not the social reality.

One of the continuing discussions among Canadians is the need for a cohesive national identity or a sense of common peoplehood. The immense size of the country, much of which is sparsely populated, and the diversity of its people have complicated this need.

In 1971, Canadian Prime Minister Pierre Trudeau presented to the House of Commons a policy of multiculturalism that sought to permit cultural groups to retain and foster their identity. Specifically, he declared that there should continue to be two official languages, French and English, but "no official culture" and no "ethnic group [taking] precedence over any other" (Labelle 1989:2). Yet it is not always possible to legislate a pluralistic society, as the case of Canada demonstrates.

The First Nation

Canada, like the United States, has had an adversarial relationship with its native peoples. However, the Canadian experience has not been as violent. During all three stages of Canadian history—French colonialism, British colonialism, and Canadian nationhood—there has been, compared with the United States, little warfare between Canadian Whites and Canadian Native Americans. Yet the legacy today is similar. Prodded by settlers, colonial governments (and later Canadian governments) drove the Native Americans from their lands. Already by the 1830s, Indian reserves were being established that were similar to the reservations in the United States. Tribal members were encouraged to renounce their status and become Canadian citizens. Assimilation was the explicit policy until recently (Champagne 1994; Waldman 1985).

The 1.4 million native peoples of Canada are collectively referred to by the government as the First Nation or Aboriginal Peoples and represent about 3 to 6 percent of the population, depending on the definition used. This population is classified into the following groups:

Status Indians: The more than 600 tribes or bands officially recognized by the government, numbering about 690,000 in 2000, of whom the majority live on Indian reserves (or reservations).

Inuit: The 62,300 people living in the northern part of the country, who typically have been called the Eskimos.

Métis: Canadians of mixed ancestry, officially numbering 218,000; depending on definitions, they range in number from 100,000 to 850,000.

Non-Status Indians: Canadians of native ancestry who, because of voluntary decisions or government rulings, have been denied registration status. The group numbers about 425,000.

The Métis and Non-Status Indians have historically enjoyed no separate legal recognition, but efforts continue to secure them special rights under the law, such as designated health, education, and welfare programs. The general public does not understand these legal distinctions, so if a Métis or Non-Status Indian "looks like an Indian," she or he is subjected to the same treatment, discriminatory or otherwise (Indian and Northern Affairs Canada and Canadian Polar Commission 2000:4).

The new Canadian Federal Constitution of 1982 included a Charter of Rights that "recognized and affirmed . . . the existing aboriginal and treaty rights" of the Canadian Native American, Inuit, and Métis peoples. This recognition received the most visibility through the efforts of the Mohawk, one of the tribes of Status Indians. At issue were land rights involving some property areas in Quebec that had spiritual significance for the Mohawk. Their protests and militant confrontations reawakened the Canadian people to the concerns of their diverse native peoples (Amnesty International 1993).

In a 1995 protest demonstration, Canadian Indians protest their living conditions on reserves by erecting teepees on Parliament Hill in Ottawa.

Some of the contemporary issues facing the First Nation of Canada are very similar to those faced by Native Americans in the United States. The Canadian Human Rights Commission has ruled that some native Inuit had their rights violated when they were forcibly relocated from northern Quebec to isolated areas in the Arctic in 1953. In response, the Department of Indian Affairs and Northern Development indicated in 1992 that it would facilitate transportation but rejected the possibility of compensation.

Another setback, also in 1992, occurred when a national referendum, the Charlottetown Agreement, was defeated. This constitutional reform package embraced a number of issues, including greater recognition of the Aboriginal Peoples. Canadian Native American and Inuit leaders expressed anger over the defeat, and Ron George, leader of the Native Council of Canada, accused those who rejected the agreement of "perpetuating apartheid in this country." However, the federal government has declared its willingness to accept the right of the Inuit and the other aboriginal people of Northern Canada to self-government (Keesing's 1992 Canada:39126; also see Champagne 1994).

The social and economic fate of contemporary Aboriginal Peoples reflects many challenges. Just 3 percent of First Nation people have a college degree, compared with 13 percent of the non-Aboriginal people. The native peoples of Canada have unemployment rates twice as high and an average income one-third lower (Statistics Canada 2001).

In a positive step, in 1999 Canada created a new territory in response to a native land claim in which the resident Inuit (formerly called Eskimos) dominated. Nunavut ("NOO-nah-voot"), meaning "our land," as the territory was called, recognizes the territorial rights of the Inuit. Admirable as this event is, observers noted it was easier to grant such economic rights and autonomy to 27,000 people in the isolated expanse of northern Canada than to the Aboriginal People of the more populated southern provinces of Canada (D. Brown 2001).

The Québécois

Assimilation and domination have been the plight of most minority groups. The French-speaking people of the province of Quebec—the Québécois, as they are known—represent a contrasting case. Since the mid-1960s, they have reasserted their identity and captured the attention of the entire nation.

Quebec accounts for about one-fourth of the nation's population and wealth. Reflecting its early settlement by the French, fully 80 percent of the province's population claims French as its first language, compared with only 24 percent in the nation as a whole (Statistics Canada 2002).

The Québécois have sought to put French Canadian culture on an equal footing with English Canadian culture in the country as a whole and to dominate in the province. At the very least, this effort has been seen as an irritant outside Quebec and has been viewed with great concern by the English-speaking minority in Quebec.

In the 1960s, the Québécois expressed the feeling that bilingual status was not enough. Even to have French recognized as one of two official languages in a nation dominated by the English-speaking population gave the Québécois second-class status in their view. With some leaders threatening to break completely with Canada and make Quebec an independent nation, Canada made French the official language of the province and the only acceptable language for commercial signs and public transactions. New residents are now required to send their children to French schools. The English-speaking residents felt as if they had been made aliens, even though many of them had roots extending back to the 1700s. These changes spurred residents to migrate from Quebec and some corporate headquarters to relocate to the neighboring English-speaking province of Ontario (Salée 1994).

The long debate over how much independence Quebec should be permitted reached a stalemate with the Meech Lake Accords. In 1987, at Meech Lake, a group of constitutional amendments was developed that would recognize Quebec as a distinct society, but the effort to pass the accords failed.

Through the past four decades of debate, the force both unifying and dividing the French-speaking people of Quebec has been the Parti Québécois. Since its establishment in 1968, the Parti Québécois has been a force in the politics of the provinces. It gained majority control of the province's assembly in 1994. The national version, Bloc Québécois, holding in 2004 about 18 percent of seats in Parliament, plays a role in the opposition coalition. The Bloc Québécois has advocated separatism: the creation of an independent nation of Quebec. Separatists contend that Quebec has the confidence, natural resources, and economic structure to stand on its own. However, not all Québécois who vote for the party favor this extreme position, although they are certainly sympathetic to preserving their language and culture.

In 1995, the people of Quebec were given a different referendum question that they would vote on alone: whether they wanted to separate from Canada and form a new nation. In a very close vote, 50.5 percent of the voters indicated a preference to remain united with Canada. The vote was particularly striking, given the confusion over how separation would be accomplished and its significance economically. Separatists vowed to keep working for secession and called for another referendum in the future, although surveys show the support for independence had dropped to 40 percent of the province by 2002. Independence for Quebec would not be easy because the Supreme Court of Canada ruled in 1998 that Quebec cannot secede without seeking the consent of the central government. Canadians opposed to separation spoke of reconciliation after the bitter election debate, but it was unclear what further concessions they were prepared to make to the separatists. Many French-speaking residents now seem to accept the steps that have been taken, but a minority still seeks full control of financial and political policies (C. Krauss 2003).

Canada is characterized by the presence of two linguistic communities: the Anglophone and the Francophone, the latter occurring largely in one province, Quebec. Outside Quebec, Canadians are opposed to separatism, and within this province, they are divided. Language and cultural issues therefore both unify and divide a nation of 32 million people.

Immigration and Race

Immigration has also been a significant social force contributing to Canadian multiculturalism. Canada, proportionately to its population, receives consistently the most

Supporters of a Quebec separatist movement participate in a rally. In 1995, a referendum calling for separation from the rest of Canada was narrowly defeated; today, support for such a drastic step appears to have declined.

immigrants of any nation. Over 18 percent of its population is foreign born, with an increasing proportion being of Asian background rather than European. New arrivals particularly gravitate to urban areas. In recent years, 53 percent of immigrants have gone to Toronto, 15 percent to Vancouver, and 13 percent to Montreal.

Canada also speaks of its **visible minorities**—persons other than Aboriginal or First Nation people who are non-White in racial background. This would include much of the immigrant population as well as the Black population. In the 2001 census, the visible minority population accounted for 13.4 percent of the population compared to less than 5 percent 20 years earlier (Statistics Canada 2003a).

People in the United States tend to view Canada's race relations in favorable terms. In part, this view reflects Canada's role as the "promised land" to slaves escaping the U.S. South and crossing the free North to Canada, where they were unlikely to be recaptured. The view of Canada as a land of positive intergroup relations is also fostered by Canadians' comparing themselves with the United States. They have long been willing to compare their best social institutions to the worst examples of racism in the United States and to pride themselves on being more virtuous and high-minded (McClain 1979).

The social reality, past and present, is quite different. Africans came in 1689 as involuntary immigrants to be enslaved by French colonists. Slavery officially continued until 1833. It never flourished because the Canadian economy did not need a large labor force, so most slaves worked as domestic servants. Blacks from the United States did flee to Canada before slavery ended, but some fugitive slaves returned after Lincoln's issuance of the Emancipation Proclamation in 1863. The early Black arrivals in Canada were greeted in a variety of ways. Often they were warmly received as fugitives from slavery, but as their numbers grew in some areas, Canadians became concerned that they would overwhelm the White population (Winks 1971).

The contemporary Black Canadian population, about 3 percent of the nation's population, consists of indigenous Afro-Canadians with several generations of roots in Canada, West Indian immigrants and their descendants, and a number of post–World War II immigrants from the United States. Immigration has become significant, especially in cities where immigrants tend to settle (Statistics Canada 2003a).

Before 1966, Canada's immigration policy alternated between restrictive and more open, as necessary to assist the economy. As in the United States, there were some very exclusionary phases based on race. From 1884 to 1923, Canada levied a Chinese "head tax" that virtually brought Chinese immigration to a halt, although earlier it had been encouraged. Subsequent policies through 1947 were not much better. Current immigration policy favors those with specific skills that make an economic contribution to the country.

Public agitation to restrict immigration has been particularly intense in response to increased pressure from Latin Americans and Asians to gain entry. A national survey of Canadians in 2002 found that 54 percent felt immigration should be reduced, and only 26 percent favored an increase. Yet three-quarters or more agreed that immigrants make an economic and cultural contribution to their country (*Migration News* 2002).

It is difficult to escape the parallels with the United States. For example, since the 1980s there has been a degree of resurgence in open racism. Its targets were Blacks, Asian immigrants, and Jewish Canadians. A government-commissioned national survey released in 2003 found that 20 percent of the visible minorities often feel discriminated against, compared to 5 percent of the rest of the population. The government and the courts have been far from silent on issues relevant to "the visible minorities" and the Aboriginal Peoples. Canadian courts have liberally interpreted their Charter of Rights and Freedoms to prevent systematic discrimination, and equal rights legislation has been passed. Yet institutional racism and continuing debates about immigration policy will remain a part of the Canadian scene for some time to come (Farnsworth 1996; McKenna 1994; Statistics Canada 2003b).

visible minorities
In Canada, persons other than Aboriginal or First Nation people who are non-white in racial background.

In 1541, Frenchman Jacques Cartier established the first European settlement along the St. Lawrence River, but within a year he withdrew because of confrontations with the Iroquois. Almost 500 years later, the descendants of the Europeans and Aboriginal Peoples are still trying to resolve Canada's identity as it is shaped by issues of ethnicity, race, and language.

Northern Ireland

Armed conflict between Protestants and Roman Catholics is difficult for many in the United States to understand. Our recent history in racial and ethnic relations makes it easy for us to recognize that societies may be torn apart by differences based on skin color or even language. But atrocities between fellow citizens who share the bond of the Christian faith, even if in name only, can strike us as incredible. Yet newspapers and television news regularly recount the horrors from Northern Ireland, a very troubled land of only 1.6 million people.

Partition

The roots of today's violence lie in the invasion of Ireland by the English (then the Anglo-Normans) in the 12th century. England, preoccupied with European enemies and hampered by resistance from the Irish, never gained complete control of the island. The northernmost area, called Ulster, received a heavy influx of Protestant settlers from Scotland and England in the 17th century after Oliver Cromwell's defeat of the Irish supporters of Britain's Roman Catholic monarch (Figure 16.3).

Ireland was united with Great Britain (England, Scotland, and Wales) in 1801 to form the United Kingdom. Despite this union, Ireland was still governed as a colony. Most of the people of Ireland found it difficult to accept union and did not consider the government in London theirs. In secret, the native Irish continued to speak Irish (or Gaelic) and worship as Roman Catholics in defiance of the Protestant British government. Protestant settlers continued to speak English and to pay homage to the British monarch after the Restoration. Unhappy with their colonial status, the Irish, as they had done for the previous seven centuries, again pushed for independence or at least **home rule** with a local Irish parliament. Protestants in Ireland and most people in Britain objected to such demands, derisively calling them "Rome rule." In the late 1800s, as home rule bills were introduced, Irish Roman Catholics marched in support, only to be confronted by angry Protestants.

A very limited home rule bill was passed in 1914, but its implementation was delayed by World War I. Tired of waiting, a small group of militant Irish nationalists declared they would accept no compromises and no more delays. What could have been an isolated incident, unsupported by the majority of Roman Catholic and Protestant Irish alike, aroused an extreme reaction from England and escalated the Easter Rebellion of 1916 into the Anglo-Irish War of 1919–1921. In 1921, a treaty was signed that provided for establishing an independent sovereign nation in the south, which evolved into today's Republic of Ireland.

From 1921 through the present, the United Kingdom has retained its control over six of the nine counties of Ulster—today's Northern Ireland. The Republic of Ireland is 95 percent Roman Catholic, but Northern Ireland, with its population 54 percent Protestant and 43 percent Roman Catholic, is still a land divided. The partition was completed, but peace was not established (Dahlburg 1998).

The Civil Rights Movement

home rule
Britain's grant of a local parliament to Ireland.

The immediate postpartition period was fairly peaceful, with fewer than 20 deaths through the late 1960s related to the Protestant–Roman Catholic conflict that had divid-

International boundaries

Administrative boundaries

Atlantic Ocean

Scotland

Glasgow

Edinburgh

North Sea

Londonderry

Northern Ireland

Belfast

Ireland

Dublin

Irish Sea

Liverpool

Wales

Cardiff

England

London

Celtic Sea

English Channel

Belgium

France

FIGURE 16.3   United Kingdom

ed the island for centuries. Britain was indifferent to Northern Ireland governance and looked the other way as the Protestants capitalized on their majority. Political districts were created that minimized the voting strength of Roman Catholics in sending representatives to Stormont, Northern Ireland's Parliament, and Protestant areas were divided to maximize electoral power. In some local elections, the abuses were more blatant, tying voting to home ownership and thereby disfranchising large numbers of Roman Catholics, who were more likely to be renters or to be living with kin (Terchek 1977).

These political problems faced by Roman Catholics were compounded by other social problems. Because they had historically worked for Protestant factory owners, the Roman Catholics were more likely to be poor, live in substandard housing, and suffer from more and longer periods of unemployment. Residential segregation and separate schools further isolated the two groups from one another (Boal et al. 1982; Conroy 1981; Whyte 1986).

The civil rights movement of Northern Ireland began with a march in Londonderry (see Figure 16.3) in 1969, with Roman Catholics joined by some sympathetic Protestants, protesting the social ills described here. Marching in defiance of a police order, the demonstrators soon were confronted by the police, and violence broke out, leaving civilians injured. A year later, Belfast protests led to an escalation of violence, and ten demonstrators were killed. British troops were ordered into Northern Ireland the next day. Within two years, a well-organized guerrilla movement, the Irish Republican Army (IRA), rose on behalf of militant Roman Catholics. Simultaneously, terrorist Unionists, paramilitary Protestant groups, surfaced. The violence continued to escalate amid futile efforts by civil rights workers to have the issues discussed. In 1971, Britain initiated the policy of internment, allowing Britain to hold suspected terrorists, mostly Roman Catholics, without making charges against them.

In late 1994, peace was made in Northern Ireland as both the militant Unionists and the IRA forces declared cease-fires. This development followed months of intense effort between Great Britain and the Republic of Ireland, which pledged to involve the militant groups in negotiations that would bring a permanent end to the violence. The Irish Republic government also agreed to end its claim on Northern Ireland. The uneasy peace had held for only a year when the IRA, critical of the exclusion of some Roman Catholic groups from peace talks, struck out at targets in England and British military installations in Northern Ireland.

The Northern Ireland Accord

The continued violence, despite cease-fires on paper, led two nations to become involved in the negotiations that before had distanced themselves from the dispute: the United States and the Republic of Ireland. Momentum for a consensus came; and on Good Friday 1998, the Northern Ireland Accord was signed, calling for a new Northern Ireland Assembly that would have Protestants and Catholics share power, unlike the Protestant-dominated parliament abolished in 1972. A new North/South Ministerial (or Cabinet Ministers) Council was called for as a forum where the Irish Republic government would meet to make policy with the new Northern Ireland Assembly. Other provisions called for amending the Irish Republic constitution where it had claimed the territory of Northern Ireland as its own (Balz 1998).

Within months of the accord, one of the most violent attacks in recent history took place. A renegade group calling itself the Real IRA bombed a shopping area, leaving 28 dead—all civilians—including Protestants, Catholics, and even residents of the Republic of Ireland. In its aftermath, some of the dissenters from the accord said enough was enough and that it was time to push for peace. The IRA leadership

The violence since 1969 in the small nation of Northern Ireland is proportionately equivalent to nearly four million dead or wounded in the United States.

Source: © 2004 STAR TRIBUNE/Minneapolis-St. Paul

Wall murals throughout Northern Ireland offer grim testimony to the long confrontation between Roman Catholics and Protestants.

announced in 2001 that it was reducing its arsenal through disarmament as a show of good faith, but this does not mean peace has been achieved in the streets. The sporadic violence now occurs in a worldwide atmosphere that has focused attention on terrorism. Both sides of the Northern Ireland conflict label the militant actions of the other side as terrorist in nature.

Even with a guarded expectation for peace, problems continue to face Northern Ireland. Both Great Britain and the European Union have pledged to economically assist the strife-torn region. Even if political equality were possible, there is the issue of the persistence of social inequality. More Roman Catholic children leave school early and are much less likely to receive a university education. Consequently, there is a significant difference in unemployment rates: Twenty-three percent of Catholic men are unemployed, compared with 9 percent of the Protestant men. As a result, more than twice as many Roman Catholic households depend on public assistance than do Protestants. As is so often the case with ethnic tension, the basic characteristic of the minority experience is unequal treatment and its economic consequences (Cairns and Darby 1998; P. Tyler 2004).

Israel and the Palestinians

In 1991, when the Gulf War ended, hopes were high in many parts of the world that a comprehensive Middle East peace plan could be hammered out. Just a decade later, after the terrorist attacks of September 11, 2001, the expectations for a lasting peace were much dimmer. The key elements in any peace plan were to resolve the conflict between Israel and its Arab neighbors and to resolve the challenge of the Palestinian refugees. Although the issues are debated in the political arena, the origins of the conflict can be found in race, ethnicity, and religion.

Nearly 2,000 years ago, the Jews were exiled from Palestine in the **Diaspora**. The exiled Jews settled throughout Europe and elsewhere in the Middle East. There, they often encountered hostility and the anti-Semitism described in Chapter 14. With the conversion of the Roman Empire to Christianity, Palestine became the site of many Christian pilgrimages. Beginning in the seventh century, Palestine gradually fell under the Muslim influence of the Arabs. By the beginning of the 20th century, tourism had become established. In addition, some Jews had migrated from Russia and established settlements that were tolerated by the Ottoman Empire, which then controlled Palestine.

Diaspora
The exile of Jews from Palestine.

Great Britain expanded its colonial control from Egypt into Palestine during World War I, driving out the Turks. Britain ruled the land but endorsed the eventual establishment of a Jewish national homeland in Palestine. The spirit of **Zionism**, the yearning to establish a Jewish state in the biblical homeland, was well under way. From the Arab perspective, Zionism meant the subjugation, if not the elimination, of the Palestinians.

Thousands of Jews came to settle from throughout the world; even so, in the 1920s, Palestine was only about 15 percent Jewish. Ethnic tension grew as the Arabs of Palestine were threatened by the Zionist fervor. Rioting grew to such a point that, in 1939, Britain yielded to Palestinian demands that Jewish immigration be stopped. This occurred at the same time as large numbers of Jews were fleeing Nazism in Europe. After World War II, Jews resumed their demand for a homeland, despite Arab objections. Britain turned to the newly formed United Nations to settle the dispute. In May 1948, the British mandate over Palestine ended, and the State of Israel was founded (Masci 2001).

The Palestinian people define themselves as the people who live in this former British mandate, along with their descendants on their fathers' side. They are viewed as an ethnic group within the larger group of Arabs. They generally speak Arabic, and most of them (97 percent) are Muslim. With a rapid rate of natural increase, the Palestinians have grown in number from 1.4 million at the end of World War II to about 7 million worldwide: 700,000 in Israel, 1.5 million in the West Bank, and 800,000 in the Gaza Strip (Third World Institute 2003:436).

Arab-Israeli Conflicts

No sooner had Israel been recognized than the Arab nations, particularly Egypt, Jordan, Iraq, Syria, and Lebanon, announced their intention to restore control to the Palestinian Arabs, by force if necessary. As hostilities broke out, the Israeli military stepped in to preserve the borders, which no Arab nation agreed to recognize. Some 60 percent of the 1.3 million Arabs fled or were expelled from Israeli territory, becoming refugees in neighboring countries. An uneasy peace followed as Israel attempted to encourage new Jewish immigration. Israel also extended the same services that were available to the Jews, such as education and health care, to the non-Jewish Israelis. The new Jewish population continued to grow under the country's Law of Return, which gave every Jew in the world the right to settle permanently as a citizen. The question of Jerusalem remained unsettled, and the city was divided into two separate sections—Israeli Jewish and Jordanian Arab—a division both sides refused to regard as permanent.

In 1967, Egypt, followed by Syria, responded to Israel's military actions to take surrounding territory in what has come to be called the Six-Day War. In the course of defeating the Arab states' military, Israel occupied the Gaza Strip and the West Bank (Figure 16.4 on p. 423). The defeat was all the more bitter for the Arabs as Israeli-held territory expanded.

The October 1973 war (called the Yom Kippur War by Jews and the Ramadan War by Arabs), launched against Israel by Egypt and Syria, did not change any boundaries, but it did lead to huge oil price increases as Arab and other oil-rich nations retaliated for the European and U.S. backing of Israel. In 1979, Egypt, through the mediation of U.S. President Carter, recognized Israel's right to exist, for which Israel returned the Sinai, but there was no suggestion that the other occupied territories would be returned to neighboring Arab states. This recognition by Egypt, following several unsuccessful Arab military attacks, signaled to the Palestinians that they were alone in their struggle against Israel (Masci 2001).

Although our primary attention here is on the Palestinians and the Jews, another significant ethnic issue is present in Israel. The Law of Return has brought to Israel Jews of varying cultural backgrounds. European Jews have been the dominant force, but a significant migration of the more religiously observant Jews from North Africa and other

Zionism
Traditional Jewish religious yearning to return to the biblical homeland, now used to refer to support for the state of Israel.

parts of the Middle East has created what sociologist Ernest Krausz (1973) called "the two nations." Not only are the various Jewish groups culturally diverse, but there are also significant socioeconomic differences: The Europeans generally are more prosperous, better represented in the Knesset (Israel's parliament), and better educated. The secular Jews feel pressure from the more traditional and ultra-Orthodox Jews, who push for a nation more reflective of Jewish customs and law. Indeed, in a 1998 survey, more Israeli Jews see the lack of unity within the state as a major shortcoming than as a failure to end the Israeli-Arab conflict (*Los Angeles Times* poll 1998; M. Miller 1998).

Intifada
The Palestinian uprising against Israeli authorities in the occupied territories.

The Intifada

The occupied territories were regarded initially by Israel as a security zone between it and its belligerent neighbors. By the 1980s, however, it was clear that they were also serving as the location of new settlements for Jews migrating to Israel, especially from Russia. Palestinians, though enjoying some political and monetary support of Arab nations, saw little likelihood of a successful military effort to eliminate Israel. Therefore, in December 1987, they began the **Intifada**, the uprising against Israel by the Palestinians in the occupied territories through attacks against soldiers, the boycott of Israeli goods, general strikes, resistance, and noncooperation with Israeli authorities. The target of this first Intifada, lasting five years, was the Israelis.

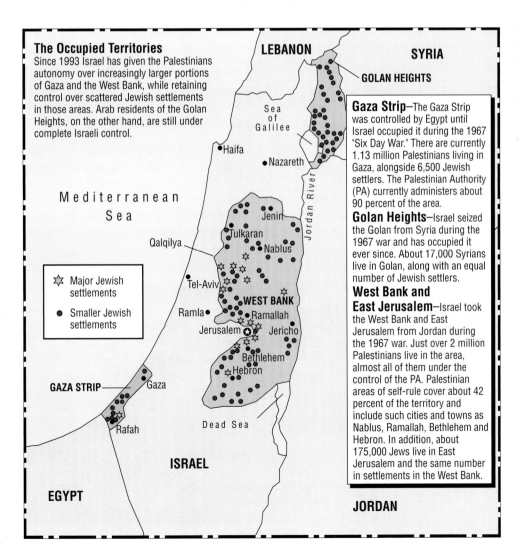

FIGURE 16.4 Israeli Settlements and Palestinian Lands

Source: Map, "Israeli Settlements and Palestinian Lands" from "Middle East Conflict" by David Masci, *CQ Researcher*, April 6, 2001. Copyright © 2001. Reproduced by permission of Copyright Clearance Center, on behalf of the publisher.

The Intifada has been a grassroots, popular movement whose growth in support was as much a surprise to the Palestine Liberation Organization (PLO) and the Arab nations as it was to Israel and its supporters. The broad range of participants in the Intifada—students, workers, union members, professionals, and business leaders—showed the unambiguous Palestinian opposition to occupation.

Despite condemnation by both the United Nations and the United States, Israel continued to expel suspected activists from the occupied territories into neighboring Arab states. The Intifada began out of the frustration of the Palestinians within Israel, but the confrontations were later encouraged by the PLO, an umbrella organization for several Palestinian factions of varying militancy.

With television news footage of Israeli soldiers appearing to attack defenseless youths, the Intifada transformed world opinion, especially in the United States. Palestinians came to be viewed as people struggling for self-determination rather than as terrorists out to destroy Israel. Instead of Israel being viewed as the "David" and its Arab neighbors "Goliath," Israel came to take on the bully role and the Palestinians the sympathetic underdog role (Hubbard 1993).

Nearly half of the world's Palestinian people live under Israeli control. Of the Israeli Palestinians, about one-third are regarded as residents, and the rest live in the occupied territories. The Diaspora of Jews that the creation of Israel was to remedy has led to the displacement of the Palestinian Arabs. From the Israeli perspective, the continued possession of these lands is vital to serve as a buffer from bordering enemies, as evidenced by Iraq's firing of 39 Scud missiles into Israel during the 1991 Gulf War. An entire generation of Israelis and Palestinians has been born since the 1967 Six-Day War. A declining number of Israelis personally recall the time when the Jews did not have a homeland. The Intifada and international reaction propelled Israel and the PLO to reach an agreement in 1993 known as the Oslo Accords.

The Search for Solutions Amid Violence

The Oslo Accords between Israeli Prime Minister Yitzhak Rabin and PLO Chairman Yasser Arafat and subsequent agreements ended the state of war and appeared to set in motion the creation of the first-ever self-governing Palestinian territory in the Gaza Strip and the West Bank. Hard-liners on both sides grew resistant to the move toward separate recognized Palestinian and Israel states. Prime Minister Rabin was assassinated at a peace rally by an Israeli who felt the government had given up too much. Suc-

Daily, Israelis—both Jews and Arabs—confront the deadly outcome of violent events. Here, the funeral of a Palestinian killed in a clash with Israeli soldiers in the West bank leads to both personal sorrow and yet another opportunity for political statements.

ceeding governments in Israel took stronger stands against relinquishing control of the occupied territories. Chairman Arafat became more ineffectual, with diminishing control over various Palestinian factions.

Despite the assurances at Oslo, Israel did not end its occupation of the Palestinian territories by 1999, justifying its actions as necessary to stop anti-Israel violence originating in Palestinian settlements. Complicating the picture was the continued growth of Israeli settlements into the West Bank (from 120,000 people in 1993 to 214,000 by 2001). Palestinians, assisted by Arabs in other countries, mounted a second Intifada beginning in September 2000, precipitated by the Israeli killing of several Palestinians at a Jerusalem mosque. This time militant Palestinians went outside the occupied territories and bombed civilian sites in Israel through a series of suicide bombings. This second Intifada, continuing through the present, has taken more Israeli lives. In the 1990s, about one Israeli died for every 25 Palestinians, but the recent violence has seen about one Israeli die for every three Palestinian deaths. Each violent episode brings a call for retaliation by the other side and desperate calls for a cease-fire from outside the region. Israel, despite worldwide denunciation, created a "security barrier" of concrete walls, ditches, and barbed wire to try to protect its Jewish settlers, which served to limit the mobility of peaceful Palestinians trying to access crops, schools, hospitals, and jobs (*The Economist* 2004b; Harman 2002; Lerner 2002).

The immediate problem is to end the violence, but any lasting peace must face a series of difficult issues, including the following:

- The status of Jerusalem. It is Israel's capital but is also viewed by Muslims as the third most holy city in the world.
- The future of the Jewish settlements in the Palestinian territories.
- The future of Palestinians and other Arabs with Israeli citizenship.
- The creation of a truly independent Palestinian national state with strong leadership.
- The future of Palestinian refugees elsewhere.

Added worries are the uneasy peace between Israel and its Arab neighbors and the sometimes interrelated events in Iraq and Iran (Rouhana and Bar-Tal 1998).

The last 60 years have witnessed significant changes: Israel has gone from a land under siege to a nation whose borders are recognized by almost everyone. Israel has come to terms with the various factions of religious and secular Jews trying to coexist. The Palestinian people have gone from disfranchisement to having territory and welcoming back others from exile. The current solution is fragile and temporary, as is any form of secession with a foundation for accommodation amid continuing violence.

Republic of South Africa

In every nation in the world, some racial, ethnic, or religious groups enjoy advantages denied to other groups. Nations differ in the extent of this denial and in whether it is supported by law or by custom. In no other industrial society has the denial been so entrenched in law as in the Republic of South Africa.

The Republic of South Africa is different from the rest of Africa because the original African peoples of the area are no longer present. Today, the country is multiracial, as shown in Table 16.2. The largest group is the Black Africans, or Bantus, who migrated from the north in the 18th century. Cape Coloureds, the product of mixed race, and Asians make up the remaining non-Whites. The small White community consists of the English and the Afrikaners, the latter descended from Dutch and other European settlers. As in all other multicultural nations we have considered, colonialism and immigration have left their mark.

TABLE 16.2
Racial Groups in the Republic of South Africa

	All Whites	Non-Whites	Black Africans	Coloureds	Asians
1904	22%	78%	67%	9%	2%
1936	21	79	69	8	2
1951	21	79	68	9	3
2003	10	90	79	9	3
2010 (proj.)	9	91	82	7	2

Note: "Non-White" totals subject to rounding error.

Sources: Author's estimates based on Statistics South Africa 2004; van den Berghe 1978:102.

The Legacy of Colonialism

The permanent settlement of South Africa by Europeans began in 1652, when the Dutch East India Company established a colony in Cape Town as a port of call for shipping vessels bound for India. The area was sparsely populated, and the original inhabitants of the Cape of Good Hope, the Hottentots and Bushmen, were pushed inland like the indigenous peoples of the New World. To fill the need for laborers, the Dutch imported slaves from areas of Africa farther north. Slavery was confined mostly to areas near towns and involved more limited numbers than in the United States. The Boers, seminomads descended from the Dutch, did not remain on the coast but trekked inland to establish vast sheep and cattle ranches. The trekkers, as they were known, regularly fought off the Black inhabitants of the interior regions. Sexual relations between Dutch men and slave and Hottentot women were quite common, giving rise to a mulatto group referred to today as Cape Coloureds.

The British entered the scene by acquiring part of South Africa in 1814, at the end of the Napoleonic Wars. The British introduced workers from India as indentured servants on sugar plantations. They had also freed the slaves by 1834, with little compensation to the Dutch slave owners, and had given Blacks almost all political and civil rights. The Boers were not happy with these developments and spent most of the 19th century in a violent struggle with the growing number of English colonists. In 1902, the British finally overwhelmed the Boers, leaving bitter memories on both sides. Once in control, however, they recognized that the superior numbers of the non-Whites were a potential threat to their power, as they had been to the power of the Afrikaners.

The growing non-White population consisted of the Coloureds, or mixed population, and the Black tribal groups, collectively called Bantus. The British gave both groups the vote but restricted the franchise to people who met certain property qualifications. **Pass laws** were introduced, placing curfews on the Bantus and limiting their geographic movement. These laws, enforced through "reference books" until 1986, were intended to prevent urban areas from becoming overcrowded with job-seeking Black Africans, a familiar occurrence in colonial Africa (van den Berghe 1965; W. Wilson 1973).

Apartheid

pass laws
Laws that controlled internal movement by non-Whites in South Africa.

apartheid
The policy of the South African government intended to maintain separation of Blacks, Coloureds, and Asians from the dominant Whites.

In 1948, South Africa was granted its independence from the United Kingdom, and the National Party, dominated by the Afrikaners, assumed control of the government. Under the leadership of this party, the rule of White supremacy, already well under way in the colonial period as custom, became more and more formalized into law. To deal with the multiracial population, the Whites devised a policy called apartheid to ensure their dominance. **Apartheid** (in Afrikaans, the language of the Afrikaners, it means "separation" or "apartness") came to mean a policy of separate development, euphemistically called multinational development by the government. At the time, these changes were regarded as cosmetic outside South Africa and by most Black South Africans.

The White ruling class was not homogeneous. The English and Afrikaners belonged to different political parties, lived apart, spoke different languages, and worshipped separately; but they shared the belief that some form of apartheid was necessary. Apartheid can perhaps be best understood as a 20th-century effort to reestablish the master-slave relationship. Blacks could not vote. They could not move throughout the country freely. They were unable to hold jobs unless the government approved. To work at approved jobs, they were forced to live in temporary quarters at great distances from their real homes. Their access to education, health care, and social services was severely limited (W. Wilson 1973).

Events took a significant turn in 1990, when South African Prime Minister F. W. De Klerk legalized 60 banned Black organizations and freed Nelson Mandela, leader of the African National Congress (ANC), after 27 years of imprisonment. Mandela's triumphant remarks after his release appear in "Listen to Our Voices."

The next year, De Klerk and Black leaders signed a National Peace Accord, pledging themselves to the establishment of a multiparty democracy and an end to violence. After a series of political defeats, De Klerk called for a referendum in 1992 to allow Whites to vote on ending apartheid. If he failed to receive popular support, he vowed to resign. A record high turnout gave a solid 68.6 percent vote favoring the continued dismantling of legal apartheid and the creation of a new constitution through negotiation. The process toward power-sharing ended symbolically when De Klerk and Mandela were jointly awarded the 1993 Nobel Peace Prize (Ottaway and Taylor 1992; Winant 2001).

A South African citizen displays the "passbook" that all non-Whites had to carry with them under Apartheid. These internal passports required obedience to a complex series of laws and regulations.

The Era of Reconciliation and Moving On

In April 1994, South Africa held its first universal election. Apartheid had ended. Nelson Mandela's ANC received 62 percent of the vote, giving him a five-year term as president. The National Party's F. W. De Klerk is serving as one of two executive deputy presidents. Mandela enjoyed the advantage of wide personal support throughout the nation. He retired in 1999 when his second term ended and was succeeded by fellow ANC leader Thabo Mbeki, who faces a daunting agenda because of the legacy of apartheid.

A significant step to help South Africa move past apartheid was the creation of the Truth and Reconciliation Commission (TRC). People were allowed to come forward and confess to horrors they had committed under apartheid from 1961 through 1993. If they were judged by the TRC to be truly remorseful, and most were, they were not subject to prosecution. If they failed to confess to all crimes they had committed, they were prosecuted. The stories gripped the country as people learned that actions taken in the name of the Afrikaner government were often worse than anyone had anticipated (Gobodo-Madikizela 2003).

The immediate relief that came with the end of apartheid has given way to greater concerns about the future of all South Africans. In "Research Focus" we consider the views expressed by contemporary South Africans.

With the emergence of the new multiracial government in South Africa, we see a country with enormous promise but many challenges that are similar to those of our own multiracial society. Some of the controversial issues facing the ANC-led government are very familiar to citizens in the United States:

Desperate poverty. Despite the growth of a small but conspicuous middle class among Black South Africans, poverty rates stand at 56 percent, compared to 4.5 percent of White South Africans.

Affirmative action. Race-based employment goals and other preference programs have been proposed, yet critics insist that such efforts constitute reverse apartheid.

Voices **Listen to Our Voices** Listen to

AFRICA, IT IS OURS!

Nelson Mandela

The following excerpts are from 71-year-old Black nationalist leader Nelson Mandela's speech, delivered in front of the Cape Town City Hall after his release from a 27-year imprisonment on February 12, 1990.

Amandla! Amandla! i-Afrika, mayibuye! [Power! Power! Africa, it is ours!]

My friends, comrades and fellow South Africans, I greet you all in the name of peace, democracy and freedom for all. I stand here before you not as a prophet but as a humble servant of you, the people.

Your tireless and heroic sacrifices have made it possible for me to be here today. I therefore place the remaining years of my life in your hands.

On this day of my release, I extend my sincere and warmest gratitude to the millions of my compatriots and those in every corner of the globe who have campaigned tirelessly for my release.

Negotiations on the dismantling of apartheid will have to address the overwhelming demand of our people for a democratic nonracial and unitary South Africa. There must be an end to white monopoly on political power.

And [there must be] a fundamental restructuring of our political and economic systems to insure that the inequalities of apartheid are addressed and our society thoroughly democratized. . . .

Our struggle has reached a decisive moment. We call on our people to seize this moment so that the process toward democracy is rapid and uninterrupted. We have waited too long for our freedom. We can no longer wait. Now is the time to intensify the struggle on all fronts.

To relax our efforts now would be a mistake which generations to come will not be able to forgive. The sight of freedom looming on the horizon should encourage us to redouble our efforts. It is only through disciplined mass action that our victory can be assured.

We call on our white compatriots to join us in the shaping of a new South Africa. The freedom movement is the political home for you, too. We call on the international community to continue the campaign to isolate the apartheid regime.

To lift sanctions now would be to run the risk of aborting the process toward the complete eradication of apartheid. Our march to freedom is irreversible. We must not allow fear to stand in our way.

Universal suffrage on a common voters' roll in a united democratic and nonracial South Africa is the only way to peace and racial harmony.

In conclusion, I wish to go to my own words during my trial in 1964. They are as true today as they were then. I wrote: I have fought against white domination, and I have fought against black domination. I have cherished the idea of a democratic and free society in which all persons live together in harmony and with equal opportunities.

It is an ideal which I hope to live for and to achieve. But if needs be, it is an ideal for which I am prepared to die. ■

Medical care. The nation is trying to confront the duality of private care for the affluent (usually Whites) and government-subsidized care (usually for people of color). AIDS has reached devastating levels, with 21.5 percent of the population having HIV/AIDS as of the beginning of 2004.

Crime. Although government-initiated violence has ended, the generations of conflict and years of intertribal attacks have created a climate for crime, illegal gun ownership, and disrespect for law enforcement.

School integration. Multiracial schools are replacing the apartheid system, but for some, the change is occurring too fast or not fast enough. While 15 percent of working-age Whites hold a college degree, only 1.5 percent of Black South Africans are so advantaged.

Focus **Research Focus** Research Focus

LISTENING TO THE PEOPLE

In the United States, we take for granted the regular release of opinion or survey data about what people think about the sensitive issues in their country. However, public opinion surveying does not typically occur in totalitarian countries such as South Africa under apartheid. Today, surveying is now a regular part of South African life; and, not too surprisingly, the subject sometimes turns to race relations.

The South African Institute of Race Relations in 2001 and the Henry Kaiser Family Foundation in 2003 commissioned national surveys to find out what adults from all racial groups thought about racism in everyday life. Reviewing these studies, the data reveal a racial divide on many issues.

Nearly two-thirds of Black Africans (65 percent) indicated in 2003 that they felt the country was headed in the right direction, while only about one-third (36 percent) of Whites felt the same way. Blacks overwhelmingly see unemployment as the major problem facing the nation, while Whites place crime and security as the top problem, with government corruption as number two. Blacks, meanwhile, do not see the government as a problem but give priority to both housing and water supply—two issues not ranked highly by their fellow White countrymen.

All South Africans—whether Black, Coloured, Indian, or White—agree that democracy is preferable to any other kind of government, has been good, and that South Africa will remain democratic. Blacks are much more likely to see the gap between the rich and poor as a threat to democracy. Blacks are more likely to see education and health care as improving over the 10 years of post-Apartheid South Africa, while Whites see it as actually getting worse. Just 19 percent of White respondents said they would consider a return to apartheid.

In summary, the survey revealed deep concern among all South Africans about a number of social and economic issues, but the specific factor of race is not viewed as the dominant problem. Yet the consciousness of racism has not vanished. The majority still see racism as a serious concern. Yet when asked, they generally see their own group as the victim of racism, with little recognition of the problems of prejudice and discrimination facing the other groups.

There seemed little doubt from this survey that, as during the apartheid era, South Africa still has a racial problem to solve. ■

Sources: Henry Kaiser Family Foundation 2004; Moein 2004; Schlemmer 2001a, 2001b.

These issues must be addressed with minimal increases in government spending as the government seeks to reverse deficit spending without an increase in taxes that would frighten away needed foreign investment. As difficult as all these challenges are, perhaps the most difficult is land reform (Dixon 2003; Goering 2003; Haub 2004; Kane-Berman 2003; South African Institute of Race Relations 2002, 2004).

The government has pledged to address the issue of land ownership. Between 1960 and 1990, the government forced 3.5 million Black South Africans from their land and often allowed Whites to settle on it. Under the 1994 Restitution of Land Rights Act, these displaced citizens can now file for a return of their land. Where feasible, the government plans to restore the original inhabitants to their land; where this is not feasible, the government is to make "just and equitable compensation." By 2004, despite tens of thousands of claims filed, only 2 percent of White-owned farm land has been transferred. The magnitude of this land reform issue cannot be minimized. Originally the goal was to achieve 30 percent of land transfer by 2004, but this has now been deferred to 2015. With its other economic problems and now the decision to invest hundreds of millions of dollars in hosting the 2010 Football (soccer) World Cup, more new land is likely to be occupied by Black South Africans through squatter arrangements than through government-approved transfer (LaFraniere and Wines 2004).

Conclusion

By looking beyond our borders, we gather new insights into the social processes that frame and define intergroup relationships. The colonial experience has played a role in all cases under consideration in this chapter, but particularly in South Africa. In Mexico and South Africa, which have long histories of multiethnic societies, intergroup sexual relations have been widespread but with different results. Mestizos in Mexico occupy a middle racial group and experience less tension, whereas in South Africa, the Cape Coloureds had freedoms under apartheid almost as limited as those of the Bantus. South Africa enforced de jure segregation, whereas Israeli communities seem to have de facto segregation. Israel's and South Africa's intergroup conflicts have involved the world community. Indigenous people figure prominently in Canada and Mexico. Complete assimilation is absent in all five societies considered in this chapter and is unlikely to occur in the near future; the legal and informal barriers to assimilation and pluralism vary for subordinate people choosing either option. Looking at the status of women in Mexico reminds us of the worldwide nature of gender stratification but also offers insight into the patterns present in developing nations.

If we add the United States to these societies, the similarities become even more striking. The problems of racial and ethnic adjustment in the United States have dominated our attention, but they parallel past and present experiences in other societies with racial, ethnic, or religious heterogeneity. The U.S. government has been involved in providing educational, financial, and legal support for programs intended to help particular racial or ethnic groups, and it continues to avoid interfering with religious freedom. Bilingual, bicultural programs in schools, autonomy for Native Americans on reservations, and increased participation in decision making by residents of ghettoes and barrios are all viewed as acceptable goals, although they are not pursued to the extent that many subordinate-group people would like.

The analysis of this chapter has reminded us of the global nature of dominant-subordinate relations along dimensions of race, ethnicity, religion, and gender. In the next chapter, we will take an overview of racial and ethnic relations but also explore social inequality along the dimensions of age, disability status, and sexual orientation.

Key Terms

apartheid   426
color gradient   411
Diaspora   421
ethnonational conflict   408

home rule   418
Intifada   423
pass laws   426

visible minorities   417
world systems theory   408
Zionism   422

Review Questions

1. Identify who the native peoples are and what their role has been in each of the societies discussed in this chapter.
2. On what levels can one speak of an identity issue facing Canada as a nation?
3. What role has secession played in Canada, Northern Ireland, and Israel?
4. How have civil uprisings affected intergroup tensions in Northern Ireland and Israel?
5. To what extent are the problems facing South Africa today a part of apartheid's legacy?

Critical Thinking

1. Social construction of race emphasizes how we create arbitrary definitions of skin color that then have social consequences. Drawing on the societies discussed, select one nation and identify how social definitions work in other ways to define group boundaries.
2. Apply the functionalist and conflict approaches of sociology first introduced in Chapter 1 to each of the societies under study in this chapter.
3. The conflicts summarized are examples of ethnonational conflicts, but how have the actions or inactions of the United States contributed to these problems?

Internet Connections—Research Navigator™

 Follow the instructions found on page 31 of this text to access the features of Research Navigator™. Once at the Web site, enter your Login Name and Password. Then, to use the ContentSelect database, enter keywords such as "Apartheid," "Intifada," and "Quebecois," and the research engine will supply relevant and recent scholarly and popular press publications. Use the *New York Times* Search-by-Subject Archive to find recent news articles related to sociology and the Link Library feature to locate relevant Web links organized by the key terms associated with this chapter

17 Overcoming Exclusion

THE EXPERIENCE OF SOCIAL DISADVANTAGE IS NOT LIMITED to groups defined by race, ethnicity, gender, or religion. Despite an improving medical and financial situation, the elderly are still as a group at a disadvantage, given the ageism in our society. People with disabilities also have sought to achieve both respect and opportunities. Although the Americans with Disabilities Act (ADA) is a significant step forward, serious advocacy efforts continue. Long-term homophobia has made it a challenge for gays and lesbians to go about their lives. Progress has been mixed; some civil rights legislation has been passed at the local level, but the federal government took positions against avowed homosexuals in the military and sought to prevent legal recognition of gay and lesbian marriage. For each of these groups, as well as the racial and ethnic minorities discussed earlier, it is easy to applaud the progress already made. However, given the level of inequality that still persists, the full agenda for further progress remains.

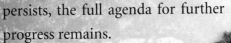

What metaphor do we use to describe a nation whose racial, ethnic, and religious minorities are on the way to becoming numerical majorities in many cities and, by 2005, in several states? For several generations, the image of the melting pot has been used as a convenient description of our culturally diverse nation. The analogy of an alchemist's cauldron was clever, even if a bit ethnocentric. It originated in the Middle Ages, when the alchemist used a melting pot to attempt to change less costly metals into gold and silver.

The Melting Pot was the title of a 1908 play by Israel Zangwill. In this play, a young Russian immigrant to the United States composes a symphony that portrays a nation that serves as a crucible (or pot) where all ethnic and racial groups melt together into a new, superior stock.

The vision of the United States as a melting pot became popular in the first part of the 20th century, particularly because it suggested that the United States had an almost divinely inspired mission to destroy artificial divisions and create a single humankind. However, the image did not mesh with reality, as the dominant group indicated its unwillingness to welcome Native Americans, African Americans, Hispanics or Latinos, Jews, and Asians, among many others, into the melting pot.

The image of the melting pot is not invoked as much today. Instead, people speak of a salad bowl to describe a country that is ethnically diverse. As we can distinguish the lettuce from the tomatoes from the peppers in a tossed salad, we can see ethnic restaurants and the persistence of foreign languages in conversations on street corners. The dressing over the ingredients is akin to the shared value system and culture, covering but not hiding the different ingredients of the salad.

Yet even the notion of a salad is wilting. Like the melting pot that came before, the image of a salad is static, certainly not indicative of the dynamic changes we see in the United States. It also fails to conjure up the myriad cultural pieces that make up the fabric or mosaic of our diverse nation.

The kaleidoscope offers another familiar and more useful analogy. Patented in 1817 by Scottish scientist Sir David Brewster, the kaleidoscope was a toy and then became a table ornament in the parlors of the rich. Users of this optical device turn a set of mirrors and observe the seemingly endless colors and patterns that are reflected off pieces of glass, tinsel, or beads. The growing popularity of the phrase "people of color" fits well with the idea of the United States as a kaleidoscope. The changing images correspond to the often-bewildering array of groups found in our country (Schaefer 1992).

The images created by a kaleidoscope are hard to describe because they change dramatically with little effort. Similarly, in the kaleidoscope of the United States, we find it a challenge to describe the dynamic multiracial nature of this republic. Yet even as we begin to understand the past, present, and future of all the many racial and ethnic groups, we recognize that there are still other people who are stigmatized in society by virtue of group membership. In this chapter, we will continue our effort to understand the people excluded in varying degrees from society by considering the cases of the aged, people with disabilities, and the gay and lesbian community.

The Aged: A Social Minority

Older people in the United States are subject to a paradox. They are a significant segment of the population who, as we shall see, often are viewed with negative stereotypes and are subject to discrimination. Yet they also have successfully organized into a potent collective force that wields significant political clout on certain social issues. Unlike other social groups subjected to differential treatment, this social category will include most of us someday. So in this one case, the notion of the elderly as "them" will eventually give way to "us."

The elderly share the characteristics of subordinate or minority groups that we introduced in Chapter 1. Specifically,

1. The elderly experience unequal treatment in employment and may face prejudice and discrimination.

2. The elderly share physical characteristics that distinguish them from younger people. In addition, their cultural preferences and leisure-time activities often differ from those of the rest of society.

3. Membership in this disadvantaged group is involuntary.

4. Older people have a strong sense of group solidarity, as reflected in senior citizens' centers, retirement communities, and advocacy organizations.

5. Older people generally are married to others of comparable age.

There is one crucial difference between older people and other subordinate groups, such as racial and ethnic minorities or women: All of us who live long will eventually assume the ascribed status of being an older person (Barron 1953; Wagley and Harris 1958).

Who Are the Elderly?

As shown in Figure 17.1, an increasing proportion of the population is composed of older people. In the 20th century, the number of people in the United States under age 65 tripled. At the same time, the number aged 65 or over increased 11-fold. Consequently, men and women aged 65 and over, who constituted only 4 percent of the population in 1900, are expected by 2050 to account for more than 20 percent of the population.

These trends are expected to continue well through the 21st century as mortality declines and the postwar baby boomers age. While the elderly population continues

 CD-ROM *Activity 11.2*

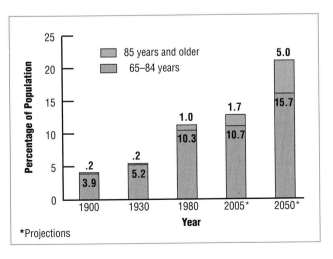

FIGURE 17.1 Actual and Projected Growth of the Elderly Population of the United States
Sources: Bureau of the Census 1975, 2003a:14.

to increase, the "oldest old" segment of the population (i.e., people 85 years old and over) is growing at an even faster rate. By 2050, the proportion of the population 85 and over will reach 4.8 percent, compared with only 1.7 percent in 2005.

Compared with the rest of the population, the elderly are more likely to be female, White, and living in certain states. Men generally have higher death rates then women at every age. As a result, elderly women outnumber men by a ratio of 3 to 2. The difference grows with advancing age, so that among the oldest-old group, women outnumber men 5 to 2. About 83 percent of the elderly are White and non-Hispanic. Although the aged population is growing more racially and ethnically diverse, the higher death rates of members of racial and ethnic minorities, coupled with immigration to the United States of younger Latinos and Asians, are likely to keep the older population more White than the nation as a whole. The aged tend to be found in larger numbers in certain states. Although California has the largest absolute number of elderly, the highest proportions are found in Florida and Pennsylvania, followed by several rural states such as Nebraska, Iowa, Maine, Montana, and the Dakotas.

Ageism

Respected gerontologist Bernice Neugarten (1996) observed that negative stereotypes of old age are strongly entrenched in a society that prides itself on being oriented toward youth and the future. In 1968, physician Robert Butler, the founding director of the National Institute on Aging, coined the term **ageism** to refer to prejudice and discrimination against the elderly. Ageism reflects a deep uneasiness among young and middle-aged people about growing old. For many, old age symbolizes disease and death; seeing the elderly serves as a reminder that they too may someday become old and infirm. By contrast, society glorifies youth, seeing it as interchangeable with beauty and the future. Ageism is so common that Robert Butler (1990:178) notes that it "knows no one century, nor culture, and is not likely to go away any time soon."

If there is any doubt how pervasive ageism is, we need only consider an experiment conducted by sociologist William Levin, as described in "Research Focus."

How do these images described in Levin's experiment develop? Partly, we tend to see the elderly only in situations that reinforce the image. For example, physicians see more sick old people, so "all old people are sick." Social workers see only the indigent; therefore, "all aged are poor." We see the aged sitting on park benches but do not notice them rushing to and from jobs or volunteer work, so "all old people are inactive with no interests to keep them involved with society." The needy aged have come to represent all the elderly in the public mind (Birren and Gribbin 1973; Neugarten 1996).

For many, old age symbolizes the stigma of disease. With ageism all too common in the Untied States, it is hardly surprising that older people are barely visible on television. In 2002, the Senate Special Committee on Aging convened a panel on the media's portrayal of older people and sharply criticized media and marketing executives for bombarding audiences with negative images of the aged. The social consequences of such images are significant. Research shows that older people who have positive perceptions of aging live an average of 7.5 years longer than those who have negative perceptions (M. Gardner 2003; Levy et al. 2002; E. Ramirez 2002).

The federal Age Discrimination in Employment Act, which went into effect in 1968, was passed to protect workers 40 years of age or older from being fired because of their age and replaced with younger workers who presumably would receive lower salaries. The Supreme Court strengthened federal protection against age discrimination in 1996, ruling unanimously that such lawsuits can be successful even if an older worker is replaced by someone older than 40. Consequently, if a firm unfairly fires a 65-year-old employee to make way for a 45-year-old, this still can constitute age discrimination.

While firing workers simply because they are old violates federal law, courts have upheld the right to lay off older workers for economic reasons. Critics contend that

ageism
Prejudice and discrimination against the elderly.

THE FACE OF AGEISM

For more than 80 years, sociologists have documented in their research how we stereotype groups of people. Using the checklist approach, studies identify how respondents tend to associate certain adjectives such as *wise* or *lazy* with certain racial and ethnic groups. Much more recently, research has documented the same stereotyping pattern when it comes to age.

"Does this person appear to you to be competent or incompetent? Generous or selfish?" Sociologist William Levin asked such questions of college students in California, Massachusetts, and Tennessee after showing them photographs of men who appeared to be about 25, 52, and 73 years old. Levin's findings confirmed that a widespread age bias is evident across the United States.

The students questioned in Levin's experiment were not told that the three photographs were of the same man at different stages of his life. Special care was taken to select old photographs that had a contemporary look. Levin asked the college students to evaluate the "three men" for a job using 19 measures. The 25-year-old man was found to be active, powerful, healthy, fast, attractive, energetic, involved, and in possession of a good memory. Students thought that the 52-year-old man had a high IQ and was reliable. By contrast, the 73-year-old man was evaluated as inactive, weak, sickly, slow, ugly, unreliable, lazy, socially isolated, and possessing a low IQ and a poor memory. Clearly, the negative stereotypes of older people evident in this study could contribute to discrimination in the paid labor force and other areas of our society. ■

Source: Levin 1988.

later the same firms hire young, cheaper workers to replace experienced older workers. When economic growth began to slow in 2001 and companies cut back on their workforces, complaints of age bias grew sharply as older workers began to suspect they were bearing a disproportionate share of the layoffs. According to the Equal Employment Opportunity Commission, between 1999 and 2004, complaints of age discrimination rose more than 41 percent. However, evidence of a countertrend has emerged. Some firms have been giving larger raises to older workers to encourage their retirement at the higher salary—a tactic that prompts younger workers to complain of age discrimination (Novelli 2004; Uchitelle 2003).

The American Association of Retired Persons (AARP) conducted an experiment in 1993 that confirmed that older people often face discrimination when applying for jobs. Comparable résumés for two applicants—one 57 years old and the other 32 years old—were sent to 775 large firms and employment agencies around the United States. In situations for which positions were available, the younger applicant received a favorable response 43 percent of the time. In contrast, the older applicant received favorable responses less than half as often (only 17 percent of the time). One Fortune 500 corporation asked the younger applicant for more information but informed the older applicant that no appropriate positions were open (Bendick et al. 1993).

Yet in contradiction to these negative stereotypes present in an ageist society, researchers have found that an older worker can be an asset for employers. According to a 1991 study, older workers can be retrained in new technologies, have lower rates of absenteeism than younger employees, and often are more effective salespeople.

Being older does not mean that employment is not available, although sometimes jobs that are open are unrelated to one's career. Here a retiree has a "second career" as a greeter at a discount department store in Fishkill, New York.

The study focused on two corporations based in the United States (the hotel chain Days Inns of America and the holding company Travelers Corporation of Hartford) and a British retail chain, all of which have long-term experience in hiring workers age 50 and over. Clearly, the findings pointed to older workers as good investments. Yet despite such studies, complaints of age bias grew during the economic slowdown beginning in 2001, when companies cut back on their workforces (Equal Employment Opportunity Commission 2001; Telsch 1991:A16).

A degree of conflict is emerging along generational lines that resemble other types of intergroup tension. Although the conflict involves neither violence nor the degree of subjugation found with other dominant-subordinate relations in the United States, a feeling still prevails that jobs and benefits for the elderly are at the expense of younger generations. Younger people are increasingly unhappy about paying Social Security taxes and underwriting the Medicare program, especially because they speculate that they themselves will never receive benefits from these fiscally insecure programs.

The Economic Picture

The elderly, like the other groups we have considered, do not form a single economic profile. The perception of "elderly" and "poor" as practically synonymous has changed in recent years to a view that the noninstitutionalized elderly are economically better off than the population as a whole. Both views are too simplistic; income varies widely among the aged.

There is significant variation in wealth and poverty among the nation's older people. Some individuals and couples find themselves poor in part because of fixed pensions and skyrocketing health care costs. As shown in Figure 17.2, poverty has declined among the elderly of all racial groups.

As a group, older people in the United States are neither homogeneous nor poor. The typical elderly person enjoys a standard of living that is much higher than at any point in the nation's past. Class differences among the elderly tend to narrow somewhat: Retirees who had middle-class incomes while younger tend to remain better off after retirement than those who had lower incomes, but the financial gap is declining. (Smith and Tillipman 2000).

The decline in poverty rates is welcome. However, advocates of the position that the elderly are receiving too much at the expense of the younger generations point to the rising affluence of the aged as evidence of an unfair economic burden placed on the young and future generations of workers.

As we can see in the previously mentioned data, the aged who are most likely to experience poverty are the same people more likely to be poor earlier in their lives:

FIGURE 17.2   Poverty Rate Among the Elderly, 2003

Note: Data for Whites (2000) is for non-Hispanic Whites.
Source: DeNavas-Walt et al. 2004:47-50.

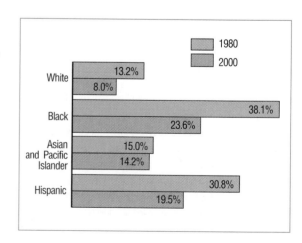

female-headed households and racial and ethnic minorities. Although overall the aged are doing well economically, poverty remains a particularly difficult problem for the thousands of elderly who are impoverished annually by paying for long-term medical care (Quadagno 2005).

Advocacy Efforts by the Elderly

As we have seen with racial, ethnic, and gender groups, efforts to bring about desired change often require the formation of political organizations and advocacy groups. This is true with the elderly and, as we will see later, is also true for people with disabilities, gay men, and lesbian women. One such group working on behalf of the elderly is the Gray Panthers. As of 1995, this organization had 40,000 members in 32 states and five foreign countries working to combat prejudice and discrimination against older people. In early 1995, Maggie Kuhn, the best known of the Gray Panthers' founders, died at age 89. Kuhn had spent the last 25 years of her life as a leader in the battle against ageism and other forms of injustice. Her desire to create an advocacy group of the elderly began when she was forced to retire at age 65 from her position on a church staff. Only two weeks before her death, she joined striking transit workers on a picket line (Folkart 1995; R. Thomas 1995).

The growing collective consciousness among older people also contributed to the establishment of the Older Women's League (OWL) in 1980. OWL focuses on access to health insurance, Social Security benefits, and pension reform. OWL leaders and the group's 15,000 members hope that the organization will serve as a critical link between the feminist movement described in Chapter 15 and activists for "gray power" (Kening 2004).

The largest organization representing the nation's elderly is the American Association of Retired Persons (AARP), which was founded in 1958 by a retired school principal who was having difficulty obtaining insurance because of age prejudice. Many of AARP's services involve discounts and insurance for its 35 million members (44 percent of American aged 50 or older); but recognizing that many elderly are still gainfully employed, it has dropped its full name, American Association of *Retired* Persons.

The potential power of AARP is enormous; it represents one out of every four registered voters in the United States. AARP has endorsed voter registration campaigns, nursing home reforms, and pension reforms. Acknowledging its difficulties in recruiting members of racial and ethnic minority groups, AARP began a Minority Affairs Initiative. The spokeswoman for this initiative, Margaret Dixon, became the AARP's first African American president in 1996 (AARP 2003).

People grow old in many different ways. Not all the elderly face the same challenges or enjoy the same resources. Whereas the AARP lobbies to protect the elderly in general, other groups work in more specific ways. For example, the National Committee to Preserve Social Security and Medicare, founded in 1982, unsuccessfully lobbied Congress to keep Medicare benefits for the ailing poor elderly. Other large special interest groups represent retired federal employees, retired teachers, and retired union workers (Quadagno 2005).

The elderly in the United States are better off today financially and physically than ever before. Many of them have strong financial assets and medical care packages that will take care of almost any need. But, as we have seen, a significant segment is impoverished, faced with the prospect of declining health and mounting medical bills. Older people of color may have to add being aged to a lifetime of discrimination. As in all other stages of the life course, the aged constitute a diverse group in the United States and around the world.

Although organizations such as the Gray Panthers, OWL, and AARP are undoubtedly valuable, the diversity of the nation's older population necessitates many different responses to the problems of the elderly. For example, older African Americans and

Hispanics tend to rely more on family members, friends, and informal social networks than on organizational support systems. Because of their lower incomes and greater incapacity resulting from poor health, older Blacks and Hispanics are more likely to need substantial assistance from family members than are older Whites. In recent years, older people of color have emerged as a distinct political force, independent of the larger elderly population, in some urban centers and in the Southwest. Advocacy groups for the aged are still in their early stages, and low-income elderly often are the least represented (Achenbaumm 1993; Neugarten 1996; Schaefer 2005).

People with Disabilities: Moving On

George Lane was scheduled to appear in court in September 1997, arising from a reckless driving misdeamenor charge following an accident that left him unable to walk. Arriving at the Polk County, Tennessee, courthouse, he found that the courtroom was on the second floor in a building without an elevator. The court refused to make any allowance, so he dragged himself up the steps only to learn the case had been postponed. Refusing to repeat the experience at the next hearing date, Lane was forced to have his attorney shuttle information back and forth from the courtroom. The court felt it was not obligated to make any accommodation to his disability, and finally, seven years later, the Supreme Court ruled 5–4 that Lane's rights had been denied (Robau 2003).

Throughout history, people have been socially disadvantaged, not because of the limits of their own skills and abilities but because assumptions are made about them based on some group characteristics. People with disabilities are such a group. The very term *disabilities* suggests lack of ability in some area, but as we shall see, society often assumes that a person with a disability is far less capable than she or he is. Furthermore, society limits the life chances of people with disabilities in ways that are unnecessary and unrelated to any physical infirmity.

Disability in Contemporary Society

CD-ROM *Activity 11.1*

Societies have always had members with disabilities. Historically, they have dealt differently with people who had physical or mental limitations, but rarely have they been treated as equals. According to the 2000 Census, an estimated 49.7 million people who were aged five and older have disabilities, or about one in six in the population. **Disability** is considered a reduced ability to perform tasks one would normally do at a given stage in life. This includes everyone from people who have difficulty carrying 10 pounds to people who use a wheelchair, crutches, or a walker. As shown in Figure 17.3, many people with disabilities are otherwise in good health (V. Freedman et al. 2004; Waldrop and Stern 2003).

The proportion of people with disabilities continues to increase. Because of advances in medicine, many people who once would have died from an accident or illness now survive. Also, as more people live longer, they are more likely to experience diseases that have disabling consequences.

Disabilities are found in all segments of the population, but racial and ethnic minorities are disproportionately more likely to experience them and also to have less access to assistance. Fewer African Americans and Hispanic people with disabilities are graduating from college compared with White people with disabilities. They also have incomes consistently lower than their White counterparts (Waldrop and Stern 2003).

Although disability knows no social class, about two-thirds of working-age people with a disability in the United States are unemployed. African Americans and Hispanics with disabilities are even more likely to be jobless. Most of them believe that they would be able to work if they were offered the opportunity or if some reasonable

disability
Reduced ability to perform tasks one would normally do at a given stage in life.

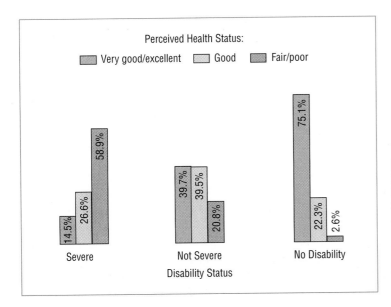

Perceived Health Status:
Very good/excellent   Good   Fair/poor

FIGURE 17.3
Perceived Health Status by Disability Status (age 25 to 64 years, percentage with specified health status)
Source: Based on 1997 Survey of Income and Program Participation as released by the Bureau of the Census in J. McNeil 2001.

Severe: 14.5%, 26.6%, 58.9%
Not Severe: 39.7%, 39.5%, 20.8%
No Disability: 75.1%, 22.3%, 2.6%

Disability Status

accommodation could be made to address the disability. These accommodations can be modest. Between 1978 and 1992, Sears Roebuck found that, on average, it cost only $126 to accommodate a worker's disability with some measures involving little or no cost, such as flexible work schedules, back-support belts, and rest periods (Kirkpatrick 1994; B. Noble 1995; Shapiro 1993).

A significant stigma is attached to having a major visible disability. Not wishing to present an image of a "disabled" president, Franklin Roosevelt enlisted the cooperation of the press corps to avoid being shown in a wheelchair or using crutches. This picture shows the President leaving a New York City townhouse in 1933, with a rare view of the president's leg braces.
Source: © New York Daily News, L. P. Reprinted with permission.

Labeling the Disabled

Labeling theorists, drawing on the work of sociologist Erving Goffman (1963), suggest that society attaches a stigma to many forms of disability and that this stigma leads to prejudicial treatment. Indeed, people with disabilities often observe that people without disabilities see them only as blind, deaf, wheelchair users, and so forth, rather than as complex human beings with individual strengths and weaknesses whose blindness or deafness is merely one aspect of their lives.

In "Listen to Our Voices," writer Kathi Wolfe discusses both the subtle and the more overt ways society assign labels to people with disabilities.

In this regard, a review of studies of women with disabilities disclosed that most academic research on the disabled does not even differentiate by gender, thereby perpetuating the view that when a disability is present, no other personal characteristic

Voices Listen to Our Voices *Listen to Our*

DEBUNK THOSE STEREOTYPES

"You must be so excited! It's great what blind people can do!" said the woman next to me at Starbucks a couple of weeks ago. I groaned inwardly as I folded my white cane and sat down with my coffee. Erik Weihenmayer had just become the first blind man to climb Mount Everest, putting him on the "Today" show and the cover of *Time* magazine. The sighted folks were inspired again, and I knew what was coming. "So?" she continued, "When are you going to climb Mount Everest?"

If this encounter had been unique, I would have laughed and shrugged the woman's misplaced admiration and silly question. But anyone who's disabled can tell you that the experience is all too common.

One of us bursts onto the cultural radar screen as a superhero, and all of us are expected to perform amazing feats.

It's hard to say which stereotype is more annoying: the disabled as helpless victims or as superheroes. It's certainly no fun to be an object of pity. At least half a dozen times in the past few years, well-meaning but

Kathi Wolfe

annoying people have thrown coins next to my plate when I've been eating at a restaurant. On the other hand, it's bad to be held up as some kind of motivational guru. I wish I had a nickel for every time someone has said that I must be so much more "insightful" than a sighted person.

Like most people, disabled and non-disabled alike, I'm neither victim nor star. I work as a freelance writer, shop, take care of family responsibilities and visit friends. But you wouldn't recognize me from the stereotypes in the media. . . .

I belong to a disabled women's support group that meets monthly. One woman just bought her first condo ("handicapped-accessible") and is deep into mortgage rates and maintenance fees. A paraplegic describes balancing her career with being a wife and the mother of an 8 year old. A baby boomer whose speech and gait are impaired is getting ready for college while ironing out her tense relationship with her own mom. Those are everyday challenges we have to surmount. They're not Everests. They're just tougher than they might be if we weren't disabled. . . .

can matter. When gender differences are recognized, such recognition may deny a person's dignity. One study found that women with disabilities were more likely to be discouraged from having children and much more likely to be advised to have hysterectomies than women without disabilities but with similar medical conditions (Fine and Asch 1981, 1988a, 1988b; Gove 1980; Karkabi 1993).

As with other subordinate statuses, the mass media have contributed to the stereotyping of people with disabilities. Too often, they are treated with a mixture of pity and fear. Nationwide charity telethons promote a negative image of the disabled as being childlike and nonproductive, suggesting that, until they are "cured," they cannot contribute to society like other people. At the very least, the poster child image proclaims that it is not okay to be disabled. By contrast, in literature and film, evil characters with disabilities—from Captain Hook to Dr. Strangelove to Freddy

Listen to Our Voices Listen to Our Voices Listen

Don't get me wrong—I like to read news reports on disabled people, at least when they're about issues—health insurance, discrimination, education—that concern me and my peers.

Just keep us in some kind of real context. Occasionally, show us not as main characters but as background characters—like a story about a subway delay or a festival that includes, but doesn't necessarily feature, folks with white canes and wheelchairs stuck on the subway or sitting in the audience. And on TV and in movies, give us some roles as regular characters—like Marlee Matlin's deaf political consultant on "The West Wing." There's been progress on this front in the last few years; I'd like to see more.

And I'd like to see stories about some of the people who really are heroes to those of us with disabilities. Like those who found a sudden demand for their previously unwanted services in World War II, and rose to the challenge. While able-bodied men were away fighting, disabled people worked in factories and offices and served as volunteers. Reporting for a 1995 article, I talked to Norma Krajczar of Morehead City, N.C. As a visually impaired teenager in Massachu-

setts, Norma was a volunteer aircraft warden; the thought was that her sensitive hearing would give her an advantage over sighted wardens in listening for enemy planes. And I learned that Akron, Ohio, became known as the "crossroads of the deaf" because of all the deaf people who came to work in tire factories converted to defense plants, making more money than they had ever been able to before. Yet, even with all the reporting that's been done recently about the Greatest Generation, you don't hear much about those folks.

Eyesight aside, I'm never going to climb Mount Everest. I'm a lover of creature comforts who freaks if the AC breaks down for 15 minutes. And as I told that woman at Starbucks, I'm terrified of heights.

I don't mean to be a grouch; I know she was trying to be nice. But next time she wants to strike up a conversation, maybe she could try something she'd say to an able-bodied person. Like, "The O's [Baltimore Orioles] are tanking again." Or, "Just what's in a Frappuccino, anyways?" I'd even settle for, "Hot enough for you?"

Now, these are things I know about. ■

Source: Wolfe 2001:23. Reprinted by permission of Kathi Wolfe.

Krueger—reinforce the view that disability is a punishment for evil. Efforts to encourage sober driving or safety in the workplace use images of people with disabilities to frighten people into the appropriate behavior.

Even the more favorable treatments of disabled characters tend to focus on courageous and inspirational characters who achieve striking personal successes against great odds, such as Tiny Tim in *A Christmas Carol* or the idiot savant in the film *Rain Man,* rather than on the impact of prejudice and discrimination on ordinary disabled people. The press coverage received by people with disabilities who excel also minimizes the day-to-day reality of most people with a disability (Bennetts 1993; Gartner and Joe 1987; Norden 1994).

Negative attitudes are not the only challenge facing people with disabilities. According to the 2000 Census, among men with any kind of disability, 60 percent are employed compared to 80 percent of men without a disability. The comparison is similar among women, with 51 of those with a disability employed compared to 67 percent of those without a reported disability (Waldrop and Stern 2003).

Through institutional discrimination, society is sometimes organized in a way that limits people with disabilities. Architectural barriers and transportation difficulties often add to the problems of disabled people when they seek and obtain employment. Simply getting around city streets can be quite difficult for people with mobility challenges. Many streets are not properly equipped with curb cuts for wheelchair users. A genuinely barrier-free building needs more than a ramp; it should also include automatic doors, raised letters and Braille on signs, and toilets that are accessible to the disabled. Even if a disabled person finds a job, and even if the job is in a barrier-free building, he or she still faces the problem of getting to work in a society where many rail stations and most buses remain inaccessible to wheelchair users and others with disabilities.

For so many people with disability, it is not just a glass ceiling they face; they are even refused entrance through the door. They face challenges to being taken seriously

as job applicants, and research shows that the problems intensify further for members of racial and ethnic minorities with disabilities. The Glass Ceiling Commission took a special look at employment opportunities for people with disabilities who are also members of racial and ethnic minorities. The analysis revealed that White people with disabilities are twice as likely to be employed full-time as African American or Hispanic people with disabilities. The primary reason for this is that minorities with disabilities experience dual sources of discrimination: subordinate group status as a member of a minority race and disability. The negative stereotype of being disabled is added on top of the stereotypes associated with racial and ethnic minorities (Braddock and Bachelder 1994).

Advocacy for Disability Rights

Until recently, the people with disabilities as a group have scarcely been thought of in any terms except perhaps pity. Often history has forgotten how deep the mistreatment has been. There has been a steadily growing effort to ensure not only the survival of people with disabilities but also the same rights as enjoyed by others. In the early 1960s, Ed Roberts and some other young adults with disabilities wanted to attend the University of California at Berkeley. Reluctant at first, the university was eventually persuaded to admit them and agreed to reserve space in the university infirmary as living quarters for disabled students. These students and others eventually established their own student center and became known as the Rolling Quads. They eventually turned their attention to the surrounding community and established the Berkeley Center for Independent Living, which became a model for hundreds of independent living centers (Brannon 1995).

By the early 1970s, following the example of the Rolling Quads, a strong social movement for disability rights had emerged across the United States, which drew on the experiences of the Black civil rights movement and the feminist movement. This movement now includes a variety of organizations; some work on behalf of people with a single disability (such as the National Federation of the Blind), and others represent people with any of many disabilities (such as New York City's Disabled in Action). The large number of disabled Vietnam veterans who joined the effort gave a boost to advocacy efforts and a growing legitimacy in larger society.

Like other advocacy and resistance efforts, women and men involved in the disability rights movement are working to challenge negative views of disabled people; to gain a greater voice for the disabled in all agency and public policy decisions that affect them; and to reshape laws, institutions, and environments so that people with disabilities can be fully integrated into mainstream society. Disability rights activists argue that there is an important distinction between organizations *for* disabled people and organizations *of* disabled people. The former include service providers, charitable associations, and parents' groups. Some activists maintain that because people with disabilities do not control these organizations, they do not give priority to the goals of independence and self-help emphasized by the disability rights movement (Scotch 1989, 2001).

Many of these organizations worked for the 1990 passage of the Americans with Disabilities Act (ADA). This law in many respects is the most sweeping antidiscrimination legislation since the 1964 Civil Rights Act. The ADA went into effect in 1992, covering people with a disability, defined as a condition that "substantially limits" a "major life activity" such as walking or seeing. It prohibits bias in employment, transportation, public accommodations, and telecommunication against people with disabilities. Businesses with more than 25 employees cannot refuse to hire a qualified disabled applicant; these companies are expected to make a "reasonable accommodation" to permit such a worker to do the job. Commercial establishments such as office buildings, hotels, theaters, supermarkets, and dry cleaners are barred from denying service to people with disabilities (Kilborn 1992).

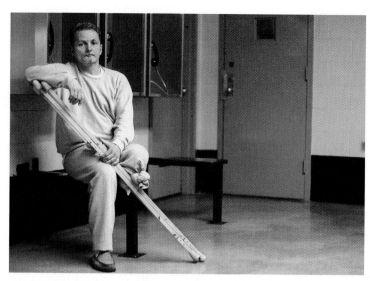

George Lane got his day in court—finally. A Tennessee courthouse held Mr. Lane's trial without him because he was unable to reach the courtroom, which was located in a building without an elevator. The court refused to accommodate him, and the Tennessee Supreme Court upheld the trial. Finally, after seven years, the U.S. Supreme Court held that the county court must hold the trial in a room that the paraplegic could reach.

The ADA represents a significant framing of the issues of people with disabilities. Basically, we can see it taking a civil rights view of disabilities that seeks to humanize the way society sees and treats people with disabilities. The ADA does not take the perspective adopted in other nations, such as Great Britain, of seeing disability as totally an entitlement issue; that is, because you have a disability, you automatically receive certain benefits. Rather, its perspective is that the disabled are being denied certain rights. As disability rights activist Mark Johnson said, "Black people fought for the right to ride in the front of the bus. We're fighting for the right to get on the bus" (Shapiro 1993:128; also see Albrecht 1995, 1997; Gooding 1994).

Colleges are being asked to reconsider what constitutes a student athlete and what competitive programs should be supported with coaches and even scholarships. While athletes with some disabilities have long participated in intercollegiate athletics, the concept of developing programs for people with disabilities is not very common. Currently, only six universities support wheelchair basketball and two track and field events for people with disabilities. Some activists are asking that colleges change their conception of what constitutes an athletic program, much like Title IX forced higher education to see women as college athletes (W. Suggs 2004).

Rethinking the rights of people with disabilities began with the ADA but has now come with the call for visitability. **Visitablity** refers to making private homes built to be accessible for visitors with disabilities. In the mid-1990s, cities such as Atlanta and Austin, Texas (as well as Great Britain) passed ordinances encouraging new homes to have at least one no-step entrance, wider doorways, grab bars in bathrooms, and other accommodations. This new idea suggests that all environments should be accessible—not just public places such as courtrooms or token handicapped-accessible accommodations in hotels but all living spaces. Many oppose such a move as unnecessary government interference; others see it as, at last, a recognition that people with disabilities should be able to move freely throughout the country (Buchholz 2003; Ragged Edge 1998).

visitability
Building private homes to be accessible for visitors with disabilities.

Activists remain encouraged since the passage of the ADA. Although the act has been in effect for only a decade, studies reveal that people with disabilities feel empowered and perceive increased access to employment opportunities. However, one must remember that civil rights activists felt a measure of optimism after passage of the major civil rights legislation more than 30 years ago (Pfeiffer 1996; Scotch 1988).

Gays and Lesbians: Coming Out for Equality

When and how did you first realize you were a heterosexual?

What do you think caused your heterosexuality?

Is it possible that your heterosexuality is just a phase you may grow out of?

Why are heterosexuals so promiscuous?

These are not questions heterosexuals are likely to hear being asked because these queries assume something is wrong with being attracted to members of the opposite sex. On the other hand, we are all accustomed to hearing homosexuals questioned about their orientation.

Homosexuality has been forbidden in most periods of Western history, but it has not always been a social issue. For example, at certain times in many societies, it was possible to acknowledge same-sex love and act on it without necessarily encountering open hostility. Yet in general, societies have barely tolerated people who have sexual intimacy in any manner other than heterosexual.

The Episcopal Church received both praise and criticism in 2003 when they named Rt. Rev. V. Gene Robinson, an openly gay man, to lead a district.

Being Gay and Lesbian in the USA

There are anecdotal accounts of public recognition of homosexuality throughout U.S. history, but it was not until the 1920s and 1930s that it became visible. By that time, clubs for gays and lesbians were growing in number, typically in urban areas. Plays, books, and organizations were created to meet the social needs of gays and lesbians. As homosexuality has become more visible, efforts to suppress it have been institutionalized. At about the same time, the U.S. Army hired psychiatrists to screen recruits for evidence of homosexuality and dismissed volunteers who were gay (P. Schwartz 1992).

The studies published by Alfred Kinsey and his research group (1948, 1953) shocked the general public when they documented that almost half of all men had had same-sex fantasies and that about one-third had experienced a homosexual encounter after childhood. Although women reported less homosexual activity, the very fact that lesbian behavior was even raised in a national discussion was unprecedented. The Kinsey reports also launched a public debate about the number of homosexuals in the United States.

Given that gay men and lesbians are severely stigmatized, accurate data are hard to obtain. Researchers for the National Health and Life Survey and the Voter News Service in their election exit polls estimate that 2 to 5 percent of U.S. adults identify themselves as gay or lesbian. An analysis of the 2000 Census estimates at least 600,000 gay households and a gay and lesbian population approaching 10 million (Dang and Frazer 2004; Laumann et al. 1994; D. Smith and Gates 2001).

Discussion and growing recognition of a sizable gay population did not lead to a consistent effort to promote understanding over the last 60 years. The general focus was to explore ways to prevent and control homosexuality as a disease, which is what psychiatrists thought it was. Well into the 1960s, discrimination against gays and lesbians was common and legal. Bars frequented by people seeking same-sex partners were raided and people jailed, with their names often published in local newspapers. Although not surprising, it was disappointing to hear that the county board in Rhea County, Tennessee, passed unanimously a measure in 2004 that allowed the county to prosecute someone for being gay or lesbian as a "crime against nature." A few days later, after recognizing the losing court battle they would face, the county commissioners rescinded the antigay motion, but clearly they did not take back their view of gays and lesbians (E. Barry 2004).

All students wish to take advantage of what college life offers. Here, students at Florida International University took the step of forming a fraternity, Gamma Lambda Mu, aimed at gay men.

Prejudice and Discrimination

Homophobia, the fear of and prejudice toward homosexuality, is present in every facet of life: the family, organized religion, the workplace, official policies, and the mass media. Like the myths and stereotypes of race and gender, those about homosexuality keep gay men and lesbian women oppressed as a group and may also keep sympathetic members of the dominant group, the heterosexual community, from joining in support.

Homophobia is considered a much more respectable form of bigotry than the voicing of ill feelings against any other oppressed groups. People still openly avoid homosexuals, and group members are stereotyped on television and in motion pictures. Although homophobia has decreased, many people still feel at ease in expressing their homophobic feelings that a homosexual lifestyle is unacceptable (F. Newport 2003).

As we will see later, gays and lesbians have made extensive efforts to make their feelings known, to ask for respect and a variety of rights, and to have their sexual orientation accepted. However, their efforts seem to have had only a modest impact on public opinion. In 2004, 46 percent of the public felt that homosexual relations should not be legal—almost the same proportion as in 1977, when it was 43 percent. Yet there is a recognition that homosexual men and women should have equal rights in terms of job opportunities. This support has increased to 88 percent in 2003, compared with 56 percent in 1977 (Gallup 2004; F. Newport 2003).

The stigmatization of gays and lesbians was seen as a major factor in the slow initial response to the presence of AIDS (acquired immunodeficiency syndrome), which, when it first appeared in the United States, overwhelmingly claimed gay men as its victims. The inattention and the reluctance to develop a national policy forced gay communities in major cities to establish self-help groups to care for the sick, educate the healthy, and lobby for more responsive public policies. The most outspoken AIDS activist group has been the AIDS Coalition to Unleash Power (ACT-UP), which has conducted controversial protests and sit-ins in the halls of government and at scientific conferences. Although initially such efforts may have siphoned away participants from the broader gay rights effort, ultimately, new constituencies of gay men and lesbians were created, along with alliances with sympathetic supporters from the heterosexual community (Adam 1995; Shilts 1982).

In some instances, antigay prejudice has led to violence. Most notable were the 1978 killings of San Francisco Supervisor Harvey Milk (at one time the nation's most prominent openly gay public official) and Mayor George Moscone (a heterosexual supporter of gay rights) by a former police officer and supervisor. The National Coalition of Anti-Violence Programs (2004) released a report documenting more than 2,000 bias-motivated incidents against lesbians and gay men in the United States in 2003. Nationwide, 27 percent of the victims hurt in these attacks suffered injury or death. In a sobering finding in this study, about 60 percent of the attacks were not reported to police.

In 1998, the nation was shocked by the unprovoked, brutal murder of Matthew Shepard, a University of Wyoming student, by two men. Subsequent investigation showed that Shepard's being gay was the reason for his attackers' murdering him rather than leaving him alone after robbing the young man. This tragic event galvanized a move to include sexual orientation as a basis of hate crimes in many states. Gay and lesbians themselves began to actively resist their treatment, sometimes working with local law enforcement agencies and prosecutors to end antigay violence (J. Cloud 2003; Jenness 1995).

Advocacy for Gay and Lesbian Rights

The first homosexual organization in the United States was founded in Chicago in 1924. Such groups grew steadily over the next 50 years, but they were primarily local and were more likely to be self-help and social rather than confrontational. The social

homophobia
The fear of and prejudice toward homosexuality.

movements of the 1950s and 1960s on behalf of African Americans and women caused lesbians and gay men also to reflect more directly on the oppression their sexual orientation caused.

The contemporary gay and lesbian movement marks its beginning in New York City on June 28, 1969. Police raided the Stonewall Inn, an after-hours gay bar, and forced patrons into the street. Instead of meekly dispersing and accepting the disruption, the patrons locked police inside the bar and rioted until police reinforcements arrived. For the next three nights, lesbians and gay men marched through the streets of New York, protesting police raids and other forms of discrimination. Within months, gay liberation groups appeared in cities and campuses throughout the United States (Duberman 1993; Humphreys 1972).

Despite the efforts of the lesbian and gay rights movement, in 1986 the Supreme Court in *Bowers v. Hardwick* ruled by a 5–4 vote that the Constitution does not protect homosexual relations between consenting adults, even in the privacy of their own homes. This position held until the court reversed itself by a 6–3 vote in *Lawrence v. Texas*. The divisiveness of the issue nationally was reflected among the justices. Justice Anthony Kennedy declared that gays are "entitled to respect for their private lives" while Justice Antonin Scalia complained that the decision indicated that the court had "largely signed on to the so-called homosexual agenda" (L. Greenhouse 2003b:A1).

In 2000, the Supreme Court hurt the gay rights movement when it ruled 5–4 that the Boy Scouts organization had a constitutional right to exclude gay members because opposition to homosexuality was part of the organization's message. The Court clearly stated in its ruling that it was not endorsing this view but supporting the right of the organization to hold this position and to limit participation based on it. Despite this and earlier Supreme Court decisions, gays and lesbians worked to establish the principle that sexual orientation should not be the basis for discrimination.

Issues involving gays and lesbians have always been present, but because of advocacy efforts, the concerns are being advanced by political leaders and the courts. In 1993, President Bill Clinton, under pressure from the gay community, reviewed the prohibition of homosexuals from the military. However, he encountered even greater pressure from opponents and eventually compromised in 1994 with the "don't ask, don't tell" policy. The policy allows lesbians and gay men to continue to serve in the military as long as they keep their homosexuality secret, but commanders can still

Despite the stability of many same-sex couples, the same people who are concerned over family instability often are opposed to legal recognition of gay and lesbian couples.

Source: Signe Wilkinson/ Cartoonists & Writer's Syndicate/cartoonweb.com

SIGNE WILKINSON, Philadelphia Daily News

investigate and dismiss military personnel if they find any evidence that they have committed homosexual acts. Indeed, according to a 2003 report, the military is discharging three or four service members every day (A. Hull 2003).

For many gay and lesbian couples, the inability to have their relationships recognized legally is the most personal restriction they have to face. Several dozen cities have begun to recognize **domestic partnerships**, defined as two unrelated adults who have chosen to share one another's lives in a relationship of mutual caring, who reside together and agree to be jointly responsible for their dependents, basic living expenses, and other common necessities. Domestic partnership benefits can apply to inheritance, parenting, pensions, taxation, housing, immigration, workplace fringe benefits, and health care. Although the advocacy efforts for legally recognizing domestic partnerships have come from the lesbian and gay community, the majority of the relationships that would benefit would be cohabiting heterosexual couples.

The most vocal debate is over whether gay and lesbian couples should be able to legally get married. Congress enacted the Defense of Marriage Act in 1996, which would deny federal recognition of same-sex marriages. Despite criticism from the gay community and those supportive of legal recognition of same-sex marriage, the measure was immensely popular with the public. Despite this action, Vermont gave same-sex couples the legal benefits of marriage through civil union in 1999. Then, in 2002, the Massachusetts Supreme Court ruled 4–3 that under the state's constitution, gay couples have the right to legally marry. In a quick response, 13 states in various 2004 elections passed amendments to their own constitutions which would prevent same-sex marriages from receiving any recognition. A 2004 survey showed that only 24 percent felt that same-sex marriages should be legal. Yet efforts in Congress to propose a constitutional amendment that would limit marriage to heterosexual couples has failed even to come to a vote (Gallup 2004b).

We have used *assimilation* throughout this book to describe the process by which individuals forsake their own heritage to become a part of a different culture. Assimilation has emerged as a hot issue in the gay community. Some argue that promoting gay marriage is merely trying to assimilate or to become like the oppressor, adopting their social conventions. Efforts to downplay overt expression of homosexuality are yet another example of assimilation. Critics of assimilation argue that equal treatment is the real issue and should not be the result of conforming to the ways of heterosexual dominant society. The debate is unlikely to be resolved soon because full acceptance of gays and lesbians is far removed from today's social and political agenda. But this discussion repeats a pattern found with every subordinate group of how to maintain one's unique identity and become part of a multicultural society (Hequembourg and Arditi 1999).

domestic partnership
Two unrelated adults who have chosen to share one another's lives in a relationship of mutual caring, who reside together, and who agree to be jointly responsible for their dependents, basic living expenses, and other common necessities.

The Glass Half Empty

A common expression makes reference to a glass half full or half empty of water. If one is thirsty, it is half empty and in need of being replenished. If one is attempting to clean up dirty dishes, it is half full. For many people, the progress of subordinate groups or minorities—the half-full glass—makes it difficult to understand calls for more programs and new reforms (needed because it is also half empty). With the passage of the ADA, why is more assistance needed for people with disabilities? Is there not enough protection against sexism, racism, and ageism?

In absolute terms, the glass of water has been filling up, but people in the early 21st century do not compare themselves with people in the 1960s. For example, Latinos and African Americans regard the appropriate reference group to be Whites today; compared with them, the glass is half empty at best.

In Figure 17.4, we show the present picture and recent changes by comparing African Americans and Hispanics with Whites. We see that the nation's largest minority groups—African Americans and Hispanics—have higher household income, complete more schooling, and enjoy longer life expectancy today than in 1975. White Americans have made similar strides in all three areas. The gap remains and, if one analyzes it closely, has actually increased in some instances. Both Blacks and Latinos in 2000 had yet to reach the income level that Whites had exceeded back in 1975. Also, Blacks today have barely matched the life expectancy that Whites had 25 years earlier. Similarly, many minority Americans remain entrenched in poverty: nearly one out of four Hispanics and African Americans.

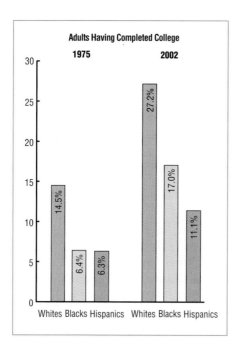

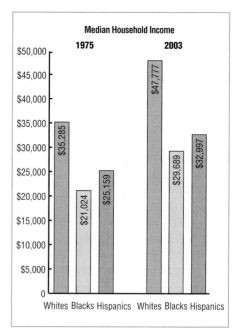

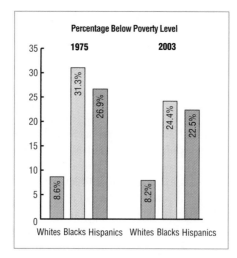

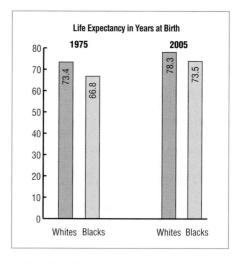

FIGURE 17.4   Recent Changes in Schooling, Income, and Life Expectancy

Note: Education data include people 25 and over. Hispanic education 1975 data estimated by author from data for 1970 and 1980. White data are for non-Hispanic (except in education).

Sources: Bureau of the Census 1988:167, 2003a: 43, 48, 183; DeNavas-Walt et al. 2004: 4,10.

Little has changed since 1975. We have chosen 1975 because that was a year for which we have comparable data for Hispanics (or Latinos), Whites, and African Americans. However, the patterns would be no different if we considered 1950, 1960, or 1970.

These data provide only the broadest overview. Detailed analyses do not yield a brighter picture. For example, 3.9 percent of all doctorates were awarded to African Americans in 1981. By 1998, the proportion had increased only to 4.5 percent. The United States continues to rely on overseas students to fill the places on the educational ladder. In 2002, the number of doctorates awarded to nonresident aliens (i.e., immigrants who gained entry for schooling with no other ties to U.S. citizens) was 150 percent that of Blacks, Asian Americans, Latinos, and American Indians *combined* (Smallwood 2003).

Conclusion

As the United States promotes racial, ethnic, and religious diversity, it strives also to impose universal criteria on employers, educators, and realtors so that subordinate racial and ethnic groups can participate fully in the larger society. In some instances, to bring about equality of results—not just equality of opportunity—programs have been developed to give competitive advantages to women and minority men. Only more recently have similar strides been made on behalf of people with disabilities. These latest answers to social inequality have provoked much controversy over how to achieve the admirable goal of a multiracial, multiethnic society, undifferentiated in opportunity and rewards.

The huge outpouring of information for the census documents the racial and ethnic diversity of the entire nation. And as we see in Figure 17.5, although the proportion of specific minorities present may be different in different regions and different communities, the tapestry of racial and ethnic groups is always close at hand wherever one is in the United States.

Relations between racial, ethnic, or religious groups take two broad forms, as situations characterized by either consensus or conflict. Consensus prevails where assimilation or fusion of groups has been completed. Consensus also prevails in a pluralistic society in the sense that members have agreed to respect differences between groups. By eliminating the contending group, extermination and expulsion also lead to a consensus society. In the study of intergroup relations, it is often easy to ignore conflict where there is a high degree of consensus because it is assumed

that an orderly society has no problems. In some instances, however, this assumption is misleading. Through long periods of history, misery inflicted on a racial, ethnic, or religious group was judged to be appropriate, if not actually divinely inspired.

In recent history, harmonious relations between all racial, ethnic, and religious groups have been widely accepted as a worthy goal. The struggle against oppression and inequality is not new. It dates back at least to the revolutions in England, France, and the American colonies in the 17th and 18th centuries. The 20th century was unique in the extension of equality to the less-privileged classes, many of whose members are racial and ethnic minorities. Conflict along racial and ethnic lines is especially bitter now because it evokes memories of slavery, colonial oppression, and overt discrimination. Today's African Americans are much more aware of slavery than contemporary poor people are of 17th-century debtors' prison.

Racial and ethnic equality implies the right of the individual to choose his or her own way of life. As Hunt and Walker (1979) observed, however, individual rights may conflict with the group consensus. Gay and lesbian marriages and accommodating the needs of people with disabilities in the workplace are the latest examples. This conflict makes the situation exceedingly complex; even if a society allows a group to select its own destiny, individual members of the group may be unable to freely pursue their own course of action. If Native Americans as a group choose to emphasize their cultural distinctiveness, individuals who want to integrate into White society may be looked on by their peers as traitors to their tribe.

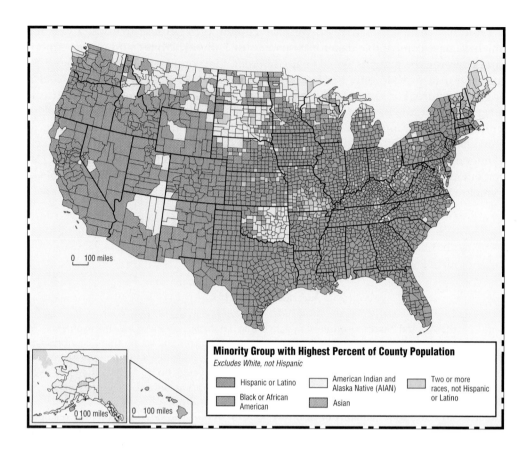

FIGURE 17.5   The Image of Diversity from Census 2000

Source: Brewer and Suchan 2001:20.

Unquestionably, the struggle for justice among racial and ethnic groups has not completely met its goals. Many people are still committed to repression, although they may see it only as the benign neglect of those less privileged. Such repression leads to the dehumanization of both the subordinated individual and the oppressor. Growth in equal rights movements and self-determination for Third World countries largely populated by non-White people has moved the world onto a course that seems irreversible. The old ethnic battle lines now renewed in Iran, Sudan, and Chechnya in Russia have only added to the tensions. Philip (1970) acknowledged that people are more willing to reject stability if preserving it means inequality.

Self-determination, whether for groups or individuals, often is impossible in societies as they are currently structured. Bringing about social equality therefore will entail significant changes in existing institutions. Because such changes are not likely to come about with everyone's willing cooperation, the social costs will be high. However, if there is a trend in racial and ethnic relations in the world

today, it is the growing belief that the social costs, however high, must be paid to achieve self-determination.

It is naive to foresee a world of societies in which one person equals one vote and all are accepted without regard to race, ethnicity, religion, gender, age, disability status, or sexual orientation. It is equally unlikely to expect to see a society, let alone a world, that is without a privileged class or prestigious jobholders. Contact between different peoples, as we have seen numerous times, precedes conflict. Contact also may initiate mutual understanding and appreciation.

In a commencement address at American University in 1963, President John F. Kennedy declared, "If we cannot end now our differences, at least we can help make the world safe for diversity" (Cleveland 1995:23). Yet today, with conflicts along ethnic, racial, and religious lines jeopardizing peace and fostering terrorism, such a goal seems very distant. What may well emerge from contemporary and future unrest is the recognition by human beings that people are fundamentally alike and share the same abilities, weaknesses, and dreams.

Key Terms

ageism   436

disability   440

domestic partnership   451

homophobia   449

visitability   446

Review Questions

1. What contributes to the changing image of diversity in the United States?
2. In what ways are the aged, people with disabilities, and gays and lesbians stereotyped?
3. What are common and differing aspects of the effort to mobilize the elderly, people with disabilities, and gay men and lesbians to achieve equality?
4. What has been the role of the federal government in the effort to achieve equality by the aged, people with disabilities, and the gay and lesbian community?
5. What does it mean to overcome exclusion?

Critical Thinking

1. Sociologists use the term *master status* to describe a status that dominates others and thereby determines a person's general position in society. To what degree can that term be applied to the three groups considered in this chapter?
2. The media—in advertisements, humor, dramas, and situation comedies—portray life in society. What are some examples, both positive and negative, of how the elderly, people with disabilities, and gays and lesbians are presented in the media that you have seen? In what ways are these groups stereotyped?
3. How might advances in technology, including innovations for the home and computer chat rooms, have a unique effect on each of the groups trying to overcome exclusion discussed in this chapter?
4. How do policy makers trying to bring about change use the model of "half full" and "half empty" either to argue for change on behalf of minorities or to use the same concepts to maintain that the status quo is adequate for addressing issues of social inequality?

Internet Connections—Research Navigator™

Follow the instructions found on page 31 of this text to access the features of Research Navigator™. Once at the Web site, enter your Login Name and Password. Then, to use the ContentSelect database, enter keywords such as "gay marriage," "Americans with Disaiblities Act," and "age discrimination," and the research engine will supply relevant and recent scholarly and popular press publications. Use the *New York Times* Search-by-Subject Archive to find recent news articles related to sociology and the Link Library feature to locate relevant Web links organized by the key terms associated with this chapter.

Internet Resource Directory

The following is a sample of the thousands of Web sites that offer information on topics discussed in this book. Most of these sites have links to other resources.

GENERAL

Hate Crimes Laws
http://www.adl.org/99hatecrime/intro.asp

U.S. Citizenship and Immigration Services
http://www.uscis.gov/graphics/

Race Traitor (constructing whiteness)
http://www.racetraitor.org

U.S. Census Bureau
http://www.census.gov
and specifically www.census.gov/pubinfo/www/hotlinks.html

U.S. Commission on Civil Rights
http://www.usccr.gov

AFRICAN AMERICANS

Black Collegian Online
http://www.black-collegian.com/

Kwanzaa Information Center
http://www.melanet.com/kwanzaa/

MelaNET (The UnCut Black Experience)
http://www.melanet.com/

ASIAN AMERICANS

Asian American Network
http://www.aan.net/

Hmong Home Page
http://www.stolaf.edu/people/cdr/hmong/

HISPANICS AND LATINOS

Latin American National Information Center
http://lanic.utexas.edu

Mexican American Studies and Research Center (University of Arizona)
http://masrc.arizona.edu/

JEWS AND JUDAISM

American Jewish Committee
http://www.ajc.org

Anti-Defamation League
http://www.adl.org

Judaism and Jewish Resources
http://shamash.org

MUSLIM AND ARAB AMERICANS

Arab American Institute
http://www.aaiusa.org/

American-Arab Anti-Discrimination Committee
http://www.adc.org

Muslim Students' Association
http://msa-natl.org

NATIVE AMERICANS

Bureau of Indian Affairs
http://www.doi.gov/bureau-indian-affairs.html

Nation of Hawai'i
http://hawaii-nation.org/

Native Web
http://www.nativeweb.org

Smithsonian National Museum of the American Indian
http://www.nmai.si.edu

WOMEN AND MEN

The Men's Issues Page
http://www.vix.com/men/

National Organization for Women
http://www.now.org

National Women's History Project
http://www.nwhp.org/

Womensnet
http://www.igc.apc.org/womensnet

OUTSIDE THE UNITED STATES

Abya Yala Net (South and Meso American Indian Rights Center)
http://abyayala.nativeweb.org

African National Congress (South Africa)
http://www.anc.org.za/

American-Israeli Cooperative Enterprise
http://www.us-israel.org/about/

Information (general) on countries (CIA World Factbook)
http://www.odci.gov/cia/publications/factbook

Peace People (Northern Ireland)
http://www.peacepeople.com

ETHNIC GROUPS AND OTHER SUBORDINATE GROUPS

Administration on Aging
http://www.aoa.dhhs.gov

American Institute of Polish Culture
http://www.ampolinstitute.org

American Irish Historical Society
http://www.aihs.org

Catholics for a Free Choice
http://www.cath4choice.org

Disability Social History Project
http://www.disabilityhistory.org

German Americans (German Embassy site)
http://www.germany-info.org/

Human Rights Web

http://www.hrweb.org

Interracial Voice (people of mixed racial background)

http://www.webcom.com/~intvoice

Polish American Association

http://www.polish.org

SeniorLink

http://www.seniorlink.com/

Society and Culture: Disabilities (Yahoo)

http://www.yahoo.com/Society_and_Culture/Disabilities/

Sons of Norway

http://www.sofn.com

THE AUTHOR

Richard T. Schaefer (for e-mail correspondence)

schaeferrt@aol.com

www.schaefersociology.net

Glossary

Parenthetical numbers refer to the pages on which the term is introduced.

abolitionists Whites and free Blacks who favored the end of slavery. (188)

absolute deprivation The minimum level of subsistence below which families or individuals should not be expected to exist. (68)

affirmative action Positive efforts to recruit subordinate group members, including women, for jobs, promotions, and educational opportunities. (81)

Afrocentric perspective An emphasis on the customs of African cultures and how they have pervaded the history, culture, and behavior of Blacks in the United States and around the world. (29)

ageism Prejudice and discrimination against the elderly. (436)

AJAs Americans of Japanese ancestry in Hawaii. (329)

amalgamation The process by which a dominant group and a subordinate group combine through intermarriage to form a new group. (22)

androgyny The state of being both masculine and feminine, aggressive and gentle. (385)

anti-Semitism Anti-Jewish prejudice or discrimination. (356)

apartheid The policy of the South African government intended to maintain separation of Blacks, Coloureds, and Asians from the dominant Whites. (212, 426)

assimilation The process by which a subordinate individual or group takes on the characteristics of the dominant group. (23)

asylees Foreigners who have already entered the United States and now seek protection because of persecution or a well-founded fear of persecution. (113)

authoritarian personality A psychological construct of a personality type likely to be prejudiced and to use others as scapegoats. (40)

bilingual education A program designed to allow students to learn academic concepts in their native language while they learn a second language. (242)

bilingualism The use of two or more languages in places of work or education and the treatment of each language as legitimate. (25, 242)

biological race The mistaken notion of a genetically isolated human group. (10)

blaming the victim Portraying the problems of racial and ethnic minorities as their fault rather than recognizing society's responsibilities. (16)

blended identity Self-image and worldview that is a combination of religious faith, cultural background based on nationality, and current residency. (290)

Bogardus scale Technique to measure social distance toward different racial and ethnic groups. (47)

borderlands The area of a common culture along the border between Mexico and the United States. (245)

bracero Contracted Mexican laborers brought to the United States during World War II. (260)

brain drain Immigration to the United States of skilled workers, professionals, and technicians who are desperately needed by their home countries. (103, 252)

Chicanismo An ideology emphasizing pride and positive identity among Mexican Americans. (265)

civil disobedience A tactic promoted by Martin Luther King, Jr., based on the belief that people have the right to disobey unjust laws under certain circumstances. (198)

civil religion The religious dimension in American life that merges the state with sacred beliefs. (136)

class As defined by Max Weber, people who share similar levels of wealth. (13, 223)

colonialism A foreign power's maintenance of political, social, economic, and cultural dominance over people for an extended period. (18)

color gradient The placement of people on a continuum from light to dark skin color rather than in distinct racial groupings by skin color. (251, 271, 411)

comparable worth *See* pay equity. (393)

conflict perspective A sociological approach that assumes that the social structure is best understood in terms of conflict or tension between competing groups. (15)

contact hypothesis An interactionist perspective stating that intergroup contact between people of equal status in noncompetitive circumstances will reduce prejudice. (56)

creationists People who support a literal interpretation of the biblical book of Genesis on the origins of the universe and argue that evolution should not be presented as established scientific thought. (143)

crossover effect An effect that appears as previously high-scoring Native American children score as below average in intelligence when tests are given in English rather than their native languages. (172)

culture of poverty A way of life that involves no future planning, no enduring commitment to marriage, and no work ethic; this culture follows the poor even when they move out of the slums or the barrio. (262)

curanderismo Hispanic folk medicine. (277)

de facto segregation Segregation that is the result of residential patterns. (212)

deficit model of ethnic identity One's ethnicity is viewed by others as a factor of subtracting away the characteristics corresponding to some ideal ethnic type. (287)

de jure segregation Children assigned to schools specifically to maintain racially separated schools. (196)

denomination A large, organized religion not officially linked with the state or government. (130)

desi Colloquial name for people who trace their ancestry to South Asia, especially India and Pakistan. (319)

Diaspora The exile of Jews from Palestine. (367, 421)

differential justice Whites being dealt with more leniently than Blacks, whether at the time of arrest, indictment, conviction, sentencing, or parole. (228)

disability Reduced ability to perform tasks one would normally do at a given stage in life. (440)

discrimination The denial of opportunities and equal rights to individuals and groups because of prejudice or for other arbitrary reasons. (37, 67)

displaced homemakers Women whose primary occupation had been homemaking but who did not find full-time employment after being divorced, separated, or widowed. (396)

domestic partnership Two unrelated adults who have chosen to share one another's lives in a relationship of mutual caring, who reside together, and who agree to be jointly responsible for their dependents, basic living expenses, and other common necessities. (451)

double jeopardy The subordinate status twice defined, as experienced by women of color. (74, 403)

dual labor market Division of the economy into two areas of employment, the secondary one of which is populated primarily by minorities working at menial jobs. (71)

dysfunction An element of society that may disrupt a social system or decrease its stability. (15)

Ebonics Distinctive dialect with a complex language structure found among many Black Americans. (188)

emigration Leaving a country to settle in another. (17)

English immersion Teaching in English by teachers who know the students' native language but use it only when students do not understand the lessons. (242)

environmental justice Efforts to ensure that hazardous substances are controlled so that all communities receive protection regardless of race or socioeconomic circumstances. (80, 178)

ethclass The merged ethnicity and class in a person's status. (135, 238)

ethnic cleansing Policy of ethnic Serbs to eliminate Muslims from parts of Bosnia. (20)

ethnic group A group set apart from others because of its national origin or distinctive cultural patterns. (7)

ethnicity paradox The maintenance of one's ethnic ties in a way that can assist with assimilation in larger society. (124)

ethnocentrism The tendency to assume that one's culture and way of life are superior to all others. (34)

ethnonational conflicts Conflicts between ethnic, racial, religious, and linguistic groups within nations replacing conflicts between nations. (408)

ethnophaulism Ethnic or racial slurs, including derisive nicknames. (37)

evacuees Japanese Americans interned in camps for the duration of World War II. (343)

exploitation theory A Marxist theory that views racial subordination in the United States as a manifestation of the class system inherent in capitalism. (41)

familism Pride and closeness in the family that result in placing family obligation and loyalty before individual needs. (276)

feminine mystique Society's view of a woman as only her children's mother and her husband's wife. (389)

feminization of poverty The trend since 1970 that has women accounting for a growing proportion of those below the poverty line. (396)

fish-ins Tribes' protests over government interference with their traditional rights to fish as they like. (163)

fringe-of-values theory Behavior that is on the border of conduct that a society regards as proper and is often carried out by subordinate groups, subjecting those groups to negative sanctions. (361)

functionalist perspective A sociological approach emphasizing how parts of a society are structured to maintain its stability. (14)

fusion A minority and a majority group combining to form a new group. (22)

gender roles Expectations regarding the proper behavior, attitudes, and activities of males and females. (385)

genocide The deliberate, systematic killing of an entire people or nation. (20)

gerrymandering Redrawing districts bizarrely to create politically advantageous outcomes. (231)

glass ceiling The barrier that blocks the promotion of a qualified worker because of gender or minority membership. (86, 394)

glass escalator The male advantage experienced in occupations dominated by women. (87)

glass wall A barrier to moving laterally in a business to positions that are more likely to lead to upward mobility. (87)

globalization Worldwide integration of government policies, cultures, social movements, and financial markets through trade, movements of people, and the exchange of ideas. (18, 111)

gook syndrome David Riesman's phrase describing Americans' tendency to stereotype Asians and to regard them as all alike and undesirable. (321)

hajj Pilgrimage to Mecca to be completed at least once in a Muslim's lifetime. (288)

halakha Jewish laws covering obligations and duties. (375)

Haoles Hawaiian term for Caucasians. (327)

hate crimes Criminal offense committed because of the offender's bias against a race, religion, ethnic/national origin group, or sexual orientation group. (35)

hijab Refers to a variety of garments that allow women to follow the guidelines of modest dress. (296)

Holocaust The state-sponsored systematic persecution and annihilation of European Jewry by Nazi Germany and its collaborators. (363)

Holocaust revisionist People who deny the Nazi effort to exterminate the Jews or who minimize the numbers killed. (363)

home rule Britain's grant of a local parliament to Ireland. (418)

hometown clubs Nonprofit organizations that maintain close ties to immigrants' hometowns in Mexico and other Latin American countries. (246)

homophobia The fear of and prejudice toward homosexuality. (449)

hui kuan Chinese American benevolent associations organized on the basis of the district of the immigrant's origin in China. (337)

ilchomose The 1.5 generation of Korean Americans—those who immigrated into the United States as children. (325)

immigration Coming into a new country as a permanent resident. (17)

income Salaries, wages, and other money received. (215)

informal economy Transfers of money, goods, or services that are not reported to the government. Common in inner-city neighborhoods and poverty-stricken rural areas. (70)

in-group virtues Proper behavior by one's own group (in-group virtues) becomes unacceptable when practiced by outsiders (out-group vices). (362)

institutional discrimination A denial of opportunities and equal rights to individuals or groups resulting from the normal operations of a society. (69)

intelligence quotient (IQ) The ratio of a person's mental age (as computed by an IQ test) to his or her chronological age, multiplied by 100. (11)

internal colonialism The treatment of subordinate peoples as colonial subjects by those in power. (19, 156)

Intifada The Palestinian uprising against Israeli authorities in the occupied territories. (423)

irregular economy *See* informal economy. (70)

Issei First-generation immigrants from Japan to the United States. (341)

jihad Struggle against the enemies of Allah, usually taken to mean one's own internal struggle. (289)

Jim Crow Southern laws passed in the late 19th century that kept Blacks in their subordinate position. (189)

Judaization The lessening importance of Judaism as a religion and the substitution of cultural traditions as the tie that binds Jews. (358)

kashrut Laws pertaining to permissible (kosher) and forbidden foods and their preparation. (372)

Kibei Japanese Americans of the *Nisei* generation sent back to Japan for schooling and to have marriages arranged. (341)

kickouts or pushouts Native American school dropouts who leave behind an unproductive academic environment. (172)

kye Rotating credit system used by Korean Americans to subsidize the start of businesses. (326)

labeling theory A sociological approach introduced by Howard Becker that attempts to explain why certain people are viewed as deviants and others engaging in the same behavior are not. (16)

La Raza "The People"—a term referring to the rich heritage of Mexican Americans and therefore used to denote a sense of pride among Mexican Americans today. (261)

life chances People's opportunities to provide themselves with material goods, positive living conditions, and favorable life experiences. (132, 276)

maquiladoras Foreign-owned companies on the Mexican side of the border with the United States. (246)

marginality The status of being between two cultures at the same time, such as the status of Jewish immigrants in the United States. (28, 377)

Marielitos People who arrived from Cuba in the third wave of Cuban immigration, most specifically those forcibly deported by way of Mariel Harbor. The term is generally reserved for refugees seen as especially undesirable. (247)

melting pot Diverse racial or ethnic groups or both, forming a new creation, a new cultural entity. (22)

middlemen minorities Groups such as Japanese Americans that typically occupy middle positions in the social and occupational stratification system. (311)

migradollars (or remittances) The money that immigrant workers send back to families in their native societies. (110)

migration A general term that describes any transfer of population. (17)

millenarian movements Movements, such as the Ghost Dance, that prophesy a cataclysm in the immediate future, to be followed by collective salvation. (155)

minority group A subordinate group whose members have significantly less control or power over their own lives than do the members of a dominant or majority group. (5)

model or ideal minority A group that, despite past prejudice and discrimination, succeeds economically, socially, and educationally without resorting to political or violent confrontations with Whites. (309)

mojados "Wetbacks"; derisive slang for Mexicans who enter illegally, supposedly by swimming the Rio Grande. (261)

mommy tax Lower salaries women receive over their lifetime because they have children. (399)

mommy track An unofficial corporate career track for women who want to divide their attention between work and family. (394)

nativism Beliefs and policies favoring native-born citizens over immigrants. (96)

naturalization Conferring of citizenship on a person after birth. (100)

neocolonialism Continuing dependence of former colonies on foreign countries. (269)

Neoricans Puerto Ricans who return to the island to settle after living on the mainland of the United States (also Nuyoricans). (268)

Nisei Children born of immigrants from Japan. (341)

normative approach The view that prejudice is influenced by societal norms and situations that encourage or discourage the tolerance of minorities. (42)

Orientalism The simplistic view of the people and history of the Orient with no recognition of change over time or the diversity within its many cultures. (284)

out-group vices Proper behavior by one's own group (in-group virtues) becomes unacceptable when practiced by outsiders (out-group vices). (362)

panethnicity The development of solidarity between ethnic subgroups, as reflected in the terms *Hispanic* or *Asian American*. (27, 237, 330)

pan-Indianism Intertribal social movements in which several tribes, joined by political goals but not by kinship, unite in a common identity. (162)

pass laws Laws that controlled internal movement by non-Whites in South Africa. (426)

pay equity The same wages for different types of work that are judged to be comparable by such measures as employee knowledge, skills, effort, responsibility, and working conditions; also called comparable worth. (393)

pentecostalism A religion similar in many respects to evangelical faiths that believes in the infusion of the Holy Spirit into services and in religious experiences such as faith healing. (279)

peoplehood Milton Gordon's term for a group with a shared feeling. (379)

pluralism Mutual respect between the various groups in a society for one another's cultures, allowing minorities to express their own culture without experiencing prejudice or hostility. (24)

powwows Native American gatherings of dancing, singing, music playing, and visiting, accompanied by competitions. (165)

prejudice A negative attitude toward an entire category of people, such as a racial or ethnic minority. (37)

principle of third-generation interest Marcus Hansen's contention that ethnic interest and awareness increase in the third generation, among the grandchildren of immigrants. (123)

racial formation A sociohistorical process by which racial categories are created, inhibited, transformed, and destroyed. (13)

racial group A group that is socially set apart because of obvious physical differences. (7)

racial profiling Any arbitrary police-initiated action based on race, ethnicity, or natural origin rather than a person's behavior. (47, 314)

racism A doctrine that one race is superior. (12)

redlining The pattern of discrimination against people trying to buy homes in minority and racially changing neighborhoods. (78, 226)

refugees People living outside their country of citizenship for fear of political or religious persecution. (112)

relative deprivation The conscious experience of a negative discrepancy between legitimate expectations and present actualities. (67, 201)

remittances (or migradollars) The monies that immigrants return to their country of origin. (110, 246)

repatriation The 1930s program of deporting Mexicans. (260)

respectable bigotry Michael Lerner's term for the social acceptance of prejudice against White ethnics, when intolerance against non-White minorities is regarded as unacceptable. (125)

restrictive covenants Private contracts or agreements that discourage or prevent minority-group members from purchasing housing in a neighborhood. (197)

reverse discrimination Actions that cause better-qualified White men to be passed over for women and minority men. (84)

riff-raff theory Also called the rotten-apple theory; the belief that the riots of the 1960s were caused by discontented youths rather than by social and economic problems facing all African Americans. (201)

rising expectations The increasing sense of frustration that legitimate needs are being blocked. (201)

Sansei The children of the *Nisei*—that is, the grandchildren of the original immigrants from Japan. (341)

scapegoating theory A person or group blamed irrationally for another person's or group's problems or difficulties. (39)

secessionist minority Groups, such as the Amish, that reject both assimilation and coexistence. (141)

second shift The double burden—work outside the home followed by child care and housework—that is faced by many women and that few men share equitably. (399)

segregation The physical separation of two groups, often imposed on a subordinate group by the dominant group. (21)

self-fulfilling prophecy The tendency to respond to and act on the basis of stereotypes, a predisposition that can lead one to validate false definitions. (16)

set-asides Programs stipulating that a minimum proportion of government contracts must be awarded to minority-owned businesses. (219, 312)

setoffs Deductions from money due in U.S. government settlements with Native Americans, equal to the cost of federal services provided to the tribe. (160)

sexism The ideology that one sex is superior to the other. (385)

sexual harassment Any unwanted and unwelcome sexual advances that interfere with a person's ability to perform a job and enjoy the benefits of a job. (395)

sinophobes People with a fear of anything associated with China. (97)

slave codes Laws that defined the low position held by slaves in the United States. (185)

slavery reparations Act of making amends for the injustices of slavery. (190)

social distance Tendency to approach or withdraw from a racial group. (47)

sociology The systematic study of social behavior and human groups. (13)

sovereignty Tribal self-rule. (166)

sovereignty movement Effort by the indigenous people of Hawaii to secure a measure of self-government and restoration of their lands. (329)

states' rights The principle, reinvoked in the late 1940s, that holds that each state is sovereign and has the right to order its own affairs without interference by the federal government. (77)

stereotypes Unreliable, exaggerated generalizations about all members of a group that do not take individual differences into account. (16, 43)

stratification A structured ranking of entire groups of people that perpetuates unequal rewards and power in a society. (13)

suffragists Women and men who worked successfully to gain women the right to vote. (388)

symbolic ethnicity Herbert Gans's term that describes emphasis on ethnic food and ethnically associated political issues rather than deeper ties to one's heritage. (124)

tongs Chinese American secret associations. (337)

total discrimination The combination of current discrimination with past discrimination created by poor schools and menial jobs. (68)

tracking The practice of placing students in specific curriculum groups on the basis of test scores and other criteria. (213, 275)

transnationals Immigrants who sustain multiple social relationships linking their societies of origin and settlement. (112)

tsu Clans established along family lines and forming a basis for social organization by Chinese Americans. (336)

underemployment Work at a job for which the worker is overqualified, involuntary part-time instead of full-time employment, or intermittent employment. (217)

underground economy *See* informal economy. (70)

victim discounting Tendency to view crime as less socially significant if the victim is viewed as less worthy. (228)

victimization surveys Annual attempts to measure crime rates by interviewing ordinary citizens who may or may not have been crime victims. (228)

visible minorities In Canada, persons other than Aboriginal or First Nation people who are non-white in racial background. (322)

Viet Kieu Vietnamese living abroad such as in the United States. (322)

visitability Building private homes to be accessible for visitors with disabilities. (446)

wealth An inclusive term encompassing all of a person's material assets, including land and other types of property. (215)

White primary Legal provisions forbidding Black voting in election primaries, which in one-party areas of the South effectively denied Blacks their right to select elected officials. (189)

world systems theory A view of the global economic system as divided between nations that control wealth and those that provide natural resources and labor. (19, 153, 273, 408)

xenophobia The fear or hatred of strangers or foreigners. (96)

yellow peril A term denoting a generalized prejudice toward Asian people and their customs. (312)

Yiddishkait Jewishness. (375)

Yonsei The fourth generation of Japanese Americans in the United States; the children of the *Sansei*. (341)

Zionism Traditional Jewish religious yearning to return to the biblical homeland, now used to refer to support for the state of Israel. (367, 422)

zoning laws Legal provisions stipulating land use and the architectural design of housing, often used to keep racial minorities and low-income people out of suburban areas. (227)

References

AARP. 2003. *AARP Home.* Accessed May 12, 2003, at www.aarp.org.
———. 2004. *Civil Rights and Labor Relations.* Princeton, NJ: Gallup Organization.

ABC News. 1992. *Primetime Live:* "True Colors." Transcript of November 26 episode.

ABDO, GENEIVE. 2004. "A Muslim Rap Finds Voice." *Chicago Tribune,* June 30, 1, 19.
———. 2004b. "New Generation Lifting Muslims." *Chicago Tribune,* September 3, 1, 8.

ABELMANN, NANCY AND JOHN LIE. 1995. *Blue Dreams: Korean Americans and the Los Angeles Riots.* Cambridge, MA: Harvard University Press.

ABRAHAM, NABEEL AND ANDREW SHYROCK. 2000. *Arab Detroit: From Margin to Mainstream.* Detroit, MI: Wayne State University Press.

ABRAHAMSON, ALAN. 1997. "School Growth: A New Chapter for U.S. Jews." *Los Angeles Times,* October 22, B2.

ABRAHAMSON, ALAN AND JUDY PASTERNAK. 1998. "For U.S. Jews, Era of Plenty Takes Many Far from Roots." *Los Angeles Times,* April 20, A1, A10–11.

ABRAHAMSON, MARK. 1996. *Urban Enclaves: Identity and Place in America.* New York: St. Martin's Press.

ABRON, JONINA M. 1986. "The Legacy of the Black Panther Party." *The Black Scholar,* November–December, 17: 33–37.

ACHENBAUMM, W. A. 1993. "Old Age." In *Encyclopedia of American Social History,* edited by Mary Kupeic Coyton, Elliot J. Gorn, and Peter W. Williams, 2051–2062. New York: Scribner's.

ACLU. 1996. *Racial Justice.* New York: American Civil Liberties Union.

ADAM, BARRY D. 1995. *The Rise of a Gay and Lesbian Movement,* rev. ed. New York: Twayne.

ADLER, PATRICIA A. AND PETER ADLER. 1998. *Peer Power: Preadolescent Culture and Identity.* New Brunswick, NJ: Rutgers University Press.

ADLER, PATRICIA A., STEVEN J. KESS, AND PETER ADLER. 1992. "Socialization to Gender Role: Popularity among Elementary School Boys and Girls." *Sociology of Education,* July, 65: 169–187.

ADORNO, T. W., ELSE FRENKEL-BRUNSWIK, DANIEL J. LEVINSON, AND R. NEVITT SANFORD. 1950. *The Authoritarian Personality.* New York: Wiley.

AGLIONBY, JOHN. 2004. US Pays Debt at Last to Vietnam War Allies. *The Guardian,* August 24, 11.

AGUIRRE JR., ADALBERTO. 2004. "Profiling Mexican American Identity." *American Behavioral Scientist,* March, 47: 928–942.

AGUILLAR-SAN JUAN, KARIN. 1998. "Creating Ethnic Places in 'Little Saigon'": History, Memory and Citizenship. Paper presented at American Sociological Association Annual Meeting, San Francisco.

AKWESASNE NOTES. 1972. "Columbus a Trader in Indian Slaves," Early Autumn, 4: 22.

ALAN GUTTMACHER INSTITUTE, THE. 2004. *An Overview of Abortion in the United States.* Accessed September 27, 2004 at www.agi-usa.org.

ALÁRCON, ODETTE. 1995. An Interview. *Research Report* (Center for Research on Women, Wellesley College), Fall, 15: 3–4.

ALBRECHT, GARY L. 1995. "Review of Disabling Laws, Enabling Acts: Disability Rights in Britain and America." *Contemporary Sociology* 24(5): 627–629.
———. 1997. "Disability Is Area Rich with Sociological Opportunity." *Footnotes,* December, 25: 6.

ALEXANDER, DELROY. 2001. "Money Flow Home to Mexico on the Rise." *Chicago Tribune,* November 10, sec. 2, 1–2.

ALLEN, JR., ERNEST. 1996. "Religious Heterodoxy and Nationalist Tradition: The Continuing Evolution of the Nation of Islam." *Black Scholar* 26(3–4): 2–34.

ALLPORT, GORDON W. 1979. *The Nature of Prejudice, 25th Anniversary Edition.* Reading, MA: Addison-Wesley.

ALONSO-ZALDIVAR, RICHARDO AND JENNIFER OLDHAN. 2002. "New Airport Screener Jobs Going Mostly to Whites." *Los Angeles Times,* September 24, A18.

ALVORD, LORI ARVISO AND ELIZABETH COHEN VAN PELT. 1999. *The Scalpel and the Silver Bear.* New York: Bantam.

ALVORD, VALERIE. 2000. "Refugees' Success Breeds Pressure, Discrimination." *USA Today,* May 1, 74.

AMERICAN INDIAN HIGHER EDUCATION CONSORTIUM. 1999. *Tribal Colleges: An Introduction.* Alexandra, VA: A.I.H.E.C.

AMERICAN JEWISH COMMITTEE. 1965. *Mutual Savings Banks of New York City.* New York: American Jewish Committee.
———. 1966a. *Mutual Savings Banks: A Follow-Up Report.* New York: American Jewish Committee.
———. 1966b. *Patterns of Exclusion from the Executive Suite: Corporate Banking.* New York: American Jewish Committee.
———. 2001. *American Jewish Year Book 2001.* New York: AJC.
———. 2002. *2001 Annual Survey of American Jewish Opinion.* New York: AJC.

AMNESTY INTERNATIONAL. 1993. *Amnesty International Report 1993.* New York: Amnesty International.

ANDERSON, DENNIS. 1998. "Judge Rules Rest of Prop. 187 Is Unconstitutional." *USA Today,* March 19, 9A.

ANGIER, NATALIE. 1993. "U.S. Opens the Door Just a Crack to Alternative Forms of Medicine." *New York Times,* January 10, 1, 13.

ANTI-DEFAMATION LEAGUE (ADL). 1996. *The Web of Hate: Extremists Exploit the Internet.* New York: Anti-Defamation League.
———. 2001. *Audit of Anti-Semitic Incidents 2000.* New York: Anti-Defamation League.

APONTE, ROBERT. 1991. "Urban Hispanic Poverty: Disaggregations and Explanations." *Social Problems,* November, 38: 516–528.

APPELBAUM, RICHARD AND PETER DREIEN. 1999. "The Campus Anti Sweatshop Movement." *The American Prospect,* September–October, 71–78.

APPLEBOME, PETER. 1996. "70 Years after Scopes Trial, Creation Debate Lives." *New York Times,* March 10, 1, 22.
———. 1997. "Dispute over Ebonics Reflects a Volatile Mix That Roils Urban Education." *New York Times,* March 1, p. 8.

ARAN, KENNETH, HERMAN ARTHUR, RAMON COLON, AND HARVEY GOLDENBERG. 1973. *Puerto Rican History and Culture: A Study Guide and Curriculum Outline.* New York: United Federation of Teachers.

ARCHULETA, GLENDA. 1998. Interview with Archuleta (Council for Energy Resource Tribes) by Richard T. Schaefer, September 18.

ARDEN, HARVEY. 1975. "The Pious Ones." *National Geographic,* August, 168: 276–298.

ANSARI, ZAFAR ISHAQ. 2004. "Islam among African Americans: An Overview." Pp. 222-267 in *Muslims' Place in the American Public Square,* edited by Zahid H. Bukhari et al. Walnut Creek, CA: Atamira Press.

ANTI-DEFAMATION LEAGUE. 2004. *Audit of Anti-Semitic Incidents, 2002.* New York, ADL.

ARIAS, ELIZABETH AND BETTY SMITH. 2003. "Deaths: Preliminary Data for 2001." *National Vital Statistics Reports* 51 (March 14).

ARANDA, ELIZABETH M. AND GUILLERMO REBOLLO-GIL. 2004. "Ethnoracism and the 'Sandwiched' Minorities." *American Behavioral Scientist,* March, 47: 910–927.

ASANTE, MOLEFI KETE. 2000. *All American: How to Cover Asian America.* San Francisco: AAJA.

ASANTE, MOLEFI KETE AND MARK T. MATTSON. 1991. *The Historical and Cultural Atlas of African Americans.* New York: Macmillan.

ASIAN AMERICAN JOURNALIST ASSOCIATION. 2000. *All-American: How to Cover Asian America.* San Francisco, CA: AAJA.

ASSOCIATED PRESS. 2003. "U.S. Withholds Approval for Nuclear Waste Storage on Indian Reservation." *New York Times,* March 11.

ASSOCIATION OF AMERICAN MEDICAL COLLEGES. 2004. *Facts— Applicants, Matriculants and Graduates.* Accessed August 5, 2004 at www.aamc.org.

AVILA, OSCAR. 2003. "Muslim Holiday Testing Schools." *Chicago Tribune,* November 24, 1, 16.

———. 2004. "The conflicting colors of Vietnam." *Chicago Tribune,* February 22, sect. 4, 1, 6.

BADGETT, M. V. LEE AND HEIDI I. HARTMANN. 1995. "The Effectiveness of Equal Employment Opportunity Policies." In *Economic Perspectives in Affirmative Action,* edited by Margaret C. Simms, 55–83. Washington, DC: Joint Center for Political and Economic Studies.

BAGBY, ISHAN. 2004. *A Portrait of Detroit Mosques: Muslim Views on Policy, Politics and Religion.* Clinton Township, MI: Institute for Social Policy and Understanding.

BAHR, HOWARD M. 1972. "An End to Invisibility." Pp. 404–412 in *Native Americans Today: Sociological Perspectives,* edited by Howard M. Bahr, Bruce A. Chadwick, and Robert C. Day. New York: Harper & Row.

BALDWIN, JAMES. 1967. "Negroes Are Anti-Semitic Because They're Anti-White." *New York Times,* May 21, 114.

BALDWIN, NEIL. 2001. *Henry Ford and the Jews: The Mass Production of Hate.* Public Affairs.

BALTZELL, E. DIGBY. 1964. *The Protestant Establishment: Aristocracy and Caste in America.* New York: Vintage Books.

BALZ, DAN. 1998. "A Helping Hand from Across the Sea." *Washington Post National Weekly Edition,* April 20, 15: 16–17.

BAMSHAD, MICHAEL J. AND STEVE E. OLSON. 2003. "Does Race Exist?" *Scientific American,* December, 78–85.

BANERJEE, NEELA. 2000. "Fighting Back against Domestic Violence: Asian American Women Organize to Break the Silence." *AsianWeek,* November 30, 22:13–15.

BARBARO, FRED. 1974. "Ethnic Resentment." *Society,* March–April 11: 67–75.

BARCLAY, WILLIAM, KRISHNA KUMAR, AND RUTH P. SIMMS. 1976. *Racial Conflict, Discrimination, and Power: Historical and Contemporary Studies.* New York: AMS Press.

BARNES, ANNIE S. 2000. *Everyday Racism: A Book for All Americans.* Naperville, IL: Sourcebooks.

BARNES, JESSICA S. AND CLAUDETTE L. BENNETT. 2002. *The Asian Population: 2000.* Census Brief C2KBR/01-16. Washington, DC: U.S. Government Printing Office.

BARRERA, MARIO, CARLOS MUNOS, AND CHARLES ORNELAS. 1972. "The Barrio as an Internal Colony." Pp. 465–549 in *People and Politics in Urban Society,* edited by Harlan Mahlan. Beverly Hills, CA: Sage Publications.

BARRETT, DAVID B. AND TODD M. JOHNSON. 2001. "Worldwide Adherents of All Religions by Six Continental Areas, Mid-2000." P. 302 in *Britannica Book of the Year 2001.* Chicago: Encyclopedia Britannica.

BARRINGER, FELICITY. 2004. "Bitter Division for Sierra Club on Immigration." *New York Times,* March 14, A1, A16.

BARRON, MILTON L. 1953. "Minority Group Characteristics of the Aged in American Society." *Journal of Gerontology,* October, 8: 477–482.

BARRY, ELLEN. 2004. "County Rescinds Vote." *Los Angeles Times,* March 19, A16.

BARTLETT, DONALD L. AND JAMES B. STEELE. 2002. "Casinos: Wheel of Misfortune." *Time,* December 10, 160: 44–53, 56–58.

BASH, HARRY M. 1979. *Sociology, Race and Ethnicity.* New York: Gordon & Breach.

———. 2001. "If I'm So White, Why Ain't I Right?: Some Methodological Misgivings on Taking Identity Ascriptions at Face Value." Paper presented at the Annual Meeting of the Midwest Sociological Society, St. Louis.

BASU, MONI. 2004. "In troubled times, U.S. Muslims Get Political." *Atlanta Journal-Constitution,* July 24, 1.

BAUER, RAYMOND A. AND ALICE H. BAUER. 1942. "Day to Day Resistance to Slavery." *Journal of Negro History,* October, 27: 388–419.

BAUM, GERALDINE. 1998. "New Power of Women Recasts Judaism." *Los Angeles Times,* April 21, A1, A14, A15.

BA-YUNUS, ILYAS AND KASSIM KONE. 2004. "Muslim Americans: A Demographic Report." Pp. 299–322 in *Muslims' Place in the American Public Square,* edited by Zahid H. Bukhari et al. Walnut Creek, CA: Atamira Press.

BELL, DERRICK. 1994. "The Freedom of Employment Act." *The Nation,* (ay 23, 258: 708, 710–714).

BELLAH, ROBERT. 1967. "Civil Religion in America." *Daedalus,* Winter, 96: 1–21.

BELT, DON. 2002. "The World of Islam." *National Geographic,* January, 76–85.

BEM, SANDRA L. AND DARYL J. BEM. 1970. "Case Study of a Nonconscious Ideology: Training the Woman to Know Her Place." Pp. 89–99 in *Beliefs, Attitudes, and Human Affairs,* edited by Daryl J. Bem. Belmont, CA: Brooks/Cole Publishing Co.

BENDICK, MARC, JR., CHARLES W. JACKSON, AND J. HORACIO ROMERO. 1993. *Employment Discrimination against Older Workers: An Experimental Study of Hiring Practices.* Washington, DC: Fair Employment Council of Greater Washington.

BENDYNA, MARY E. AND PAUL M. PEARL. 2000. *Political Preferences of American Catholics at the Time of Election 2000.* Washington, DC: Center for Applied Research in the Apostolate, Georgetown University.

BENNETT, LERONE, JR. 1966. *Before the Mayflower,* rev. ed. Baltimore: Penguin.

BENNETT, PHILLIP. 1993. "Ethnic Labels Fail to Keep Up with Reality." *The Cincinnati Enquirer,* November 18, A10.

BENNETT, VIVIENNE. 1995. "Gender, Class, and Water: Women and the Politics of Water Service in Monterrey, Mexico." *Latin American Perspective,* September, 22: 76–99.

BENNETTS, LESLIE. 1993. "Jerry vs. the Kids." *Vanity Fair,* September, 56: 83–84, 86, 90, 92, 94, 96, 98.

BERLIN, IRA. 1998. *Many Thousands Gone: The First Two Centuries of Slavery in North America.* Cambridge, MA: Harvard University Press.

BERLIN, IRA, MARC FAVREAU, AND STEVEN F. MILLER. 1998. *Remembering Slavery: African Americans Talk about Their Personal Experiences of Slavery and Emancipation.* Cambridge, MA: Harvard University Press.

BERTRAND, MARIANE AND SENDHIL MULLAINATHAN. 2003. *Are Emily and Greg More Employable than Lakisha and Jamal? A Field Experiment on Labor Market Discrimination.* Cambridge, MA: National Bureau of Economic Research.

BIGELOW, REBECCA. 1992. "Certain Inalienable Rights." *Friends Journal,* November, 38: 6–8.

BILLSON, JANET MANCINI 1988. "No Owner of Soil: The Concept of Marginality Revisited on Its Sixtieth Birthday." *International Review of Modern Sociology,* Autumn, 18: 183–204.

BIRREN, JAMES E. AND KATHY GRIBBIN. 1993. "The Elderly." In *Outsiders USA,* edited by Don Spiegel and Patricia Keith-Spiegel. San Francisco: Rinehart Press.

BLACKSTOCK, NELSON. 1976. *COINTELPRO: The FBI's Secret War on Political Freedom.* New York: Vintage Press.

BLAUNER, ROBERT. 1969. "Internal Colonialism and Ghetto Revolt." *Social Problem,* Spring, 16: 393–408.

———. 1972. *Racial Oppression in America.* New York: Harper & Row.

BLOCH, HANNAH. 1996. "Cutting Off the Brains." *Time,* February 5, 147: 46.

BLOOM, LEONARD. 1971. *The Social Psychology of Race Relations.* Cambridge, MA: Schenkman.

BOAL, FREDERICK W., J. DOUGLAS, AND H. NEVILLE. 1982. *Integration and Division: Geographical Perspectives on the Northern Ireland Problems.* New York: Academic Press.

BOBO, LAWRENCE, JAMES R. KLUEGEL, AND RYAN A. SMITH. 1997. "Laissez-Faire Racism: The Crystallization of a Kinder, Gentler, Antiblack Ideology." Pp. 15–42 in *Racial Attitudes in the 1990s: Continuity and Change,* edited by Steven A. Tuch and Jack K. Martin. Westport, CT: Praeger.

BOEHM, MIKE. 2004. "Repeating the History." *Los Angeles Times,* February 20, E2.

BOGARDUS, EMORY. 1968. "Comparing Racial Distance in Ethiopia, South Africa, and the United States." *Sociology and Social Research,* January, 52:149–156.

BOHLAND, JAMES R. 1982. "Indian Residential Segregation in the Urban Southwest: 1970 and 1980." *Social Science Quarterly,* December, 63: 749–761.

BONACICH, EDNA. 1972. "A Theory of Ethnic Antagonism: The Split Labor Market." *American Sociological Review,* October, 37: 547–559.

———. 1976. "Advanced Capitalism and Black/White Race Relations in the United States: A Split Labor Market Interpretation." *American Sociological Review,* February, 41: 34–51.

———. 1988. "The Social Costs of Immigrant Entrepreneurship." *Amerasia,* Spring, 14: 119–128.

———. AND APPELBAUM, RICHARD. 2000. *Behind the Label: Inequality in the Los Angeles Apparel Industry.* Berkeley: University of California Press.

———. AND JOHN MODELL. 1981. *The Economic Basis of Ethnic Solidarity.* Berkeley: University of California Press.

BONFANTE, JORDAN. 1995. "The Catholic Paradox." *Time,* October 9, 146: 64–68.

BONILLA-SILVA, EDUARDO. 1996. "Rethinking Racism: Toward a Structural Interpretation." *American Sociological Review,* June, 62: 465–480.

———. 2002. "The Linguistics of Color Blind Racism: How to Talk Nasty about Blacks without Sounding Racist." *Critical Sociology,* No. 1–2, 28: 41–64.

BONUS, RICK. 2000. *Locating Filipino Americans: Ethnicity and the Cultural Politics of Space.* Philadelphia, PA: Temple University Press.

BOSITIS, DAVID A. 1996. "The Farrakhan Factor." *Washington Post National Weekly Edition,* December 16, 14: 24.

———. 2003. "Black Elected Officials Reach Historic Highs." *Focus* 31, November/December, 3-4.

BORK, ROBERT H. 1995. "What to Do About the First Amendment." *Commentary* 99, February, 23–29.

BOUDREAUX, RUHID. 2002. "Indian Rights Law Is Upheld in Mexico." *Los Angeles Times,* September 7, A3.

BOWLES, SCOTT. 2000. "Bans on Racial Profiling Gain Steam." *USA Today,* June 2, 3A.

BOWMAN, TOM. 1998. "Evangelicals Allege Bias in U.S. Navy, Marine Chaplain Corps." *Baltimore Sun,* August 23, A12.

BOWSER, BENJAMIN AND RAYMOND G. HUNT, EDS. 1996. *Impacts of Racism on White Americans.* Beverly Hills, CA: Sage Publications.

BOXALL, BETTINA. 2001. "Asian Indians Remake Silicon Valley." *Los Angeles Times,* July 6, A1, A26.

BOYER, EDWARD J. 1996. "Life in a New Land: Illegal Immigrant Who Fled Deputies Reaches Goal: A Job in U.S." *Chicago Tribune,* May 7, 131, B8.

BRACHEAR, MANYA A. 2003. "Muslim-Run Food Pantry Feeds Body and Soul." *New York Times,* December 14, sect. 4, 1, 5.

BRADDOCK, D., AND BACHELDER, L. 1994. *The Glass Ceiling and Persons with Disabilities.* Washington, DC: The Glass Ceiling Commission.

BRANNON, RUTH. 1995. "The Use of the Concept of Disability Culture: A Historian's View." *Disability Studies Quarterly,* Fall, 15: 3–15.

BRAXTON, GREG. 1999. "A Mad Dash for Diversity." *Los Angeles Times,* August 9, F1, F10.

BREWER, CYNTHIA A. AND TRUDY A. SUCHAN. 2001. *Mapping Census 2000: The Geography of U.S. Diversity.* Washington, DC: U.S. Government Printing Office.

BRIGGS, DAVID. 1996. "Greeley Poll Says Catholics Want Democratic Church." *Chicago Tribune,* May 31, sect. 2, 9.

BRIGGS, KENNETH A. 1978. Jewish Leader Urges a Program to Convert 'Seekers' to Judaism. *New York Times,* December 3, 1, 37.

BRIMMER, ANDREW. 1995. "The Economic Cost of Discrimination against Black Americans." Pp. 9–29 in *Economic Perspectives in Affirmative Action,* edited by Margaret C. Simms. Washington, DC: Joint Center for Political and Economic Studies.

BRITTINGHAM, ANGELA AND G. PATRICIA DE LA CRUZ. 2004. "Ancestry 2000." *Census 2000 Brief c2kbr-35.* Washington, DC: U.S. Government Printing Office.

BRODIE, MOLLYANN, ANNIE STEFFENSON, JAMIE VALDEZ, REBECCA LEVIN, AND ROBERTO SURO. 2000. *2002 National Survey of Latinos.* Menlo Park, CA: Henry J. Kaiser Foundation and Pew Hispanic Center.

BROOKE, JAMES. 1995. "Attacks on U.S. Muslims Surge Even as Their Faith Holds." *New York Times,* August 28, A1, B7.

———. 1998. "Indians Striving to Save Their Languages." *New York Times,* April 9, A1, A20.

BROOKS-GUNN, JEANNE, PAMELA K. KLEBANOV, AND GREG J. DUNCAN. 1996. "Ethnic Differences in Children's Intelligence Test Scores: Role of Economic Deprivation, Home Environment, and Maternal Characteristics." *Child Development,* April, 67: 396–408.

BROWN, DEE. 1971. *Bury My Heart at Wounded Knee.* New York: Holt, Rinehart & Winston.

BROWN, DeNEEN L. 2001. "Canada's Inuit Struggle to Keep Old Culture Alive." *Chicago Tribune,* July 17, 8.

BROWN, PATRICIA LEIGH. 2003. "For the Muslim Prom Queen, There Are No Kings Allowed." *New York Times,* June 9, A1, A24.

BROWNE, IRENE, ED. 2001. *Latinas and African American Women at Work: Race, Gender, and Economic Inequality.* New York: Russell Sage Foundation.

BROWNSTEIN, ANDREW. 2001. "A Battle over a Name in the Land of the Sioux." *Chronicle of Higher Education,* February 23, 47: A46–A49.

BRYSON, KEN AND LYNNE M. CASPER. 1999. *Co-resident Grandparents and Grandchildren.* Current Population Reports Ser. 823, No. 198. Washington, DC: U.S. Government Printing Office.

BUCHHOLZ, BARBARA BALLINGER. 2003. "Expanded access." *Chicago Tribune,* January 26, sect. 16, 1R, 5R.

BUDIG, MICHELLE J. 2002. "Male Advantage and the Gender Composition of Jobs: Who Rides the Glass Escalator?" *Social Problems* 49(2): 258–277.

BUDIG, MICHELLE J. AND PAULA ENGLAND. 2001. "The Wage Penalty for Motherhood." *American Sociological Review* 66, April, 204–225.

BULLARD, ROBERT D. 1990. "Ecological Inequalities and the New South: Black Communities under Siege." *Journal of Ethnic Studies,* Winter, 17:101–115.

BUNCHE CENTER. 2003. *Prime Time in Black and White: Not Much Is New for 2002.* Bunche Research Report 1 (1).

BUREAU OF THE CENSUS. 1975. *Historical Statistics of the United States, Colonial Times to 1970.* Washington, DC: U.S. Government Printing Office.

———. 1981. *Statistical Abstract of the United States, 1981.* Washington, DC: U.S. Government Printing Office.

———. 1988. *Statistical Abstract of the United States, 1988.* Washington, DC: U.S. Government Printing Office.

———. 1996. *Statistical Abstract of the United States, 1996.* Washington, DC: U.S. Government Printing Office.

———. 2001a. *Profile of the Foreign-Born Population in the United States.* Washington, DC: U.S. Government Printing Office.

———. 2001b. *Black Population in the U.S.: March 2000,* PPL-142. Accessed March 8, 2002, at http://www.census.gov.

———. 2001c. Census 2000 PHC-T.6., *Population by Race and Hispanic or Latino Origin in the United States.* Accessed February 5, 2001, at http://www.census.gov.

———. 2001e. *March 2001 Current Population Survey.* From Table HINC-01. Accessed February 1, 2002, at http://www. census.gov/hhes/www/income.html.

———. 2001g. QT-02. *Profile of Selected Social Characteristics.* Accessed February 5, 2002, at http://factfinder.census.gov.

———. 2001h. (NP-D1-A) *Projections of the Resident Population by Age, Sex, Race, and Hispanic Origin: 1999 to 2100.* Washington, DC: U.S. Government Printing Office.

———. 2001j. *Statistical Abstract of the United States, 2001.* Washington, DC: U.S. Government Printing Office.

———. 2002b. *Table 1. United States—Race and Hispanic Origin: 1790–1990:* Internet Release Date: September 13, 2002.

———. 2002c. March 2002. "Current Population Survey." From Table HINC-03. Accessed October 18, 2002, at http://www.census.gov.

———. 2003a. *Statistical Abstract of the United States, 2003.* Washington DC: U.S. Government Printing Office.

———. 2003b. *Detailed List of Languages Spoken at Home for the Population 5 Years Ago Over by State: 2000*. Released February 5, 2003. Accessed August 1, 2003, at www.census/gov/population/www/cen2000/phc-t20.html.

———. 2003c. *Florida Leads in Growth of School-Age Population: Census Bureau Estimates Also Show Increasing State Diversity*. September 18, 2003 News Release, Table 3.

———. 2004a. *Statistical Abstract of the United States, 2004*. Washington DC: U.S. Government Printing Office.

———. 2004b. *U.S. Interim Projections by Age, Sex, Race, and Hispanic Origin*. Released March 18, 2004 at www.census.gov/ipc/www/usinterimproj.

———. 2004e. *July 1, 2003 State and County Characteristics*. Accessed September 30, 2004, at www.census.gov.

———. 2004h. *Housing Vacancies and Homeownership*. Released February 26, 2004. Accessed August 5, at www.census.gov.

———. 2004f. *Facts and Features: Opening of the National Museum of the American Indian*. Publication CB04-FF SE.13. Reload September 21, 2004 at ww.census.gov.

———. 2004p. *American Fact Finder: Census 2000 Survey File 3 (SF3)-Sample Data, Tables P19 and P20*. Accessed August 11, 2004, at http://factfinder.census.gov.

BUREAU OF CITIZENSHIP AND IMMIGRATION SERVICES. 2003a. *Fiscal Year 2002 Yearbook of Immigrant Statistics*. www.bcis.gov.

———. 2003b. *100 Sample U.S. History and Government Questions with Answers*. Accessed October 20, 2003, at www.immigration.gov/graphics/services/natL/negvire.htm.

BUREAU OF INDIAN AFFAIRS. 1970. *Answers to Your Questions about Indians*. Washington, DC: U.S. Government Printing Office.

———. 1986. *American Indians Today: Answers to Your Questions*. Washington, DC: U.S. Government Printing Office.

———. 1988. *Report of BIA Education: Excellence in Indian Education through the Effective School Process*. Washington, DC: U.S. Government Printing Office.

BUREAU OF LABOR STATISTICS. 2004a. *Women in the Labor Force: A Databook*. Washington, DC: U.S. Government Printing Office.

———. 2004b. *Time-Use Survey*. Accessed September 14, 2004, at www.bls.gov/tus.

BURGESS, MIKE. 1992. American Indian Religious Freedom Act Hearings. *News from Indian Country*, Late December, 8–9.

BUSH, GEORGE W. 2001. *Islam Is Peace*. Accessed October 16, 2004, at www.whitehouse.gov/news/releases.

BUSINESS AND PROFESSIONAL WOMEN. 2002. *Equal Pay Day 2002 Legislative Bankguard*, April 14, 2002, at http://www.bpwusa.org/Content/FairPay/Docy/NCPE.

BUTLER, JOHN SIBLEY. 1996. "The Return of Open Debate." *Society*, March/April, 39: 11–18.

BUTLER, ROBERT N. 1990. "A Disease Called Ageism." *Journal of the American Geriatrics Society*, February, 38: 178–180.

CAIRNS, ED AND JOHN DARBY. 1998. "The Conflict in Northern Ireland." *American Psychologist* 56(7): 754–760.

CAMARILLO, ALBERT. 1993. "Latin Americans: Mexican Americans and Central Americans." Pp. 855–872 in *Encyclopedia of American Social History*, edited by Mary Koplec Coyton, Elliot J. Gorn, and Peter W. Williams. New York: Charles Scribner.

CANAK, WILLIAM AND LAURA SWANSON. 1998. *Modern Mexico*. New York: McGraw-Hill.

CAINKAR, LOUISE. 2005. "The Middle East Diaspora: Arabs and Assyrians in The New Chicago." In *The New Chicago*, edited by John Koval et al. Philadelphia, PA: Temple University Press.

CANEDY, DANA. 2003. "Navy Leaves a Battered Island and Puerto Ricans Cheer." *New York Times*, May 2, A20.

CAPPS, RANDY, KU LEIGHTON, AND MICHAEL FIX. 2002. *How Are Immigrants Faring After Welfare Reform? Preliminary Evidence from Los Angeles and New York City*. Washington, DC: Urban Institute.

CARD, DAVID, JOHN DiNARDO, AND EUGENA ESTES. 1998. "The More Things Change: Immigrants and the Children of Immigrants in the 1940s, the 1970s, and the 1990s." Paper presented at the Joint Center for Poverty Research, Northwestern University of Chicago, April 9.

CARNEGIE FOUNDATION FOR THE ADVANCEMENT OF TEACHING. 1990. "Native Americans and Higher Education: New Mood of Optimism." *Change*, January–February, 27–30.

CARLSON, DARREN K. 2004. "Racial Profiling Seen as Pervasive, Unjust," July 30, at www.gallup.com.

CARRELL, MICHAEL R., NORBERT F. ELBERT, AND ROBERT D. HATFIELD. 2000. *Human Resource Management: Strategies for Managing a Diverse and Global Workforce*. 6th ed. Orlando, FL: Dryden Press.

CARRIER, JIM. 2000. *Ten Ways to Fight Hate, 2nd ed.* Montgomery, AL: Tolerance.org.

CARROLL, SUSAN J. 2004. "Women in State Government: Historical Overview and Current Trends." In *The Book of the States, 2004*. Lexington, KY: The Council of State Governments.

CART, JULIE. 2001. "Natives Brace for a Paradise Loss." *Los Angeles Times*, May 23, A15.

CARTER, BILL. 2001. "'Los Simpsons': Don't Have a Vaca, Man." *New York Times*, February 18, sec. WK, p. 3.

CARVAJAL, DOREEN. 1996. "Diversity Pays Off in a Babel of Yellow Pages." *New York Times*, December 3, 1, 23.

CASTAÑEDA, JORGE G. 1995. "Ferocious Differences." *Atlantic Monthly*, July, 276: 68–69, 71–76.

———. 1996. "A Tale of Two Islands." *Los Angeles Times*, February 12, p. B5.

CATALANO, SHANNAN. 2004. *Crime Victimization, 2003*. Washington, DC: U.S. Government Printing Office.

CATALYST. 2001. "Women Satisfied with Current Job in Financial Industry but Barriers Still Exist." Press Release July 25, 2001. Accessed January 31, 2002, at http://www.catalystwomen.org.

CBS NEW YORK. 2003. "Shame On You: Rockstar Video Games." Accessed November 15, 2003, at cbsnewyork.com.

CERAR, K. MELISSA. 1995. *Teenage Refugees from Nicaragua Speak Out*. New York: Rosen Publishing.

CHAMPAGNE, DUANE. 1994. *Native America. Portrait of the Peoples*. Detroit: Visible Ink.

CERT. 2004. *CERT Member Tribes*. Accessed August 3, 2004, at www.cert.com.

CHANG, PATRICIA M. Y. 1997. "Female Clergy in the Contemporary Protestant Church: A Current Assessment." *Journal for the Scientific Study of Religion*, December, 36: 565–573.

CHASE-DUNN, CHRISTOPHER AND THOMAS D. HALL. 1998. "World-Systems in North America: Networks, Rise and Fall and Pulsations of Trade in Stateless Systems." *American Indian Culture and Research Journal* 22(1): 23–72.

CHAWLA, MADHU S. 1992. "Racial Hatred." Pp. 116–117 in *Asian Americans*, edited by Joann Faung Jean Lee. New York: The New Press.

CHEN, DAVID W. AND SOMINI SENGUPTA. 2001. "Not Yet Citizens but Eager to Fight for the U.S." *New York Times*, October 22, A1, B2.

CHIDEYA, FARAI. 1993. "Endangered Family." *Newsweek*, August 30, 122:16–27.

CHILDREN NOW. 1998. *A Different World: Children's Perceptions of Race, Class, and the Media*. Oakland, CA: Children Now.

———. 2004. *2003-04 Fall Colors Prime Time Diversity Report*. Oakland, CA: Children Now.

CHIN, KO-LIN. 1996. *Chinatown Gangs: Extortion, Enterprise, and Ethnicity*. New York: Oxford University Press.

CHIROT, DANIEL AND EDWARDS, JENNIFER. 2003. "Making Sense of the Senseless: Understanding Genocide." *Contexts*, Spring, 12–19.

CHRISTOPULOS, DIANA. 1974. "Puerto Rico in the Twentieth Century: A Historical Survey. Pp. 123–163 in *Puerto Rico and Puerto Ricans: Studies in History and Society*, edited by Adalberto Lopez and James Petras. New York: Wiley.

CLARK, KENNETH B. AND MAMIE P. CLARK. 1947. "Racial Identification and Preferences in Negro Children." Pp. 169–178 in *Readings in Social Psychology*, edited by Theodore M. Newcomb and Eugene L. Hartley, eds. New York: Holt, Rinehart & Winston.

CLARY, MIKE. 1997a. "Black, Cuban Racial Chasm Splits Miami." *Los Angeles Times*, March 23, pp. A1, A20.

———. 1997b. "A City That Still Is Consumed by Castro." *Los Angeles Times*, January 1, A1, A26.

CLEAVER, KATHLEEN. 1982. "How TV Wrecked the Black Panthers." *Channels*, November–December, 98–99.

CLEMETSON, LYNETTE. 2003. "Arab-Americans Gain a Higher Political Profile." *New York Times*, October 19.

———. 2004. "Some Younger U.S. Arabs Reassert Ethnicity." *New York Times,* January 11, 12.

CLEVELAND, HARLAN. 1995. "The Limits to Cultural Diversity." *Futurist,* March–April, 29: 19, 22–26, 43–44.

CLOUD, JOHN. 2003. "The New Face of Gay Power." *Time,* October 13, 162: 52–56.

CLYMER, ADAM. 2002b. "Court Allows a New Approach to Redrawing Districts by Race." *New York Times,* June 27, A1, A18.

COATES, RODNEY D. 2004. "Critical Racial and Ethnic Studies—Profiling and Reparations. *American Behavioral Scientist,* March, 47: 873–878.

COCKBURN, ANDREW. 2003. "True Colors: Divided Loyalty in Puerto Rico." *203,* March, 34-55.

COGNARD-BLACK, ANDREW J. 2004. "Will They Stay, or Will They Go?" Sex- Atypical Among Token Men Who Teach. *Sociological Quarterly* 45(1): 113–139.

COHEN, STEVEN M. 1988. *American Assimilation or Jewish Revival?* Bloomington: Indiana University Press.

———. 1991. *Content or Continuity? Alternative Bases for Commitment.* New York: American Jewish Committee.

COHON, SAMUEL M. 1995. "Not in Our Town. The Courage to Resist Hatred." *The Chronicle,* 6–9, 36, 38, 44, 48–50.

COLE, DAVID. 1999. *No Equal Justice: Race and Class in the American Criminal Justice System.* New York: The New Press.

COLEMAN, JAMES S., ERNEST Q. CAMPBELL, CAROL J. HOBSON, JAMES McPARTLAND, ALEXANDER M. MOOD, FREDERIC D. WEINFOLD, AND ROBERT L. LINK. 1966. *Equality of Educational Opportunity.* Washington, DC: U.S. Office of Education.

COMAS-DÍAZ, LILLIAN, M. BRINTON LYKES, AND RENATO D. ALARCÓN. 1998. "Ethnic Conflict and the Psychology of Liberation in Guatemala, Peru, and Puerto Rico." *American Psychologist,* July, 53: 778–792.

COMER, JAMES P. AND ALVIN F. POUSSAINT. 1992. *Raising Black Children.* New York: Plume.

COMMISSION ON CIVIL RIGHTS 1980. *Characters in Textbooks: A Review of the Literature.* Washington, DC: U.S. Government Printing Office.

———. 1981. *Affirmative Action in the 1980s: Dismantling the Process of Discrimination.* Washington, DC: U.S. Government Printing Office.

COMMISSION ON WARTIME RELOCATION AND INTERNMENT OF CIVILIANS. 1982a. *Recommendations.* Washington, DC: U.S. Government Printing Office.

———. 1982b. *Report.* Washington, DC: U.S. Government Printing Office.

COMMITTEE OF 100. 2001. *American Attitudes towards Chinese Americans and Asian Immigrants.* New York: Committee of 100.

CONLEY, DALTON. 2002. "Forty Acres and a Mule: What if Americans Pay Reparations?" *Contexts,* Fall, 1:13–20.

CONLIN, MICHELLE. 2003. "The New Gender Gap." *Business Week,* May 26.

CONNOR, WALTER. 1994. *Ethnonationalism: The Quest for Understanding.* Princeton, NJ: Princeton University Press.

CONROY, JOHN. 1981. "Ulster's Lost Generation." *New York Times Magazine,* August 2, 16–21, 70–72, 74–75.

CONVER, BILL. 1976. "Group Chairman Lists Problems Endangering Jewish Family." *Peoria Journal Star,* December 4, A2.

"CONVERTS TO JUDAISM." 1982. *New York Times,* August 29, 23.

CONYERS, JAMES L., JR. 1996. "A Case Study of Social Stratification: An Afrocentric Edification." *Western Journal of Black Studies,* Spring, 20: 9–15.

COOPER, ABRAHAM AND HAROLD BRACKMAN. 2001. "Holocaust Deniers Spread Their Lies in the Middle East." *USA Today,* March 8, 15A.

COOPER, RICHARD S., CHARLES N. ROTIMI, AND RYK WARD. 1999. "The Puzzle of Hypertension in African Americans." *Scientific American,* February, 56–63.

CORNACCHIA, EUGENE J. AND DALE C. NELSON. 1992. "Historical Differences in the Political Experiences of American Blacks and White Ethnics: Revisiting an Unresolved Controversy." *Ethnic and Racial Studies* January, 15: 102–124.

CORNELIUS, WAYNE A. 1996. "Economics, Culture, and the Politics of Restricting Immigration." *Chronicle of Higher Education,* November 15, 43: B4–B5.

CORNELL, STEPHEN. 1984. "Crisis and Response in Indian–White Relations: 1960–1984." *Social Problems,* October, 32: 44–59.

———. 1996. "The Variable Ties That Bind: Content and Circumstance in Ethnic Processes." *Ethnic and Racial Studies,* April, 19: 265–289.

CORNELL, STEPHEN AND JOSEPH P. KALT. 1990. "Pathways from Poverty: Economic Development and Institution-Building on American Indian Reservations." *American Indian Culture and Research Journal* 14(1): 89–125.

———. 2003. *Alaska Native Self-Government and Service Delivery: What Works?* Tucson: Native Nations Institute for Leadership, Management, and Policy.

CORRELL, JOSHUA ET AL. 2002. "The Police Officer's Dilemma: Using Ethnicity to Disambiguate Potentially Threatening Individuals." *Journal of Personality and Social Psychology* 83(6): 1314–1329.

COSE, ELLIS. 1993. *The Rage of a Privileged Class.* New York: HarperCollins.

COSER, LEWIS A. 1956. *The Functions of Social Conflict.* New York: Free Press.

COSER, LEWIS A. AND ROSE LAUB COSER. 1974. *Greedy Institutions.* New York: Free Press.

COUNCIL ON AMERICAN-ISLAMIC RELATIONS. 2004. *Poll: 1-in-4 Americans Holds Anti-Muslim Views.* Accessed October 7, 2004, at www.cair-net.org.

COUNCIL ON SCIENTIFIC AFFAIRS. 1991. "Hispanic Health in the United States." *Journal of the American Medical Association,* January 9, 265: 248–252.

COX, JAMES. 2002. "Activists Challenge Corporations That They Say Are Tied to Slavery." *USA Today,* February 21, 1A, 8A, 9A.

COX, OLIVER C. 1942. "The Modern Caste School of Social Relations." *Social Forces,* December, 21: 218–226.

DAHLBURG, JOHN-THOR. 1998. "Deal Okd to End 30 Years of 'Trouble' in Northern Ireland." *Los Angeles Times,* April 11, A1, A8–A9.

———. 2001. "A New World for Haitians." *Los Angeles Times,* September 4, A1, A9.

———. 2004a. "The Spanish-Speaking Heritage of the State Now Reflects All of Latin America, Not Just Cuba." *Los Angeles Times,* June 28, A1, A12.

———. 2004b. "The Cuban Americans Rush to Visit Kin While They Can." *Los Angeles Times,* June 30, A27.

DAITZ, BEN. 2003. "Navajo Miners Battle a Deadly Legacy of Yellow Dust." *New York Times,* May 13, D5, D8.

DANG, ALAIN AND SOMJEM FRNZER. 2004. *Black Same-Sex Households in the United States.* Washington, DC: National Gay and Lesbian Task Force Policy Institutes.

DANIELS, ROGER. 1972. *Concentration Camps, USA.* New York: Holt, Rinehart & Winston.

———. 1990. *Coming to America.* New York: HarperCollins.

DANNIN, ROBERT. 2002. *Black Pilgrimage to Islam.* Cambridge, England: Oxford University Press.

DART, BOB. 1998. Preserving America: Lancaster County, PA. *Atlanta Journal and Constitution,* June 28.

DART, JOHN. 1997. "Poll Studies Chinese Americans, Religion." *Los Angeles Times,* July 5, B5.

DAVID, GARY C. 2003. "Rethinking Who's an Arab American: Arab-American Studies in the New Millennium." *Al-Jadid,* Fall, 9.

———. 2004a. "Being Arab and Becoming Americanized: Forms of Mediated Assimilation in Metropolitan Detroit." Pp. 125–142 in *Muslim Minorities in the West,* edited by Yvonne Yazbeck Haddad and Jane I. Smith, Lanham, MD: Rowman and Littlefield.

———. 2004b. Scholarship on Arab Americans Distorted Past 9/11. *Al-Jadid,* Winter/Spring, 26–27.

———. AND KENNETH KAHTAN AYOUBY. 2004. "Perpetual Suspects and Permanent Others: Arab Americans and the War and Terrorism." Pp. 30–71 in *Guerras e Imigracioes,* edited by Marco Aurélio Machado de Oliveira. Universida de Federal de Mato Grosso Do Sul.

———. 2005. "Studying the Exotic Other in the Classroom: The Portrayal of Arab Americans in Educational Source Materials." *Multicultural Perspectives.* Forthcoming.

DÁVILA, ARLENE. 2001. *Latinos, Inc.: The Marketing and Making of a People.* Berkeley: University of California Press.

DAVIS, JAMES AND TOM W. SMITH. 2001. *General Social Surveys, 1972–2000*. Storrs, CT: The Roper Center.

DAWSON, MICHAEL C. AND ROVANA POPOFF. 2004. "Reparations: Justice and Greed in Black and White." *DuBois Review* 1(1): 47–91.

DAY, JENNIFER CHEESEMAN AND KELLY HOLDER. 2004. "Voting and Registration in the Election of November 2002." *Current Population Reports* Ser. P20. No. 552. Washington, DC: U.S. Government Printing Office.

DE ANDA, ROBERTO M. 2004. *Chicanas and Chicanos in Contemporary Society.* 2nd ed. Lanham MD: Rowman and Littlefield & Bacon.

DEATH PENALTY INFORMATION CENTER. 2004. *Facts About the Death Penalty,* January 30. Washington, DC: DPIC.

DE LA CRUZ, SR. PATRICIA AND ANGELA BRITTINGHAM. 2003. "The Arab Population: 2000." *Census 2000 Brief* Sr. C2KBR. No. 23. Washington, DC: U.S. Government Printing Office.

DEL OLMO, FRANK. 2003. "Slow Motion Carnage at the Border." *Los Angeles Times,* May 18, M5.

DE LA GARZA, RODOLFO O., LOUIS DESIPIO, F. CHRIS GARCIA, JOHN GARCIA, AND ANGELO FALCON. 1992. *Latino Voices: Mexican, Puerto Rican, and Cuban Perspectives on American Politics.* Boulder, CO: Westview Press.

DELLAPERGOLA, SERGIO. 2001. World Jewish Population, 2001. Pp. 532–569 in *American Jewish Yearbook 2001,* edited by David Singer and Lawrence Grossman. New York: American Jewish Committee.

DELORIA, VINE, JR. 1969. *Custer Died for Your Sins: An Indian Manifesto.* New York: Avon.

———. 1971. *Of Utmost Good Faith.* New York: Bantam.

———. 1992. "Secularism, Civil Religion, and the Religious Freedom of American Indians." *American Indian Culture and Research Journal* 16(2): 9–20.

———. 1995. *Red Earth, White Lies.* New York: Scribner's.

———. 2004. "Promises Made, Promises Broken." Pp. 143–159 in *Native Universe: Voices of Indian America,* edited by Gerald McMaster and Clifford E. Trofzer. Washington, DC: National Geographic.

DELORIA, VINE, JR. AND CLIFFORD M. LYTLE. 1983. *American Indians, American Justice.* Austin: University of Texas Press.

DENAVAS-WALT, CARMEN, BERNADETTE PROCTOR, AND ROBERT J. MILLS. 2004. *Income, Poverty and Health Insurance 2003.* Washington, DC: U.S. Government Printing Office.

DEPALMA, ANTHONY. 1995. "Racism? Mexico's in Denial." *New York Times,* June 11, E4.

DEPARTMENT OF ENERGY. 2000. *Final Report: Task Force against Racial Profiling.* Washington, DC: U.S. Government Printing Office.

DEPARTMENT OF JUSTICE. 2000. *The Civil Liberties Act of 1988: Redress for Japanese Americans.* Accessed June 29, 2000, at http://www.usdoj.gov/crt/ora/main.html.

———. 2001a. *Report to the Congress of the United States: A Review of Restrictions on Persons of Italian Ancestry During World War II.* Accessed February 1, 2002 at http://www.house.gov/judiciary/Italians.pdf.

———. 2001b. *Uniform Crime Reports 2000.* Washington, DC: U.S. Government Printing Office.

———. 2003a. *Uniform Crime Reports, 2003.* Washington, DC: U.S. Government Printing Office.

———. 2003b. *Fact Sheet for Hate Crime Statistics, 2002.* News release November 12, 2003. Accessible at www.fbi.gov.

———. 2004. *Uniform Crime Reports 2004.* Washington, DC: U.S. Government Printing Office.

DEPARTMENT OF LABOR. 1965. *The Negro Family: The Case for National Action.* Washington, DC: U.S. Government Printing Office.

———. 1980. *Perspectives on Working Women: A Databook.* Washington, DC: U.S. Government Printing Office.

———. 1995. *Good for Business: Making Full Use of the Nation's Capital.* Washington, DC: U.S. Government Printing Office.

———. 1998. *Work and Elder Care: Facts for Caregivers and Their Employers.* Accessed November 20, 1998, at http://www.dol.gov/dol/wb/public/wb_pubs/elderc.htm.

———. 2001. *Working in the 21st Century.* Washington, DC: U.S. Government Printing Office.

DEUTSCHER, IRWIN, FRED P. PESTELLO, AND H. FRANCES PESTELLO. 1993. *Sentiments and Acts.* New York: Aldine de Gruyter.

DIAMOND, JARED. 2003. "Globalization, Then." *Los Angeles Times,* September 14, M1, M3.

DINNERSTEIN, LEONARD. 1994. *Anti-Semitism in America.* New York: Oxford University Press.

DIONNE, E. J., JR. 1988. "Jackson Share of Votes by Whites Triples in '88." *New York Times,* June 13, B7.

DISCH, ESTELLE. 1997. *Reconstructing Gender: A Multicultural Anthology.* Mountain View, CA: Mayfield.

DIXON, ROBYN. 2003. "Crime in South Africa More Vexing and Vicious." *Los Angeles Times,* May 4,. A1, A5.

DOLAN, MAURA. 2000. "State Justices Deal New Set Back to Affirmative Action." *Los Angeles Times,* December 1.

DOMINO, JOHN C. 1995. *Sexual Harassment and the Courts.* New York: HarperCollins.

DORRIS, MICHAEL 1988. "For the Indians, No Thanksgiving." *New York Times,* November 24, A23.

DOYLE, JAMES A. AND MICHELE A. PALUDI. 1998. *Sex and Gender: The Human Experience,* 4th ed. New York: McGraw-Hill.

DRABELLE, DENNIS. 1997. "The Trade of the Tribes." *Washington Post National Weekly Edition,* September 8, 14: 34.

DU BOIS, W. E. B. 1903. *The Souls of Black Folks: Essays and Sketches.* Reprinted in 1961 by New York: Facade Publications.

———. 1935. Does the Negro Need Separate Schools? *Journal of Negro Education,* July, 1: 328–335.

———. 1939. *Black Folk: Then and Now.* New York: Holt, Rinehart & Winston.

———. 1952. *Battle for Peace: The Story of My 83rd Birthday.* New York: Masses and Mainstream.

———. 1961. *The Souls of Black Folk.* New York: Fawcett.

———. 1968. *Dusk of Dawn.* New York: Schocken.

———. 1969a. *An ABC of Color.* New York: International Publications.

———. 1969b. *The Suppression of the African Slave-Trade to the United States of America, 1638–1870.* New York: Schocken.

———. 1970. *The Negro American Family.* Cambridge, MA: MIT Press.

———. 1996. *The Philadelphia Negro: A Social Study.* Philadelphia: University of Pennsylvania Press (originally published in 1899).

DUBERMAN, MARTIN. 1993. *Stonewall.* New York: Dutton.

DUDLEY, CARL S. AND DAVID A. ROOZEN. 2001. *Faith Communities Today.* Hartford, CT: Hartford Seminary.

DUFF, JOHN B. 1971. *The Irish in the United States.* Belmont, CA: Wadsworth.

DUNN, ASHLEY. 1994. "Southeast Asians Highly Dependent on Welfare in U.S." *New York Times,* May 19, A1, A20.

DURANT, THOMAS J., JR. AND JOYCE S. LOUDEN. 1986. "The Black Middle Class in America: Historical and Contemporary Perspectives." *Phylon,* December, 47: 253–263.

DYSON, MICHAEL ERIC. 1995. *Making Malcolm: The Myth and Meaning of Malcolm X.* New York: Oxford University Press.

EARLY, GERALD. 1994. Defining Afrocentrism. *Journal of Blacks in Higher Education* 1 (Winter), p. 46.

ECKSTROM, KEVIN. 2001. "New, Diverse Take Spot on Catholic Altars." *Chicago Tribune,* August 31, 8.

———. 2004. "An Amish Exception." *The Economist,* February 7, 33.

———. 2004B. "Who's Winning the Fight?" *The Economist,* July 3, 38.

———. 2004C. "Indigenous People in South America: A Political Awakening." *The Economist,* February 21, 35–37.

EDMONDS, PATRICIA. 1995. "Gambling's Backers Find It Isn't a Sure Bet." *USA Today,* December 29, A1, A2.

EGAN, TIMOTHY. 1998. "New Prosperity Brings New Conflict to Indian Country." *New York Times,* March 8, 1, 22.

———. 2000. "New Prosperity Brings New Conflict to Indian Country." *New York Times,* March 8, 1, 22.

EITLE, TAMELA MCNULTY. 2002. "Special Education on Racial Segregation: Understanding Variation in the Representation of Black Students in Educable Mentally Handicapped Programs." *Sociological Quarterly* 43(4): 575–605.

EL NASSER, HAYA. 1996. "Census Predicts California Will Grow 56% by 2025." *USA Today,* October 23, 7A.

———. 1997. "Varied Heritage Claimed and Extolled by Millions." *USA Today*, May 8, 1A, 2A.

———. 2003. "Black America's New Diversity." *USA Today*, February 7, 3A.

ELKINS, STANLEY. 1959. *Slavery: A Problem in American Institutional and Intellectual Life*. Chicago: University of Chicago Press.

ELLINGWOOD, KEN. 2001. "Results of Crackdown at Border Called Mixed." *Los Angeles Times*, August 4, 39.

ELLIS, RICHARD N. 1972. *The Western American Indian: Case Studies in Tribal History*. Lincoln: University of Nebraska Press.

ENG, MONICA. 1998. "Chinese-Americans Have Their Own Ways of Paying Respect." *Chicago Tribune*, May 28, sec. 5, 1, 2.

ENGEN, RODNEY L., SARA STERN, AND GEORGE S. BRIDGES. 2002. "Racial Disparities in the Punishment of Youth: A Theoretical and Empirical Assessment of the Literature." *Social Problems* 49(2): 194–220.

EPSTEIN, CYNTHIA FUCHS. 1999. "The Major Myth of the Women's Movement." *Dissent*, Fall, 83–111.

EQUAL EMPLOYMENT OPPORTUNITY COMMISSION. 2001. *Age Discrimination in Employment Act (ADEA) Changes FY 1992–FY 2000*. Accessed December 10, 2001, at http://www.eeoc.gov/stats/adea.html.

ESCHBACH, KARL AND KALMAN APPLEBAUM. 2000. "Who Goes to Powwows? Evidence from the Survey of American Indians and Alaskan Natives." *American Indian Culture and Research Journal* 24(2): 65–83.

ESPIRITU, YEN LE. 1992. *Asian American Panethnicity: Bridging Institutions and Identities*. Philadelphia: Temple University Press.

———. 1996. "Colonial Oppression, Labour Importation, and Group Formation: Filipinos in the United States." *Ethnic and Racial Studies*, January, 19: 29–48.

ESPIRITU, YEN LE AND DIANE L. WOLF. 2001. "The Paradox of Assimilation: Children of Filipino Immigrants in San Diego." Pp. 157–186 in *Ethnicities: Children of Immigrants in America*, edited by Ruben G. Rumbaut and Alejandro Portes. Berkeley: University of California Press.

FAIR US. 2003. *Issue Brief*. Accessed August 24 at www.fairus.org/html/newsroom.html.

FARKAS, STEVE. 2003. "*What Immigrants Say About Life in the United States.*" Washington DC: Migration Policy Institute.

FARNSWORTH, CLYDE H. 1996. "Canada's Justice System Faces Charges of Racism." *New York Times*, January 28, 3.

FEAGIN, JOE R., HERNÁN VERA, AND PINAR BATUR. 2000. *White Racism*. 2nd ed. New York: Routledge.

FERREE, MYRA MARX AND BETH B. HESS. 1994. *Controversy and Coalition: The New Feminist Movement across Three Decades of Change*, rev. ed. New York: Twayne.

FIELDS, JASON. 2003. *Children's Living Arrangements and Characteristics: March 2002*. Current Population Reports Ser. P20, No. 547. Washington, DC: U.S. Government Printing Office.

FINDER, ALAN. 1994. "Muslim Gave Racist Speech, Jackson Says." *New York Times*, January 23, 21.

FINE, MICHELLE AND ADRIENNE ASCH. 1981. "Disabled Women: Sexism without the Pedestal." *Journal of Sociology and Social Welfare*, July, 8: 233–248.

———. 1988a. "Disability beyond Stigma: Social Interaction, Discrimination, and Activism." *Journal of Social Issues* 44(1): 3–21.

———. 1988b. *Women with Disabilities: Essays in Psychology, Culture, and Politics*. Philadelphia: Temple University Press.

———. 1995. "Despite Tough Laws, Sweatshops Flourish." *New York Times*, February 6, A1, B4.

FINESTEIN, ISRAEL. 1988. "The Future of American Jewry." *The Jewish Journal of Sociology*, December, 30:121–125.

FING, JING, SHANTHA MADHAVAN, AND MICHAEL H. ALDERMAN. 1996. "The Association between Birthplace and Mortality from Cardiovascular Causes among Black and White Residents of New York City." *New England Journal of Medicine*, November 21, 335: 1545–1551.

FISHMAN, JOSHUA A., ROBERT G. HAYDEN, AND MARY E. WARSHAVER. 1966. "The Non-English and the Ethnic Group Press, 1910–1960." Pp. 51–74 in *Language Loyalty in the United States*, edited by Joshua A. Fishman. London: Mouton.

FIX, MICHAEL, WENDY ZIMMERMAN, AND JEFFERY S. PASSEL. 2001. *The Integration of Immigrant Families in the United States*. Washington, DC: The Urban Institute.

FIXICO, DONALD L. 1988. "The Federal Policy of Termination and Relocation, 1945–1960." Pp. 260–277 in *The American Indian Experience*, edited by Phillip Weeks. Arlington Heights, IL: Forum Press.

FLEISCHMAN, JEFFREY. 2004. "New Anti-Semitism Stirs Old Anxieties." *Los Angeles Times*, March 27, A1, A6.

FLETCHER, MICHAEL A. 2002. "A Report Card in Historically Black Colleges." *Washington Post National Weekly Edition*, December 9, 20: 31.

FLEXNER, ELEANOR. 1959. *Century of Struggle: The Women's Rights Movement in the United States*. Cambridge, MA: Harvard University Press.

FOERSTRER, AMY. 2004. "Race, Identity, and Belonging: 'Blackness' and the Struggle for Solidarity in a Multiethnic Labor Union." *Social Problems* 51(3): 386–409.

FOLKHART, BART A. 1995. "Maggie Kuhn, 89; Iconoclastic Founder of Gray Panthers." *Los Angeles Times*, April 23, A34.

FONG, STANLEY L. M. 1965. "Assimilation of Chinese in America: Changes in Orientation and Perception." *American Journal of Sociology*, November, 71: 265–273.

———. 1973. "Assimilation and Changing Social Roles of Chinese Americans." *Journal of Social Issues* 29(2): 115–127.

———. 2002. *The Contemporary Asian American Experience: Beyond the Model Minority*. 2nd ed. Upper Saddle River, NJ: Prentice Hall.

FOX, ELAINE. 1992. "Crossing the Bridge: Adaptive Strategies among Navajo Health Care Workers." *Free Inquiry in Creative Sociology*, May, 20: 25–34.

FOX, STEPHEN. 1990. *The Unknown Internment*. Boston: Twayne.

FRANKEL, BRUCE. 1995. "N.Y.'s 'Jewish Rosa Parks' Wins Bus Battle." *USA Today*, March 17, p. 4A.

FRANKENBERG, ERICA, CHUNGMEI LEE, AND GARY ORFIELD. 2003. *A Multiracial Society with Segregated Schools: Are We Losing the Dream?* Cambridge, MA: Civil Rights Project, Harvard University.

FRANKLIN, JOHN HOPE AND ALFRED A. MOSS, JR. 2000. *From Slavery to Freedom: A History of African Americans*, 8th ed. New York: McGraw-Hill.

FRAZIER, E. FRANKLIN. 1957. *Black Bourgeois: The Rise of a New Middle Class*. New York: Free Press.

———. 1964. *The Negro Church in America*. New York: Schocken.

FREEDMAN, DONNA. 2001. "Talking the Talk." *Chicago Tribune*, July 13, sec. 13, 1.

FREEDMAN, SAMUEL G. 2003. "Sex and the City Celebrates Judaism." *USA Today*, July 17, 13A.

———. 2004. "Latino Parents Decry Bilingual Programs." *New York Times*, July 14, A21.

FREEDMAN, VICKI A., LINDA G. MARTIN, AND ROBERT F. SCHOENI. 2004. "Disability in America." *Population Bulletin*, September.

FREEMAN, JO. 1973. "The Origins of the Women's Liberation Movement." *American Journal of Sociology*, January, 78: 792–811.

———. 1975. *The Politics of Women's Liberation*. New York: David McKay.

———. 1983. "On the Origins of Social Movements. Pp. 1–30 in *Social Movements of the Sixties and Seventies*, edited by Jo Freeman. New York: Longman.

FRIEDAN, BETTY. 1963. *The Feminine Mystique*. New York: Dell.

———. 1981. *The Second Stage*. New York: Summit Books.

———. 1991. "Back to the Feminine Mystique?" *The Humanist*, January–February, 51: 26–27.

FRIEDMAN, GEORGES. 1967. *The End of the Jewish People?* Garden City, New York: Doubleday.

FRIENDS COMMITTEE ON NATIONAL LEGISLATION. 1993. "American Indian Religious Freedom." *News from Indian Country*, Mid-February, 8.

FUCHS, ESTELLE AND ROBERT J. HAVIGHURST. 1972. *To Live on This Earth: American Indian Education*. Garden City, NY: Doubleday.

FULLER, CHEVON. 1998. "Service Redlining." *Civil Rights Journal*, Fall, 3: 33–36.

"FUTURE OF JEWISH DAY SCHOOLS THREATENED BY FINANCES, IDEOLOGY." 2000. *Religion Watch*, January, 4.

GALARZA, ERNESTO. 1964. *Merchants of Labor: The Mexican Bracero Story*. Santa Barbara, CA: McNally & Loften.

GALLUP. 2002. *Poll Topics and Trends: Race.* Accessed January 28, 2002, at http://www.gallup.com/poll/topics/race.asp.

————. 2004a. *Poll Topics and Trends: Religion.* Accessed August 2, 2004, at www.gallup.com.

————. 2004b. *Focus on Gay and Lesbian Marriages.* Accessed April 14, 2004, at www.gallup.com.

GALLUP, GEORGE H. 1972. *The Gallup Poll, Public Opinion, 1935–1971.* New York: Random House.

GALLUP POLL MONTHLY. 1995. Gallup Short Subjects, December, 363: 38–48.

GANS, HERBERT J. 1956. "American Jewry: Present and Future." *Commentary,* May, 21: 424–425.

————. 1979. "Symbolic Ethnicity: The Future of Ethnic Groups and Cultures in America." *Ethnic and Racial Studies,* January, 2: 1–20.

————. 1995. *The War against the Poor: The Underclass and Antipoverty Policy.* New York: Basic Books.

GARDNER, MARILYN. 2003. "This View of Seniors Just Doesn't 'Ad' Up." *Christian Science Monitor,* January 15, 15.

GARFINKEL, HERBERT. 1959. *When Negroes March.* New York: Atheneum.

GARNER, ROBERTA. 1996. *Contemporary Movements and Ideologies.* New York: McGraw-Hill.

GARTNER, ALAN AND TOM JOE, EDS. 1987. *Images of the Disabled, Disabled Images.* New York: Praeger.

GARY, LAWRENCE E., LULA A. BEATTY, GRETA L. BERRY, AND MARY D. PRICE. 1983. *Stable Black Families: Final Report.* Washington, DC: Institute for Urban Affairs and Research, Howard University.

GERBER, DAVID A. 1993. *Nativism, Anti-Catholicism, and Anti-Semitism.* New York: Scribner's.

GERTH, H. H. AND C. WRIGHT MILLS. 1958. *From Max Weber: Essays in Sociology.* New York: Galaxy Books.

GETLIN, JOSH. 1998. "Leaving an Impact on American Culture." *Los Angeles Times,* April 22, A1, A26, A27.

GIAGO, TIM. 2001. "National Media Should Stop Using Obscene Words." *The Denver Post,* January 21, 6H.

GIBBS, NANCY. 2001. "A Whole New World." *Time,* June 11, 36–45.

GILENS, MARTIN. 1996. "'Race Coding' and White Opposition to Welfare." *American Political Science Review,* September, 90: 593–604.

GITTLER, JOSEPH B., ED. 1981. *Jewish Life in the United States: Perspectives from the Social Sciences.* New York: New York University Press.

GLADWELL, MALCOLM. 1996. "Discrimination: It's Just a Bus Stop Away." *Washington Post National Weekly Edition,* February 19, 13: 33.

GLANCY, DIANE. 1998. "When the Boats Arrived." Hungry Mind Review. *The National Book Magazine,* Spring, 7.

GLANZ, JAMES. 2000. "Amid Race Profiling Claims, Asian Americans Avoid Labs." *New York Times,* July 25, A1, A12.

GLAZER, NATHAN. 1971. "The Issue of Cultural Pluralism in America Today." Pp. 2–8 in *Pluralism beyond Frontier: Report of the San Francisco Consultation on Ethnicity,.* San Francisco: American Jewish Committee.

————. 1990. American Jewry or American Judaism? *Society,* November–December, 28:14–20.

GLAZER, NATHAN AND DANIEL PATRICK MOYNIHAN. 1970. *Beyond the Melting Pot: The Negroes, Puerto Ricans, Jews, Italians, and Irish of New York City.* 2nd ed. Cambridge: MIT Press.

GLEASON, PHILIP. 1980. "American Identity and Americanization." Pp. 31–58 in *Harvard Encyclopedia of American Ethnic Groups,* edited by Stephen Therstromm. Cambridge: Belknap Press of Harvard University Press.

GLIONNA, JOHN M. 2004. "Finding a Voice in Politics." *Los Angeles Times,* May 22, A1, A22.

GOBODO-MADIKIZELA, PUMLA. 2003. *A Human Being Died That Night.* New York: Houghton Mifflin.

GOERING, JOHN M. 1971. "The Emergence of Ethnic Interests: A Case of Serendipity." *Social Forces,* March, 48: 379–384.

GOERING, LAURIE. 2003. "S. Africa Seeks to Empower Excluded Class. *Chicago Tribune,* October 14, 4.

GOFFMAN, ERVING. 1963. *Stigma: Notes on Management of Spoiled Identity.* Englewood Cliffs, NJ: Prentice Hall.

GOLD, MICHAEL. 1965. *Jews without Money.* New York: Avon.

GOLD, STEVEN J. 2001. *Arab Americans in Detroit.* Accessed October 15, 2004, at www.commurb.org/features/sgold/detroit.html.

GOLDSCHEIDER, CALVIN. 2003. "Are American Jews Vanishing Again?" *Contexts,* Winter, 18–24.

GOLDSTEIN, SIDNEY AND CALVIN GOLDSCHEIDER. 1968. *Jewish Americans: Three Generations in a Jewish Community.* Englewood Cliffs, NJ: Prentice Hall.

GOMPERS, SAMUEL AND HERMAN GUSTADT. 1908. *Meat vs. Rice: American Manhood against Asiatic Coolieism: Which Shall Survive?* San Francisco: Asiatic Exclusion League.

GOODNOUGH, ABBY. 2004. "Honor for Dr. King Splits Florida City, and Faces Reversal." *New York Times,* May 10, A1, A20.

GOODING, CAROLINE. 1994. *Disabling Laws, Enabling Acts: Disability Rights in Britain and America.* Boulder, CO: Westview.

GOODSTEIN, LAURIE. 2001. "As Attacks' Impact Recedes a Return to Religion as Usual." *New York Times,* November 26, A1, B6.

————. 2004. "Muslim Women Seeking a Place in the Mosque." *New York Times,* July 22, A1, A16.

GORDON, ANTHONY AND RICHARD M. HOROWITZ. 1997. "Will Your Grandchildren Be Jewish?" Unpub. research based on a 1990 National Jewish Population Survey and the 1991 New York Jewish Population Study.

GORDON, MILTON M. 1964. *Assimilation in American Life: The Role of Race, Religion, and National Origins.* New York: Oxford University Press.

————. 1996. "Liberal versus Corporate Pluralism." *Society,* March/April, 33: 37–40.

GORDON, WENDELL. 1975. "A Case for a Less Restrictive Border Policy." *Social Science Quarterly,* December, 56: 485–491.

GORMAN, TOM. 2002. "Tribe Offers Up Its Land to Store Nuclear Waste." *Los Angeles Times,* May 29, A1, A15.

GOULDNER, ALVIN. 1970. *The Coming Crisis in Western Sociology.* New York: Basic Books.

GOVE, WALTER R. 1980. *The Labeling of Deviance,* 2nd ed. Beverly Hills, CA: Sage Publications.

GRAHAM, LAWRENCE OTIS. 1995. *Member of the Club: Reflections on Life in a Racially Polarized World.* New York: HarperCollins.

GRAHAM, WADE. 1996. "Masters of the Game: How the U.S. Protects the Traffic in Cheap Mexican Labor." *Harper's* 293, July, 35–50.

GRATTET, RYKEN AND VALERIE JENNESS. 2001. "The Birth and Maturation of Hate Crime Policy in the United States." *American Behavioral Scientist,* December, 45: 668–696.

GRAY-LITTLE, BERNADETTE AND ADAM R. HAFDAHL. 2000. "Factors Influencing Racial Comparisons of Self-Esteem: A Qualitative Review." *Psychological Bulletin* 126(1): 26–54.

GREELEY, ANDREW M. 1974a. *Ethnicity in the United States: A Preliminary Reconnaissance.* New York: Wiley.

————. 1974b. "Political Participation among Ethnic Groups in the United States: A Preliminary Reconnaissance." *American Journal of Sociology* 80 (July), pp. 170–204.

————. 1977. *The American Catholic.* New York: Basic Books.

GREENHOUSE, LINDA. 1996. "Case on Government Interface in Religion Tied to Separation of Powers." *New York Times,* October 16, C23.

————. 2003a. "Justices Back Affirmative Action by 5–4. But Wider Vote Bans a Racial Point System." *New York Times,* June 24, A1, A25.

————. 2003b. "Justices, 6-3, Legalize Gay Sexual Conduct in Sweeping Reversal of Courts '86 Ruling." *New York Times,* June 27, A1, A16-A17.

GREENHOUSE, STEVEN. 2001. "Fear and Poverty Sicken Many Migrant Workers in the U.S." *New York Times,* May 13, 14.

GREENWALD, ANTHONY G., MARK A. OAKES, AND HUNTER HOFFMAN. 2003. "Targets of Discrimination: Effects of Race on Responses to Weapon Holders." *Journal of Experimental Social Psychology,* July, 39: 399–405.

GRIECO, ELIZABETH M. 2001. *The Native Hawaiian and Other Pacific Islander Population 2000.* Brief C2KBR/01-14. Washington, DC: U.S. Government Printing Office.

GRIECO, ELIZABETH M. AND RACHEL C. CASSIDY. 2001. "Overview of Race and Hispanic Origin." *Current Population Reports* Ser. CENBR/01-1. Washington, DC: U.S. Government Printing Office.

GRIMSHAW, ALLEN D. 1969. *Racial Violence in the United States.* Chicago: Aldine.

GRODSKY, ERIC AND DEVAH PAGER. 2001. "The Structure of Disadvantage: Individual and Occupational Determinants of the Black-White Wage Gap." *American Sociological Review,* August, 66: 542–567.

GROSS, JANE. 1989. "Diversity Hinders Asians' Power in U.S." *New York Times,* June 25, A22.

GUERIN-GONZALES, CAMILLE. 1994. *Mexican Workers and American Dreams.* New Brunswick, NJ: Rutgers University Press.

GUEST, KENNETH J. 2003. *God in Chinatown: Religion and Survival in New York's Evolving Immigrant Community.* New York, New York: University Press.

GUGLIELMO, JENNIFER AND SALENO SALVATORE, EDS. 2003. *Are Italians White?* New York: Routledge.

GUZMÁN, BETSY. 2001. *The Hispanic Population.* Census 2000 Brief Series C2kBR/01-3. Washington, DC: U.S. Government Printing Office.

HAAK, GERALD O. 1970. "Co-opting the Oppressors: The Case of the Japanese-Americans." *Society,* October, 7: 23–31.

HACKER, ANDREW. 1995. *Two Nations: Black and White, Separate, Hostile, and Unequal,* expanded and updated ed. New York: Ballantine.

HACKER, HELEN MAYER. 1951. "Women as a Minority Group." *Social Forces,* October, 30: 60–69.

———. 1974. "Women as a Minority Group: Twenty Years Later." Pp. 124–134 in *Who Discriminates against Women,* edited by Florence Denmark, Beverly Hills, CA: Sage Publications.

HAERI, SHAYKH FADHILALLA. 2004. *The Thoughtful Guide to Islam.* Alresford UK: O Books.

HAGAN, WILLIAM T. 1961. *American Indians.* Chicago: University of Chicago Press.

HALLINAN, MAUREEN T. 2003. *Ability Grouping and Student Learning.* Pp: 95–140 in Brookings Papers on Education Policy, edited by Diane Ravitch. Washington, DC: Brookings Institution Press.

HANSEN, MARCUS LEE. 1952. "The Third Generation in America." *Commentary,* November, 14: 493–500.

HARLAN, LOUIS R. 1972. *Booker T. Washington: The Making of a Black Leader.* New York: Oxford University Press.

HARMAN, DANNA. 2002. "In Crisis, Israel Rallies behind Settlers." *Christian Science Monitor,* April 26, 1, 9.

HARRIS, DAVID A. 1987. "Japan and the Jews." *Morning Freiheit,* November 8, 1, 3.

HARRIS, HAMIL R. AND PAUL FARHI. 2004. "Debate Continues as Cosby Again Criticizes Black Youths." *Washington Post,* July 3, A1.

HASSABALLA, HESHAM A. 2004. "The Koran Commands Muslims to Use Vote." *Chicago Tribune,* September 12, sec. 2, 1, 6.

HAUB, CARL. 2004. *2004 World Population Data Sheet.* Washington, DC: U.S. Population Reference Bureau.

HAWAII DEPARTMENT OF HEALTH. 2001. *Annual Statistics 2000,* A46–A55. Accessed March 20, 2002, at http://www.hawaii.gov.

HAWKINS, HUGH. 1962. *Booker T. Washington and His Critics: The Problem of Negro Leadership.* Boston: Heath.

HAYNES, V. DION. 2003. "Immigration, Safety Issues Clash." *Chicago Tribune,* November 29, 31.

HAYS, KRISTEN L. 1994. "Topeka Comes Full Circle." *Modern Maturity,* April–May, 34.

HECHINGER, FRED M. 1987. "Bilingual Programs." *New York Times,* April 7, C10.

HEER, DAVID M. AND AMGRA GROSSBARD-SHECTMAN. 1981. "The Impact of the Female Marriage Squeeze and the Contraceptive Revolution on Sex Roles and the Women's Liberation Movement in the United States, 1960 to 1975." *Journal of Marriage and the Family,* February, 43: 49–76.

HEIN, JEREMY. 2000. "Interpersonal Discrimination against Hmong Americans: Parallels and Variation in Microlevel Racial Inequality." *Sociological Quarterly* 41(3): 413–429.

HEMLOCK, DOREEN A. 1996. "Puerto Rico Loses Its Edge." *New York Times,* September 21, 17, 30.

HENNESSEY, KATHLEEN. 2004. "Rare Town Where Voters Don't Have to Be Citizens." *Los Angeles Times,* July 22, A23.

HENRY, WILLIAM A., III. 1994. "Pride and Prejudice." *Time,* February 28, 143: 21–27.

HENTOFF, NICHOLAS. 1984. "Dennis Banks and the Road Block to Indian Ground." *Village Voice,* October, 29: 19–23.

HEQUEMBOURG, AMY AND JORGE ARDITI. 1999. "Fractured Resistances: The Debate over Assimilationism among Gays and Lesbians in the United States." *Sociological Quarterly* 40(4): 663–680.

HERBERG, WILL. 1983. *Protestant–Catholic–Jew: An Essay in American Religious Sociology,* rev. ed. Chicago: University of Chicago Press.

HERO, RODNEY. 1995. *Latinos and U.S. Politics.* New York: HarperCollins.

HERRNSTEIN, RICHARD J. AND CHARLES MURRAY. 1994. *The Bell Curve: Intelligence and Class Structure in American Life.* New York: Free Press.

HERSKOVITS, MELVILLE J. 1930. *The Anthropometry of the American Negro.* New York: Columbia University Press.

———. 1941. *The Myth of the Negro Past.* New York: Harper.

HICKMAN, MATTHEW J. 2003. *Tribal Law Enforcement, 2000.* Bureau of Justice Statistics Fact Sheet (January).

HIGHAM, JOHN. 1966. "American Anti-Semitism Historically Reconsidered." Pp. 237–258 in *Jews in the Mind of America,* edited by Charles Herbert Stember. New York: Basic Books.

HILL, HERBERT. 1967. "The Racial Practices of Organized Labor: The Age of Gompers and After." Pp. 365–402 in *Employment, Race, and Poverty,* edited by Arthur M. Ross and Herbert Hill. New York: Harcourt, Brace & World.

HILL, ROBERT B. 1999. *The Strengths of African American Families: Twenty-Five Years Later.* Lanham, MD: University Press of America.

HILBERG, SOLESTE AND RONALD G. THARP. 2002. *Theoretical Perspectives, Research Findings, and Classroom Implications of the Learning Styles of American Indian and Alaska Native Students.* Washington, DC: Eric Digest.

HIMMELFARB, HAROLD S. 1982. "Research on American Jewish Identity and Identification: Progress, Pitfalls, and Prospects." Pp. 56–95 in *Understanding American Jewry,* edited by Marshall Sklare. New Brunswick, NJ: Transaction Books.

HIRSCHMAN, CHARLES. 1983. "America's Melting Pot Reconsidered." Pp. 397–423 in *Annual Review of Sociology 1983,* edited by Ralph H. Turner. Palo Alto, CA: Annual Reviews.

HIRSLEY, MICHAEL. 1991. "Religious Display Needs Firm Count." *Chicago Tribune,* December 20, Section 2, 10.

HOCHSCHILD, ARLIE RUSSELL. 1990. "The Second Shift: Employed Women Are Putting in Another Day of Work at Home. *Utne Reader,* March–April, 38: 66–73.

———. 1997. "Time for Change." *Ms.,* September/October, pp. 8: 39–40.

HOCHSCHILD, ARLIE RUSSELL AND ANNE MACHUNG. 1989. *The Second Shift.* New York: Viking.

HOCHSCHILD, JENNIFER L. 1995. *Facing Up to the American Dream: Race, Class, and the Soul of the Nation.* Princeton, NJ: Rutgers University Press.

HOFFER, THOMAS B. ET AL. 2001. *Doctorate Recipients from United States Universities: Summary Report 2000.* Chicago: National Opinion Research Center.

HOLFORD, DAVID M. 1975. "The Subversion of the Indian Land Allotment System, 1887–1934." *Indian Historian,* Spring, 8: 11–21.

HOLMES, STEVEN A. 1996. "Anti-Immigrant Mood Moves Asians to Organize." *New York Times,* January 3, A1, A11.

HOOKS, BELL. 1994. "Black Students Who Reject Feminism." *The Chronicle of Higher Education,* July 13, 60: A44.

HOSOKAWA, BILL. 1969. *Nisei: The Quiet Americans.* New York: Morrow.

HUBBARD, AMY S. 1993. "U.S. Jewish Community Responses to the Changing Strategy of the Palestinian Nationalist Movement: A Pilot Study." Paper presented at the Annual Meeting of the Eastern Sociological Society, Boston.

HUDGINS, JOHN L. 1992. "The Strengths of Black Families Revisited." *The Urban League Review,* Winter, 15: 9–20.

HUGHES, MICHAEL. 1998. "Symbolic Racism, Old-Fashioned Racism, and Whites' Opposition to Affirmative Action." Pp. 45–75 in *Racial Attitudes in the 1990s: Continuity and Change,* edited by Steven A. Tuch and Jack K. Martin. Westport, CT: Praeger.

HULL, ANNE. 2003. Translating "Don't Ask, Don't Tell." *Washington Post National Weekly Edition,* December 21: 30–31.

HUMAN RIGHTS WATCH. 1998. *Losing the Vote: The Impact of Felony Disenfranchisement Laws in the United States.* Washington, DC: Human Rights Watch.

———. 2002. "Florida Ex-Offenders Barred from Vote Decisive in Election." Accessed February 1, 2002, at http://www.hrw.org/campaign/elections/results.htm.

HUMPHREYS, LAUD. 1972. *Out of the Closets.* Englewood Cliffs, NJ: Prentice Hall.

HUNT, LARRY L. 1999. "Hispanic Protestantism in the United States: Trends by Decade and Generation." *Social Forces* 77(4): 1601–1624.

HURH, WON MOO. 1994. "Majority Americans' Perception of Koreans in the United States: Implications of Ethnic Images and Stereotypes." Pp. 3–21 in *Korean Americans: Conflict and Harmony,* edited by H. Kwon. Chicago: Center for Korean Studies.

———. 1998. *The Korean Americans.* Westport, CT: Greenwood Press.

HURH, WON MOO and KWANG CHUNG KIM. 1982. "Race Relations Paradigms and Korean American Research: A Sociology of Knowledge Perspective." Pp. 219–255 in *Koreans in Los Angeles,* edited by E. Yu, E. Phillips, and E. Yang. Los Angeles: Center for Korean American and Korean Studies, California State University.

———. 1984. *Korean Immigrants in America: A Structural Analysis of Ethnic Confinement and Adhesive Adaptation.* Cranbury, NJ: Fairleigh Dickinson University Press.

———. 1989. "The 'Success' Image of Asian Americans: Its Validity, and Its Practical and Theoretical Implications." *Ethnic and Racial Studies,* October, 12: 512–538.

IGNATIEV, NOEL. 1994. "Treason to Whiteness Is Loyalty to Humanity." Interview with Noel Ignatiev. *Utne Reader,* November/December, 83–86.

———. 1995. *How the Irish Became White.* New York: Routledge.

"ILLITERACY IS NOT ALL ALIKE." 1917a. *New York Times,* February 8, 12.

IMMIGRATION AND NATURALIZATION SERVICE. 2002. *1999 Statistical Yearbook of the Immigration and Naturalization Service.* Washington, DC: United States Government Printing Office.

IMMIGRATION AND REFUGEE SERVICES OF AMERICA. 2004. *Reference Reports* 25 (1).

INDIAN HEALTH SERVICE. 1995. *Trends in Indian Health 1995.* Washington, DC: Indian Health Service.

INDIAN AND NORTHERN AFFAIRS CANADA AND CANADIAN POLAR COMMISSION. 2000. *2000–2001 Estimates.* Ottawa: Canadian Government Publishing.

INDIAN COUNTRY. 1999. "Parents Ask for Both Traditional and Modern Medical Treatments." May 24, B2.

INDIANZ.COM. 2004. *Tribal authority over the Indians still unsettled question.* Accessed August 9, 2004, at www.Indianz.com.

INOUE, MIYAKO. 1989. "Japanese Americans in St. Louis: From Internees to Professionals." *City and Society,* December, 3: 142–152.

INSTITUTE FOR SOCIAL POLICY AND UNDERSTANDING. 2004. *The USA Patriot Act: Impact on the Arab and Muslim American Community.* Clinton Township, MI: ISPU.

INSTITUTE FOR SOCIAL RESEARCH. 2002. "U.S. Husbands Are Doing More Housework While Wives Are Doing Less." March 12 Press Release. Ann Arbor, MI: ISR.

INSTITUTES OF MEDICINE. 1999. *Towards Environmental Justice.* Washington, DC: National Academy Press.

INTER-PARLIAMENTARY UNION. 2004. *Women in National Parliaments.* Accessed October 4, 2004, at http://www.ipu.org.

ISHII-KUNTZ, MASAKO. 1997. "Intergenerational Relationships among Chinese, Japanese and Korean Americans." *Family Relations* 46(1): 23–32.

ISSACSON, JASON and RICHARD FOLTIN. 2001. *Election 2000: Post Election.* New York: American Jewish Committee.

ITANO, NICOLE. 1997. "Lawsuit Draws Little Support from Student Body." *Yale Daily News,* October 31.

JAHER, FREDERIC CAPLE. 1994. *A Scapegoat in the New Wilderness.* Cambridge, MA: Harvard University Press.

JAMES, KEITH, ET AL. 1995. "School Achievement and Dropout among Anglo and Indian Females and Males: A Comparative Examination." *American Indian Culture and Research Journal* 19(3): 181–206.

JAMIESON, AMIE, HYON B. SHIN, AND JENNIFER DAY. 2002. "Voting and Registration in the Election of November 2000." *Current Population Reports* Ser. P20, No. 542. Washington, DC: U.S. Government Printing Office.

JENNESS, VALERIE. 1995. "Hate Crimes in the United States: The Transformation of Injured Persons into Victims and the Extension of Victim Status to Multiple Constituencies." Pp. 213–237 in *Images of Issues: Typifying Contemporary Social Problems,* edited by Joel Best. 2nd ed.. New York: Aldine de Gruyter.

JOHNSON, KEVIN. 1992. "German Ancestry Is Strong Beneath Milwaukee Surface." *USA Today,* August 4, 9A.

JOHNSON, PETER. 2001. "Minorities Lose Time on Network News." *USA Today,* February 28, 4 D.

JOHNSON, TROY R. 1996. "Roots of Contemporary Native American Activism." *American Indian Culture and Research Journal* 20(2): 127–154.

JOLIDON, LAURENCE. 1991. "Battle Builds over Indians' Fishing Rights." *USA Today,* March 21, 1A–2A.

JONES, DALE E., SHERRI DOTY, JAMES E. HORSCH, RICHARD HOUSEAL, MAC LYNN, JOHN P. MARCUM, KENNETH M. SANCHAGRIN, AND RICHARD H. TAYLOR. 2002. *Religious Congregations and Membership in the United States 2000: An Enumeration by Region, State, and County Based on Data Reported by 149 Religious Bodies.* Nashville, TN: Glenmary Research Center.

JONES, DEL. 2003. "Few Women in Fortune 500's Top Tiers." *USA Today,* January 27, B1, B2.

JONES, JAMES T., IV. 1988. "Harassment Is Too Often Part of the Job." *USA Today,* August 8, 5D.

JONES, JEFFREY M. 2003a. "Nearly Half of Americans Say Immigration Levels Should be Decreased." Poll Analysis, July 10, 2003. Accessed August 6, 2003, at www.gallup.com.

———. 2003b. "Majority of American Say Anti-Semitism a Problem in U.S." Released June 11, 2003, at www.gallup.com.

JONES, NICHOLAS and AMY SYMENS SMITH. 2001. *The Two or More Races Population: 2000.* Series C2KBR/01-6. Washington, DC: U.S. Government Printing Office.

JONES, TIM. 2003. "In Wausau, Hmong at Another Crossroads." *Chicago Tribune,* June 16, 8.

KAGAN, JEROME. 1971. "The Magical Aura of the IQ." *Saturday Review of Literature,* December 4, 4: 92–93.

KAHNG, ANTHONY. 1978. "EEO in America." *Equal Opportunity Forum,* July, 5: 22–23.

KAISER FAMILY FOUNDATION. 2004. *South Africa at Ten Years of Democracy.* Washington, DC: Washington Post/ Kaiser Family Foundation/ Harvard University at www.kff.org/kaiserpolls/southafrica.cfm.

KAISER, ROB. 2004. "Chicago OKs Set Aside Charges." *Chicago Tribune,* May 27, sec. 3, 1.

KALITA, S. MITRA. 2003. *Suburban Sahibs: Three Immigrant Families and Their Passage from India to America.* New Brunswick, NJ: Rutgers University Press.

KALT, JOSEPH P. AND JOSEPH W. SINGER. 2004. *Myths and Realities of Tribal Sovereignty: The Law and Economics of Indian Self-Rule.* Cambridge, MA: Harvard University Native American Program.

KANAMINE, LINDA. 1992. "Amid Crushing Poverty, Glimmers of Hope." *USA Today,* November 30, 7A.

———. 1994. "Tribal Leaders Now Feel They 'Can Be Heard.'" *USA Today,* April 28, 1A–2A.

KANE-BERMAN, JOHN. 2003. *South Africa Survey 2002/2003.* Johannesburg: South Africa Institute of Race Relations.

KANELLOS, NICHOLAS. 1994. *The Hispanic Almanac: From Columbus to Corporate America.* Detroit: Visible Ink Press.

KANG, K. CONNIE. 1996. "Filipinos Happy with Life in U.S., but Lack United Voice." *Los Angeles Times,* January 26, A1, A20.

KANG, K. CONNIE and LISA RICHARDSON. 2002. "We Can't All Get Along Yet." *Los Angeles Times,* April 27, A1, A18–A19.

KAPUR, DEUESH AND JOHN MCHALE. 2003. "Migration's New Payoff." *Foreign Policy,* November/December, 48–57.

KARKABI, BARBARA. 1993. "Researcher in Houston Surveys Disabled Women about Sexuality." *Austin American–Statesman,* May 26, E8.

KASER, TOM. 1977. "Hawaii's Schools: An Ethnic Survey." *Integrated Education*, May–June, 15: 31–36.

KAUFMAN, GAYLE AND PETER UHLENBERG. 2000. "The Influence of the Work Effort of Married Men and Women." *Social Forces* 78(3): 931–949.

KEEN, JUDY AND RICHARD BENEDETTO. 2001. "Republican Party on a Crusade to Win Over Hispanic Americans." *USA Today*, August 7, A1, A2.

"KEESING'S 1992 Canada: Rejection of Charlottetown Constitutional Reform Package." *Keesing's Record of World Events*, October, 39126.

KEILMAN, JOHN. 2002. "Hispanic Healers Popular, Untested." *Chicago Tribune*, January 21, 1, 7.

KELLY, DAVID. 2003. "Spanish Spoken Here—and Hmong, Narago, Arabic." *Chicago Tribune*, March 5, 16.

KENING, DAN. 2004. "OWL Keeps an Eye Out for Issues Affecting Women." *Chicago Tribune*, March 12, sec. 9, 1,12.

KERSHAW, SARAH. 2003. "Immigrants Now Embrace Homes for Elderly." *New York Times*, October 20, A1, A10.

KIBRIA, NAZLI. 2002. *Becoming Asian American: Second-Generation Chinese and Korean American Identities*. Baltimore, MD: Johns Hopkins Press.

KIEH, GEORGE KLAY, JR. 1995. "Malcolm X and Pan-Africanism." *Western Journal of Black Studies* 19(4): 293–299.

KILBORN, PETER T. 1992. "Big Change Likely as Law Bans Bias toward Disabled." *New York Times*, July 19, 1, 24.

KILLIAN, CAITLIN. 2003. "The Other Side of the Veil: North Africa Women in France Respond to the Headscarf Affair." *Gender and Society*, August, 17: 567–590.

KILLIAN, LEWIS M. 1975. *The Impossible Revolution, Phase 2: Black Power and the American Dream*. New York: Random House.

KILSON, MARTIN. 1995. "Affirmative Action." *Dissent*, Fall, 42: 469–470.

KIM, KILJOONG. 2005. "The Korean Presence in Chicago." In *The New Chicago*, edited by John Koval et al. Philadelphia, PA: Temple University Press.

KIM, KWANG CHUNG AND SHIN KIM. 1998. "Korean Middleman Merchants: A Conceptual Revision of Middleman Minority Theory." Paper presented at Midwest Sociological Society Annual Meeting, April 2.

KIMURA, YUKIKO. 1988. *Issei: Japanese Immigrants in Hawaii*. Honolulu: University of Hawaii Press.

KING, MARTIN LUTHER, JR. 1958. *Stride Towards Freedom: The Montgomery Story*. New York: Harper.

———. 1963. *Why We Can't Wait*. New York: Mentor.

———. 1967. *Where Do We Go from Here: Chaos or Community?* New York: Harper & Row.

———. 1971. "I Have a Dream." Pp. 346–351 in *Black Protest Thought in the Twentieth Century*, edited by August Meier, Elliott Rudwick, and Francis L. Broderick. Indianapolis: Bobbs-Merrill.

KING, PETER. 2004a. "Still Living in the Shadow of a September Day." *Los Angeles Times*, August 3, A1, A12, A13.

———. 2004b. "Their Spiritual Thirst Found a Desert Spring." *Los Angeles Times*, August 4, A1, A16, A17.

———. 2004c. "Private Moments in the Public Eye." *Los Angeles Times*, August 5, A1, A16, A17.

KING, RYAN S. AND MARC MAVER. 2004. *The Vanishing Black Electorate: Felony Disenfranchisement in Atlanta, Georgia*. Washington, DC: The Sentencing Report.

KINLOCH, GRAHAM C. 1974. *The Dynamics of Race Relations: A Sociological Analysis*. New York: McGraw-Hill.

KINSEY, ALFRED G., WARDELL B. POMEROY, AND CLYDE E. MARTIN. 1948. *Sexual Behavior in the Human Male*. Philadelphia: Saunders.

———, AND PAUL H. GEBHARD. 1953. *Sexual Behavior in the Human Female*. Philadelphia: Saunders.

KINZER, STEPHEN. 2000. "Museums and Tribes: A Tricky Truce." *New York Times*, December 24, sec. 2,. 1, 39.

KIRKPATRICK, P. 1994. "Triple Jeopardy: Disability, Race and Poverty in America." *Poverty and Race* 3:1–8.

KITAGAWA, EVELYN. 1972. "Socioeconomic Differences in the United States and Some Implications for Population Policy." Pp. 87–110 in *Demographic and Social Aspects of Population Growth*, edited by Charles F. Westoff and Robert Parke, Jr. Washington, DC: U.S. Government Printing Office.

KITANO, HARRY H. L. 1976. *Japanese Americans: The Evolution of a Subculture*, 2nd ed. Englewood Cliffs, NJ: Prentice Hall.

———. 1980. Japanese. In *Harvard Encyclopedia of American Ethnic Groups*, edited by Stephen Thernstrom. Cambridge, MA: Belknap Press of Harvard University Press.

KITSUSE, JOHN I. AND LEONARD BROOM. 1956. *The Managed Casualty: The Japanese American Family in World War II*. Berkeley: University of California Press.

KLAUSNER, SAMUEL Z. 1988. "Anti-Semitism in the Executive Suite: Yesterday, Today, and Tomorrow." *Moment*, September, 13: 32–39, 55.

KNUDSON, THOMAS J. 1987. "Zoning the Reservations for Enterprise." *New York Times*, January 25, E4.

KONG, DEBORAH. 2002. "Home for Asian Elderly Defies Past." *Chicago Tribune*, January 2, 9.

KORECKI, NATASHA. 2003. "Rebuilding Mexico from the Suburbs." *Daily Herald*, (Arlington Heights, IL), November 20.

KOSMIN, BARRY A. 1991. *The National Survey of Religious Identification*. New York: City University of New York.

———. AND SEYMOUR P. LACHMAN. 1993. *One Nation Under God: Religion in Contemporary American Society*. New York: Harmony Books.

———, EGON MAYER, AND ARIELA KEYSAR. 2001. American Religious Identification Survey 2001. New York Graduate Center of the City University of New York.

KOZLOWICZ, JOHN. 2001. *Regaining the Language*. Accessed February 10, 2002, at http://www.hocakworak.com.

KRAUSS, CLIFFORD. 2002. "Immigrant Families Are Courted to Revive Canada's Culture." *New York Times*, October 2, A1, A8.

———. 2003. "Immigrant Families Quebec Seeking to End Its Old Cultural Divide." *New York Times*, April 13, A6.

KRAYBILL, DONALD B. 2001. *The Riddle of Amish Culture*, rev. ed. Baltimore, MD: Johns Hopkins University Press.

KRAYBILL, DONALD B. AND STEVEN M. NOLT. 1995. *Amish Enterprises: From Plows to Profits*. Baltimore, MD: Johns Hopkins Press.

KRUEGER, ALAN B. 2002. "Economic Scene." *New York Times*, December 11, C2.

KUGEL, SETH. 2004. "Destination, Neza York." *New York Times*, February 15, 4.

KUNITZ, STEPHEN J. 1996. "The History and Politics of U.S. Health Care Policy for American Indians and Alaskan Natives." *American Journal of Public Health*, October, 86: 1464–1473.

KWON, HO-YOUN, KWAG CHUNG KEM, AND R. STEPHEN WARNER, EDS. 2001. *Korean Americans and Their Religions: Pilgrims and Missionaries from a Different Shore*. Philadelphia: Pennsylvania State University Press.

KWONG, PETER. 1994. "The Wages of Fear." *Village Voice*, April 26, 39: 25–29.

LABELLE, HUGUETTE. 1989. "Multiculturalism and Government." Pp. 1–7 in *Multiculturalism and Intergroup Relations*, edited by James S. Frideres. New York: Greenwood Press.

LACY, DAN. 1972. *The White Use of Blacks in America*. New York: McGraw-Hill.

LADERMAN, GARY AND LUIS LEÓN, EDS. 2003. "Islam in America." Pp. 123–148 in *Religion and American Cultures*. Santa Barbara, CA: ABC Clio.

LADNER, JOYCE. 1967. "What 'Black Power' Means to Negroes in Mississippi." *Transaction*, November, 5: 6–15.

LAFRANIERE, SHARON AND MICHAEL WINES. 2004. "Africa Puzzle: Landless Blacks and White Forms." *New York Times*, January 6, A1, A10.

LAL, BARBARA BALLIS. 1995. "Symbolic Interaction Theories." *American Behavioral Scientist*, January, 38: 421–441.

LAMB, DAVID. 1997. "Viet Kieu: A Bridge between 2 Worlds." *Los Angeles Times*, November 4, A1, A8.

LANDALE, NANCY S. AND NIMFA B. OGENA. 1995. "Migration and Union Dissolution among Puerto Rican Women." *International Migration Review*, Fall, 29: 671–692.

———, AND R. S. OROPESA. 2002. "White, Clack, or Puerto Rican? Racial Self-Identification among Mainland and Island Puerto Ricans." *Social Forces* 81(1): 231–254.

———, ———. AND BRIDGET K. GORMAN. 2000. "Migration and Infant Death: Assimilation or Selective Migration among Puerto Ricans?" *American Sociological Review*, December, 65: 888–909.

LANDRY, BART. 1987. *The New Black Middle Class.* Berkeley: University of California Press.

LAPIERE, RICHARD T. 1934. Attitudes vs. Actions. *Social Forces,* October, 13: 230–237.

———. 1969. "Comment of Irwin Deutscher's Looking Backward." *American Sociologist,* February, 4: 41–42.

LAREAU, ANNETTE. 2002. "Juvenile Inequality: Social Class and Childrearing in Black Families and White Families." *American Sociological Review,* October, 67: 747–776.

LAU, YVONNE. 2005a. "Chicago's Chinese Americans: From Chinatown and Beyond." In *The New Chicago* edited by John Koval et al. Philadelphia, PA: Temple University Press.

———. 2005b. "Filipino Americans in Chicago: Success at What Cost?" In *The New Chicago,* edited by John Koval et al. Philadelphia, PA: Temple University Press.

LAUERMAN, CONNIE. 1993. "Tribal Wave." *Chicago Tribune,* April 5, sec. 2, 1–2.

LAUMANN, EDWARD O., JOHN H. GAGNON, ROBERT T. MICHAEL, AND STUART MICHAELS. 1994. *The Social Organization of Sexuality: Sexual Practices in the United States.* Chicago: University of Chicago Press.

LAVENDER, ABRAHAM D., ED. 1977. *A Coat of Many Colors: Jewish Subcommunities in the United States.* Westport, CT: Greenwood Press.

LAXSON, JOAN D. 1991. "'We' See 'Them': Tourism and Native Americans." *Annals of Tourism Research* 18(3): 365–391.

LEAVITT, PAUL. 2002. "Bush Calls Agent Kicked Off Flight 'Honorable Fellow.'" *USA Today,* January 8.

LEE, DON. 1992. "A Sense of Identity." *Kansas City Star,* April 4, E1, E7.

LEE, JENNIFER. 2001. "Manhattan's Chinatown Reeling from the Effects of September 11." *New York Times,* November 21, B1, B9.

LEE, SHARON M. 1998. "Asian Americans: Diverse and Growing." *Population Bulletin* 53, June.

LEEHOTZ, ROBERT. 1995. "Is Concept of Race a Relic?" *Los Angeles Times,* April 15, A1, A14.

LEINWAND, DONNA. 2004. "Muslims See New Opposition to Building Mosques Since 9/11." *USA Today,* March 9, A1, A2.

LEM, KIM. 1976. "Asian American Employment." *Civil Rights Digest,* Fall, 9: 12–21.

LEMANN, NICHOLAS. 1986a. "The Origins of the Underclass." *The Atlantic Monthly,* June, 258: 31–43, 47–55.

———. 1986b. "The Origins of the Underclass." *The Atlantic Monthly,* July, 258: 54–68.

LEONARD, KAREN ISAKSEN. 1997. *The South Asian Americans.* Westport, CT: Greenwood Press.

———. 2003. *Muslims in the United States: The State of Research.* New York: Russell Sage Foundation.

LERNER, MICHAEL. 1969. "Respectable Bigotry." *American Scholar,* August, 38: 606–617.

———. 1993. "Jews Are Not White." *Village Voice,* May 18, 38: 33–34.

———. 2002. "Israel's Jewish Critics Aren't 'Self-Hating.'" *Los Angeles Times,* April 28, M2.

LESSINGER, JOHANNA. 1995. *From the Ganges to the Hudson: Indian Immigrants in New York City.* Boston: Allyn & Bacon.

LEVIN, WILLIAM C. 1988. "Age Stereotyping: College Student Evaluations." *Research on Aging,* March, 10: 134–148.

LEVINE, NAOMI AND MARTIN HOCHBAUM, EDS. 1974. *Poor Jews: An American Awakening.* New Brunswick, NJ: Transaction Books.

LEVITT, PEGGY. 2004. "Salsa and Ketchup: Transnational Migrants Struggle Two Worlds." *Contexts,* Spring, 20–26.

LEVY, BECCA R., MARTIN D. SLADE, SUZANNE R. KUNKEL, AND STANISLAV V. KASL. 2002. "Longevity Increased by Positive Self-Perceptions of Aging." *Journal of Personality and Social Psychology* 83(2): 261–270.

LEVY, JACQUES E. 1975. *César Chávez: Autobiography of La Causa.* New York: Norton.

LEWINSON, PAUL. 1965. *Race, Class, and Party: A History of Negro Suffrage and White Politics in the South.* New York: Universal Library.

LEWIS, NEIL A. 2003. "Secrecy Is Barked on 9/11 Detainees." *New York Times,* June 18, A1, A16.

LEWIS, OSCAR. 1959. *Five Families: Mexican Case Studies in the Culture of Poverty.* New York: Basic Books.

———. 1965. *La Vida: A Puerto Rican Family in the Culture of Poverty—San Juan and New York.* New York: Random House.

———. 1966. "The Culture of Poverty." *Scientific American,* October, 19–25.

LEWIS MUMFORD CENTER. 2001. *Ethnic Diversity Grows, Neighborhood Integration Is at a Standstill.* Albany, NY: Lewis Mumford Center.

LI, WEN LANG. 1976. "Chinese Americans: Exclusion from the Melting Pot." Pp. 297–324 in Anthony Dworkin and Rosalind Dworkin, eds., *Minority Report.* New York: Praeger.

LICHTBLAU, ERIC. 2003. "Bush Issues Racial Profiling Ban But Exempts Security Information." *New York Times,* June 18, A1, A16.

LIEBMAN, CHARLES S. 1973. *The Ambivalent American Jew.* Philadelphia: Jewish Publication Society of America.

LIGHT, IVAN H. 1973. *Ethnic Enterprise in America: Business and Welfare among Chinese, Japanese, and Blacks.* Berkeley: University of California Press.

LIGHT, IVAN H., GEORGES SABAGH, MENDI BOZORGMEHR, AND CLAUDIA DER-MARTIROSIAN. 1994. "Beyond the Ethnic Enclave Economy." *Social Problems,* February, 41: 65–80.

LIN, JAN. 1998. *Reconstructing Chinatown: Ethnic Enclave, Global Change.* Minneapolis: University of Minnesota Press.

LIN, SAM CHU. 1996. "Painful Memories." *AsianWeek,* July 12, 17: 10.

LINCOLN, C. ERIC. 1994. *The Black Muslims in America,* 3rd ed. Grand Rapids, MI: William B. Eerdmans.

LIND, ANDREW W. 1946. *Hawaii's Japanese: An Experiment in Democracy.* Princeton, NJ: Princeton University Press.

———. 1969. *Hawaii: The Last of the Magic Isles.* London: Oxford University Press.

LINDNER, EILEEN, ED. 2004. *Yearbook of American and Canadian Churches 2004.* Nashville: Abingden Press.

LINDSLEY, SHERYL L. 1998. "Organizational Interventions to Prejudice." Pp. 302–310 in *Communicating Prejudice,* edited by Michael L. Hecht. Thousand Oaks, CA: Sage Publications.

LINTHICUM, LESLIE. 1993. "Navajo School Working to Revive Language." *News from Indian Country,* Late June, 5.

LOBDELL, WILLIAM. 2001. "Latino Exodus from Catholic Church Rising, Study Says." *Los Angeles Times,* May 5, B1, B7.

LODDER, LEEANN, SCOTT MCFARLAND, DIANA WHITE. 2003. *Racial Preference and Suburban Employment Opportunities.* Chicago: Chicago Urban League.

LOGAN, JOHN R. 2001. *The New Latinos: Who They Are, Where They Are.* Albany: Lewis Mumford Center for Comparative Urban and Regional Research, State University of New York at Albany.

———. 2003. *How Race Counts for Hispanic Americans.* New York: Mumford Center.

LOGAN, JOHN R., ALBA RICHARD D., AND WERQUAN ZHANG. 2002. "Immigrant Enclaves and Ethnic Communities in New York and Los Angeles." *American Sociological Review,* April, 67: 299–322.

LOGAN, RAYFORD W. 1954. *The Negro in American Life and Thought: The Nadir, 1877–1901.* New York: Dial Press.

LOMAX, LOUIS E. 1971. *The Negro Revolt,* rev. ed. New York: Harper & Row.

LOPATA, HELENA ZNANIECKA. 1993. *Polish Americans.* Rutgers, NJ: Transaction Books.

LOPEZ, DAVID AND YEN ESPIRITU. 1990. "Panethnicity in the United States: A Theoretical Framework." *Ethnic and Racial Studies,* April, 13: 198–224.

LOPEZ, JULIE AMPARANO. 1992. "Women Face Glass Walls as Well as Ceilings." *Wall Street Journal,* March 3.

LOS ANGELES TIMES POLL. 1997. Hong Kong Transition Project Survey. Los Angeles: Los Angeles Times.

———. 1998. *American and Israeli Jews.* Los Angeles: *Los Angeles Times* and *Yedioth Ahronoth.*

LOURY, GLENN C. 1996. "Joy and Doubt on the Mall." *Utne Reader,* January–February, 73: 70–73.

LOTKE, ERIC. 2004. "Racial Disparity in the Justice System: More Than the Sum of Its Parts." *Focus,* May/June, 32: 3–4.

LOUIE, ANDREA. 2004. *Chineseness across Borders: Renegotiation Chinese Identities in China and the United States.* Durham, N.C.: Duke University Press.

LUCE, CLARE BOOTHE. 1975. "Refugees and Guilt." *New York Times,* May 11, E19.

LUCONI, STEFANO. 2001. *From Paesani to White Ethnics: The Italian Experience in Philadelphia*. Albany: State University Press of New York.

LUDWIG, JACK. *Has the Civil Rights Movement Overcome?* Accessed July 15, 2004, at www.gallup.com.

LUKER, KRISTIN. 1984. *Abortion and the Politics of Motherhood*. Berkeley: University of California Press.

LYMAN, STANFORD M. 1974. *Chinese Americans*. New York: Random House.

———. 1986. *Chinatown and Little Tokyo*. Milwood, NY: Associated Faculty Press.

LYNCH, DAVID J. 2000. "Papal Visit Elicits Painful Ambivalence." *USA Today*, March 24, 12A.

MACK, RAYMOND W. 1996. "Whose Affirmative Action?" *Society*, March/April, 33: 41–43.

MACRAE, NEIL C., STANGOR, CHARLES, AND HEWSTONE, MILES. 1996. *Stereotypes and Stereotyping*. New York: Guilford Press.

MAJOR, ALINE K., AIRLEN EGLEY, JR., JAMES C. HOWELL, BARBARA MENDENHALL, AND TROY ARMSTRONG. 2004. *Youth Gangs in Indian Country*. Washington, DC: Office of Juvenile Justice and Delinquency Prevention.

MALCOLM X. 1964. *The Autobiography of Malcolm X*. New York: Grove Press.

MALKIN, MICHELLE. 2004. *In Defense of the Interment: The Case for Racial Profiling in World War II and the War on Terror*. Regency Books.

MANDELA, NELSON. 1990. "Africa, It Is Ours." *New York Times*, February 12, A10.

MANDELBAUM, ROBB. 2000. "Sour Grapes." *New York Times*, December 10, 62.

MANING, ANITA. 1997. "Troubled Waters: Environmental Racism Suit Makes Waves." *USA Today*, July 31, A1.

MANNING, ROBERT D. 1995. "Multiculturalism in the United States: Clashing Concepts, Changing Demographics, and Competing Cultures." *International Journal of Group Tensions*, Summer, 117–168.

MARABLE, MANNING. 2000. *How Capitalism Underdeveloped Black America*, updated ed. Boston: South End Press.

MARSHALL, PATRICK. 2001. "Religion in Schools." *CQ Research*, July 12, 11: 1–24.

MARSHALL, THOM. 2004. "Times Have Changed: Jap Road Finally Comes to End." *Houston Chronicle*, July 20.

MARTIN, JOEL W. 2001. *The Land Looks After Us: A History of Native American Religion*. New York: Oxford University Press.

MARTIN, PHILIP AND JONAS WIDGREN. 1996. "International Migration: A Global Challenge." *Population Bulletin* 5, April.

MARTINEZ, MICHAEL. 2004. "Experts: Plan May Cut Border Deaths." *Chicago Tribune*, January 11, 8.

MARX, KARL AND FREDERICK ENGELS. 1955. *Selected Works in Two Volumes*. Moscow: Foreign Languages Publishing House.

MASCI, DAVID. 2001. "Middle East Conflict." *CQ Researcher*, April 6, 11: 273–296.

MASON, HEATHER. 2003. *Does Bilingual Education Translate to Success?* Accessed July 8, 2003, at www.gallup.com.

MASON, PHILIP. 1970. *Race Relations*. London: Oxford University Press.

MASSEY, DOUGLAS DAWSON. 2004. "Reparations Segregation and Stratification: A Biosocial Perspective." *Dubois Review* 1(1): 7–25.

MASSEY, DOUGLAS S. AND NANCY A. DENTON. 1993. *American Apartheid: Segregation and the Making of the Underclass*. Cambridge, MA: Harvard University Press.

MATTHIESSEN, PETER. 1991. *In the Spirit of Crazy Horse*. New York: Peking.

MATZA, DAVID. 1964. *Delinquency and Drift*. New York: Wiley.

MAUER, MARC. 2004. "Disenfranchising Felons Hurts Entire Communities." *Focus*, May/June, 32: 5–6.

MAURO, TONY. 1995. "Ruling Helps Communities Set Guidelines." *USA Today*, December 21, A1, A2.

MAYER, EGON. 2001. *American Religious Identification Survey*. New York: The Graduate Center of the City University of New York.

MAYKOVICH, MINAKO KUROKAWA. 1972a. *Japanese American Identity Dilemma*. Tokyo: Waseda University Press.

———. 1972b. "Reciprocity in Racial Stereotypes: White, Black and Yellow." *American Journal of Sociology*, March, 77: 876–877.

MCCLAIN, PAULA DENICE. 1979. *Alienation and Resistance: The Political Behavior of Afro-Canadians*. Palo Alto, CA: R & E Research Associates.

MCCLOUD, AMINAH BEVERLY. 1995. *African American Islam*. New York: Routledge.

———. 2004. "Conceptual Discourse: Living as a Muslim in a Pluralistic Society." Pp. 73–83 in *Muslims Place in the American Public Square*, edited by Zahid H. Bukhari et al. Walnut Creek, CA: Altamira Press.

MCCOY, RON. 2004. Truth-in-Marketing. "Law Indian Arts and Crafts Act Regulations Published." *American Indian Art Magazine*, Spring, 29: 84–85.

MCDEVITT, JACK, JACK LEVIN, AND SUSAN BENNETT. 2002. "Hate crime Offenders: An Expanded Typology." *Journal of Social Issues*, Summer, 58: 303–317.

MCDONALD, LEANDER, RICHARD L. LUDTKE, AND ALAN ALLERY. 2002. *Long Term Care and Health Needs of America's Native American Elders*. Fargo, ND: National Resource Center on Native American Aging.

MCINTOSH, IAN S. AND DAVID MAYBURY-LEWIS. 2001. "Cultural Survival on 'Cultural Survival.'" *Cultural Survival Quarterly*, Spring, 25: 4–5.

MCINTOSH, PEGGY. 1988. *White Privilege: Unpacking the Invisible Knapsack*. Wellesley, MA: Wellesley College Center for Research on Women.

MCKENNA, IAN. 1994. "Legal Protection against Racial Discrimination Law in Canada." *New Community*, April, 20: 415–436.

MCKINNON, JESSE. 2003. *The Black Population in the United States: March 2002*. Current Population Reports Ser. P20, No. 541. Washington, DC: U.S. Government Printing Office.

MCNEIL, JACK. 2001. "Americans with Disabilities." *Current Population Reports* Ser. P70, No. 73. Washington, DC: U.S. Government Printing Office.

MCNICKLE, D'ARCY. 1973. *Native American Tribalism: Indian Survivals and Renewals*. New York: Oxford University Press.

MEHTA, CHIRAG, NIK THEODORE, ILIANA MORA, AND JENNIFER WADE. 2002. *Chicago's Undocumented Immigrants: An Analysis of Wage, Working Conditions, and Economic Contributions*. Chicago, IL: Center for Urban Economic Development, University of Illinois at Chicago.

MEIER, AUGUST AND ELLIOTT RUDWICK. 1966. *From Plantation to Ghetto: An Interpretive History of American Negroes*. New York: Hill & Wang.

MEIER, MATT S. AND FELICIANO RIVERA. 1972. *The Chicanos: A History of Mexican Americans*. New York: Hill & Wang.

MELÉNDEZ, EDWIN. 1994. "Puerto Rico Migration and Occupational Selectivity, 1982–1981." *International Migration Review*, Spring, 28: 49–67.

MERTON, ROBERT K. 1949. "Discrimination and the American Creed." Pp. 99–126 in *Discrimination and National Welfare*, edited by Robert M. MacIver. New York: Harper & Row.

———. 1976. *Sociological Ambivalence and Other Essays*. New York: Free Press.

MESSNER, MICHAEL A. 1997. *Politics of Masculinities: Men in Movements*. Thousand Oaks, CA: Sage.

MEYERS, GUSTAVUS. 1943. *History of Bigotry in the United States*. Rev. by Henry M. Christman, 1960. New York: Capricorn Books.

MIGRATION NEWS. 1998. Mexico, Dual Nationality, 5, April. Accessed at http://migration.ucdavis.edu.

———. 2000. *Hometown Clubs*, 7, July. Accessed at http://migrationnews.ucdavis.edu.

———. 2002a. Canada: Polls Data, April. Accessed at http://migration.ucdavis.edu.

———. 2002b. *Income, Education, Politics*, October. Accessed at http://migrationnews.ucdavis.edu.

———. 2002c. *Mexico: Bush IDs Remittances*, December. Accessed at http://migrationnews.ucdavis.edu.

———. 2003a. *Sanctions, Borders, and Refugees*, July. Accessed at http://migrationnews.ucdavis.edu.

———. 2003b *DHS: 9/11 Aftermath, Visas*, July. Accessed at http://migrationnews.ucdavis.edu.

———. 2004 *NAFTA at 10*. January 11. Accessed at http://migrationnews.ucdavis.edu.

MIHESUAH, DEVON A., ED. 2000. *Reparation Reader: Who Owns American Indian Remains?* Lincoln: University of Nebraska Press.

MILLER, DAVID L. AND RICHARD T. SCHAEFER. 1998. "Promise Keepers and Race: The Stand in the Gap Rally, Washington, DC, 1997." Paper presented at the annual meeting of the Midwest Sociological Society, April, Kansas City, MO.

MILLER, MARJORIE. 1998. "Cultural Battles Fall along a Religious Divide." *Los Angeles Times,* April 12, 59.

MILLER, NORMAN. 2002. "Personalization and the Promise of Contact Theory." *Journal of Social Issues,* Summer, 58: 387–410.

MILLS, ROBERT J. AND BHANDARI SHAILESH. 2003. *Health Insurance in the United States: 2002.* Current Population Reports, Series P60 (223), Washington, DC: U.S. Government Printing Office.

MIN, PYONG GAP. 1995. *Asian Americans: Contemporary Trends and Issues.* Thousand Oaks, CA: Sage.

MINTON, TODD D. 2002. "Jails in Indian Country, 2001." *Bureau of Justice Statistics Bulletin,* May.

MITCHEL, GARY. 1996. "Native Languages Go Silent." *News from the Indian Country,* Late April, 10: 1A, 7A.

MIYAMOTO, S. FRANK. 1973. "The Forced Evacuation of the Japanese Minority during World War II." *Journal of Social Issues* 29(2): 11–31.

MOFFAT, SUSAN. 1995. "Minorities Found More Likely to Live Near Toxic Sites." *Los Angeles Times,* August 30, B1, B3.

MOGELONSKY, MARCIA. 1995. "Asian–Indian Americans." *American Demographics,* August, 17: 32–39.

MONAGHAN, PETER. 2002. "Rescuing a History from Obscurity." *Chronicle of Higher Education,* April 19, A18-A19.

MONTAGU, ASHLEY. 1972. *Statement on Race.* New York: Oxford University Press.

MOORE, DAVID W. 2002. "Americans' View of Influences of Religion Settling Back to pre-September 11th Levels." *Gallup Poll Tuesday Briefly,* December 31, 2002. Accessed at www.gallup.com.

MOORE, JOAN W. 1970. "Colonialism: The Case of the Mexican Americans." *Social Problems,* Spring, 17: 463–472.

MOORE, JOAN W. AND HARRY PACHON. 1985. *Hispanics in the United States.* Englewood Cliffs, NJ: Prentice Hall.

———, ———. AND RAQUEL PINDERHUGHES, EDS. 1993. *In the Barrios: Latinos and the Underclass Debate.* New York: Sage.

MOORE, STEPHEN. 1998. *A Fiscal Report of the Newest Americans.* Washington, DC: National Immigration Forum and Cato Institute.

MOQUIN, WAYNE AND CHARLES VAN DOREN, EDS. 1971. *A Documentary History of the Mexican Americans.* New York: Praeger.

MORIN, RICHARD. 2004. "A Decade of Democracy." *Washington Post National Weekly Edition,* April 5, 11.

MORRIS, MILTON D. AND GARY E. RUBIN. 1993. "The Turbulent Friendship: Black–Jewish Relations in the 1990s." *Annals,* November, 42–60.

MORSE, SAMUEL F. B. 1835. *Foreign Conspiracy against the Liberties of United States.* New York: Leavitt, Lord.

MOSKOS, CHARLES C. AND JOHN SIBLEY BUTLER, EDS. 1996. *All That We Can Be: Black Leadership and Racial Integration the Army Way.* New York: Basic Books.

MOULDER, FRANCES V. 1996. "Teaching about Race and Ethnicity: A Message of Despair or a Message of Hope?" Paper presented at the Annual Meeting of the American Sociological Association, New York City.

MUI, YIAN Q. 2001. "Videos Revive Viet Memories." *Chicago Tribune,* July 19, 8B.

MULLER, ELI. 2001. "Orthodox Jews Relieved by 'Yale 5' Loss." *Yale Daily News,* January 12.

MURPHY, DEAN. 2004. "Imagining Life without Illegal Immigrants." *New York Times,* January 11.

MUSCHKIN, CLARA G. 1993. "Consequences of Return Migrant Status for Employment in Puerto Rico." *International Migration Review,* Spring, 27: 79–102.

"MUSLIMS IN THE AMERICAN PUBLIC SQUARE." 2001. *American Muslim Poll.* Washington, DC: Project MAPS.

MYRDAL, GUNNAR. 1944. *An American Dilemma: The Negro Problem and Modern Democracy.* New York: Harper.

NABOKOV, PETER. 1970. *Tijerina and the Courthouse Raid,* 2nd ed. Berkeley, CA: Ramparts Press.

NAFF, ALIKA. 1980. *Arabs.* In *Harvard Encyclopedia and Asian Ethnic Groups,* edited by Richard Thernstrom. Cambridge, MA: Harvard University Press.

NAGEL, JOANE. 1988. "The Roots of Red Power: Demographic and Organizational Bases of American Indian Activism 1950–1990." Paper presented at the Annual Meeting of the American Sociological Association, Atlanta.

———. 1996. *American Indian Ethnic Renewal: Red Power and the Resurgence of Identity and Culture.* New York: Oxford University Press.

NASH, MANNING. 1962. "Race and the Ideology of Race." *Current Anthropology,* June, pp. 3: 285–288.

NATIONAL ADVISORY COMMISSION ON CIVIL DISORDERS. 1968. *Report.* New York: Bantam.

NATIONAL ASIAN PACIFIC AMERICAN LEGAL CONSORTIUM. 2002. *Backlash: When America Turned on its Own.* Washington, DC: NAPALC.

NATIONAL COALITION OF ANTI-VIOLENCE COALITIONS. 2004. *Anti-LGBT Violence in 2003.* New York: National Coalition of Anti-Violence Programs.

NATIONAL CONFERENCE OF CHRISTIANS AND JEWS (NCCJ). 1994. *Taking America's Pulse.* New York: NCCJ.

NATIONAL INDIAN GAMING ASSOCIATION. 2004a. *Indian Gaming Facts.* Accessed September 27, 2004, at www.indiangaming.org.

———. 2004b. *Tribal Government Gaming: The Native American Success Story—An Analysis of the Economic Impact of Tribal Government Gaming in 2003.* Washington, DC: National Indian Gaming Association.

NATIONAL ITALIAN AMERICAN FOUNDATION. 2001. *National Survey: American Teen-Agers and Stereotyping.* Accessed October 1, 2003, at www.niaf.org.

NATIONAL ORGANIZATION FOR MEN AGAINST SEXISM. 2003. *NOMAS Home.* Accessed May 11 at www.nomas.org. National Women's Political Caucus. 2002. *About NWPC.* Accessed April 14, 2002, at http://www.nwpc.org/abort_home.html.

NAVARRO, MIREYA. 1995. "Puerto Rico Reeling under Scourge of Drugs and Rising Gang Violence." *New York Times,* July 23, p. 11.

———. 1998. "With a Vote for 'None of the Above,' Puerto Ricans Endorse Island's Status Quo." *New York Times,* December 14, A12.

———. 1999. "Miami's Generations of Exiles Side by Side, Yet Worlds Apart." *New York Times,* January 11, A1, A25.

———. 2000. "Puerto Rican Presence Wanes in New York." *New York Times,* February 28, A1, A20.

———. 2004. "Young Japanese-Americans Honor Ethnic Roots." *New York Times,* August 2, A1, A15.

NEUGARTEN, BERNICE L. 1996. *The Meanings of Age. Selected Papers of Bernice L. Neugarten.* Ed. with a forward by Dail A. Neugarten.

"A NEW POLL." 2004. *Religion Watch,* September, 3–4.

NEWPORT, FRANK. 2003. *Six out of 10 Americans Say Homosexual Relations Should Be Recognized as Legal.* Accessed May 15, 2003, at www.gallup.com.

NEW YORK TIMES. 1917a. Illiteracy Is Not All Alike. (February 8), p. 12.

———. 1917b. The Immigration Bill Veto. (January 31), p. 210.

———. 1982. Converts to Judaism. (August 29), p. 23.

NEWMAN, WILLIAM M. 1973. *American Pluralism: A Study of Minority Groups and Social Theory.* New York: Harper & Row.

NG, KWAI HANG. 1999. Chinese Christian, Christian Chinese? Ethnicity and Religion: An Ethnographic Study of a Chinese Protestant Church. Paper presented at Conference on Sociological Ethnography, Evanston.

———. 2003. "Seeking the Christian Tutelage: Agency and Culture in Chinese Immigrants' Conversion to Christianity." *Sociology of Religion* 63(2): 195–214.

NIE, NORMAN H., BARBARA CURRIE, AND ANDREW M. GREELEY. 1974. "Political Attitudes among American Ethnics: A Study of Perceptual Distortion." *Ethnicity,* December, 1:317–343.

NIEBUHR, GUSTAV. 1998. "Southern Baptists Declare Wife Should 'Submit' to Her Husband." *New York Times,* June 10, A1, A20.

NIELSEN, JOYCE MCCARL, GLENDA WALDEN, AND CHARLOTTE A. KUNKEL. 2000. "Gendered Heteronormality: Empirical Illusions in Everyday Life." *Sociological Quarterly* 41(2): 283–296.

NISHI, SETSUKO MATSUNAGA. 1995. "Japanese Americans." Pp. 95–133 in *Asian Americans: Contemporary Trends and Issues,* edited by Pyong Gap Min. Thousand Oaks, CA: Sage Publications.

NOBLE, BARBARA PRESLEY. 1995. "A Level Playing Field, for Just $121." *New York Times,* March 5, F21.

NOEL, DONALD L. 1972. *The Origins of American Slavery and Racism.* Columbus, OH: Charles Merrill Publishing Co.

NORDEN, MARTIN E. 1994. *The Cinema of Isolation: A History of Physical Disability in the Movies.* New Brunswick, NJ: Rutgers University Press.

NOVAK, MICHAEL. 1996. *Unmeltable Ethnics: Politics and Culture in American Life,* 2nd. ed. New Brunswick, NJ: Transaction Books.

NOVELLI, WILLIAM D. 2004. "Common Sense: The Case for Age Discrimination Law." Pp. 4, 7 in *Global Report on Aging.* Washington, DC: AARP.

O'CONNOR, ANNE-MARIE. 1998. "Church's New Wave of Change." *Los Angeles Times,* March 25, A1, A16.

———. 1999. "Roar of Soccer at Coliseum." *Los Angeles Times,* April 29, A1.

OAKES, JAMES. 1993. "Slavery." Pp. 1407–1419 in *Encyclopedia of American Social History,* edited by Mary Kupiec Clayton, Elliot J. Gorn, and Peter W. Williams. New York: Scribner's.

OBERSCHALL, ANTHONY. 1968. "The Los Angeles Riot of August 1965." *Social Problems,* Winter, 15: 322–341.

O'CONNOR, ANNE-MARIE. 1998. "Church's New Wave of Change." *Los Angeles Times,* March 25, A1, A16.

OGUNWOLE, STELLA V. 2002. *The American Indian and Alaskan Native Population.* Census 2000 Brief C2KBR/01:15. Washington, DC, U.S. Government Printing Office.

OHNUMA, KEIKO. 1991. "Study Finds Asians Unhappy at CSU." *AsianWeek,* August 8, 12: 5.

OLIVER, MELVIN L. AND THOMAS M. SHAPIRO. 1996. *Black Wealth/White Wealth: New Perspective on Racial Inequality.* New York: Routledge.

OLMOS, EDWARD JAMES, LEA YBARRA, AND MANUEL MONTERREY. 1999. *Americanos: Latino Life in the United States.* Boston: Little, Brown.

OLZAK, SUSAN. 1998. "Ethnic Protest in Core and Periphery States." *Ethnic and Racial Studie,* March, 21: 187–217.

OMI, MICHAEL AND HOWARD WINANT. 1994. *Racial Formation in the United States,* 2nd ed. New York: Routledge.

O'NEILL, WILLIAM. 1969. *Everyone Was Brave: The Rise and Fall of Feminism in America.* Chicago: Quadrangle.

ONISHI, NORIMITSU. 1995. "Japanese in America Looking beyond Past to Shape Future." *New York Times,* December 25, 1.

ORFIELD, GARY. 2002. *Schools More Separate: Consequences of a Decade of Resegregation.* Cambridge, MA: The Civil Rights Project, Harvard University.

———. AND HOLLY J. LIEBOWITZ, EDS. 1999. *Religion, Race, and Justice in a Changing America.* New York: The Twentieth Century Fund.

———. SUSAN E. EATON, AND THE HARVARD PROJECT ON SCHOOL SEGREGATION. 1996. *Dismantling Desegregation: The Quiet Reversal of Brown v. Board of Education.* New York: The New Press.

ORLOV, ANN AND REED UEDA. 1980. "Central and South Americans." Pp. 210–217 in *Harvard Encyclopedia of American Ethnic Groups,* edited by Stephan Thernstrom. Cambridge, MA: Belknap Press of Harvard University Press.

OTTAWAY, DAVID S. AND PAUL TAYLOR. 1992. "A Minority Decides to Stand Aside for Majority Rule." *Washington Post National Weekly Edition,* April 5, 9: 17.

OWEN, CAROLYN A., HOWARD C. EISNER, AND THOMAS R. McFAUL. 1981. "A Half-Century of Social Distance Research: National Replication of the Bogardus Studies." *Sociology and Social Research,* October, 66: 80–97.

PADGET, MARTIN. 2004. *Indian Country: Travels in the American Southwest, 1840–1935.* Albuquerque, NM: University of New Mexico Press.

PAGER, DEVAH. 2003. "The Mark of a Criminal." *American Journal of Sociology* 108: 937–975.

PAIK, NANCY. 2001. *One Nation: Islam in America.* Accessed March 15, 2001, at http://www.channelonenews.com/special/islam/media.html.

PARAL, ROB. 2004. "Health Worker Shortages and the Potential of Immigration Policy." *Immigration Policy in Focus* 3, February.

PARK, ROBERT E. 1928. "Human Migration and the Marginal Man." *American Journal of Sociology.* May, 33: 881–893.

———. 1950. *Race and Culture: Essays in the Sociology of Contemporary Man.* New York: Free Press.

PARK, ROBERT E. AND ERNEST W. BURGESS. 1921. *Introduction to the Science of Sociology.* Chicago: University of Chicago Press.

PARKER, LAURA. 2001. "USA Just Wouldn't Work without Immigrant Labor." *USA Today,* July 23, A1, A2.

PARMELEE, LISA FERRARO. 2002. *Intergroup Relations Before and After 9/11.* New York: National Conference for Community and Justice.

PARRISH, MICHAEL. 1995. "Betting on Hard Labour and a Plot of Land." *Los Angeles Times,* July 7, A1, A20.

PARSONS, TALCOTT AND ROBERT BALES. 1955. *Family, Socialization and Interaction Processes.* Glencoe, IL: Free Press.

PATTILLO-McCOY, MARY. 1998. "Church Culture as a Strategy of Action in the Black Community." *American Sociological Review,* December, 63: 767–784.

———. 1999. *Black Picket Fences: Privilege and Peril among the Black Middle Class.* Chicago: University of Chicago Press.

PAYNE, CHARLES M. 1995. *I've Got the Light of Freedom.* Berkeley: University of California Press.

PEASE, JOHN AND LEE MARTIN. 1997. "Want Ads and Jobs for the Poor: A Glaring Mismatch." *Sociological Forum* 12(4): 545–564.

PECKHAM, PAT. 2002. "Hmong's Resettlement Changes Agency's Focus." *Wausau Daily Herald,* February 10, 1A, 2A.

PEEK, LORI. 2002. *Religious and Ethnic Issues after September 11, 2001: Examining Muslim University Student Expenses.* Boulder: University of Colorado, Natural Hazards Research and Applications Information Center.

PERÉZ, LINSANDRO. 2001. "Growing Up in Cuban Miami: Immigrants, the Enclave, and New Generations." Pp. 91–125 in *Ethnicities,* edited by Ruben G. Rumbaut and Alejandro Portes. Berkeley: University of California Press.

PERUSSE, ROLAND I. 1990. *The United States and Puerto Rico: The Struggle for Equality.* Malabor, FL: Robert E. Krieger Publishing Company.

PESSAR, PATRICIA R. 1995. *A Visa for a Dream: Dominicans in the United States.* Boston: Allyn & Bacon.

PETERSON, WILLIAM. 1971. *Japanese Americans: Oppression and Success.* New York: Random House.

PEW CHARITABLE TRUSTS. 2000. "Jews and the American Public Square Data." Accessed May 23, 2001, at http://www.pewtrusts.org.

PEW RESEARCH CENTER. 2004. *Beliefs that Jews Were Responsible for Christ's Death Increases.* Washington, DC: Pew Research Center.

PEWEWARDY, CORNEL. 1998. "Our Children Can't Wait: Recapturing the Essence of Indigenous Schools in the United States." *Cultural Survival Quarterly,* Spring, 29–34.

PFEIFFER, DAVID. 1996. "A Critical Review of ADA Implementation Studies Which Use Empirical Data." *Disability Studies Quarterly,* Winter, 16: 30–47.

PIDO, ANTONIO J. A. 1986. *The Filipinos in America.* New York: Center for Migration Studies.

PINDERHUGHES, RAQUEL 1996. "The Impact of Race on Environmental Quality: An Empirical and Theoretical Discussion." *Sociological Perspectives,* Summer, 39: 231–248.

PINKNEY, ALPHONSO. 1975. *Black Americans,* 2nd ed. Englewood Cliffs, NJ: Prentice Hall.

———. 1984. *The Myth of Black Progress.* New York: Cambridge University Press.

———. 2001. *Black Americans,* 5th ed. Upper Saddle River, NJ: Prentice Hall.

PLECK, ELIZABETH H. 1993. "Gender Roles and Relations." Pp. 1945–1960 in *Encyclopedia of American Social History,* edited by Mary Kupiec Clayton, Elliot J. Gorn, and Peter W. Williams. New York: Scribner's.

POLAKOVIC, GARY. 2001. "Latinos, Poor Live Closer to Sources of Air Pollution." *Los Angeles Times,* October 18, B1, B12.

POSADAS, BARBARA M. 1999. *The Filipino Americans.* Westport, CT: Greenwood Press.

POTTER, EDUARDO. "What Unions Can Gain From Immigrations." *New York Times,* March 28, Business Section, 3.

POWELL-HOPSON, DARLENE AND DEREK HOPSON. 1988. "Implications of Doll Color Preferences among Black Preschool Children and White Preschool Children." *Journal of Black Psychology,* February, 14: 57–63.

Presserr, Harriet B. 2003. "Race-Ethnic and Gender Differences in Nonstandard Work Shifts." *Work and Occupations,* November, 30: 412–439.

ProEnglish Language Association. 2002a. *Making English Our Official Language.* Accessed March 22, 2002, at http://www.proenglish.org/issues/offeng/states.html.

———. 2002b. "Rep. Stump (R-AZ) Introduces the Strongest Official English Bill to Date." *ProEnglish Advocate,* Winter, 1.

Public Broadcasting System. 1998. *Weekend Edition*: National Public Radio with Eric Westervelt and Scott Simon, May 30.

Purdy, Matthew. 2001. "Ignoring and Then Embracing the Truth about Racial Profiling." *New York Times,* March 11, p.

Quadagno, Jill. 2005. *Aging and the Life Course: An Introduction to Social Gerontology,* 3rd ed. New York: McGraw-Hill.

Rabinove, Samuel. 1970. "Private Club Discrimination and the Law." *Civil Rights Digest,* Spring, 3: 28–33.

Rachlin, Carol. 1970. "Tight Shoe Night: Oklahoma Indians Today." Pp. 160–183 in *The American Indian Today,* edited by Stuart Levine and Nancy Oestreich Lurie. Baltimore: Penguin.

Ragged Edge. 1998. "Austin, Texas Becomes Second City in the Nation to Require Basic Access in Single-Family Homes." (November/December), p. 5.

Rainey, James. 2000. "Farm Workers Union Ends 16-Year Boycott of Grapes." *Los Angeles Times,* November 22, A3, A36, A37.

Ramirez, Eddy. 2002. "Ageism in the Media Is Seen as Harmful to Health of the Elderly." *Los Angeles Times,* September 5, A20.

Ramirez, Margaret. 2000. "Study Finds Segregation of Latinos in Catholic Church." *Los Angeles Times,* March 1, A1, A24.

Ramirez, Roberto R. and Patricia de la Cruz. 2003. *The Hispanic Population in the United States: March 2003.* Current Population Reports Ser. P20, No. 545. Washington, DC: U.S. Government Printing Office.

Rangaswamy, Padma. 2005. "Asian Indians in Chicago." In *The New Chicago,* edited by John Koval et al. Philadelphia, PA: Temple University Press.

Rawick, George P. 1972. *From Sundown to Sunup: The Making of the Black Community.* Westport, CT: Greenwood Press.

Raybon, Patricia. 1989. "A Case for 'Severe Bias.'" *Newsweek,* October 2, 114: 11.

Read, Jen'nan Ghazal. 2003. "The Source of Gender Role Attitudes Among Christian and Muslim Arab-American Women." *Sociology of Religion,* Summer, 64: 207–222.

Reese, Debbie. 1996. "Teaching Young Children about Native Americans." *ERIC Digest,* May, ED0-PS-96-3.

Reeves, Terrance and Claudette Bennett. 2003. "The Asian and Pacific Islander Population in the United States: March 2002." *Current Population Reports.* Ser. P20. No. 540. Washington, DC: U.S. Government Printing Office.

Religion Watch. 1995a. "Women Religious Leadership Facing Mainline Decline, Conservative Growth." November, 11: 1–3.

———. 1995b. "Reform Synagogues Increasingly Adopting Orthodox Practices."1995b. *Religion Watch,* March, 10: 7.

———. 2000. "Future of Jewish Day Schools Threatened by Finances, Ideology." (January), p. 4.

———. 2004. "A New Poll." (September): p. 3-4.

Religious Diversity News. 2004. "The Oklahoma Headscarf Case." Accessed October 16, 2004, at www.pluralism.org.

Remini, Robert V. 2001. *Andrew Jackson and His Indian Wars.* New York: Viking.

Reskin, Barbara F. 1998. *The Realities of Affirmative Action in Employment.* Washington, DC: American Sociological Association.

Reyhner, Jon. 2001a. "Cultural Survival vs. Forced Assimilation." *Cultural Survival Quarterly,* Summer, 25: 22–25.

———. 2001b. "Family, Community, and School Impacts on American Indian and Alaskan Native Students Success." Paper presented at the annual meeting of the National Indian Education Association, October 29.

Richmond, Anthony H. 2002. "Globalization: Implications for Immigrants and Refugees." *Ethnic and Racial Studies,* September, 25: 707–727.

Rivera, George, Jr. 1988. "Hispanic Folk Medicine Utilization in Urban Colorado." *Sociology and Social Research,* July, 72: 237–241.

Rivera-Batiz, Francisco and Carlos E. Santiago. 1996. *Island Paradox: Puerto Rico in the 1990s.* New York: Russell Sage Foundation.

Robau, Dori. 2004. *Tennessee v. Lane, George, et al.* Accessed October 10, 2004, atjournalism.medill.northwestern.edu/docket/.

Roberts, D. F. 1955. "The Dynamics of Racial Intermixture in the American Negro: Some Anthropological Considerations." *American Journal of Human Genetics,* December, 7: 361–367.

Rodríguez, Clara E. 1989. *Puerto Ricans: Born in the USA.* Boston: Unwin Hyman.

———. 2000. *Changing Race: Latinos, the Census, and the History of Ethnicity in the United States.* New York: New York University Press.

———, ed. 1997. *Latin Looks: Image of Latinas and Latinos in the U.S. Media.* Boulder, CO: Westview Press.

Rodríguez, Robert. 1994. "Immigrant Bashing: Latinos Besieged by Public Policy Bias." *Black Issues in Higher Education,* February 24, 10: 31–34.

Roediger, David R. 1994. *Towards the Abolition of Whiteness: Essays on Race, Politics, and Working Class History (Haymarket).* New York: Verso Books.

Rohter, Larry. 1993. "Trade Pact Threatens Puerto Rico's Economic Rise." *New York Times,* January 3, 1, 14.

Romney, Lee. 2004 "Chinese Americans Emerge as a Political Power in S.F." *Los Angeles Times,* February 1, B1, B12.

Rosales, F. Arturo. 1996. *Chicano! The History of the Mexican American Civil Rights Movement.* Houston, TX: Arte Público Press.

Rose, Arnold. 1951. *The Roots of Prejudice.* Paris: UNESCO.

Rosenbaum, James E. and Patricia Meaden. 1992. "Harassment and Acceptance of Low-Income Black Youth in White Suburban Schools." Paper presented at the Annual Meeting of the American Sociological Association, Pittsburgh.

Rosenberg, Tom. 2000. "Changing My Name after 60 Years." *Newsweek,* July 17, 136: 10.

Rosin, Hanna. 2002. "To Be Arab and American." *Washington Post National Weekly Edition.* November 18, 20: 9.

Rossi, Alice S. 1964. "Equality between the Sexes: An Immodest Proposal." *Daedalus,* Spring, 93: 607–652.

Rouhana, Nadim N. and Daniel Bar-Tal. 1998. "Psychological Dynamics of Intractable Ethnonational Conflicts: The Israeli–Palestinian Case." *American Psychologist,* July, 761–770.

Rudrappa, Sharmila. 2004. *Ethnic Routes to Becoming American: Indian Immigrants and the Cultures of Citizenship.* New Brunswick, NJ: Rutgers University Press.

Rudwick, Elliott. 1957. "The Niagara Movement." *Journal of Negro History,* July, 42: 177–200.

Rusk, David. 2001. *The "Segregation Tax": The Cost of Racial Segregation to Black Homeowners.* Washington, DC: Brookings Institution.

Ryan, William. 1976. *Blaming the Victim,* rev. ed. New York: Random House.

Saad, Lydia. 1998. "America Divided Over Status of Puerto Rico." *Gallup Poll Monthly,* March, p. 390: 278.

Sachs, Susan. 2001. "For Newcomers, a Homey New Chinatown." *New York Times,* July 22, A1, A44.

Sadker, Myra Pollack and David Miller Sadker. 2003. *Teachers, Schools, and Sociology.* 6th ed. New York: McGraw-Hill.

Sahagun, Louis. 2004. "Tribes Fear Backlash to Prosperity." *Los Angeles Times,* May 3, B1, B6.

Said, Edward. 1978. *Orientalism.* New York: Viking.

St. Espada, Martín. 2000. "!Viva Vieques!" *The Progressive,* July, 64: 27–29.

Salée, Daniel. 1994. "Identity Politics and Multiculturalism in Quebec." *Cultural Survival Quarterly,* Summer–Fall, 89–94.

Salopek, Paul. 1996. "Assimilation Puts Tribal Cultures at Loss for Words." *Chicago Tribune,* February 25, 1, 13.

Salzberger, Ronald P. and Mary G. Turck. 2004. *Reparations for Slavery: A Reader.* London: Rowman and Little Field.

Samhan, Helen. 2001. "Arab Americans." In *Grolier's Multimedia Encyclopedia.* Accessed March 15, 2001, at http://www.grolier.com.

Sanchez, Rene. 1998. "The Winter of Their Discontent." *Washington Post National Weekly Edition,* December, 16: 20.

SANDERS, IRWIN T. AND EWA T. MORAWSKA. 1975. *Polish-American Community Life: A Survey of Research.* Boston: Community Sociology Training Program.

SAVAGE, DAVID G. 1995. "Plan to Boost Firms Owned by Minorities Is Assailed." *Los Angeles Times*, April 2, A14.

SCHAEFER, RICHARD T. 1971. "The Ku Klux Klan: Continuity and Change." *Phylon,* Summer, 32: 143–157.

———. 1976. *The Extent and Content of Racial Prejudice in Great Britain.* San Francisco: R & E Research Associates.

———. 1980. "The Management of Secrecy: The Ku Klux Klan's Successful Secret." Pp. 161–177 in Stanton K. Tefft, ed., *Secrecy: A Cross-Cultural Perspective.* New York: Human Sciences Press.

———. 1986. "Racial Prejudice in a Capitalist State: What Has Happened to the American Creed?" *Phylon,* September, 47: 192–198.

———. 1996. "Education and Prejudice: Unraveling the Relationship." *Sociological Quarterly,* January, 37: 1–16.

———. 2005. *Sociology.* 9th ed. New York, McGraw-Hill.

SCHAEFER, RICHARD T. AND SANDRA L. SCHAEFER. 1975. "Reluctant Welcome: U.S. Responses to the South Vietnamese Refugees." *New Community,* Autumn, 4: 366–370.

SCHLEMMER, LAURENCE. 2001a. "Between a Rainbow and a Hard Place." *Fast Facts,* December, 2–12.

———. 2001b. "Race Relations and Racism in Everyday Life." *Fast Facts,* September, 2–12.

SCHMIDLEY, DIANNE. 2003. "The Foreign-Born Population in the United States: March 2002." *Current Population Reports Ser. P20 No. 539.* Washington DC: U.S. Government Printing Office.

SCHMIDT, WILLIAM E. 1988. "Religious Leaders Try to Heal Rift in Chicago." *New York Times,* November 27, 14.

SCHODOLSKI, VINCENT J. 2002. "Demographic Shift Pits Blacks against Latinos." *Chicago Tribune,* April 25, 1, 12.

SCHULZ, AMY J. 1998. "Navajo Women and the Politics of Identity." *Social Problems,* August, 45: 336–352.

SCHWARTZ, ALEX. 2001. *The State of Minority Access to Home Mortgage Lending: A Profile of the New York Metropolitan Area.* Washington: Brooking Institution Center on Urban and Metropolitan Policy.

SCHWARTZ, FELICE. 1989. "Management Women and the New Facts of Life." *Harvard Business Review,* January–February, 67: 65–76.

SCHWARTZ, FELICE AND JEAN ZIMMERMAN. 1992. *Breaking with Tradition: Women and Work, The New Facts of Life.* New York: Warner Books.

SCHWARTZ, JIM AND JEFFERY SCHECKNER. 2001. "Jewish Population in the United States." Pp. 253–277 in *American Jewish Yearbook 2001,* edited by David Singer and Lawrence Grossman. New York: American Jewish Committee.

SCHWARTZ, JOHN. 1994. "Preserving Endangered Speeches." *Washington Post National Weekly Edition,* March 21, 11: 38.

SCHWARTZ, PEPPER. 1992. "Sex as a Social Problem." Pp. 794–819 in *Social Problems,* edited by Craig Calhoun and George Ritzer. New York: McGraw-Hill.

SCOTT, JANNY. 2003. "Debating White Private Clubs Are Acceptable and Private." *New York Times,* December 8, Sec. 7, 5.

SCOTCH, RICHARD K. 1988. "Disability as the Basis for a Social Movement: Advocacy and the Politics of Definition." *Journal of Social Issues* 44(1): 159–172.

———. 1989. "Politics and Policy in the History of the Disability Rights Movement." *The Milbank Quarterly,* Supplement 2, 6: 380–400.

———. 2001. *From Good Will to Civil Rights: Transforming Federal Disability Policy,* 2nd ed. Philadelphia: University of California Press.

SEAGER, JON. 2003. *The Penguin Atlas of Women in the World.* Rev. Ed. Old Steine, UYK: Penguin.

SEARS, DAVID O. AND J. B.MCCONAHAY. 1969. "Participation in the Los Angeles Riot." *Social Problems,* Summer, 17: 3–20.

———. 1970. "Racial Socialization, Comparison Levels, and the Watts Riot." *Journal of Social Issues,* Winter, 26: 121–140.

———. 1973. *The Politics of Violence: The New Urban Blacks and the Watts Riots.* Boston: Houghton-Mifflin.

SEIBERT, DEBORAH. 2002. Interview with Author. *Wausau Daily Herald* Staff Member, March 27.

SELZER, MICHAEL. 1972. *"Kike": Anti-Semitism in America.* New York: Meridian.

SENGUPTA, SOMINI. 1997. "Asians' Advances Academically Are Found to Obscure a Need." *New York Times,* November 9, 17.

SERVIN, MANUEL P. 1974. "The Beginnings of California's Anti-Mexican Prejudice." Pp. 2–26 in Manuel P. Servin, ed. *An Awakened Minority: The Mexican Americans,* 2nd ed. Beverly Hills, CA: Glencoe Press.

SHAFFER, GWEN. 1994. "Asian Americans Organize for Justice." *Environmental Action,* Winter 1994, 25: 30–33.

SHAHEEN, JACK. 2003. "Reel Bad Arabs: How Hollywood Vilifies a People." *Annals,* July, 558: 171–193.

SHANKLIN, EUGENIA. 1994. *Anthropology and Race.* Belmont, CA: Wadsworth.

SHAPIRO, JOSEPH P. 1993. *No Pity: People with Disabilities Forging a New Civil Rights Movement.* New York: Times Books.

SHAPIRO, THOMAS M. 2004. *The Hidden Cost of Being African American: How Wealth Perpetuates Inequality.* New York: Oxford University Press.

SHERIF, MUSAFER AND CAROLYN SHERIF. 1969. *Social Psychology.* New York: Harper & Row.

SHERKAT, DARREN E. AND CHRISTOPHER G. ELLISON. 1999. "Recent Developments and Current Controversies in the Sociology of Religion." Pp. 363–394 in *Annual Review of Sociology 1999,* edited by Karen S. Cook and John Hagan. Palo Alto, CA: Annual Reviews.

SHERMAN, C. BEZALEL. 1974. "Immigration and Emigration: The Jewish Case." Pp. 51–55 in *The Jew in American Society,* edited by Marshall Sklare. New York: Behrman House.

SHILTS, RANDY. 1982. *The Mayor of Castro Street: The Life and Times of Harvey Milk.* New York: St. Martin's.

SHUSTER, BETH. 1996. "Consulate Takes Activist Role for Mexicans in U.S." *Los Angeles Times,* April 9, A1, A18–A19.

SIGELMAN, LEE. 1995. "Blacks, Whites, and Anti-Semitism." *Sociological Quarterly* 36(4): 649–656.

SIGELMAN, LEE AND STEVEN A. TUCH. 1997. "Metastereotypes: Blacks' Perception of Whites' Stereotypes of Blacks." *Public Opinion Quarterly,* Spring, 61: 87–101.

SILBERMAN, CHARLES E. 1971. *Crisis in the Classroom: The Remaking of American Education.* New York: Random House.

SILVERMAN, ROBERT MARK. 2003. "Race, Consumer Characteristics, and Hiring Preferences: The South Side of Chicago." *Research in Community Sociology* 8: 159–179.

SIMON, STEPHANIE. 2004. "Muslim Call to Prayer Stirs a Midwest Town," *Los Angeles Times,* May 8, A17.

SIMPSON, JACQUELINE C. 1995. "Pluralism: The Evolution of a Nebulous Concept." *American Behavioral Scientist,* January, 38: 459–477.

SINGER, AUDREY. 2004. *The Rise of New Immigrant Gateways.* Washington, DC: The Brookings Institute.

SKLARE, MARSHALL. 1971. *America's Jews.* New York: Random House.

SKRENTRY, JOHN DAVID. 1996. *The Ironies of Affirmative Action.* Chicago: University of Chicago Press.

SLAVIN, ROBERT E. AND ALAN CHEUNG. 2003. *Effective Reading Programs for English Language Learners.* Baltimore, MD: Center for Research on the Education of Students Placed at Risk, Johns Hopkins University.

SLAVIN, STEVEN AND MARY PRADT. 1979. "Anti-Semitism in Banking." *The Bankers Magazine,* July–August, 162: 19–21.

———. 1982. *The Einstein Syndrome: Corporate Anti-Semitism in America Today.* Washington DC: University Press of America.

SLOAN, GEORGE. 1980. "30 Pekin High School Students Walk Out of Classes." *Peoria Journal Star,* September 4, 4.

SMALLWOOD, SCOTT. 2003. "American Women Surpass Men in Earning Doctorates." *Chronicle of Higher Education,* December 12, A10.

SMITH, DAN. 2003. *The Penguin State of the World Atlas.* 7th ed. London: Penguin Books.

SMITH, DAVID M. AND GARY J. GATES. 2001. *Gay and Lesbian Families in the United States: Same-Sex Unmarried Partner Households.* Washington, DC: Human Rights Campaign.

SMITH, DENISE AND HAVA TILLIPMAN. 2000. "The Older Population in the United States." *Current Population Reports Ser. P20-532.* Washington, DC: U.S. Government Printing Office.

SMITH, JAMES F. 2001. "Mexico's Forgotten Find Cause for New Hope." *Los Angeles Times,* February 23, A1, A12, A13.

SMITH, PAUL CHAAT AND ROBERT ALLEN WARRIOR. 1996. *Like a Hurricane: The Indian Movement from Alcatraz to Wounded Knee.* New York: The New Press.

SMITH, TOM W. 2000. *Taking America's Pulse II: A Survey of Intergroup Relations.* New York: National Conference for Community and Justice.

——. 2001. *Religious Diversity in America: The Emergence of Muslims, Buddhists, Hindus, and Others.* New York: American Jewish Committee.

SNELL, TRACY L. 2001. "Capital Punishment 2000." *Bureau of Justice Statistics Bulletin,* December.

SNIDERMAN, PAUL M. AND EDWARD G. CARMINES. 1997. *Reaching Beyond Race.* Cambridge, MA: Harvard University Press.

SNIPP, C. MATTHEW. 1989. *American Indians: The First of This Land.* New York: Sage.

SOCIETY FOR HUMAN RESOURCE MANAGEMENT. 2002. "Diversity aspects covered in corporate America." *New York Times Magazine,* August 15, 100.

SOMNERS, CHRISTINA HOFF. 1994. *Who Stole Feminism?* New York: McGraw-Hill.

SONG, TAE-HYON. 1991. "Social Contact and Ethnic Distance between Koreans and the U.S. Whites in the United States." Paper, Western Illinois University, Macomb.

SOO, JULIE D. 1999. "Strained Relations: Why Chinatown's Venerable Associations Are Ending Up in Court." *AsianWeek,* January 14, 15–18.

SORENSEN, ELAINE. 1994. *Comparable Worth. Is It a Worthy Policy?* Princeton, NJ: Princeton University Press.

SOUTH AFRICA INSTITUTE OF RACE RELATIONS. 2002. "What We Have Learned." *Fast Facts,* November, 2–8.

——. 2004. "Poverty Levels: People Living in Poverty." *Fast Facts,* August, 13.

SOUTHERN, DAVID W. 1987. *Gunnar Myrdal and Black–White Relations.* Baton Rouge: Louisiana State University.

SOUTHERN POVERTY LAW CENTER. 2004. "Active Hate Groups in the United States in 2003." *Intelligence Report,* Spring.

SQUITIERI, TOM. 1999. "FALN Brought Bloody Battle into American Streets." *USA Today,* September 21, 15A.

STAMPP, KENNETH M. 1956. *The Peculiar Institution: Slavery in the Ante-Bellum South.* New York: Random House.

STARK, RODNEY AND CHARLES GLOCK. 1968. *American Piety: The Nature of Religious Commitment.* Berkeley: University of California Press.

STARKS, CAROLYN. 2002. "Sitting Here in Limbo." *Chicago Tribune,* March 26.

STATE OF HAWAII. 2001. *2000 State of Hawaii Data Book.* Honolulu: Department of Business, Economic Development and Tourism.

STATISTICS CANADA. 2001. *Aboriginal Peoples in Canada.* Ottawa: Canadian Centre for Justice

——. 2002. *Population.* Accessed May 13, 2002, at http://www.statcan.ca/english.

——. 2003a. *2001 Census: Analysis Serves Canada's Ethnocultural Portrait: The Changing Mosaic.* Ottawa: Statistics Canada.

——. 2003b. *Ethnic Diversity Survey: Portrait of a Multicultural Society.* Ottawa: Statistics Canada.

STATISTICS SOUTH AFRICA. 2004. *Key Finds at Mid-2004.* Accessed October 9, 2004, at www.statsaa.gov.za.

STATON, RON. 2004. "Still Fighting for National Hawaiian Recognition." *Asian Week,* January 22, 8.

STEINER, STAN. 1976. *The Vanishing White Man.* New York: Harper & Row.

STERN, KENNETH S. 2001. "Lying about the Holocaust." *Intelligence Report,* Fall, 50–55.

STEWART, JOCELYN Y. 2002. "Groups Fight Increased Bias Against Arabs." *Los Angeles Times,* July 8, B3.

STODDARD, ELLYN R. 1973. *Mexican Americans.* New York: Random House.

——. 1976a. "A Conceptual Analysis of the 'Alien Invasion': Institutionalized Support of Illegal Mexican Aliens in the U.S." *International Migration Review,* Summer, 10: 157–189.

——. 1976b. "Illegal Mexican Labor in the Borderlands: Institutionalized Support of an Unlawful Practice." *Pacific Sociological Review,* April, 19: 175–210.

STOLL, MICHAEL A. 2004. *The American People: Census 2000.* New York, NY: Russell Sage.

STONEQUIST, EVERETT V. 1937. *The Marginal Man: A Study in Personality and Culture Conflict.* New York: Scribner's.

STOOPS, NICOLE. 2004. "Educational Attainment in the United States: 2003." *Current Population Reports* P20. No. 550. Washington, DC: U.S. Government Printing Office.

STOUT, DAVID. 2000. "At Indian Bureau, A Milestone and an Apology." *New York Times,* September 9, A47.

STRAUSS, GARY. 2002. "Good Old Boys' Network Still Rules Corporate Boards." *USA Today,* November 1, B1, B2.

SUGGS, WELCH. 2002. "Title IX at 30." *Chronicle of Higher Education,* June 21, 48: A38–A42.

——. 2004. "'Varsity' With an Asterisk." *Chronicle of Higher Education,* February 13, A35–A37.

SULLIVAN, CHERYL. 1986. "Seeking Self-Sufficiency." *Christian Science Monitor,* June 25, 16–17.

SUNG, BETTY LEE. 1967. *Mountains of Gold: The Story of the Chinese in America.* New York: Macmillan.

SURO, ROBERTO. 1998. *Strangers among Us: Latino Lives in a Changing America.* New York: Vintage Books.

SWAGERTY, WILLIAM R. 1983. "Native Peoples and Early European Contacts." Pp. 15–16 in *Encyclopedia of American Social History,* edited by Mary Kupiec Clayton, Elliot J. Gorn, and Peter W. Williams. New York: Scribner's.

SWANSON, STEVENSON. 2004. "Chinatown: Hopes for a Mini-boom." *Chicago Tribune,* August 1, 1, 5.

SWARNS, CHRISTINA. 2004. "The Uneven Scales of Capital Justice." *American Prospect,* July, A14–A15.

SWARTZ, JON. 2003. "Internet Firms Woo Hispanics." *USA Today,* January 27, 3B.

SZEGEDY-MASZAK, MARIANNE. 2001. "Guess Who's Footing the 'Mommy Tax?'" *U.S. News and World Report,* March 19, 130: 48.

TAFOYA, SONYA M., HANS JOHNSON, AND LAURA E. HILL. 2004. *Who Chooses to Choose Two?* New York: Russell Sage Foundation and Population Reference Bureau.

TAKAKI, RONALD. 1989. *Strangers from a Different Shore: A History of Asian Americans.* Boston: Little, Brown.

TAKEZAWA, YASUKO I. 1991. "Children of Inmates: The Effects of the Redress Movement among Third Generation Japanese Americans." *Qualitative Sociology,* Spring, 14: 39–56.

TALBOT, MARGARET. 1997. "Getting Credit for Being White." *New York Times Magazine,* November 30, 116–119.

TAYLOR, STUART, JR. 1987. "High Court Backs Basing Promotion on a Racial Quota." *New York Times,* February 26, 1, 14.

——. 1988. "Justices Back New York Law Ending Sex Bias by Big Clubs." *New York Times,* June 21, A1, A18.

TAYLOR, T. SHAUN. 2004. "Blacks Find Progress Slow in Joining Trade Unions." *Chicago Tribune,* August 1, 1, 12-13.

TELSCH, KATHLEEN. 1991. "New Study of Older Workers Finds They Can Become Good Investments." *New York Times,* May 21, A16.

TEN BROCK, JACOBUS, EDWARD N. BARNHART, AND FLOYD W. MATSON. 1954. *Prejudice, War and the Constitution.* Berkeley: University of California Press.

TERCHEK, RONALD J. 1977. "Conflict and Cleavage in Northern Ireland." *The Annals,* September, 47–59.

THERRIEN, MELISSA AND ROBERTO R. RAMIREZ. 2001. "The Hispanic Population in the United States, March 2000." *Current Population Reports* Ser. P20, No. 535. Washington, DC: U.S. Government Printing Office.

THIRD WORLD JOURNALISTS. 1994. *Third World Guide 93/94.* Toronto: Garamond Press.

THOMAS, CURLEW O. AND BARBARA BOSTON THOMAS. 1984. "Blacks' Socioeconomic Status and the Civil Rights Movement's Decline, 1970–1979: An Examination of Some Hypotheses." *Phylon,* March, 45: 40–51.

THOMAS, DOROTHY S. AND RICHARD S. NISHIMOTO. 1946. *The Spoilage: Japanese-American Evacuation and Resettlement.* Berkeley: University of California Press.

THOMAS, ROBERT M., JR. 1995. "Maggie Kuhn, 89, the Founder of the Gray Panthers, Is Dead." *New York Times,* April 23, 47.

THOMAS, WILLIAM ISAAC. 1923. *The Unadjusted Girl.* Boston: Little, Brown.

THOMPSON, GINGER. 2001. "Fallout of U.S. Recession Drifts South into Mexico." *New York Times*, December 26, C1, C2.

———. 2003. "Money Sent Home by Mexicans Is Booming." *New York Times*, October 28, p. A12.

THORNTON, RUSSELL. 1981. "Demographic Antecedents of the 1890 Ghost Dance." *American Sociological Review*, February, 46: 88–96.

———. 1991. "North American Indians and the Demography of Contact." Paper presented at the Annual Meeting of the American Sociological Association, Cincinnati.

THORSON, JAMES. 1995. *Aging in a Changing Society*. Belmont, CA: Wadsworth.

THRUPKAEW, NOY. 2002. "The Myth of the Model Minority." *The American Prospect*, April 8, 13: 38–47.

TIME. 1974. Are You a Jew? 104 (September 2), pp. 56, 59.

TIZON, THOMAS ALEX. 2004. "Internment Lesson Plan Is Under Attack." *Los Angeles Times*, September 12, A21.

TOMASKOVIC-DEVEY, DONALD. 1993. "The Gender and Race Composition of Jobs and the Male/Female, White/Black Pay Gaps." *Social Forces*, September, 72: 45–76.

TOMLINSON, T. M. 1969. "The Development of a Riot Ideology among Urban Negroes." Pp. 226–235 in *Racial Violence in the United States*, edited by Allen D. Grimshaw. Chicago: Aldine.

TONG, BENSON. 2000. *The Chinese Americans*. Westport, CT: Greenwood Press.

TOOSSI, MITRA. 2002. "Accepting of Change: The U.S. Labor Force, 1950–2050." *Monthly Labor Review*, May, 15–28.

TORRIERO, E.A. 2004. "Political Strife Hits Hmong in St. Paul." *Chicago Tribune*, June 14, 12.

TRAN, QUYNH-GIANG. 2001. "Black Men's Pay in Top Jobs Lags." *Chicago Tribune*, August 15, 1, 13.

TUCKER, M. BELINDA AND CLAUDIA MITCHELL-KERNAN, EDS. 1995. *The Decline in Marriage among African Americans*. New York: Russell Sage.

TURE, KWAME AND CHARLES HAMILTON. 1992. *Black Power: The Politics of Liberation*. New York: Vintage Books.

TURNER, MARGERY AUSTIN, FRED FREIBURG, ERIN GODFREY, CLARK HERBIG, DIANE K. LEVY, AND ROBIN R. SMITH. 2002. *All Other Things Being Equal: A Paired Testing Study of Mortgage Lending Institutions*. Washington, DC: Urban Institute.

TURNER, RALPH H. 1994. "Race Riots Past and Present: A Cultural-Collective Approach." *Symbolic Interaction* 17(3): 309–324.

TURNER, RICHARD BRENT. 2003. *Islam in the African-American Experience*. 2nd ed. Bloomington, IN: Indiana University Press.

TURNER, WALLACE. 1972. "New Hawaii Economy Stirs Minority Upset." *New York Times*, August 13, 1, 46.

TYLER, GUS. 1972. "White Worker/Blue Mood." *Dissent*, Winter, 190: 190–196.

TYLER, PATRICK. 2004. "Strife Drops, and Belfast Builds Again With Hope." *New York Times*, September 16.

TYLER, S. LYMAN. 1973. *A History of Indian Policy*. Washington, DC: U.S. Government Printing Office.

UNITED JEWISH COMMUNITIES. 2003. *The National Jewish Population Survey 2000–01*. New York: United Jewish Community.

UPI. 1997. "Carrier to Change Offensive Manual." *Chicago Defender*, August 21, 10.

U.S. COMMITTEE FOR REFUGEES. 2003. *World Refugee Survey 2003*. Washington, DC: U.S. Committee for Refugees.

U.S. ENGLISH. 2004. *Official English: States with Official English Laws*. Accessed August 11, 2004, at us-english.org/inc/official/states.asp.

USDANSKY, MARGARET L. 1992. "Old Ethnic Influences Still Play in Cities." *USA Today*, August 4, 9A.

VALENTINE, CHARLES A. 1968. *Culture and Poverty: Critique and Counter-Proposals*. Chicago: University of Chicago Press.

VAN AUSDALE, DEBRA AND JOE R. FEAGIN. 2002. *The First R: How Children Learn Race and Racism*. New York: Rowman & Littlefield.

VAN DEN BERGHE, PIERRE L. 1965. *South Africa: A Study in Conflict*. Middletown, CT: Wesleyan University.

———. 1978. *Race and Racism: A Comparative Perspective*, 2nd ed. New York: Wiley.

VARADARAJAN, TUNKO. 1999. "A Patel Motel Cartel?" *New York Times Magazine*, July 4, 36–39.

VEGA, WILLIAM A. ET AL. 1986. "Cohesion and Adaptability in Mexican-American and Anglo Families." *Journal of Marriage and Family*, November, 48: 857–867.

VERHOVEK, SAM HOVE. 1997. "Racial Tensions in Suit Slowing Drive for 'Environmental Justice.'" *New York Times*, September 7, 1, 16.

VIGIL, MAURILIO. 1990. "The Ethnic Organization as an Instrument of Political and Social Change: MALDEF, a Case Study." *The Journal of Ethnic Studies*, Spring, 18: 15–31.

WAGLEY, CHARLES AND MARVIN HARRIS. 1958. *Minorities in the New World: Six Case Studies*. New York: Columbia University Press.

WAGNER, ANGIE. 2004. "Invisible Indian Tribes." *Fort Lauderdale Sun-Sentential*, May 23.

WAITZKIN, HOWARD. 1986. *The Second Sickness: Contradictions of Capitalistic Health Care*. Rev. ed. New York: Free Press.

WALDMAN, CARL. 1985. *Atlas of North American Indians*. New York: Facts on File.

WALLER, DAVID. 1996. "Friendly Fire: When Environmentalists Dehumanize American Indians." *American Indian Culture and Research Journal* 20(2): 107–126.

WALLERSTEIN, IMMANUEL. 1974. *The Modern World System*. New York: Academic Press.

———. 2004. *World-Systems Analysis: An Introduction*. Durham, ND: Duke University Press.

WALZER, SUSAN. 1996. "Thinking about the Baby: Gender and Divisions of Infant Care." *Social Problems*, May, 43: 219–234.

WANG, L. LING-CHI. 1991. "Roots and Changing Identity of the Chinese in the United States." *Daedalus* Spring, 120: 181–206.

WARD, DEBORAH L. 1996. "Native Hawaiian Vote: The 'Aes Have It." *Ka Wai Ola O Oha*, October 1996.

WARNER, SAM BASS, JR. 1968. *The Private City: Philadelphia in Three Periods of Its Growth*. Philadelphia: University of Pennsylvania Press.

WARNER, W. LLOYD AND LEO SROLE. 1945. *The Social Systems of American Ethnic Groups*. New Haven, CT: Yale University Press.

WASHBURN, WILCOMB E. 1984. "A Fifty-Year Perspective on the Indian Reorganization Act." *American Anthropologist*, June, 86: 279–289.

WARREN, JEVE. 2000. "Poll: Custody Fight Sharply Divides Dade." *Miami Herald*, April 9, 1A, 24A.

WASHINGTON, BOOKER T. 1900. *Up from Slavery: An Autobiography*. New York: A. L. Burt.

WATANABE, TERESA. 2004. "Anti-Muslim Incidents Rise, Study Finds." *Los Angeles Times*, May 31, B1, B8.

WATERS, MARY. 1990. *Ethnic Options. Choosing Identities in America*. Berkeley: University of California Press.

WAUSAU SCHOOL DISTRICT. 2001. *Wausau School District. Wausau Daily Herald: Community*. Accessed March 27, 2002, at http://wausaudailyherald.com.

WAX, MURRAY L. 1971. *Indian Americans: Unity and Diversity*. Englewood Cliffs, NJ: Prentice Hall.

WAX, MURRAY L. AND ROBERT W. BUCHANAN. 1975. *Solving "the Indian Problem": The White Man's Burdensome Business*. New York: New York Times Book Company.

WEBER, MAX [1913–1922]. 1947. *The Theory of Social and Economic Organization*. Translated by A. Henderson and T. Parsons. New York: Free Press.

WEGLYN, MICHI. 1976. *Years of Infamy: The Untold Story of America's Concentration Camps*. New York: Quill Paperbacks.

WEI, WILLIAM. 1993. *The Asian American Movement*. Philadelphia: Temple University Press.

WEINBERG, DANIEL H. 2004. *Evidence from Census 2000 about Earnings by Detailed Occupation for Men and Women*. CENSR-15. Washington, DC: U.S. Government Printing Office.

WEINER, TIM. 2004. "Of Gringos and Old Grudges: This Land is Their Land." *New York Times*, January 9, A4.

WERTSMAN, VLADIMA. 2001. "Arab Americans: A Comparative and Critical Analysis of Leading Reference Sources." *Multicultural Review*, June, 42–47.

WESSEL, DAVID. 2001. "Hidden Costs of Brain Drain." *Wall Street Journal*, March 1, 1.

WELLINGTON, ALISON J. 1994. "Accounting for the Male/Female Wage Gap among Whites: 1976 and 1985." *American Sociological Review*, December, 59: 839–848.

WELLS, ROBERT N., JR. 1989. "Native Americans' Needs Overlooked by Colleges." Paper, Canton, New York: St. Lawrence University.

———. 1991. "Indian Education from the Tribal Perspective: A Survey of American Indian Tribal Leaders." Paper, Canton, New York: St. Lawrence University.

WERNICK, ROBERT. 1996. "The Rise, and Fall, of a Fervid Third Party." *Smithsonian*, November, 27: 150–152, 154–158.

WERTHEIMER, JACK. 1996. *Conservative Synagogues and Their Members*. New York: Jewish Theological Seminary of America.

WHITE, JACK E. 1997. "I'm Just Who I Am." *Time*, May 5, 149: 32–34, 36.

WHITMAN, DAVID. 1987. "For Latinos, a Growing Divide." *U.S. News and World Report*, August 10, 103: 47–49.

WHYTE, JOHN H. 1986. "How Is the Boundary Maintained between the Two Communities in Northern Ireland?" *Ethnic and Racial Studies*, April, 9: 219–234.

WICKHAM, DEWAYNE. 1993. "Subtle Racism Thrives." *USA Today*, October 25, 2A.

WIESEL, ELIE. 1960. *Night*. New York: Bantam.

WILGOREN, JODI. 2001. "On Campus and on Knees, Facing Mecca." *New York Times*, February 15, A1, A26.

WILKINSON, GLEN A. 1966. "Indian Tribal Claims before the Court of Claims." *Georgetown Law Journal*, December, 55: 511–528.

WILLETO, ANGELA A. A. 1999. "Navajo Culture and Female Influences on Academic Success: Traditional Is Not a Significant Predictor of Achievement among Young Navajos." *Journal of American Indian Education*, Winter, 38: 1–24.

WILLIAMS, DAVID R. AND CHIQUITEA COLLINS. 2004. "Reparations: A Viable Strategy to Address the Enigma of African American Health." *American Behavioral Scientist*, March, 47: 977–1000.

WILLIAMS, L. SUSAN, SANDRA D. ALVAREZ, AND KEVIN S. ANDRADO HAUCK. 2002. "My Name is Not Maria: Young Latinas Seeking Home in the Heartland." *Social Problems* 49(4): 563–584.

WILLIAMS, PATRICIA J. 1997. *Of Race and Risk. The Nation Digital Edition*, December 12, 1997. Accessed at http://www. then-ation.com

WILLIE, CHARLES V. 1978. "The Inclining Significance of Race." *Society*, July–August, 15: 10, 12–13.

———. 1979. *The Caste and Class Controversy*. Bayside, NY: General Hall.

WILSON, JAMES Q. AND EDWARD C. BANFIELD. 1964. "Public Regardingness as a Value Premise in Voting Behavior." *American Political Science Review*, December, 58: 876–887.

WILSON, JOHN. 1973. *Introduction to Social Movements*. New York: Basic Books.

WILSON, WILLIAM J. 1973. *Power, Racism and Privilege: Race Relations in Theoretical and Sociohistorical Perspectives*. New York: Macmillan.

———. 1980. *The Declining Significance of Race: Blacks and Changing American Institutions*, 2nd ed. Chicago: University of Chicago Press.

———. 1988. "The Ghetto Underclass and the Social Transformation of the Inner City." *The Black Scholar* May–June, 19: 10–17.

———. 1996. *When Work Disappears: The World of the New Urban Poor*. New York: Knopf.

———. 2003. "There Goes the Neighborhood. *New York Times*, June 16, A19.

WINANT, HOWARD. 1994. *Racial Conditions: Politics, Theory, Comparisons*. Minneapolis: University of Minnesota Press.

———. 2001. *The World Is a Ghetto: Race and Democracy Since World War II*. New York: Basic Books.

WINKLER, KAREN. 1990. "Researcher's Examination of California's Poor Latino Population Prompts Debate over the Traditional Definitions of the Underclass." *Chronicle of Higher Education*, October 10, 37: A5, A8.

WINKS, ROBIN W. 1971. *The Blacks in Canada: A History*. Montreal, Quebec: McGill-Queen's University Press.

WINSEMAN, ALBERT L. 2004. *U.S. Churches Looking for a Few White Men*. Accessed July 27, 2004, at www.gallup.com.

WITT, SHIRLEY HILL. 1970. "Nationalistic Trends among American Indians." Pp. 93–127 in *The American Indian Today, edited by* Stuart Levine and Nancy Oestreich Lurie. Baltimore: Penguin.

WOLFE, ANN G. 1972. "The Invisible Jewish Poor." *Journal of Jewish Communal Services* 48(3): 259–265.

WOLFE, KATHI. 2001. "Debunk Those Stereotypes." *Washington Post National Weekly Edition*, July 9, 18: 23.

"WOMEN RELIGIOUS LEADERSHIP FACING MAINLINE DECLINE, CONSERVATIVE GROWTH." 1995a. *Religion Watch*, November, 11: 1–3.

WOMEN WORK. 1998. *Women Work: Poverty Persists*. Washington, DC: Women Work.

WONG, MORRISON G. 1995. "Chinese Americans." Pp. 58–94 in *Asian Americans: Contemporary Trends and Issues,* edited by Pyong Gap Min. Thousand Oaks, CA: Sage Publications.

WOO, ELAINE. 1996. "Immigrants, U.S. Peers Differ Starkly on Schools." *Los Angeles Times*, February 22, A1, A19.

WOODSON, CARTER G. 1968. *The African Background Outlined*. Washington, DC: Association Press, 1936. Reprinted New York: Negro Universities Press.

WOODWARD, C. VANN. 1974. *The Strange Career of Jim Crow,* 3rd ed. New York: Oxford University Press.

WOOTON, BARBARA H. 1997. "Gender Differences in Occupational Employment." *Monthly Labor Review* April, 120: 15–24.

WRIGHT, PAUL AND ROBERT W. GARDNER. 1983. *Ethnicity, Birthplace, and Achievement: The Changing Hawaii Mosaic*. Honolulu: East–West Population Institute.

WU, FRANK M. 2002. *Yellow: Race in America beyond Black and White*. New York: Basic Books.

WYMAN, MARK. 1993. *Round-Trip to America. The Immigrants Return to Europe, 1830–1930*. Ithaca, NY: Cornell University Press.

YANCEY, GEORGE. 2003. *Who Is White? Latinos, Asians, and the New Black-Nonblack Divide*. Boulder, CO: Lynne Rienner.

YBARRA, MICHAEL J. 1996. "Limitations of Statuses: In the Light of Today." *New York Times*, June 9, E4.

YEE, ALBERT H. 1973. "Myopic Perceptions and Textbooks: Chinese Americans' Search for Identity." *Journal of Social Issues* 29(2): 99–113.

YINGER, JOHN. 1995. *Closed Doors, Opportunities Lost: The Continuing Costs of Housing Discrimination*. New York: Russell Sage Foundation.

YOUNG, JEFFREY R. 2003. "Researchers Change Racial Bias on the SAT." *Chronicle of Higher Education*, October 10, A34–A35.

ZAMBRANA, RUTH E., ED. 1995. *Understanding Latino Families: Scholarship, Policy, and Practice*. Thousand Oaks, CA: Sage.

ZAREMBRO, ALAN. 2004. "Physician, Remake Thyself: Lured by Higher Pay and Heavy Recruiting, Philippine Doctors Are Getting Additional Degrees and Starting Over in the U.S. as Nurses." *Los Angeles Times,* January 10, A1, A10.

ZHAO, YILU. 2002. "Chinatown Gentrifies, and Evicts." *New York Times*, August 23, A13.

ZHOU, MIN AND CARL L. BANKSTON, III. 1998. *Growing Up American: How Vietnamese Children Adapt to Life in the United States*. New York: Russell Sage Foundation.

ZHOU, MIN. 2004. "Are Asian Americans Becoming 'White?'" *Contexts*, Winter, 29–37.

ZHOU, MIN. AND YOSHINORI KAMO. 1994. "An Analysis of Earnings Patterns for Chinese, Japanese, and Non-Hispanic White Males in the United States." *Sociological Quarterly* 35(4): 581–602.

ZIA, HELEN. 2000. *Asian American Dreams: The Emergence of an American People*. New York: Farrar, Straus & Giroux.

ZOGBY, JAMES J. 1998. *Arab Americans Challenge Official Violations*. Accessed October 17, 2000, at http://www.arabaai.org/newsandviews/washingtonwatch/032898.html.

———. 2001. *Arab American Attitudes and the September 11 Attacks*. Washington DC: Arab American Institute Foundation.

ZOGBY, JAMES J. 2003. *Arab Pendulum Swings on Civil Liberties*. Accessed July 20, 2004, at www.aaiusa.org/wwatch/112403.htm.

Photo Credits

Chapter 1 Page 2 (from top): © John Henley/Corbis; © Gary D. Landsman/Corbis; © Kim Kulilsh/Corbis; © Rolf Bruderer/Corbis; 2–3: © Steve Chenn/Corbis/Bettmann; 3 (from top): Dex Images/Corbis/Bettmann; © Ariel Skelley/Corbis; 9: Getty Images Inc.—Hulton Archive Photos; 10: Cartoon by Don Wright. Copyright 2006 Tribune Media Services. Reprinted with permission; 13: Tony Freeman/PhotoEdit; 14: Los Angeles Times Syndicate; 19: Getty Images, Inc.—Liaison; 24: Stock Boston; 29: The Image Works.

Chapter 2 Page 32 (from top): Roger Ressmeyer/CORBIS—NY; Bob Kirst/CORBIS—NY; Bettmann/CORBIS—NY; Jim McDonald/CORBIS—NY; 32–33: Todd Gipstein/CORBIS—NY; 33 (from top): Scott Houston/CORBIS—NY; Kai Pfaffentach/CORBIS—NY; 34: The Phillips Collection, Washington, D.C., ARS (Artists Rights Society, Inc.); 40: Bernard J. "Barney" Gallagher; 41: Charles Wilson Peale/Jennifer Warburg; 43: Joe Heller/Green Bay Press-Gazette; 44: The Lakota Journal, Editorial; 46: AP Wide World Photos; 55: Jeff Stahler. Reprinted by permission of Newspaper Enterprise Association, Inc.

Chapter 3 Page 64 (from top): Dorothea Lang/CORBIS—NY; Matthew McVay/CORBIS—NY; Phillip Gould/CORBIS—NY; Ed Kashi/CORBIS—NY; 64–65: Bettmann/CORBIS—NY; 65 (from top): Patrick Robert/Corbis/Sygma; Mark Peterson/CORBIS—NY; 66: Ted Hardin; 71: Judy Gelles/Stock Boston; 72: Harvard University KSG Wiener Center; 76: Bachmann/Stock Boston; 78: Copley News Service; 80: Mark Ludak/The Image Works; 85: Signe Wilkinson, Cartoonists & Writers Syndicate/cartoonweb.com.

Chapter 4 Page 90 (from top): © David H. Wells/Corbis; © Dave Bartruff/Corbis; © Morton Beebe/Corbis; © Janet Jarman/Corbis; 90–91: © Corbis; 91 (from top): © Catherine Karnow/Corbis; © David Turnley/Corbis; 97: © Bettmann/CORBIS; 99: Courtesy of the Library of Congress; 103: Takeshi Takahara/Photo Researchers, Inc.; 105: UE/Huck—Konopacki Cartoons; 106: Courtesy of The New York Times Company; 109: Copley News Service; 112: Corbis/Bettmann; 113: AP Wide World Photos.

Chapter 5 Page 116 (from top): © Gabe Palmer/Corbis; Corbis Royalty Free; © Bettmann/Corbis; © Jean-Paul Pelissier/Reuters/Corbis; 116–117: © Nik Wheeler/Corbis; 117 (from top): Corbis/Bettmann; © Nathan Benn/Corbis; 120: Diane Glancy; 122: Jose Luis Pelaez, Inc./CORBIS—NY; 124: Joel Gordon Photography; 127: Paula Lerner/Woodfin Camp & Associates; 136: Agence France Presse/Getty Images; 137: The Chicago Tribune; 140: AP Wide World Photos; 142: King Features Syndicate; 144: AP Wide World Photos.

Chapter 6 Page 148 (from top): Will Hart/Photo Edit Don Wiechec/CORBIS—NY; Steve Widstrand/CORBIS—NY; Staffan Widstrand/CORBIS—NY; Tom Bean/CORBIS—NY; 148–149: George Lee White/CORBIS—NY; 149 (from top): © John Running/Black Star Publishing/PictureQuest; 151: Lawrence Migdale/Stock Boston; 154: Jeff Kerr; 155: Alexander Gardner/The Newberry Library; 157: AP Wide World Photos; 160: John Running/Stock Boston; 162: Spencer Grant/Stock Boston; 169: Miguel Gandert/CORBIS—NY; 171: Sara Wiles; 176: AP Wide World Photos; 177: Jim Steinberg/Photo Researchers, Inc.

Chapter 7 Page 182 (from top): Richard T. Nowitz/CORBIS—NY; CORBIS—NY; Annie Griffiths Belt/CORBIS—NY; Bettmann/CORBIS—NY; 182–183: Flip Schulke/CORBIS—NY; 183 (from top): William Philpott/CORBIS—NY; David Turnley/CORBIS—NY; 188: The Granger Collection, New York; 190: By permission of Mike Luckovich and Creators Syndicate, Inc.; 191: Bob Daemmrich/The Image Works; 193: AP Wide World Photos; 195: Margaret Bourke-White/Getty Images/Time Life Pictures; 196: Corbis/Bettmann; 199: Dan Budnik/Woodfin Camp & Associates; 201: AP Wide World Photos; 205: Courtesy The Balch Institute Collections, The Historical Society of Pennsylvania.

Chapter 8 Page 208 (from top): Bob Daemmrich/The Image Works; Rolf Bruderer/CORBIS—NY; Radu Sigheti/CORBIS—NY; 208–209: James L. Amos/CORBIS—NY; 209 (from top): Alan Jones/Australian Pictures/Corbis; Ariel Skelley/CORBIS—NY; 213: Howard University; 215: Michael Grecco/Icon International; 221: Jose Galvez/PhotoEdit; 223: PhotoEdit; 224: Columbia Law School; 227: Bob Daemmrich/Stock Boston; 230: Greg Gibson/AP Wide World Photos.

Chapter 9 Page 234 (from top): Bill Gentle/CORBIS—NY; Hans Georg Roth/CORBIS—NY; Larry Hirshowitz/CORBIS—NY; Reuters/Corbis; 234–235: Gideon Mendel/CORBIS—NY; 235 (from top): Jose Luis Pelaez/CORBIS—NY; Stephanie Maze/CORBIS—NY; 238: Jeff Greenberg/PhotoEdit; 244: Philadelphia Business Journal; 245 (top): AP Wide World Photos; 245 (margin): Bob Daemmrich/The Image Works; 248: Richard T. Schaefer; 251: AP Wide World Photos; 253: AP Wide World Photos.

Chapter 10 Page 256 (from top): Jose Luis Pelaez/CORBIS—NY; Charles Lenars/CORBIS—NY; Stephen Frink/CORBIS—NY; Jose Luis Pelaez/CORBIS—NY; 256-257: Wolfgang Kaehler/CORBIS—NY; 257 (from top): Bo Zaunders/CORBIS—NY; Douglas Peebles/CORBIS—NY; 259: Robert Frerck/Odyssey Productions, Inc.; 261: Jeff Greenberg/Visuals Unlimited; 264: Lester

Sloan/Woodfin Camp & Associates; **265:** © Gary Huck/UE/Huck—Konopacki Labor Cartoons; **270:** Paul Fusco/Magnum Photos, Inc.; **271:** Steve Benson. Reprinted by permission of United Feature Syndicate, Inc.; **272:** Frank Espada/Professor Martin Espada; **274:** Bill Aron/PhotoEdit.

Chapter 11 Page 282 (from top): © John Van Hasselt/ Corbis Sygma; © Cheryl Diaz Meyer/Dallas Morning News/Corbis; © Ed Kashi/Corbis; © Bettmann/Corbis; **282–283:** © Hulton-Deutsch Collection/Corbis; **283 (from top):** © Sherwin Crasto/ Reuters/Corbis; © Ricki Rosen/ Corbis Saba; **288:** Charles Wilson Peale, "Yarrow Mamout." Courtesy of The Historical Society of Pennsylvania Collection, Atwater Kent Museum of Philadelphia; **289:** A. Ramey/Stock Boston; **292:** Pictorial Parade/Getty Images, Inc.; **294:** Photo courtesy of Wow Publishing, Inc.; **295 (margin):** Bill Aron/PhotoEdit; **295 (bottom):** Brian Vander Brug/Los Angeles Times Syndicate; **298:** Ed Kashi/CORBIS—NY; **301:** Arab American Institute; **303:** Lawrence K. Ho/Los Angeles Times Syndicate.

Chapter 12 Page 306 (from top): Richard Ellis/ Corbis/Sygma; Kelly Mooney/CORBIS—NY; Kelly Mooney/CORBIS—NY; Anne W. Krause/CORBIS—NY; **306–307:** Craig Aurness/CORBIS—NY; **307 (from top):** Annie Griffiths Belt/CORBIS—NY; Corbis Royalty Free; **311:** © 2001 Oliver Chin. Reprinted by permission of Oliver Chin; **313:** Fabian Falcon/Stock Boston; **315:** Tak Toyoshima; **317:** AP Wide World Photos; **319:** John Lee/The Chicago Tribune; **323 (left):** Lawrence Migdale/Lawrence Migdale/Pix; **323 (right):** Index Stock Imagery, Inc.; **324:** Mike Roemer; **330:** Corbis/ Bettmann.

Chapter 13 Page 332 (from top): Reed Kaestner/ CORBIS—NY; David Paterson/CORBIS—NY; Phil Schermeister/CORBIS—NY; Nik Wheeler/CORBIS—NY; **332–333:** Corbis Royalty Free; **333 (from top):** Piere Vauthey/CORBIS—NY; Catherine Karnow/CORBIS—NY; **336:** John Sotomayor/New York Times; **337:** David Turnely/Corbis/Bettmann; **339:** Rob Lewine/Corbis/ Bettmann; **345:** Division of Rare and Manuscript Collections, Cornell University Library; **348:** AP Wide World Photos; **350:** Corbis/Bettmann.

Chapter 14 Page 354 (from top): Annie Griffiths Belt/CORBIS—NY; Nathan Benn/CORBIS—NY; Najlah Feanny/CORBIS—NY; Bettman/CORBIS—NY; **354–355:** Corbis Royalty Free; **355 (from top):** Richard T. Nowitz/CORBIS—NY; David Wells/CORBIS—NY; **361:** Corbis/Bettmann; **364:** Ulf Anderson/SIPA Press; **367:** AP Wide World Photos; **371:** Bill Aron/PhotoEdit; **373:** H. Gans/The Image Works; **375:** A. Ramey/Stock Boston; **379:** Bill Aron/PhotoEdit.

Chapter 15 Page 382 (from top): © Nathan Benn/ Corbis; © Earl & Nazima Kowall/Corbis; © LWA-Dann Tardif/Corbis; © Patrik Giardino/Corbis; **382–383:** © Bettmann/Corbis; **383 (from top):** © Jack Hollingsworth/ Corbis; © Jose Luis Pelaez, Inc./Corbis; **385:** Photofest; **387:** Photo Researchers, Inc.; **389:** Edios Interactive; **390:** © Sigrid Estrada; **392:** AP Wide World Photos; **397:** AP Wide World Photos; **398:** Kirk Anderson, www.kirk-toons.com.

Chapter 16 Page 406 (from top): Charles Lenars/ Corbis/Bettmann; © Christie's Images/CORBIS; © Lindsay Hebberd/CORBIS; © Brooks Kraft/Corbis; **406–407:** © John Garrett/Corbis; **407 (from top):** © Richard A. Cooke/Corbis; © Jonathan Blair/Corbis; **412:** Wesley Bocxe/Photo Researchers, Inc.; **414:** Andrew Wallace/Getty Images, Inc.—Liaison; **416:** Rick Friedman/Black Star; **420:** Star Tribune; **421:** Stepane Compoint/Corbis/Sygma; **424:** ANAX/Imapress/The Image Works; **427:** Corbis/Bettmann; **428:** Louis Gubb/The Image Works.

Chapter 17 Page 432 (from top): © Hulton-Deutsch Collection/CORBIS; © Ed Eckstein/CORBIS; © Bob Krist/CORBIS; © Norbert Schaefer/CORBIS; **432–433:** © Richard Hamilton Smith/CORBIS; **433 (from top):** © Neal Preston/CORBIS; © Cat Gwyn/CORBIS; **438:** Jack Kurtz/The Image Works; **441:** © New York Daily News, L. P. Reprinted with permission; **442:** Kathi Wolfe; **444:** Copley News Service; **446:** AP Wide World Photos; **447:** AP Wide World Photos; **448:** Brian Smith/Corbis/ Outline; **450:** Signe Wilkinson/Cartoonists/Cartoonists & Writers Syndicate/cartoonweb.com.

Index

Italicized letters "f" and "t" following numbers indicate figures and tables, respectively.

SINGLE PC LICENSE AGREEMENT AND LIMITED WARRANTY

READ THIS LICENSE CAREFULLY BEFORE OPENING THIS PACKAGE. BY OPENING THIS PACKAGE, YOU ARE AGREEING TO THE TERMS AND CONDITIONS OF THIS LICENSE. IF YOU DO NOT AGREE, DO NOT OPEN THE PACKAGE. PROMPTLY RETURN THE UNOPENED PACKAGE AND ALL ACCOMPANYING ITEMS TO THE PLACE YOU OBTAINED THEM [[FOR A FULL REFUND OF ANY SUMS YOU HAVE PAID FOR THE SOFTWARE]]. *THESE TERMS APPLY TO ALL LICENSED SOFTWARE ON THE DISK EXCEPT THAT THE TERMS FOR USE OF ANY SHAREWARE OR FREEWARE ON THE DISKETTES ARE AS SET FORTH IN THE ELECTRONIC LICENSE LOCATED ON THE DISK:*

1. **GRANT OF LICENSE and OWNERSHIP:** The enclosed computer programs <<and data>> ("Software") are licensed, not sold, to you by Pearson Education, Inc. publishing as Prentice Hall ("We" or the "Company") and in consideration [[of your payment of the license fee, which is part of the price you paid]] [[of your purchase or adoption of the accompanying Company textbooks and/or other materials,]] and your agreement to these terms. We reserve any rights not granted to you. You own only the disk(s) but we and/or our licensors own the Software itself. This license allows you to use and display your copy of the Software on a single computer (i.e., with a single CPU) at a single location for <u>academic</u> use only, so long as you comply with the terms of this Agreement. You may make one copy for back up, or transfer your copy to another CPU, provided that the Software is usable on only one computer.

2. **RESTRICTIONS:** You may <u>not</u> transfer or distribute the Software or documentation to anyone else. Except for backup, you may <u>not</u> copy the documentation or the Software. You may <u>not</u> network the Software or otherwise use it on more than one computer or computer terminal at the same time. You may <u>not</u> reverse engineer, disassemble, decompile, modify, adapt, translate, or create derivative works based on the Software or the Documentation. You may be held legally responsible for any copying or copyright infringement that is caused by your failure to abide by the terms of these restrictions.

3. **TERMINATION:** This license is effective until terminated. This license will terminate automatically without notice from the Company if you fail to comply with any provisions or limitations of this license. Upon termination, you shall destroy the Documentation and all copies of the Software. All provisions of this Agreement as to limitation and disclaimer of warranties, limitation of liability, remedies or damages, and our ownership rights shall survive termination.

4. **LIMITED WARRANTY AND DISCLAIMER OF WARRANTY:** Company warrants that for a period of 60 days from the date you purchase this SOFTWARE (or purchase or adopt the accompanying textbook), the Software, when properly installed and used in accordance with the Documentation, will operate in substantial conformity with the description of the Software set forth in the Documentation, and that for a period of 30 days the disk(s) on which the Software is delivered shall be free from defects in materials and workmanship under normal use. The Company does <u>not</u> warrant that the Software will meet your requirements or that the operation of the Software will be uninterrupted or error-free. Your only remedy and the Company's only obligation under these limited warranties is, at the Company's option, return of the disk for a refund of any amounts paid for it by you or replacement of the disk. THIS LIMITED WARRANTY IS THE ONLY WARRANTY PROVIDED BY THE COMPANY AND ITS LICENSORS, AND THE COMPANY AND ITS LICENSORS DISCLAIM ALL OTHER WARRANTIES, EXPRESS OR IMPLIED, INCLUDING WITHOUT LIMITATION, THE IMPLIED WARRANTIES OF MERCHANTABILITY AND FITNESS FOR A PARTICULAR PURPOSE. THE COMPANY DOES NOT WARRANT, GUARANTEE OR MAKE ANY REPRESENTATION REGARDING THE ACCURACY, RELIABILITY, CURRENTNESS, USE, OR RESULTS OF USE, OF THE SOFTWARE.

5. **LIMITATION OF REMEDIES AND DAMAGES:** IN NO EVENT, SHALL THE COMPANY OR ITS EMPLOYEES, AGENTS, LICENSORS, OR CONTRACTORS BE LIABLE FOR ANY INCIDENTAL, INDIRECT, SPECIAL, OR CONSEQUENTIAL DAMAGES ARISING OUT OF OR IN CONNECTION WITH THIS LICENSE OR THE SOFTWARE, INCLUDING FOR LOSS OF USE, LOSS OF DATA, LOSS OF INCOME OR PROFIT, OR OTHER LOSSES, SUSTAINED AS A RESULT OF INJURY TO ANY PERSON, OR LOSS OF OR DAMAGE TO PROPERTY, OR CLAIMS OF THIRD PARTIES, EVEN IF THE COMPANY OR AN AUTHORIZED REPRESENTATIVE OF THE COMPANY HAS BEEN ADVISED OF THE POSSIBILITY OF SUCH DAMAGES. IN NO EVENT SHALL THE LIABILITY OF THE COMPANY FOR DAMAGES WITH RESPECT TO THE SOFTWARE EXCEED THE AMOUNTS ACTUALLY PAID BY YOU, IF ANY, FOR THE SOFTWARE OR THE ACCOMPANYING TEXTBOOK. BECAUSE SOME JURISDICTIONS DO NOT ALLOW THE LIMITATION OF LIABILITY IN CERTAIN CIRCUMSTANCES, THE ABOVE LIMITATIONS MAY NOT ALWAYS APPLY TO YOU.

6. **GENERAL:** THIS AGREEMENT SHALL BE CONSTRUED IN ACCORDANCE WITH THE LAWS OF THE UNITED STATES OF AMERICA AND THE STATE OF NEW YORK, APPLICABLE TO CONTRACTS MADE IN NEW YORK, AND SHALL BENEFIT THE COMPANY, ITS AFFILIATES AND ASSIGNEES. HIS AGREEMENT IS THE COMPLETE AND EXCLUSIVE STATEMENT OF THE AGREEMENT BETWEEN YOU AND THE COMPANY AND SUPERSEDES ALL PROPOSALS OR PRIOR AGREEMENTS, ORAL, OR WRITTEN, AND ANY OTHER COMMUNICATIONS BETWEEN YOU AND THE COMPANY OR ANY REPRESENTATIVE OF THE COMPANY RELATING TO THE SUBJECT MATTER OF THIS AGREEMENT. If you are a U.S. Government user, this Software is licensed with "restricted rights" as set forth in subparagraphs (a)-(d) of the Commercial Computer-Restricted Rights clause at FAR 52.227-19 or in subparagraphs (c)(1)(ii) of the Rights in Technical Data and Computer Software clause at DFARS 252.227-7013, and similar clauses, as applicable.

Should you have any questions concerning this agreement or if you wish to contact the Company for any reason, please contact in writing: Social Sciences Media Editor, Prentice Hall, One Lake Street Upper Saddle River, NJ 07458.